KU-246-095

Edited by Derek S. Pugh

Organization Theory

Selected Readings

FOURTH EDITION

PENGUIN BOOKS

PENGUIN BOOKS

Published by the Penguin Group
Penguin Books Ltd, 80 Strand, London WC2R 0RL, England
Penguin Putnam Inc., 375 Hudson Street, New York, New York 10014, USA
Penguin Books Australia Ltd, 250 Camberwell Road, Camberwell, Victoria 3124, Australia
Penguin Books Canada Ltd, 10 Alcorn Avenue, Toronto, Ontario, Canada M4V 3B2
Penguin Books India (P) Ltd, 11 Community Centre, Panchsheel Park, New Delhi – 110 017, India
Penguin Books (NZ) Ltd, Cnr Rosedale and Airborne Roads, Albany, Auckland, New Zealand
Penguin Books (South Africa) (Pty) Ltd, 24 Sturdee Avenue, Rosebank 2196, South Africa

Penguin Books Ltd, Registered Offices: 80 Strand, London WC2R 0RL, England

www.penguin.com

First published 1971
Second edition 1984
Reprinted in Pelican Books 1985
Reprinted in Penguin Books 1987
Third edition 1990
Fourth edition 1997
7

Set in 9.75/11.5 pt Postscript Monotype Bembo by
Rowland Phototypesetting Ltd, Bury St Edmunds, Suffolk
Printed in England by Clays Ltd, St Ives plc

PENGUIN BUSINESS

ORGANIZATION THEORY

Derek S. Pugh is Emeritus Professor of International Management at the Open University Business School. He is co-author, with David J. Hickson, of *Writers on Organizations* and *Management Worldwide*, both published by Penguin.

For my children, Helena, Jonathan and Rosalind,
who already spend most of their waking lives
in formal organizations

Contents

Introduction to the Fourth Edition

The continuance in print since 1971 of earlier editions of this volume attests to the established importance of organization theory in the concerns of managers and management educators. Focal issues and the ideas about them have, of course, changed over this period and it is now appropriate to offer a fourth edition. This set of readings – issued to accompany the fifth edition of the companion introductory text *Writers on Organizations* by D. S. Pugh and D. J. Hickson (Penguin Books, 1997) – has been thoroughly revised and almost half of the present selection represents new contributions to the subject.

We live in an organizational world. Most of us cannot, even from childhood, escape from belonging to formal organizations. We begin with schools, youth clubs and religious congregations and progress to colleges, sports teams and political parties. As consumers, clients and customers we are continually served by large formal organizations: television networks, banks, the National Health Service, multiple chain stores and oil companies. As citizens we are on the receiving end of local, regional, national and, increasingly, international government. Finally, and most important, the jobs on which our livelihoods depend exist in formal organizations.

If we are to gain an insight into, and perhaps some control over, our situation in these arrangements, we need to develop our understanding of how such organizations function and why the people within them behave as they do. Every act of a worker, supervisor, shop steward or managing director rests on interpretations about what has happened and conjectures about what will happen. Attempts to gain understanding entirely based on our own experiences will inevitably be of limited use as we meet new experiences. We therefore need information and ideas to enable us to generalize effectively to unknown situations encountered for the first time – that is to say we need theories. Theory and practice are inseparable. To neglect a wider understanding, in a vain attempt to be non-theoretical, merely reduces our range of options. As a cynic once put it: claiming to be practical and down-to-earth merely means that you are using *old-fashioned* theories.

Organization theory is the body of thinking and writing which addresses itself to the problem of how to organize. The basis of selection for this wide-ranging volume has been to include those writers whose work has had a clear impact on thinking, practice and research in the subject. They have all stimulated work by others, some of it in support of their theories, some of it highly critical. Their views are the subject of much current debate. In every case the readings are primary sources, so that the reader may be in a position to sample the direct impact of the writer's work.

More specifically, organization theory can be defined as the study of the structure, functioning and performance of organizations and the behaviour of groups and individuals within them. The subject has a long history which can be traced back, for example, to the Old Testament, when decentralization through the appointment of judges was undertaken to relieve the load on Moses, the chief executive. The first English textbooks appeared in the thirteenth century, e.g. Robert Grosseteste, *The Rules of Saint Robert*. It is, however, in the present century that the rise of large-scale industrial and commercial enterprises has led to a continuous stream of organizational writing. It is also in this century that the impact of social-science thinking has built up until it has become a major force. It is still, though, a heterogeneous study, with the systematic analysis of sociologists, psychologists and economists mingling with distilled practical experience of managers, administrators and consultants.

These writers have attempted to draw together information and distil theories of how organizations function and how they should be managed. Their writings have been theoretical in the sense that they have tried to discover generalizations applicable to all organizations. They all believe that it is necessary continually to examine, criticize and update thinking about the organization and how it functions if it is to develop and not to decay.

The concept of organizational behaviour is basic to this field. From this point of view the task of management can be considered as the organization of individuals' behaviour in relation to the physical means and resources to achieve the desired goal. The basic problem in this subject to which all writing may be related is: '*How much* organization and control of behaviour is necessary for efficient functioning?' It is in the implied answer to this question on the control of organizational behaviour that two sides of a continuing debate may be usefully distinguished. On the one hand there are those who may be called the 'organizers', who maintain that more and better control is necessary for efficiency. They point to the advantage of specialization and clear job definitions, standard routines and clear lines of authority. Later more sophisticated theorists argue for the need to inculcate values of hard work, commitment to the task, belief in the worth of the product, and to develop a common culture which encourages enterprise, professionalism and respect for the customer. It is in the conscious full control by management of the structure, functioning and culture of the organization that effectiveness is achieved.

On the other hand there are those who, in this context, may be called the 'behaviouralists', who maintain that the continuing attempt to increase control over behaviour is self-defeating; that the inevitable rigidity in functioning, apathy in performance, and counter-control through informal relationships, means that increased efficiency does not necessarily occur with increased control. Even when it does it is only in the short term and at the cost of internal conflict and greatly reducing the individual's ability to be creative or innovative and thus the organization's capacity to cope with the inevitable environmental changes which take place. These theorists argue that in a world of environmental flux, there must be autonomy and trust given to members if they are to show the flexibility required.

It is around this continuing dilemma that the study of organization theory takes place. It is a dilemma because, of course, both sides of the discussion are right. It is not possible to opt for one view *to the exclusion of* the other, and it is one of the basic tasks of management to determine the optimum degree of control necessary to operate efficiently. The nature of such control, the processes used to achieve it, and its effects – positive *and* negative – on the individual organizational member are crucial parts of management decision-making. The various writers in this volume examine the many factors which affect the achievement of efficient organizational performance, and seek to determine how such organizational effectiveness can be obtained.

This volume has been arranged, inevitably somewhat arbitrarily, into five separate but highly interrelated sections: organization structure, the organization in its environment, management and decision-making, people in organizations, and organizational change and learning. Each section has a short introduction to the readings selected.

D. S. Pugh,
Open University Business School,
1997

PART ONE

The Structure of Organizations

All organizations have to make provision for continuing activities directed toward the achievement of given aims. Regularities in activities such as task allocation, coordination and supervision are established which constitute the organization's structure. The contributors to this section examine in a systematic way, comparatively across numbers of organizations, the structural differences encountered and ask what are the causes of these various forms.

Weber (Reading 1) analysed three general types of organization stemming from the bases for wielding authority, and drew attention to the fact that in modern society the bureaucratic type has become dominant because, he considered, of its greater technical efficiency. In doing so he formed the starting point of a series of studies designed to examine the nature and functioning of bureaucracy.

Pugh (Reading 2) describes work carried out with his colleagues which examines in detail the management structures of modern organizations. Measures of the degree of specialization, standardization and centralization of the authority structures which characterize organizations are obtained and the effects of contextual factors such as size, technology, ownership and interdependence with other organizations demonstrated.

Williamson (Reading 3) examines the complex nature of the modern corporation. He argues that the development of its structure is due to the need to economize on the transaction costs which are incurred in information processing. In certain situations within the corporation this leads to hierarchical control, in others to market relationships.

Bartlett and Ghoshal (Reading 4) focus on those corporations which operate internationally. They argue that the major constraint limiting such companies from operating effectively on a global basis is their inadequate organizational capabilities. They therefore need to develop into transnational organizations.

Handy (Reading 5) suggests that it is unnecessary for the modern organization to exist as a physical entity with buildings, personnel, etc. in a

1

particular location. When the members are linked by modern information technology, it becomes a virtual organization. This has large implications for the way that it is structured and managed.

1   M. Weber

Legitimate Authority and Bureaucracy

From *The Theory of Social and Economic Organisation*, Free Press, 1947, translated and edited by A. M. Henderson and T. Parsons, pp. 328–40. (Footnotes as in the translation. German original published in 1924)

The three pure types of legitimate authority

There are three pure types of legitimate authority. The validity of their claims to legitimacy may be based on:

1. Rational grounds – resting on a belief in the 'legality' of patterns of normative rules and the right of those elevated to authority under such rules to issue commands (legal authority).
2. Traditional grounds – resting on an established belief in the sanctity of immemorial traditions and the legitimacy of the status of those exercising authority under them (traditional authority); or finally,
3. Charismatic grounds – resting on devotion to the specific and exceptional sanctity, heroism or exemplary character of an individual person, and of the normative patterns or order revealed or ordained by him (charismatic authority).

In the case of legal authority, obedience is owed to the legally established impersonal order. It extends to the persons exercising the authority of office under it only by virtue of the formal legality of their commands and only within the scope of authority of the office. In the case of traditional authority, obedience is owed to the *person* of the chief who occupies the traditionally sanctioned position of authority and who is (within its sphere) bound by tradition. But here the obligation of obedience is not based on the impersonal order, but is a matter of personal loyalty within the area of accustomed obligations. In the case of charismatic authority, it is the charismatically qualified leader as such who is obeyed by virtue of

3

personal trust in him and his revelation, his heroism or his exemplary qualities so far as they fall within the scope of the individual's belief in his charisma.

1. The usefulness of the above classification can only be judged by its results in promoting systematic analysis. The concept of 'charisma' ('the gift of grace') is taken from the vocabulary of early Christianity. For the Christian religious organization Rudolf Sohm, in his *Kirchenrecht*, was the first to clarify the substance of the concept, even though he did not use the same terminology. Others (for instance, Hollin, *Enthusiasmus und Bussgewalt*) have clarified certain important consequences of it. It is thus nothing new.

2. The fact that none of these three ideal types, the elucidation of which will occupy the following pages, is usually to be found in historical cases in 'pure' form, is naturally not a valid objection to attempting their conceptual formulation in the sharpest possible form. In this respect the present case is no different from many others. Later on the transformation of pure charisma by the process of routinization will be discussed and thereby the relevance of the concept to the understanding of empirical systems of authority considerably increased. But even so it may be said of every empirically historical phenomenon of authority that is not likely to be 'as an open book'. Analysis in terms of sociological types has, after all, as compared with purely empirical historical investigation, certain advantages which should not be minimized. That is, it can in the particular case of a concrete form of authority determine what conforms to or approximates such types as 'charisma', 'hereditary charisma', 'the charisma of office', 'patriarchy', 'bureaucracy', the authority of status groups,[1] and in doing so it can work with relatively unambiguous concepts. But the idea that the whole of concrete historical reality can be exhausted in the conceptual scheme about to be developed is as far from the author's thoughts as anything could be.

---

1. *Ständische*. There is no really acceptable English rendering to this term – Ed.

Legal authority with a bureaucratic administrative staff[2]

Legal authority: The pure type with employment of a bureaucratic administrative staff

The effectiveness of legal authority rests on the acceptance of the validity of the following mutually interdependent ideas.

1. That any given legal norm may be established by agreement or by imposition, on grounds of expediency or rational values or both, with a claim to obedience at least on the part of the members of the corporate group. This is, however, usually extended to include all persons within the sphere of authority or of power in question – which in the case of territorial bodies is the territorial area – who stand in certain social relationships or carry out forms of social action which in the order governing the corporate group have been declared to be relevant.

2. That every body of law consists essentially in a consistent system of abstract rules, which have normally been intentionally established. Furthermore, administration of law is held to consist in the application of these rules to particular cases; the administrative process in the rational pursuit of the interests which are specified in the order governing the corporate group within the limits laid down by legal precepts and following principles which are capable of generalized formulation and are approved in the order governing the group, or at least not disapproved in it.

3. That thus the typical person in authority occupies an 'office'. In the action associated with his status, including the commands he issues to others, he is subject to an impersonal order to which his actions are oriented. This is true not only for persons exercising legal authority who are in the usual sense 'officials', but, for instance, for the elected president of a state.

4. That the person who obeys authority does so, as it is usually stated, only in his capacity as a 'member' of the corporate group and what he obeys is only 'the law'. He may in this connection be the member of an association, of a territorial commune, of a church, or a citizen of a state.

5. In conformity with point 3, it is held that the members of the corporate group, in so far as they obey a person in authority, do not owe this obedience to him as an individual, but to the impersonal order. Hence, it

---

2. The specifically modern type of administration has intentionally been taken as a point of departure in order to make it possible later to contrast the others with it.

follows that there is an obligation to obedience only within the sphere of the rationally delimited authority which, in terms of the order, has been conferred upon him.

The following may thus be said to be the fundamental categories of rational legal authority:

1. A continuous organization of official functions bound by rules.

2. A specified sphere of competence. This involves (a) a sphere of obligations to perform functions which has been marked off as part of a systematic division of labour. (b) The provision of the incumbent with the necessary authority to carry out these functions. (c) That the necessary means of compulsion are clearly defined and their use is subject to definite conditions. A unit exercising authority which is organized in this way will be called an 'administrative organ'.[3]

There are administrative organs in this sense in large-scale private organizations, in parties and armies, as well as in the state and the church. An elected president, a cabinet of ministers, or a body of elected representatives also in this sense constitute administrative organs. This is not, however, the place to discuss these concepts. Not every administrative organ is provided with compulsory powers. But this distinction is not important for present purposes.

3. The organization of offices follows the principle of hierarchy; that is, each lower office is under the control and supervision of a higher one. There is a right of appeal and of statement of grievances from the lower to the higher. Hierarchies differ in respect to whether and in what cases complaints can lead to a ruling from an authority at various points higher in the scale, and as to whether changes are imposed from higher up or the responsibility for such changes is left to the lower office, the conduct of which was the subject of complaint.

4. The rules which regulate the conduct of an office may be technical rules or norms.[4] In both cases, if their application is to be fully rational, specialized training is necessary. It is thus normally true that only a person who has demonstrated an adequate technical training is qualified to be a

3. *Behörde.*
4. Weber does not explain this distinction. By a 'technical rule' he probably means a prescribed course of action which is dictated primarily on grounds touching efficiency of the performance of the immediate functions, while by 'norms' he probably means rules which limit conduct on grounds other than those of efficiency. Of course, in one sense all rules are norms in that they are prescriptions for conduct, conformity with which is problematic – Ed.

member of the administrative staff of such an organized group, and hence only such persons are eligible for appointment to official positions. The administrative staff of a rational corporate group thus typically consists of 'officials', whether the organization be devoted to political, religious, economic – in particular, capitalistic – or other ends.

5. In the rational type it is a matter of principle that the members of the administrative staff should be completely separated from ownership of the means of production or administration. Officials, employees and workers attached to the administrative staff do not themselves own the non-human means of production and administration. These are rather provided for their use in kind or in money, and the official is obligated to render an accounting of their use. There exists, furthermore, in principle complete separation of the property belonging to the organization, which is controlled within the sphere of office, and the personal property of the official, which is available for his own private uses. There is a corresponding separation of the place in which official functions are carried out, the 'office' in the sense of premises, from living quarters.

6. In the rational type case, there is also a complete absence of appropriation of his official position by the incumbent. Where 'rights' to an office exist, as in the case of judges, and recently of an increasing proportion of officials and even of workers, they do not normally serve the purpose of appropriation by the official, but of securing the purely objective and independent character of the conduct of the office so that it is oriented only to the relevant norms.

7. Administrative acts, decisions and rules are formulated and recorded in writing, even in cases where oral discussion is the rule or is even mandatory. This applies at least to preliminary discussions and proposals, to final decisions and to all sorts of orders and rules. The combination of written documents and a continuous organization of official functions constitutes the 'office'[5] which is the central focus of all types of modern corporate action.

---

5. *Bureau.* It has seemed necessary to use the English word 'office' in three different meanings, which are distinguished in Weber's discussion by at least two terms. The first is *Amt*, which means 'office' in the sense of the institutionally defined status of a person. The second is the 'work premises' as in the expression 'he spent the afternoon in his office'. For this Weber uses *Bureau*, as also for the third meaning which he has just defined, the 'organized work process of a group'. In this last sense an office is a particular type of 'organization', or *Betrieb* in Weber's sense. This use is established in English in such expressions as 'the District Attorney's Office has such and such functions'. Which of the three meanings is involved in a given case will generally be clear from the context – Ed.

8. Legal authority can be exercised in a wide variety of different forms which will be distinguished and discussed later. The following analysis will be deliberately confined for the most part to the aspect of imperative coordination in the structure of the administrative staff. It will consist in an analysis in terms of ideal types of officialdom or 'bureaucracy'.

In the above outline no mention has been made of the kind of supreme head appropriate to a system of legal authority. This is a consequence of certain considerations which can only be made entirely understandable at a later stage in the analysis. There are very important types of rational imperative coordination which, with respect to the ultimate source of authority, belong to other categories. This is true of the hereditary charismatic type, as illustrated by hereditary monarchy, and of the pure charismatic type of a president chosen by plebiscite. Other cases involve rational elements at important points but are made up of a combination of bureaucratic and charismatic components, as is true of the cabinet form of government. Still others are subject to the authority of the chief of other corporate groups, whether their character be charismatic or bureaucratic; thus the formal head of a government department under a parliamentary regime may be a minister who occupies his position because of his authority in a party. The type of rational, legal administrative staff is capable of application in all kinds of situations and contexts. It is the most important mechanism for the administration of everyday profane affairs. For in that sphere, the exercise of authority and, more broadly, imperative coordination, consists precisely in administration.

The purest type of exercise of legal authority is that which employs a bureaucratic administrative staff. Only the supreme chief of the organization occupies his position of authority by virtue of appropriation, of election or of having been designated for the succession. But even *his* authority consists in a sphere of legal 'competence'. The whole administrative staff under the supreme authority then consists, in the purest type, of individual officials who are appointed and function according to the following criteria:[6]

1. They are personally free and subject to authority only with respect to their impersonal official obligations.
2. They are organized in a clearly defined hierarchy of offices.
3. Each office has a clearly defined sphere of competence in the legal sense.

6. This characterization applies to the 'monocratic' as opposed to the 'collegial' type, which will be discussed below [not included].

4. The office is filled by a free contractual relationship. Thus, in principle, there is free selection.
5. Candidates are selected on the basis of technical qualifications. In the most rational case, this is tested by examination or guaranteed by diplomas certifying technical training, or both. They are *appointed*, not elected.
6. They are remunerated by fixed salaries in money, for the most part with a right to pensions. Only under certain circumstances does the employing authority, especially in private organizations, have a right to terminate the appointment, but the official is always free to resign. The salary scale is primarily graded according to rank in the hierarchy: but in addition to this criterion, the responsibility of the position and the requirements of the incumbent's social status may be taken into account.
7. The office is treated as the sole, or at least the primary, occupation of the incumbent.
8. It constitutes a career. There is a system of 'promotion' according to seniority or to achievement, or both. Promotion is dependent on the judgement of superiors.
9. The official works entirely separated from ownership of the means of administration and without appropriation of his position.
10. He is subject to strict and systematic discipline and control in the conduct of the office.

This type of organization is in principle applicable with equal facility to a wide variety of different fields. It may be applied in profit-making business or in charitable organizations, or in any number of other types of private enterprises serving ideal or material ends. It is equally applicable to political and to religious organizations. With varying degrees of approximation to a pure type, its historical existence can be demonstrated in all these fields.

1. For example, this type of bureaucracy is found in private clinics, as well as in endowed hospitals or the hospitals maintained by religious orders. Bureaucratic organization has played a major role in the Catholic Church. It is well illustrated by the administrative role of the priesthood[7] in the modern church, which has expropriated almost all of the old church benefices, which were in former days to a large extent subject to private appropriation. It is also illustrated by the conception of the universal

7. *Kaplanokratie.*

Episcopate, which is thought of as formally constituting a universal legal competence in religious matters. Similarly, the doctrine of Papal infallibility is thought of as in fact involving a universal competence, but only one which functions *ex cathedra* in the sphere of the office, thus implying the typical distinction between the sphere of office and that of the private affairs of the incumbent. The same phenomena are found in the large-scale capitalistic enterprise; and the larger it is, the greater their role. And this is not less true of political parties, which will be discussed separately. Finally, the modern army is essentially a bureaucratic organization administered by that peculiar type of military functionary, the 'officer'.

2. Bureaucratic authority is carried out in its purest form where it is most clearly dominated by the principle of appointment. There is no such thing as a hierarchy of elected officials in the same sense as there is a hierarchical organization of appointed officials. In the first place, election makes it impossible to attain a stringency of discipline even approaching that in the appointed type. For it is open to a subordinate official to compete for elective honours on the same terms as his superiors, and his prospects are not dependent on the superior's judgement.[8]

3. Appointment by free contract, which makes free selection possible, is essential to modern bureaucracy. Where there is a hierarchical organization with impersonal spheres of competence, but occupied by unfree officials – like slaves or dependants, who, however, function in a formally bureaucratic manner – the term 'patrimonial bureaucracy' will be used.

4. The role of technical qualifications in bureaucratic organizations is continually increasing. Even an official in a party or a trade-union organization is in need of specialized knowledge, though it is usually of an empirical character, developed by experience, rather than by formal training. In the modern state, the only 'offices' for which no technical qualifications are required are those of ministers and presidents. This only goes to prove that they are 'officials' only in a formal sense, and not substantively, as is true of the managing director or president of a large business corporation. There is no question but that the 'position' of the capitalistic entrepreneur is as definitely appropriated as is that of a monarch. Thus at the top of a bureaucratic organization, there is necessarily an element which is at least not purely bureaucratic. The category of bureaucracy is one applying only to the exercise of control by means of a particular kind of administrative staff.

8. On elective officials.

5. The bureaucratic official normally receives a fixed salary. By contrast, sources of income which are privately appropriated will be called 'benefices'.[9] Bureaucratic salaries are also normally paid in money. Though this is not essential to the concept of bureaucracy, it is the arrangement which best fits the pure type. Payments in kind are apt to have the character of benefices, and the receipt of a benefice normally implies the appropriation of opportunities for earnings and of positions. There are, however, gradual transitions in this field with many intermediate types. Appropriation by virtue of leasing or sale of offices or the pledge of income from office are phenomena foreign to the pure type of bureaucracy.

6. 'Offices' which do not constitute the incumbent's principal occupation, in particular 'honorary' offices, belong in other categories. The typical 'bureaucratic' official occupies the office as his principal occupation.

7. With respect to the separation of the official from ownership of the means of administration, the situation is essentially the same in the field of public administration and in private bureaucratic organizations, such as the large-scale capitalistic enterprise.

8. Collegial bodies will be discussed separately below [not included]. At the present time they are rapidly decreasing in importance in favour of types of organization which are in fact, and for the most part formally as well, subject to the authority of a single head. For instance, the collegial 'governments' in Prussia have long since given way to the monocratic 'district president'.[10] The decisive factor in this development has been the need for rapid, clear decisions, free of the necessity of compromise between different opinions and also free of shifting majorities.

9. The modern army officer is a type of appointed official who is clearly marked off by certain class distinctions. This will be discussed elsewhere [not included]. In this respect such officers differ radically from elected military leaders, from charismatic *condottieri*, from the type of officers who recruit and lead mercenary armies as a capitalistic enterprise, and, finally, from the incumbents of commissions which have been purchased. There may be gradual transitions between these types. The patrimonial 'retainer', who is separated from the means of carrying out his function, and the proprietor of a mercenary army for capitalistic purposes have, along with the private capitalistic entrepreneur, been pioneers in the organization

9. *Pfrüden.*
10. *Regierungspräsident.*

of the modern type of bureaucracy. This will be discussed in detail below.[11]

The monocratic type of bureaucratic administration

Experience tends universally to show that the purely bureaucratic type of administrative organization – that is, the monocratic variety of bureaucracy – is, from a purely technical point of view, capable of attaining the highest degree of efficiency and is in this sense formally the most rational known means of carrying out imperative control over human beings. It is superior to any other form in precision, in stability, in the stringency of its discipline, and in its reliability. It thus makes possible a particularly high degree of calculability of results for the heads of the organization and for those acting in relation to it. It is finally superior both in intensive efficiency and in the scope of its operations, and is formally capable of application to all kinds of administrative tasks.

The development of the modern form of the organization of corporate groups in all fields is nothing less than identical with the development and continual spread of bureaucratic administration. This is true of church and state, of armies, political parties, economic enterprises, organizations to promote all kinds of causes, private associations, clubs, and many others. Its development is, to take the most striking case, the most crucial phenomenon of the modern Western state. However many forms there may be which do not appear to fit this pattern, such as collegial representative bodies, parliamentary committees, soviets, honorary officers, lay judges, and what not, and however much people may complain about the 'evils of bureaucracy', it would be sheer illusion to think for a moment that continuous administrative work can be carried out in any field except by means of officials working in offices. The whole pattern of everyday life is cut to fit this framework. For bureaucratic administration is, other things being equal, always, from a formal, technical point of view, the most rational type. For the needs of mass administration today, it is completely indispensable. The choice is only that between bureaucracy and dilettantism in the field of administration.

11. The parts of Weber's work included in this translation contain only fragmentary discussions of military organization. It was a subject in which Weber was greatly interested and to which he attributed great importance for social phenomena generally. This factor is one on which, for the ancient world, he laid great stress in his important study, *Agrarverhält-nisse im Altertum*. Though at various points in the rest of *Wirtschaft und Gesellschaft* the subject comes up, it is probable that he intended to treat it systematically but that this was never done – Ed.

The primary source of the superiority of bureaucratic administration lies in the role of technical knowledge which, through the development of modern technology and business methods in the production of goods, has become completely indispensable. In this respect, it makes no difference whether the economic system is organized on a capitalistic or a socialistic basis. Indeed, if in the latter case a comparable level of technical efficiency were to be achieved, it would mean a tremendous increase in the importance of specialized bureaucracy.

When those subject to bureaucratic control seek to escape the influence of the existing bureaucratic apparatus, this is normally possible only by creating an organization of their own which is equally subject to the process of bureaucratization. Similarly the existing bureaucratic apparatus is driven to continue functioning by the most powerful interests which are material and objective, but also ideal in character. Without it, a society like our own – with a separation of officials, employees, and workers from ownership of the means of administration, dependent on discipline and on technical training – could no longer function. The only exception would be those groups, such as the peasantry, who are still in possession of their own means of subsistence. Even in case of revolution by force or of occupation by an enemy, the bureaucratic machinery will normally continue to function just as it has for the previous legal government.

The question is always who controls the existing bureaucratic machinery. And such control is possible only in a very limited degree to persons who are not technical specialists. Generally speaking, the trained permanent official is more likely to get his way in the long run than his nominal superior, the Cabinet minister, who is not a specialist.

Though by no means alone, the capitalistic system has undeniably played a major role in the development of bureaucracy. Indeed, without it capitalistic production could not continue and any rational type of socialism would have simply to take it over and increase its importance. Its development, largely under capitalistic auspices, has created an urgent need for stable, strict, intensive, and calculable administration. It is this need which gives bureaucracy a crucial role in our society as the central element in any kind of large-scale administration. Only by reversion in every field – political, religious, economic, etc. – to small-scale organization would it be possible to any considerable extent to escape its influence. On the one hand, capitalism in its modern stages of development strongly tends to foster the development of bureaucracy, though both capitalism and bureaucracy have arisen from many different historical sources. Conversely, capitalism is the most rational economic basis for bureaucratic administration and enables it to develop in the most rational form, especially because, from a fiscal point of view, it supplies the necessary money resources.

Along with these fiscal conditions of efficient bureaucratic administration, there are certain extremely important conditions in the field of communication and transportation. The precision of its functioning requires the services of the railway, the telegraph and the telephone, and becomes increasingly dependent on them. A socialistic form of organization would not alter this fact. It would be a question whether in a socialistic system it would be possible to provide conditions for carrying out as stringent bureaucratic organization as has been possible in a capitalistic order. For socialism would, in fact, require a still higher degree of formal bureaucratization than capitalism. If this should prove not to be possible, it would demonstrate the existence of another of those fundamental elements of irrationality in social systems – a conflict between formal and substantive rationality of the sort which sociology so often encounters.

Bureaucratic administration means fundamentally the exercise of control on the basis of knowledge. This is the feature of it which makes it specifically rational. This consists on the one hand in technical knowledge which, by itself, is sufficient to ensure it a position of extraordinary power. But in addition to this, bureaucratic organizations, or the holders of power who make use of them, have the tendency to increase their power still further by the knowledge growing out of experience in the service. For they acquire through the conduct of office a special knowledge of facts and have available a store of documentary material peculiar to themselves. While not peculiar to bureaucratic organizations, the concept of 'official secrets' is certainly typical of them. It stands in relation to technical knowledge in somewhat the same position as commercial secrets do to technological training. It is a product of the striving for power.

Bureaucracy is superior in knowledge, including both technical knowledge and knowledge of the concrete fact within its own sphere or interest, which is usually confined to the interests of a private business – a capitalistic enterprise. The capitalistic entrepreneur is, in our society, the only type who has been able to maintain at least relative immunity from subjection to the control of rational bureaucratic knowledge. All the rest of the population have tended to be organized in large-scale corporate groups which are inevitably subject to bureaucratic control. This is as inevitable as the dominance of precision machinery in the mass production of goods.

The following are the principal more general social consequences of bureaucratic control:

1. The tendency to 'levelling' in the interests of the broadest possible basis of recruitment in terms of technical competence.
2. The tendency to plutocracy growing out of the interest in the greatest possible length of technical training. Today this often lasts up to the age of thirty.
3. The dominance of a spirit of formalistic impersonality, *sine ira et studio*, without hatred or passion, and hence without affection or enthusiasm. The dominant norms are concepts of straightforward duty without regard to personal considerations. Everyone is subject to formal equality of treatment; that is, everyone in the same empirical situation. This is the spirit in which the ideal official conducts his office.

The development of bureaucracy greatly favours the levelling of social classes and this can be shown historically to be the normal tendency. Conversely, every process of social levelling creates a favourable situation for the development of bureaucracy; for it tends to eliminate class privileges, which include the appropriation of means of administration and the appropriation of authority as well as the occupation of offices on an honorary basis or as an avocation by virtue of wealth. This combination everywhere inevitably foreshadows the development of mass democracy, which will be discussed in another connection.

The 'spirit' of rational bureaucracy has normally the following general characteristics:

1. Formalism, which is promoted by all the interests which are concerned with the security of their own personal situation, whatever this may consist in. Otherwise the door would be open to arbitrariness and hence formalism is the line of least resistance.

2. There is another tendency, which is apparently in contradiction to the above, a contradiction which is in part genuine. It is the tendency of officials to treat their official function from what is substantively a utilitarian point of view in the interest of the welfare of those under their authority. But this utilitarian tendency is generally expressed in the enactment of corresponding regulatory measures which themselves have a formal character and tend to be treated in a formalistic spirit. This tendency to substantive rationality is supported by all those subject to authority who are not included in the class mentioned above as interested in the security of advantages already controlled. The problems which open up at this point belong in the theory of 'democracy'.

2 D. S. Pugh

Does Context Determine Form?

From 'The measurement of organization structures: does context determine form?', *Organizational Dynamics*, spring 1973, pp. 19–34

This article will give some answers, admittedly partial and preliminary, to the following questions. Are there any general principles of organization structure to which all organizations should adhere? Or does the context of the organization – its size, ownership, geographical location, technology of manufacture – determine what structure is appropriate? And how much latitude does the management of a company have in designing the organization initially and tampering with it later on? Obviously, the questions are interdependent. If the context of the organization is crucial to determining the suitable structure, then management operates within fairly rigid constraints: it can either recognize the structure predetermined by the context and make its decisions accordingly, or it can fail to recognize the structure indicated by the context, make the wrong decisions and impair the effectiveness and even the survival of the organization. This assumes, of course, that management retains the freedom to make the wrong decisions on structure.

Even more obviously, these questions are difficult to answer. Let us begin with the fact that systematic and reliable information on organizational structure is scarce. We have a plethora of formal organization charts that conceal as much as they reveal and a quantity of unsynthesized case material. What we need is a precise formulation of the characteristics of organization structure and the development of measuring scales with which to assess differences quantitatively.

We do know something about the decisions that top managers face on organizations. For example, should authority be centralized? Centralization may help maintain a consistent policy, but it may also inhibit initiative lower down the hierarchy. Again, should managerial tasks be highly

16

specialized? The technical complexity of business life means that considerable advantages can accrue from allowing people to specialize in a limited field. On the other hand, these advantages may be achieved at the expense of their commitment to the overall objectives of the company.

Should a company lay down a large number of standard rules and procedures for employees to follow? These may ensure a certain uniformity of performance, but they may also produce frustration – and a tendency to hide behind the rules. Should the organization structure be 'tall' or 'flat'? Flat structures – with relatively few hierarchical levels – allow communications to pass easily up and down, but managers may become overloaded with too many direct subordinates. Tall structures allow managers to devote more time to subordinates, but may well overextend lines of command and distort communication.

All these choices involve benefits and costs. It also seems reasonable to suppose that the extent and importance of the costs and benefits will vary according to the situation of the company. All too often in the past these issues have been debated dogmatically in an 'either/or' fashion without reference to size, technology, product range, market conditions or corporate objectives. Operationally, the important question is: to what *degree* should organizational characteristics such as those above be present in different types of companies? To answer this question there must obviously be accurate comparative measures of centralization of authority, specialization of task, standardization of procedure, and so on, to set beside measurement of size, technology, ownership, business environment and level of performance. A programme of research aimed at identifying such measurements – of organization structure, operating context and performance – was inaugurated in the Industrial Administration Research Unit of the University of Aston a number of years ago, and continues in the Organizational Behaviour Research Group at the London Business School and elsewhere. The object of the research is threefold:

1. To discover in what ways an organization structures its activities.

2. To see whether or not it is possible to create statistically valid and reliable methods of measuring structural differences between organizations.

3. To examine what constraints the organization's context (i.e. its size, technology of manufacture, diffusion of ownership, etc.) imposes on the management structure.

Formal analysis of organization structure

Measurement must begin with ideas about which characteristics should be measured. In the field of organization structure the problem is not the absence of such ideas to distil from the range of academic discourse, but rather variables that can be clearly defined for scientific study.

From the literature available we have selected six primary variables or dimensions of organization structure:

Specialization: the degree to which an organization's activities are divided into specialized roles.

Standardization: the degree to which an organization lays down standard rules and procedures.

Standardization of employment practices: the degree to which an organization has standardized employment practices.

Formalization: the degree to which instructions, procedures, etc. are written down.

Centralization: the degree to which the authority to make certain decisions is located at the top of the management hierarchy.

Configuration: the 'shape' of the organization's role structure, e.g. whether the management chain of command is long or short, whether superiors have limited span of control – relatively few subordinates – or broad span of control – a relatively large number of subordinates – and whether there is a large or small percentage of specialized or support personnel. Configuration is a blanket term used to cover all three variables.

We need to distinguish between the two forms of standardization because they are far from synonymous. High standardization of employment practices, for example, is a distinctive feature of personnel bureaucracies but not of work-flow bureaucracies.

In our surveys we have limited ourselves to work organizations employing more than 150 people – a work organization being defined as one that employs (that is, pays) its members. We constructed scales from data on a first sample of fifty-two such organizations, including firms making motor-car bumpers and milk-chocolate buttons, municipal organizations that repaired roads or taught arithmetic, large department stores, small insurance companies, and so on. Several further samples duplicated the original investigation and increased the number of organizations to over two hundred.

Our problem was how to apply our six dimensions; how to go beyond individual experience and scholarship to the systematic study of existing organizations. We decided to use scales measuring the six dimensions of any organization, so that the positions of a particular organization on those scales form a profile of the organization.

Our approach to developing comparative scales was also guided by the need to demonstrate that the items forming a scale 'hang together', that is, that they are in some sense cumulative. We can represent an organization's comparative position on a characteristic by a numerical score, in the same way as an IQ score represents an individual's comparative intelligence. But just as an IQ is a sample of a person's intelligence taken for comparative purposes and does not detract from his uniqueness as a functioning individual, so our scales, being likewise comparative samples, do not detract from the uniqueness of each organization's functioning. They do, however, indicate limits within which the unique variations take place.

We began by interviewing at length the chief executive of the organization, who may be a works manager, an area superintendent or a chairman. There followed a series of interviews with department heads of varying status, as many as were necessary to obtain the information required. Interviews were conducted with standard schedules listing what had to be found out.

We were concerned to make sure that variables concerned both manufacturing and non-manufacturing organizations. We therefore asked each organization, for example, for which given list of potentially standard routines it had standardized procedure. (See Table 1 for sample questions in the six dimensions.)

On the other hand, because this was descriptive data about structure and was not personal to the respondent, we made no attempt to standardize the interview procedures themselves. At the same time, we tried to obtain documentary evidence to substantiate the verbal descriptions.

Analysis of six structural profiles

For purposes of discussion we have selected six organizations and have constructed the structural profiles for each one. Two are governmental organizations. The other four are in the private sector of the economy but the nature of the ownership varies drastically: one is family owned; another

Table 1. Sample questions in six dimensions

Specialization
1. Are the following activities performed by specialists, i.e. those exclusively engaged in the activities and not in the line chain of authority?
   (*a*) Activities to develop, legitimize and symbolize the organizational purpose (e.g. public relations, advertising).
   (*b*) Activities to dispose of, distribute and service the output (e.g. sales, service).
   (*c*) Activities to obtain and control materials and equipment (e.g. buying, stock control).
   (*d*) Activities to devise new outputs, equipment, processes (e.g. R&D, development).
   (*e*) Activities to develop and transform human resources (e.g. training, education).
   (*f*) Activities to acquire information on the operational field (e.g. market research).
2. What professional qualifications do these specialists hold?

Standardization
1. How closely defined is a typical operative's task (e.g. custom, apprenticeship, rate fixing, work study)?
2. Are there specific procedures to ensure the perpetuation of the organization (e.g. R&D programmes, systematic market research)?
3. How detailed is the marketing policy (e.g. general aims only, specific policy worked out and adhered to)?
4. How detailed are the costing and stock-control systems (e.g. stock taking: yearly, monthly, etc.; costing: historical job costing, budgeting, standard cost system)?

Standardization of employment practices
1. Is there a central recruiting and interviewing procedure?
2. Is there a standard selection procedure for foremen and managers?
3. Is there a standard discipline procedure with set offences and penalties?

Formalization
1. Is there an employee handbook or rulebook?
2. Is there an organization chart?
3. Are there any written terms of reference or job descriptions? For which grades of employees?
4. Are there agenda and minutes for workflow (e.g. production) meetings?

Centralization
Which level in the hierarchy has the authority to
   (*a*) decide which supplies of materials are to be used?
   (*b*) decide the price of the output?
   (*c*) alter the responsibilities or areas of work of departments?
   (*d*) decide marketing territories to be covered?

Configuration
1. What is the chief executive's span of control?
2. What is the average number of direct workers per first-line supervisor?
3. What is the percentage of indirect personnel (i.e. employees with no direct or supervisory responsibility for work on the output)?
4. What is the percentage of employees in each functional specialism (e.g. sales and service, design and development, market research)?

---

is owned jointly by a family and its employees; the third is a subsidiary of a large publicly owned company; the fourth is a medium-sized publicly held company. The number of employees also varies widely from 16,500 in the municipal organization to only 1,200 in the manufacturing organization owned by the central government. We selected these six from the many available in order to demonstrate the sort of distinctive profiles we obtain for particular organizations and to underscore the way in which we can make useful comparisons about organizations on this basis.

With all this diversity, it is not too surprising that no two profiles look alike. What is surprising, and deserves further comment, are the similarities in some of the six dimensions between several of the six organizations (see Figure 1).

Organization A is a municipal department responsible for a public service. But it is far from being the classic form of bureaucracy described by Weber. By definition, such a bureaucracy would have an extremely high-score pattern on all our scales. That is, it would be highly specialized with many

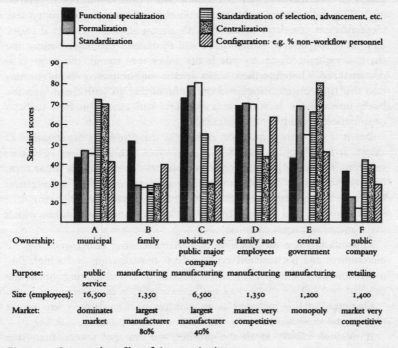

Figure 1 Structural profiles of six organizations

narrowly defined specialist 'officers', highly standardized in its procedures and highly formalized, with documents prescribing all activities and recording them in the files as precedents. If everything has to be referred upwards for decision, then it would also score as highly centralized. In configuration it would have a high proportion of 'supportive', administrative or 'nonworkflow' personnel. But clearly this example does not fit the pattern completely; it is below standard in both specialization and configuration, which demonstrates the effectiveness of this method of determining empirically what profile actually exists, in overcoming stereotyped thinking.

Organization B represents a relatively unstructured family firm, relying more on traditional ways of doing things. Although it has the specialities usual in manufacturing industry (and hence a comparatively high specialization score) it has minimized standardized procedure and formalized paperwork.

Organization C represents 'big business'. It is the subsidiary of a very large company, and its profile shows the effects of size: generally, very high scores on specialization, standardization and formalization, but decentralized. The distinctively different relationship of centralization is typical. Centralization correlates *negatively* with almost all other structural scales. The more specialized, standardized and formalized the organization, the *less* it is centralized; or, to put it the other way round, the more it is decentralized. Therefore these scales do not confirm the common assumption that large organizations and the routines that go with them 'pass the buck' upwards for decision with elaborate staff offices; in fact, such an organization is relatively decentralized.

But it is not only a question of size, as the profile of organization D shows. It has the same number of employees as organization B, yet its structure is in striking contrast and is closer to that of a much larger firm. Clearly the policies and attitudes of the management of an organization may have a considerable effect on its structure, even though factors like size, technology and form of ownership set the framework within which the management must function.

Organization E is an example of a manufacturing unit owned by the government and is characterized by a high centralization and a high formalization score. Comparison of the profiles of D and E brings home the fact that two organizations may be 'bureaucratic' in quite different ways.

Organization F is included as an example of the relatively low scores often found in retailing.

If we look closely at all the profiles, we can spot several that have pronounced features in common. For example, organizations C and D both score high on functional specialization, formalization and standardization. Moreover, by using the statistical method of principal components analysis, we emerged with comparatively few composite scores that sum up the structural characteristics of each organization. Plotting the composite scores reveals several closely related clusters, four of which we will discuss in detail. (See Figure 2 for a visual representation of the clusters.)

The reader may already have recognized the first cluster from studying the six profiles in Figure 1. It indicates that high specialization, high standardization and high formalization form a pattern that prevails in large-scale manufacturing industry. Among the examples are factories in the vehicle-assembly industry, those processing metals and those mass producing food-stuffs and confectionery. Organizations like these have gone a long way in regulating their employees' work by specifying their specialized roles, the procedures they are to follow in carrying out these roles and the documentation involved in what they have to do. In short, the pattern of scores

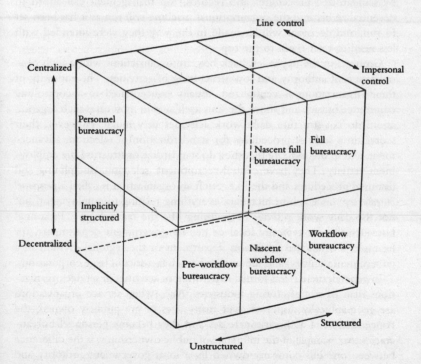

Figure 2   Relationships between the clusters

among specialization, standardization and formalization denotes the range and pattern of structuring. Manufacturing industry therefore tends to have highly structured work activities: production schedules, quality-inspection procedures, returns of output per worker and per machine, firms recording maintenance jobs, etc. We can call this the *workflow bureaucracy* kind of organization. In Figure 1, organizations C and D follow this pattern. This kind of organization (placed in the lower right front box in Figure 2) usually has a high percentage of 'non-workflow' personnel (employees not directly engaged in production). Many of these are in the large specialized sections such as production planning and scheduling, quality inspection and testing, work study, and research and development, which generate standardization and formalization.

To some it may be surprising that the workflow-structured organization is relatively decentralized. The explanation appears to be that when the responsibilities of specialized roles are laid down, and activities are regulated by standardized procedures and records, top management can afford to decentralize because the organizational machine will run as it has been set to run, and decisions will be made in the way they were intended with less need to refer them to the top.

Grouped in the upper left back box are organizations with a high centralization of authority and low structuring of activities. The authority of these organizations is centralized, usually concentrated in a controlling committee outside and above the unit itself, and in most cases such organizations do not structure daily work activities very much. However, their scores on a scale of procedures for standardization of selection, advancement, and so on, indicate that they do standardize or structure the employment activity. They have central recruitment, selection, disciplining and dismissal procedures and the like. Such an organization is called a *personnel bureaucracy*, since it bureaucratizes everything relating to employment, but not the daily work activity to anything like the same degree. Personnel bureaucracies are typically local or central government departments (for example, a municipal education department or the regional division of a government ministry) and the smaller branch factories of large corporations.

In general, there is less formal structuring of activities in service organizations than in manufacturing industries. Also, when service organizations are geographically dispersed over many sites or are publicly owned, the concentration of authority increases and they become personnel bureaucracies. An example of the influence of public ownership was the difference between one bus company owned by a local government authority and another, at the time one of the largest remaining 'private' transport organizations in the country. The central government, through a holding corporation, owned fifty per cent of the equity of the private company, but took no direct part in its operations. They had identical technologies (scores of 6 each on the scale of workflow integration) and were in the same size range (8,618 and 6,300 employees); therefore they are very close in structural profile, except for the higher concentration of authority in the municipal undertaking, which reflects its high dependence on local government.

A cluster of organizations can be seen in the lower left back box, which at first glance are low on both structuring and centralization. This minimal structuring and dispersed authority suggests unregulated chaos. Not so; instead, this indicates that such organizations score low on the structural characteristics because the scales reflect overt regulation. We call such an organization an *implicitly structured organization*. These organizations are run not by explicit regulation but by implicitly transmitted custom, a common condition in small organizations where management and ownership overlap. On investigation, this hypothesis was supported. These implicitly structured organizations are comparatively small factories (within the size range of the sample); they tend to be independent of external links and their scores on concentration of ownership indicate that the operating control of the organization has remained with the directors who own them.

The upper right front box of Figure 2 includes those organizations that are high on both structuring and centralization and which therefore show the characteristics of a workflow bureaucracy (for example, standardization of task-control procedures), as in large manufacturing corporations, together with the characteristics of personnel bureaucracy (for example, centralized authority for decision-making), as in government departments. This was in fact found to be the case. A central government branch factory, government-owned public services and nationalized industries fit this pattern. Thus, we may regard them as examples of *full bureaucracy*.

Analysis of organizational context

Once we have measured organization structure, the question arises: 'Do organizations of different size have different kinds of structure?' Similarly, organizations can range from being technologically very advanced to being very simple, or from being owned and controlled by one man to being owned by many people and controlled (i.e. actually run) by none of them. Clearly we must employ as much vigour in measuring the non-structural or contextual aspects of organizations as we did in measuring the structural factors. To guide the measuring, we have identified the principal dimensions of context as follows:

Origin and history: whether an organization was privately founded and the kinds of changes in ownership, locations, etc. it has experienced.

Ownership and control: the kind of ownership (e.g. private or public) and its concentration in a few hands or dispersion into many.

Size: the number of employees, net assets, market position, etc.

Charter: the number and range of goods and services.

Technology: the degree of integration achieved in an organization's work process.

Location: the number of geographically dispersed operating sites.

Interdependence: the extent to which an organization depends on customers, suppliers, trade unions, any owning groups, etc. Table 2 lists some examples of the information that was obtained.

Exploring structure and context

It has now become possible to explore the relationship between structural and contextual characteristics in a wide range of work organizations. How far, for example, is specialization a function of size? Note that the question is not 'Is specialization a result of large size or is it not?' We are now in a position to rephrase the question: *To what extent* is size associated with specialization? The correlation between size and overall role-specialization in the first sample was 0·75 – size is thus the most important single element. But what part do other factors play? The correlation of 'workflow integration' – a scale that has been developed for measuring comparative technology (see Table 2) – and overall specialization was 0·38. This is not very large in itself, but since there is no relationship between size and technology (correlation of 0·08), we should expect an analysis using both dimensions to produce a higher relationship than size alone. This is in fact what happens, and the multiple correlation of size to technology and specialization is 0·81. Thus, knowing an organization's score on our scales of size *and* technology, we can predict to within relatively close limits what its specialization score will be. Likewise, knowing an organization's dependence on other organizations and its geographical dispersion over sites tells

Table 2. Some contextual scales

Workflow integration
A highly workflow-integrated technology is signified by:
1. Automatic repeat-cycle equipment, self adjusting.
2. Single-purpose equipment.
3. Fixed 'line' or sequence of operations.
4. Single input point at commencement of 'line'.
5. No waiting time between operations.
6. No 'buffer stocks' between operations.
7. Breakdown anywhere stops workflow immediately.
8. Outputs of workflow (production) segments/departments become inputs of others, i.e. flow from department to department throughout.
9. Operations evaluated by measurement techniques against precise specifications.
A technology low in workflow integration is at the opposite extreme on these items.

Vertical integration (component scale of dependence)
1. Integration with suppliers: ownership and tied supply/long contracts/single orders.
2. Sensitivity of outputs volume to consumer influence: outputs for schedule and call off/orders/stock.
3. Integration with customers: ownership and tied market/long-term contracts/regular contracts/single orders.
4. Dependence of organization on its largest customer: sole/major/medium/minor outlet.
5. Dependence of largest customer on organization: sole/major/medium/minor supplier.

Dependence
1. Status of organizational unit: branch/head branch/legal subsidiary/principal unit.
2. Unit size as a percentage of parent-group size.
3. Representation on policy-making boards.
4. Number of specialist services contracted out.
5. Vertical integration.

---

us a great deal about the likely centralization of authority in its structure (multiple correlation of 0·75).

These relationships between context and structure we have found to be reasonably stable in surveys of different samples. Where differences in the relationships have been found they have been easily related to the varying characteristics of the sample studied. In general, the framework has been adequate for thinking about the degree of constraint that contextual factors place on the design of organizational structures. The degree of constraint appears to be substantial (about 50 per cent of the variability between structures may be directly related to contextual features such as size, technology, interdependence, etc.) but it allows considerable opportunities for choice and variation in particular organizations based on the attitudes and views of top management.

In other words, context is a determining factor – perhaps overall the determining factor – which designs, shapes and modifies the structure of any organization. But within these contextual limits top management has plenty of leeway left to make its influence felt – 50 per cent is a major margin of freedom. With this approach we can discuss a number of basic issues of organizational design, such as those indicated at the beginning of this article. And we can conduct the discussion on the basis of a number of comparative empirical findings, which inevitably underline the range of variation possible, rather than merely on individual views and experiences, which inevitably tend towards dogmatic over-generalization. The two issues we will focus on are the relationship between size and formalization (paperwork procedures) and the effects of technology on organization structure.

Formalization of procedures

Using the measures that we have developed we can explore systematically the relationship between a structural feature of organization, such as the degree of formalization of paperwork procedures, and a contextual one, such as the size of operation (indicated by the number of personnel employed).

Formalization indicates the extent to which rules, procedures, instructions and communications are written down. How does the weight of documentation vary from organization to organization? Definitions of thirty-eight documents have been assembled, each of which can be used by any known work organization. They range from, for example, organization charts, memo forms, agendas and minutes to written terms of reference, job descriptions, records of maintenance performed, statements of tasks done or to be done on the output, handbooks and manuals of procedures. Scores range from 4 in a single-product foodstuffs factory where there are few such documents to 49 in a metals-processing plant where each routine procedure is documented in detail.

A wide range of differences in paperwork usage is found in all our surveys. What relation does this have to the size of organization? The correlations found range from 0·55 to 0·83 in different samples, demonstrating a strong tendency for the two to be mutually implicit while still allowing for many exceptions. Figure 3 gives examples of three typical organizations and also of two organizations that have considerably less paperwork, and two that have considerably more, than would be expected from their size alone.

Three typical organizations

Size:	large (6,500 employees)	medium (2,900)	small (300)
Ownership:	limited company	municipal	subsidiary of a limited company
Purpose:	manufacturing	public service	food manufacturing
Formalization score:	49	27	4

Four unusual organizations

Size:	large (16,500)	small (300)
Ownership:	municipal	government
Purpose:	professional service	manufacturing
Formalization score:	25	37

Size:	medium (1,400)	medium (1,400)
Ownership:	family	family
Purpose:	retailing	manufacturing
Formalization score:	7	45

Figure 3 Formalization: examples from seven organizations

The four unusual organizations emphasize the range of variation possible and lead us to look for factors other than size in explanation. Ownership patterns may play a part, the government-owned plant having more formalization than would be expected, the family retail firm having less. But the family manufacturing firm has considerably more, so the attitudes of its top management and their belief in the necessity for formal procedures become relevant. Similarly, the presence of professional staff in the municipal service is accompanied by the belief that they do not require such a high degree of control over their jobs because of their professional training.

One further important factor relating to formalization is clear: in our comparative surveys of international samples we have found that formalization is the one aspect of structure that clearly distinguishes US and Canadian organizations from British ones. Size for size, North American organizations have a formalization score that is on average 50 per cent greater than their British counterparts. Since the relationship with size holds up in both cultures, and since in general American organizations are bigger than British ones, the average American manager is subjected to considerably more control through paperwork procedures than his British opposite number. The reason for this cultural difference we can only speculate on. It may be that in the more homogeneous British culture more can be taken for granted, whereas in the more heterogeneous American culture controls, even in smaller organizations, must be spelled out formally to be effective.

The effects of technology on organizations

Does technology determine organization? Is the form of organization in a chemical plant, for instance, dictated by the fact that it is a chemical plant: that is, by its highly automated equipment and continuous-flow procedures? And is the organization of a batch-production engineering factory shaped by the way its work is done: that is, by its rows of machine tools and its varying batches?

These are contentious questions. They also ask how far the number of levels of management, the centralization of major decisions, the proliferation of standard procedures, the development of specialist 'service' sections and the many other features of the structure of an organization depend on its technology.

In a study that has had considerable impact on both management- and behavioural-science writers, Joan Woodward in *Management and Technology* maintains that 'It was possible to trace a cause-and-effect relationship between a system of production and its associated organizational pattern and, as a result, to predict what the organizational requirements of a firm were likely to be, given its production system.'

Woodward took this view as a result of comparing as many as eighty firms on a unit and small batch, large batch and mass, and flow process classification. She found, for example, that the line of command from the chief executive of each firm was shortest in unit and small batch firms, lengthened in large batch and mass, and was longest in process firms. Another example of this relationship was the ratio of managers to total personnel, which also increased from unit to process technology.

In contrast, it appeared that the spans of control of the first-line production supervisors were widest in large batch and mass production (an average of forty-six), but dropped away in unit and small batch to an average of twenty-one and in process industries to an average of fourteen. Other suggested examples of this pattern were clear definition of duties and amount of paperwork, which were also greatest in large batch and mass technology.

Woodward's study immediately raised the question as to whether it was possible to develop general management principles of organization, as advocated by such writers as Fayol, Urwick, Gulick and Brown. Woodward maintained that this was now no longer possible. The principles that they had advocated, such as the necessity of clear lines of authority and responsibility (one man, one boss, etc.) and limited spans of control for effective supervision, might well apply in large batch and mass-production firms, since they rested primarily on the experience of managers and consultants in this range of technology. But outside this range, in unit and jobbing and process technologies, different principles would probably be required.

The studies that we have carried out include replications of the Woodward work, since technology is one of a range of contextual factors that we examined. Equipped with a much more comprehensive analysis of organization structure than Woodward we can explore more systematically what are the *relative* effects of technology on organization structure.

In addition to using Woodward's categories, the present research programme also developed a measure of technology based on the items in Table 2 and labelled *Workflow integration*. This discriminates between organizations on the basis of the rigidity or flexibility of the sequence of operations carried out by the equipment on the work. This has affinities with the Woodward classification but is not equivalent to it. Thus it was possible to examine the relationships of these two measures with the dimensions of organization structure.

Did the organizations with the most process-oriented technologies have the largest scores on specialization of management roles, standardization of procedures, etc.? In the first study, taking manufacturing organizations only, a correlation of 0.52 was found between Woodward technology and standardization. This would suggest considerable support for the proposition that the technology of manufacture has considerable bearing on the management structure. But the advantage of a survey that takes a range of factors into account becomes immediately apparent when we consider their relationship. The correlation of size to specialization is 0.83 and to standardization 0.65, both of which are considerably higher than technology relationships. When we recall that size and technology are correlated among manufacturing organizations, and the effects of size are discounted by the technique known as partial correlation, then the remaining relationships between technology and structure are slight indeed (0.26 with specialization, 0.07 with standardization). In general, our studies have confirmed that the relationships of technology to the main structural dimensions in manufacturing organizations are always very small and play a secondary role relative to other contextual features such as size and interdependence with other organizations (such as owning group, customers, suppliers, etc.). Technology is shown to be related to manufacturing organization structures in a number of highly specific job ratios that we consider under *Configuration* in Table 1.

The ratio of subordinates to first-line supervisors is the only point at which the Woodward results and the present results agree exactly. Supervisors have most subordinates in large batch and mass production. This is where each foreman often has forty or fifty workers turning out large quantities of standard items, whereas in jobbing or in process plants he has a smaller group. Hence the proportion of employees in inspection work and maintenance work is also greatest at the large batch stage and lowest in both unit production and processing. The proportion in production control is highest from unit or jobbing to the mass stage, dropping away in process technologies where production control is built into the processes themselves and does not require the clerical and progress-chasing effort imposed by complex assemblies.

The detailed examination of these features is interesting, but it is of much less consequence than their implications taken as a whole. What is distinctive about them, as against the range of organizational characteristics not related to technology?

The first-mentioned characteristic of the ratio of subordinates to first-line supervisors is an element of organization at the level of the operative and his immediate boss. Obviously, the number of men a supervisor requires to run a row of lathes differs from the number he requires to run the more continuous integrated workflow of an automatic transfer machine. Thus the subordinate/supervisor ratio is an aspect of organization that reflects activities directly bound up with the technology itself. Also, it is the variety of equipment and products in batch production that demands larger numbers of inspectors and of maintenance personnel; unit and process technologies are less demanding in this respect. It is the complexity of technology both in variety of equipment and in sequences of operations that requires relatively larger numbers of production-control personnel than the more automated types of process technology.

The point is made more clearly by the contrast with activities such as accounting or market research, which are not directly implicated in the work technology itself: here, research results show no connection with technological factors.

As a result, it may be suggested that the connections between the workflow-integration measure of technology and the numbers engaged in employment and in purchasing and warehousing may be due to the intermediate position of these activities. They are closer to the production work itself than, for example, accounting, but not as close as inspection.

Among the extensive range of organizational features studied, therefore, only those directly centred on the production workflow itself show any connection with technology; these are all 'job counts' of employees on production-linked activities. Away from the shop floor, technology appears to have little influence on organizational structure.

Further developments

Our continuing research programme is exploring new areas. For example, what changes in organization structure takes place over time? In one small study we have already undertaken, fourteen organizations were re-studied after a period of four to five years. The organizations were all manufacturing firms and workflow bureaucracies in terms of Figure 2. There was an overall decrease in size from 5 to 10 per cent, as measured by number of employees, but the other contextual features remained constant. In spite of this stability there was a clear tendency for structuring scores to increase (more specialization, standardization, formalization), but for centralization to decrease. If within certain limits imposed by the organization's context top management is able to accentuate one of two broad strategies of control, *either* retaining most decision-making at the top and tolerating wider spans of control *or* delegating decisions to lower-level specialists and relying on procedures and forms to maintain control, then on this evidence they are consistently choosing the second alternative, at least in manufacturing.

Clearly, more evidence is required before the significance of this trend can be evaluated. And evidence is also required on the *processes* by which organization structures are changed. What are the interdepartmental power struggles, the interpersonal conflicts, the pressures for and resistance to proposed changes that make up the evolving structure as it responds to changes in the organization's context? Studies have already been carried out that show a clear relationship of structure to organizational climate and morale. One study, for example, has shown that greater structuring of activities is accompanied by more formal interpersonal relationships and that greater centralization of authority leads to a greater degree of 'social distance' between the levels in an organization: social distance being the degree to which a manager regards his supervisor as a superior and not as a colleague as well. These important structural constraints need to be more fully investigated.

Implications of the research

It has long been realized that an organization's context is important in the development of its structure. What is surprising is the magnitude of the relationships outlined above. People often speak as if the personalities of the founder and directors of a business had been the most important influence in creating the present organization. Other people point to historical crises or the vagaries of government policy as being the stimuli that caused the business to develop in a particular way. Though we would certainly expect personality, events and policies to play their part, the fact that information relating solely to an organization's context enables us to make such accurate predictions indicates that context is more important than is generally realized.

The manager of the future will have available to him ever-increasing amounts of information, and will be anxious to know what signals he should primarily attend to. If he knows what is crucial to organization functioning he can manage by exception. What types and amounts of environmental change can occur before internal adjustments must be made to maintain performance?

The fact that there is now available a reliable system of comparative measures of organization context and structure enables the many managers who have collaborated in these surveys to place their organizations in relation to others more easily and to work towards evaluating the costs and benefits of the forms of management structure that could help them to meet the challenges of the future.

Bibliography

The full details of the research described in this paper are given in:

D. S. PUGH and D. J. HICKSON (1976), *Organizational Structure in its Context: The Aston Programme I*, Gower Publishing.

D. S. PUGH and C. R. HININGS (eds.) (1976), *Organizational Structure Extensions and Replications: The Aston Programme II*, Gower Publishing.

D. S. PUGH and R. L. PAYNE (eds.) (1977), *Organizational Behaviour in its Context: The Aston Programme III*, Gower Publishing.

D. J. HICKSON and C. J. McMILLAN (eds.) (1981), *Organization and Nation: The Aston Programme IV*, Gower Publishing.

3   O. E. Williamson

The Modern Corporation

From *The Economic Institutions of Capitalism: Firms, Markets, Relational Contracting*, The Free Press, 1985, chapter 11

There is virtual unanimity for the proposition that the modern corporation is a complex and important economic institution. There is much less agreement on what its attributes are and on how and why it has successively evolved to take on its current configuration. While I agree that there have been a number of contributing factors, I submit that the modern corporation is mainly to be understood as the product of a series of organizational innovations that have had the purpose and effect of economizing on transaction costs.

Note that I do not argue that the modern corporation is to be understood exclusively in those terms. Clearly there have been other contributing factors, of which the quest for monopoly gains is one and the imperatives of technology are another. Those mainly have a bearing on market shares and on the absolute size of specific technological units, however; the distribution of economic activity, as between firms and markets, and the internal organization (including both the shape and the aggregate size) of the firm are not explained, except perhaps in trivial ways, in those terms. Inasmuch as shape and composition are core issues, a theory of the modern corporation that does not address them is, at best, seriously incomplete.

Specifically, the study of the modern corporation should extend beyond vertical integration to concern itself with and provide consistent explanations for the following features of the organization of economic activity: What economic purposes are served by the widespread adoption of divisionalization? What ramifications, if any, does internal organization have for the longstanding dilemma posed by the separation of ownership from control? Can the 'puzzle' of the conglomerate be unravelled? Do similar considerations apply in assessing multinational enterprise? Can an underlying rationale be provided for the reported association between technological innovation and direct foreign investment?

Key legal features of the corporation – limited liability and the transferability of ownership – are taken as given. Failure to discuss them does not reflect a judgment that they are either irrelevant or uninteresting. The main focus of this chapter, however, is on the internal organization of the corporation. Since any of a number of internal structures is consistent with these legal features, an explanation for the specific organizational innovations that were actually adopted evidently resides elsewhere. Among the more significant of those innovations, and the ones addressed here, are the development of line-and-staff organization by the railroads; selective forward integration by manufacturers into distribution; the development of the divisionalized corporate form; the evolution of the conglomerate; and the appearance of the multinational enterprise. The first three changes have been studied by business historians, the contributions of Chandler (1962; 1977) being the most ambitious and notable.

Railroad organization in the nineteenth century is examined in section 1. The multidivisional structure is described and interpreted in section 2. Conglomerate organization and multinational organization are treated in section 3. The central proposition repeated throughout is this: Organization form matters.

1. Railroad organization

The 1840s mark the beginning of a great wave of organizational change that has evolved into the modern corporation (Chandler, 1977). According to Stuart Bruchey, the fifteenth-century merchant of Venice would have understood the form of organization and methods of managing men, records, and investment used by Baltimore merchants in 1790 (1956, pp. 370–71). Those practices evidently remained quite serviceable until after the 1840s. The two most significant developments were the appearance of the railroads and, in response, forward integration by manufacturers into distribution. Selective forward integration is described and interpreted in Chapter 5. The experience of the railroads has yet to be addressed.

Although a number of technological developments – including the telegraph (Chandler, 1977, p. 189), the development of continuous process machinery (pp. 252–3), the refinement of interchangeable parts manufacture (pp. 75–7), and related mass manufacturing techniques (chap. 8) – contributed to organizational changes in the second half of the nineteenth century, none was more important than the railroads (Porter and Livesay, 1971, p. 55). Not only did the railroads pose distinctive organizational problems of their own, but the incentive to integrate forward from manufacturing into distribution would have been much less without the low-cost, reliable, all-weather transportation afforded by the railroads.

The appearance and purported importance of the railroads have been matters of great interest to economic historians. But with very few exceptions the organizational – as opposed to the technological – significance of the railroads has been neglected. Thus Robert Fogel (1964) and Albert Fishlow (1965) 'investigated the railroad as a construction activity and as a means of transport, but not as an organizational form. As with most economists, the internal workings of the railroad organizations were ignored. This appears to be the result of an implicit assumption that the organization form used to accomplish an objective does not matter' (Temin, 1981, p. 3).

The economic success of the railroads entailed more, however, than the substitution of one technology (rails) for another (canals). Rather, organizational aspects also required attention. As Chandler puts it:

[The] safe, regular reliable movement of goods and passengers, as well as the continuing maintenance and repair of locomotives, rolling stock, and track, roadbed, stations, roundhouses, and other equipment, required the creation of a sizable administrative organization. It meant the employment of a set of managers to supervise these functional activities over an extensive geographical area; and the appointment of an administrative command of middle and top executives to monitor, evaluate, and coordinate the work of managers responsible for the day-to-day operations. It meant, too, the formulation of brand new types of internal administrative procedures and accounting and statistical controls. Hence, the operational requirements of the railroads demanded the creation of the first administrative hierarchies in American business. [1977, p. 87]

To be sure, that can be disputed. Markets, after all, can and do perform many of those functions. What is it about the 'operational requirements' of the railroads that was responsible for the displacement of markets by hierarchies? Does similar reasoning apply to other transportation systems, such as trucking?

The 'natural' railroad units, as they first evolved, were lines of about fifty miles in length. Those roads employed about fifty workers and were administered by a superintendent and several managers of functional activities (Chandler, 1977, p. 96). That was adequate as long as traffic flows were uncomplicated and short hauls prevailed. The full promise of the railroads could be realized, however, only if traffic densities were increased and longer hauls introduced. How was that to be effected?

In principle, successive end-to-end systems could be joined by contract. The resulting contracts would be tightly bilateral, however, since investments in site-specific assets by each party were considerable. Contracting difficulties of two kinds would have to be faced. Not only would the railroads need to reach agreement on how to deal with a series of complex operating matters – equipment utilization, costing, and maintenance; adapting cooperatively to unanticipated disturbances; assigning responsibility for customer complaints, breakdown, and so on – but problems of customers contracting with a set of autonomous end-to-end suppliers would have to be worked out.

There were several possibilities. One would be to be patient: The marvel of the market would work things out. A second would be to move to the opposite extreme and coordinate through comprehensive planning. A third would be to evolve organizational innovations located in between.

David Evans and Sanford Grossman interpret the railroad response in market terms. They note that 'market systems in which property ownership is dispersed among numerous self-interested businesses and individuals have demonstrated a remarkable ability to coordinate the provision of goods and services' (1983, p. 96), and they specifically apply this argument to the railroads:

The experience of the railroads in the 19th century ... demonstrates how the market system encourages physical coordination. Many separate companies built segments of our railroad system during the mid-19th century. By interconnecting with each other and enabling produce and passengers to transfer easily between railroads, these companies were able to increase revenues and profits. [Evans and Grossman, 1983, p. 103]

Evans and Grossman support this by reference to the study by George Taylor and Irene Neu, who reported that traffic between New York City and Boston moved easily over tracks owned by four different companies in 1861 (Taylor and Neu, 1956, p. 19). They also cite Chandler in support of their argument that 'the market provides strong incentives for physical coordination without common ownership' (Evans and Grossman, 1983, p. 104, n. 22).

Evidently there is more to railroad organization than 'physical coordination,' however. Otherwise the natural railroad units of fifty miles in length would have remained intact. And there is also more to railroad organization than unified ownership. Thus the Western and Albany road, which was just over 150 miles in length and was built in three sections, each operated as a separate division with its own set of functional managers, experienced severe problems (Chandler, 1977, pp. 96–7). As a consequence a new organizational form was fashioned whereby the first 'formal administrative structure manned by full-time salaried managers' in the United States appeared (pp. 97–8).

That structure was progressively perfected. The organizational innovation that the railroads eventually evolved is characterized by Chandler as the 'decentralized line-and-staff concept of organization.' It provided that 'the managers on the line of authority were responsible for ordering men involved with the basic function of the enterprise, and other functional managers (the staff executives) were responsible for setting standards' (Chandler, 1977, p. 106). Geographic divisions were defined, and the superintendents in charge were held responsible for the 'day-to-day movement of trains and traffic by an express delegation of authority' (p. 102). The division superintendents were on the 'direct line of authority from the president through the general superintendent' (p. 106), and the functional managers within the geographic divisions – who dealt with transportation, motive power, maintenance of way, passenger, freight, and accounting – reported to them rather than to their functional superiors at the central office (pp. 106–7). That administrative apparatus permitted individual railroads to operate thousands of miles of track by 1893.[1]

To be sure, that falls well short of central planning. Moreover, the contractual difficulties posed by coordination and efficient utilization to which Chandler referred were not the only factors that elicited the large system response. Chandler also gives great weight to the strategic purposes served (1977, chap. 5). The latter, however, also has contractual origins: Unable to control prices and allocate traffic through interfirm organization, the railroads were driven to merger. Thus whereas there is a widely held view that express or tacit collusion is easy to effectuate – John Kenneth Galbraith opines that 'the firm, in tacit collaboration with other firms in the industry, has wholly sufficient power to set and maintain prices' (1967, p. 200) – that is repeatedly refuted by the evidence. The history of cartel failures among the railroads is especially instructive. The early railroads evolved a series of progressively more elaborate interfirm structures in an effort to curb competitive pricing. The first involved informal alliances, which worked well until 'the volume of through traffic began to fall off and competitive pressures increased.' With the onset of the depression in 1873 there began an 'increasingly desperate search for traffic . . . Secret

1. Each of the ten largest railroads operated more than five thousand miles of track in 1893 (Chandler, 1977, p. 168).

rebating intensified. Soon roads were openly reducing rates.' The railroads thereupon decided to 'transform weak, tenuous alliances into strong, carefully organized, well-managed federations' (Chandler, 1977, pp. 134, 137). The membership of the federations was expanded, and other federations in other geographic regions appeared. As Albert Fink, who headed up the largest such federation realized, however, 'the only bond which holds this government together is the intelligence and good faith of the parties composing it' (Chandler, 1977, p. 140). To rectify that weakness, Fink urged the railroads to seek legislation that would give the actions of the federation legal standing.

Lack of legal sanctions means that loyal members of the cartel must exact penalties against deviants in the market place. Unless such disciplinary actions (mainly price cuts) can be localized, every member of the cartel, loyalist and defector alike, suffers. That is a very severe (if little remarked) limitation on the efficacy of cartels. Inasmuch as national legislation was not forthcoming, Fink and his associates 'found to their sorrow that they could not rely on the intelligence and good faith of railroad executives' (Chandler, 1977, p. 141). In the end, the railroads turned to merger. The high-powered incentives of autonomous ownership evidently presented too strong a temptation for cheating in an industry where sunk costs were substantial.

The railroad industry thus progressed from small, end-to-end units with fifty miles of track to systems of several hundred and, eventually, to several thousand miles of track. Market coordination was thus supplanted by administrative organization in substantial degree:

The fast-freight lines, the cooperatives, and finally the traffic departments of the larger roads had completed the transformation from market coordination to administrative coordination in American overland transportation. A multitude of commission agents, freight forwarders, and express companies, as well as stage and wagon companies, and canal, river, lake, and coastal shipping lines disappeared. In their place stood a small number of large multi-unit railroad enterprises . . . By the 1880s the transformation begun in the 1840s was virtually completed. [Chandler, 1977, p. 130]

To be sure, transaction cost economics does not predict the final configuration in detail. It is nevertheless noteworthy that (1) efficient technological units were very small in relation to efficient economic units in this industry, which is to say that organizational rather than technological factors were responsible for the creation of large systems; (2) transaction cost economics predicts that severe problems will arise in attempting to coordinate autonomous end-to-end systems that are characterized by site specificity by contract;[2] and (3) the limits of cartels also have organizational origins and are evident upon posing problems of interfirm organization in contracting terms. That the trucking industry, which does not have the same site specificity (mainly roadbed) features, should differ from the railroad industry in significant respects is furthermore predicted by transaction cost reasoning. (Indeed, the absence of site-specific investments in the trucking industry make it a much better candidate than the railroads to illustrate the Evans and Grossman argument that market coordination is a marvel.[3] If Chandler's account is accurate, the railroad industry illustrates the importance of hierarchy.)

Operating the large railroad systems was possible only upon solving administrative complexities which greatly exceeded those faced by earlier business enterprises. As discussed below, the hierarchical structure that the railroad managers crafted was broadly consistent with the principles of efficient hierarchical decomposition stated by Simon. Thus, support activities (lower-frequency dynamics) were split off from operations (higher-frequency dynamics), and the linkages within each of those classes of activity were stronger than the linkages between. The organizational innovation, in Chandler's judgment, paved the way for modern business enterprise.

2. The M-form innovation

2.1 The transformation

The most significant organizational innovation of the twentieth century was the development in the 1920s of the multidivisional structure. That development was little noted and not widely appreciated, however, as late as 1960. Leading management texts extolled the virtues of 'basic depart-

---

2 . Other types of specific assets also influenced railroad organization. In particular, although steam locomotives were assets on wheels, they required an inordinate amount of preventive and corrective maintenance. A resale market in steam locomotives was impaired by the acquired knowledge embedded in the mechanics familiar with the idiosyncratic attributes of each. (The diesel locomotive, by comparison, was less idiosyncratic in maintenance cost respects.)

3. Trucking is also a much better candidate for deregulation than the railroads. To be sure, no one is urging a return of the railroads to their regulatory status of 1980. That there is greater dissatisfaction with deregulation of the railroads than with trucking is, however, predictable upon examining their transaction cost features. See Christopher Conte, 'Push for tighter U.S. supervision of railroads is a threat to success of Reagan deregulators,' *Wall Street Journal*, January 7, 1985, p. 50.

mentation' and 'line and staff authority relationships,' but the special importance of multidivisionalization went unremarked.[4]

Chandler's pathbreaking study of business history, *Strategy and Structure*, simply bypassed this management literature. He advanced the thesis that 'changing developments in business organization presented a challenging area for comparative analysis' and observed that 'the study of [organizational] innovation seemed to furnish the proper focus for such an investigation' (Chandler, 1962 [1966 edition], p. 2). Having identified the multidivisional structure as one of the most important such innovations, he proceeded to trace its origins, identify the factors that gave rise to its appearance, and describe the subsequent diffusion of that organization form. It was uninformed and untenable to argue that organization form was of no account after the appearance of Chandler's book.

The leading figures in the creation of the multidivisional (or M-form) structure were Pierre S. du Pont and Alfred P. Sloan; the period was the early 1930s; the firms were du Pont and General Motors; and the organizational strain of trying to cope with economic adversity under the old structure was the occasion to innovate in both. The structures of the two companies, however, were different.

Du Pont was operating under the centralized, functionally departmentalized or unitary (U-form) structure. General Motors, by contrast, had been operated more like a holding company (H-form) by William Durant, whose genius in perceiving market opportunities in the automobile industry (Livesay, 1979, pp. 232–4) evidently did not extend to organization. John Lee Pratt, who served as an assistant to Durant and as chairman of the Appropriations Committee after Du Pont took an equity position in General Motors, observed that 'under Mr. Durant's regime we were never able to get things under control' (Chandler, 1966, p. 154). A leading reason is that the Executive Committee, which consisted of Division Managers, was highly politicized: 'When one of them had a project, why he would vote for his fellow members; if they would vote for his project, he would vote for theirs. It was a sort of horse trading' (Pratt, quoted by Chandler, 1966, p. 154).

Chandler summarizes the defects of the large U-form enterprise in the following way:

The inherent weakness in the centralized, functionally departmentalized operating company ... became critical only when the administrative load on the senior

---

4. The treatment of these matters by Harold Koontz and Cyril O'Donnell (1955) is representative.

executives increased to such an extent that they were unable to handle their entrepreneurial responsibilities efficiently. This situation arose when the operations of the enterprise became too complex and the problems of coordination, appraisal, and policy formulation too intricate for a small number of top officers to handle both long-run, entrepreneurial, and short-run operational administrative activities. [1966, pp. 382–3]

The ability of the management to handle the volume and complexity of the demands placed upon it became strained and even collapsed. Unable meaningfully to identify with or contribute to the realization of global goals, managers in each of the functional parts attended to what they perceived to be operational subgoals instead (Chandler, 1966, p. 156). In the language of transaction cost economics, bounds on rationality were reached as the U-form structure labored under a communication overload while the pursuit of subgoals by the functional parts (sales, engineering, production) was partly a manifestation of opportunism.

The M-form structure fashioned by du Pont and Sloan involved the creation of semiautonomous operating divisions (mainly profit centers) organized along product, brand, or geographic lines. The operating affairs of each were managed separately. More than a change in decomposition rules was needed, however, for the M-form to be fully effective. Du Pont and Sloan also created a general office 'consisting of a number of powerful general executives and large advisory and financial staffs' (Chandler, 1977, p. 460) to monitor divisional performance, allocate resources among divisions, and engage in strategic planning. The reasons for the success of the M-form innovation are summarized by Chandler:

The basic reason for its success was simply that it clearly removed the executives responsible for the destiny of the entire enterprise from the more routine operational activities, and so gave them the time, information, and even psychological commitment for long-term planning and appraisal . . .

[The] new structure left the broad strategic decisions as to the allocation of existing resources and the acquisition of new ones in the hands of a top team of generalists. Relieved of operating duties and tactical decisions, a general executive was less likely to reflect the position of just one part of the whole. [1966, pp. 382–3]

In contrast with the holding company – which is also a divisionalized form but has little general office capability and hence is little more than a corporate shell – the M-form organization adds (1) a strategic planning and resource allocation capability and (2) monitoring and control apparatus. As a consequence, cash flows are reallocated among divisions to favor high-yield uses, and internal incentive and control instruments are exercised in a discriminating way. In short, the M-form corporation takes on many of the properties of (and is usefully regarded as) a miniature capital market,[5] which is a much more ambitious concept of the corporation than the term 'holding company' contemplates.

2.2 An information processing interpretation

Most recent treatments of the corporation nevertheless accord scant attention to the architecture of the firm and focus entirely on incentive features instead. In fact, however, organization form matters even in a firm in which incentive problems attributable to opportunism are missing. The studies of hierarchy by W. Ross Ashby (1960) and by Herbert Simon (1962) are germane.

Ashby established that all adaptive systems that have a capacity to respond to a bimodal distribution of disturbances – some being disturbances in degree; other being disturbances in kind – will be characterized by double feedback. The rudimentary model is shown in Figure 11-1. Disturbances in degree are handled in the primary feedback loop (or operating part) within the context of extant decision rules. Disturbances in kind involve longer-run adjustments in which parameter changes are introduced or new rules are developed in the secondary (or strategic) feedback loop. The second feedback loop is needed because the repertoire of the primary loop is limited – which is a concession to bounded rationality. Evolutionary systems that are subject to such bimodal disturbances will, under natural selection, necessarily develop two readily distinguishable feedbacks (Ashby, 1960, p. 131).

Simon's discussion of the organizational division of decision-making labor in the firm is in the same spirit. From 'the information processing point of view, division of labor means factoring the total system of decisions that need to be made into relatively independent subsystems, each one of which can be designed with only minimal concern for its interaction with the others' (Simon, 1973, p. 270). That applies to both technical and temporal aspects of the organization. In both respects the object is to recognize and give effect to conditions of near decomposability. That is accomplished by grouping the operating parts into separable entities within which interactions are strong and between which they are weak and by making temporal distinctions of a strategic versus operating kind. Problems are thus factored in such a way that the higher-frequency (or short-run)

---

5. Richard Heflebower (1960) and Armen Alchian (1969) also impute capital market resource allocation and control functions to the M-form corporation.

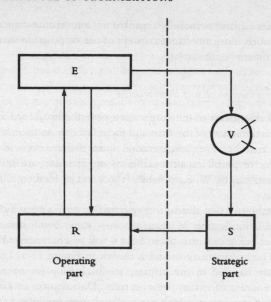

Figure 11-1 Double feedback

dynamics are associated with the operating parts while the lower-frequency (or long-run) dynamics are associated with the strategic system (Simon, 1962, p. 477). Those operating and strategic distinctions correspond with the lower and higher levels in the organizational hierarchy, respectively. They furthermore correspond with the primary and secondary feedback loops to which Ashby referred.

2.3 Governance

Effective divisionalization requires more than mere decomposition. Otherwise the H-form would have been an adequate answer to the strains that appear as the (indecomposable) U-form structure was scaled up.

Indeed, in a team theory world in which managers are assumed to share identical preferences, the problem of organization is precisely one of decomposing the enterprise in efficient information processing respects (Marschak and Radner, 1972; Geanakoplos and Milgrom, 1984). As noted in Chapter 2, team theory combines the assumption of bounded rationality with non-self-interest-seeking. If, however, the managers of the firm are given to opportunism, additional problems of incentive alignment, decision review, auditing, dispute resolution, and the like must be confronted. Those who invented the M-form structure were aware of those needs and made provision for them.

Opportunism in the H-form enterprise can take several forms. For one thing, subsidiaries that have preemptive claims against their own earnings are unlikely to return those resources to the center but will 'reinvest' to excess instead.[6] Additionally, since the secondary feedback loop has limited competence to evaluate performance, costs are apt to escalate. If subsidiaries enjoy relief from market tests because of corporate cross-subsidization, moreover, further cost excesses will appear. Finally, partisan decision-making of the kind that Pratt associated with General Motors in the Durant era may appear.

The M-form structure removes the general office executives from partisan involvement in the functional parts and assigns operating responsibilities to the divisions. The general office, moreover, is supported by an elite staff that has the capacity to evaluate divisional performance. Not only, therefore, is the goal structure altered in favor of enterprise-wide considerations, but an improved information base permits rewards and penalties to be assigned to divisions on a more discriminating basis, and resources can be reallocated within the firm from less to more productive uses. A concept of the firm as an internal capital market thus emerges.

Effective multidivisionalization thus involves the general office in the following set of activities: (1) the identification of separable economic activities within the firm; (2) according quasi-autonomous standing (usually of a profit center nature) to each; (3) monitoring the efficiency performance of each division; (4) awarding incentives; (5) allocating cash flows to high-yield uses; and (6) performing strategic planning (diversification, acquisition, divestiture, and related activities) in other respects. The M-form structure is thus one that *combines* the divisionalization concept with an internal control and strategic decision-making capability.

2.4 An isomorphism

Although the economic correspondences are imperfect, it is nevertheless of interest that the U-form, H-form, and M-form structures bear a formal

6. To be sure, the H-form firm could encourage divisions to invest in one another. Serious problems of information display, evaluation, auditing, and the like are posed for which a central agency is apt to enjoy advantages, however – which is to say that internal resource allocation among divisions can benefit from the support of a general office.

relation to the basic contracting schema set out in Chapter 1. Figure 11-2 displays the parallel relations.

Thus whereas the contracting schema was developed in terms of two production technologies ($k = 0$ and $k > 0$), the organizational distinction to be made is between two information processing technologies (centralized and decentralized, respectively). Given the requisite preconditions[7] and assuming the absence of opportunism, the $k > 0$/decentralized technologies

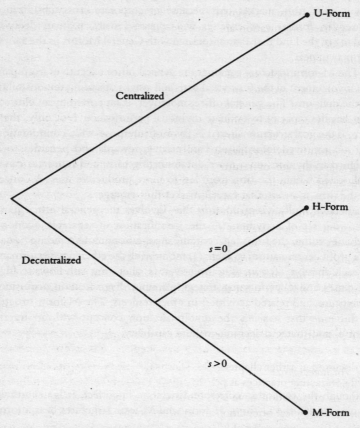

Figure 11-2   Organizational choices

7. The preconditions in the production technology case go to specifying the stochastic structure of demand. In the information technology case, the issue is one of firm size and complexity. (The M-form structure is unneeded in small and simple firms.)

will yield a superior result. But the $k > 0$/decentralized technologies also pose serious hazards of opportunism. Unless safeguards can be devised, the full benefits of the $k > 0$/decentralized technologies will go unrealized.

The $s = 0$ condition reflects a refusal to safeguard a contract for which nonredeployable assets are at hazard. The organizational correspondence is the H-form firm. The $s > 0$ conditions reflects a decision to provide protective governance. The M-form firm is the organizational counterpart for contractual safeguards. Thus the full benefits of the $k > 0$/decentralized organization are achieved only if $s > 0$/M-form governance is provided.

Indeed, the contracting analogy can be carried further by regarding investors who supply capital to a firm as the counterpart of the suppliers of intermediate product in the nonstandard contracting context. Recall that suppliers of intermediate product were willing to employ any technology and would accept any contract for which expected breakeven could be projected. The same is true of suppliers of capital: They will invest in any firm with any organization form on terms such that a competitive (risk-adjusted) rate of return can be projected. This, however, merely reflects the outcome of a competitive market process. More germane to our purposes here is the following. Although firms that employ an inferior (U-form) information technology or that do not safeguard the superior technology against the hazards of opportunism (H-form) may still be able to raise capital if their product line is sufficiently strong (e.g. they enjoy patent protection), they could raise capital on better terms if a superior information technology supported by safeguards were to be employed – which is what the M-form structure adds to decentralization.

3. Applications: conglomerate and multinational enterprise

As discussed in earlier chapters, the inhospitality tradition regarded nonstandard contracting practices as presumptively unlawful. Nonstandard internal forms of organization have also been regarded with deep suspicion. The same technological orientation to economic organization plainly informed both of those approaches. Unless a clear-cut technological justification for the contracting practices or organizational structure in question could be discerned, antitrust specialists were quick to ascribe antisocial purpose and effect. Transaction cost economics regards nonstandard forms of market and internal organization differently. For one thing, anticompetitive concerns ought to be reserved for the subset of conditions for which a condition of preexisting monopoly power exists. For another, the possibility that economies of transaction cost are realized ought to be admitted. Rather, therefore, than regard organizational innovations with suspicion and hostility, such innovations are assessed on the merits instead. Real economies of all kinds, transaction cost included, warrant respect.

3.1 The conglomerate

The conglomerate form of organization has been subject to a variety of interpretations. Some of them are sketched here, after which a transaction cost interpretation is advanced. The matter of tradeoffs is then briefly addressed.

a. EARLIER INTERPRETATIONS   The antitrust enforcement agencies were among the first to venture an unfavorable assessment of the conglomerate. Thus the staff of the Federal Trade Commission held:

With the economic power which it secures through its operation in many diverse fields, the giant conglomerate may attain an almost impregnable position. Threatened with competition in any one of its various activities, it may well sell below cost in that field, offsetting its losses through profits made in its other lines – a practice which is frequently explained as one of meeting competition. The conglomerate corporation is thus in a position to strike out with great force against smaller business. [US Federal Trade Commission, 1948, p. 59]

Robert Solo subsequently characterized the conglomerate corporation as a 'truly dangerous phenomenon' and argued that it 'will probably subvert management effectiveness and organizational rationale for generations' (1972, pp. 47–8). Others advised that the large conglomerate was a hazard to competition 'in every line of commerce in every section of the country' (Blake, 1973, p. 567). Bogeyman economics became fashionable. Procter & Gamble, for example, was repeatedly described as a 'brooding omnipresence' in a court of law.[8] Even those who regarded the conglomerate form more sympathetically referred to it as a puzzle (Posner, 1972, p. 204).

To be sure, Morris Adelman (1961) advanced a more favorable interpretation. He observed that the conglomerate form of organization had attractive portfolio diversification properties. But why should the conglomerate

8. The phrase was repeatedly used by expert economists for the plaintiff in *Purex* v. *Procter & Gamble*, which was a private antitrust suit in which Purex claimed that the resources of Procter & Gamble put a scare into Purex in its rivalry with Clorox. The district court decided against Purex. 419 F. Supp. 931 (C.D. Cal. 1976).

appear in the 1960s rather than much earlier? After all, holding companies, which long predated the conglomerate, can accomplish portfolio diversification. And individual stockholders, through mutual funds and otherwise, are able to diversify their own portfolios. At best the portfolio diversification thesis is a very incomplete explanation for the postwar wave of conglomerate mergers.[9]

b. AN INTERNAL CAPITAL MARKET INTERPRETATION As set out previously, Alfred P. Sloan, Jr, and his associates at General Motors were among the first to perceive the merits of the M-form structure. But while the divisionalization concept was well understood and carefully implemented within General Motors, those same executives were fixated on the notion that General Motors was an automobile company.

Thus Sloan remarked that 'tetraethyl lead was clearly a misfit for GM. It was a chemical product, rather than a mechanical one. And it had to go to market as part of the gasoline and thus required a gasoline distribution system.'[10] Accordingly, although GM retained an investment position, the Ethyl Corporation became a free-standing entity rather than an operating division (Sloan, 1964, p. 224). Similarly, although Durant had acquired Frigidaire and Frigidaire's market share of refrigerators exceeded 50 percent in the 1920s, the position was allowed to deteriorate as rivals developed market positions in other major appliances (radios, ranges, washers, etc.) while Frigidaire concentrated on refrigerators. The suggestion that GM get into air conditioners 'did not register on us, and the proposal was not . . . adopted' (Sloan, 1964, p. 361). As Richard Burton and Arthur Kuhn conclude, GM's 'deep and myopic involvement in the automobile sector of the economy [prevented] product diversification opportunities in other market areas – even in product lines where GM had already achieved substantial penetration – [from being] recognized' (1979, pp. 10–11).

The conglomerate form of organization, whereby the corporation consciously took on a diversified character and nurtured its various parts, evidently required a conceptual break in the mind-set of Sloan and other prewar business leaders. That occurred gradually, more by evolution than by grand design (Sobel, 1974, p. 377), and it involved a new group of organizational innovators – of which Royal Little was one (Sobel, 1974).

9. Homemade diversification is not a perfect substitute for conglomerate diversification, because bankruptcy has real costs that the firm, but not individuals, can reduce by portfolio diversification. Bankruptcy costs have not sharply increased in the past thirty years, however, so those differences do not explain the appearance of the conglomerate during that interval.

10. Quoted by Burton and Kuhn (1979, p. 6).

The natural growth of conglomerates, which would occur as the techniques for managing diverse assets were refined, was accelerated as antitrust enforcement against horizontal and vertical mergers became progressively more severe. Conglomerate acquisitions – in terms of numbers, assets acquired, and as a proportion of total acquisitions – grew rapidly with the result that 'pure' conglomerate mergers, which in the period 1948–53 constituted only 3 percent of the assets acquired by merger, had grown to 49 percent by 1973–7 (Scherer, 1980, p. 124).

As developed more fully elsewhere (Williamson, 1975, pp. 158–62), the conglomerate is best understood as a logical outgrowth of the M-form mode for organizing complex economic affairs. Thus once the merits of the M-form structure for managing separable, albeit related, lines of business (e.g. a series of automobile or a series of chemical divisions) were recognized and digested, its extension to manage less closely related activities was natural. That is not to say that the management of product variety is without problems of its own. But the basic M-form logic, whereby strategic and operating decisions are distinguished and responsibilities are separated, carried over. The conglomerates in which M-form principles of organization are respected are usefully thought of as internal capital markets whereby cash flows from diverse sources are concentrated and directed to high-yield uses.

The conglomerate is noteworthy, however, not merely because it permitted the M-form structure to take that diversification step. Equally interesting are the unanticipated systems consequences that developed as a byproduct. Thus once it was clear that the corporation could manage diverse assets in an effective way, the possibility of takeover by tender offer suggested itself. The issues here are developed in Chapter 12.

C. TRADEOFFS   The term 'M-form' is reserved for those divisionalized firms in which the general office is engaged in periodic auditing and decision review and is actively involved in the internal resource allocation process. Cash flows, therefore, are subject to an internal investment competition rather than automatically reinvested at their source. The affirmative assessment of the conglomerate as a miniature capital market presumes that the firm is operated in such a way. Not all conglomerates were. In particular, firms that in the 1960s were referred to as 'go-go' conglomerates did not respect M-form principles. Their merits, if they had any, presumably resided elsewhere.

Inasmuch, however, as the organizational logic of the M-form structure runs very deep – serving, as it does, both to economize on bounded rationality (the information processing interpretation) and safeguard the internal resource allocation process against the hazards of opportunism (which is what the general office concept adds), the rationale for conglomerate structures in which M-form principles are violated is gravely suspect. Indeed, one would expect, and events have borne the expectation out, that the 'go-go' conglomerates would become unglued when adversity set in – as it did in the late 1960s. Those firms found it necessary to reorganize along M-form lines, to simplify their product lines, or to do both.

Note in that connection that the M-form conglomerate engages in a depth-for-breadth tradeoff. As Alchian and Demsetz put it: 'Efficient production into heterogeneous resources is not a result of having *better* resources but in knowing more *accurately* the relative productive performance of those resources' (1972, p. 789; emphasis in original). Plainly, diversification can be taken to excess. As the capacity to engage knowledgeably in internal resource allocation becomes strained, problems of misallocation and opportunism intrude. That conglomerate firms voluntarily engage in divestiture is presumably explained by that condition.

Lest I be misunderstood, I do not mean to suggest that opportunities to express managerial preferences in ways that conflict with the preferences of the stockholders have been extinguished as a result of the conglomerate form. The continuing tension between management and stockholder interests is reflected in numerous efforts that incumbent managements have taken to protect target firms against takeover (Cary, 1969; Williamson, 1979a, Benston, 1980). Changes in internal organization have nevertheless relieved managerial discretion concerns. A study of the economic institutions of capitalism that makes no allowance for organization form changes and their capital market ramifications will naturally overlook the possibility that the corporate control dilemma posed by Berle and Means has since been alleviated more by internal than it has by regulatory or external organizational reforms.[11]

11. Hostility to the conglomerate form nevertheless continues. See Samuel Loescher (1984). Also, the Antitrust Division of the United States Department of Justice argued in 1978 that Occidental Petroleum should not be permitted to acquire the Mead Corporation because that would permit Mead to make 'efficient and cost effective' investments in greenfield plants to the disadvantage of Mead's less efficient rivals. For a discussion of the government's use of 'creative lawyering' to deter conglomerate mergers, see Williamson (1979b, pp. 69–73).

Antitrust caveats apply wherever an acquiring firm is properly characterized as one of a very few most likely potential entrants (Williamson, 1975, pp. 165–70). Also, although very large conglomerates might be regarded as objectionable from a populist political standpoint, such arguments should be advanced in a frankly political way (rather than masqueraded in economic garb) and treated in the context of giant-size firms quite generally.

3.2 Multinational enterprise

The discussion of the multinational enterprise (MNE) that follows deals mainly with recent developments and, among them, emphasizes organizational aspects – particularly those associated with technology transfer in manufacturing industries. As Mira Wilkins has reported, direct foreign investment, expressed as a percentage of GNP, was in the range of 7 to 8 percent in 1914, 1929 and 1970 (Wilkins, 1974, p. 437). Both the character of this investment and, relatedly, the organization structure within which this investment took place were changing, however. It is not accidental that the term MNE was coined neither in 1914 nor in 1929 but is of much more recent origin.

Thus whereas the ratio of the book value of US foreign investments in manufacturing as compared with all other (petroleum, trade, mining, public utilities) was 0·47 in 1950, that had increased to 0·71 in 1970 (Wilkins, 1974, p. 329). Also, 'what impressed Europeans about American plants in Europe and the United States [in 1929] was mass production, standardization, and scientific management; in the 1960s, Europeans were remarking that America's superiority was based on technological and managerial advantage [and] that this expertise was being exported via direct investment' (Wilkins, 1974, p. 436).

The spread of the multinational corporation in the post-World War II period has given rise to considerable scrutiny, some puzzlement, and even some alarm (Tsurumi, 1977, p. 74). One of the reasons for this unsettled state of affairs is that transaction cost economizing and organization form issues have been relatively neglected in efforts to assess MNE activity.[12]

Organization form is relevant in two related respects. First is the matter of US-based as against foreign-based investment rates. Yoshi Tsurumi reports in this connection that the rate of foreign direct investments by US firms increased rapidly after 1953, peaked in the mid-1960s, and has leveled off and declined since (Tsurumi, 1977, p. 97). The pattern of foreign direct investments by foreign firms, by contrast, has lagged that of the United States by about a decade (pp. 91–2).

Recall that the conglomerate uses the M-form structure to extend asset management from specialized to diversified lines of commerce. The MNE counterpart is the use of the M-form structure to extend asset management from a domestic base to include foreign operations. Thus the domestic M-form strategy for decomposing complex business structures

---

12. An important exception is the work of Buckley and Casson (1976).

into semi-autonomous operating units was subsequently applied to the management of foreign subsidiaries. The transformation of the corporation along M-form lines came earlier in the United States than in Europe and elsewhere. US corporations were for that reason better qualified to engage in foreign direct investments at an earlier date than were foreign-based firms. Only as the latter took on the M-form structure did that multinational management capability appear. The pattern of foreign direct investments recorded by Tsurumi and reported above is consistent with the temporal differences of US and foreign firms in adopting the M-form structure.

That US corporations possessed an M-form capability earlier than their foreign counterparts does not, however, establish that they used it to organize foreign investment. John Stopford and Louis Wells have studied that issue. They report that while initial foreign investments were usually organized as autonomous subsidiaries, divisional status within an M-form structure invariably appeared as the size and complexity of foreign operations increased (Stopford and Wells, 1972, p. 21). The transformation usually followed the organization of domestic operations along M-form lines (p. 24). The adoption of a 'global' strategy or 'worldwide perspective' – whereby 'strategic planning and major policy decisions' are made in the central office of the enterprise (p. 25) – could be accomplished only within a multidivisional framework.

Even more interesting than those organization form issues is the fact that foreign direct investments by US firms have been concentrated in a few industries. Manufacturing industries that have made substantial foreign direct investments include chemicals, drugs, automobiles, food processing, electronics, electrical and nonelectrical machinery, nonferrous metals, and rubber. Tobacco, textiles and apparel, furniture, printing, glass, steel, and aircraft have, by comparison, done little foreign direct investment (Tsurumi, 1977, p. 87)

Stephen Hymer's 'dual' explanation for the multinational enterprise is of interest in this connection. Thus Hymer observes that direct foreign investment 'allows business firms to transfer capital, technology, and organizational skill from one country to another. It is also an instrument for restraining competition between firms of different nations' (Hymer, 1970, p. 443).

Hymer is surely correct that the MNE can service both of those purposes, and examples of both kinds can doubtless be found. It is nevertheless useful to ask whether the overall character of MNE investment, in terms of its distribution among industries, is more consistent with the efficiency purposes to which Hymer refers (transfer of capital, technology, and organizational skill) or with the oligopolistic restraint hypothesis. Adopting a transaction cost orientation discloses that the observed pattern of investment is more consistent with the efficiency part of Hymer's dual explanation.

For one thing, oligopolistic purposes can presumably be realized by portfolio investment coupled with a limited degree of management involvement to segregate markets. Put differently, direct foreign investment and the organization of foreign subsidiaries within an M-form structure are not needed to effect competitive restraints. Furthermore, if competitive restraints were mainly responsible for those investments, then presumably all concentrated industries – which would include tobacco, glass, and steel – rather than those associated with rapid technical progress, would be active in MNE creation. Finally, although many of the leading US firms that engaged in foreign direct investment enjoyed 'market power,' that was by no means true for all.

By contrast, the pattern of foreign direct investments reported by Tsurumi appears to be consistent with a transaction cost economizing interpretation. Raymond Vernon's 1971 study of the Fortune 500 corporations disclosed that 187 of them had a substantial multinational presence. R&D expenditures as a percentage of sales were higher among those 187 than among the remaining firms in the Fortune 500 group. Furthermore, according to Vernon, firms that went multinational tended to be technological innovators at the time of making their initial foreign direct investments.

That raises the question of the attributes of firms and markets for accomplishing technology transfer. The difficulties with transferring technology across a market interface are of three kinds: recognition, disclosure, and team organization (Arrow, 1962; Williamson, 1975, pp. 31–3, 203–7; Teece, 1977).[13] Of those three, recognition is probably the least severe. To be sure, foreign firms may sometimes fail to perceive the opportunities to apply technological developments originated elsewhere. But enterprising domestic firms that have made the advance can be expected to identify at least some of the potential applications abroad.

Suppose, therefore, that recognition problems are set aside and consider disclosure. Attempts to transfer technology by contract can break down because of the 'paradox of information.' A very severe information asymmetry problem exists, on which account the less informed party (in this

---

13. Our argument is similar to that advanced by Buckley and Casson (1976).

instance the buyer) must be wary of opportunistic representations by the seller.[14] Although sometimes the asymmetry can be overcome by sufficient *ex ante* disclosure (and veracity checks thereon), that may shift rather than solve the difficulty. The fundamental paradox of information is that 'its value for the purchaser is not known until he has the information, but then he has in effect acquired it without cost' (Arrow, 1971, p. 152).

Suppose, *arguendo*, that buyers concede value and are prepared to pay for information in the seller's possession. The incentive to trade is then clear, and for some items this will suffice. The formula for a chemical compound or the blueprints for a special device may be all that is needed to effect the transfer. Frequently, however, and probably often, new knowledge is diffusely distributed and is poorly defined (Nelson, 1981). Where the requisite information is distributed among a number of individuals all of whom understand their speciality in only a tacit, intuitive way[15] a simple contract to transfer the technology cannot be devised.

Transfer need not cease, however, because simple contracts are not feasible. If the benefits of technology transfer are sufficiently great, exchange may be accomplished either by devising a complex trade or through direct foreign investment. Which will be employed depends on the circumstances. If only a one-time (or very occasional) transfer of technology is contemplated, direct foreign investment is a somewhat extreme response.[16] The complex contractual alternative is to negotiate a tie-in sale whereby the technology and associated knowhow are transferred as a package. Since the knowhow is concentrated in the human assets who are already familiar with the technology, this entails the creation of a 'consulting team' by the seller to accompany the physical technology transfer – the object being to overcome startup difficulties and to familiarize the employees of the foreign firm, through teaching and demonstration, with the idiosyncrasies of the operation.[17]

14. Markets for information are apt to be especially costly and/or hazardous when transmission across a national boundary is attempted. Language differences naturally complicate the communication problem, and differences in the technological base compound those difficulties. If, moreover, as is commonly the case, cultural differences foster suspicion, the trust needed to support informational exchange may be lacking. Not only will contract negotiations be more complex and costly on that account, but execution will be subject to more formal and costly procedures than would occur under a regime of greater trust.

15. On this, see Polanyi (1962).

16. This is an implication of transaction cost reasoning in which the frequency dimension has explanatory power.

17. On the importance of on-site observation and of teaching-by-doing, see Polanyi (1962), Doeringer and Piore (1971, pp. 15–16), and Williamson, Wachter, and Harris (1975).

Inasmuch as many of the contingencies that arise in the execution of such contracts will be unforeseen, and as it will be too costly to work out appropriate *ex ante* responses for others, such consulting contracts are subject to considerable strain. Where a succession of transfers is contemplated, which is to say when the frequency shifts from occasional to recurring, complex contracting is apt to give way to direct foreign investment. A more harmonious and efficient exchange relation – better disclosure, easier reconciliation of differences, more complete crosscultural adaptation, more effective team organization and reconfiguration – predictably results from the substitution of an internal governance relation for bilateral trading under those recurrent trading circumstances where assets, of which complex technology transfer is an example, have a highly specific character.

The upshot is that while puzzlement with and concerns over MNEs will surely continue,[18] a transaction cost interpretation of the phenomenon sheds insight on the following conspicuous features of multinational investment: (1) the reported concentration of foreign direct investment in manufacturing industries where technology transfer is of special importance; (2) the organization of those investments within M-form structures; and (3) the differential timing of foreign direct investment between US and foreign manufacturing enterprises (which difference also has organization form origins).[19]

4. Concluding remarks

There is widespread agreement, among economists and noneconomists alike, with the proposition that the modern corporation is an important and complex economic institution. Such agreement is mainly explained by the obtrusive size of the largest firms. The economic factors that lie behind the size, shape, and performance of the modern corporation, however, are poorly understood.

The puzzlement is not of recent origin. Edward Mason complained more than twenty years ago that 'the functioning of the corporate system

18. For recent summaries of and contributions to this literature, see Caves (1982) and Hennart and Wilkins (1983).

19. The argument can be extended to deal with such observations as those of Mansfield, Romeo, and Wagner (1979), who report that firms use subsidiaries to transfer their newest technology overseas but rely on licensing or joint ventures for older technology. The transaction cost argument is that the latter are more well defined, hence are more easily reduced to contract, and require less firm-specific know-how to effect successful transfer.

has not to date been adequately explained ... The man of action may be content with a system that works. But one who reflects on the properties or characteristics of this system cannot help asking why it works and whether it will continue to work' (1959, p. 4). The predicament to which Mason refers is, I submit, largely the product of two different (but not unrelated) intellectual traditions. The first holds that the structural features of the corporation are irrelevant. The neoclassical theory of the firm that populates intermediate theory textbooks is consistent with this view. Structural differences are suppressed as the firm is described as a production function to which a profit maximization objective has been assigned. The second has public policy roots – the inhospitality tradition to which I referred earlier. The distinctive structural features of the corporation are here believed to be the result of unwanted (anticompetitive) intrusions into market processes.

The transaction cost approach differs from both. Unlike neoclassical analysis, internal organization is specifically held to be important. Unlike the inhospitality tradition, structural differences are presumed to arise primarily in the service of transaction cost economizing.

The progressive evolution of the modern corporation records the imprint of transaction cost economizing at every stage. The railroads, which were the 'first modern business enterprises' (Chandler, 1977, p. 120), devised the line-and-staff structure when coordination of end-to-end systems by contract broke down and older and simpler structures were unable to manage the resulting networks. Transaction costs rather than technology were plainly driving those developments. Forward integration out of manufacturing into distribution was widespread at the turn of the century. As discussed in Chapter 5, integration occurred selectively rather than comprehensively and in a manner that is broadly consistent with transaction cost reasoning.

The two leading corporate forms that were in place in 1920 were the function (or U-form) and holding company (H form) structures. Both experienced internal inefficiency and managerial discretion distortions as firms grew in size and complexity. Viewing internal organization within a nexus of contract perspective, the implicit contracts were too cumbersome on the one hand (the U-form case) and too incomplete on the other (the H-form condition). Faced with the need either to retrench or to develop a new set of internal contracting relationships, organizational innovators devised the M-form structure.

The resulting structure recognized essential decomposability, thus rectifying the overcentralization condition in the U-form enterprise. The M-form furthermore effected a split between operating and strategic decision-making and reserved the latter for the general office. Providing the general office with an internal incentive and control capability was required lest the potential benefits of the division of effort be dissipated. Such a capacity had been lacking in the H-form organization and contributed to problematic performance therein.

This argument bears a resemblance to the two technology problem discussed in earlier chapters. The two technologies under review here are the centralized and decentralized modes of organization. The first corresponds to the U-form; the second can be either H or M. The contractual difference between the latter two is that safeguards against opportunism are more fully developed in the M-form. Investors will presumably be prepared to supply capital on superior terms, therefore, to a large, diversified M-form corporation than they would to an equivalent H-form firm. In the degree to which the M-form is in fact the fitter, natural selection, which includes competition in the capital market, favors this result.

The M-form innovation introduced by General Motors and du Pont (and subsequently imitated by others) thus served both technical and internal governance purposes – in that it served both to economize on bounded rationality and attenuate opportunism. Specifically, operating decisions were no longer forced to the top but were resolved at the divisional level, which relieved the communication load. Strategic decisions were reserved for the general office, which reduced partisan political input into the resource allocation process. And the internal auditing and control techniques to which the general office had access served to overcome information impactedness conditions and permit fine tuning controls to be exercised over the operating parts.

The M-form structure, which was originally adopted by firms in relatively specialized lines of commerce, was subsequently extended to manage diversified assets (the conglomerate) and foreign direct investments (MNE). A breadth-for-depth tradeoff is involved in the former case, as the firm selectively internalizes functions ordinarily associated with the capital market. MNE activity has also been selective – being concentrated in the more technologically progressive industries where higher rates of R&D are reported and technology transfer arguably poses greater difficulties. This pattern of foreign direct investment cannot be explained by a monopoly hypothesis but is consistent with transaction cost reasoning.

To be sure, the interpretation of the modern corporation set out in this chapter and elsewhere in this book deals only with salient features. There is both room for and need of refinement. It nevertheless makes headway against the rationality puzzlement to which Mason referred and which has troubled other students of the modern corporation. The basic proposition is this: Organization form deserves to be taken seriously. Once that is acknowledged, transaction cost economizing becomes a very large part of the argument.

Bibliography

ADELMAN, M. A. (1961), 'The antimerger act, 1950–1960', *American Economic Review*, 51, pp. 236–44

ALCHIAN, A. (1969), 'Corporate management and property rights', in: H. G. Manne (ed.), *Economic Policy and Regulation of Corporate Securities*, Washington DC, American Institute for Public Policy Research

ALCHIAN, A., and DEMSETZ, H. (1972), 'Production, information costs and economic organization', *American Economic Review*, 62, pp. 777–95

ARROW, K. J. (1962), 'Economic welfare and the allocation of resources of invention', in: National Bureau of Economic Research (ed.), *The Rate and Direction of Inventive Activity: Economic and Social Factors*, Princeton University Press

ARROW, K. J. (1971), *Essays in the Theory of Risk-Bearing*, Chicago, Markham

ASHBY, W. ROSS (1960), *Design for a Brain*, Wiley

BENSTON, G. J. (1980), *Conglomerate Mergers: Causes, Consequences and Remedies*, Washington DC, American Institute for Public Policy Research

BLAKE, H. M. (1973), 'Conglomerate mergers and the antitrust laws', *Columbia Law Review*, 73, 555–92

BRUCHEY, S. W. (1956), *Robert Oliver, Merchant of Baltimore, 1783–1819*, Johns Hopkins Press

BUCKLEY, P. J., and CASSON, M. (1976), *The Future of Multi-National Enterprise*, Holmes & Meier, Macmillan.

BURTON, R. H., and KUHN, A. J. (1979), *Strategy Follows Structure: The Missing Link of Their Intertwined Relation*, Fuqua School of Business, Duke University (Working Paper no. 260)

CARY, W. (1969), 'Corporate devices used to insulate management from attack', *Antitrust Law Journal*, 39, pp. 318–33

CAVES, R. E. (1982), *Multinational Enterprises and Economic Analysis*, Cambridge University Press.

CHANDLER, A. D. (1962), *Strategy and Structure*, MIT Press

CHANDLER, A. D. (1966), *Strategy and Structure*, Doubleday

CHANDLER, A. D. (1977), *The Invisible Hand: The Managerial Revolution in American Business*, Harvard University Press

DOERINGER, P., and PIORE, M. (1971), *Internal Labor Markets and Manpower Analysis*, D. C. Heath

EVANS, D., and GROSSMAN, S. (1983), 'Integration', in: D. Evans (ed.), *Breaking Up Bell*, North-Holland Publishing

FISHLOW, A. (1965), *American Railroads and the Transformation of the Antebellum Economy*, Harvard University Press

FOGEL, R. (1964), *Railroads and American Economic Growth: Essays in Econometric History*, Johns Hopkins Press

GALBRAITH, J. K. (1967), *The New Industrial State*, Houghton-Mifflin

GEANAKOPLOS, J., and MILGROM, P. (1984), Information, Planning and Control in Hierarchies (unpublished paper)

HEFLEBOWER, R. B. (1960), 'Observations on decentralization in large enterprises', *Journal of Industrial Economics*, 9, pp. 7–22

HENNART, J.-F., and WILKINS, M. (1983), Multinational Enterprise, Transaction Costs and the Markets and Hierarchies Hypothesis, unpublished MS, Florida International University

HYMER, S. (1970), 'The efficiency (contradictions) of multinational corporations', *American Economic Review*, 60, pp. 441–8

KOONTZ, H., and O'DONNELL, C. (1955), *Principles of Management: An Analysis of Managerial Functions*, McGraw-Hill

LIVESAY, H. C. (1979), *American Made: Men Who Shaped the American Economy*, Little, Brown

LOESCHER, S. (1984), 'Bureaucratic measurement, shuttling stock shares and shortened time horizons', *Quarterly Review of Economics and Business*, 24, pp. 8–23

MANSFIELD, E., ROMEO, A., and WAGNER, S. (1979), 'Foreign trade and U.S. research and development', *Review of Economics and Statistics*, 61, pp. 49–57

MARSCHAK, J., and RADNER, R. (1972), *Economic Theory of Teams*, Yale University Press

MASON, E. (1959), *The Corporation in Modern Society*, Harvard University Press

NELSON, R. R. (1981), 'Assessing private enterprise: an exegesis of tangled doctrine', *Bell Journal of Economics*, spring

POLANYI, M. (1962), *Personal Knowledge: Towards a Post-Critical Philosophy*, Harper & Row

PORTER, G., and LIVESAY, H. C. (1971), *Merchants and Manufacturers: Studies in the Changing Structure of Nineteenth-Century Marketing*, Johns Hopkins Press

POSNER, R. A. (1972), 'The appropriate scope of regulation in the cable television industry', *Bell Journal of Economics and Management Science*, 3, pp. 98–129

SCHERER, F. M. (1980), *Industrial Market Structure and Economic Performance*, Rand McNally

SIMON, H. A. (1962), 'The architecture of complexity', *Proceedings of the American Philosophical Society*, 106, pp. 467–82

SIMON, H. A. (1973), 'Applying information technology to organization design', *Public Administration Review*, 33, pp. 268–78

SLOAN, A. P. (1964), *My Years with General Motors*, MacFadden

SOBEL, R. (1974), *The Entrepreneurs*, Weybright & Talley

SOLO, R. (1972), 'New maths and old sterilities', *Saturday Review*, 22 January, pp. 47–8

STOPFORD, J. M., and WELLS, L. T. (1972), *Managing the Multinational Enterprise: Organization of the Firm and Ownership of the Subsidiaries*, Basic Books

TAYLOR, G., and NEU, I. (1956), *The American Railroad Network*, Harvard University Press

TEECE, D. J. (1977), 'Technology transfer by multinational firms', *Economic Journal*, 87, pp. 242-61

TEMIN, P. (1981), 'The future of the new economic history', *Journal of Interdisciplinary History*, 12, pp. 179-97

TSURUMI, Y. (1977), *Multinational Management*, Ballinger

US FEDERAL TRADE COMMISSION (1948), *Report of the Federal Trade Commission on the Merger Movement: A Summary Report*, Washington DC, US Government Printing Office

VERNON, R. (1971), *Sovereignty at Bay*, Basic Books

WILKINS, M. (1974), *The Maturing of the Multinational Enterprise: American Business Abroad from 1914 to 1970*, Harvard University Press

WILLIAMSON, O. E. (1975), *Markets and Hierarchies: Analysis and Antitrust Implications*, Free Press

WILLIAMSON, O. E. (1979a), 'Assessing vertical market restrictions', *University of Pennsylvania Law Review*, 127, pp. 953-93

WILLIAMSON, O. E. (1979b), 'On the governance of the modern corporation', *Hofstra Law Review*, 8, pp. 63-78

WILLIAMSON, O. E., WACHTER, M. L., and HARRIS, J. E. (1975), 'Understanding the employment relation: the analysis of idiosyncratic exchange', *Bell Journal of Economics*, 6, pp. 250-80

4   C. A. Bartlett and S. Ghoshal

The Transnational Organization

From 'Managing across borders: new organizational responses', *Sloan Management Review*, fall 1987, pp. 43–53

In a companion article (summer 1987), we described how recent changes in the international operating environment have forced companies to optimize *efficiency*, *responsiveness*, and *learning* simultaneously in their worldwide operations. To companies that previously concentrated on developing and managing one of these capabilities, this new challenge implied not only a total strategic reorientation but a major change in organizational capability, as well.

Implementing such a complex, three-pronged strategic objective would be difficult under any circumstances, but in a worldwide company the task is complicated even further. The very act of 'going international' multiplies a company's organizational complexity. Typically, doing so requires adding a third dimension to the existing business- and function-oriented management structure. It is difficult enough balancing product divisions that bring efficiency and focus to domestic product-market strategies with corporate staffs whose functional expertise allows them to play an important counterbalance and control role. The thought of adding capable, geographically oriented management – and maintaining a three-way balance of organizational perspectives and capabilities among product, function, and area – is intimidating to most managers. The difficulty is increased because the resolution of tensions among product, function, and area managers must be accomplished in an organization whose operating units are often divided by distance and time and whose key members are separated by culture and language.

From unidimensional to multidimensional capabilities

Faced with the task of building multiple strategic capabilities in highly complex organizations, managers in almost every company we studied made the simplifying assumption that they were faced with a series of dichotomous choices.[1] They discussed the relative merits of pursuing a strategy of national responsiveness as opposed to one based on global integration; they considered whether key assets and resources should be centralized or decentralized; and they debated the need for strong central control versus greater subsidiary autonomy. How a company resolved these dilemmas typically reflected influences exerted and choices made during its historical development. In telecommunications, ITT's need to develop an organization responsive to national political demands and local specification differences was as important to its survival in the pre- and post-World War II era as was NEC's need to build its highly centralized technological manufacturing and marketing skills and resources in order to expand abroad in the same industry in the 1960s and 1970s.

When new competitive challenges emerged, however, such unidimensional biases became strategically limiting. As ITT demonstrated by its outstanding historic success and NEC showed by its more delayed international expansion, strong *geographic management* is essential for development of dispersed responsiveness. Geographic management allows worldwide companies to sense, analyze, and respond to the needs of different national markets.

Effective competitors also need to build strong *business management* with global product responsibilities if they are to achieve global efficiency and integration. These managers act as champions of manufacturing rationalization, product standardization, and low-cost global sourcing. (As the telecommunications switching industry globalized, NEC's organizational capability in this area gave it a major competitive advantage.) Unencumbered by either territorial or functional loyalties, central product groups remain sensitive to overall competitive issues and become agents to facilitate changes that, though painful, are necessary for competitive viability.

Finally, a strong, worldwide *functional management* allows an organization to build and transfer its core competencies – a capability vital to worldwide learning. Links between functional managers allow the company to accumulate specialized knowledge and skills and to apply them wherever they are required in the worldwide operations. Functional management acts as the repository of organizational learning and as the prime mover for its consolidation and circulation within the company. It was for want of a strongly linked research and technical function across subsidiaries that ITT failed in its attempt to coordinate the development and diffusion of its System 12 digital switch.

Thus, to respond to the needs for efficiency, responsiveness, and learning *simultaneously*, the company must develop a multidimensional organization in which the effectiveness of each management group is maintained *and* in which each group is prevented from dominating the others. As we saw in company after company, the most difficult challenge for managers trying to respond to broad, emerging strategic demands was to develop the new elements of multidimensional organization without eroding the effectiveness of their current unidimensional capability.

Overcoming simplifying assumptions

For all nine companies at the core of our study, the challenge of breaking down biases and building a truly multidimensional organization proved difficult. Behind the pervasive either/or mentality that led to the development of unidimensional capabilities, we identified three simplifying assumptions that blocked the necessary organizational development. The need to reduce organizational and strategic complexity has made these assumptions almost universal in worldwide companies, regardless of industry, national origin, or management culture.

– There is a widespread, often implicit assumption that roles of different organizational units are uniform and symmetrical; different businesses should be managed in the same way, as should different functions and national operations.
– Most companies, some consciously, most unconsciously, create internal interunit relationships on clear patterns of dependence or independence, on the assumption that such relationships *should* be clear and unambiguous.
– Finally, there is the assumption that one of corporate management's principal tasks is to institutionalize clearly understood mechanisms for decision-making and to implement simple means of exercising control.

Those companies most successful in developing truly multidimensional organizations were the ones that challenged these assumptions and replaced them with some very different attitudes and norms. Instead of treating different businesses, functions, and subsidiaries similarly, they systematically *differentiated* tasks and responsibilities. Instead of seeking organizational clarity by basing relationships on dependence or independence, they built and managed *interdependence* among the different units of companies. And instead of considering control their key task, corporate managers searched for complex mechanisms to *coordinate and coopt* the differentiated and interdependent organizational units into sharing a vision of the company's strategic tasks. These are the central organizational characteristics of what we described in the earlier article as transnational corporations – those most effective in managing across borders in today's environment of intense competition and rapid, often discontinuous change.

From symmetry to differentiation

Like many other companies we studied, Unilever built its international operations under an implicit assumption of organizational symmetry. Managers of diverse local operating companies in products ranging from packaged foods to chemicals and detergents all reported to strongly independent national managers, who in turn reported through regional directors to the board. In the post-World War II era, the company began to recognize a need to supplement this geographically dominated structure with an organizational ability to capture potential economies and to transfer learning across national boundaries. To meet this need, a few product-coordination groups were formed at the corporate center. But the assumption of organizational symmetry ensured that all businesses were similarly managed, and the number of coordination groups grew from three in 1962 to six in 1969 and to ten by 1977.

By the mid-1970s, however, the entrenched organizational symmetry was being threatened. Global economic disruption caused by the oil crisis dramatically highlighted the very substantial differences in the company's businesses and markets and forced management to recognize the need to differentiate its organizational structures and administrative processes. While standardization, coordination, and integration paid high dividends in the chemical and detergent businesses, for example, important differences in local tastes and national cultures impeded the same degree of coordination in foods. As a result, the roles, responsibilities, and powers of the central product-coordination groups eventually began to diverge as the company tried to shake off the constraint of the symmetry assumption.

But as Unilever tackled the challenge of managing some businesses in a more globally coordinated manner, it was confronted with the question of what to coordinate. Historically, the company's philosophy of decentralized capabilities and delegated responsibilities resulted in most national subsidiaries' becoming fully integrated, self-sufficient operations. While they were free to draw on product technology, manufacturing capabilities, and marketing expertise developed at the center, they were not required to do so, and most units chose to develop, manufacture, and market products as they thought appropriate. Thus functions, too, tended to be managed symmetrically.

Over time, decentralization of all functional responsibilities became increasingly difficult to support. In the 1970s, for example, when arch-competitor Procter & Gamble's subsidiaries were launching a new generation of laundry detergents based on the rape seed formula created by the parent company, most of Unilever's national detergent companies responded with their own products. The cost of developing thirteen different formulations was extremely high, and management soon recognized that not one was as good as P&G's centrally developed product. For the sake of cost control and competitive effectiveness, Unilever had to break with tradition and begin centralizing European product development. The company has since created a system in which central coordination is more normal, although very different for different functions such as basic research, product development, manufacturing, marketing, and sales.

Just as they saw the need to change symmetrical structures and homogeneous processes imposed on different businesses and functions, most companies we observed eventually recognized the importance of differentiating the management of diverse geographic operations. Despite the fact that various national subsidiaries operated with very different external environments and internal constraints, they all traditionally reported through the same channels, operated under similar planning and control systems, and worked under a set of common and generalized mandates.

Increasingly, however, managers recognized that such symmetrical treatment can constrain strategic capabilities. At Unilever, for example, it became clear that Europe's highly competitive markets and closely linked economies meant that its operating companies in that region required more coordination and control than those in, say, Latin America. Little by little, management increased the product-coordination groups' role in Europe until they had direct line responsibility for all operating companies in their businesses. Elsewhere, however, national management maintained its historic line management role, and product coordinators acted only as advisers. Unilever has thus moved in sequence from a symmetrical organization to a much more differentiated one: differentiating by product, then by function, and finally by geography.

Recently, within Europe, differentiation by national units has proceeded even further. Operations in 'key countries' such as France, Germany, and the United Kingdom are allowed to retain considerably more autonomy than those in 'receiver countries' such as Switzerland, Sweden, Holland, and Denmark. While the company's overall commitment to decentralization is maintained, 'receiver countries' have gradually become more dependent on the center for direction and support, particularly in the areas of product development and competitive strategy.

Figure 1 is a schematic representation of the different ways in which Unilever manages its diverse businesses, functions, and markets.[2] The vertical axis represents the level of global integration, and hence of central coordination; the horizontal axis represents the extent of national differentiation, and consequently of the desired influence of subsidiaries in strategic and operational decisions.

The detergent business must be managed in a more globally integrated manner than packaged foods, but also needs a more nationally differentiated strategy than the chemicals business. But not all tasks need to be managed in this differentiated yet coordinated manner: there is little need for national differentiation in research or for global coordination of sales management. And even those functions such as marketing that exhibit the more complex simultaneous demands need not be managed in this way in all national markets. Marketing strategy for export sales can be highly coordinated, while approaches taken in closed markets like India and Brazil can be managed locally. Only in key strategic markets like Germany, the UK, and France is there a need for differentiated yet coordinated marketing strategies. This flexible and differentiated management approach stands in marked contrast to the standardized, symmetrical approach implied in Unilever's earlier blanket commitment to decentralized responsibility.

But Unilever is far from unique. In all of the companies we studied, senior management was working to differentiate its organizational structure and processes in increasingly sophisticated ways.[3] For example, Philips's consumer electronics division began experimenting with an organization differentiated by product life-cycle stage — high-tech products like CD players being managed with very different strategies and organization processes from those for stable high-volume products like color TVs, which, in turn, were managed differently from mature and declining products like portable radios. Procter & Gamble is differentiating the roles of its subsidiaries by giving some of them responsibilities as 'lead countries' in product strategy development, then rotating that leadership role from product to product.[4] Matsushita differentiates the way it manages its worldwide operations not on the basis of geography, but on the unit's strategic role. (Single-product, wholly owned manufacturing units, the A Group, are

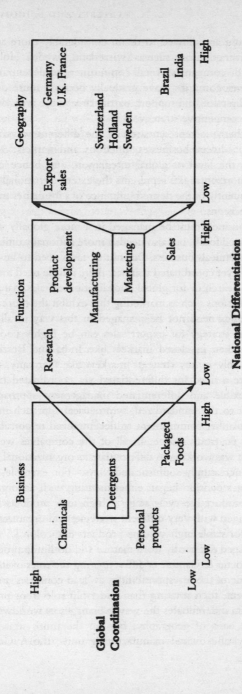

Figure 1 Unilever's differentiated organization

managed differently from multiproduct, multifunction companies, the B Group, and from simple sales and marketing subs, the C Group.) L. M. Ericsson, which had centralized most of the basic research on its digital switch, is now decentralizing development and applications responsibilities to a few key country subsidiaries that have the capability to contribute.[5]

Thus, instead of deciding the overall roles of product, functional, and geographic management on the basis of simplistic dichotomies such as global versus domestic businesses or centralized versus decentralized organizations, many companies are creating different levels of influence for different groups as they perform different activities. Doing this allows the relatively underdeveloped management perspectives to be built in a gradual, complementary manner rather than in the sudden, adversarial environment often associated with either/or choices. Internal heterogeneity has made the change from unidimensional to multidimensional organization easier by breaking the problem up into many small, differentiated parts and by allowing for a step-by-step process of organizational change.

From dependence or independence to interdependence

The limitations of the assumption of clarity in organizational relationships eventually confronted top managers in the Japanese soap and detergent company Kao. In the early 1980s they began to recognize that their foreign subsidiaries' strong dependence on the parent company provided significant benefits of global efficiency only at the cost of less sensitivity and responsiveness to local market needs. For example, when investigating the reason for the company's slow penetration of the shampoo market in Thailand despite offering a technologically superior product, headquarters managers found that the subsidiary had adopted the product positioning, packaging, and pricing policies developed for the Japanese domestic market. Since local management had been unable to make the necessary local adaptations, managers were brought in from headquarters to identify the source of the problem and to make necessary changes in the marketing mix.

In other companies we studied – Unilever and ITT, for example – clarity or organizational relationships was achieved by giving foreign subsidiaries substantial independence. But, as our earlier discussion of Unilever illustrated, such organizational clarity was achieved at the cost of substantial inefficiency; individual subsidiaries often reinvented the wheel or operated at suboptimal scale.

New strategic demands make organizational models of simple interunit dependence *or* independence inappropriate. The reality of today's world-wide competitive environment demands collaborative information sharing and problem solving, cooperative support and resource sharing, and collective action and implementation. Independent units risk being picked off one-by-one by competitors whose coordinated global approach gives them two important strategic advantages – the ability to integrate research, manufacturing, and other scale-efficient operations, and the opportunity to cross-subsidize the losses from battles in one market with funds generated by profitable operations in home markets or protected environments.[6] The desire to capture such strategic benefits was one of Philips's main motivations as it attempted to coordinate the competitive responses of historically independent national organizations.

On the other hand, foreign operations totally dependent on a central unit must deal with problems reaching beyond the loss of local market responsiveness described in the Kao example. They also risk being unable to respond effectively to strong national competitors or to sense potentially important local market or technical intelligence. This was the problem Procter & Gamble's Japan subsidiary faced in an environment where local competitors began challenging P&G's previously secure position with successive, innovative product changes and novel market strategies, particularly in the disposable diapers business. After suffering major losses in market share, management recognized that a local operation focused primarily on implementing the company's classic marketing strategy was no longer sufficient; the Japanese subsidiary needed the freedom and incentive to be more innovative. Not only to ensure the viability of the Japanese subsidiary, but also to protect its global strategic position, P&G realized it had to expand the role of the local unit and change its relationship with the parent company to enhance two-way learning and mutual support.

But it is not easy to change relationships of dependence or independence that have been built up over a long history. Many companies have tried to address the increasing need for interunit collaboration by adding layer upon layer of administrative mechanisms to foster greater cooperation. Top managers have extolled the virtues of teamwork and have even created special departments to audit management response to this need. In most cases these efforts to obtain cooperation by fiat or by administrative mechanisms have been disappointing. The independent units have feigned compliance while fiercely protecting their independence. The dependent units have found that the new cooperative spirit implies little more than the right to agree with those on whom they depend.

Yet some companies have gradually developed the capability to achieve such cooperation and to build what Rosabeth Kanter calls an 'integrative organization.'[7] Of the companies we studied, the most successful did so not by creating new units, but by changing the basis of the relationships among product, functional, and geographic management groups. From relations based on dependence or independence, they moved to relations based on formidable levels of explicit, genuine interdependence. In essence, they made integration and collaboration self-enforcing by making it necessary for each group to cooperate in order to achieve its own interests. Companies were able to create such interdependencies in many ways, as two brief examples will illustrate.

– NEC has developed reciprocal relationships among different parts of its organizations by creating a series of internal quasi markets. It builds cooperation between the R&D function and the different product groups by allocating only a part of the R&D budget directly to the company's several central laboratories. This portion is used to support basic and applied research in core technologies of potential value to the corporation as a whole. The remaining funds are allocated to the product groups to support research programs that reflect their priorities. In response to the product divisions' proposed projects, each research group puts forward proposals that it feels will lead to the desired product or process improvements. What follows is a negotiation process that results in the product divisions' 'buying' some of the proposals put up by the laboratories, while different R&D groups adopt some of the projects demanded by the product managers. In other words, NEC has created an internal market for ensuring that research is relevant to market needs. (A similar process seems to have had comparable success at Matsushita.)[8]

– Procter & Gamble employs an entirely different approach to creating and managing interdependencies. In Europe, for example, it formed a number of Eurobrand teams for developing product-market strategies for different product lines.[9] Each team is headed by the general manager of a subsidiary that has a particularly well-developed competence in that business. It also includes the appropriate product and advertising managers from the other subsidiaries and relevant functional managers from the company's European headquarters. Each team's effectiveness clearly depends on the involvement and support provided by its members and, more important, by the organizational units they represent. Historically, the company's various subsidiaries had little incentive to cooperate. Now, however, the success of each team – and the reputation of the general manager heading it – depends on the support of other subsidiaries; this has made cooperation self-enforcing. Each general manager is aware that the level of support and commitment he can expect from the other members of the Eurobrand team depends on the support and contribution the product managers from his subsidiaries provide to the other teams. The interdependencies of these Eurobrand teams were able to foster teamwork driven by individual interests.

In observing many such examples of companies building and extending interdependence among units, we were able to identify three important flows that seem to be at the center of the emerging organizational relationships. Most fundamental was the product interdependence that most companies were building as they specialized and integrated their worldwide manufacturing operations to achieve greater efficiency, while retaining sourcing flexibility and sensitivity to host country interests.[10] The resulting *flow of parts, components, and finished goods* increased the interdependence of the worldwide operations in an obvious and fundamental manner.

We also observed companies developing a resource interdependence that often contrasted sharply with earlier policies that had either encouraged local self-sufficiency or required the centralization of all surplus resources. Systems such as NEC's internal quasi markets were designed to develop a greater *flow of funds, skills, and other scarce resources* among organizational units.

Finally, the worldwide diffusion of technology, the development of international markets, and the globalization of competitive strategies have meant that vital strategic information now exists in many different locations worldwide. Furthermore, the growing dispersion of assets and delegation of responsibilities to foreign operations have resulted in the development of local knowledge and expertise that has implications for the broader organization. With these changes, the need to manage the *flow of intelligence, ideas, and knowledge* has become central to the learning process and has reinforced the growing interdependence of worldwide operations, as P&G's Eurobrand teams illustrate.

It is important to emphasize that the relationships we are highlighting are different from the interdependencies commonly observed in multiunit organizations. Traditionally, MNC managers have attempted to highlight what has been called 'pooled interdependence' to make subunit managers responsive to global rather than local interests. (Before the Euroteam approach, for instance, P&G's European vice president often tried to convince independent-minded subsidiary managers to transfer surplus generated funds to other more needy subsidiaries, in the overall corporate interest, arguing that, 'Someday when you're in need they might be able to fund a major product launch for you.')

As the example illustrates, pooled interdependence is often too broad and amorphous to affect day-to-day management behavior. The interdependencies we described earlier are more clearly reciprocal, and each unit's ability to achieve its goals is made conditional upon its willingness to help other units achieve their own goals. Such interdependencies more effectively promote the organization's ability to share the perspectives and link the resources of different components, and thereby to expand its organizational capabilities.[11]

From control to coordination and cooption

The simplifying assumptions of organizational symmetry and dependence (or independence) had allowed the management processes in many companies to be dominated by simple controls – tight operational controls in subsidiaries dependent on the center, and a looser system of administrative or financial controls in decentralized units.[12] When companies began to challenge the assumptions underlying organizational relationships, however, they found they also had to adapt their management processes. The growing interdependence of organizational units strained the simple control-dominated systems and underlined the need to supplement existing processes with more sophisticated ones. Furthermore, the differentiation of organizational tasks and roles amplified the diversity of management perspectives and capabilities and forced management to differentiate management processes.

As organizations became, at the same time, more diverse and more interdependent, there was an explosion in the number of issues that had to be linked, reconciled, or integrated. The rapidly increasing flows of goods, resources, and information among organizational units increased the need for *coordination* as a central management function. But the costs of coordination are high, both in financial and human terms, and coordinating capabilities are always limited. Most companies, though, tended to concentrate on a primary means of coordination and control – 'the company's way of doing things.' (At ITT it was through 'the system,' as Harold Geneen used to call his sophisticated set of controls, while at Kao it was primarily through centralization of decisions.) Clearly, there was a need to develop multiple means of coordination, to rank the demands for coordination, and to allocate the scarce coordinating resources. The way in which one of our sample companies developed its portfolio of coordinative processes illustrates the point well.

During the late 1970s and early 1980s, Philips had gradually developed some sophisticated means of coordination. This greatly helped the company shape its historically evolved, nationally centered organization into the kind of multidimensional organization it needed to be in the 1980s. Coordinating the flow of goods in a global sourcing network is a highly complex logistical task, but one that can often be formalized and delegated to middle and lower-level management. By standardizing product specifications and rationalizing sourcing patterns through designating certain plants as international production centers (IPCs), Philips facilitated goods-flow coordination. By making these flows reasonably constant and forecastable, the company could manage them almost entirely through formal systems and processes. These became the main coordination mechanisms in the company's attempt to increase the integration of worldwide sourcing of products and components.

Coordinating the flow of financial, technical, and human resources, however, was not so easily routinized. Philips saw the allocation of these scarce resources as a reflection of key strategic choices and therefore managed the coordination process by centralizing many decisions. The board became heavily involved in major capital budgeting decisions; the product divisions reasserted control over product development, a process once jealously guarded by the national organizations; and the influential corporate staff bureau played a major role in personnel assignments and transfers.

But while goods flows could be coordinated through formalization, and resource flows through centralization, critical information flows were much more difficult to manage. The rapid globalization of the consumer electronics industry in the 1970s forced Philips to recognize the need to move strategic information and proprietary knowledge around the company much more quickly. While some routine data could be transferred through normal information systems, much of the information was so diverse and changeable that establishing formal processes was impossible. While some core knowledge had to be stored and transferred through corporate management, the sheer volume and complexity of information – and the need for its rapid diffusion – limited the ability to coordinate through centralization. Philips found that the most effective way to manage complex flows of information and knowledge was through various socialization processes: the transfer of people, the encouragement of informal communication channels that fostered information exchange, or the creation of forums that facilitated interunit learning.

Perhaps most well known is the company's constant worldwide transfer and rotation of a group of senior managers (once referred to internally as the 'Dutch Mafia,' but today a more international group) as a means of transferring critical knowledge and experience throughout the organization. Philips also made more extensive use of committees and task forces than any other company we studied. Although the frequent meetings and constant travel were expensive, the company benefited not only from information exchange but also from the development of personal contacts that grew into vital information channels.

In other companies, we saw a similar broadening of administrative processes as managers learned to operate with previously underutilized means of coordination. Unilever's heavy reliance on the socialization of managers to provide the coordination 'glue' was supplemented by the growing role of the central product-coordination departments. In contrast, NEC reduced central management's coordination role by developing formal systems and social processes in a way that created a more robust and flexible coordinative capability.

Having developed diverse new means of coordination, management's main task is to carefully ration their usage and application. As the Philips example illustrates, it is important to distinguish where tasks can be formalized and managed through systems, where social linkages can be fostered to encourage informal agreements and cooperation, and where the coordination task is so vital or sensitive that it must use the scarce resource of central management arbitration.[13]

While the growing interdependence of organizational units forces the development of more complex administrative processes, the differentiation of roles and responsibilities forces management to change the way it uses the new coordination and control mechanisms. Even though they recognize the growing diversity of tasks facing them, a surprising number of companies have had great difficulty in differentiating the way they manage products, functions, or geographic units. The simplicity of applying a single planning and control system across businesses and the political acceptability of defining uniform job descriptions for all subsidiary heads were often allowed to outweigh the clear evidence that the relevant business characteristics and subsidiary roles were vastly different.

We have described briefly how companies began to remedy this situation by differentiating roles and responsibilities within the organization. Depending on their internal capabilities and on the strategic importance of their external environments, organizational units might be asked to take on roles ranging from that of strategic leader with primary corporatewide responsibility for a particular business or function, to simple implementer responsible only for executing strategies and decisions developed elsewhere.

Clearly, these roles must be managed in quite different ways. The unit with strategic leadership responsibility must be given freedom to develop responsibility in an entrepreneurial fashion, yet must also be strongly supported by headquarters. For this unit, operating controls may be light and quite routine, but coordination of information and resource flows to and from the unit will probably require intensive involvement from senior management. In contrast, units with implementation responsibility might be managed through tight operating controls, with standardized systems used to handle much of the coordination – primarily of goods flows. Because the tasks are more routine, the use of scarce coordinating resources could be minimized.

Differentiating organizational roles and management processes can have a fragmenting and sometimes demotivating effect, however. Nowhere was this more clearly illustrated than in the many companies that unquestioningly assigned units the 'dog' and 'cash cow' roles defined by the Boston Consulting Group's growth-share matrix in the 1970s.[14] Their experience showed that there is another equally important corporate management task that complements and facilitates coordinate effectiveness. We call this task *cooption*: the process of uniting the organization with a common understanding of, identification with, and commitment to the corporation's objectives, priorities, and values.

A clear example of the importance of cooption was provided by the contrast between ITT and NEC managers. At ITT, corporate objectives were communicated more in financial than in strategic terms, and the company's national entities identified almost exclusively with their local environment. When corporate management tried to superimpose a more unified and integrated global strategy, its local subsidiaries neither understood nor accepted the need to do so. For years they resisted giving up their autonomy, and management was unable to replace the interunit rivalry with a more cooperative and collaborative process.

In contrast, NEC developed an explicitly defined and clearly communicated global strategy enshrined in the company's 'C&C' motto – a corporatewide dedication to building business and basing competitive strategy on the strong link between computers and communications. For over a decade, the C&C philosophy was constantly interpreted, refined, elaborated, and eventually institutionalized in organizational units dedicated to various C&C missions (e.g., the C&C Systems Research Laboratories, the C&C Corporate Planning Committee, and eventually the C&C Systems

Division). Top management recognized that one of its major tasks was to inculcate the worldwide organization with an understanding of the C&C strategy and philosophy and to raise managers' consciousness about the global implications of competing in these converging businesses. By the mid-1980s, the company was confident that every NEC employee in every operating unit had a clear understanding of NEC's global strategy as well as of his or her role in it. Indeed, it was this homogeneity that allowed the company to begin the successful decentralization of its strategic tasks and the differentiation of its management processes.

Thus the management process that distinguished transnational organizations from simpler unidimensional forms was one in which control was made less dominant by the increased importance of interunit integration and collaboration. These new processes required corporate management to supplement its control role with the more subtle tasks of coordination and cooption, giving rise to a much more complex and sophisticated management process.

Sustaining a dynamic balance: role of the 'mind matrix'

Developing multidimensional perspectives and capabilities does not mean that product, functional, and geographic management must have the same level of influence on all key decisions. Quite the contrary. It means that the organization must possess a differentiated influence structure – one in which different groups have different roles for different activities. These roles cannot be fixed but must change continually to respond to new environmental demands and evolving industry characteristics. Not only is it necessary to prevent any one perspective from dominating the others, it is equally important not to be locked into a model of operation that prevents reassignment of responsibilities, realignment of relationships, and rebalancing of power distribution. This ability to manage the multi-dimensional organization capability in a flexible manner is the hallmark of a transnational company.

In the change processes we have described, managers were clearly employing some powerful organizational tools to create and control the desired flexible management process. They used the classic tool of formal structure to strengthen, weaken, or shift roles and responsibilities over time, and they employed management systems effectively to redirect corporate resources and to channel information in a way that shifted the balance of power. By controlling the ebb and flow of responsibilities, and by rebalancing power relationships, they were able to prevent any of the multidimensional perspectives from atrophying. Simultaneously, they prevented the establishment of entrenched power bases.

But the most successful companies had an additional element at the core of their management processes. We were always conscious that a substantial amount of senior management attention focused on the *individual* members of the organization. NEC's continual efforts to inculcate all corporate members with a common vision of goals and priorities; P&G's careful assignment of managers to teams and task forces to broaden their perspectives; Philips's frequent use of conferences and meetings as forums to reconcile differences; and Unilever's extensive use of training as a powerful socialization process and its well-planned career path management that provided diverse experience across businesses, functions, and geographic locations – all are examples of companies trying to develop multidimensional perspectives and flexible approaches at the level of the individual manager.

What is critical, then, is not just the structure, but also the mentality of those who constitute the structure. The common thread that holds together the diverse tasks we have described is a managerial mindset that understands the need for multiple strategic capabilities, that is able to view problems from both local and global perspectives, and that accepts the importance of a flexible approach. This pattern suggests that managers should resist the temptation to view their task in the traditional terms of building a formal global matrix structure – an organizational form that in practice has proven extraordinarily difficult to manage in the international environment. They might be better guided by the perspective of one top manager who described the challenge as 'creating a matrix in the minds of managers.'

Our study has led us to conclude that a company's ability to develop transnational organizational capability and management mentality will be the key factor that separates the winners from the mere survivors in the emerging international environment.

References

1. The findings presented in this article are based on a three-year research project on the organization and management of multinational corporations. A description of the three-phase study and of the nine American, European, and Japanese MNCs that made up the core of the clinical research stage is contained in the companion article, 'Managing across borders: new strategic requirements'

(summer 1987). Complete findings [are] presented in . . . *Managing across Borders: The Transnational Solution* (Boston: Harvard Business School Press, 1989).

2. This global integration/national responsiveness framework was first applied to the analysis of MNC tasks by Prahalad. See C. K. Prahalad, 'The Strategic Process in a Multinational Corporation' (Boston: Harvard Business School, unpublished doctoral dissertation, 1976).

3. Working with a group of Swedish companies, Hedlund has come to similar conclusions. He describes MNCs with dispersed capabilities and differentiated operations as 'heterarchies.' See G. Hedlund, 'The hypermodern MNC – a heterarchy?', *Human Resource Management*, spring 1986, pp. 9–35.

4. Rugman and Poynter have observed a similar phenomenon in the trend toward assigning mature national subsidiaries worldwide responsibility for products with worldwide markets. See A. M. Rugman and T. A. Poynter, 'World product mandates: how will multinationals respond?', *Business Quarterly*, October 1982, pp. 54–61.

5. This issue of differentiation in the roles and responsibilities of MNC subsidiaries has been discussed and a normative framework for creating such differentiation has been proposed in C. A. Bartlett and S. Ghoshal, 'Tap your subsidiaries for global reach,' *Harvard Business Review*, November–December 1986, pp. 87–94.

6. Such global competitive strategies have been described extensively by many authors. See, for example, T. Hout, M. E. Porter, and E. Rudden, 'How global companies win out,' *Harvard Business Review*, September–October 1982, pp. 98–108; and G. Hamel and C. K. Prahalad, 'Do you really have a global strategy?', *Harvard Business Review*, July–August 1985, pp. 139–48.

7. See R. M. Kanter, *The Change Masters* (New York, Simon & Schuster, 1983).

8. The use of such internal quasi market mechanisms as a means of managing interdependencies has been richly described by Westney and Sakakibara. See D. E. Westney and K. Sakakibara, 'The role of Japan-based R&D in global technology strategy,' *Technology in Society*, 7, 1985, pp. 315–30.

9. For a full description of the development of Eurobrand in P&G, see C. A. Bartlett, 'Procter & Gamble Europe: Vizir launch' (Boston, Harvard Business School, Case Services no. 9-384-139).

10. Kogut provides an excellent discussion on how multinational corporations can develop operational flexibility using a worldwide configuration of specialized resource capabilities linked through an integrated management system. See B. Kogut, 'Designing global strategies: profiting from operational flexibility,' *Sloan Management Review*, fall 1985, pp. 27–38.

11. The distinction among sequential, reciprocal, and pooled interdependencies has been made in J. D. Thompson, *Organizations in Action* (New York, McGraw-Hill, 1967).

12. The role of headquarters management in establishing control over worldwide operations and the means by which it is done have been richly described in Y. L. Doz and C. K. Prahalad, 'Headquarters Influence and Strategic Control in MNCs,' *Sloan Management Review*, fall 1981, pp. 15–30.

13. The use of centralization, formalization, and socialization as means of coordination has been discussed by many authors, including P. M. Blau and R. A. Schoenherr, *The Structure of Organizations* (New York, Basic Books, 1971); and W. G. Ouchi, 'Markets, Bureaucracies, and Clans,' *Administrative Science Quarterly*, 25, March 1980, pp. 129–41.

In the specific context of the multinational corporation, the process implications of these mechanisms were described by Bartlett in a model that distinguished 'substantive decision management,' 'temporary coalition management,' and 'decision context management' as alternative management process modes in MNCs. See C. A. Bartlett, 'Multinational Structural Evolution: The Changing Decision Environments' (Boston, Harvard Business School, unpublished doctoral dissertation, 1979).

See also the contributions of G. Hudlund, T. Kogono, and L. Leksell in *The Management of Headquarters – Subsidiary Relationships in MNCs*, ed. L. Otterbeck (London, Gower Publishing, 1981); and Doz and Prahalad (fall 1981).

14. See P. Haspeslagh, 'Portfolio planning: uses and limits,' *Harvard Business Review*, January–February 1982, pp. 58–73.

5   C. Handy

The Virtual Organization

From 'Trust and the virtual organization', *Harvard Business Review*, May–
June 1995, pp. 40–50

Not long ago, I found myself in the Laurentian Library, which Michelangelo built in Florence for the Medicis nearly 500 years ago. It is a special
place, filled with the scent of learning; a place more restful and more
uplifting, in many ways, than the Church of San Lorenzo, in whose cloister
it stands. The Laurentian is no longer used as a library, however. It is
visited only by tourists, and, as for its contents, they could all be fitted
onto one CD-ROM disc.

Was this, I wondered, a symbol of what was coming to all our organizations? Their buildings turned into museums for tourists, their work on
discs? And would we not lose something thereby, because, for all their
probable efficiency, videoconferencing and cruising the Internet are not
the same as working in Michelangelo's library?

Only the week before, in fact, I had been with a group of librarians,
discussing the future of their modern-day libraries. Computer screens and
keyboards, they agreed, were taking over from shelves of books and jour-
nals. A publisher revealed that he was no longer going to print and publish
his journal but would instead enter it into the database of subscribing
organizations. In that case, said one of those present, we need never visit
a library again; we can get all that we want from the screen in our room.
At the University of Virginia, added another, the change is already happening; all you need to access the library is a password and a modem. The library
of the University of Dubrovnik was destroyed, someone else reported, but
the gift of a computer terminal, linked to a host of foreign databases, more
than compensated.

I watched the expressions of those in the room as they took in the
implications of what was being said. They were coming face-to-face with

83

the idea of the virtual library: a library as a concept, not a place; an activity, not a building. For the librarians, who were accustomed to seeing themselves as guardians of a special place, the idea was either frightening or exciting, depending on their ages and attitudes.

Libraries, whose lifeblood is information, were always likely to be among the first to confront the challenge and opportunity of virtuality, but as businesses become ever more dependent on information, they come up against the same dilemmas. An office is, at heart, an interpretative library geared to a particular purpose, and more and more of our economic activity is a churning of information, ideas, and intelligence in all their infinite variety – an invitation to virtuality.

It is easy to be seduced by the technological possibilities of the virtual organization, but the managerial and personal implications may cause us to rethink what we mean by an organization. At its simplest, the managerial dilemma comes down to the question, How do you manage people whom you do not see? The simple answer is, By trusting them, but the apparent simplicity disguises a turnaround in organizational thinking. The rules of trust are both obvious and well established, but they do not sit easily with a managerial tradition that believes efficiency and control are closely linked and that you can't have one without a lot of the other. Organizationally, we have to wonder whether a company is, in the future, going to be anything more than the box of contracts that some companies now seem to be. Is a box of contracts a sustainable basis for getting the work done in our society, or is it not, in fact, a recipe for disintegration? For society as a whole, the challenge will be to make sure that virtuality brings benefits to all and not just to a favored few. Organizations and, in particular, business organizations, are the linchpins of society. That gives them responsibilities beyond themselves, responsibilities that virtuality throws into high relief.

The virtuality dimension

If one ignores the technology, there is nothing new, conceptually, in the idea of an activity without a building as its home. Where information is the raw material of work, it has never been necessary to have all the people in the same place at the same time. A network of salespeople is the most common example – so ordinary and everyday an example that we would not think of giving it such a grandiose title as a virtual organization. Yet salespeople operate on their own, out of no common place – out of sight but not, one hopes, out of touch or, for that matter, out of line.

Journalism provides other examples. I myself fill an occasional slot on the BBC morning radio program *Today*. For many years, I did not meet my director, nor have I ever met any members of the production team. I communicate by telephone from wherever I happen to be, and my contributions are often broadcast from remote, unmanned studios. It is not in any way unusual.

The Open University in Great Britain, with counterparts all over the world, is perhaps the most ambitious example of a concept without a place. The Open University has a home base, to be sure, but none of the students and few of the faculty are to be found there. Its home base is merely the administrative hub of an unseen and sprawling empire. Its business school is already the largest in Europe, although few of the students have ever met any of the faculty or any of the other students. They used to meet at short residential summer schools, using the campuses of more traditional universities. This year, however, the university has created its first truly virtual summer school. The students will participate from their homes or places of work via E-mail, mobile phone, and videoconferencing. They will never be together in the same place at the same time. The technology has been provided by the university, which has thoughtfully included the mobile phone for students so that, as they sit with their computers beside them, still connected to their land telephone lines, they may converse with supervisors.

In my part of Great Britain, the central library in Norwich, serving the eastern region of the country, burned to the ground last summer. The librarian is considering replacing the grand building with a network of tiny libraries in every hamlet and town throughout the region, each linked to a central facility and, indeed, to every library in the world if need be. As in Dubrovnik, disaster can help us leap into the future before we ever intended. What will hold our librarian back, however, is not the technology or the money – both are potentially available – but the hearts and minds of his staff and his political masters. That's because what people cannot see they often cannot contemplate.

Business is creeping along behind such exemplars from the public sector. Large parts of organizations are now made up of ad hoc miniorganizations, projects collated for a particular time and purpose, drawing their participants from both inside and outside the parent organization. The projects often have no one place to call their own. They exist as activities not as buildings, their only visible sign is an E-mail address. Inside the buildings that *do* exist, so-called hot-desking is increasingly common. In international business, videoconferencing is the norm. The trains in Great Britain double as mobile offices, with the commuter's doze interrupted by the ringing of personal phones and the bleeping of portable computers.

One day soon, when everyone has a personal phone, the phone will no longer belong to a place. That will be more dramatically different than it sounds. We will be able to call anyone without knowing where they are or what they are doing. The office as the home of our telephone – with a secretary to answer it and a line plugged into the 'wall – will become an antiquated and very expensive notion. An office that is available 168 hours a week but occupied for perhaps 20 is a luxury that organizations can ill afford. If there is an office in the future, it will be more like a clubhouse: a place for meeting, eating, and greeting, with rooms reserved for activities, not for particular people.

Virtuality, however, isn't always as much fun as it is supposed to be. A room of one's own, or at least a desk of one's own, has been the executive security blanket for a century or more. A sense of place is as important to most of us as a sense of purpose. E-mail and voice mail have many attractions, including immediacy, but they are not the same as watching the eyes of others. The loneliness of the long-distance executive is well documented. Even office politics and gossip have their attractions, if only as an antidote to the monotony of much of what goes on in the name of work. Few are going to be eager advocates of virtuality when it really means that work is what you do, not where you go.

The managerial dilemmas

Like it or not, the mixture of economics and technology means that more and more of us will be spending time in virtual space – out of sight, if not out of touch. No longer will our colleagues be down the corridor, available for an unscheduled meeting or a quick progress check. Most meetings will have to be scheduled, even those on video, and will therefore become more infrequent. We will have to learn how to run organizations without meetings.

We will also have to get accustomed to working with and managing those whom we do not see, except on rare and prearranged occasions. That is harder than it sounds. I once sat with a features writer of a daily paper. She was interviewing me in the newsroom, a place filled with smoke, noise, telephones, and the sweat of a hundred journalists. I had to perch on the edge of her desk – there was nowhere else.

'Couldn't we have done this somewhere else?' I said over the hubbub. 'Like at your home?'

'I wish we could,' she said. 'Indeed, I would do so much of my work a lot better if I could do it where it suited me. I could send it down the wire just as easily from home, or wherever, as from here.'

'Why don't you, then?' I asked with surprise.

'Because *they* want me where they can see me.' And she pointed down the long room to where two men sat behind large plateglass windows. They were the editors, she explained, and they liked to be able to see what everyone was doing, to check the work, or to interrupt it whenever they needed to give out a new assignment.

'The truth is,' she said, 'they don't trust us.'

Trust is the heart of the matter. That seems obvious and trite, yet most of our organizations tend to be arranged on the assumption that people cannot be trusted or relied on, even in tiny matters. Oversight systems are set up to prevent anyone from doing the wrong thing, whether by accident or design.

The other day, a courier could not find my family's remote cottage. He called his base on his radio, and the base called us to ask directions. He was just around the corner, but his base managed to omit a vital part of the directions. So he called them again, and they called us again. Then the courier repeated the cycle a third time to ask whether we had a dangerous dog. When he eventually arrived, we asked whether it would not have been simpler and less aggravating to everyone if he had called us directly from the roadside telephone booth where he had been parked. 'I can't do that,' he said, 'because they won't refund any money I spend.' 'But it's only pennies!' I exclaimed. 'I know,' he said, 'but that only shows how little they trust us!'

Writ large, that sort of attitude creates a paraphernalia of systems, checkers, and checkers checking checkers – expensive and deadening. Some commentators have argued that *audit mania* (the urge to have some independent inspection) is a virus infecting our society. It exists, they suggest, because we no longer trust people to act for anything but their own short-term interests. That attitude becomes a self-fulfilling prophecy. 'If they don't trust me,' employees say to themselves, 'Why should I bother to put their needs before mine?' If it is even partly true that a lack of trust makes employees untrustworthy, it does not bode well for the future of virtuality in organizations. If we are to enjoy the efficiencies and other benefits of the virtual organization, we will have to rediscover how to run organizations based more on trust than on control. Virtuality requires trust to make it work: Technology on its own is not enough.

The rules of trust

Common sense tells us that there are seven cardinal principles of trust we should keep in mind:

Trust is not blind. It is unwise to trust people whom you do not know well, whom you have not observed in action over time, and who are not committed to the same goals. In practice, it is hard to know more than fifty people that well. Those fifty can each, in turn, know another fifty, and so on. Large organizations are not therefore incompatible with the principle of trust, but they have to be made up of relatively constant, smaller groupings. The idea that people should move around as much and as fast as possible in order to get more exposure and more experience – what the Japanese call the horizontal fast track – can mean that there is no time to learn to trust anyone and, in the end, no point, because the organization starts to replace trust with systems of control.

My title in one large organization was MKR/32. In that capacity, I wrote memos to FIN/41 or PRO/23. I rarely heard any names, and I never met the people behind those titles. I had no reason to trust them and, frankly, no desire to. I was a 'temporary role occupant,' in the jargon of the time, a role occupant in an organization of command and control, based on the premise that no one could really be trusted. I left after a year. Such places can be prisons for the human soul.

Trust needs boundaries. Unlimited trust is, in practice, unrealistic. By trust, organizations really mean confidence, a confidence in someone's competence and in his or her commitment to a goal. Define that goal, and the individual or the team can be left to get on with it. Control is then after the event, when the results are assessed. It is not a matter of granting permission before the event. Freedom within boundaries works best, however, when the work unit is self-contained, having the capability within it to solve its own problems. Trust-based organizations are, as a result, reengineering their work, pulling back from the old reductionist models of organization, in which everything was divided into its component parts or functions. At first sight, the new holistic designs for the units of the organization look more expensive because they duplicate functions and do not necessarily replicate each other. The energy and effectiveness released by the freedom within boundaries more than compensates, however. To succeed, reengineering must be built on trust. When it fails, it is because trust is absent.

Trust demands learning. An organizational architecture made up of relatively independent and constant groupings, pushes the organization toward the sort of federal structure that is becoming more common everywhere. A necessary condition of constancy, however, is an ability to change: If one set of people cannot be exchanged for another set when circumstances alter, then the first set must adapt or die. The constant groups must always be flexible enough to change when times and customers demand it. They must also keep themselves abreast of change, forever exploring new options and new technologies. They must create a real learning culture. The choice of people for these groups is therefore crucial. Every individual has to be capable of self-renewal. Recruitment and placement become key, along with the choice of group leaders. Such topics will require the serious attention of senior management. They should not be delegated to a lower echelon of human resources.

Trust is tough. The reality is, however, that even the best recruiters and the best judges of character will get it wrong sometimes. When trust proves to be misplaced – not because people are deceitful or malicious but because they do not live up to expectations or cannot be relied on to do what is needed – then those people have to go. Where you cannot trust, you have to become a checker once more, with all the systems of control that involves. Therefore, for the sake of the whole, the individual must leave. Trust has to be ruthless. It is incompatible with any promise of a job for life. After all, who can be so sure of their recruitment procedures that they are prepared to trust forever those whom they select? It is because trust is so important but so risky, that organizations tend to restrict their core commitments to a smaller group of what I call *trusties*. But that policy in turn pushes the organization toward a core/periphery model, one that can, if practitioners are not careful, degenerate into a set of purely formal contractual relationships with all the outsiders. Nothing is simple; there is paradox everywhere.

Trust needs bonding. Self-contained units responsible for delivering specified results are the necessary building blocks of an organization based on trust, but long-lasting groups of trusties can create their own problems, those of organizations within the organization. For the whole to work, the goals of the smaller units have to gel with the goals of the whole. The blossoming of vision and mission statements is one attempt to deal with integration, as are campaigns for total quality or excellence. Such things matter. Or rather, if they did not exist, their absence would matter. They are not, however, enough in themselves. They need to be backed up by exhortation and personal example. Anita Roddick holds her spreading Body Shop together by what can best be called 'personal infection,' pouring her energies into the reinforcement of her values and beliefs through every medium she can find. It is always a dangerous strategy to personalize a mission, in case the person stumbles or falls, as the Body Shop nearly did last year after unfavorable publicity, but organizations based on trust need that sort of personal statement from their leaders. Trust is not and never can be an impersonal commodity.

Trust needs touch. Visionary leaders, no matter how articulate, are not enough. A shared commitment still requires personal contact to make it real. To augment John Naisbitt's telling phrase, high tech has to be balanced by high touch to build high-trust organizations. Paradoxically, the more virtual an organization becomes, the more its people need to meet in person. The meetings, however, are different. They are more about process than task, more concerned that people get to know each other than that they deliver. Videoconferences are more task focused, but they are easier and more productive if the individuals know each other as people, not just as images on the screen. Work and play, therefore, alternate in many of the corporate get-togethers that now fill the conference resorts out of season. These are not perks for the privileged; they are the necessary lubricants of virtuality, occasions not only for getting to know each other and for meeting the leaders but also for reinforcing corporate goals and rethinking corporate strategies. As one who delivers the occasional 'cabaret' at such occasions, I am always surprised to find how few of the participants have met each other in person, even if they have worked together before. I am then further surprised by how quickly a common mood develops. You can almost watch the culture grow, and you wonder how they could have worked effectively without it.

Trust requires leaders. At their best, the units in good trust-based organizations hardly have to be managed, but they do need a multiplicity of leaders. I once teased an English audience by comparing a team of Englishmen to a rowing crew on the river – eight men going backward as fast as they can without talking to each other, steered by the one person who can't row! I thought it quite witty at the time, but I was corrected after the session by one of the participants, who had once been an Olympic oarsman. 'How do you think we could go backward so fast without communicating, steered by this little fellow in the stern, if we didn't know each other very well, didn't have total confidence to do our jobs and a shared commitment – almost a passion – for the same goal? It is the perfect formula for a team.'

I had to admit it – he was right. 'But tell me,' I said to him, 'who is the manager of this team?' 'There isn't one,' he replied, after thinking about it. 'Unless that is what you call our part-time administrator back in the office.' Manager, he was reminding me, is a low-status title in organizations of colleagues.

'Well, then, who is the leader?'

'That depends,' he said. 'When we are racing, it is the little chap who is steering, because he is the only one who can see where we are going. But there is also the stroke, who sets the standard for all of us. He is a leader, too, in a way. But off the river, it's the captain of the crew, who selects us, bonds us together, builds our commitment to our goal and our dedication. Lastly, in training, there is our coach, who is undoubtedly the main influence on our work. So you see,' he concluded, 'there isn't a simple answer to your question.'

A rowing crew, I realized, has to be based on trust if it is to have any chance of success. And if any member of that crew does not pull his weight, then he does not deserve the confidence of the others and must be asked to leave. Nor can all the leadership requirements be discharged by one person, no matter how great or how good.

The organization's dilemma

Racing crews row for the sake of glory, but it is not as clear what motivates the people in the virtual organizations of business. Why should the now smaller core of trusted individuals give so much of their lives and time and talent to an organization that they work for but do not live in, an organization that, significantly, someone else owns, someone whom they almost certainly do not know and have never met, because, for the most part, that someone is not an individual at all but an institution owned, in turn, by other anonymous people?

That question had a clear answer in times past. The organization was the instrument of its owners, and the individual was the instrument of the organization. The implied and the legal contracts were both instrumental. The individual was a hired hand, a human resource, employed to work the assets of the organization. Good pay, good prospects, and a challenging job were enough for most. The human resource, however, is now the human asset, not the human cost. That is not just refined semantics, it is the literal financial truth. The market value of the top 200 businesses on the London Stock Exchange is on average three times the worth of the visible fixed assets. In the case of the high-tech high fliers, it can be up to 20 times. If that means anything, it means that the market is valuing the intangible assets many times higher than the tangible ones. Whether those intangible assets are the research in a company's pipeline, the brands, the know-how, or the networks of experience, they amount in the end to one thing: the people.

Those people can and often do walk out the door. Whole teams of analysts nowadays shift themselves from one financial institution to another at the glint of a golden handshake or the lure of new pastures. If laborers are worthy of their hire, there is no reason to suppose that they won't go where the hire looks better. The assets of the new information-based corporations are, as a result, increasingly fragile. It is hard to measure assets in the present, harder still to gauge their future. Investing in information-based businesses will be even more of a gamble than it has been in the past.

The consequences of increased gambling are predictable: Investors will be in more of a hurry to get their money back; managers will be under pressure to milk their assets while they still have them; horizons will shrink; and the result will be that, even if the assets don't walk, they will wilt. Under those pressures, even inspired, articulate leaders will be hard-pressed to hold the virtual corporation together.

When labourers become assets, the underlying contract with the organization has to change. Trust inevitably requires some sense of mutuality, of reciprocal loyalty. Virtual organizations, which feed on information, ideas, and intelligence (which in turn are vested in the heads and hearts of people), cannot escape the dilemma. One answer is to turn the laborers into members; that is, to turn the instrumental contract into a membership contract for the smaller core. Members have rights. They also have responsibilities. Their rights include a share in the governance of the community to which they belong. No one can buy a club against the wishes of its members. Major capital investments and strategic initiatives require the agreement of the members. The terms and conditions of membership require members' agreement. Their responsibilities center on the need to make the business grow, because without growth there will be no striving and, ultimately, no point. Growth, however, can mean growth in quality, size, profitability, or desirability, and maybe in all four. People who think of themselves as members have more of an interest in the future of the business and its growth than those who are only its hired help.

Giving membership rights to key people is not the same as giving them ownership, but those membership rights inevitably diminish the powers of the owners. Shareholders become investors rather than owners. They are entitled to a reasonable return on their money – a return that takes the risk into account – but they are not entitled, for instance, to sell the company over the heads of its members or to dictate to management, unless the financial returns start to evaporate. Major investors, however, who tend to be long-term investors, might also be included in the extended family of the business. Such a shift in the governance of the corporation would bring Anglo-American businesses more into line with the businesses of continental Europe or Japan. Companies there, paradoxically perhaps, are seeking to give more power to the investors as a discipline for the members and their management and as a way of increasing the financial base. The principle of requisite balance would suggest that all groups should meet halfway, and they probably will, as the world of business becomes increasingly linked and interdependent.

The concept of membership, when made real, would replace the sense of belonging to a *place* with a sense of belonging to a *community*, even if that community were a largely virtual one. A sense of belonging is something humans need if they are to commit themselves to more than simple selfishness. Families and family businesses know something about the sense of belonging and the motivating force of collective pride in the family tradition, as well as the responsibilities that go with belonging. Families, at their best, are communities built on mutual trust. If the family could be extended to include key contributors, the sense of belonging would be properly inclusive. Without some real sense of belonging, virtuality looks like a very precarious state and a perilous base for the next phase of capitalism, whatever the economic and technological advantages.

Society's dilemma

An economy that adds value through information, ideas, and intelligence – the Three I Economy – offers a way out of the apparent clash between material growth and environmental erosion. Information, ideas, and intelligence consume few of the earth's resources. Virtuality will redesign our cities with fewer skyscrapers and fewer commuters, making a quieter and perhaps a gentler world. Our aspirations for growth in a Three I Economy would increasingly be more a matter for the mind than for the body. The growth sectors would be education in all its varied forms, health care, the arts and entertainment, leisure, travel, and sports. As the economic statistics show, the new growth is already happening, and the organizations that deliver it tend to be small groups of colleagues united by mutual trust. Small, growing companies often serve today's young people, who aspire to better music systems and computers rather than to faster cars or flashier clothes. The younger generation also relishes employment in the new and freer organizations.

Not all people do, however. If the Three I Economy is to take off in the First World and thus give hope of a sustainable future to others, everyone needs to be able to participate. Currently, there is in every country of the First World a growing underclass that knows little about the concepts behind the Three I Economy. For members of that underclass, such concepts are a joke. They want hamburgers and heating, not computers. In the short term, maybe, they should be helped with their hamburgers and heating, but they also need a hand up into the Three I Economy. Virtuality will be a recipe for a divided society unless we help everyone, and a society divided will not long survive. We have to take from the present to ensure our future, instead of borrowing from the future to ensure our present, as most countries do today.

Everyone has something to contribute to a Three I Economy. There is no unteachable group. Talent in some form or another exists in all human beings, it only needs to be detected and developed. Naturally, early education is crucial, but our future should not be determined by the time we are sixteen. Work can be a great laboratory of learning, and organizations, therefore, hold one of the keys to the future of society. But if they concentrate their efforts only on their core members, they will be throwing away that key. Who else will help those who are outside the organization – the independents, the part-timers, and the small contractors and suppliers?

Already, in the European Union, one half of the available workforce is outside the organization, not in full-time jobs. If organizations do not embrace the concept of an extended family and include their associated workers in their plans for their human assets, the workforce will become increasingly useless to them and to themselves. If a trust-based organization means trust for some and the old instrumental contract for the less able, then trust will become a dirty word, a synonym for selfishness. Some see the peripheral workforce as the responsibility of government – to train, to employ, or, if all else fails, to support. Governments, however, have their limits. They can pass laws, they can regulate, and they can sometimes find money to empower others; but they cannot and should not try to do it all themselves. They need help from the rest of society.

The hope for the future that is contained within the virtual organization will end in disillusionment unless we can mobilize society to think beyond itself to save itself. Governments in a democracy can move only as fast as the opinion leaders in society. Business has always been a major leader of opinion, but if business minds its own business exclusively or if it takes virtuality to extremes and becomes a mere broker or box of contracts, then it will have failed society. In the end, its search for wealth will have destroyed wealth.

PART TWO

The Organization in Its Environment

All organizations are situated in an environment, be that business, governmental, educational or voluntary service. In this environment are other organizations and people with whom transactions have to take place. These will include suppliers, clients or customers, and competitors. In addition there will be more general aspects of the environment which will have important effects, such as legal, technological, cultural and ethical developments. The contributors to this section have been concerned to analyse how the need to function successfully in different environments has led organizations to adopt different structures and strategies.

Burns (Reading 6) highlights the limitations of formal bureaucracies which are only appropriate to stable environmental conditions. Changing situations require organismic (earlier called 'organic') systems. In these, authority, task allocation and communication are extremely flexible in contrast to the rigid rules and procedures of bureaucracy.

Lawrence and Lorsch (Reading 7) continue the exploration of the relationship of the organization's structure to the environment which it faces. They analyse the degree of structural differentiation necessary for a firm to function in a particular environment and the consequent integration mechanisms required for it to be a high performer.

Pfeffer and Salancik (Reading 8) argue for a 'resource dependence perspective' which sees all organizational functioning as resulting from the organization's dependence on other institutions in its environment.

Miles and Snow (Reading 9) demonstrate that organizations to be successful must achieve a strategic fit between their environments and their management strategies and structures.

Hannan and Freeman (Reading 10) take an ecological and evolutionary view of organizational functioning. Their studies of organizational 'births and deaths' lead them to argue that the chances of organizations thriving and surviving depend primarily upon the pressures of their particular environmental 'niches'.

Hofstede (Reading 11) conducted a major worldwide study of the values of employees in fifty different countries of an American multinational

97

corporation – later publicly identified as IBM. His work underlines the importance of national culture to organizational behaviour. This environmental feature is particularly important in the ever more frequent international activities of organizations. Hofstede questions, therefore, how far American theories – which have been so dominant in management thinking – can be applied in other countries.

6   T. Burns

Mechanistic and Organismic Structures

From 'Industry in a new age', *New Society*, 31 January 1963, pp. 17–20

Industry has a long past. We are now near the end of the second century of industrialism in its recognizably modern form. To be conscious of the history of an institution like the industrial concern is to become alive to two essential considerations. First, that like any other institution – government, the church, the family, military forces, for example – industry has undergone substantial changes in its organizational form as well as in its activities, tasks and objectives. Secondly, and in consequence, unless we realize that industrial organization is still in the process of development, we are liable to be trapped into trying to use out-of-date organizational systems for coping with entirely new situations.

A sense of the past – and the very recent past – is essential to anyone who is trying to perceive the here-and-now of industrial organization. What is happening now is part of a continuing development. A study of this process will at least help firms avoid the traps they often fall into when they try to confront a situation of the newest kind with an organizational system appropriate to an earlier phase of industrial development. Adaptation to new challenge is not an automatic process: there are many factors against it.

What we recognize as industrialism is the product of two technologies, material and social. It has developed in spasmodic fashion from the rudimentary forms of the eighteenth century by alternate advances in first one technology and then the other.

The elementary form of industrialism is Adam Smith's conjunction of the division of labour traditional in advanced society with the extension of its advantages by 'those machines by which labour is so much facilitated and enlarged'.

The modern industrial system was founded at a time when the perception

99

by early mechanical scientists that natural events 'obeyed' certain laws became widely diffused – in the eighteenth century. Samuel Smiles' legend that Arkwright was first struck by the feasibility of mechanical spinning 'by accidentally observing a hot piece of iron become elongated by passing between iron rollers' may be fiction, but it reflects truly the commonplace terms in which the new habits of scientific thought could be used by craftsmen-inventors, who saw not just an interesting analogy but one process obeying a law which might also apply to a different and entirely new process.

At the same time as Adam Smith was observing the archetypal form of the two technologies, a third step was being taken: the creation of the first successful factory by Strutt and Arkwright. By 1835 Ure could already discount the basic principles of division of labour as outdated and misleading. The industrial system was simply the factory system as developed by Arkwright: the term 'factory' meaning 'the combined operation of many work people, adult and young, in tending with assiduous skill a system of productive machines continuously impelled by a central power. It is the constant aim and tendency of every improvement in machinery to supersede human labour altogether.'

Factory organization stayed for three generations at the point at which Arkwright had left it. Marx's account contains the same essentials: a collection of machines in a building all driven by one prime mover, and, preferably, of the same type and engaged on the same process. Attending the machines were men and women who themselves were attended by 'feeders', most of them children, who fetched and carried away materials. There was also a 'superior, but numerically unimportant' class of maintenance and repair workers. All of these worked under a master, with perhaps a chief workman or foreman. The primitive social technology of the factory system still confined it, even by the 1850s, largely to the mass production of textiles.

Technical developments in transport and communications, the impact of the international exhibitions in London and Paris, free trade, the armaments revolutions supported by the development of machine tools and of steel, and chemical technology (in Germany first) all combined during the 1850s and 1860s to form the springboard, in material technology, of the next advance in the social techniques of industrial organization.

As yet, there is no account of how that advance took place. All that can be said is that with the extension of the factory system into engineering and chemicals, iron and steel processing, food manufacture and clothing, an organizational development took place which provided for the conduct and control of many complex series of production processes within the same plant. One overt sign of this development is the increase in the number of salaried officials employed in industry. The proportion of 'administrative employees' to 'production employees' in British manufacturing industry had risen to 8·6 per cent by 1907 and to 20 per cent by 1948. Similar increases took place in western Europe and the United States.

The growth in the numbers of industrial administrative officials, or managers, reflects the growth of organizational structures. Production department managers, sales managers, accountants, cashiers, inspectors, training officers, publicity managers, and the rest emerged as specialized parts of the general management function as industrial concerns increased in size. Their jobs were created, in fact, out of the eighteenth-century master's, either directly or at one or two removes. This gives them and the whole social structure which contains their newly created roles its hierarchical character. It is indeed a patrimonial structure. All rights and powers at every level derive from the boss; fealty, or 'responsibility', is owed to him; all benefits are 'as if' dispensed by him. The bond is more easily and more often broken than in pre-feudal polities, but loyalty to the concern, to employers, is still regarded not only as proper, but as essential to the preservation of the system.

Chester Barnard makes this point with unusual emphasis: 'The most important single contribution required of the executive, certainly the most universal qualification, is loyalty, domination by the organization personality.' More recently, A. W. Gouldner has pointed out 'much of W. H. Whyte's recent study of Organization Man is a discussion of the efforts by industry to attach managerial loyalty to the corporation'.

The development of the bureaucratic system made possible the increase in scale of undertakings characteristic of the first part of this century. It had other aspects. The divorce of ownership and management, although by no means absolute, went far enough to render survival of the enterprise (and the survival of the existing management) at least as important a consideration as making the best profit. Profit itself wears a different aspect in the large-scale corporation.

More important, the growth of bureaucracy – the social technology which made possible the second stage of industrialism – was only feasible because the development of material technology was held relatively steady. An industry based on major technological advances shows a high death-rate among enterprises in its early years; growth occurs when the rate of technical advance slows down. What happens is that consumer demand tends to be standardized through publicity and price reductions, and technical progress is consequently restrained. This enables companies to maintain relatively stable conditions, in which large-scale production is built up by converting manufacturing processes into routine cycles of activity for machines or semi-skilled assembly hands.

Under such conditions, not only could a given industrial company grow in size, not only could the actual manufacturing processes be routinized, mechanized and quickened, but the various management functions also could be broken down into specialisms and routines. Thus developed specialized management tasks: those of ensuring employee cooperation, of coordinating different departments, of planning and monitoring.

It is this second phase of industrialism which now dominates the institutional life of western societies. But while the greater part of the industrial system is in this second, bureaucratic phase of the historical development (and some older and smaller establishments remain in the first), it is now becoming clear that we have entered a third phase during the past two or three decades. J. K. Galbraith, in his *Affluent Society*, has described the new, more insecure relationship with the consumer which appears as production catches up and overtakes spontaneous domestic demand. The 'propensity to consume' has had to be stimulated by advertising, by styling, and by marketing promotions guided by research into the habits, motives, and potential 'needs' of consumers. At the same time, partly in an effort to maintain expansion, partly because of the stimulus of government spending on new military equipment, industry has admitted a sizeable influx of new technical developments.

There are signs that industry organized according to principles of bureaucracy – by now traditional – is no longer able to accommodate the new elements of industrial life in the affluent second half of the twentieth century. These new demands are made by large-scale research and development and by industry's new relationship with its markets. Both demand a much greater flexibility in internal organization, much higher levels of commitment to the commercial aims of the company from all its members, and an even higher proportion of administrators, controllers, and monitors to operatives.

Recently, with G. M. Stalker, I made an attempt to elucidate the situation of concerns in the electronics industry which were confronted with rapidly changing commercial circumstances and a much faster rate of technical progress. I found it necessary to posit two 'ideal types' of working organization, the one mechanistic, adapted to relatively stable conditions, the other, 'organismic', adapted to conditions of change.

In mechanistic systems the problems and tasks which face the concern as a whole are, typically, broken down into specialisms. Each individual carries out his assigned task as something apart from the overall purpose of the company as a whole. 'Somebody at the top' is responsible for seeing that his work is relevant to that of others. The technical methods, duties, and powers attached to each post are precisely defined, and a high value is placed on precision and demarcation. Interaction within the working organization follows vertical lines – i.e. between superiors and subordinates. How a man operates and what he does is prescribed by his functional role and governed by instructions and decisions issued by superiors. This hierarchy of command is maintained by the assumption that the only man who knows – or should know – all about the company is the man at the top. He is the only one, therefore, who knows exactly how the human resources should be properly disposed. The management system, usually visualized as the complex hierarchy familiar in organization charts, operates as a simple control system, with information flowing upwards through a succession of filters, and decisions and instructions flowing downwards through a succession of amplifiers.

Mechanistic systems are, in fact, the 'rational bureaucracy' of an earlier generation of students of organization. For the individual, it provides an ordered world of work. His own decisions and actions occur within a stable constellation of jobs, skills, specialized knowledge, and sectional responsibilities. In a textile mill, or any factory which sees itself turning out any standardized product for a familiar and steady market, one finds decision making at all levels prescribed by the familiar.

As one descends through the levels of management, one finds more limited information and less understanding of the human capacities of other members of the firm. One also finds each person's task more and more clearly defined by his superior. Beyond a certain limit he has insufficient authority, insufficient information, and usually insufficient technical ability to be able to make decisions. He is informed quite clearly when this limit occurs; beyond it, he has one course open – to report to his superior.

Organismic systems are adapted to unstable conditions, when new and unfamiliar problems and requirements continually arise which cannot be broken down and distributed among specialist roles within a hierarchy. Jobs lose much of their formal definition. The definitive and enduring demarcation of functions becomes impossible. Responsibilities and functions, and even methods and powers, have to be constantly redefined through interaction with others participating in common tasks or in the solution of common problems. Each individual has to do his job with knowledge of overall purpose and situation of the company as a whole. Interaction runs laterally as much as vertically, and communication between people of different rank tends to resemble 'lateral' consultation rather than 'vertical' command. Omniscience can no longer be imputed to the boss at the top.

The head of one successful electronics concern, at the very beginning of the first interview of the whole study, attacked the idea of the organization chart as inapplicable in his concern and as a dangerous method of thinking. The first requirement of a management, according to him, was that it should make the fullest use of the capacities of its members; any individual's job should be as little defined as possible, so that it would 'shape itself' to his special abilities and initiative.

In this company, insistence on the least possible specification for managerial positions was much more in evidence than any devices for ensuring adequate interaction within the system. This did occur, but it was often due to physical conditions rather than to order by top management. A single-storeyed building housed the entire company, two thousand strong, from laboratories to canteen. Access to anyone was, therefore, physically simple and direct; it was easier to walk across to the laboratory door, the office door, or the factory door and look about for the person one wanted, than even to telephone. Written communication inside the factory was actively discouraged. More important than the physical set-up however was the need of each individual manager for interaction with others, in order to get his own functions defined, since these were not specified from above.

For the individual, the important part of the difference between the mechanistic and the organismic is in the degree of his commitment to the working organization. Mechanistic systems tell him what he has to attend to, and how, and also tell him what he does *not* have to bother with, what is *not* his affair, what is *not* expected of him – what he can post elsewhere as the responsibility of others. In organismic systems, such boundaries disappear. The individual is expected to regard himself as fully implicated in the discharge of any task appearing over his horizon. He has not merely to exercise a special competence, but to commit himself to the success of the concern's undertakings as a whole.

Mechanistic and organismic systems of management[1]

A mechanistic management system is appropriate to stable conditions. It is characterized by:

1. The *specialized differentiation* of functional tasks into which the problems and tasks facing the concern as a whole are broken down.
2. The *abstract nature* of each individual task, which is pursued with techniques and purposes more or less distinct from those of the concern as a whole.
3. The reconciliation, for each level in the hierarchy, of these distinct performances by the *immediate superiors*.
4. The *precise definition* of rights and obligations and technical methods attached to each functional role.
5. The *translation of rights* and obligations and methods into the responsibilities of a functional position.
6. *Hierarchic structure* of control, authority, and communication.
7. A reinforcement of the hierarchic structure by the location of *knowledge* of actualities exclusively *at the top* of the hierarchy.
8. A tendency for *vertical interaction* between members of the concern, i.e. between superior and subordinate.
9. A tendency for operations and working behaviour to be *governed by superiors*.
10. *Insistence on loyalty* to the concern and obedience to superiors as a condition of membership.
11. A greater importance and prestige attaching to *internal* (local) than to general (cosmopolitan) knowledge, experience and skill.

The organismic form is appropriate to changing conditions, which give rise constantly to fresh problems and unforeseen requirements for action which cannot be broken down or distributed automatically arising from the functional roles defined within a hierarchic structure. It is characterized by:

1. The *contributive nature* of special knowledge and experience to the common task of the concern.
2. The *realistic* nature of the individual task, which is seen as set by the total situation of the concern.

1. Source: Burns and Stalker (1961).

3. The adjustment and *continual redefinition* of individual tasks through interaction with others.
4. The *shedding of responsibility* as a limited field of rights, obligations, and methods. (Problems may not be posted upwards, downwards or sideways.)
5. The *spread of commitment* to the concern beyond any technical definition.
6. A *network structure* of control, authority, and communication.
7. Omniscience no longer imputed to the head of the concern; *knowledge* may be located anywhere in the network; this location becoming the centre of authority.
8. A *lateral* rather than a vertical direction of communication through the organization.
9. A content of communication which consists of *information and advice* rather than instructions and decisions.
10. *Commitment* to the concern's tasks and to the 'technological ethos' of material progress and expansion is more highly valued than loyalty.
11. Importance and prestige attach to *affiliations and expertise* valid in the industrial and technical and commercial milieux external to the firm.

In studying the electronics industry in Britain, we were occupied for the most part with companies which had been started a generation or more ago, well within the time period of the second phase of industrialization. They were equipped at the outset with working organizations designed by mechanistic principles. The ideology of formal bureaucracy seemed so deeply ingrained in industrial management that the common reaction to unfamiliar and novel conditions was to redefine, in more precise and rigorous terms, the roles and working relationships obtaining within management, along orthodox lines of organization charts and organization manuals. The formal structure was reinforced, not adapted. In these concerns the effort to make the orthodox bureaucratic system work produced what can best be described as pathological forms of the mechanistic system.

Three of these pathological systems are described below. All three were responses to the need for finding answers to new and unfamiliar problems and for making decisions in new circumstances of uncertainty.

First, there is the *ambiguous figure* system. In a mechanistic organization, the normal procedure for dealing with any matter lying outside the boundaries of one individual's functional responsibility is to refer it to the point in the system where such responsibility is known to reside, or, failing that, to lay it before one's superior. If conditions are changing rapidly such episodes occur frequently; in many instances, the immediate superior has to put such matters higher up still. A sizeable volume of matters for solution and decision can thus find their way to the head of the concern. There can, and frequently does, develop a system by which a large number of executives find – or claim – that they can only get matters settled by going to the top man.

So, in some places we studied, an ambiguous system developed of an official hierarchy, and a clandestine or open system of pair relationships between the head of the concern and some dozens of persons at different positions below him in the management. The head of the concern was overloaded with work, and senior managers whose standing depended on the mechanistic formal system felt aggrieved at being bypassed. The managing director told himself – or brought in consultants to tell him – to delegate responsibility and decision-making. The organization chart would be redrawn. But inevitably, this strategy promoted its own counter measures from the beneficiaries of the old, latent system as the stream of novel and unfamiliar problems built up anew.

The conflict between managers who saw their standing and prospects depending on the ascendancy of the old system or the new deflected attention and effort into internal politics. All of this bore heavily on the time and effective effort the head of the company was free to apply to his proper function, the more so because political moves focused on controlling access to him.

Secondly, the *mechanistic jungle*. Some companies simply grew more branches of the bureaucratic hierarchy. Most of the problems which appeared in all these firms with pathological mechanisms manifested themselves as difficulties in communications. These were met, typically, by creating special intermediaries and interpreters: methods engineers, standardization groups, contract managers, post design engineers. Underlying this familiar strategy were two equally familiar clichés of managerial thinking. The first is to look for the solution of a problem, especially a problem of communication, in 'bringing somebody in' to deal with it. A new job, or possibly a whole new department, may then be created, which depends for its survival on the perpetuation of the difficulty. The second attitude probably comes from the traditions of productive management: a development engineer is not doing the job he is paid for unless he is at his drawing board, drawing, and so on. Higher management has the same instinctive reaction when it finds people moving about the works, when individuals it wants are not 'in their place'. There, managers cannot trust subordinates when they are not demonstrably and physically 'on the job'. Their response, therefore, when there was an admitted need for 'better communication' was to tether functionaries to their posts and to appoint persons who would specialize in 'liaison'.

The third kind of pathological response is the *super-personal* or committee system. It was encountered only rarely in the electronics firms we studied; it appeared sporadically in many of them, but it was feared as the characteristic disease of government administration. The committee is a traditional device whereby *temporary* commitments over and above those encapsulated in a single functional role may be contained within the system and discharged without enlarging the demands on individual functionaries, or upsetting the balance of power.

Committees are often set up where new kinds of work and/or unfamiliar problems seem to involve decisions, responsibilities, and powers beyond the capabilities or deserts of any one man or department. Bureaucratic hierarchies are most prone to this defect. Here most considerations, most of the time, are subordinated to the career structure afforded by the concern (a situation by no means confined to the civil service or even to universities). The difficulty of filling a job calling for unfamiliar responsibility is overcome by creating a super-person – a committee.

Why do companies not adapt to new situations by changing their working organization from mechanistic to organismic? The answer seems to lie in the fact that the individual member of the concern is not only committed to the working organization as a whole. In addition, he is a member of a group or a department with sectional interests in conflict with those of other groups, and all of these individuals are deeply concerned with the position they occupy, relative to others, and their future security or betterment are matters of deep concern.

In regard to sectional commitments, he may be, and usually is, concerned to extend the control he has over his own situation, to increase the value of his personal contribution, and to have his resources possibly more thoroughly exploited and certainly more highly rewarded. He often tries to increase his personal power by attaching himself to parties of people who represent the same kind of ability and wish to enhance its exchange value, or to cabals who seek to control or influence the exercise of patronage in the firm. The interest groups so formed are quite often identical with a department, or the dominant groups in it, and their political leaders are heads of departments, or accepted activist leaders, or elected representatives (e.g. shop stewards). They become involved in issues of internal politics arising from the conflicting demands such as those on allocation of capital, on direction of others, and on patronage.

Apart from this sectional loyalty, an individual usually considers his own career at least as important as the well-being of the firm, and while there may be little incompatibility in his serving the ends of both, occasions do arise when personal interests outweigh the firm's interests, or even a clear conflict arises.

If we accept the notion that a large number, if not all, of the members of a firm have commitments of this kind to themselves, then it is apparent that the resulting relationships and conduct are adjusted to other self-motivated relationships and conduct throughout the concern. We can therefore speak of the new career structure of the concern, as well as of its working organization and political system. Any concern will contain these three systems. All three will interact: particularly, the political system and career structure will influence the constitution and operation of the working organization.

(There are two qualifications to be made here. The tripartite system of commitments is not exhaustive, and is not necessarily self-balancing. Besides commitments to the concern, to 'political' groups, and to his own career prospects, each member of a concern is involved in a multiplicity of relationships. Some arise out of social origin and culture. Others are generated by the encounters which are governed, or seem to be governed, by a desire for the comfort of friendship, or the satisfactions which come from popularity and personal esteem, or those other rewards of inspiring respect, apprehension or alarm. All relationships of this sociable kind, since they represent social values, involve the parties in commitments.)

Neither political nor career preoccupations operate overtly, or even, in some cases, consciously. They give rise to intricate manoeuvres and counter moves, all of them expressed through decisions, or in discussions about decisions, concerning the organization and the policies of the firm. Since sectional interests and preoccupations with advancement only display themselves in terms of the working organization, that organization becomes more or less adjusted to serving the ends of the political and career system rather than those of the concern. Interlocking systems of commitments – to sectional interests and to individual status – generate strong forces. These divert organizations from purposive adaptation. Out of date mechanistic organizations are perpetuated and pathological systems develop, usually because of one or the other of two things: internal politics and the career structure.

Reference

BURNS, T., and STALKER, G. M. (1961), *The Management of Innovation*, Tavistock

7   P. R. Lawrence and J. W. Lorsch

High-performing Organizations in Three Environments

From *Organization and Environment*, Harvard University Press, 1967, chapter 6

In this chapter we shall summarize and amplify the answers we have found to the major question of this study: What types of organization are most effective under different environmental conditions? By comparing three high-performing organizations we can arrive at a more concise understanding of how their internal differences were related to their ability to deal effectively with different sets of environmental conditions. This comparison also provides a more complete picture of each organization, to allow the reader to move beyond the numerical measures and gain a fuller appreciation of the distinct characters of these three effective organizations. While our focus will be on the high performers, we shall draw occasionally on our findings about the other organizations for help in clarifying our conclusions.

It may seem, in this summary, that we are describing 'ideal types' of organizations, which can cope effectively with different environmental conditions. This inference is not valid for two reasons. First, we believe that the major contribution of this study is not the identification of any 'type' of organization that seems to be effective under a particular set of conditions. Rather, it is the increased understanding of a complex set of interrelationships among internal organizational states and processes and external environmental demands. It is these relationships that we shall explain further in this chapter. Second, although all three high-performing organizations were effective in dealing with their particular environments, it would be naive to assume that they were ideal. Each one had problems. One characteristic that the top managers in these organizations seemed to have in common was a constant search for ways to improve their organization's functioning.

Organizational states and environmental demands

In each industry, as we have seen, the high-performing organization came nearer to meeting the demands of its environment than its less effective competitors. The most successful organizations tended to maintain states of differentiation and integration consistent with the diversity of the parts of the environment and the required interdependence of these parts. The differences in the demands of these three environments meant that the high-performing plastics organization was more highly differentiated than the high-performing food organization, which in turn was more differentiated than the high-performing container organization. Simultaneously, all three high-performing organizations were achieving approximately the same degree of integration.

To illustrate the varying states of differentiation among these three organizations, we can use hypothetical encounters among managers in both the plastics and the container high-performing organizations. In the plastics organization we might find a sales manager discussing a potential new product with a fundamental research scientist and an integrator. In this discussion the sales manager is concerned with the needs of the customer. What performance characteristics must a new product have to perform in the customer's machinery? How much can the customer afford to pay? How long can the material be stored without deteriorating? Further, our sales manager, while talking about these matters, may be thinking about more pressing current problems. Should he lower the price on an existing product? Did the material shipped to another customer meet his specifications? Is he going to meet this quarter's sales targets?

By contrast, our fundamental scientist is concerned about a different order of problems. Will this new product provide a scientific challenge? To get the desired result, could he change the molecular structure of a known material without affecting its stability? What difficulties will he encounter in solving these problems? Will this be a more interesting project to work on than another he heard about last week? Will he receive some professional recognition if he is successful in solving the problem? Thus our sales manager and our fundamental scientist not only have quite different goal orientations, but they are thinking about different time dimensions

– the sales manager about what is going on today and in the next few months; the scientist, how he will spend the next few years.

But these are not the only ways in which these two specialists are different. The sales manager may be outgoing and concerned with maintaining a warm, friendly relationship with the scientist. He may be put off because the scientist seems withdrawn and disinclined to talk about anything other than the problems in which he is interested. He may also be annoyed that the scientist seems to have such freedom in choosing what he will work on. Furthermore, the scientist is probably often late for appointments, which, from the salesman's point of view, is no way to run a business. Our scientist, for his part, may feel uncomfortable because the salesman seems to be pressing for immediate answers to technical questions that will take a long time to investigate. All these discomforts are concrete manifestations of the relatively wide differences between these two men in respect to their working and thinking styles and the departmental structures to which each is accustomed.

Between these different points of view stands our integrator. If he is effective, he will understand and to some extent share the viewpoints of both specialists and will be working to help them communicate with each other. We do not want to dwell on his role at this point, but the mere fact that he is present is a result of the great differences among specialists in his organization.

In the high-performing container organization we might find a research scientist meeting with a plant manager to determine how to solve a quality problem. The plant manager talks about getting the problem solved as quickly as possible, in order to reduce the spoilage rate. He is probably thinking about how this problem will affect his ability to meet the current production schedule and to operate within cost constraints. The researcher is also seeking an immediate answer to the problem. He is concerned not with its theoretical niceties, but with how he can find an immediate applied solution. What adjustments in materials or machine procedures can he suggest to get the desired effect? In fact, these specialists may share a concern with finding the most feasible solution. They also operate in a similar, short-term time dimension. The differences in their interpersonal style are also not too large. Both are primarily concerned with getting the job done, and neither finds the other's style of behavior strange. They are also accustomed to quite similar organizational practices. Both see that they are rewarded for quite specific short-run accomplishments, and both might be feeling similar pressures from their superiors to get the job done. In essence, these two specialists, while somewhat different in their thinking and behavior patterns, would not find it uncomfortable or difficult to work together in seeking a joint solution to a problem. Thus they would need no integrator.

These two hypothetical examples show clearly that the differentiation in the plastics organization is much greater than in the equally effective container concern. The high-performing food organization fell between the extremes of differentiation represented by the other two organizations. These examples illustrate another important point stressed earlier: that the states of differentiation and integration within any organization are antagonistic. Other things (such as the determinants of conflict resolution) being equal, the more highly differentiated the units of an organization are, the more difficult it will be to achieve integration among them. The implications of this finding for our comparison of these three high-performing organizations should be clear. Achieving integration becomes more problematic as we move from the relatively undifferentiated container organization, past the moderately differentiated food organization, to the highly differentiated plastics organization. The organizational problems of achieving the required states of both differentiation and integration are more difficult for a firm in the plastics industry than for one in the container industry. The next issue on which we shall compare these three organizations, then, is the devices they use to resolve conflict and achieve effective integration in the face of these varying degrees of differentiation.

Integrative devices

Each of these high-performing organizations used a different combination of devices for achieving integration. As the reader will recall, the plastics organization had established a special department, one of whose primary activities was the integration of effort among the basic functional units (Table 1). In addition, this organization had an elaborate set of permanent integrating teams, each made up of members from the various functional units and the integrating department. The purpose of these teams was to provide a formal setting in which interdepartmental conflicts could be resolved and decisions reached. Finally, this organization also placed a great deal of reliance on direct contact among managers at all levels, whether or not they were on a formal team, as a further means of reaching joint decisions. As Table 1 suggests, this organization, the most highly differentiated of the three high performers, had the most elaborate set of formal

Table 1. Comparison of integrative devices in three high-performing organizations

	Plastics	Food	Container
Degree of differentiation*	10.7	8.0	5.7
Major integrative devices	1. Integrative department	1. Individual integrators	1. Direct managerial contact
	2. Permanent cross-functional teams at three levels of management	2. Temporary cross-functional teams	2. Managerial hierarchy
	3. Direct managerial contact	3. Direct managerial contact	3. Paper system
	4. Managerial hierarchy	4. Managerial hierarchy	
	5. Paper system	5. Paper system	

* High score means greater actual differentiation.

mechanisms for achieving integration and in addition also relied heavily on direct contact between managers.

The food organization had somewhat less complex formal integrative devices. Managers within the various functional departments were assigned integrating roles. Occasionally, when the need for collaboration became especially urgent around a particular issue, temporary teams, made up of specialists from the various units involved, were formed. Managers in this organization also relied heavily on direct contact with their colleagues in other units. In this organization the managerial manpower devoted to integration was less than that in the plastics organization. Yet, compared with the container firm, the food organization was devoting a large amount of managerial time and effort to this activity.

Integration in the container organization was achieved primarily through the managerial hierarchy, with some reliance on direct contact among functional managers and on paperwork systems that helped to resolve the more routine scheduling question. Having little differentiation, this organization was able to achieve integration by relying largely on the formal chain of command. We are not implying that the other two organizations did not use this method at all. As Table 1 suggests, some integration did occur through the hierarchy as well as through paper systems in both of these organizations. But the great differences among functional managers seemed to necessitate the use of additional integrating devices in these two organizations.

From this discussion we can see another partial determinant of effective conflict resolution. This is the appropriateness of the choice that management makes about formal integrating devices. The comparison of these devices in these three high-performing organizations indicates that, if they are going to facilitate the process of conflict resolution, they should be fairly elaborate when the organization is highly differentiated and integration is thus more difficult. But when the units in the organization are not highly differentiated, simpler devices seem to work quite effectively. As we have already seen, however, the appropriate choice of an integrating device is not in itself sufficient to assure effective settlement of differences. All the plastics and food organizations, regardless of performance level, had some type of integrating device besides the managerial hierarchy. These devices were not equally helpful in interdepartmental decision-making because, as we have pointed out, some of the organizations did not meet many of the other partial determinants of effective conflict resolution. However, there was evidence in all organizations that these devices did serve some useful purpose. To at least a minimal extent they helped to bridge the gap between highly differentiated functional departments. By contrast, in the low-performing container organization there was no evidence that the integrating unit was serving a useful purpose. Given the low differentiation within the organization, there seemed to be no necessity for an integrating department.

This comparison of the integrating devices in the three high-performing organizations points up the relationship between the types of integrating mechanisms and the other partial determinants of effective conflict resolution. We have stressed earlier that these determinants are interdependent. Even though we have not been able to trace the relationship systematically, this statement seems to include the final partial determinant, the choice of integrative devices. In all these organizations the choice of integrative devices clearly affected the level at which decisions were made as well as the relative influence of the various basic units.

We should also remember that any one of these determinants is only partial and that they should be seen as immediate determinants only. We have not explored the causes underlying them.

Comparison of effective conflict-resolving practices

Because of differences in the demands of each environment and the related differences in integrative devices, each of these high-performing organizations had developed some different procedures and practices for resolving interdepartmental conflict. However, certain important determinants of effective conflict resolution prevailed in all three organizations. We shall first examine the differences, then explore the similarities.

Differences in conflict resolution

The three effective companies differed in the relative influence of the various departments in reaching interdepartmental decisions. In the plastics organization it was the integrating department that had the highest influence. This was consistent with the conditions in that organization's environment. The high degree of differentiation and the complexity of problems made it necessary for the members of the integrating unit to have a strong voice in interdepartmental decisions. Their great influence meant that they could work effectively among the specialist managers in resolving interdepartmental issues.

In the food organization the research and marketing units had the highest influence. This too was in line with environmental demands and with the type of integrating device employed. Since there was no integrating unit, the two departments dealing with the important market and scientific sectors of the environment needed high influence if they were effectively to resolve conflicts around issues of innovation. However, as we also indicated earlier, there was ample evidence that within these two units the individuals who were formally designated as integrators did have much influence on decisions.

The pattern of departmental influence in the container organization contributed to the effective resolution of conflict for similar reasons. Here the members of the sales and production departments had the highest influence. This was appropriate, since the top managers in these two departments had to settle differences over scheduling and customer service problems. If these managers or their subordinates had felt that the views of their departments were not being given adequate consideration, they would have been less effective in solving problems and implementing decisions.

Here again we have been restating comparatively the findings reported in earlier chapters. Such reiteration helps us to understand how this factor of relative departmental influence contributes to performance in different environments. Each high-performing organization had its own pattern, but each of these was consistent with the demands of the most critical competitive issue.

A second important difference among these three organizations in respect to conflict resolution lay in the pattern of total and hierarchical influence. The food and plastics organizations had higher total influence than their less effective competitors, and, related to this, the influence on decisions was distributed fairly evenly through several levels (Figure 1). The lower-level and middle-level managers who had the necessary detailed knowledge also had the influence necessary to make relevant decisions. In fact, they seemed to have as much influence on decisions as their top-level superiors. In the container industry, on the other hand, total influence in the high performer was lower than in the low performer, and the decision-making influence was significantly more concentrated at the upper management levels. This was consistent with the conditions in this environment. Since

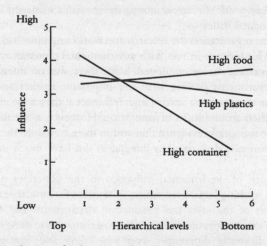

Figure 1 Distribution of influence in three high-performing organizations.

(Lines fitted by least-square method. The difference in the slope of the lines between the high-performing food and the high-performing container organization was significant at 0.001. This difference between the high-performing plastics and the high-performing container organizations was significant at 0.005. There was no significant difference between the food and plastics organizations.)

the information required to make decisions (especially the crucial scheduling decisions) was available at the top of the organization, it made sense for many decisions to be reached at this level, where the positional authority also resided.

The importance of the differences in these influence lines can be better understood if we let some of the managers in each organization speak for themselves. In the plastics organization lower and middle managers described their involvement in decisions in this way:

When we have a disagreement, ninety-nine times out of a hundred we argue it out and decide ourselves. We never go up above except in extreme cases.

We have disagreements, but they don't block progress, and they do get resolved by us. I would say on our team we have never had a problem which had to be taken up with somebody above us.

We could use these teams to buck it up to the higher management, but I think this would be a weak committee and a weak individual, and I am not willing to give my freedom up. They give you all the rope you need. If you need their help, they are there; if you don't need them, don't bother them.

The last manager quoted went on to substantiate a point made by many of his colleagues: while lower and middle managers made most decisions at their own level, they also recognized that major issues, which might have implications for products other than their own, should be discussed with higher management. But this discussion always took place *after* they had agreed on the best course of action for their own products.

Over and over, these lower and middle managers indicated their own responsibility for decisions and their feeling that to ask their superiors to resolve conflicts would be to acknowledge their own inadequacy. A higher-level manager stressed that this was also the view at his level:

Top management has told these fellows, 'We want you to decide what is best for your business, and we want you to run it. We don't want to tell you how to run it.' We assume that nobody in the company knows as much about a business as the men on that team.

This same flavor was evident in remarks gathered in the food organization. Here, too, middle and lower managers stressed their own involvement in decisions.

Given these facts, the reader may be wondering about the activities of the upper echelons of management in the plastics and food organizations. If they were not involved in these decisions, what were they doing? While we made no detailed study of their activity, the data collected in interviews indicated clearly that they had plenty to keep them busy. First, they had the problems of administering their respective functional units. Second, they reviewed decisions made by their subordinates to make certain that the specialists working on one part of the product line were not doing anything that would adversely affect another part. In addition, in their dynamic environments they are constantly concerned with the search for new and longer-range opportunities, which would fall outside the purview of any of their subordinates. In this regard we found that in all the effective organizations the managers' time-horizons became longer-ranged as one moved up the hierarchy. This tendency was particularly marked in the plastics and food organizations. This, too, suggested that top executives in the food and plastics organizations were heavily involved in longer-range issues and problems.

The tone of comments by managers in the container organization about who made decisions was dramatically different from that in the other two organizations. The middle and lower managers in the container organization emphasized the chief executive's and the other officers' role in decision making:

My primary contact is with [sales vice-president and the chief executive]. This contact is around who we are going to give the containers to, because of our oversold position. They will determine which ones we are going to take care of . . . Actually, what you really need though is [the chief executive's] decision. I usually start out these kinds of conflicts with [the production scheduling manager], but when somebody has to get heard, it ends up with [the chief executive]. Usually I am in contact with him three or four times a day.

When there is a problem I try to tell [production vice-president] the facts and make some recommendations. He makes the decisions or takes it up to [the chief executive]. He doesn't get reversed very often. Sometimes he may say to me, 'I agree with you, go ahead and do it,' and then [the chief executive] will change it.

The sales vice-president explained his own involvement, emphasizing application of the available facts:

[The chief executive] holds a weekly scheduling meeting on Monday, which includes him, myself, the scheduling manager, and a couple of the sales managers, depending upon what the crucial problems are. The scheduling manager has prepared the schedule on Friday. On Monday we tear it apart. This business is like playing an organ. You've got to hit the right keys, or it just doesn't sound right. The keys we play with are on the production schedule. In these meetings, though, the final decision rests with [the chief executive]. He gets the facts from us, and we influence the decision, but if there is any doubt, he decides.

All these comments serve to underline the differences in the distribution of influence between plastics and foods on the one hand and containers on the other. These differences directly reflect differences in their respective environments.

Similarities in conflict resolution

So far, we have accentuated the important differences in these organizations in terms of the determinants of conflict resolution. Let us now look at some similarities. First, however, we should stress again that the differences actually stemmed from a fundamental similarity: each of these organizations had developed conflict-resolving practices consistent with its environment.

The first major similarity among these organizations is in the basis of influence of the managers most centrally involved in achieving integration and resolving conflict. In all three organizations these managers, whatever their level, had reputations in the company for being highly competent and knowledgeable. Their large voice in interdepartmental decisions was seen as legitimate by other managers because of this competence. To return to the point made earlier, the positional influence of the managers assigned the task of helping to resolve interdepartmental conflict was consistent with their influence based on competence. Unlike the situation in some of the low-performing organizations, these two important sources of influence coincided in all these effective organizations. This point is illustrated by comments about the competence of the managers centrally concerned with conflict resolution in each organization.

In the container company, as we indicated earlier, the chief executive was regarded as extremely knowledgeable about the various facets of the business. As one manager expressed it:

The fact is, as I understand it, that he is almost a legend in the industry. He knows every function in this company better than any of the people who are supposed to be handling that function.

But the chief executive was not the only one who had this respect. Managers in this organization also emphasized the knowledge and ability of the other top executives. A research engineer described the competence of the research director:

I think another thing related to the close supervision I receive is the nature of the [research director]. He is an exceptional kind of guy, and he seems to know all the details and everything going on in the plant, and in the lab. He is continually amazing people in this regard.

A similar point was made about the production vice-president by one of his plant managers:

Oh yes, I hear from [the production vice-president], but if he wants you, you are in trouble. You hear from him for sure, if your figures are too far off. He is pretty understanding. If you can explain, he understands. He also can really help you out on a serious production problem. He can tell you what to do. He knows just how far a job should be run before it should be pulled off.

In this organization, as these comments suggest, the knowledge and expertise of the top managers gained them respect from their subordinates and legitimated their strong influence over decisions. In the foods and plastics organizations the knowledge-based influence worked in a similar manner to justify the high influence of the middle managers centrally involved in helping to resolve interdepartmental conflict. Comments similar to those cited in earlier chapters may help to highlight this point. An integrator in the food organization explained the importance of expertise in his job:

Generally, the way I solve these problems is through man-to-man contact. I think face-to-face contact is the very best thing. Also, what we [the integrators] find is that most people develop a heavy respect for expertise, and this is what we turn to when we need to work out an issue with the fellows in other departments.

Similarly, a fundamental research scientist in the plastics organization indicated (as did many others in this organization) that he believed the members of the integrating unit to be competent, which helped them to achieve collaboration:

I believe we have a good setup in [the integrating unit]. They do an excellent job of bringing the industry problems back to somebody who can do something about them. They do an excellent job of taking the projects out and finding uses for them. In recent years I think it has been staffed with competent men.

In all three high-performing organizations, then, our data suggest a consistency in three factors that helped those primarily responsible for achieving integration to settle interdepartmental disputes. The managers who were assigned the responsibility for resolving conflict were at a level in the organization where they had the knowledge and information required to reach interdepartmental decisions and they were regarded as competent by their associates. Thus (a) *positional influence*, (b) *influence based on competence*, and (c) *the actual knowledge and information required to make decisions* all coincided. While there was this similarity, as we pointed out above, the level at which influence and knowledge were concentrated varied among the organizations because of differences in the certainty of their respective environments.

A second important similarity in these three organizations lay in the mode of behavior employed to resolve conflict. All three, as we have seen, relied heavily on open confrontation. The managers involved in settling conflicts were accustomed to open discussion of all related issues and to working through differences until they found what they appeared to be an optimal solution. This was so regardless of the level at which the conflicts were handled. Typical comments from managers in each of the three organizations illustrate this point more vividly than the numerical data reported earlier. A researcher in the plastics organization described how he and his colleagues resolved conflicts:

I haven't gotten into any disagreements yet where we let emotions stand in the way. We just go to the data and prove out which is right. If there is still some question about it, somebody can do the work to re-examine it. Emotions come up now and then. However, we usually have group decisions, so if I am not getting anywhere, I have to work it out with the others.

A production engineer in the food organization expressed a similar viewpoint:

We often will disagree as to basic equipment. When we can't agree on what equipment to use, we will collaborate on some tests [with research], and sometimes we will run it both ways to find out what is the best way. Actually, the way this works out, one of their fellows and I will be at each other's desk doing a lot of scratching with a pencil trying to figure out the best answer and to support our point of view. We will finally agree on what is the best way to go. It is a decision we reach together.

The director of research in the container organization discussed his role in the resolution of conflict with the chief executive:

I am sure a lot of people would say this is a one-man company. Sure, [the chief executive] keeps close tabs on the dollars, and I must keep good score for him in regard to everything we spend. He is pretty gentle with me and I have no run-ins with him. He talked to me this morning about a problem, and I knew that regardless of whether I said yes or disagreed with him he would have gone along and taken my advice. He likes to complain a lot, and holler and bellow and be like a wild bull, but he gives up when he sees a good case. He'll ask for a real good story, and we have to give it to him, but if it *is* a good story, he will go along with us.

We should emphasize several important points about this comment. It and similar remarks from the major executives in the container organization indicated that while the chief executive was strong and dominant, he expected to have all points of view and pertinent information discussed before making a decision. These responses likewise indicated that there was give and take in these discussions and that the other major executives often influence the outcome, if the facts supported their point of view. It is also worth noting, as a comment from a plant manager in this organization suggests, that lower managers used the same method to resolve conflicts:

I'm an easy-going sort of fellow, but I get mad sometimes. When we get something to fight about, we just say it, face the problem, and it is over. We get the issue out on the table and solve it. It has to be done that way. [The production vice-president] does it that way. We all follow his lead.

While these statements all deal with technical issues, we could cite similar comments concerning marketing problems. The important fact to emphasize is that these three organizations relied on confrontation as a mode for resolving interdepartmental conflict to a greater extent than all but one of the other organizations (the low-performing food organization). This fact does not seem unrelated to the importance of competence and knowledge as a basis of influence for the managers primarily responsible for resolving conflicts. High value was traditionally placed on knowledge and expertise in all three organizations. Consequently, managers were very willing to see disagreements settled on this basis.

This reliance on confrontation suggests another important characteristic of all three organizations: managers must have had sufficient trust in their colleagues and, particularly in the case of the container organization, in their superiors to discuss openly their own points of view as they related to the issues at hand. They seemed to feel no great concern that expressing disagreement with someone else's position (even a superior's) would be damaging to their careers. This feeling of trust apparently fostered effective problem solving and decision making.

Summary comparison of the high-performing organizations

The plastics organization, which functioned in the most dynamic and diverse of the three environments, was consequently most highly differentiated of the three high-performing organizations. Since this condition could create major problems in maintaining the required state of integration, this organization, as we have seen, had developed an elaborate set of formal devices (both an integrating unit and cross-functional teams) to facilitate the resolution of conflict and the achievement of integration. Because market and scientific factors were uncertain and complex, the lower and middle echelons of management had to be involved in reaching joint departmental decisions; these managers were centrally involved in the resolution of conflict. This organization also met all the determinants of effective conflict resolution. The integrators had balanced orientations and felt that they were being rewarded for the total performance of their product group. Relative to the functional managers they had high influence, which was based on their competence and knowledge. In resolving conflict all the managers relied heavily on open confrontation.

In contrast to the plastics organization, the container organization was in a relatively stable and homogeneous environment. Thus its functional units were not highly differentiated, which meant that the only formal integrating device required was the managerial hierarchy. But in using this device this organization also met the determinants of effective conflict resolution. The sales and production units, which were centrally involved in the crucial decisions related to scheduling and delivery, both felt that they had much influence over decisions. Around these issues influence was concentrated at the top of the organization, where top managers could centrally collect the relevant information to reach decisions. Middle managers, particularly those dealing with technical matters, did have some influence. The great influence of the top managers stemmed not only from their position, but also from their competence and knowledge. Finally, conflicts between departments were resolved and decisions reached through problem-solving behavior.

In these two paragraphs we have described two quite different organizations, each of which is well equipped to deal with its own external environment. Another way to understand the contrasts between them is to examine the major sources of satisfaction and of stress for the executives in each. While we made no systematic effort to collect such data in the plastics organization, the contrast between the two organizations can be clearly seen from interview comments of the managers in each organization. Managers in both organizations were generally quite well satisfied with their situations, but they were finding satisfaction for some quite different reasons. In the plastics organization an important source of satisfaction was the active involvement in decisions. Middle managers often expressed the feeling that they were running their own firms. One product manager in the sales department put it this way:

Our present organization allows us as individuals to more formally play a role in decision-making, which we didn't do before. Now, with the teams, we can make a decision which will affect the profit. We can see the results of our efforts more realistically than we could before. Now that it has management approval, it has a nice flavor. It's nice to be doing something they approve of. The product manager has no formal authority. But putting him on the team gives him some sort of authority. I'm not sure what kind of authority it is, but it makes my job more meaningful . . . Of course, we all recognize that the other guys on the team are depending upon our effort, so we make an effort to produce.

Managers in the container organization, however, indicated that they liked their jobs for quite a different reason – because they knew where to get a decision made. One manager expressed it in this manner:

He [the chief executive] does all the scheduling himself, and in essence what you have is a large organization run by one man. This is a refreshing switch from the organization where I had previously worked. I find this very beneficial. If I want something decided, I can go right to him and get a direct decision. You tell him what you want to do, and he will tell you right then and there whether he will let you do it or whether he won't.

The sources of dissatisfaction and stress in the two organizations were also different. A manager in the plastics organization described some of the points of concern to him:

I worked for another company which was different, where there were fairly definite lines of authority. This place was quite a revelation to me. In my old company we always knew whose jobs things were. Occasionally here we run into situations where we don't know whose jobs things are . . . All of these meetings take a lot of time. I used to spend eight hours by myself, and I thought I could get more things done. I feel now that I spend time on committees instead of making autocratic decisions, but this isn't really a disadvantage, as we do get better solutions . . . Also, there can be conflict between your position as a functional manager and as a team manager. The more empathy with others you have, the worse it gets.

What disturbed this manager and a few others was the ambiguity of responsibility and relationships in this organization. Many managers often had dual loyalties – to their functional superiors and to their team colleagues. They had to decide themselves what needed to be done. The involvement of many managers in interdepartmental decision making made these difficulties unavoidable, and it also meant that managers who had a low tolerance for ambiguity and uncertainty did not always enjoy their work.

By contrast, the few managers in the container organization who expressed dissatisfaction were most concerned because upper managers seemed to be so involved in their activities. As one man said:

Your boss is telling you to check something, and then he jumps down your throat five minutes later. They should know what you are doing and try to give you some answers, or else they should let you do it . . . I know this job involves a lot of pressure, particularly because at first you are just getting ignored around here and then they are jumping on you, and the pressure is really acute. Somebody has to be the whipping boy around here, and that is just part of this job.

These data suggest two things. The first is quite obvious – that these two organizations were quite different places in which to work. The second inference is more speculative. There is some suggestion, from the tone of the interviews, that the managers in the two organizations had somewhat different personality needs. Those in the plastics organization seemed to prefer more independence and had a greater tolerance for ambiguity, while those in the container company were perhaps better satisfied with greater dependence upon authority and were more bothered by ambiguity. While there may have been these differences in personality needs, each organization (as well as the food organization) seemed to provide a setting in which many members could gain a sense of competence in their job. This provided them with important sources of satisfaction. The fact that so few managers in either organization did express any dissatisfaction with such different organizational climates would suggest that this is so. While we have no way to confirm this speculation, it does raise again the importance of the point made earlier, that the organization must fit not only the demands of the environment, but also the needs of its members.

In any case, the contrast between the plastic and the container organizations is very sharp. In a sense, they represent opposite ends on a continuum, one dealing with a very dynamic and diverse environment, where innovation is the dominant issue, the other with a very stable and homogeneous environment, where regularity and consistency of operations were important. The food organization, as our discussion has suggested, was in many ways like the plastic organization. The differences between them seemed to be more of degree than of kind. While the food environment was not so dynamic and diverse as that of plastic, it seemed to be towards that end of the continuum. The integrating devices, although not so elaborate as those in the plastics organization, were of the same nature, designed to provide linkage at the middle- and lower-managerial levels. The two organizations met most of the same determinants of effective conflict resolution. The major difference between them was that the plastics organization appeared to be devoting more of its managerial manpower to devices that facilitated the resolution of conflict. The important point, however, is that the food organization, like the other effective organizations, had developed a set of internal states and characteristics consistent with the demands of its particular environment.

We should, however, recognize one limit to this conclusion. Each of these organizations had developed characteristics that were in tune with the demands of its *present* environment. Whether these same characteristics will provide long-run viability depends, of course, on whether the environmental demands change in the future. Given the widely observed tendency toward greater scientific, technological, and market changes, the plastics and food organizations would seem to be in a more favorable position to maintain their high performance. Major technological or market changes in the container industry would almost certainly create serious problems for the high-performing container organization. This suggests that the managements in stable industries must develop within their organizations some capabilities for watching for environmental changes and preparing to adapt to them. It also suggests that in the future more and more organizations may resemble the high-performing plastics and food organizations.

A contingency theory of organizations

From this comparison we have seen that it is possible to understand the differences in the internal states and processes of these three effective organizations on the basis of the differences in their external environments. This, along with the comparison between the high performers and the other organizations in each environment, has provided us with some important leads as to, what characteristics organizations must have in order to cope effectively with different environmental demands. These findings suggest a contingency theory of organization which recognizes their systemic nature. The basic assumption underlying such a theory, which the findings of this study strongly support, is that organizational variables are in a complex interrelationship with one another and with conditions in the environment.

In this study we have found an important relationship among external variables (the certainty and diversity of the environment, and the strategic environmental issue), internal states of differentiation and integration, and the process of conflict resolution. If an organization's internal states and processes are consistent with external demands, the findings of this study suggest that it will be effective in dealing with its environment.

More specifically, we have found that the state of differentiation in the effective organization was consistent with the diversity of the parts of the environment, while the state of integration achieved was consistent with the environmental demand for interdependence. But our findings have also indicated that the states of differentiation and integration are inversely related. The more differentiated an organization, the more difficult it is to achieve integration. To overcome this problem, the effective organization has integrating devices consistent with the diversity of the environment. The more diverse the environment, and the more differentiated the organization, the more elaborate the integrating devices.

The process of conflict resolution in the effective organization is also related to these organizational and environmental variables. The locus of influence to resolve conflict is at a level where the required knowledge about the environment is available. The more unpredictable and uncertain the parts of the environment, the lower in the organizational hierarchy this tends to be. Similarly, the relative influence of the various functional departments varies, depending on which of them is vitally involved in the dominant issues posed by the environment. These are the ways in which the determinants of effective conflict resolution are contingent on variations in the environment. Four other determinants, however, seem to be interrelated only with other organizational variables and are present in effective organizations in all environments. Two of these are the confrontation of conflict and influence based on competence and expertise. The other two factors are only present in those effective organizations that have established special integrating roles outside the managerial hierarchy – a balanced orientation for the integrators and a feeling on their part that they are rewarded for achieving an effectively unified effort. Our findings indicate that when an organization meets most of these determinants of effective conflict resolution, both the general ones and those specific to its environment, it will be able to maintain the required states of differentiation and integration.

This contingency theory of organizations suggests the major relationships that managers should think about as they design and plan organizations to deal with specific environmental conditions. It clearly indicates that managers can no longer be concerned about the one best way to organize. Rather, this contingency theory, as supported and supplemented by the findings of other recent research studies, provides at least the beginning of a conceptual framework with which to design organizations according to the tasks they are trying to perform.

8 J. Pfeffer and G. R. Salancik

The Design and Management of Externally Controlled Organizations

From *The External Control of Organizations: A Resource Dependence Perspective*, Harper & Row, 1978, chapter 10

To understand organizational behavior, one must understand how the organization relates to other social actors in its environment. Organizations comply with the demands of others, or they act to manage the dependencies that create constraints on organizational actions. While not novel, the theoretical position advanced here differs from many other writings about organizations. The perspective developed denies the validity of the conceptualization of organizations as self-directed, autonomous actors pursuing their own ends and instead argues that organizations are other-directed, involved in a constant struggle for autonomy and discretion, confronted with constraint and external control.

Most current writers give only token consideration to the environmental context of organizations. The environment is there, somewhere outside the organization, and the idea is mentioned that environments constrain or affect organizations. It is sometimes mentioned that organizational environments are becoming more turbulent and this will presumably foster more decentralized management structures. Environment, and particularly environmental turbulence and uncertainty, is used as an arguing point by those wishing to promulgate their advocacy of participation. After this, the task of management is considered. Somehow, the things to be managed are usually within the organization, assumed to be under its control, and often have to do with the direction of low-level hired personnel. When authors get down to the task of describing the running of the organization, the relevance of the environment fades. Yet, the idea that organizational actions are socially constrained means that part of the explanations for behavior can be found in the social context.

130

We take the view of externally controlled organizations much more seriously. This chapter will recapitulate the arguments derived from this perspective and then explore the role of management, the design of organizations, the design of organizational environments, and the likely future of organizational structures. In many instances, our theoretical orientation leads to expectations and recommendations discrepant with the dominant literature. While we have no particular style of management to promote and no appealing phrases like 'human relations,' 'human resources,' or 'participation' to use to summarize our thoughts, we would suggest that the ideas developed are likely to be more empirically verifiable and more descriptive of the actual operation of interacting social actors.

A resource dependence perspective

To survive, organizations require resources. Typically, acquiring resources means the organization must interact with others who control those resources. In that sense, organizations depend on their environments. Because the organization does not control the resources it needs, resource acquisition may be problematic and uncertain. Others who control resources may be undependable, particularly when resources are scarce. Organizations transact with others for necessary resources, and control over resources provides others with power over the organization. Survival of the organization is partially explained by the ability to cope with environmental contingencies; negotiating exchanges to ensure the continuation of needed resources is the focus of much organizational action.

Organizations themselves are the interlocking of the behaviors of the various participants that comprise the organization. Activities and behaviors, not social actors, are organized into structures. Because social actors can have some activities included in different structures, inclusion in an organization is typically partial. In this context, organizational boundaries can be defined by the organization's control over the actions of participants relative to the control of other social entities over these same activities. Control is the ability to initiate or terminate actions at one's discretion. An organization's control over activities is never absolute because there are always competing claims for the control of given activities. Attempts are made, however, to stabilize activities by institutionalizing exchanges into formal roles and using other control mechanisms. The set of interlocked activities controlled by the organization constitutes the organization. The organization's most important sources of control to achieve interlocked structures of behavior are the ability to empower individuals to act on its behalf and to regulate the use, access, and allocation of organizationally generated resources.

Organizations are coalitions of varying interests. Participants can, and frequently do, have incompatible preferences and goals. The question of whose interests are to prevail in organizational actions is crucial to determining those actions. Power is overlooked too frequently by attending to issues of effectiveness and efficiency. Effectiveness and organizational performance can be evaluated only by asking whose interests are being served.

Organizations, in addition to being coalitions of interests, are markets in which influence and control are transacted. When an organization is created, activities and outcome potential are created. Organizations, or the energy represented in organizations, are resources. It is in the interests of those who require resources to attempt to control and influence the organization. Participants attempt to exchange their own resources, their performance, for more control over the collective effort, and then, they use that control to initiate actions for their own interests. In organizations as in other social systems, power organizes around critical and scarce resources. To the extent participants furnish resources that are more critical and scarce, they obtain more control over the organization. Of course, the determination of what is critical and scarce is itself open to change and definition. Power is, therefore, determined by the definition of social reality created by participants as well as by their control over resources.

Participants differ in the extent to which the organization controls their activities. Some participants provide resources but are not tightly bound to the organization. These actors, which may be other organizations, groups, or individuals, constitute the social environment or context of the organization. To the extent that these actors control critical resources and certain other conditions are met, they are in a position to influence the actions of organizations. In this sense, we can speak of the social control of organizations. The conditions that facilitate this control of the organization include:

1. The possession of some resource by the social actor.
2. The importance of the resource to the focal organization; its criticality for the organization's activities and survival.
3. The inability of the focal organization to obtain the resource elsewhere.
4. The visibility of the behavior or activity being controlled.
5. The social actor's discretion in the allocation, access, and use of the critical resource.

6. The focal organization's discretion and capability to take the desired action.
7. The focal organization's lack of control over resources critical to the social actor.
8. The ability of the social actor to make its preferences known to the focal organization.

Each of these conditions can be altered by the parties to the relationship. The focal organization can attempt to avoid these conditions, and thereby enhance its discretion. The social actor seeking control over the organization can act to increase the conditions, and thereby increase its control over the organization. Organizations interacting with one another are involved in a dynamic sequence of actions and reactions leading to variations in control and discretion. Strategies of achieving control or discretion and sequences of interactions have rarely been examined.

The study of Israeli managers and their attitudes toward compliance with governmental demands, and the examination of the response of United States defense contractors to affirmative-action pressures both support the idea that organizations are externally controlled. Organizational responses were predicted from the situation of resource interdependence confronting the various organizations.

Organizational environments, however, are not objective realities. Environments become known through a process of enactment in which perceptions, attention, and interpretation come to define the context for the organization. Enactments of dependencies, contingencies, and external demands are in part determined by organizational structures, information systems, and the distribution of power and control within organizations.

Assessments which are inconsistent with the actual potency and demands of various participants may be made by organizations. The cognitive and perceptual processes of individuals and the design of most information systems focus attention on familiar historical events, most frequently events that have occurred within the organization. Coupled with a tendency to attribute organizational outcomes to the actions of individuals within the organization, these characteristics of information processing tend to lead most organizations to look within their own domains for the definition and solution of problems. In addition, the contest for control within the organization intervenes to affect the enactment of organizational environments. Since coping with critical contingencies is an important determinant of influence, subunits will seek to enact environments to favor their position. Adjustments to environmental demands follow when visible problems erode the position of those in the dominant coalition. Such adjustments are slowed by the ability of those in power to institutionalize their control over the organization. When the organization's conceptions and responses to environmental constraints become too inappropriate, resource acquisition becomes increasingly difficult. We suggested a systematic procedure for assessing organizational environments and for evaluating the potential consequences of various organizational activities.

The fact of competing demands, even if correctly perceived, makes the management of organizations difficult. It is clearly easier to satisfy a single criterion, or a mutually compatible set of criteria, than to attempt to meet the conflicting demands of a variety of participants. Compliance to demands is not a satisfactory answer, since compliance with some demands must mean noncompliance with others. Organizations require some discretion to adjust to contingencies as they develop. If behaviors are already completely controlled, future adjustments are more difficult. For this reason, organizations attempt to avoid influence and constraint by restricting the flow of information about them and their activities, denying the legitimacy of demands made upon them, diversifying their dependencies, and manipulating information to increase their own legitimacy.

At the same time organizations seek to avoid being controlled, they seek stability and certainty in their own resource exchanges. Indeed, it is usually in the interests of all participants to stabilize organizational resource exchanges and ensure the organization's survival. The organization, thus, confronts a dilemma. On the one hand, future adaptation requires the ability to change and the discretion to modify actions. On the other hand, the requirements for certainty and stability necessitate the development of interorganizational structures of coordinated behaviors – interorganizational organizations. The price for inclusion in any collective structure is the loss of discretion and control over one's activities. Ironically, to gain some control over the activities of another organization, the focal organization must surrender some of its own autonomy.

Organizations seek to avoid dependencies and external control and, at the same time, to shape their own contexts and retain their autonomy for independent action. The dilemma between the maintenance of discretion and the reduction of uncertainty leads to the performance of contradictory activities. The dilemma of autonomy versus certainty has been noted by Thompson and McEwen (1958) and is an important characteristic of organizational actions taken with respect to the environment. The demands for certainty and the quest for discretion and autonomy lead to the various actions we have described – merger, joint ventures, cooptation, growth, political involvement, the restriction on the distribution of information. All these activities can be understood from the same resource dependence framework.

To say that context affects organizational actions is to say little. The question is how context affects organizations, and the answer requires specifying some process for environmental effects. One model linking organizational environments with organizational actions suggests that environmental contingencies affect the distribution of power and control in the organization. In turn, power affects succession to leadership positions in the organization, and organizational leaders – the members of the dominant coalition – shape organizational actions and structures. This model suggests that executive succession both reflects environmental contingencies and helps the organization manage its interdependence with other social actors.

We have attempted to illustrate how a large number of phenomena can be understood within the resource dependence perspective. The empirical studies reviewed clearly only begin to investigate the various themes and ideas developed within this perspective. Many implications of our model of external control remain unexamined – the use of secrecy to avoid influence and reduce conflict, the limitation of discretion to avoid external control, the attempt to define for elements in the environment their demands and satisfaction, are only a few examples. It is clear that the environment, the context of the organization, is more important than many writers have implied by restricting their attention to the effects of uncertainty on decentralized decision-making.

Three managerial roles

. . . The three roles of management – symbolic, responsive, and discretionary – differ in the way organizational constraints and actions are related. In the symbolic role, actions are unrelated to constraints. The organization's outcomes are determined primarily by its context and the administrator's actions have little effect. In the responsive role, organizational actions are developed in response to the demands from the environment. Managers form actions according to the interdependencies they confront, and constraint and action are directly related. In the discretionary role, constraints and environments are managed to suit the interests of the organization. Management's function is to direct the organization toward more favorable environments and to manage and establish negotiated environments favorable to the organization. All three roles are typically involved in the management of organizations.

The symbolic role of management

The manager is a symbol of the organization and its success or failure, a scapegoat, and a symbol of personal or individual control over social actions and outcomes. The symbolic role of management derives in part from a belief in personal causation as opposed to environmental determinism, a belief which is both pervasive and important to concepts of human action (e.g. Kelley, 1971; Lieberson and O'Connor, 1972). As a symbol of control and personal causation, managers and organizational leaders can be used as scapegoats, rewarded when things go well and fired when they go poorly. The knowledge that someone is in charge and that the fate of the organization depends on that person offers the promise of change in organizational activities and fortunes. When problems emerge, the solution is simple and easy – replace the manager. Such changes may not be accomplished readily, as the administrator's power and ability to control the interpretation of organizational outcomes can maintain tenure in office.

Organizations and social systems go to great lengths to invest managers with symbolic value. Leaders may be provided with special perquisites and designations of authority which serve not only to reward the leader but also to remind others of this person's importance by focusing their attention on him. When one leader leaves office, the search for the new leader may be elaborate, involving committees, elections, inaugurations, and the expenditure of time and resources. All of these activities tend to cause observers to attribute great consequences to the occupant of the particular administrative position. In this sense, the symbolic role of management is critical whether or not the manager actually accounts for variance in organizational results. The symbol of control and personal causation provides the prospect of stability for the social system. Belief in the importance of leaders would, logically, lead to the replacement of leaders when things went badly. But, while there is some disruption when turnover occurs, the disruption and alteration of organizational activities is clearly less than if the organization were redesigned and undertook new activities in new environments.

Beliefs in the potency of individual administrators, created through mythologies, symbols, and activities designed to create such beliefs, may be held by outsiders as well as by those individuals whose activities are structured within the organization. Not privy to information about the constraints on administrators, outsiders may have an even greater tendency to see organizational actions as under the control of one or a few persons. The various external interests will focus on the leader and attempt to influence the organization through him or her.

In creating the symbolic role of the manager, the organization also creates a mechanism for dealing with external demands. When external demands cannot be met because of constraints on the organization, the administrator can be removed. Replacing the leader, who has come to symbolize the organization to the various interest groups, may be sufficient to relieve pressures on the organization. As long as all believe that the administrator actually affects the organization, then replacement signals a change taken in response to external demands. The change communicates an intent to comply, and this intent may be as useful as actual compliance for satisfying external organizations.

Changing administrators offers a way of altering appearances, thereby removing external pressure, without losing much discretion. If the manager has little effect on organizational outcomes, his or her replacement will not change much, particularly if a person with similar views is chosen as the replacement. The manager is, therefore, a convenient target for external influences, and provides the organization with a relatively simple way of responding to external demands.

The argument that one of the manager's important roles is to serve as a symbol is a functionalist argument. Explication of the functions served (such as providing stability) must await additional research on the process of symbol creation and the actions taken to invest managers with the appearance of control over outcomes and activities. For the present, we can note that the capability of replacing managers who have been invested with symbolic importance affords the organization the possibility of coping with competing demands and constraints.

The belief in personal causation of events is also lodged in our legal system. Organizations are typically not criminally liable, only individual managers are. The electrical generating equipment price-fixing case of the early 1960s illustrates well the manager as a symbol. Manufacturing generating equipment was a business with high fixed costs. When demand fell, price wars tended to occur. In an attempt to stabilize their environment, managers from the major manufacturers met and attempted to fix prices and allocate markets. Such attempts were often unsuccessful and were at least in part a consequence of the structure of the industry. Managers were acting because of environmental contingencies and, it might be presumed, because of pressures from superiors for higher and more stable operating results. When the conspiracy was uncovered, the colluding managers were prosecuted, fined, occasionally imprisoned, and in almost every instance, fired by the employing organizations. While the firms themselves were liable for treble-damage suits, the managers faced ruined careers. More recently, officials in Lockheed and Gulf Oil were removed following disclosures of bribery of foreign political officials. The corporations, by firing their agents, could claim that such illegal actions were not condoned and would not be permitted. More of the onus for the action was shifted to the individuals involved, who were fired and thereby separated from the company.

The symbolic role of management involves the process by which causality for events is attributed to various actors or external factors (e.g. Kelley, 1971). Studies of processes of attribution, including attention to the role of salient and relevant information, the differences in perceptions between actors and observers (Jones and Nisbett, 1971), and the tendency for persons to attribute control to personal actions (e.g. Langer, 1975) are all relevant for explaining the processes by which beliefs in the causal importance of administrators are created. The symbolic role of management is both important and empirically explainable.

The responsive role of management

If managers were only symbols, it would not matter what they did. Such a position obviously underestimates the actual consequences of administrative action. Even though administrators or organizational leaders may not have tremendous effects on actions and outcomes (Salancik and Pfeffer, 1977), they do account for some variance. There are two roles of management that can be identified with this position of managerial impact, the responsive role and the discretionary role. By responsive role we mean that the manager is a processor and responder to the demands and constraints confronting the organization. In this role, the manager assesses the context, determines how to adapt the organization to meet the constraints of the context, and implements the adaptation.

The conceptualization of managers as responders must be carefully distinguished from the view of the all-knowing, all-seeing leader who directs organizational actions unconstrained by the context. To manage the organization's relationship with its environment, the manager in the responsive role must perceive the demands and dependencies confronting the organization, and then adjust the organization accordingly. To say that a leader is responsive to the demands of others is to say that the activities of the leader are structured and shaped by others. The responsive role of management posits the function of management as being an assimilator and processor of demands. Such a view is at variance with the image of great managerial leaders directing the organization, making decisions, and, through the sheer force of will, transforming organizations to achieve success.

The most appropriate activity of the responsive manager is not developing appropriate actions but deciding which demands to heed and which to reject. The actions to be taken are provided by the various participants and interests in the organization and its environment. There is no shortage of suggestions, if not demands, concerning what the organization should be doing. The manager's function is to decide which of these to follow. The choice is critical for organizational survival, for in responding to demands the organization necessarily gives up discretion. Our prediction is that administrators respond to demands as a function of the interdependence with a given other social actor, the more likely the organization is to follow its demands. To maintain support from important suppliers of resources, organizations constrain their actions to comply with the request of those with resource control. It is clear that such a course requires being aware of the situation of interdependence and the demands of those with whom the organization is interdependent.

Management is frequently described as decision-making. This, of course, is correct. But the emphasis in such a view is often misplaced, focusing almost exclusively on choice. Choice, however, is only one step in the decision process. Prior to the exercise of choice, information about the environment and possible consequences of alternative actions must be acquired and processed. Once this is done, the choice is usually obvious. Instead of describing management as decision-making, we could describe management as information gathering and be both consistent with the original position and possibly more descriptive of the actual emphasis of managers (e.g. Mintzberg, 1973). Decisions are made in a social context, and this context must inevitably constrain decisions if the decisions are to be effective in that context. The responsive role of management is not inconsistent with the more widely seen view of management as decision-making. Rather, this role emphasizes the importance of processing and responding to the organization's context. The critical factor is that constraints are imposed on the actor.

The discretionary role of management

As we have noted before, managers not only adapt their organizations to the context, but may take actions to modify the environment to which the organization then responds. In addition to a responsive role of management, therefore, we can speak of a discretionary role. Managerial action focuses on altering the system of constraints and dependencies confronting the organization. This discretionary role of management is involved when we think of organizations merging, lobbying, coopting, and doing all the various things that alter the interdependencies confronted by the organization.

In some respects, the discretionary role of management is not inconsistent with the responsive role. Both require accurate assessment of environmental constraints and contingencies. Whether one is going to respond to the environment or change it, effective action is more likely if the context is accurately perceived. Both the responsive and discretionary roles of management, then, emphasize the importance of the information-processing tasks and the criticality of the accuracy of the manager's perception, his or her model of reality.

The discretionary role, however, places more emphasis on the possibility for managerial action actually to change the organization's context. The discretionary role is more fitting to some organizations than others. Only a few have enough resources and scale to attempt to alter their contexts in a significant fashion. For millions of small business organizations, voluntary associations, and nonprofit organizations, such change of the environment is virtually out of the question.

The three roles of management we have described are certainly not mutually exclusive. At some time all may be enacted. At one point, management may serve a symbolic value; while at others, it may respond to environmental demands; while at still others, it may engage in actions to modify the environment. Although each perspective may emphasize a slightly different set of skills and activities, all are potentially important. The critical issues involve the circumstances under which one or the other role is likely to predominate and the factors that appear to be associated with successfully performing each of the managerial roles.

Specifying these three roles does not mean that they can inevitably be handled to bring success to the organization. If there is one image we wish to provide the reader, it is that success is in the hands of many actors outside the control of the organization. Organizations exist in interdependent environments and require the interlocking of activities to survive. Control over this interlocking or structuring of activities is never in the hands of a single actor such as a manager. Books about how to manage or how to succeed are ill-advised because they give the impression that there is some set of rules or procedures that will guarantee success. The essence of the concept of interdependence means that this cannot be the case. In any interdependent situation, outcomes are at least partially in the control of other social actors, and the successful outcomes achieved through performing various managerial roles derive in part from actions taken by others outside the manager's control.

Designing externally controlled organizations

This is not a treatise on organizational design. However, some implications of the resource-dependence perspective for design are worthy of consideration, if only because the adequacy and value of the perspective can be assessed. We will consider four implications: the design of scanning systems; designs for loosening dependencies; designs for managing conflicting demands and constraints; and designs of chief-executive positions.

Scanning the environment

Whether management plays a responsive role or attempts to alter the organization's environment, good information about the context will be required. Most organizations follow the easy course. Available data are collected and processed; information more difficult to gather is ignored. The information most frequently generated for other purposes – usually for accounting for the organization's internal operations – is all too frequently the only information available in the organization. Few organizations systematically seek out information about their context.

Academic literature on environmental scanning is notably sparse (e.g. Aguilar, 1967). Any recommendation, therefore, must be tentative; there is an insufficient empirical base on which to develop strong conclusions. Most writers will assert that since organizational environments are important, it is critical to scan them. Yet, the fact is that organizations typically do not do much environmental scanning. One must either question the advice or question the common practices of organizations. That there is so little literature in this area reinforces our conclusion that the allusion to the environment is frequently pro forma and seldom follows up the open systems perspective with anything remotely useful from a managerial or theoretical perspective. It may also be that scanning the environment is, in fact, not that necessary. One can imagine some advantage to ignoring environmental change. Knowing about the change puts the organization in the position of having to respond to it. It may be better to ignore changes rather than risk overresponding to every small, insignificant environmental fluctuation.

Scanning systems face two problems: how to register needed information, and how to act upon the information. Both problems affect the organization's ability to either adapt to or change the environment. Part of the problem of scanning environmental elements was implied in our earlier discussion about enactment. Subunits established to scan a particular part of the environment typically hire persons with expertise limited to one narrow segment. A market research department employs MBA or PhD business graduates trained in marketing, survey research, and statistics. The firm will survey consumers, often a dominant focus in marketing training, and test-market various products. The firm will probably have excellent information about alternative communication channels, their costs and effectiveness, as well as all kinds of attitudinal data about potential consumers for the product. Communications data are prevalent in part because other organizations (advertising agencies, the media) collect them and make them available. What the firm is not likely to have are data on whether the product is stocked anywhere, whether the sales force is doing an adequate job promoting the product, or what kind of shelf space or display it is getting. After all, the performance of the sales force is a topic for industrial psychologists interested in motivation, while issues of distribution are the responsibility of those specializing in marketing channels.

A scanning unit frequently attends to only one portion of the environment. Yet, the environment has multiple facets. The obvious solution is to establish multiple scanning units or scanning units that have within them a variety of interests, backgrounds, and types of expertise. Although this solution is useful to overcome the problem of missing important aspects of the environment, the establishment of multiple scanning units does nothing to overcome, and may actually worsen, the second problem of acting on the information.

The greater problem in coping with organizational environments is that the needed information is not in the hands of those making the decisions or is not used by these persons. The causes of these difficulties are many and varied. One problem is that information is typically collected by staff departments (marketing research, long-range planning, etc.) and must be used by line personnel. Conflicts are common between line and staff.

Information collected by specialized experts, with unique vocabularies and sophisticated methodological approaches, produces reports couched in terminology unfamiliar to the line managers who must use the information. Communication is difficult. Differences in perspective, vocabulary, and expertise all bar the use of information collected about organizational environments.

An additional problem is that those who provide information collect what they believe to be important. There is no assurance that similar judgments of importance hold for operating managers. Staff members may fail to ask managers what information is needed, and the information collected may be important only to those who collected it. This problem is not easily solved. A decision-maker may be unable to predict what information he needs or would use. A likely response to the question of what information is needed is the information he has used in the past, obviously constrained by availability. Moreover, it is not clear that the manager is the best judge of what is needed, since he operates on the basis of what he has done before. Persons develop styles of operating and decision-making; changing these styles may be difficult. Persons accustomed to making decisions using certain information are not likely to suddenly use new information, especially information they did not request.

A third problem facing operating managers and staff is that both implicitly may perceive information collection and acquisition as affecting their relative power and status. It is the case that if one controls the information used in decision-making, one can control decision outcomes. To the extent that managers rely on staff, they lose discretion and admit the importance of the staff and the need for them. One way for managers to retain power is to ignore the staff information. For their part, the staff attempt to have their reports heeded to illustrate their importance and power within the organization. The contest for control over decision-making is what is involved, and this contest is frequently exacerbated by the differences in backgrounds and ages of the parties involved.

The environmental perspective argues for the need for information about environments. Specialized scanning units, however, may be ineffective in meeting that need. Specialized units collect specialized information, so that to develop a comprehensive view of the environment, a variety of units may be required. At the same time, operating managers may use the collected information only under duress, and the problems of obtaining the attention of the managers are increased as the number of scanning units writing reports increases. Many reports are filed and forgotten, and few become incorporated in organizational decision-making. Scanning highlights and narrows the organization's attention, so that the assignment of specific individuals to scan specific environmental segments may leave the organization more isolated and less informed than before. The scanners focus on routinized, quantitative data-collection, prepare reports filled with jargon and complexity, and then struggle with operating personnel to have their efforts considered.

In writing of environmental enactment, we noted the difficulty of planning. Planning scanning systems is no less difficult, since such an activity presumes the organization already knows what it needs to know. We argue that the problem is not one of not having the necessary information. The expertise required to manage the organization's interdependence is often present in the organization. It is already possessed by the various operating managers themselves. Constantly confronted with problems from their own interactions with the environment, it is unlikely they are unaware of that environment. More probably, they are unable to consider the situation and its implications taking an overall, longer-range view. Unfortunately, operating managers are most often involved in immediate, short-run problem solving (Mintzberg, 1973), and therefore they seldom have the time or the inclination to engage in any kind of planning.

While the organization as a whole may possess the requisite information, the information may be widely dispersed throughout the organization in a variety of different functional areas and positions. One effective strategy for keeping up on major changes would be to bring together the various sources of expertise within the organization in a focused format to use this expertise in planning and decision-making. Such techniques as the Delphi (Linstone and Turoff, 1975) and Nominal Group Technique (Delbeca, Van de Ven, and Gustafson, 1975), in which participants, chosen for their expertise, are systematically queried about judgments, potential actions, and forecasts, provide some advantages over the use of specialized staff departments. Commitment to the decisions and forecasts may be increased because operating personnel are themselves involved. The planning and decision-making, moreover, can be done in language, and using data, familiar to the persons involved.

Loosening dependencies

The external control of organizational behavior comes about, in part, from the organization's dependence on specific others. Discretion permits the organization to adapt to contingencies and to alter activities as conditions change. It is likely that the maintenance of discretion should be a crucial organizational activity. Some latitude in the organization's behavior will be useful and organizations will seek to minimize external control.

The loosening of external controls can be accomplished, we have suggested, through the loosening of dependences. Organizations are controlled by an external source to the extent they depend on that source for a large proportion of input or output. Dependence diminishes through diversification. Organizations with many small suppliers are potentially less controlled than ones with a few major suppliers. From the above considerations, it might appear that organizational designs that reduce organizational dependencies would be highly differentiated structures, organizations performing a variety of activities in a variety of contexts. If diversification loosens dependence and provides the focal organization with more discretion, and if discretion is both sought and useful for survival and adaptation, then it should be the case that over time more diversified structures should emerge, particularly for those organizations dealing with concentrated input or output markets. This result might occur either because less diversified organizations were more likely to fail or because organizations systematically adapted and became more diversified.

It does appear that there have been trends toward increasing diversification. Consider Berman's (1973) history of merger waves. The first wave was described as an attempt to consolidate and control markets. In this first wave, many of the giant enterprises which today control sectors of the economy were created. Various steel producers combined to form US Steel, and tobacco manufacturers combined to form the major tobacco firms. In the second wave of merger, vertical integration was accomplished with the organizations extending to take over sources of supply and distributors. The third major wave involved conglomerate mergers, or mergers made for purposes of diversification, involving firms such as Tenneco, Gulf and Western Industries, and LTV. Such a pattern of merger activity would suggest that organizations first secure their competitive position, then attempt to manage interdependence with supply and distribution channels, and finally, turn their attention to diversification to diminish the external control of others over their activities. The situation is more complex, however. These different merger movements took place under different legal conditions. Vertical integration followed the passage and more vigorous enforcement of the Sherman Act, and the conglomerate mergers followed the passage of more stringent antimerger regulations. The regulations themselves were in response to the perceived threat of economic concentration posed by earlier mergers. While legal constraints may provide some explanation for the pattern of activities undertaken by industrial firms, other types of organizations not subject to antitrust laws have also diversified. Downs (1967), for instance, has noted that public agencies expand their domains and take on additional activities to ensure their survival. Such expansion provides the agencies with more independence.

Coping with conflicting demands

The pursuit of diversification or organizational growth, both designed to lessen dependence on elements of the organization's environment, will probably lead to an increase in the number of groups and organizations interested in the focal organization. This can increase the diversity and number of demands on the organization. Size, however, is not the critical variable affecting the complexity of demands. Even small, less diversified organizations are confronted by a variety of interests with different preferences for organizational action. Rather, the critical variable is the extent to which the organization represents a resource or potential tool to be used by others. The more useful the resources of an organization are to others, the more demands the organization will face. According to the theoretical perspective we have developed, organizational designs which disperse dependence through the environment also link the organization to more elements which might seek to use it in their service, creating more competing and conflicting interests.

Fortunately, the very differentiation that reduces the organization's dependence on external groups also helps the organization manage the conflicting demands thus created. First, diversification, while not reducing demands, does reduce the organization's need to respond to any given demand. By dispersing dependency among numerous others, the impact of the organization's not responding to given demands is reduced. A second advantage, obtained through the creation of a differentiated, loosely coupled organizational structure, is that various groups may be satisfied simultaneously. The critical factor is that the diverse interests be loosely coupled and not interdependent within the organization. When interests are not tightly interconnected and there is no need for actions to be consistent with all interests simultaneously, then it is possible to satisfy conflicting demands by establishing subunits to cope with each interest. Consumers may demand better quality products and more control over product policies. In response, the organization may establish a consumer affairs department. Demands are registered and consumers or their organizations are provided with access and a feeling of participation. At the same time, workers wanting more control can appeal to the personnel or industrial relations department, while minorities can articulate their interests through affirmative-action offices. This differentiation process can go on indefinitely, subject only to the constraint imposed by limited resources. Thompson (1967) has argued that organizations do exactly what we have described – establish subunits to deal with homogeneous subsegments of the environment.

Structural differentiation, from this perspective, derives not directly as a consequence of organizational size but as a function of the number and importance of different interests that must be coopted. This number may, in turn, be related to organizational size. And size, in turn, may be a function of growing differentiation and diversification. Differentiating an organization to simultaneously satisfy multiple constituencies is a practice evident in many organizations. Universities, for example, establish research institutes to obtain money from various sources, academic departments to serve disciplinary interests, and various student and community service units to meet the demands of those groups.

It is important to note that differentiation provides a satisfactory solution to the problem of competing demands only when the differentiated subunits are themselves relatively independent. Each subunit must be in a position to take actions unconstrained by the actions taken by other subunits. Loose-coupling assists organizations in coping with their environments by permitting new subunits to absorb protest without a requirement to rationalize the relationship among all the various subunits. Of course, it is also true that if subunits are loosely coupled then most organizational practices will be buffered from changes created by any single subunit in response to interest group demands. The organization can thus make small accommodation to interest groups without redirecting the activities of the entire organization. A consumer affairs department can deal with complaints about the product with a letter and a free sample, but the production and development departments remain unaffected.

A second benefit achieved by establishing a special department to handle particular subsegments of the environment is that each subsegment becomes partially coopted. The interest group or organization develops an interest in the subunit with which it deals. Since the established subunit is the primary access to the organization, its survival becomes defined as critical for the interest group's purposes. As a consequence, the external interest may make less extreme demands on the subunit and become interested in preserving its limited access and representation within the organization. The differentiation of organizational structures to cope with homogeneous environmental elements can both buffer the organization and lessen the force of the external influences.

Another strategy for coping with interdependence with external groups making conflicting demands is through the use of slack resources (Galbraith, 1973). Organizations can more readily cope with conflicting demands when they have sufficient resources, so that many demands can be at least partially satisfied simultaneously. Organizational slack, frequently apparent in the form of extra profits or resources, is useful not only to make the owners and managers happy but to facilitate managing the environment of competing demands. Conflict is reduced when interdependence is reduced, and interdependence is reduced when resources are plentiful. As we already noted, the elaboration of structure to include differentiated, loosely coupled subunits to cope with the various environmental elements also requires resources to support the various subunits thereby created. Again, then, the importance of slack resources for managing conflicting demands is evident.

The structural solution to conflicting demands is a differentiated organization of loosely coupled subunits, each of which deals with special environmental interests, and each of which is only slightly interdependent with other subunits within the organization. This solution depends on the availability of slack resources, for without slack, subunits could not be loosely connected and could not respond to their immediate environments without affecting the entire system.

Neither the differentiation of the organization into subunits nor the diversification of activities reduces the organization's dependence on the environment. What such actions accomplish is to alter the nature of the interdependence and structure organizational dependence so that it is more readily managed. By having numerous interests make demands on the organization, the organization reduces its need to respond to any specific interest because each represents only a small part of the total organization and its activities. While there are still resource acquisition consequences of not complying, the effects are diminished.

Moreover, diversification shifts interdependence from the organization's relationship with the environment to greater interdependence among elements in the environment. By making previously unrelated activities or markets now related under a single management or control structure, diversification makes previously unrelated environmental subsegments more interdependent. Linked through the organization, environment subsegments now compete with each other as well as facing competition within the subsegment. If there are insufficient slack resources across the entire economy, such interlocking of organizations can actually cause problems. Organizations dealing with a large set of diverse environmental elements without sufficient slack resources face difficulties in managing and resolving the competing groups therefore confronted.

The chief-executive position

We have argued that environments affect organizational change through alteration of the distribution of influence and consequent changes in administrators. As a symbol of the organization and its policies, administrators can be removed when participants demand it as a condition for continuing to support the organization. If it is indeed true that adaptation to environmental interests comes about in part through changes in administration, then the institutionalization of power and control can be seen as detrimental to the organization's ability to cope with the environment. Structures which inhibit the institutionalization of power should survive change more readily. Structures which permit power to be maintained beyond the point of being useful to the organization are less likely to be adaptable.

While the trend in organizational forms has been to more diversified structures and activities, the trend in organizational power structures, appears to be in the direction of increasing centralization. In industry, stock companies are increasingly owned by diffuse ownership interests or by trust departments and pension funds that are unwilling and unable to exercise strong influence on management. As a result, managers have acquired more control over the organization. The diffusion of control over a number of small investors enhances the manager's ability to institutionalize his power. Earlier, we noted that there was some tendency for turnover in administrators to be reduced when the corporation was management-controlled compared to the situation where managers faced a few, nonmanaging dominant ownership interests. It is likely to be true in general that the diffusion of the organization's activities will permit more centralized administrator control. This is because any single other group or organization now has less interest in the total organization and its activities and, therefore, should be less willing to spend the resources and effort necessary to control the organization. Such reasoning may be another explanation for the emergence of differentiated, diffused organizational structures.

If differentiation in organizational structures is useful for dealing with competing demands, it would be logically possible to extend that argument and suggest the usefulness of differentiation even in the chief-executive position. Instead of having a single chief executive or chief administrator, the organization might have several, each with his or her own expertise and the ability to cope with some segment of the environment. Multiple chief executives have seldom been tried, and when tried, have often not succeeded. In part, this is because the idea of multiple chief-executive officers, while useful for dealing with the various environments confronted by the organization, is inconsistent with the concept of the administrator as the symbol of organizational action. After all, when we want to fire the administrator for some problem in the organization, we would prefer to fire one, clearly visible, target rather than several persons who share responsibility and through this sharing avoid responsibility.

One way of achieving both accountability and adaptability may be to have a single figurehead but have the actual organizational control lodged in a multiparty executive position. This would require giving each executive an independent and sufficient power base to survive the struggle for dominance which would undoubtedly ensue. Of course, such an organizational design is completely at variance with the traditional prescriptions for unity of command. Indeed, the type of political decision-making likely to be produced by the structure we have described may be viewed as irrational or inefficient. Of course, the trade-off must be made between some loss of order and efficiency to achieve the capability of organizational adaptability.

In the absence of the ability or desire to establish multiple centers of control and authority, the next best solution requires ensuring that executives can be replaced easily when environmental conditions require new skills or a new symbol. Such replacement is obviously facilitated when power is decentralized in the organizations, or when the chief executive cannot control the appointment of all subordinates so as to people the organization with dedicated loyalists. Overlapping political districts common to some US cities represent an example of this form of shared power. The mayor controls the hiring of some personnel, but other boards and commissions control other hiring.

Power is also more likely to be institutionalized when the executive controls the definition of reality through a control over the information system in the organization. It is interesting that authors have not more frequently noted the connection between decentralization of authority and the decentralization of information systems. The connection is direct. If the chief executive is allowed to control the social distribution of information through secrecy and selective presentation of information, then he can control the definition of the situation. By defining organizational contingencies, his power can be institutionalized beyond both the formal authority structure and the contingencies of the environment.

The institutionalization of control is a process that has not been empirically examined and is only imperfectly understood. Yet, it is clear that organizational responsiveness will increase when power and control are not institutionalized and new skills, competencies, and interests can emerge with changing environmental contingencies.

At the same time, stability and predictability in the organization is desirable. After all, continual change would be as destructive as no change at all. Thus, some institutionalization of power and control is necessary to achieve stability. It prevents the organization from changing to meet minor environmental contingencies of short duration. However, it is likely that most organizations err on the side of stability. Those in control, certainly, would favor such a position.

Organizational and political structures

Many of the structural attributes described as desirable for organizational adaptability and for coping with an environment of conflicting demands and interests are represented in political organizations in the United States. Institutionalization of control is inhibited by the requirement for confronting elections, and multiple control structures are designed into the system by providing at the federal level the three branches of government and the host of commissions and boards, and at other governmental levels through overlapping, autonomous political districts and organizations. Structural elaboration into various departments and committees permits various interests to be heeded, while the existence of organizational slack and a loosely coupled system facilitates the absorption of protest and the incorporation of change without profoundly disturbing the entire system.

We are not the first to note structural parallels between political organization and other types of organization or the similarities in their governance and adaptation. To carry the analogy to its logical conclusion, however, suggests that one should design organizations with features of representative political structures, particularly when adaptation rather than stability or efficiency is of primary concern. Even current writing about decentralization and delegation typically speaks of such passing of power as a gift, conferred upon lower level participants. Despite awareness of surface similarities, there remain fundamental differences in the control structure of representative democracies and those of formal organizations. The belief in the requirement for absolute authority and unity of command prevents the development of designs which incorporate representative forms of control. We suspect it is mainly when the problems confronted by formal organizations become increasingly the management of conflicting demands and adaptation to changing social contexts that structural similarities to political organizations emerge.

Designing organizational environments

If organizational actions are responses to their environments, then the external perspective on organizational functioning argues strongly that organizational behavior is determined through the design of organizational environments. The focus for attempts to change organizations, it would appear, should be the context of the organizations. By changing the context, the behavior of the organizations can be changed. The profoundly important topic of designing organizational environments is almost completely neglected. The idea of changing organizations by changing their environments is scarcely found in the literature on organizational change.

Among the few social scientists who have not neglected environmental design as a way of affecting organizational behavior are economists. Their basic model presumes that persons seek their self-interest, and therefore, environments must be so structured that in seeking their own interests, individual actors also behave so as to increase social welfare. Such a realization of the importance of the design of context for determining behavior is in refreshing contrast to the frequently encountered prescriptions for training, T-groups, or other individually oriented internal-change approaches advocated most frequently by organizational-behavior authors.

The analogy we would like to make is between our perspective and social psychology. In the study of human behavior, originally time was spent attempting to predict and analyse behavior using concepts that presumably were related to the internal state of the individual, such as personality, motivation, and attitudes. Growing evidence, however, indicated that persons, regardless of individual differences, would respond similarly to similar environmental conditions. This outcome suggests that behavior could be controlled by its context, through the use of appropriate reinforcers as in operant conditioning or through other physical and social designs. Similarly, the analysis of organizational behavior has focused on internal states of organizations, their climate, leadership, even structures. Yet, if organizations are affected by their social contexts, one might expect that one efficacious way to accomplish organization change would be through the redesign of that context. This is the position we are advocating.

The appropriate design for organizational environments depends, of course, upon what activities and interests are to be served. Consider the problem of collusion among business firms. Price-fixing cases have involved pharmaceutical companies, chemical firms, food processors, and many other industries and firms. Collusion, while a violation of the antitrust laws, is a dominant form of behavior. Even when there is not overt collusion, organizations may attempt to achieve the benefits of collusion – the creation of collective structures of behavior – through joint ventures, trade associations, mergers, director interlocks, and other devices. These interfirm structures may serve the interests of the various participants quite well. Indeed, if the interests were not served, the structures would probably not persist. However, economists have argued that the welfare of all participants and the efficient allocation of resources in an economic system is best served when competition prevails. If we accept the economists' position, then what can be done to assure competition?

It is clear what can not be done. Legislating against collusion, attempting to legally restrict mergers or joint ventures, is probably not an effective solution. First, such laws must be obeyed to have any impact. Reid (1968) has noted that few mergers are ever prosecuted given the limited resources of the antitrust agencies. Price-fixing conspiracies are only occasionally uncovered, and when found out, the companies are frequently permitted to plead 'no contest', which leaves the burden of proving ultimate guilt on those who would sue for treble damages. Second, laws typically attack one type of presumably anticompetitive practice at a time. This leaves the organization with the option of developing substitutes for the practice now proscribed. Pate (1969) noted that when the antimerger laws were strengthened, more joint ventures were formed. And, Pfeffer (1976) has argued that tightening up restrictions against joint ventures would probably just cause the organizations affected to develop alternative methods for accomplishing interfirm coordination. In many ways, passing a law is a symbolic act like firing a manager. It provides the feeling that something has been done but does not affect the source of the activity.

If behavior is affected by its context, then a more adequate strategy to change behavior would involve redesigning the context. In the present case, we have seen that the tendency for firms to attempt to develop interfirm organizations is most pronounced when concentration is intermediate, a result which helped explain mergers and joint ventures among competitors, director interlocks among competing firms, and the movement of executives. If the policy outcome desired is to diminish this activity, the most effective strategy would involve making the industry less concentrated by creating new competitors either by breaking up existing firms into smaller companies or by encouraging the founding of new enterprises in the same industry.

Or, consider another example. Employment agencies, both private and state services, have frequently assisted employing firms in pursuing discriminatory hiring policies by sending applicants of only one sex or race as requested. There have been some efforts to enforce nondiscrimination regulations by threatening to take away the agency's license to operate and by actually investigating and fining the offending agencies. If the situation is examined carefully, however, the futility of such efforts can be seen. Employment agencies are numerous and the cost of entry into the business is relatively low. Because there are so many agencies and so many persons typically looking for work, what is scarce are job orders, the positions to be filled given to the agency by an employer. If the agency does not go along with the employer's request, the employer can simply move the hiring to another of the many agencies available. In the case of the state employment services, legislatures evaluate them according to placements, so again the organizations compete for job orders. In this instance, the behavior is predicted by the context. The employers have power with respect to the agencies and can obtain the behaviors they desire. Applying enforcement against the agencies only puts them in an untenable position but does not resolve their problem. Enforcement directed against the employer organizations is much more likely to change the situation of discriminatory referrals.

We could provide numerous other examples, but the point should be clear. Behavior is a consequence of the context confronting the organization. The design and change of organizational behavior, therefore, can profitably be approached from the perspective of analyzing and designing the context to produce the desired activities. Of course, such a strategy of organizational change is more difficult than attempting to enforce the law against single organizations or preaching values and norms. On the other hand, it is more likely to be effective. If behavior is externally controlled, then the design of the external system of constraints and controls is the place to begin to determine organizational actions and structures.

Organizational futures

The literature is littered with predictions about what future organizations will look like and how they will operate and be managed. The fact that most of these predictions have not been realized is, we believe, a consequence of the inadequate theoretical base underlying them. We would like to conclude our exposition of the resource-dependence perspective by considering one of the more frequently seen predictions concerning organizational futures and then consider what the evidence we have developed suggests about this forecast.

Recently, humanists such as Warren Bennis, Abraham Maslow, and Douglas McGregor have predicted the demise of bureaucracy as an organizational form. In a climate of social values that stress participation and democracy, bureaucracies, with their centralized structures of authority and control, are anachronistic. With a more skilled and more educated work force, with increasingly sophisticated technologies, the prediction has been that professional, rather than bureaucratic, organizational forms would emerge. Power would be based on skills and knowledge, and, consistent with the professional model, self-control or collegial control would be emphasized over control by the organizational hierarchy. Unfettered by inappropriate strategies of motivation and rigid, dehumanizing structures, the new workers, educated and creative, would adjust their activities to the needs of the organization and realize their creative potential in the process.

Originally, this prediction was based more on beliefs and values than on anything else. But then, these authors discovered the environment and found, they thought, a whole new, empirically based foundation for their beliefs and the associated application of those beliefs, organizational development. Miles has summarized this argument quite well:

The environment, as they (OD theorists) see it, is becoming increasingly turbulent and this, they argue, makes it especially important that organizations adopt the kinds of structure and processes mentioned above . . . OD writers tend to believe that the linkages among the elements in most organizational environments are becoming more numerous and more complex, that the rate of change in environmental conditions is increasing, and that traditional bureaucratic structures are becoming less and less adequate. It is argued that new and more adaptive structures and processes are required and that these in turn demand new levels of interpersonal skill and awareness which OD (organization development) can best provide (1974: 170–71).

Unfortunately, the issue of what effects uncertainty has on the structure of organizations, and even if uncertainty is increasing, is more complicated than suggested by numbered systems (Likert, 1967) and two-category archetypes (McGregor, 1960). We attempt below to provide some thought about these complexities, not because we envision better views of the future but because different futures appear more probable.

A recurrent theme has been that organizations attempt to manage or avoid uncertainty. Rather than accepting uncertainty as an unavoidable fate, organizations seek to create around themselves more stable and predictable environments. Thus, to forecast increasingly turbulent and unpredictable environments is to simultaneously predict attempts to create negotiated, predictable environments. Greater turbulence produces greater efforts to manage the environment. The implied contradiction in that statement can be understood by considering the nature of interdependence in social systems and how interdependence changes form without changing in magnitude.

We have described how organizations cope with the uncertainty created by interdependence by managing interdependence through interorganizational coordination. By law, collusion, merger, cooptation, and other strategies, organizations seek to avoid uncertainty arising from their need to acquire and maintain resources. Managing interdependence, however, does not avoid interdependence. Indeed, it is the case that the solution to one problem frequently creates different difficulties. The typical solution to problems of interdependence is to structure and coordinate the organization's behavior more closely with other organizations. This strategy, however, creates its own problems.

For example, steel manufacturers depend upon coal as a resource. Seeking to remove uncertainty of supply, the manufacturers may integrate backward and purchase coal mines or coal companies. Although the purchase of a coal mine reduces the organization's dependence on uncertain suppliers, the dependence on coal itself has not been eliminated. In fact, if major technological changes in steel manufacturing eliminate the need for coal, the vertical integrated firm with its own source of coal may be less able to change. And, as a consequence of being more heavily invested in resources used in the manufacture of steel, the organization is now more dependent on the steel market. Also, since the merged organization is presumably larger, capital requirements may be greater, as is the organization's visibility to regulators and others who will make demands of it.

Solving the uncertainty deriving from interdependence with suppliers leads the organization to create an environment which makes it even more important to stabilize the other elements in the environment. To assure markets, the organization may press to have laws passed restricting competition. The organization may invite major clients or financial institutions to sit on its board of directors, or it may invest in joint ventures in partnership with major competitors. The immediate effects of these efforts may be to stabilize the flow of resources to the steel manufacturer and reduce the uncertainty confronted by the organization in the short run.

A closer examination of the situation, however, reveals that the interdependence and uncertainty has merely been shifted, not eliminated. By merging with coal companies, the organization's problematic dependence is shifted from one resource to others and from suppliers to markets. By restricting competition through legislation, the organization now depends on legislators. The organization becomes more connected to elements of its environment, and the environment itself becomes more interconnected over time as various organizations engage in these strategies. The more tightly connected the system becomes, the more the fate of each is linked to the fate of all other organizations. Linked to a particular financial institution for capital, the steel manufacturer now needs the survival and health of that particular financial institution. Linked to a particular legislator, the company requires the political survival and health of that person.

If one considers the consequences of the actions for other organizations, it is even more evident how interdependence is shifted rather than eliminated. The steel manufacturer who acquired the coal company gains control over the supply and leaves other steel firms less able to acquire their own coal. The others become more interdependent with other suppliers and may find it necessary increasingly to coordinate their behaviors. Essentially, the merging organization has shifted the costs of interdependence to other parts of the system. The same thing occurs when market coordination occurs; the interdependence of sellers is shifted to make buyers more interdependent and more dependent on the sellers as a collectivity.

The only changes which alter the amount of interdependence are those which (a) increase the amount of available resources, and (b) decrease the number of contenders for those resources. If there is a scarcity of some resources, the fact that one organization stabilizes its acquisition of the resources through some form of social coordination does not alter the fact of the scarcity. It solves one organization's problem by transferring the problem to others. One can see this illustrated in the seventies 'energy crisis' (more properly, a shortage of inexpensive oil). Most of the changes made in response to that crisis were attempts to redistribute the problem of not having enough cheap oil. Some organizations stored reserves in larger amounts, while others sought new forms of energy. However, the changes that reduce conditions of scarcity are those that lead to new sources of energy or less use of energy; other changes merely reallocate the cost of scarcity.

Social systems can be evaluated according to how the burdens and costs of interdependence are allocated. Those who suffer the costs are those with the least power in the social system, and indeed, social power becomes defined and determined in the process of managing interdependence. Power is the ability to organize activities to minimize uncertainties and costs, and as mentioned previously, power is inevitably organized around the most critical and scarce resources in the social system. Solutions to problems of interdependence require the concentration of power. Strategies to manage interdependence require interlocking activities with others, and such interlocking produces concentrated power. Those organizations not involved in the resultant structure are less powerful and less able to cope with their problems of interdependence.

Because the problems facing one organization are generally due to the activities of another organization it is inevitable that the solutions to problems involve interlocking activities among the organizations, and an attempt to influence the other organization's activities to the focal organization's benefit. This interlocking of activities develops a concentration of power. Those who are least powerful in a social system are those who are least able to organize and structure the activities of other social actors for their own interests. The resulting environment is one which is increasingly structured and interlocked, coordinated, comprised of larger and larger organizations and greater concentrations of social power. The burdens of interdependence are shifted to the less organized and less powerful actors. In the modern economic environment, the least organized group of social actors are consumers, and contrary to the view of consumers portrayed in some economic and marketing theories, the consumer is increasingly likely to bear the cost of interdependence in the economic system. One might think that a solution to the consumers' problems is to concentrate power, and many actions of consumer interest groups are attempts to accomplish just that. However, while coordination makes the consumer more powerful, it also makes influence more possible. It is easier to target influence to affect a few organizations than millions of independent actors. Thus, ironically, the very structuring of activities that produces social power makes the social actors so interconnected that they are more likely targets for influence.

If all organizations attempted to solve their own problems of critical uncertainties and dependencies by interlocking behaviors with others, the resulting environment would be one of more tightly coordinated organizational action. Decision structures developed for initiating and coordinating actions must, of necessity, become more centralized with greater concentrations of power. The system is too complex, too interconnected, and too potent to rely on haphazard adjustments made by its components.

Therefore, the net result of various organizational actions would appear to be the creation of larger organizations operating in environments that are increasingly regulated and politically controlled. A single organization's larger size and increased commitment to given areas of activity make it less able to adapt and means that any failure is more consequential. Thus, there is increased need for coordination with other critical actors. This increased need for coordination leads to an increasingly interconnected environment in which power is increasingly concentrated. One might project from this that the environment that will evolve will be a stable and cooperative set of actors. Such will be the case as long as none of the parties have interests which conflict, and this circumstance is more likely to the extent that resources are plentiful. If there is a scarcity of critical resources, the consequence of greater interconnectedness is greater uncertainty. The response to that uncertainty will be even more interlocking of behavior and an even greater concentration of power.

This scenario does not suggest an increase in decentralized, participative management structures as a result of turbulent organizational environments. Rather, we would suggest that uncertainty will result in greater efforts at coordination, which require the concentration of power and decision discretion. We would argue that in the first place, uncertainty is managed so that the prediction of increasing environmental uncertainty is questionable. In the second place, increasing interconnectedness is likely to be met with increasingly concentrated decision-structures, not decentralized structures as many have predicted. There is some evidence that external pressure is accompanied by decision centralization (Hamblin, 1958; Korten, 1962; Pfeffer and Leblebici, 1973). If turbulence and uncertainty is perceived as stress or pressure, then centralization is a more correct prediction than decentralization.

Before we can have confidence in the preceding description, there are a number of other variables that must be considered. Ultimately, the need for coordination is a function of environmental munificence. Scarcity is not itself a given, but depends in part on the definition of the organization's requirements and the number of organizations contending for those resources. Definitions of required resources can change and do so as organizations adapt to their environments. A second unknown is the extent to which power can be increasingly concentrated. At some point, concentration must cease as the cost of coordination becomes too high, threatening the survival of individual social actors and posing too great a loss of autonomy consistent with survival. Moreover, the ability to coordinate must have limits also, perhaps determined by the ability to see the relationship between sets of actors and activities.

Unfortunately, speculations about the evolution of social systems require facts and knowledge that are not presently available. Because it has not been studied, there is little information about how organizational responses and environments evolve over time. The cycle of contextual effect, organizational response, and new contexts must be examined more fully in the future to describe adequately the external control of organizations.

References

AGUILAR, F. J. (1967), *Scanning the Business Environment*, Macmillan

BERMAN, L. (1973), 'What we learned from the great frenzy', *Fortune*, 87, pp. 70–73 ff.

DELBECA, A. L., VAN DE VEN, A. H., and GUSTAFSON, D. H. (1975), *Group Techniques for Program Planning*, Scott, Foresman

DOWNS, A. (1967), *Inside Bureaucracy*, Little, Brown

GALBRAITH, J. (1973), *Designing Complex Organizations*, Addison-Wesley

HAMBLIN, R. L. (1958), 'Leadership and crisis', *Sociometry*, 21, pp. 322–35

JONES, E. E., and NISBETT, R. E. (1971), *The Actor and the Observer: Divergent Perceptions of the Causes of Behavior*, General Learning Press

KELLEY, H. H. (1971), *Attribution in Social Interaction*, General Learning Press

KORTEN, D. C. (1962), 'Situational determinants of leadership structure', *Journal of Conflict Resolution*, 6, pp. 222–35

LANGER, E. (1975), 'The illusion of control', *Journal of Personality and Social Psychology*, 32, pp. 311–28

LIEBERSON, S., and O'CONNOR, J. F. (1972), 'Leadership and organizational performance: a study of large corporations', *American Sociological Review*, 37, pp. 117–30

LIKERT, R. (1967), *The Human Organization: Its Management and Value*, McGraw-Hill

LINSTONE, H. A., and TUROFF, M. (1975), *The Delphi Method: Techniques and Applications*, Addison-Wesley

MCGREGOR, D. (1960), *The Human Side of Enterprise*, McGraw-Hill

MILES, R. E. (1974), 'Organization development', in G. STRAUSS, R. E. MILES, C. C. SNOW, and A. S. TANNENBAUM (eds.), *Organizational Behavior: Research and Issues*, Industrial Relations Research Association

MINTZBERG, H. (1973), *The Nature of Managerial Work*, Harper & Row

PATE, J. L. (1969), 'Joint venture activity, 1960–1968', *Economic Review, Federal Reserve Bank of Cleveland*, pp. 16–23

PFEFFER, J. (1976), 'Patterns of joint venture activity: implications for antitrust policy', Testimony presented before the Subcommittee on Monopolies and Commercial Law of the House Committee on the Judiciary, February 11, 1976

PFEFFER, J., and LEBLEBICI, H. (1973), 'The effect of competition on some dimensions of organizational structure', *Social Forces*, 52, pp. 268–79

REID, S. R. (1968), *Mergers, Managers, and the Economy*, McGraw-Hill

SALANCIK, G. R., and PFEFFER, J. (1977), 'Constraints on administrator discretion: the limited influence of mayors on city budgets', *Urban Affairs Quarterly*

THOMPSON, J. D. (1967), *Organizations in Action*, McGraw-Hill

THOMPSON, J. D., and MCEWEN, W. J. (1958), 'Organizational goals and environment', *American Sociological Review*, 23, pp. 23–31

9   R. E. Miles and C. C. Snow

Organizational Fit

From 'Fit, failure and the hall of fame', *California Management Review*, 1984, vol. 26, no. 3, pp. 10–28

There is currently a convergence of attention and concern among managers and management scholars across basic issues of organizational success and failure. Whether attention is focused on the very survival of organizations in aging industries, the pursuit of excellence in mature industries, or the preparation of organizations for the rapidly approaching challenges of the twenty-first century, the concern is real and highly motivated. US managers and organizations have been indicted for low productivity, and management scholars have recognized the fragmentation of their literature and called for a new synthesis.

Clearly, neither organizational success nor failure has an easy explanation. Nevertheless, it is becoming increasingly evident that a simple though profound core concept is at the heart of many organization and management research findings as well as many of the proposed remedies for industrial and organizational renewal. The concept is that of *fit* among an organization's strategy, structure, and management processes.

Successful organizations achieve strategic fit with their market environment and support their strategies with appropriately designed structures and management processes. Less successful organizations typically exhibit poor fit externally and/or internally. A conceptual framework can be built upon the process of fit that will prove valuable to both managers and management scholars as they sift through current theories, perspectives, and prescriptions in search of an operational consensus. The main features of such a framework are structured around four main points:

1. *Minimal* fit among strategy, structure, and process is essential to all organizations operating in competitive environments. If a misfit occurs for a prolonged period, the result usually is failure.

2. *Tight* fit, both internally and externally, is associated with excellence. Tight fit is the underlying causal dynamic producing sustained, excellent performance and a strong corporate culture.

3. *Early* fit, the discovery and articulation of a new pattern of strategy, structure, and process, frequently results in performance records which in sporting circles would merit Hall of Fame status. The invention or early application of a new organization form may provide a more powerful competitive advantage than a market or technological breakthrough.

4. *Fragile* fit involves vulnerability to both shifting external conditions and to inadvertent internal unraveling. Even Hall of Fame organizations may become victims of deteriorating fit.

Minimal fit, misfit and failure

The concept of fit plays an undeniably important role in managerial behavior and organizational analysis. Fit is a process as well as a state — a dynamic search that seeks to *align* the organization with its environment and to *arrange* resources internally in support of that alignment. In practical terms, the basic alignment mechanism is *strategy*, and the internal arrangements are *organization structure* and *management processes*. Because in a changing environment it is very difficult to keep these major organizational components tightly integrated, perfect fit is most often a condition to be striven for rather than accomplished.

Although fit is seldom referred to explicitly, it has appeared as the hallmark of successful organizations in a variety of settings and circumstances. For example, in our own studies of organizational behavior in many widely different industries, we have regularly found that organizations of different types can be successful provided that their particular configuration of strategy, structure, and process is internally and externally consistent (R. E. Miles and C. C. Snow, 1978). In his landmark historical analysis, Alfred Chandler (1962) found that the companies now recognized as the pioneers of the divisional organization structure were among the first to identify emerging markets, develop diversification strategies to meet these market needs, and to revamp their organization structures to fit the new strategies. In their study of the management of innovation in electronics firms, Tom Burns and G. M. Stalker (1961) found that organizations pursuing innovation strategies had to use flexible, organic structures and management processes; rigid, mechanistic approaches did not fit with such strategies.

Finally, in another highly acclaimed study, Paul Lawrence and Jay Lorsch (1967) found that successful organizations in three quite different industries were those that were sufficiently differentiated to deal with the complexities of their industrial environments while simultaneously being tightly integrated internally.

These and other studies conducted by organization theorists have essentially, if not directly, reaffirmed the importance of fit. In addition, recent research in sociology and economics has supported the idea that achieving at least minimal fit is closely associated with organizational success. Industrial economists have identified a set of generic strategies that generally fit most industries, as well as some of the organizational and managerial characteristics associated with these strategies (M. E. Porter (1980)). Sociologists, borrowing concepts and theories from biology, have examined, within different populations of organizations, certain features that fit (or do not fit) particular environments (see M. T. Hannan and J. H. Freeman (1977), and H. E. Aldrich (1979)). In sum, the concept of fit may at first glance appear to be obvious, but many studies from several disciplines indicate that while fit is fundamental to organizational success, it is enormously difficult to achieve and/or maintain.

Fit and survival

It is appropriate to distinguish between degree of fit as well as the nature of fit, specifically that *minimal fit is required for organizational survival*. Under some circumstances, organizations that are 'misfits' in their industries may survive, but sooner or later they must adjust their behavior or fail. For example, in one of our studies, the objective was to determine if certain strategies were both feasible and effective in different industries (C. C. Snow and L. E. Hrebiniak, 1980). The industries selected for study were air transportation, autos, plastics, and semiconductors. We found that in general some strategies were effective and others were not. Organizations that we called 'Defenders', 'Prospectors', and 'Analyzers' were all effective; i.e. they met the test of minimal fit in each industry. On the other hand, organizations identified as 'Reactors' were generally ineffective, except in the air transportation industry which was highly regulated at the time (1975). 'Reactors' are organizations that have either a poorly articulated strategy, a strategy inappropriate for the industrial environment, or an organization structure and management system that does not fit the strategy. The findings from this study suggest that in competitive industries, there is a set of feasible strategies (e.g. Defender, Prospector, Analyzer) each of which can be effective. Moreover, misfits – organizations whose behavior lies outside the feasible set – tend to perform poorly unless they are in a 'protected' environment such as that provided by government regulation.

Fit and misfit

The line of demarcation between minimal fit and misfit, however, is not obvious. No whistles blow, warning an organization that its internal or external fit is coming undone. The process is more likely to be marked by a general deterioration whose speed is affected by competitive circumstances. For example, an in-depth study of the major firms in the tobacco industry during the years 1950–1975 illustrates the point (R. H. Miles, 1980). Few American industries have experienced the degree of negative pressure that was exerted on the tobacco industry during these years, and the experiences of four companies (Philip Morris, R. J. Reynolds, American Brands, Liggett & Meyers) pointedly show how organizations struggle to maintain an alignment with their shifting environments over time.

Each of the companies responded differently to severe, uncontrollable jolts such as the Sloan–Kettering Report linking smoking to cancer (1953), the Surgeon General's Report reaffirming this conclusion (1964), and events leading to and concluding with a ban on broadcast advertising of cigarettes (1970). Philip Morris, relying on a Prospector strategy, engaged in a series of product and market innovations that propelled the company from last among the major firms in 1950 market shares to first today. R. J. Reynolds largely pursued an Analyzer strategy – rarely the first mover in product-market innovations but always an early adopter of the successful innovations of its competitors – and today it ranks a close second to Philip Morris. Both of these companies currently exhibit a minimal if not strong fit with environmental conditions in the tobacco industry.

American Brands followed a Defender strategy in which it tried to maintain its traditional approach in the face of these environmental changes. This strategy essentially amounted to continued reliance on nonfiltered cigarettes even though the filtered cigarette market segment was growing steadily. American Brands, probably wanting not to cannibalize its sales of nonfiltered cigarettes, was at least ten years behind Philip Morris and R. J. Reynolds in entering the filtered cigarette market, and, during this period, the company fell from first to fourth place in overall market share. The company's internal fit among strategy, structure, and process was a good one throughout the mid-1950s to mid-1960s, but its strategic fit with the market underwent a gradual decline. Certainly, in retrospect, one could argue that American Brands was a misfit during this time, and the firm paid for it in declining performance.

Lastly, Liggett & Meyers behaved almost as a classic Reactor throughout this twenty-five-year period. It demonstrated substantially less internal consistency than its competition, fared poorly in its product-market strategy, and doggedly hung on to its approach despite unfavorable performance. Described by one source as 'always too late with too little', Liggett & Meyers in the late 1970s was searching for someone to purchase its tobacco business. Here was a misfit bordering on failure.

In the case of the tobacco industry, major environmental changes resulted in declining fit and performance for one company and near failure for another. Organizational misfit does not, however, have to come from external changes; it can result from internal shifts generated by the organization itself. To illustrate internally generated misfit, consider the well-known case of organizational disintegration and resurrection, the Chrysler Corporation.[1]

From a strong position as the country's second largest automobile manufacturer in the 1930s, Chrysler arguably began to decline in the post-World War II period when it changed its strategy without significantly altering its organization structure or management processes. Prior to the 1950s, Chrysler kept its capital base as small as possible, subcontracted out a substantial part of its production, and rode its suppliers hard to keep costs down. But then Chrysler decided to emulate both General Motors and Ford, even to the point of matching their product lines model for model. From the early 1960s until its Federal bailout in the 1970s, Chrysler seemed determined to be a full-line, worldwide, direct competitor of Ford and General Motors.

To support this product-market strategy, however, Chrysler was late in forming a subsidiary to monitor its distributors, late in making the necessary foreign acquisitions and often late in designing its greatly broadened product line which was done mostly by a single, centralized engineering group. In fact, Chrysler largely remained a functionally departmentalized and centralized organization long after it adopted a strategy of diversification. Managerial problems in the areas of cost control, inventory, and production merely added to the misfit between Chrysler's strategy and its structure

1. The description of Chrysler Corporation was adapted from James Brian Quinn (1977), *Chrysler Corporation*, copyrighted case, The Amos Tuck School of Business Administration, Dartmouth College.

and management system. Despite its recent public attention and economic rebound, the company has not yet achieved stable performance.

In sum, the consequence of misfit is declining performance if not complete failure. Organizational misfits can be protected by a benign environment, sometimes for lengthy periods of time, but minimal fit is required for survival in competitive environments. However, minimal fit, as the term implies, does not guarantee excellent performance.

Tight fit: the foundation for excellence

Corporate excellence requires more than minimal fit. Truly outstanding performance, achieved by many companies, is associated with tight fit – both externally with the environment and internally among strategy, structure, and management process. In fact, *tight fit is the causal force* at work when organizational excellence is said to be caused by various managerial and organizational characteristics.

In the late 1940s and early 1950s, Peter Drucker (1954) studied a number of top US corporations, including General Motors, General Electric, IBM, and Sears, Roebuck. Based on his observations, Drucker associated the widely acclaimed achievements of these organizations with such managerial characteristics as delegation and joint goal setting (Management by Objectives) and with organizational characteristics emphasizing the decentralization of operating decisions. He saw overstaffing as a threat to corporate responsiveness and argued that the best performance comes when jobs are enriched rather than narrowed. Finally, he felt that the overall key to the success of these companies was that they knew what business they were in, what their competencies were, and how to keep their efforts focused on their goals.

Some thirty years later, Thomas Peters and Robert Waterman (1983, chapter 3) studied sixty-two US companies and produced their own checklist of characteristics associated with corporate excellence. As had Drucker before them, they noted that organizations with records of sustained high performance tended to have a clear business focus, a bias for action, and lean structures and staffs that facilitated the pursuit of strategy.

Drucker clearly acknowledged the importance of organization structure and was convinced at the time that the federally decentralized (i.e. multidivision) organization structure was the design of the future. He did not, however, probe the relationship between alternative strategies and their appropriate structures and management processes. Similarly, while Peters and Waterman stressed structural leanness and responsiveness as universally valuable characteristics, they also noted the requirement of achieving a close fit among the seven 'Ss' of strategy, structure, skills, systems, style, shared values, and staff (people). Again, however, Peters and Waterman did not discuss the possible alternative organization forms appropriate for different strategies. In our view, the observations of Drucker, Peters, and Waterman are accurate and extremely valuable. The discovery thirty years apart of the association of similar characteristics with organizational excellence is a powerful argument for the validity of that association – but it is not an explanation of why that association exists nor of the causal force that may be involved.

Both the managerial and organizational characteristics described by these observers, and the outstanding performance achieved by the organizations that they have examined, are the result of the achievement – by discovery or by design – of tight fit. That is, such characteristics as convergence on a set of core business values – doing what one does best, a lean action-oriented structure that provides opportunities for the full use of people's capabilities at all levels, etc. – essentially flow from the achievement of tight fit with the environment and among strategy, structure, and process. In short, the causal dynamic of tight fit tends to operate in four stages:

1. The discovery of the basic structure and management processes necessary to support a chosen strategy creates a *gestalt* that becomes so obvious and compelling that complex organizational and managerial demands appear to be simple.
2. *Simplicity* leads to widespread understanding which reinforces and sustains fit. Organization structure and key management processes such as reward and control systems 'teach' managers and employees the appropriate attitudes and behaviors for maintaining focus on strategic requirements.
3. Simplicity *reduces the need for elaborate coordinating mechanisms*, thereby creating slack resources that can be reallocated elsewhere in the system.
4. As outstanding performance is achieved and sustained, its *association* with the process by which it is attained is reinforced, and this serves to simplify the basic fit among strategy, structure, and the process.

It should be emphasized that we do not specify 'finding the right strategy' as an important element of this causal linkage. In fact, finding strategy-structure-process fit is usually far more important and problematic. It may be that there is less to strategy than meets the eye. At any moment, in any given industry, it is likely that several organizations are considering the same strategic moves: to diversify, retrench, acquire other firms, etc. For example, in the 1920s, the top executives of Sears, Roebuck did not have a secret crystal ball that forecast the effects of the automobile on retail trade. Indeed most organizations – including Sears's major competitor, Montgomery Ward – saw similar trends. It was the case, however, that well ahead of competitors Sears developed a structure that would allow it to operate as a high-quality, low-cost, nationwide retailing organization.

It is valuable, of course, that the chosen strategy be articulated – for example, Sears pursued the image of 'a hometown store with nationwide purchasing power'. Nevertheless, it is when the blueprint of how to achieve such strategic goals is drawn that real understanding begins to emerge throughout the system. As clarity involving means emerges, that which was enormously complex and apparently beyond accomplishment, now seems straightforward and easy to achieve.

The process of searching for, discovering, and achieving tight fit is pervasive. At the individual level, for instance, learning to drive a car, fly an airplane, or serve a tennis ball are all activities that at first appear complex and difficult to learn but once mastered seem to be relatively simple. Mastery occurs, however, only when the *gestalt* is apprehended, felt, and understood. The same learning process occurs within organizations. The Baltimore Orioles, for example, believe they know how and why they won the recent World Series and have enjoyed success over the years. Strategy, structure, and process fit and are well understood by members at all levels of the organization. From the front office to the manager, coaches, and players (including those in the farm system), it seems clear how one goes about building a world-champion team. Much of the same could be said for Proctor & Gamble, Johnson & Johnson, Minnesota Mining & Manufacturing, McDonald's, Schlumberger, and other excellent companies.

In sum, what we are suggesting is that focus, leanness, action, involvement, identification, etc. are likely *products* of tight fit. Fit simplifies complex organizational and managerial arrangements, and simple systems facilitate leanness, action, and many other observed manifestations of excellence. As one understands the system, one feels more a part of it, and as one's role becomes clear to self and others, participation is facilitated, almost demanded. Closeness and understanding provide a common culture, and stories and myths emerge that perpetuate key aspects of culture.

Early fit: a key to the hall of fame?

To this point we have argued that minimal fit is necessary for an organization's survival and that tight fit is associated with excellent performance. We now suggest that *early fit – the discovery and articulation of a new organization form – can lead to sustained excellence* over considerable periods of time and thus a place in some mythical Hall of Fame.

Picking a Hall of Fame company is difficult. In sports, Hall of Fame performers are individuals who have been selected only after their careers are over, and sometimes selection is preceded by an interval of several years so that the decision is relatively objective, based on complete information, and final. Organizations, on the other hand, are ongoing systems; therefore, any given Hall of Fame nominee might immediately have one or more 'off' years. Nevertheless, some organizations would be likely to appear on every pundit's Hall of Fame list, and we believe that most of these organizations would share the characteristic of an early organizational breakthrough that was not quickly or easily matched by their competitors at the time.

There are, of course, many ways that companies can achieve a competitive advantage. For example, obtaining a patent on a particular product or technology gives a firm an edge on its competitors. Cornering the supply of a key raw material through location or judicious buying may permit a company to dominate a particular business. An innovative product design or the development of a new distribution channel can provide an organization with a competitive lead that is difficult to overcome. Yet all of these competitive advantages are more or less temporary – sooner or later competitors will imitate and improve upon the innovation and the advantage will disappear. Such abilities, therefore, do not guarantee induction into the Hall of Fame.

Sustained corporate excellence seems to have at least one necessary condition: the invention or early application of – and rapid tight fit around – a new organization form. Achieving early fit succeeds over the proprietary advantages mentioned above because a new organization form cannot be completely copied in the short or even intermediate run. In this century, certain firms would appear to merit Hall of Fame nomination based on broad criteria such as product excellence, management performance, market share and responsiveness, and the like. We will discuss five of our own nominees all of which meet these criteria but also share the characteristic of early fit through invention or application of a new organization form: Carnegie Steel, General Motors, Sears, Roebuck, Hewlett-Packard, and IBM.

Carnegie Steel

Carnegie Steel was one of the first companies to employ the fully-integrated functional organization form complete with centralized management and technical specialization.[2] In his early thirties, Andrew Carnegie left a position with the railroad to concentrate on manufacturing steel rails. Convinced that the management methods he and others had pioneered on the railroad could also be applied to the manufacturing sector, Carnegie essentially started the modern steel business in the US and he played a major role in forging the world's first billion-dollar corporation, US Steel.

At the heart of Carnegie Steel's success was its reliance on centralized management (particularly cost accounting and control) and full vertical integration. Carnegie recognized early the benefits of vertical integration in the fragmented, geographically dispersed steel industry in the latter half of the nineteenth century; his company integrated backward into the purchase of ore deposits and the production of coke, as well as forward into manufacture of finished steel products. Vertical integration permitted a new external alignment in the steel industry: substantially larger market areas could now be served much more quickly, efficiently, and profitably. Carnegie Steel supplemented its functional organization structure with careful plant design and transportation logistics, continuous technological improvements, successful (though limited) product diversification, and innovative human resources management practices and labor relations. Thus, internally, there was rapid development of a tight fit between management processes and the company's pioneering strategy and structure.

Carnegie Steel, of course, did not invent the vertically integrated, functional organization form; elements of this model were already available. However, the company's early and complete use of this form dramatically altered the steel business in a way that was not matched by competitors for decades. (See Table 1 for the evolution of major organization forms and our prediction of the next new form.)

---

2. The description of Carnegie Steel was adapted from Paul R. Lawrence and Davis Dyer (1983), *Renewing American Industry*, Free Press, chapter 3.

Table 1. Evolution of organization forms

	Product-market strategy	Organization structure	Inventor or early user	Core activating and control mechanisms
1800	Single product or service. Local/regional markets	Agency	Numerous small owner-managed firms	Personal direction and control
1850	Limited, standardized product or service line. Regional/national markets	Functional	Carnegie Steel	Central plan and budgets
1900	Diversified, changing product or service line. National/ international markets	Divisional	General Motors, Sears, Roebuck, Hewlett-Packard	Corporate policies and division profit centers
1950	Standard and innovative products or services. Stable and changing markets	Matrix	Several aerospace and electronics firms (e.g. NASA, TRW, IBM, Texas Instruments)	Temporary teams and lateral resource allocation devices such as internal markets, joint planning systems, etc.
2000	Product or service design. Global, changing markets	Dynamic network	International/ construction firms; Global consumer goods companies: Selected electronics and computer firms (e.g., IBM)	Broker-assembled temporary structures with shared information systems as basis for trust and coordination

General Motors

General Motors has the strongest claim as the inventor of the 'federally decentralized' or divisional organization structure. Among the early automobile makers, William C. Durant was one of the strongest believers in the enormous potential market for the moderately-priced car.[3] Acting on his beliefs, Durant put together a group of companies engaged in the making and selling of automobiles, parts, and accessories. In 1919, the total combined assets of Durant's General Motors made it the fifth largest company in the US. But although Durant had spotted a potentially large

3. The description of General Motors was adapted from A. D. Chandler, Jr (1962), chapter 3.

opportunity, and had moved rapidly to create an industrial empire to take advantage of it, he had little interest in developing an organization structure and management system for the enterprise he had created.

Indeed, in combining individual firms into General Motors, Durant relied on the same organizational approach of volume production and vertical integration that he had used in his previous managerial positions and that was popular at the time. However, this approach led to little more than an expanding agglomeration of different companies making automobiles, parts, accessories, trucks, tractors, and even refrigerators. An unforeseen collapse in the demand for automobiles in 1920 precipitated a financial crisis at General Motors, which was quickly followed by Durant's retirement as President. Pierre du Pont, who had been in semi-retirement from the chemical company, agreed to take the presidency of GM. One of du Pont's first actions was to approve a plan devised by Alfred P. Sloan, a high-level GM executive whose family firm had been purchased by Durant, that defined an organization structure for General Motors.

Sloan's plan, which went into effect in early 1921, called for a general office to coordinate, appraise, and set broad goals and policies for the numerous, loosely controlled operating divisions of GM. The general officers individually were to supervise and coordinate different groups of divisions and collectively were to help make policy for the corporation as a whole. Staff specialists were to advise and serve both the division managers and the general officers and to provide business and financial information necessary for appraising the performance of the individual units and for formulating overall policy. Although most of Sloan's proposals had been carried out by the end of 1921, it was not until 1925 that the original plan resulted in a smooth-running organization. The multidivisional decentralized structure allowed GM to diversify a standard product, the automobile, to meet a variety of consumer needs and tastes while maintaining overall corporate financial synergy.

From 1924 to 1927, General Motors' market share rose from 19 to 43 per cent. Unlike its major competitor, Ford, which was devastated by the Depression, GM's profits grew steadily throughout the Depression and World War II. It has been the leading automobile manufacturer in the world since its implementation of the divisional structure and for years was the corporate model of similar structural changes in other large American industrial enterprises.

Sears, Roebuck

Just as General Motors can make a strong claim to the invention of the divisional structure for product diversification, Sears, Roebuck can claim to have been one of the earliest users of this structure outside of manufacturing. Sears has long enjoyed its reputation as the world's most successful retailer.[4] Since its inception in 1895, Sears has undergone two periods where it achieved an 'early fit' among its competitors. The first phase of the Sears story began in 1895 when Julius Rosenwald, a consummate administrator, joined Richard Sears, a brilliant merchandiser, and together they built a company catering to the American farmer. Sears, Roebuck's Chicago mail-order plant was a major innovation in the retailing business. Designed by Otto Doering in 1903, this modern mass-production plant preceded by five years Henry Ford's acclaimed automobile assembly line, and it ushered in the 'distribution revolution' that was so vital a factor in early twentieth-century America's economic growth.

The second phase of the Sears story began in 1924 when Robert E. Wood left Montgomery Ward to join the company. Since farmers could now travel to cities in their automobiles and the urban population was more affluent, retail selling through local stores appeared to be more promising than mail-order sales. Promoted to President in 1928, Wood, with his new hand-picked management team, moved ahead rapidly to create a nationwide retail organization. Montgomery Ward and other retail chains of the period (e.g. J. C. Penney, Eaton's, Woolworth's, Grant's, Kresge's) have not been able to this day to match Sears's performance.

The organization form developed at Sears bore many similarities to GM's multidivisional structure, but it was geared toward retailing rather than manufacturing. Whereas GM diversified by product, Sears diversified by geographic territory. Each of the territorial units became fully fledged, autonomous divisions with their managers responsible for overall operating results, and the Chicago headquarters remained a central office with staff specialists and general executives. Sears's ultimate tight internal and external fit was not accomplished nearly as rapidly as those of Carnegie Steel or General Motors, but it was achieved by Sears before its competitors and gave the company a competitive advantage that has not, until recently, been seriously threatened.

4. The description of Sears, Roebuck was adapted from A. D. Chandler, Jr (1962), chapter 5 and from Peter F. Drucker (1954), chapter 4.

Hewlett-Packard

The decentralized, divisional structure developed by General Motors and Sears (along with a few other outstanding companies such as Du Pont and Standard Oil of New Jersey) flourished in the 1950s under the spotlight of publicity from management consulting firms and from academics like Peter Drucker. For most companies, however, the divisional structure did not serve as a proprietary advantage but merely as a necessary means of maintaining alignment with a market demanding diversity. Nevertheless, one outstanding company has taken this organization structure to new heights in its pursuit of leading-edge technological developments in an emerging industry. The company is Hewlett-Packard and the industry, of course, is electronics. Founded in 1939 by William Hewlett and David Packard, this company is the world's largest manufacturer of test and measurement instruments as well as a major producer of small computers. The company is noted for its strong corporate culture and nearly continuous high performance in a very demanding industrial environment.

From the beginning, Hewlett-Packard has pursued a strategy that brings the products of scientific research into industrial application while maintaining the collegial atmosphere of a university laboratory. This means that the firm concentrates on advanced technology and offers mostly state-of-the-art products to a variety of industrial and consumer markets. A given product line and market are actively pursued as long as the company has a distinctive technological or design advantage. When products reach the stage where successful competition depends primarily on low costs and prices, Hewlett-Packard often moves out of the arena and turns its attention to a new design or an entirely new product. As a company that achieved early fit, its technological diversification rivals General Motors' product diversification and Sears's territorial diversification.

Hewlett-Packard's strategy of technological innovation is supported by an organization structure and management system that may be unparalleled in flexibility. The fundamental business unit is the product division, an integrated, self-sustaining organization with a great deal of independence. New divisions arise when a particular product line becomes large enough to support its continued growth out of the profit it generates. Also, new divisions tend to emerge when a single division gets so large that the people involved start to lose their identification with the product line. Most human-resources management practices – especially those concerning hiring, placement, and rewards – are appropriately matched with the company's structural and strategic decentralization.

International Business Machines

Any Hall of Fame list must include IBM.[5] One of the largest producers of calculating, computing, and office machinery, IBM is arguably the best managed company in the United States, perhaps the world. Paradoxically, IBM's nomination to the Hall of Fame cannot be based on the invention of a particular organization form – nor, for that matter, a management innovation or technological breakthrough. The company is simply good at everything it does; it is a polydextrous organization that is consistently quick to adopt and refine any approach that it can use to its advantage.

The company was born when Thomas Watson, Sr, joined the Computing-Recording Corporation in 1914 and renamed it International Business Machines in 1924. However, the modern IBM dates to the stewardship of Thomas Watson, Jr, who was chief executive officer from 1956 to 1971. Today IBM is the most profitable US industrial company, and its form of organization is a combination of time-honored and advanced approaches.

IBM takes advantage of two key characteristics of the functional organization, vertical integration and production efficiency. For example, IBM is the world's largest manufacturer of memory chips and installs its entire output in its own machines. And beginning in the late 1970s, a series of huge capital improvements has made IBM one of the most automated and lowest-cost producers in the industry.

IBM has also relied to a limited extent on acquisitions, a characteristic most often associated with the divisional organization. Unlike many large conglomerates, the company is very selective about its acquisitions, the most recent of which is intended to help IBM create the futuristic electronic office.

Finally, IBM uses a variety of the most advanced approaches to organization and management. First, the company has created at least fifteen internal new ventures groups in the last few years to explore new business opportunities. The new units are independently run, but they can draw on IBM resources. Second, the company has increased its use of subcontracting. In its most recent product venture, the personal computer, IBM relied largely on parts obtained from outside suppliers and is selling the machine through retail outlets like Sears and ComputerLand as well as its own sales network. Software for the machine was developed by inviting

5. The description of IBM was adapted from 'The colossus that works', *Time*, July 11, 1983, pp. 44-54.

numerous software firms to supply ideas and materials. Third, besides being a vigorous competitor, IBM has formed many successful cooperative agreements with other companies, especially in Japan and Europe. It is generally acknowledged that substantially more cooperative arrangements involving business firms, as well as governments and universities, will be needed in coming years to supplement traditional competitive practices. And, lastly, IBM is international in scope. It is the leading computer firm in virtually every one of the approximately 130 countries where it does business.

In sum, a close, current look at the Hall of Fame companies just described would probably not uncover the maintenance of perfect fit. As suggested earlier, even these organizations are vulnerable to external and internal slippage, perhaps even distortion. Therefore, it is important to explore the processes by which tight fit may be eroded.

The fragility of fit

As noted earlier, fit is a process as well as a state. Environmental factors outside an organization's control are constantly changing and may require incremental or major strategic adjustment. Strategic change, in turn, is likely to require changes in organization structure and/or management processes. When environmental jolts are extreme, some organizations may be unwilling or unable to adjust – recall the earlier examples from the tobacco industry and witness the recent plight of several airline companies under deregulation.

However, environmental change is not the only cause of alignment deterioration. For example, misfit may occur when organizations voluntarily change their strategies but fail to follow through with appropriate structural and managerial adjustments, as illustrated by the case of Chrysler. An even more intriguing alignment-threatening process is also demonstrable, one which may well account for more deterioration of fit than either environmental jolts or unsupported strategic changes. This process involves voluntary internal structure and process changes that are made without concern for their longer-run consequences for strategy and market responsiveness. Although usually subtle and long-term in its development, this process of internal unraveling underscores the point that an organization's fit at any given time may be quite fragile.

Recall the earlier description of how the discovery of tight fit results in system simplicity: when strategy, structure, and process are completely aligned, both goals and means are visible, and task requirements are obvious and compelling. Resources previously required for coordination or troubleshooting can be redeployed in the primary system, and even tighter fit may result. However, as the spotlight of tight fit illuminates the overall system for everyone to see and understand, its bright glare may also begin to highlight the organization's inherent deficiencies. That is, each pattern of fit has its own distinct contribution to make. For example, the functional organization form is ideal for efficient production of standard goods or services and the divisional form is most appropriate for diversification. Each form not only has its own strengths but also its own built-in limitations. The form best suited for efficiency is vulnerable to market change, and the form suited to diversification is sometimes clearly redundant.

As the pattern of fit becomes increasingly clear to managers and employees of excellent (tight fit) companies, they can easily describe why the organization prospers. But at least some members of these same companies can also point to the system's shortcomings. For example, in a vertically integrated, centralized, functional organization, perceptive managers will advocate the creation of task forces, project groups, or even separate divisions to facilitate quick development of new products or services. Conversely, one can anticipate in a decentralized, divisional structure that cost-conscious managers will suggest standardizing certain components or services across divisions in order to reduce redundancy and achieve scale economies. Most organizations regularly make minor adjustments in their structures and processes to accommodate demands for which their systems were not designed. In some organizations, however, what begins as a limited adjustment may over time grow into a crippling, step-by-step unraveling of the entire system. Moreover, this may occur without conscious long-term planning or even awareness. Two brief examples, both associated with companies on our Hall of Fame list, serve as illustrations.

At General Motors, once Sloan's federally decentralized structure was fully in place, managers began to recommend standardization of various product components and production processes. Some aspects of engineering and production had been coordinated across divisions from the beginning, but the advocates of full-scale standardization finally began to override the divisional structure in the 1950s. Many readers may recall the 'scandal' that occurred when buyers discovered that the General Motors' engine in their cars had not been made by that division and, in some cases, even by a division of lower status. In fact, those engines had been manufactured according to policies that reflected increasing interdivisional coordination and centralization of decision making. During the 1950s and 1960s when

General Motors appeared invulnerable to competition – foreign or domestic – the cost of increased centralization and coordination was probably not visible. It almost appeared that the company could have its diversity and its cost savings, too. One wonders how much more rapidly General Motors might have responded to the challenge of foreign competition if it had been able to do so by simply aiming the operations of one autonomous division toward Japan and another toward Europe. In general, the more attention that is devoted to the known shortcomings of a particular organization form, the more likely is the possibility of unraveling a successful fit.

Could a similar process occur at Hewlett-Packard? In recent months, the company has been beset with problems caused by its decentralized management system and entrepreneurial culture, including overlapping products, lagging development of new technology, and a piecemeal approach to key markets.[6] The response to these problems was the launching of several programs to improve planning, coordinate marketing, and strengthen the firm's computer-related research and development efforts.

Hewlett-Packard's current CEO, John Young, recognizes that these organizational changes involve trade-offs; the benefits obtained from cross-divisional coordination have to be weighted against the threats to the entrepreneurial spirit of the various divisions. That is, the use of program managers and strategic coordinators to align product designs, to force the divisions to share components, and to coordinate pricing and marketing strategies has generated a number of successful cross-divisional development projects. However, these successes have been offset by a wave of manager and engineer defections to other companies. Thus, only time will tell if this reorganization improves the company's internal fit or begins to unravel the core threads among strategy, structure, and process that have produced Hewlett-Packard's success.

The moral of these examples is not that managers of excellent companies should not try to improve performance. Rather, it is that rearranging organization structure and management systems may in some cases preclude an organization from pursuing its desired strategy. Managers of truly outstanding companies recognize the strengths and limitations of alternative organization forms, and they will not undo a crucial link among strategy, structure, or process in order to 'solve' predictable problems.

6. 'Can John Young redesign Hewlett-Packard?', *Business Week*, December 6, 1982, pp. 72–8.

Future fit: a new organization form

Our argument concerning the effects of minimal, tight, and early fit on organizational performance is based on the belief that the search for fit has been visible in organizations for at least the past one hundred years. But will this search continue in the future? We believe it will. In fact, many managers are now considering a new organization form and are experimenting with its major components and processes in their organizations. The reality of this new form, therefore, simply awaits articulation and understanding.

In this century, there have been three major breakthroughs in the way organizations have been designed and managed (see again Table 1). The first breakthrough occurred at the turn of the century in the form of the functional organization. Prior to that time, small firms had relied on an informal structure in which the owner-manager's immediate subordinates acted as all-purpose 'agents' of the chief executive, solving whatever problems arose. There was very little of the technical specialization found in today's organizations. The functional form allowed those companies that adopted it to become very large and to specialize in a limited set of products and markets. Next came the divisional form, which facilitated even more organizational growth, but, more importantly, it facilitated diversification in both products and markets. The third breakthrough was the matrix structure in which elements of the functional and divisional forms were combined into a single system able to accommodate both standard and innovative products or projects.

Now a promising new organization form is emerging, one that appears to fit the fast-approaching conditions of the twenty-first century. As was true of previous forms, elements of this new form are sprouting in several companies and industries simultaneously.

1. *Large construction firms.* The construction industry has long been known for its use of subcontracting to accomplish large, complex tasks. Today, the size and complexity of a construction project can be immense, as evidenced by the multinational consortium of companies building an entire city in Saudi Arabia. Under such circumstances, companies must be able to form a network of reliable subcontractors, many of them large firms which have not worked together before. Some companies, therefore, have found it advantageous to focus only on the overall design and management of a project, leaving the actual construction to their affiliates.

2. *Global consumer goods companies*. Standardized products such as clothes, cameras, and watches can be designed, manufactured, and marketed throughout the world. Companies engaged in this type of business are prime examples of the 'world enterprise': buying raw materials wherever they are cheapest, manufacturing wherever costs are lowest, and selling wherever the products will bring the highest price. To do so, however, requires many different brokers – individuals and groups who bring together complementary resources. All of the participants in the process – designers, suppliers, manufacturers, distributors, etc. – must be coupled into a smooth-running operation even though they are continents apart.

3. *Electronics and computer firms*. Certain firms in these industries already are dealing with conditions that in the future will be widespread: rapid change, demassification, high technology, information abundance, and so on.[7] In these companies, product life cycles are often short and all firms live under the constant threat of technological innovations that can change the structure of the industry. Individual firms must constantly redesign their processes around new products. Across the industry, spin-off firms are continually emerging. Thus, a common development model includes venture capitalists working with high-technology entrepreneurs in the development, manufacture, and distribution of innovative products or services.

Across these three examples, some key characteristics of the new organization form are clearly visible. Organizations of the future are likely to be *vertically disaggregated*: functions typically encompassed within a single organization will instead be performed in independent organizations. That is, the functions of product design and development, manufacturing, and distribution, ordinarily integrated by a plan and controlled directly by managers, will instead be brought together by *brokers* and held in temporary alignment by a variety of *market mechanisms*.

For example, one form of a vertically disaggregated organization held together by a market mechanism is the franchise system, symbolized by McDonald's or H&R Block. In a franchise system, both the product or service and its basic recipe are provided by the parent corporation to a local management group. Such a model, however, seems appropriate only for a limited set of standard goods or services. In our view, a more flexible

---

7. For a discussion of these conditions, see Alvin Toffler (1981), *The Third Wave*, Bantam Books; and John Naisbitt (1983), *Megatrends: Ten New Directions Transforming Our Lives*, Warner Books.

and comprehensive approach – and hence a better analog of the organization of the future – is the 'designer' system associated with companies such as Yves St. Laurent or Gucci. In these companies, design skills can be applied in a variety of arenas, from electronics to household goods to personal products or services. Similarly, production expertise can be contracted for and applied to a wide array of products or services, as can skills in marketing and distribution. Thus, we expect the twenty-first century firm to be a temporary organization, brought together by an entrepreneur with the aid of brokers and maintained by a network of contractual ties. In some instances, a single entrepreneur will play a lead role and subcontract for various services. This same individual may also serve as a consultant to others attempting to form their own organizational networks. In other cases, linkages among equals may be created by request through various brokers specializing in a particular service.

Given these characteristics, we have found it useful to refer to this emerging form as the *dynamic network* organization. However, the full realization of this new type of organization awaits the development of a core activating and control mechanism comparable to those that energized the previous organization forms (e.g. the profit center in the divisional form). Our prediction is that this mechanism essentially will be a broad-access computerized information system. Note that most of today's temporary organizations (e.g. a general contractor) have been put together on the basis of lengthy experience among the key participants. Under future conditions of high complexity and rapid change, however, participants in the network organization will first have to be identified, trust between the parties will be a major issue, and fixed-fee contracts specified in advance will usually not be feasible. Therefore, as a substitute for lengthy trust-building processes, participants will have to agree on a general structure of payment for value added and then hook themselves together in a full-disclosure information system so that contributions can be mutually and instantaneously verified. Properly constructed, the dynamic network organization will display the technical expertise of the functional form, the market focus of the divisional form, and the efficient use of resources characteristic of the matrix. And, especially important, it will be able to quickly reshape itself whenever necessary.

Conclusion

The United States is in a period of economic challenge and organizational upheaval. There are myriad prescriptions for industrial and organizational renewal, and many of the factors linked to organizational success are being rediscovered today after a thirty-year hiatus. Our own analysis, however, indicates that these characteristics, while important, are merely manifestations of a more fundamental, dynamic process called fit – the search for an organization form that is both internally and externally consistent. We have argued that minimal fit is necessary for survival, tight fit is associated with corporate excellence, and early fit provides a competitive advantage that can lead to the organization Hall of Fame. Tomorrow's Hall of Fame companies are working on new organization forms today.

References

ALDRICH, H. E. (1979), *Organizations and Environments*, Prentice-Hall

BURNS, T., and STALKER, G. M. (1961), *The Management of Innovation*, Tavistock

CHANDLER, A. D., JR (1962), *Strategy and Structure*, Doubleday

DRUCKER, P. F. (1954), *The Practice of Management*, Harper & Row

HANNAN, M. T. and FREEMAN, J. H. (1977), 'The population ecology of organizations', *American Journal of Sociology*, vol. 82 (March), pp. 929–64

LAWRENCE, P. R., and LORSCH, J. W. (1967), *Organization and Environment*, Harvard Graduate School of Business Administration

MILES, R. E., and SNOW, C. C. (1978), *Organizational Strategy, Structure and Process*, McGraw-Hill

MILES, R. H. (1980), *Coffin Nails and Corporate Strategies*, Prentice-Hall

PETERS, T. J., and WATERMAN, R. H. (1983), *In Search of Excellence: Lessons from America's Best Run Companies*, Free Press

PORTER, M. E. (1980), *Competitive Strategy*, Free Press

SNOW, C. C., and HREBINIAK, L. E. (1980), 'Strategy, distinctive competence, and organizational performance', *Administrative Science Quarterly*, vol. 25 (June), pp. 317–36

10 M. T. Hannan and J. Freeman

The Population Ecology of Organizations[1]

From 'The population of ecology of organizations', *American Journal of Sociology*, 1977, vol. 82, pp. 929–64

I. Introduction

Analysis of the effects of environment on organizational structure has moved to a central place in organizations theory and research in recent years. This shift has opened a number of exciting possibilities. As yet nothing like the full promise of the shift has been realized. We believe that the lack of development is due in part to a failure to bring ecological models to bear on questions that are preeminently ecological. We argue for a reformulation of the problem in population ecology terms.

Although there is a wide variety of ecological perspectives, they all focus on selection. That is, they attribute patterns in nature to the action of selection processes. The bulk of the literature on organizations subscribes to a different view, which we call the adaptation perspective.[2] According

1. This research was supported in part by grants from the National Science Foundation (GS-32065) and the Spencer Foundation. Helpful comments were provided by Amos Hawley, François Nielsen, John Meyer, Marshall Meyer, Jeffrey Pfeffer, and Howard Aldrich.

2. There is a subtle relationship between selection and adaptation. Adaptive learning for individuals usually consists of selection among behavioral responses. Adaptation for a population involves selection among types of members. More generally, processes involving selection can usually be recast at a higher level of analysis as adaptation processes. However, once the unit of analysis is chosen there is no ambiguity in distinguishing selection from adaptation. Organizations often adapt to environmental conditions in concert and this suggests a systems effect. Though few theorists would deny the existence of such systems effects, most do not make them a subject of central concern. It is important to notice that, from the point of view embraced by sociologists whose interests focus on the broader social system, selection in favor of organizations with one set of properties to the disfavor of those with others is often an adaptive process. Societies and communities which consist in part of formal organizations adapt partly through processes that adjust the mixture of various kinds of organizations found

to the adaptation perspective, subunits of the organization, usually managers or dominant coalitions, scan the relevant environment for opportunities and threats, formulate strategic responses, and adjust organizational structure appropriately.

The adaptation perspective is seen most clearly in the literature on management. Contributors to it usually assume a hierarchy of authority and control that locates decisions concerning the organization as a whole at the top. It follows, then, that organizations are affected by their environments according to the ways in which managers or leaders formulate strategies, make decisions, and implement them. Particularly successful managers are able either to buffer their organizations from environmental disturbances or to arrange smooth adjustments that require minimal disruption of organizational structure.

A similar perspective, often worded differently, dominates the sociological literature on the subject. It plays a central role in Parsons's (1956) functional analysis of organization–environment relations and it is found in the more strictly Weberian tradition (see Selznick, 1957). It is interesting to note that, while functionalists have been interested in system effects and have based much of the logic of their approach on survival imperatives, they have not dealt with selection phenomena. This is probably a reaction against organization theory which reflects social Darwinism.

Exchange theorists have also embraced the adaptation perspective (Levine and White, 1961). And it is natural that theories emphasizing decision making take the adaptation view (March and Simon, 1958; Cyert and March, 1963). Even Thompson's (1967) celebrated marriage of open-systems and closed-systems thinking embraced the adaptation perspective explicitly (see particularly the second half of Thompson's book).

Clearly, leaders of organizations do formulate strategies and organizations do adapt to environmental contingencies. As a result at least some of the relationship between structure and environment must reflect adaptive behavior or learning. But there is no reason to presume that the great structural variability among organizations reflects only or even primarily adaptation.

There are a number of obvious limitations on the ability of organizations to adapt. That is, there are a number of processes that generate structural inertia. The stronger the pressures, the lower the organizations' adaptive

within them. Whereas a complete theory of organization and environment would have to consider both adaptation and selection, recognizing that they are complementary processes, our purpose here is to show what can be learned from studying selection alone (see Aldrich and Pfeffer [1976] for a synthetic review of the literature focusing on these different perspectives).

flexibility and the more likely that the logic of environmental selection is appropriate. As a consequence, the issue of structural inertia is central to the choice between adaptation and selection models.

The possibility that organization structure contains a large inertial component was suggested by Burns and Stalker (1961) and Stinchcombe (1965). But, on the whole the subject has been ignored. A number of relevant propositions can be found in the organizations literature, however.

Inertial pressures arise from both internal structural arrangements and environmental constraints. A minimal list of the constraints arising from internal considerations follows.

1. An organization's investment in plant, equipment, and specialized personnel constitutes assets that are not easily transferable to other tasks or functions. The ways in which such sunk costs constrain adaptation options are so obvious that they need not be discussed further.

2. Organizational decision makers also face constraints on the information they receive. Much of what we know about the flow of information through organizational structures tells us that leaders do not obtain anything close to full information on activities within the organization and environmental contingencies facing the subunits.

3. Internal political constraints are even more important. When organizations alter structure, political equilibria are disturbed. As long as the pool of resources is fixed, structural change almost always involves redistribution of resources across subunits. Such redistribution upsets the prevailing system of exchange among subunits (or subunit leaders). So at least some subunits are likely to resist any proposed reorganization. Moreover, the benefits of structural reorganization are likely to be both generalized (designed to benefit the organization as a whole) and long-run. Any negative political response will tend to generate short-run costs that are high enough that organizational leaders will forego the planned reorganization. (For a more extensive discussion of the ways in which the internal political economy of organizations impedes change or adaptation, see Downs [1967] and Zald [1970].)

4. Finally, organizations face constraints generated by their own history. Once standards of procedure and the allocation of tasks and authority have become the subject of normative agreement, the costs of change are greatly increased. Normative agreements constrain adaptation in at least two ways. First, they provide a justification and an organizing principle for those elements that wish to resist reorganization (i.e., they can resist in terms of a shared principle). Second, normative agreements preclude the serious

consideration of many alternative responses. For example, few research-oriented universities seriously consider adapting to declining enrollments by eliminating the teaching function. To entertain this option would be to challenge central organizational norms.[3]

The external pressures toward inertia seem to be at least as strong. They include at least the following factors.

1. Legal and fiscal barriers to entry and exit from markets (broadly defined) are numerous. Discussions of organizational behavior typically emphasize barriers to entry (state licensed monopoly positions, etc.). Barriers to exit are equally interesting. There are an increasing number of instances in which political decisions prevent firms from abandoning certain activities. All such constraints on entry and exit limit the breadth of adaptation possibilities.

2. Internal constraints upon the availability of information are paralleled by external constraints. The acquisition of information about relevant environments is costly particularly in turbulent situations where the information is most essential. In addition, the type of specialists employed by the organization constrains both the nature of the information it is likely to obtain (see Granovetter, 1973) and the kind of specialized information it can process and utilize.

3. Legitimacy constraints also emanate from the environment. Any legitimacy an organization has been able to generate constitutes an asset in manipulating the environment. To the extent that adaptation (e.g., eliminating undergraduate instruction in public universities) violates the legitimacy claims, it incurs considerable costs. So external legitimacy considerations also tend to limit adaptation.

4. Finally, there is the collective rationality problem. One of the most difficult issues in contemporary economics concerns general equilibria. If one can find an optimal strategy for some individual buyer or seller in a competitive market, it does not necessarily follow that there is a general equilibrium once all players start trading. More generally, it is difficult to establish that a strategy that is rational for a single decision maker will be rational if adopted by a large number of decision makers. A number of solutions to this problem have been proposed in competitive market theory, but we know of no treatment of the problem for organizations generally. Until such a treatment is established we should not presume that a course

3. Meyer's (1970) discussion of an organization's charter adds further support to the argument that normative agreements arrived at early in an organization's history constrain greatly the organization's range of adaptation to environmental constraints.

of action that is adaptive for a single organization facing some changing environment will be adaptive for many competing organizations adopting a similar strategy.

A number of these inertial pressures can be accommodated within the adaptation framework. That is, one can modify and limit the perspective in order to consider choices within the constrained set of alternatives. But to do so greatly limits the scope of one's investigation. We argue that in order to deal with the various inertial pressures the adaptation perspective must be supplemented with a selection orientation.

We consider first two broad issues that are preliminary to ecological modeling. The first concerns appropriate units of analysis. Typical analyses of the relation of organizations to environments take the point of view of a single organization facing an environment. We argue for an explicit focus on populations of organizations. The second broad issue concerns the applicability of population ecology models to the study of human social organization. Our substantive proposal begins with Hawley's (1950, 1968) classic statement on human ecology. We seek to extend Hawley's work in two ways: by using explicit competition models to specify the process producing isomorphism between organizational structure and environmental demands, and by using niche theory to extend the problem to dynamic environments. We argue that Hawley's perspective, modified and extended in these ways, serves as a useful starting point for population ecology theories of organizations.

II. Population thinking in the study of organization–environment relations

Little attention is paid in the organizations literature to issues concerning proper units of analysis (Freeman, 1975). In fact, choice of unit is treated so casually as to suggest that it is not an issue. We suspect that the opposite is true – that the choice of unit involves subtle issues and has far-reaching consequences for research activity. For instance, in the case at hand, it determines which of several ecological literatures can be brought to bear on the study of organization–environment relations.

The comparison of unit choice facing the organizational analyst with that facing the bioecologist is instructive. To oversimplify somewhat, ecological analysis is conducted at three levels: individual, population, and community. Events at one level almost always have consequences at other levels. Despite this interdependence, population events cannot be reduced to individual events (since individuals do not reflect the full genetic variability of the population) and community events cannot be simply reduced to population events. Both the latter employ a population perspective which is not appropriate at the individual level.

The situation faced by the organizations analyst is more complex. Instead of three levels of analysis, he faces at least five: (1) members, (2) subunits, (3) individual organizations, (4) populations of organizations, and (5) communities of (populations of) organizations. Levels 3–5 can be seen as corresponding to the three levels discussed for general ecology, with the individual organization taking the place of the individual organism. The added complexity arises because organizations are more nearly decomposable into constituent parts than are organisms. Individual members and subunits may move from organization to organization in a manner which has no parallel in nonhuman organization.

Instances of theory and research dealing with the effects of environments on organizations are found at all five levels. For example, Crozier's well-known analysis of the effects of culture on bureaucracy focuses on the cultural materials members bring to organizations (1964). At the other end of the continuum we find analyses of 'organizational fields' (Turk, 1970; Aldrich and Reiss, 1976). But, the most common focus is on *the* organization and *its* environment. In fact, this choice is so widespread that there appears to be a tacit understanding that individual organizations are the appropriate units for the study of organization–environment relations.

We argue for a parallel development of theory and research at the population (and, ultimately, the community) level. Because of the differing opinions about levels of analysis, 'population' has at least two referents. Conventional treatments of human ecology suggest that the populations relevant to the study of organization–environment relations are those aggregates of members attached to the organization or, perhaps, served by the organization. In this sense, the organization is viewed as analogue to a community: it has collective means of adapting to environmental situations. The unit character of a population so defined depends on shared fate. All members share to some extent in the consequences of organizational success or failure.

We use the term population in a second sense: to refer to aggregates of organizations rather than members. Populations of organizations must be alike in some respect, that is, they must have some unit character. Unfortunately, identifying a population of organizations is no simple matter. The ecological approach suggests that one focus on common fate with respect to environmental variations. Since all organizations are distinctive, no two are affected identically by any given exogenous shock. Nevertheless, we can identify classes of organizations which are relatively homogeneous in terms of environmental vulnerability. Notice that the populations of interest may change somewhat from investigation to investigation depending on the analyst's concern. Populations of organizations referred to are not immutable objects in nature but are abstractions useful for theoretical purposes.

If we are to follow the lead of population biologists, we must identify an analogue to the biologist's notion of species. Various species are defined ultimately in terms of genetic structure. As Monod (1971) indicates, it is useful to think of the genetic content of any species as a blueprint. The blueprint contains the rules for transforming energy into structure. Consequently all of the adaptive capacity of a species is summarized in the blueprint. If we are to identify a species analogue for organizations, we must search for such blueprints. These will consist of rules or procedures for obtaining and acting upon inputs in order to produce an organizational product or response.

The type of blueprint one identifies depends on substantive concerns. For example, Marschak and Radner (1972) employ the term 'organizational form'[4] to characterize the key elements of the blueprint as seen within a decision-making framework. For them the blueprint or form has two functions: an information function that describes the rules used in obtaining, processing, and transmitting information about the states of external environments, and an activity function that states the rules used in acting on received information so as to produce an organizational response. To the extent that one can identify classes of organizations that differ with regard to these two functions, one can establish classes or forms of organization.

Since our concerns extend beyond decision making, however, we find Marschak and Radner's definition of forms too limiting. In fact, there is no reason to limit a priori the variety of rules or functions that may define relevant blueprints. So for us, an organizational form is a blueprint for organizational action, for transforming inputs into outputs. The blueprint can usually be inferred, albeit in somewhat different ways, by examining any of the following: (1) the formal structure of the organization in the narrow sense – tables of organization, written rules of operation, etc.;

4. The term 'organizational form' is used widely in the sociological literature (see Stinchcombe, 1965).

(2) the patterns of activity within the organization – what actually gets done by whom; or (3) the normative order – the ways of organizing that are defined as right and proper by both members and relevant sectors of the environment.

To complete the species analogue, we must search for qualitative differences among forms. It seems most likely that we will find such differences in the first and third areas listed above, formal structure and normative order. The latter offers particularly intriguing possibilities. Whenever the history of an organization, its politics, and its social structure are encoded in a normative claim (e.g., professionalization and collegial authority), one can use these claims to identify forms and define populations for research.

Having defined the organizational form, we can provide a more precise definition of a population of organizations. Just as the organizational analyst must choose a unit of analysis, so must he choose a system for study. Systems relevant to the study of organization–environment relations are usually defined by geography, by political boundaries, by market or product considerations, etc. Given a systems definition, a population of organizations consists of all the organizations within a particular boundary that have a common form. That is, the population is the form as it exists or is realized within a specified system.

Both uses of the term population (and the ecological theories implied thereby) are likely to prove beneficial to the study of organizational structure. The first, more common, view suggests that organizational structure ought to be viewed as an outcome of a collective adaptive process. According to this view, structure and change ought to depend on the adaptiveness of subunits and on the differential access of subunits to environmental resources. The second view ignores the adaptive activities of elements within the organization except as they constitute organizational structure. It focuses on the organization as an adapting unit. Certainly both perspectives are needed. We are concerned here only with the latter, however.

Finally, we would like to identify the properties of populations most interesting to population ecologists. The main concern in this regard was expressed clearly by Elton (1927): 'In solving ecological problems we are concerned with *what animals do* in their capacity as whole, living animals, not as dead animals or as a series of parts of animals. We have next to study the circumstances under which they do those things, and, most important of all, the limiting factors which prevent them from doing certain other things. By solving these questions it is possible to discover the reasons for *the distribution and numbers of animals in nature.*' Hutchinson (1959) in the subtitle to his famous essay, 'Homage to Santa Rosalia,' expressed the main focus even more succinctly: 'Why Are There So Many Kinds of Animals?' Taking our lead from these distinguished ecologists, we suggest that a population ecology of organizations must seek to understand the distributions of organizations across environmental conditions and the limitations on organizational structures in different environments, and more generally seek to answer the question, Why are there so many kinds of organizations?

III. Discontinuities in ecological analysis

Utilization of models from ecology in the study of organizations poses a number of analytic challenges involving differences between human and nonhuman organizations with regard to their essential ingredients. Consider, first, the nongenetic transmission of information. Biological analyses are greatly simplified by the fact that most useful information concerning adaptation to the environment (which information we call structure) is transmitted genetically. Genetic processes are so nearly invariant that extreme continuity in structure is the rule. The small number of imperfections generates structural changes, which, if accepted by the environment, will be transmitted with near invariance. The extreme structural invariance of species greatly simplifies the problem of delimiting and identifying populations. More important, the adaptiveness of structure can be unambiguously identified with net reproduction rates. When a population with given properties increases its net reproduction rate following an environmental change, it follows that it is being selected for. This is why modern biologists have narrowed the definition of fitness to the net reproductive rate of population.

Human social organization presumably reflects a greater degree of learning or adaptation. As a result it is more difficult to define fitness in a precise way. Under at least some conditions, organizations may undergo such extreme structural change that they shift from one form to another. As a result, extreme adaptation may give rise to observed changes that mimic selection. This is particularly problematic when the various organizational forms are similar on many dimensions.

We have argued previously (Hannan and Freeman, 1974) for a composite measure of fitness that includes both selection (actual loss of organizations) and mobility among forms (extreme adaptation). Fitness would then be defined as the probability that a given form of organization would persist in a certain environment. We continue to believe that such an approach has value, but we now believe that it is premature to combine adaptation and selection processes. The first order of business is to study selection processes for those situations in which inertial pressures are sufficiently strong that mobility among forms is unlikely.

Furthermore, it is worth noting that the capacity to adapt is itself subject to evolution (i.e., to systematic selection). As we argue below, organizations develop the capacity to adapt at the cost of lowered performance levels in stable environments. Whether or not such adaptable organizational forms will survive (i.e., resist selection) depends on the nature of the environment and the competitive situation. Therefore, a selection point of view treats high levels of adaptability as particular evolutionary outcomes.

There is a second sense in which human ecology appears to differ from bioecology. Blau and Scott (1962) point out that, unlike the usual biological situation, individual organizations (and populations of organizations) have the potential to expand almost without limit. The expandability of primitive elements is a problem because of our focus on the distribution of organizational forms over environments. A given form (e.g., formal bureaucracy) can expand throughout some system, market, or activity, either because one bureaucracy grows or because many bureaucracies are founded. Either process will generate an increase in the prevalence of bureaucratic organizational activity. A literal application of population ecology theory to the problem of organizational change would involve simply counting relative numbers in populations. Such a procedure may miss a phenomenon of central interest to the organizational analyst. Winter (1964), in discussing the analytic problem raised here, suggests distinguishing between survival, which describes the fate of individual organizations, and viability, which describes the 'share of market' of a given organizational form.

We find at least as much merit in another perspective on the issue of size. Many theorists have asserted that structural change attends growth; in other words, a single organization cannot grow indefinitely and still maintain its original form. For instance, a mouse could not possibly maintain the same proportion of body weight to skeletal structure while growing as big as a house. It would neither look like a mouse nor operate physiologically like a mouse. Boulding (1953) and Haire (1959) argue that the same is true for organizations, Caplow (1957), building on work by Graicunas (1933) and others, argues that the ability of each member of an organization to carry on face-to-face interactions with each of the others declines with the number of organizational participants. This creates a shift in the nature of interactions such that they assume a more impersonal, formal style. Blau and a number of coauthors have argued for similar causal effects of size on structure (Blau and Scott, 1962, pp. 223–42; Blau and Schoenherr, 1971; Blau, 1972). If it is true that organizational form changes with size, selection mechanisms may indeed operate with regard to the size distribution. When big organizations prevail it may be useful to view this as a special case of selection, in which the movement from 'small form' to 'large form' is theoretically indistinguishable from the dissolution ('death') of small organizations and their replacement by (the 'birth' of) large organizations.

In sum, we have identified a number of challenges. The first concerns the two sources of change, selection and adaptive learning. We feel that the organizations literature has overemphasized the latter at the expense of the former. Much more is known about decision-making practices, forecasting, and the like than about selection in populations of organizations. The second challenge involves the distinction between selection and viability. Whether such a distinction is necessary depends on the results of research on size which is currently being pursued by many organization researchers.

IV. The principle of isomorphism

In the best developed statement of the principles of human ecology, Hawley (1968) answers the question of why there are so many kinds of organizations. According to Hawley, the diversity of organizational forms is isomorphic to the diversity of environments. In each distinguishable environmental configuration one finds, in equilibrium, only that organizational form optimally adapted to the demands of the environment. Each unit experiences constraints which force it to resemble other units with the same set of constraints. Hawley's explanation places heavy emphasis on communication patterns and structural complements of those patterns: '[organization units] must submit to standard terms of communication and to standard procedures in consequence of which they develop similar internal arrangements within limits imposed by their respective sizes' (1968, p. 334).

While the proposition seems completely sound from an ecological perspective, it does not address a number of interesting considerations. There are at least two respects in which the isomorphism formulation must be modified and extended if it is to provide satisfactory answers to the question posed. The first modification concerns the mechanism or mechanisms responsible for equilibrium. In this respect, the principle of isomorphism must be supplemented by a criterion of selection and a competition theory. The second modification deals with the fact that the principle of isomorphism neither speaks to issues of optimum adaptation to changing environments nor recognizes that populations of organizations often face multiple environments which impose somewhat inconsistent demands. An understanding of the constraints on organizational forms seems to require modeling of multiple, dynamic environments. Of course, we cannot fully extend Hawley's principle here. We attempt only to outline the main issues and suggest particular extensions.

V. Competition theory

The first of the needed extensions is a specification of the optimization process responsible for isomorphism. We have already discussed two mechanisms: selection and adaptive learning. Isomorphism can result either because nonoptimal forms are selected out of a community of organizations or because organizational decision makers learn optimal responses and adjust organizational behavior accordingly. We continue to focus on the first of these processes: selection.

Consideration of optimization raises two issues: Who is optimizing, and what is being optimized? It is quite commonly held, as in the theory of the firm, that organizational decision makers optimize profit over sets of organizational actions. From a population ecology perspective, it is the environment which optimizes.[5] Whether or not individual organizations are consciously adapting, the environment selects out optimal combinations of organizations. So if there is a rationality involved, it is the 'rationality' of natural selection. Organizational rationality and environmental rationality may coincide in the instance of firms in competitive markets. In this case, the optimal behavior of each firm is to maximize profit and the rule used by the environment (market, in this case) is to select out profit maximizers. Friedman (1953) makes use of this observation to propose a justification of the theory of the firm in terms of the principles of evolution. However, Winter (1964) has argued convincingly that the actual situation is much more complicated than this and that it is most unusual for individual rationality and environmental or market rationality to lead to the same optima. When the two rationalities do not agree, we are concerned with the optimizing behavior of the environment.

5. In biological applications, one assumes that power (in the physical sense) is optimized by natural selection in accordance with the so-called Darwin–Lotka law. For the case of human social organization, one might argue that selection optimizes the utilization of a specific set of resources including but not restricted to the power and the time of members.

A focus on selection invites an emphasis on competition. Organizational forms presumably fail to flourish in certain environmental circumstances because other forms successfully compete with them for essential resources. As long as the resources which sustain organizations are finite and populations have unlimited capacity to expand, competition must ensue.

Hawley (1950, pp. 201–3) following Durkheim (1947) among others, places a heavy emphasis on competition as a determinant of patterns of social organization. The distinctive feature of his model is the emphasis on the indirect nature of the process: 'The action of all on the common supply gives rise to a reciprocal relation between each unit and all the others, if only from the fact that what one gets reduces by that amount what the others can obtain . . . without this element of indirection, that is, unless units affect one another through affecting a common limited supply, competition does not exist' (Hawley, 1950, p. 202). In Hawley's model, competition processes typically involve four stages: (1) demand for resources exceeds supply; (2) competitors become more similar as standard conditions of competition bring forth a uniform response; (3) selection eliminates the weakest competitors; and (4) deposed competitors differentiate either territorially or functionally, yielding a more complex division of labor.

It is surprising that there is almost no reliance on competitive mechanisms in Hawley's later work. In particular, as we noted above, the rationale given for the isomorphism principle uses an adaptation logic. We propose to balance that treatment by adding an explicit focus on competition as a mechanism producing isomorphism.[6] In so doing, we can bring a rich set of formal models to bear on the problem.

The first step in constructing an ecological model of competition is to state the nature of the population growth process. At a minimum we wish the model to incorporate the idea that resources available at any moment for each form of organization are finite and fixed. This corresponds with Hawley's notion of limited supply and Stinchcombe's (1965) argument that human communities have limited 'capacities for organizing.' We also wish to incorporate the view that the rate at which units are added to populations of organizations depends on how much of the fixed capacity has already been exhausted. The greater the unexhausted capacity in an environment, the faster should be the rate of growth of populations of organizations. But the rate at which populations of organizations can expand into unused

6. We include only the first and third of Hawley's stages in our model of competition. We prefer to treat uniformity of response and community diversity as consequences of combinations of certain competitive processes and environmental features.

capacity varies among forms of organization. So there are two distinctive ecological considerations: the capacity of the environment to support forms of organization and the rate at which the populations grow (or decline) when the environmental support changes.

In order to state the model formally, it is helpful to begin with the control function that Hummon, Doreian, and Teuter (1975) use to add dynamic considerations to Blau's theory of size and differentiation. The control model states that the rate of change in the size of any unit (here a population of organizations) varies proportionately with the difference between existing size, X, and the equilibrium level of size, X^*, permitted in that environment. Then one possible representation would be

$$\frac{dX}{dt} = f(X^* - X) = r(X^* - X). \tag{1}$$

In (1) X^* and r represent the limited supply or environmental capacity and the structural ability of the population of organizations to respond to changes in the environment, respectively.

A particular form of the general growth model in (1) underlies most population ecology work on competition. This is the logistic growth model (for per capita growth):

$$\frac{dX_1}{dt} = r_1 X_1 \left(\frac{k_1 - X_1}{k_1} \right) \tag{2}$$

where X_1 denotes population size, k_1 is the capacity of the environment to support X_1 (this parameter is usually called the carrying capacity), and r_1 is the so-called natural rate of increase of the population or the rate at which the population grows when it is far below the carrying capacity.

As we indicated above, both k and r are ecological parameters of fundamental importance. Our research group has begun to compare various forms of organization by estimating the parameters of models like (2) for each form of organization. We have been successful to date in relating structural features of organizations such as complexity of core activity to variations in r and k (Nielsen and Hannan, 1977; Freeman and Brittain, 1977). This work, together with that of Hummon et al. (1975), gives us confidence that the model in (1) and/or (2) gives a good approximation of the growth of populations of organizations.

Up to this point we have presumed that the limits on growth reflect the finite nature of the environment (e.g., community wealth and mix of occupational skills). It is now time to reintroduce competition. According to Hawley, competition enters indirectly when the competitors lower the fixed supply. We can model this by following the lead of bioecologists and extending the logistic growth model. For example, consider a second population of organizations whose size is denoted by X_2. The two populations are said to compete if the addition of units of either decreases the rate of growth of the other. This will be the case when both populations are sustained by the same types of resources. Then the appropriate model is represented in the following system of growth equations (known as the Lotka–Volterra equations for competing populations):

$$\frac{dX_1}{dt} = r_1 X_1 \left(\frac{k_1 - X_1 - \alpha_{12} X_2}{k_1} \right)$$

$$\frac{dX_2}{dt} = r_2 X_2 \left(\frac{k_2 - X_2 - \alpha_{21} X_1}{k_2} \right)$$

(3)

The coefficients α_{12} and α_{21}, called competition coefficients, denote the magnitude of the effect of increases in one population on the growth of the other. In this simple formulation, the only consequence of competition is to lower the carrying capacity of the environment for a population of organizations.

Analysis of (3) produces interesting qualitative results. It is not difficult to show that a stable two-population equilibrium exists for the system in (3) only if

$$\frac{1}{\alpha_{21}} < \frac{k_2}{k_1} < \alpha_{12}.$$

(4)

Therefore, very similar populations (i.e., populations with competition coefficients near unity) can coexist only under a very precise k_2/k_1 ratio. As a result, when $\alpha_{12} = \alpha_{21} = 1$, no two-population equilibrium can be stable; any exogenous shock will result in the elimination of one of the populations. This result supports the generality of the widely cited 'principle of competitive exclusion' (Gause, 1934).[7] According to this principle, no two populations can continuously occupy the same niche. Populations are said to occupy the same niche to the extent that they depend on identical environmental resources. If they are identical, then the addition of an element to X_2 has the same consequences for growth in X_1 as does the addition of an element to X_1; in other words, the competition coefficients are unity. The broad conclusion is that the greater the similarity of two resource-limited competitors, the less feasible is it that a single environment can support both of them in equilibrium.

7. This so-called principle has mostly suggestive value (see MacArthur [1972, pp. 43–6] for a penetrating critique of attempts to derive quantitative implications from Gause's principle; most of these criticisms do not apply to the qualitative inferences we consider).

If two populations of organizations sustained by identical environmental resources differ in some organizational characteristic, that population with the characteristic less fit to environmental contingencies will tend to be eliminated. The stable equilibrium will then contain only one population which can be said to be isomorphic to the environment.

In order to see the implications of the model for organizational diversity, we extend the Lotka−Volterra system to include M competitors:

$$\frac{dX_i}{dt} = r_i X_i (k_i - X_i - \Sigma \alpha_{ij} X_j)/k_i \quad (i = 1, \ldots, M). \tag{5}$$

The general system (5) has a community equilibrium:

$$k_i = X_i + \Sigma \alpha_{ij} X_j \quad (i = 1, \ldots, M). \tag{6}$$

These equations can be expressed in matrix form:

$$k = A x, \tag{7}$$

where x and k are $(M \times 1)$ column vectors and A is the community matrix:

$$A = \begin{pmatrix} 1 & \alpha_{12} & \cdot & \cdot & \alpha_{1m} \\ \alpha_{21} & 1 & & & \cdot \\ \cdot & & & & \cdot \\ \cdot & & & & \cdot \\ \alpha_{m1} & \cdot & \cdot & \cdot & 1 \end{pmatrix}$$

whose elements are the competition coefficients.

The so-called theory of community structure entails the analysis of the equilibrium behavior of the system of equation (7) from the perspective of postulated competition processes.[8] The results, though stated in terms of species diversity, are quite general. In particular, one can show that when growth in population is constrained only by resource availability, the number of distinct resources sets an upper bound on diversity in the system.[9] Even more generally, the upper bound on diversity is equal to the number of distinct resources plus the number of additional constraints on growth (Levin, 1970).

It is difficult to apply either result directly in order to calculate the upper bound on diversity even in the nonhuman context. The chief difficulty is that of identifying distinct constraints. A good deal of empirical work is

8. We restrict attention to the case in which all entries of A are nonnegative. Negative entries are appropriate for predator/prey (or more generally, host/parasite) relations. The typical result for this case is cyclical population growth.

9. A more precise statement of the theorem is that no stable equilibrium exists for a system of M competitors and $N < M$ resources (MacArthur and Levins, 1964).

required if one is to judge how different two constraints must be in order to have distinct consequences for community equilibria. The theorems do, however, imply useful qualitative results. If one can identify environmental changes which add constraints to a system or eliminate them, one can conclude that the upper bound of diversity is increased or decreased.

This broad qualitative result has a number of potential applications to the research problems of interest. For example, the expansion of markets and of state control mechanisms through social systems tends to have the consequence of eliminating or reducing the number of constraints which are idiosyncratic to local environments. Viewed from the perspective of the larger system, the process of expansion of the economic and political center should, then, tend to replace some local constraints with more uniform ones. As long as the local environments were heterogeneous at the outset, expansion of the center ought to reduce the number of constraints on organization in the whole system.

The theory just discussed implies on the one hand that the change in constraint structure ought to lower organizational diversity through the elimination of some population.[10] One can imagine, on the other hand, that in some local environments, the combination of unaltered local constraints and new larger system constraints might increase the total number of constraints in the local system. In that case, organizational diversity in those local environments should increase. Such an increase would result in the creation or adoption of new organizational forms.

The increasingly important role of the state in regulating economic and social action provides numerous opportunities for analyzing the impact of changes in constraint structures on the diversity of organizational forms. Consider the impact of licensing laws, minimum wage, health, and safety legislation, affirmative action, and other regulations on organizational action. When such regulations are applied to the full range of organizations in broad areas of activity they undoubtedly alter the size distributions of organizations. Most often they select out the smallest organizations. But it is not difficult to imagine situations in which medium-sized organizations (more precisely, those with some minimum level of complexity) would be more adversely affected. Besides altering size distributions, such regulations undoubtedly affect the diversity of organizational arrangements in other ways. Here one could analyze the impact of state action on the diversity of accounting systems within industries, curricula within universities,

10. For a more comprehensive statement of this argument with reference to ethnic organization, see Hannan (1975).

departmental structures within hospitals, etc. In each case it would be essential to determine whether the newly imposed constraint replaced lower level constraints, in which case diversity should decline, or whether the constraint cumulated with the existing constraints, in which case organizational diversity would be likely to increase.

To indicate the richness of the simple competition theory we have proposed we will briefly discuss another sort of empirical test. We noted above that research on regulation might concern itself with impacts on distributions of organizations by size. The classical model of organizational size distributions (Simon and Bonini, 1958) proposes the following simple process. A number of organizations begin with the same small size. Some fraction are able to make or borrow some useful technical or organizational innovation that permits them to grow to some larger size. During some specified time period the process repeats itself with the same fraction making the innovation required to attain a larger size. Such a growth process eventually yields the lognormal distribution that characterizes so many size distributions.

Competition theory suggests a refinement of this classical model. If, as we argued earlier, large changes in organizational size are accompanied by structural changes (changes in form), organizations of very different size in the same area of activity will tend to exhibit different forms. As a consequence of these structural differences, they will tend to depend on different sets of environmental resource (and constraints). That is, within any area of activity, patterns of resource use will tend to be specialized to segments of the size distribution. This being the case, organizations will compete most intensely with similar size organizations. Also, competition between pairs of organizations within an activity will be a decreasing function of the distance separating them on the size gradient. For example, small local banks compete most with other small banks, to a lesser extent with medium-scale regional banks, and hardly at all with international banks. Under these conditions, significant alterations in the size distribution indicate selection for and against certain organizational forms closely associated with regard to size.

Now let us return to the classical model. When large-sized organizations emerge they pose a competitive threat to medium-sized but hardly any threat to small organizations. In fact, the rise of large organizations may increase the survival chances of small ones in a manner not anticipated in the classical model. When the large organizations enter, those in the middle of the size distribution are trapped. Whatever strategy they adopt to fight off the challenge of the larger form makes them more vulnerable in competition with small organizations and vice versa. That is, at least in a stable environment the two ends of the size distribution ought to outcompete the middle (see below). So in a longitudinal analysis of organizational size distributions we would expect to see the number of medium-sized organizations decline upon the entry of larger organizations. Also, we would expect the fortunes of small organizations to improve as their competitors are removed from the environment. This reasoning holds generally for competition along a single gradient: those in the middle will be eliminated in stable environments (MacArthur, 1972, pp. 43–6).

VI. Niche theory

The principle of isomorphism implies that social organizations in equilibrium will exhibit structural features that are specialized to salient features of the resource environment. As long as the environment is stable and certain, we see no difficulty with this proposition. But does it hold when the environment shifts either predictably or unpredictably among several alternative configurations? Though the issues raised by attempting to answer this question are complex, doing so is crucial to developing adequate models of organizational–environment relations.

Intuition suggests that isomorphism holds as a good approximation only in stable environments. Faced with unstable environments, organizations ought to develop a generalist structure that is not optimally adapted to any single environmental configuration but is optimal over an entire set of configurations. In other words, we ought to find specialized organizations in stable and certain environments and generalist organizations in unstable and uncertain environments. Whether or not this simple proposition holds for social organizations, only empirical research will tell. However, a variety of population ecology models suggests that it is too simplistic. We cannot hope in one paper to develop fully the arguments involved. Instead we indicate the main lines of development with reference to one rather evocative perspective developed by Levins (1962, 1968): the theory of niche width.

The concept of 'niche,' initially borrowed by biologists from early social science, plays a central role in ecological theory. This is not the place for an extended discussion of the multiple uses of the concept (see Whittaker and Levin, 1976). The model which follows uses Hutchinson's (1957) formulation. From this point of view the (realized) niche of a population is defined as that area in constraint space (the space whose dimensions are

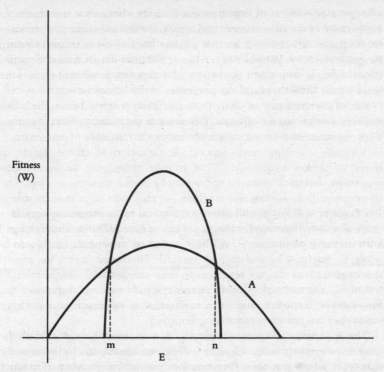

Fitness (W)

B

A

m   n

E

Figure 1   Fitness functions (niches) for specialists and generalists

levels of resources, etc.) in which the population outcompetes all other local populations. The niche, then, consists of all those combinations of resource levels at which the population can survive and reproduce itself.

Each population occupies a distinct niche. For present purposes it suffices to consider cases where pairs of populations differ with respect to a single environmental dimension, E, and are alike with respect to all others. Then relative competitive positions can be simply summarized as in figure 1. As we have drawn this figure, one population, A, occupies a very broad niche, whereas the other, B, has concentrated its fitness, denoted W, on a very narrow band of environmental variation. This distinction, which is usually referred to as generalism versus specialism, is crucial to biological ecology and to a population ecology of organizations.

In essence, the distinction between specialism and generalism refers to whether a population of organizations flourishes because it maximizes its exploitation of the environment and accepts the risk of having that environment change or because it accepts a lower level of exploitation in return for greater security. Whether or not the equilibrium distribution of organizational forms is dominated by the specialist depends, as we will see, on the shape of the fitness sets and on properties of the environment.

Part of the efficiency resulting from specialism is derived from the lower requirements for excess capacity. Given some uncertainty, most organizations maintain some excess capacity to insure the reliability of performance. In a rapidly changing environment, the definition of excess capacity is likely to change frequently. What is used today may become excess tomorrow, and what is excess today may be crucial tomorrow. Organizations operating in environments where the transition from state to state is less frequent will (in equilibrium) have to maintain excess capacity in a given allocational pattern for longer periods of time. Whereas those charged with assessing performance will be tempted to view such allocations as wasteful, they may be essential for survival. Thompson (1967) has argued that organizations allocate resources to units charged with the function of insulating core technology from environmentally induced disruption. So, for example, manufacturing firms may retain or employ legal staffs even when they are not currently facing litigation.

The importance of excess capacity is not completely bound up with the issue of how much excess capacity will be maintained. It also involves the manner in which it is used. Organizations may insure reliable performance by creating specialized units, as Thompson (1967) suggests, or they may allocate excess capacity to organizational roles, by employing personnel with skills and abilities which exceed the routine requirements of their jobs. This is one of the important reasons for using professionals in organizations. Professionals use more resources not only because they tend to be paid more, but also because organizations must allow them more discretion (including the freedom to respond to outside reference groups). Organizations, in turn, become more flexible by employing professionals. They increase their capacity to deal with a variable environment and the contingencies it produces. For example, hospitals and their patients often employ obstetricians and pediatricians in their delivery rooms even though the normal delivery of babies can be performed equally well, and perhaps even better, by midwives. The skills of the medical doctor represent excess capacity to insure reliable performance should delivery not be normal. Usually, the pediatrician examines the infant immediately after birth to see if there is any abnormality requiring immediate action. If the mother is suffering dangerous consequences from giving birth, and the child is also in need of attention, the presence of the pediatrician insures that the obstetrician will not have to choose between them in allocating his attention.

Excess capacity may also be allocated to the development and maintenance of procedural systems. When the certainty of a given environmental state is high, organizational operations should be routine, and coordination can be accomplished by formalized rules and the investment of resources in training incumbents to follow those formalized procedures. If in fact the environment were unchanging ($p = 1$), all participants were procedurally skilled, and the procedures were perfectly tuned, there would be no need for any control structure at all, except to monitor behavior. However, when certainty is low, organizational operations are less routine. Under these circumstances, a greater allocation of resources to develop and maintain procedural systems is counterproductive and optimal organizational forms will allocate resources to less formalized systems capable of more innovative responses (e.g., committees and teams). In this case, excess capacity is represented by the increased time it takes such structures to make decisions and by increased coordination costs.

The point here is that populations of organizational forms will be selected for or against depending upon the amount of excess capacity they maintain and how they allocate it. It may or may not be rational for any particular organization to adopt one pattern or another. What would seem like waste to anyone assessing performance at one time may be the difference between survival and failure later. Similarly, organizations may survive because high levels of professionalization produce coordination by mutual adjustment despite a somewhat chaotic appearance. Others, in which everyone seems to know precisely what he is doing at all times, may fail. Under a given set of environmental circumstances the fundamental ecological question is: which forms thrive and which forms disappear.

Generalism may be observed in a population of organizations, then, either in its reliance upon a wide variety of resources simultaneously or in its maintenance of excess capacity at any given time. This excess capacity allows such organizations to change in order to take advantage of resources which become more readily available. Corporations which maintain an unusually large proportion of their total assets in fluid form ('slack,' in terms of theory of the firm; Penrose, 1959; Cyert and March, 1963) are generalizing. In either case, generalism is costly. Under stable environmental circumstances, generalists will be outcompeted by specialists. And at any given point in time, a static analysis will reveal excess capacity. An implication – shifting our focus to individual generalists – is that outside agents will often mistake excess capacity for waste.

We can investigate the evolution of niche width if we make the assumption that areas under the fitness curve are equal, and that specialists differ from generalists in how they distribute the fixed quantity of fitness over environmental outcomes. Specialists outcompete generalists over the range of outcomes to which they have specialized (because of the fixed level of fitness assumption). As long as the environmental variation remains within that interval (the interval $[m, n]$ in fig. 1), generalists have no adaptive advantage and will be selected against. Alternatively, if the environment is only occasionally within the interval, specialists will fare less well than generalists. These brief comments make clear the importance of environmental variation for the evolution of niche width.

To simplify further, consider an environment which can take on only two states and in every period falls in state one with probability p and in state two with probability $q = (1 - p)$. Assume further that variations in environmental states are Bernoulli trials (independent from period to period). For this situation Levins (1962, 1968) has shown that optimal niche width depends on p and the 'distance' between the two states of the environment.

To see this, we change focus slightly. Since each organization faces two environments, its fitness depends on fitness in the pair. We can summarize the adaptive potential of each organization by plotting these pairs of values (fitness in state 1 and in state 2) in a new space whose axes are fitness in each of the states, as in figure 2. In this representation, each point denotes the fitness of a distinct organizational form. The cloud of points is termed the 'fitness set.' We presume that all of the naturally possible adaptations are represented in the fitness set.

Our interest is in determining which points in the fitness set will be favored by natural selection. Notice first that all points interior to the set are inferior in terms of fitness to at least some point on the boundary of the set. In this sense the boundary, drawn as a continuous line, represents the optimal possibilities. Since natural selection maximizes fitness, it must choose points on the boundary. This narrows our search to seeking which form(s) on the boundary will be favored.

As figure 2b is drawn, no organizational form does particularly well in both states of the environment – no form has high levels of fitness in both. This will be the case when the two states are 'far apart' in the sense that they impose very different adaptive contingencies on organizations. In such cases (see Levins, 1968), the fitness set will be concave. When the 'distance'

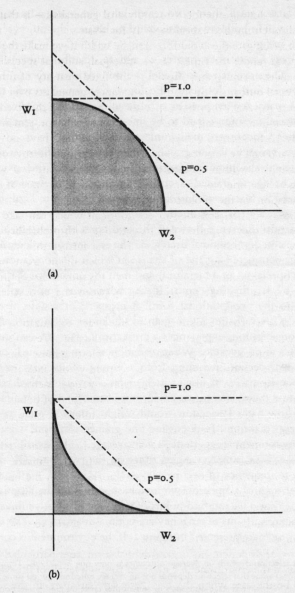

Figure 2 Optimal adaptation in fine-grained environment; *a*, convex fitness set;
b concave fitness set

between states is small, there is no reason why certain organizational forms cannot do well in both environments. In such cases, the fitness set will be convex, as in figure 2a.

The fitness functions in figures 2a and 2b describe different adaptive situations. The next step is to model the optimization process. To do so we introduce a further distinction. Ecologists have found it useful to distinguish both spatial and temporal environmental variation according to grain. Environmental variation is said to be fine-grained when a typical element (organization) encounters many units or replications. From a temporal perspective, variation is fine-grained when typical durations in states are short relative to the lifetime of organizations. Otherwise, the environment is said to be coarse-grained. Demand for products or services is often characterized by fine-grained variation whereas changes in legal structures are more typically coarse-grained.

The essential difference between the two types of environmental variation is the cost of suboptimal strategies. The problem of ecological adaptation can be considered a game of chance in which the population chooses a strategy (specialism or generalism) and then the environment chooses an outcome (by, say, flipping a coin). If the environment 'comes up' in a state favorable to the organizational form, it prospers; otherwise, it declines. However, if the variation is fine-grained (durations are short), each population of organizations experiences a great many trials and environment is experienced as an average. When variation is coarse-grained, however, the period of decline stemming from a wrong choice may exceed the organizational capacity to sustain itself under unfavorable conditions.

To capture these differences, Levins introduced an adaptive function to represent how natural selection would weight fitness in each state under the different conditions. In discussing fine-grained variation, we suggested that the environment is experienced as an average.[11] The appropriate adaptive function, then, simply weights fitness in the two states (W_1 and W_2) according to frequency of occurrence: $A(W_1, W_2) = pW_1 + qW_2$. In order to consider optimal adaptation we merely superimpose the adaptive function on the fitness set and find points of tangency of adaptive function and fitness functions. Points of tangency are optimal adaptations. The solutions for various cases are presented in figure 2. If the environment is completely

11. That selection depends on average outcomes is only one hypothesis. Templeton and Rothman (1974) argue that selection depends not on average outcomes but on some minimum level of fitness. Whether average outcomes or some other criterion guides selection in populations of organizations is open to question. We follow Levins in order to keep the exposition simple.

stable (i.e., $p = 1$), then specialism is optimal. If the environment is maximally uncertain (i.e., $p = \cdot 5$), generalism is optimal in the convex case (when the demands of the different environments are not too dissimilar) but not in the concave case. In fact, as the model is developed, specialism always wins out in the concave case.

Consider first the cases in which the environment is stable (i.e., $p = 1$). Not surprisingly, specialism is optimal. The results for unstable environments diverge. When the fitness set is convex (i.e., the demands of the different environmental states are similar and/or complementary), generalism is optimal. But when the environmental demands differ (and the fitness set is concave), specialism is optimal. This is not as strange a result as it first appears. When the environment changes rapidly among quite different states, the cost of generalism is high. Since the demands in the different states are dissimilar, considerable structural management is required of generalists. But since the environment changes rapidly, these organizations will spend most of their time and energies adjusting structure. It is apparently better under such conditions to adopt a specialized structure and 'ride out' the adverse environments.

The case of coarse-grained environments is somewhat more complex. Our intuitive understanding is that since the duration of an environmental state is long, maladaptation ought to be given greater weight. That is, the costs of maladaptation greatly outweigh any advantage incurred by the correct choice. One adaptive function which gives this result is the log-linear model used by Levins: $A(W_1, W_2) = W_1^p W_2^q$. The method of finding optimal adaptations is the same. The results are found in figure 3. Only one case differs from what we found for fine-gr.. led environments: the combination of uncertain and coarse-grained variation with concave fitness sets. We saw above that when such variation is fine-grained, it is better to specialize. When the duration of environmental states is long, however, the costs of this strategy are great. Long periods of nonadaptation will threaten the survival of the organization. In addition, the fact that the environment changes less often means that generalists need not spend most of their time and energies altering structure. Thus generalism is the optimal strategy in this case as we see in figure 3b.

The combination of coarse-grained environmental variation and concave fitness sets raises a further possibility. The optimal adaptation in the face of environmental uncertainty possesses fairly low levels of fitness in either state. It seems clear that there must be a better solution. Levins discusses this case in depth and concludes that for the biological case with genetic transmission of structure 'polymorphism' or genetically maintained

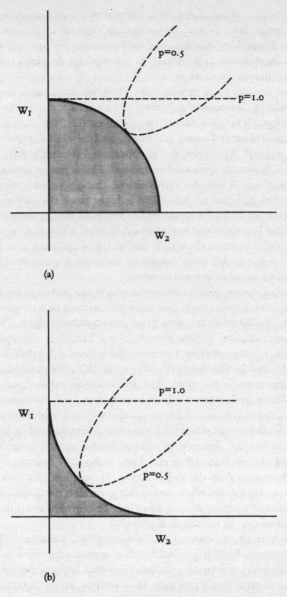

Figure 3   Optimal adaptation in coarse-grained environments; a, convex fitness set; b, concave fitness set

population heterogeneity will be selected for. The suggestion is that populations combine types (differing, say, in color, blood type, etc.) some of which are specialized to state 1 and some to state 2. With such a combination at least a portion of the population will always flourish and maintain the genetic diversity which allows it to continue to flourish when the environment changes state. The set of all such heterogeneous populations (composed of proportions of specialists to each of the two environments) can be represented in the fitness diagrams as a straight line joining the most extreme points with all combinations falling within this line.

Coarse-grained and uncertain variation favors a distinct form of generalism: polymorphism. We do not have to search very far to find an analogous outcome. Organizations may federate in such a way that supra-organizations consisting of heterogeneous collections of specialist organizations pool resources. When the environment is uncertain and coarse-grained and subunits difficult to set up and tear down, the costs of maintaining the unwieldy structure imposed by federation may be more than offset by the fact that at least a portion of the amalgamated organization will do well no matter what the state of the environment. In terms of the model suggested above there are no other situations in which such federated organizations have a competitive advantage. And even in this case, the only time during which they have such an advantage is when coarse-grained variation is uncertain.

Such an amalgamated 'holding company' pattern may be observed in modern universities. Enrollment and research support wax and wane over time as do the yield on invested endowment securities and the beneficence of legislatures. Some of these resources follow predictable cycles. Others do not. But it is extremely expensive to build up and dismantle academic units. It is costly not only in money but also in the energies consumed by political conflict. Consequently, universities are constantly 'taxing' subunits with plentiful environments to subsidize less fortunate subunits. It is common, for instance, for universities to allocate faculty positions according to some fixed master plan, undersupporting the rapidly growing departments and maintaining excess faculty in others. This partial explanation of the unwieldy structures that encompass liberal arts departments, professional schools, research laboratories, etc., is at least as persuasive as explanations that emphasize intellectual interdependence among units.

Much more can be said concerning applications of niche theory to organization–environment relations. We have focused on a simple version highlighting the interplay between competition and environmental variation in the determination of optimal adaptive structure in order to show that the principle of isomorphism needs considerable expansion to deal with multiple environmental outcomes and their associated uncertainty. The literature in ecology to which we have made reference is growing exponentially at the moment and new results and models are appearing monthly. The products of these developments provide students of organizations with a rich potential for the study of organization–environment relations.

Consider an example. In his analysis of bureaucratic and craft administration or production, Stinchcombe (1959) argued that construction firms do not rely upon bureaucratically organized administrative staffs because of seasonal fluctuations in demand. Administrative staffs constitute an overhead cost which remains roughly constant over the year. The advantage of the otherwise costly (in terms of salaries) craft administration is that coordination of work is accomplished through a reliance upon prior socialization of craftsmen and upon organization. Since employment levels can more easily be increased or decreased with demand under a craft system, administrative costs are more easily altered to meet demand.

The fundamental source of this pattern is the seasonal variation in construction. In ecological terms, the demand environment is coarse-grained. In addition, the two states defined by season are quite different, resulting in a concave fitness curve. Craft-administered housing construction firms are probably quite inefficient when demand is at its peak and when the kind of housing under construction is standardized. In such situations, we would expect this form of organization to face stiff competition from other firms. For instance, in regions where housing construction is less seasonal, modular housing, mobile homes, and prefabricated housing are more likely to flourish and we would expect the construction business to be more highly bureaucratized.

Another variation in demand is to be found in the business cycle. While seasonal fluctuations are stable (uncertainty is low), interest rates, labor relations, and materials costs are more difficult to predict. Variations of this sort should favor a generalist mode of adaptation. That is, when environments are coarse-grained, characterized by concave fitness curves, and uncertain, populations of organizations will be more likely to survive if they hedge their bets by seeking a wider variety of resource bases. For this reason, we think, craft-administered construction organizations are frequently general contractors who not only build houses but engage in other kinds of construction as well (shopping plazas, office buildings, etc.). In comparison, modular housing is cheaper and the units are installed on rented space. Consequently, interest rates are less important. Since organizations producing this kind of housing do not employ craftsmen but use the cheapest and least skilled labor they can obtain, labor relations are less problematical. It may also be that their reliance on different materials (e.g., sheet aluminum) contributes to a lower level of uncertainty. In consequence, we would expect this form of organization to be more highly specialized in its adaptation (of course there are technical factors which also contribute to this as well).

Craft-administered construction firms are set up in such a way that they can adapt rapidly to changes in demand, and they can adapt to different construction problems by varying the mix of skills represented in their work force. Bureaucratically administered construction firms are more specialized and as a result they are efficient only when demand is high, and very inefficient when it is low. We also believe that they tend to be more specialized with regard to type of construction. Craft-administered organizations sacrifice efficient exploitation of their niche for flexibility. Bureaucratic organizations choose the opposite strategy. This formulation is an extension of Stinchcombe's and serves to show that his argument is essentially ecological.

VII. Discussion

Our aim in this paper has been to move toward an application of modern population ecology theory to the study of organization–environment relations. For us, the central question is, why are there so many kinds of organizations? Phrasing the question in this way opens the possibility of applying a rich variety of formal models to the analysis of the effects of environmental variations of organizational structure.

We begin with Hawley's classical formulation of human ecology. However, we recognize that ecological theory has progressed enormously since sociologists last systematically applied ideas from bioecology to social organization. Nonetheless, Hawley's theoretical perspective remains a very useful point of departure. In particular we concentrate on the principle of isomorphism. This principle asserts that there is a one-to-one correspondence between structural elements of social organization and those units that mediate flows of essential resources into the system. It explains the variations in organizational forms in equilibrium. But any observed isomorphism can arise from purposeful adaptation of organizations to the common constraints they face or because nonisomorphic organizations are selected against. Surely both processes are at work in most social systems. We believe that the organizations literature has emphasized the former to the exclusion of the latter.

We suspect that careful empirical research will reveal that for wide classes of organizations there are very strong inertial pressures on structure arising both from internal arrangements (e.g., internal politics) and the environment (e.g., public legitimation of organizational activity). To claim otherwise is to ignore the most obvious feature of organizational life. Failing churches do not become retail stores; nor do firms transform themselves into churches. Even within broad areas of organizational action, such as higher education and labor union activity, there appear to be substantial obstacles to fundamental structural change. Research is needed on this issue. But until we see evidence to the contrary, we will continue to doubt that the major features of the world of organizations arise through learning or adaptation. Given these doubts, it is important to explore an evolutionary explanation of the principle of isomorphism. That is, we wish to embed the principle of isomorphism within an explicit selection framework.

In order to add selection processes we propose a competition theory using Lotka−Volterra models. This theory relies on growth models that appear suitable for representing both organizational development and the growth of populations of organizations. Recent work by bioecologists on Lotka−Volterra systems yields propositions that have immediate relevance for the study of organization−environment relations. These results concern the effects of changes in the number and mixture of constraints upon systems with regard to the upper bound of the diversity of forms of organization. We propose that such propositions can be tested by examining the impact of varieties of state regulation both on size distributions and on the diversity of organizational forms within broadly defined areas of activity (e.g., medical care, higher education, and newspaper publishing).

A more important extension of Hawley's work introduces dynamic considerations. The fundamental issue here concerns the meaning of isomorphism in situations in which the environment to which units are adapted is changing and uncertain. Should 'rational' organizations attempt to develop specialized isomorphic structural relations with one of the possible environmental states? Or should they adopt a more plastic strategy and institute more generalized structural features? The isomorphism principle does not speak to these issues.

We suggest that the concrete implication of generalism for organizations is the accumulation and retention of varieties of excess capacity. To retain the flexibility of structure required for adaptation to different environmental outcomes requires that some capacities be held in reserve and not committed to action. Generalists will always be outperformed by specialists who, with the same levels of resources, happen to have hit upon their optimal environment. Consequently, in any cross-section the generalists will appear inefficient because excess capacity will often be judged waste. Nonetheless, organizational slack is a pervasive feature of many types of organizations. The question then arises: what types of environments favor generalists? Answering this question comprehensively takes one a long way toward understanding the dynamic of organization–environment relations.

We begin addressing this question in the suggestive framework of Levins's (1962, 1968) fitness-set theory. This is one of a class of recent theories that relates the nature of environmental uncertainty to optimal levels of structural specialism. Levins argues that along with uncertainty one must consider the grain of the environment or the lumpiness of environmental outcomes. The theory indicates that specialism is always favored in stable or certain environments. This is no surprise. But contrary to the view widely held in the organizations literature, the theory also indicates that generalism is not always optimal in uncertain environments. When the environment shifts uncertainly among states that place very different demands on the organization, and the duration of environmental states is short relative to the life of the organization (variation is fine-grained), populations of organizations that specialize will be favored over those that generalize. This is because organizations that attempt to adapt to each environmental outcome will spend most of their time adjusting structure and very little time in organizational action directed at other ends.

Stated in these terms, the proposition appears obvious. However, when one reads the literature on organization–environment relations, one finds that it was not so obvious. Most important, the proposition follows from a simple explicit model that has the capacity to unify a wide variety of propositions relating environmental variations to organizational structure.

We have identified some of the leading conceptual and methodological obstacles to applying population ecology models to the study of organization–environment relations. We pointed to differences between human and nonhuman social organization in terms of mechanisms of structural invariance and structural change, associated problems of delimiting populations of organizations, and difficulties in defining fitness for populations of expandable units. In each case we have merely sketched the issues and proposed short-run simplifications which would facilitate the application of existing models. Clearly, each issue deserves careful scrutiny.

At the moment we are frustrated at least as much by the lack of empirical information on rates of selection in populations of organizations as by the unresolved issues just mentioned. Census data are presented in a manner that renders the calculation of failure rates impossible; and little longitudinal research on populations of organizations has been reported. We do, however, have some information on rates of selection. We know, for example, that failure rates for small businesses are high. By recent estimates upwards of 8 per cent of small business firms in the United States fail each year (Hollander, 1967; Bolton, 1971; see also Churchill, 1955).

In part this high failure rate reflects what Stinchcombe (1965) called the liability of newness. Many new organizations attempt to enter niches that have already been filled by organizations that have amassed social, economic, and political resources that make them difficult to dislodge. It is important to determine whether there is any selective disadvantage of smallness not of newness.

We doubt that many readers will dispute the contention that failure rates are high for new and/or small organizations. However, much of the sociological literature and virtually all of the critical literature on large organizations tacitly accepts the view that such organizations are not subject to strong selection pressures. While we do not yet have the empirical data to judge this hypothesis, we can make several comments. First, we do not dispute that the largest organizations individually and collectively exercise strong dominance over most of the organizations that constitute their environments. But it does not follow from the observation that such organizations are strong in any one period that they will be strong in every period. Thus, it is interesting to know how firmly embedded are the largest and most powerful organizations. Consider the so-called Fortune 500, the largest publicly owned industrial firms in the United States. We contrasted the lists for 1955 and 1975 (adjusting for pure name changes). Of those on the list in 1955, only 268 (53·6 per cent) were still listed in 1975. One hundred and twenty-two had disappeared through merger, 109 had slipped off the '500,' and one (a firm specializing in Cuban sugar!) had been liquidated. The number whose relative sales growth caused them to be dropped from the list is quite impressive in that the large number of mergers had opened many slots on the list. So we see that, whereas actual liquidation was rare for the largest industrial firms in the United States over a twenty-year period, there was a good deal of volatility with regard to position in this pseudodominance structure because of both mergers and slipping sales.[12]

12. From at least some perspectives, mergers can be viewed as changes in form. This will almost certainly be the case when the organizations merged have very different structures. These data also indicate a strong selective advantage for a conglomerate form of industrial organization.

Second, the choice of time perspective is important. Even the largest and most powerful organizations fail to survive over long periods. For example, of the thousands of firms in business in the United States during the Revolution, only thirteen survive as autonomous firms and seven as recognizable divisions of firms (*Nation's Business*, 1976). Presumably one needs a longer time perspective to study the population ecology of the largest and most dominant organizations.

Third, studying small organizations is not such a bad idea. The sociological literature has concentrated on the largest organizations for obvious design reasons. But, if inertial pressures on certain aspects of structure are strong enough, intense selection among small organizations may greatly constrain the variety observable among large organizations. At least some elements of structure change with size (as we argued in Section III) and the pressure toward inertia should not be overemphasized. Nonetheless we see much value in studies of the organizational life cycle that would inform us as to which aspects of structure get locked in during which phases of the cycle. For example, we conjecture that a critical period is that during which the organization grows beyond the control of a single owner/ manager. At this time the manner in which authority is delegated, if at all, seems likely to have a lasting impact on organizational structure. This is the period during which an organization becomes less an extension of one or a few dominant individuals and more an organization per se with a life of its own. If the selection pressures at this point are as intense as anecdotal evidence suggests they are, selection models will prove very useful in accounting for the varieties of forms among the whole range of organizations.

The optimism of the previous paragraph should be tempered by the realization that when one examines the largest and most dominant organizations, one is usually considering only a small number of organizations. The smaller the number, the less useful are models that depend on the type of random mechanisms that underlie population ecology models.

Fourth, we must consider what one anonymous reader, caught up in the spirit of our paper, called the anti-eugenic actions of the state in saving firms such as Lockheed from failure. This is a dramatic instance of the way in which large dominant organizations can create linkages with other large and powerful ones so as to reduce selection pressures. If such moves are effective, they alter the pattern of selection. In our view the selection pressure is bumped up to a higher level. So instead of individual organizations failing, entire networks fail. The general consequence of a large number of linkages of this sort is an increase in the instability of the entire system (Simon, 1962, 1973; May, 1973), and therefore we should see boom and bust cycles of organizational outcomes. Selection models retain relevance, then, even when the systems of organizations are tightly coupled (see Hannan, 1976).

Finally, some readers of earlier drafts have (some approvingly, some disapprovingly) treated our arguments as metaphoric. This is not what we intend. In a fundamental sense all theoretical activity involves metaphoric activity (although admittedly the term 'analogue' comes closer than does 'metaphor'). The use of metaphors or analogues enters into the formulation of 'if . . . then' statements. For example, certain molecular genetic models draw an analogy between DNA surfaces and crystal structures. The latter have simple well-behaved geometric structures amenable to strong topological (mathematical) analysis. No one argues that DNA proteins are crystals; but to the extent that their surfaces have certain crystal-like properties, the mathematical model used to analyze crystals will shed light on the genetic structure. This is, as we understand it, the general strategy of model building.

We have, for example, used results that rely on the application of certain logistic differential equations, the Lotka–Volterra equations. No known population (of animals, or of organizations) grows in exactly the manner specified by this mathematic model (and this fact has caused numerous naturalists to argue that the model is biologically meaningless). What the equations do is to model the growth path of populations that exist on finite resources in a closed system (where population growth in the absence of competition is logistic and the presence of competing populations lowers carrying capacities in that system). To the extent that the interactions of populations of *Paramecium aureilia* and *P. caudatum* (Gause's experiment) meet the conditions of the model, the model explains certain key features of population dynamics and the relationship of environmental variations to structure. To the extent that the interactions of populations of rational–legal bureaucracies and populations of patrimonial bureaucracies also meet the conditions of the model, the model explains the same important phenomena. Neither the protozoa nor the bureaucracies behave exactly as the model stipulates. The model is an abstraction that will lead to insight whenever the stated conditions are approximated.

Throughout we make a strong continuity-of-nature hypothesis. We propose that, whenever the stated conditions hold, the models lead to valuable insights regardless of whether the populations under study are composed of protozoans or organizations. We do not argue 'metaphorically.' That is, we do *not* argue as follows: an empirical regularity is found to hold for certain protozoans; because we hypothesized that populations of organizations are like populations of protozoans in essential ways, we propose that the generalizations derived from the latter will hold for organizations as well. This is the kind of reasoning by which biological propositions have most often entered sociological arguments (e.g., the famous – or infamous – organismic analogy advanced by Spencer).

Instead of applying biological laws to human social organization, we advocate the application of population ecology theories. As we have indicated at a number of points, these theories are quite general and must be modified for any concrete application (sociological *or* biological). Our purpose has been twofold. First, we sketched some of the alterations in perspective required if population ecology theories are to be applied to the study of organizations. Second, we wished to stimulate a reopening of the lines of communication between sociology and ecology. It is ironic that Hawley's (1944, p. 399) diagnosis of some thirty years ago remains apt today: 'Probably most of the difficulties which beset human ecology may be traced to the isolation of the subject from the mainstream of ecological thought.'

References

ALDRICH, Howard E., and PFEFFER, Jeffrey (1976), 'Environments of organizations,' *Annual Review of Sociology*, 2, pp. 79–105

ALDRICH, Howard E., and REISS, Albert J. (1976), 'Continuities in the study of ecological succession: changes in the race composition of neighborhoods and their businesses,' *American Journal of Sociology*, 81 (January), pp. 846–66

BLAU, Peter M. (1972), 'Interdependence and hierarchy in organizations,' *Social Science Research*, 1 (April), pp. 1–24

BLAU, Peter M., and SCHOENHERR, Richard A. (1971), *The Structure of Organizations*, New York, Basic Books

BLAU, Peter M., and SCOTT, W. Richard (1962), *Formal Organizations*, San Francisco, Chandler

BOLTON, J. E. (1971), *Small Firms*, Report of the Committee of Inquiry on Small Firms, London, Her Majesty's Stationery Office

BOULDING, Kenneth (1953), 'Toward a general theory of growth,' *Canadian Journal of Economics and Political Science*, 19, pp. 326–40

BURNS, Tom, and STALKER, G. M. (1961), *The Management of Innovation*, London, Tavistock

CAPLOW, Theodore (1957), 'Organizational size,' *Administrative Science Quarterly*, 1 (March), pp. 484–505

CHURCHILL, Betty C. (1955), 'Age and life expectancy of business firms,' *Survey of Current Business*, 35 (December), pp. 15–19

CROZIER, Michel (1964), *The Bureaucratic Phenomenon*, Chicago, University of Chicago Press

CYERT, Richard M., and MARCH, James G. (1963), *A Behavioral Theory of the Firm*, Englewood Cliffs, NJ, Prentice-Hall

DOWNS, Anthony (1967), *Inside Bureaucracy*, Boston, Little, Brown

DURKHEIM, E. (1947), *The Division of Labor in Society*, trans. G. Simpson. Glencoe, Ill., Free Press

ELTON, C. (1927), *Animal Ecology*, London, Sidgwick & Jackson

FREEMAN, John (1975), 'The unit problem in organizational research,' presented at the annual meeting of the American Sociological Association, San Francisco

FREEMAN, John, and BRITTAIN, Jack (1977), 'Union merger processes and industrial environments,' *Industrial Relations*, in press

FRIEDMAN, Milton (1953), *Essays on Positive Economics*, Chicago, University of Chicago Press

GAUSE, G. F. (1934), *The Struggle for Existence*, Baltimore, Md, Williams & Wilkins

GRAICUNAS, V. A. (1933), 'Relationship in organizations,' *Bulletin of the International Management Institute* (March), pp. 183–7

GRANOVETTER, Mark S. (1973), 'The strength of weak ties,' *American Journal of Sociology*, 78 (May), pp. 1360–80

HAIRE, Mason (1959), 'Biological models and empirical histories of the growth of organizations,' pp. 272–306 in *Modern Organization Theory*, ed. Mason Haire, New York, Wiley

HANNAN, Michael T. (1975), 'The dynamics of ethnic boundaries.' Unpublished

HANNAN, Michael T. (1976), 'Modeling stability and complexity in networks of organizations,' presented at the annual meeting of the American Sociological Association, New York

HANNAN, Michael T., and FREEMAN, John (1974), 'Environment and the structure of organizations,' presented at the annual meeting of the American Sociological Association, Montreal

HAWLEY, Amos H. (1944), 'Ecology and human ecology,' *Social Forces*, 22 (May), pp. 398–405

HAWLEY, Amos H. (1950), *Human Ecology: A Theory of Community Structure*, New York, Ronald

HAWLEY, Amos H. (1968), 'Human ecology,' pp. 328–37 in *International Encyclopedia of the Social Sciences*, ed. David L. Sills, New York, Macmillan

HOLLANDER, Edward O. (ed.) (1967), *The Future of Small Business*, New York, Praeger

HUMMON, Norman P., DOREIAN, Patrick, and TEUTER, Klaus (1975), 'A structural control model of organizational change,' *American Sociological Review*, 40 (December), pp. 812–24

HUTCHINSON, G. Evelyn (1957), 'Concluding remarks,' *Cold Spring Habor Symposium on Quantitative Biology*, 22, pp. 415–27

HUTCHINSON, G. Evelyn (1959), 'Homage to Santa Rosalia, or why are there so many kinds of animals?', *American Naturalist*, 93, pp. 145–59

LEVIN, Simon A. (1970), 'Community equilibrium and stability: an extension of the competitive exclusion principle,' *American Naturalist*, 104 (September–October), pp. 413–23

LEVINE, Sol, and WHITE, Paul E. (1961), 'Exchange as a framework for the study of interorganizational relationships,' *Administrative Science Quarterly*, 5 (March), pp. 583–601

LEVINS, Richard (1962), 'Theory of fitness in a heterogeneous environment I. The fitness set and adaptive function,' *American Naturalist*, 96 (November–December), pp. 361–78

LEVINS, Richard (1968), *Evolution in Changing Environments*, Princeton, NJ, Princeton University Press

MACARTHUR, Robert H. (1972), *Geographical Ecology: Patterns in the Distribution of Species*, Princeton, NJ, Princeton University Press

MACARTHUR, Robert H., and LEVINS, Richard (1964), 'Competition, habitat selection and character displacement in patchy environment,' *Proceedings of the National Academy of Sciences*, 51, pp. 1207–10

MARCH, James G., and SIMON, Herbert (1958), *Organizations*, New York, Wiley

MARSCHAK, Jacob, and RADNER, Roy (1972), *Economic Theory of Teams*, New Haven, Conn., Yale University Press

MAY, Robert M. (1973), *Stability and Complexity in Model Ecosystems*, Princeton, NJ, Princeton University Press

MEYER, John W. (1970), 'The charter: conditions of diffuse socialization in schools,' pp. 564–78 in *Social Processes and Social Structures*, ed. W. Richard Scott, New York, Holt, Rinehart & Winston

MONOD, Jacques (1971), *Chance and Necessity*, New York, Vintage

Nation's Business (1976), 'America's oldest companies,' 64 (July), pp. 36–7

NIELSEN, François, and HANNAN, Michael T. (1977), 'The expansion of national educational systems: tests of a population ecology model,' *American Sociological Review*, in press

PARSONS, Talcott (1956), 'Suggestions for a sociological approach to the theory of organizations, I,' *Administrative Science Quarterly*, 1 (March), pp. 63–85

PENROSE, Edith T. (1959), *The Theory of the Growth of the Firm*, New York, Wiley

SELZNICK, Philip (1957), *Leadership in Administration*, New York, Row, Peterson

SIMON, Herbert A. (1962), 'The architecture of complexity,' *Proceedings of the American Philosophical Society*, 106 (December), pp. 467–82

SIMON, Herbert A. (1973), 'The organization of complex systems,' pp. 1–28 in *Hierarchy Theory: The Challenge of Complex Systems*, ed. H. Patee, New York, Braziller

SIMON, Herbert A., and BONINI, C. P. (1958), 'The size distribution of business firms,' *American Economic Review*, 48 (September), pp. 607–17

STINCHCOMBE, Arthur L. (1959), 'Bureaucratic and craft administration of production,' *Administrative Science Quarterly*, 4 (June), pp. 168–87

STINCHCOMBE, Arthur L. (1965), 'Social structure and organizations,' pp. 153–93 in *Handbook of Organizations*, ed. James G. March, Chicago, Rand McNally

TEMPLETON, Alan R., and ROTHMAN, Edward A. (1974), 'Evolution of heterogenous environments,' *American Naturalist*, 108 (July–August), pp. 409–28

THOMPSON, James D. (1967), *Organizations in Action*, New York, McGraw-Hill

TURK, Herman (1970), 'Interorganizational networks in urban society: initial perspectives and comparative research,' *American Sociological Review*, 35 (February), pp. 1–19

WHITTAKER, Robert N., and LEVIN, Simon (eds.) (1976), *Niche: Theory and Application*, Stroudsberg, Pa, Dowden, Hutchinson & Ross

WINTER, Sidney G., Jr. (1964), 'Economic "natural selection" and the theory of the firm,' *Yale Economic Essays*, 4, pp. 224–72

ZALD, Mayer (1970), 'Political economy: a framework for analysis,' pp. 221–61 in *Power in Organizations*, ed. M. N. Zald, Nashville, Tenn., Valderbilt University Press

11 G. Hofstede

Motivation, Leadership and Organization: Do American Theories Apply Abroad?[1]

From *Organizational Dynamics*, summer 1980, pp. 42–63

A well-known experiment used in organizational behavior courses involves showing the class an ambiguous picture – one that can be interpreted in two different ways. One such picture represents either an attractive young girl or an ugly old woman, depending on the way you look at it. Some of my colleagues and I use the experiment, which demonstrates how different people in the same situation may perceive quite different things. We start by asking half of the class to close their eyes while we show the other half a slightly altered version of the picture – one in which only the young girl can be seen – for only five seconds. Then we ask those who just saw the young girl's picture to close their eyes while we give the other half of the class a five-second look at a version in which only the old woman can be seen. After this preparation we show the ambiguous picture to everyone at the same time.

The results are amazing – most of those 'conditioned' by seeing the young girl first see only the young girl in the ambiguous picture, and those 'conditioned' by seeing the old woman tend to see only the old woman. We then ask one of those who perceive the old woman to explain to one of those who perceive the young girl what he or she sees, and vice versa, until everyone finally sees both images in the picture. Each

---

1. This article is based on research carried out by the author in the period 1973–8 at the European Institute for Advanced Studies in Management, Brussels. The article itself was sponsored by executive search consultants Berndtson International SA, Brussels. The author acknowledges the helpful comments of Mark Cantley, André Laurent, Ernest G. Miller and Jennifer Robinson on an earlier version of it.

group usually finds it very difficult to get its views across to the other one and sometimes there's considerable irritation at how 'stupid' the other group is.

Cultural conditioning

I use this experiment to introduce a discussion on cultural conditioning. Basically, it shows that in five seconds I can condition half a class to see something different from what the other half sees. If this is so in the simple classroom situation, how much stronger should differences in perception of the same reality be between people who have been conditioned by different education and life experience not for five seconds, but for twenty, thirty, or forty years?

I define culture as the collective mental programming of the people in an environment. Culture is not a characteristic of individuals; it encompasses a number of people who were conditioned by the same education and life experience. When we speak of the culture of a group, a tribe, a geographical region, a national minority, or a nation, culture refers to the collective mental programming that these people have in common; the programming that is different from that of other groups, tribes, regions, minorities or majorities, or nations.

Culture, in this sense of collective mental programming, is often difficult to change; if it does so at all, it changes slowly. This is so not only because it exists in the minds of the people but, if it is shared by a number of people, because it has become crystallized in the institutions these people have built together: their family structures, educational structures, religious organizations, associations, forms of government, work organizations, law, literature, settlement patterns, buildings and even, as I hope to show, scientific theories. All of these reflect common beliefs that derive from the common culture.

One well-known mechanism by which culturally determined beliefs perpetuate themselves is the *self-fulfilling prophecy*. If, for example, it is believed that people from a certain minority are irresponsible, the institutions in such an environment will not admit these people into positions of responsibility. Never being given responsibility, the members of the minority will be unable to learn it and very probably will actually behave irresponsibly; so everybody remains caught in the belief. Another example: if it is believed that all people are ultimately motivated by a desire to accumulate wealth, those who do not want to accumulate wealth are considered deviant. Rather than be considered deviant, people in such an environment will usually justify their economic success, thereby reinforcing the belief that wealth was their motivation.

Although we are all conditioned by cultural influences at many different levels – family, social, group, geographical region, professional environment – this article deals specifically with the influence of our national environment: that is, our country. Most countries' inhabitants share a national character that is more clearly apparent to foreigners than to the nationals themselves; it represents the cultural mental programming that the nationals tend to have in common. It has its roots in a common history, or rather a shared set of beliefs about the country's history, and it is reinforced because the nation shares among its members many culture-shaping institutions: a government, an army, laws, an education system, a TV network. Most people within a country communicate quite rarely with people outside, much less so than with people from other groups within their own country. One of the problems of the young Third World nations is the integration of culturally diverse groups into a common 'mental programming' that distinguishes the nation as a whole.

National culture in four dimensions

The concept of national culture or national character has suffered from vagueness. There has been little consensus on what represents the national culture of, for example, Americans, Mexicans, French, or Japanese. We seem to lack even the terminology to describe it. Over a period of six years, I have been involved in a large research project on national cultures. For a set of forty independent nations, I have tried to determine empirically the main criteria by which their national cultures differed. I found four such criteria, which I label dimensions: these are Power Distance, Uncertainty Avoidance, Individualism–Collectivism, and Masculinity–Femininity. The dimensions of national culture are best understood by comparison with the dimensions of personality we use when we describe individuals' behavior. In recruiting, an organization often tries to get an impression of a candidate's dimensions of personality, such an intelligence (high–low); energy level (active–passive); and emotional stability (stable–unstable). These distinctions can be refined through the use of certain tests, but it's essential to have a set of criteria whereby the characteristics of individuals can be meaningfully described. The dimensions of national culture I use represent a corresponding set of criteria for describing national cultures.[2]

Characterizing a national culture does not, of course, mean that every person in the nation has all the characteristics assigned to that culture.

2. The research data: The four dimensions of national culture were found through a combination of theoretical reasoning and massive statistical analysis, in what is most likely the largest survey material ever obtained with a single questionnaire. This survey material was collected between 1967 and 1973 among employees of subsidiaries of one large US-based multinational corporation [subsequently identified as IBM – Ed.] in forty countries around the globe. The total data bank contains more than 116,000 questionnaires collected from virtually everyone in the corporation, from unskilled workers to research PhDs and top managers. Moreover, data were collected twice during a period from 1967 to 1969 and a repeat survey during 1971 to 1973. Out of a total of about 150 different survey questions (of the precoded answer type), about sixty deal with the respondents' beliefs and values; these were analyzed for the present study. The questionnaire was administered in the language of each country; a total of twenty language versions had to be made. On the basis of these data, each of the forty countries could be given an index score for each of the four dimensions.

I was wondering at first whether differences found among employees of one single corporation could be used to detect truly national culture differences. I also wondered what effect the translation of the questionnaire could have had. With this in mind, I administered a number of the same questions in 1971–1973 to an international group of about 400 managers from different public and private organizations following management development courses in Lausanne, Switzerland. This time, all received the questionnaire in English. In spite of the different mix of respondents and the different language used, I found largely the same differences between countries in the manager group that I found among the multinational personnel. Then I started looking for other studies, comparing aspects of national character across a number of countries on the basis of surveys using other questions and other respondents (such as students) or on representative public opinion polls. I found thirteen such studies; these compared between five and nineteen countries at a time. The results of these studies showed a statistically significant similarity (correlation) with one or more of the four dimensions. Finally, I also looked for national indicators (such as per capita national income, inequality of income distribution, and government spending on development aid) that could logically be supposed to be related to one or more of the dimensions. I found thirty-one such indicators – of which the values were available for between five and forty countries – that were correlated in a statistically significant way with at least one of the dimensions. All these additional studies (for which the data were collected by other people, not by me) helped make the picture of the four dimensions more complete. Interestingly, very few of these studies had even been related to each other before, but the four dimensions provide a framework that shows how they can be fit together like pieces of a huge puzzle. The fact that data obtained with a single multinational corporation have the power to uncover the secrets of entire national cultures can be understood when it's known that the respondents form well-matched samples for their nations: they are employed by the same firm (or its subsidiary); their jobs are similar (I consistently compared the same occupations across the different countries); and their age categories and sex composition were similar – only their nationalities differed. Therefore, if we look at the differences in survey answers between multinational employees in countries A, B, C, and so on, the general factor that can account for the differences in the answers is national culture.

Therefore, in describing national cultures we refer to the common elements within each nation – the national norms – but we are not describing individuals. This should be kept in mind when interpreting the four dimensions explained in the following paragraphs.

Power Distance

The first dimension of national culture is called *Power Distance*. It indicates the extent to which a society accepts the fact that power in institutions and organizations is distributed unequally. It's reflected in the values of the

Table 1. The Power Distance dimension

Small Power Distance	Large Power Distance
Inequality in society should be minimized.	There should be an order of inequality in this world in which everybody has a rightful place; high and low are protected by this order.
All people should be interdependent.	A few people should be independent; most should be dependent.
Hierarchy means an inequality of roles established for convenience.	Hierarchy means existential inequality.
Superiors consider subordinates to be 'people like me'.	Superiors consider subordinates to be a different kind of people.
Subordinates consider superiors to be 'people like me'.	Subordinates consider superiors as a different kind of people.
Superiors are accessible.	Superiors are inaccessible.
The use of power should be legitimate and is subject to the judgment as to whether it is good or evil.	Power is a basic fact of society that antedates good or evil. Its legitimacy is irrelevant.
All should have equal rights.	Power-holders are entitled to privileges.
Those in power should try to look less powerful than they are.	Those in power should try to look as powerful as possible.
The system is to blame.	The underdog is to blame.
The way to change a social system is to redistribute power.	The way to change a social system is to dethrone those in power.
People at various power levels feel less threatened and more prepared to trust people.	Other people are a potential threat to one's power and can rarely be trusted.
Latent harmony exists between the powerful and the powerless.	Latent conflict exists between the powerful and the powerless.
Cooperation among the powerless can be based on solidarity.	Cooperation among the powerless is difficult to attain because of their low-faith-in-people norm.

less powerful members of society as well as in those of the more powerful ones. A fuller picture of the difference between small Power Distance and large Power Distance societies is shown in Table 1. Of course, this shows only the extremes; most countries fall somewhere in between.

Uncertainty Avoidance

The second dimension, *Uncertainty Avoidance*, indicates the extent to which a society feels threatened by uncertain and ambiguous situations and tries to avoid these situations by providing greater career stability, establishing more formal rules, not tolerating deviant ideas and behaviors, and believing

Table 2. The Uncertainty Avoidance dimension

Weak Uncertainty Avoidance	Strong Uncertainty Avoidance
The uncertainty inherent in life is more easily accepted and each day is taken as it comes.	The uncertainty inherent in life is felt as a continuous threat that must be fought.
Ease and lower stress are experienced.	Higher anxiety and stress are experienced.
Time is free.	Time is money.
Hard work, as such, is not a virtue.	There is an inner urge to work hard.
Aggressive behavior is frowned upon.	Aggressive behavior of self and others is accepted.
Less showing of emotions is preferred.	More showing of emotions is preferred.
Conflict and competition can be contained on the level of fair play and used constructively.	Conflict and competition can unleash aggression and should therefore be avoided.
More acceptance of dissent is entailed.	A strong need for consensus is involved.
Deviation is not considered threatening; greater tolerance is shown.	Deviant persons and ideas are dangerous; intolerance holds sway.
The ambience is one of less nationalism.	Nationalism is pervasive.
More positive feelings towards younger people are seen.	Younger people are suspect.
There is more willingness to take risks in life.	There is great concern with security in life.
The accent is on relativism, empiricism.	The search is for ultimate, absolute truths and values.
There should be as few rules as possible.	There is a need for written rules and regulations.
If rules cannot be kept, we should change them.	If rules cannot be kept, we are sinners and should repent.
Belief is placed in generalists and common sense.	Belief is placed in experts and their knowledge.
The authorities are there to serve the citizens.	Ordinary citizens are incompetent compared with the authorities.

in absolute truths and the attainment of expertise. Nevertheless, societies in which uncertainty avoidance is strong are also characterized by a higher level of anxiety and aggressiveness that creates, among other things, a strong inner urge in people to work hard. (See Table 2.)

Individualism – Collectivism

The third dimension encompasses *Individualism* and its opposite, *Collectivism*. Individualism implies a loosely knit social framework in which people are supposed to take care of themselves and of their immediate families only, while collectivism is characterized by a tight social framework in which people distinguish between in-groups and out-groups; they expect their in-group (relatives, clan, organizations) to look after them, and in exchange for that they feel they owe absolute loyalty to it. A fuller picture of this dimension is presented in Table 3.

Table 3. The Individualism dimension

Collectivist	Individualist
In society, people are born into extended families or clans who protect them in exchange for loyalty.	In society, everybody is supposed to take care of himself/herself and his/her immediate family.
'We' consciousness holds sway.	'I' consciousness holds sway.
Identity is based in the social system.	Identity is based in the individual.
There is emotional dependence of individual on organizations and institutions.	There is emotional independence of individual from organizations or institutions.
The involvement with organizations is moral.	The involvement with organizations is calculative.
The emphasis is on belonging to organizations; membership is the ideal	The emphasis is on individual initiative and achievement; leadership is the ideal.
Private life is invaded by organizations and clans to which one belongs; opinions are predetermined.	Everybody has a right to a private life and opinion.
Expertise, order, duty, and security are provided by organization or clan.	Autonomy, variety, pleasure, and individual financial security are sought in the system.
Friendships are predetermined by stable social relationships, but there is need for prestige within these relationships.	The need is for specific friendships.
Belief is placed in group decisions.	Belief is placed in individual decisions.
Value standards differ for in-groups and out-groups (particularism).	Value standards should apply to all (universalism).

Masculinity

The fourth dimension is called *Masculinity* even though, in concept, it encompasses its opposite pole, *Femininity*. Measurements in terms of this dimension express the extent to which the dominant values in society are 'masculine' – that is, assertiveness, the acquisition of money and things, and *not* caring for others, the quality of life, or people. These values were labeled 'masculine' because, *within* nearly all societies, men scored higher in terms of the values' positive sense than of their negative sense (in terms of assertiveness, for example, rather than its lack) – even though the society as a whole might veer toward the 'feminine' pole. Interestingly, the more an entire society scores to the masculine side, the wider the gap between its 'men's' and 'women's' values (see Table 4).

Table 4. The Masculinity dimension

Feminine	Masculine
Men needn't be assertive, but can also assume nurturing roles.	Men should be assertive. Women should be nurturing.
Sex roles in society are more fluid.	Sex roles in society are clearly differentiated.
There should be equality between the sexes.	Men should dominate in society.
Quality of life is important.	Performance is what counts.
You work in order to live.	You live in order to work.
People and environment are important.	Money and things are important.
Interdependence is the ideal.	Independence is the ideal.
Service provides the motivation.	Ambition provides the drive.
One sympathizes with the unfortunate.	One admires the successful achiever.
Small and slow are beautiful.	Big and fast are beautiful.
Unisex and androgyny are ideal.	Ostentatious manliness ('machismo') is appreciated.

A set of cultural maps of the world

Research data were obtained by comparing the beliefs and values of employees within the subsidiaries of one large multinational corporation in forty countries around the world. These countries represent the wealthy countries of the West and the larger, more prosperous of the Third World countries. The Eastern bloc countries are missing, but data are available for Yugoslavia (where the corporation is represented by a local, self-managed company under Yugoslavian law). It was possible, on the basis of mean answers of employees on a number of key questions, to assign an index value to each country on each dimension. As described earlier, these index values appear to be related in a statistically significant way to a vast amount of other data about these countries, including both research results from other samples and national indicator figures.

Because of the difficulty of representing four dimensions in a single diagram, the position of the countries on the dimensions is shown in Figures 1, 2, and 3 for two dimensions at a time. The vertical and horizontal axes and the circles around clusters of countries have been drawn subjectively, in order to show the degree of proximity of geographically or historically related countries. The three diagrams thus represent a composite set of cultural maps of the world.

Of the three 'maps', those in Figure 1 (Power Distance by Uncertainty Avoidance) and Figure 3 (Masculinity by Uncertainty Avoidance) show a scattering of countries in all corners – that is, all combinations of index values occur. Figure 2 (Power Distance by Individualism), however, shows one empty corner: the combination of small Power Distance and Collectivism does not occur. In fact, there is a tendency for large Power Distance to be associated with Collectivism and for small Power Distance with Individualism. However, there is a third factor that should be taken into account here: national wealth. Both small Power Distance and Individualism go together with greater national wealth (per capita gross national product). The relationship between Individualism and Wealth is quite strong, as Figure 2 shows. In the upper part (Collectivist) we find only the poorer countries, with Japan as a borderline exception. In the lower part (Individualist), we find only the wealthier countries. If we look at the

---

The 40 Countries
(Showing Abbreviations used in Figures 1, 2, and 3.)

ARG	Argentina	FRA	France	JAP	Japan	SIN	Singapore
AUL	Australia	GBR	Great Britain	MEX	Mexico	SPA	Spain
AUT	Austria	GER	Germany (West)	NET	Netherlands	SWE	Sweden
BEL	Belgium	GRE	Greece	NOR	Norway	SWI	Switzerland
BRA	Brazil	HOK	Hong Kong	NZL	New Zealand	TAI	Taiwan
CAN	Canada	IND	India	PAK	Pakistan	THA	Thailand
CHL	Chile	IRA	Iran	PER	Peru	TUR	Turkey
COL	Colombia	IRE	Ireland	PHI	Philippines	USA	United States
DEN	Denmark	ISR	Israel	POR	Portugal	VEN	Venezuela
FIN	Finland	ITA	Italy	SAF	South Africa	YUG	Yugoslavia

poorer and the wealthier countries separately, there is no longer any relationship between Power Distance and Individualism.

The cultural relativity of management theories

Of particular interest in the context of this discussion is the relative position of the United States on the four dimensions. Here is how the United States rates:

On *Power Distance* at rank 25 out of the 40 countries, it is below average but it is not as low as a number of other wealthy countries.

On *Uncertainty Avoidance* at rank 31 out of 40, it is well below average.

On *Individualism* at rank 1 out of 40, the United States is the single most individualist country of the entire set (followed closely by Australia and Great Britain).

On *Masculinity* at rank 12 out of 40, it is well above average.

For about sixty years, the United States has been the world's largest producer and exporter of management theories covering such key areas as motivation, leadership, and organization. Before that, the centers of theorizing about what we now call 'management' lay in the Old World. We can trace the history of management thought as far back as we want – at least to parts of the Old Testament of the Bible, and to ancient Greece (Plato's *The Laws* and *The Republic*, 350 BC). Sixteenth-century European 'management' theorists include Niccolò Machiavelli (Italy) and Thomas More (England); early twentieth-century theorists include Max Weber (Germany) and Henri Fayol (France).

Today we are all culturally conditioned. We see the world in the way we have learned to see it. Only to a limited extent can we, in our thinking, step out of the boundaries imposed by our cultural conditioning. This applies to the author of a theory as much as it does to the ordinary citizen: theories reflect the cultural environment in which they were written. If this is true, Italian, British, German, and French theories reflect the culture of the Italy, Britain, Germany, and France of their day, and American theories reflect the culture of the United States of their day. Since most present-day theorists are middle-class intellectuals, their theories reflect a national, intellectual, middle-class, culture background.

Now we ask the question: To what extent do theories developed in one country and reflecting the cultural boundaries of that country apply to other countries? Do American management theories apply in Japan? In India? No management theorist, to my knowledge, has ever explicitly addressed himself or herself to this issue. Most probably assume that their theories are universally valid. The availability of a conceptual framework built on four dimensions of natural culture, in conjunction with the cultural maps of the world, makes it possible to see more clearly where and to what extent theories developed in one country are likely to apply elsewhere. In the remaining sections of this chapter I shall look from this viewpoint at most popular American theories of management in the areas of motivation, leadership, and organization.

Motivation

Why do people behave as they do? There is a great variety of theories of human motivation. According to Sigmund Freud, we are impelled to act by unconscious forces within us, which he called our id. Our conscious conception of ourselves – our ego – tries to control these forces, and an equally unconscious internal pilot – our superego – criticizes the thoughts and acts of our ego and causes feelings of guilt and anxiety when the ego seems to be giving in to the id. The superego is the product of early socialization, mainly learned from our parents when we were young children.

Freud's work has been extremely influential in psychology, but he is rarely quoted in the context of management theories. The latter almost exclusively refer to motivation theories developed later in the United States, particularly those of David McClelland, Abraham Maslow, Frederick Herzberg, and Victor Vroom. According to McClelland (1976), we perform because we have a need to achieve (the achievement motive). More recently, McClelland (1975) has also paid a lot of attention to the power motive. Maslow has postulated a hierarchy of human needs, from 'basic' to 'higher': most basic are physiological needs, followed by security, social needs, esteem needs and, finally, a need for 'self-actualization'. The latter incorporates McClelland's theory of achievement, but is defined in broader terms. Maslow's theory of the hierarchy of needs postulates that a higher need will become active only if the lower needs are sufficiently satisfied. Our acting is basically a rational activity by which we expect to fulfill successive levels of needs. Herzberg's two-factory theory of motivation (cf. Reading 18) distinguishes between hygiene factors (largely corresponding to Maslow's more basic needs – physiological, security, social) and

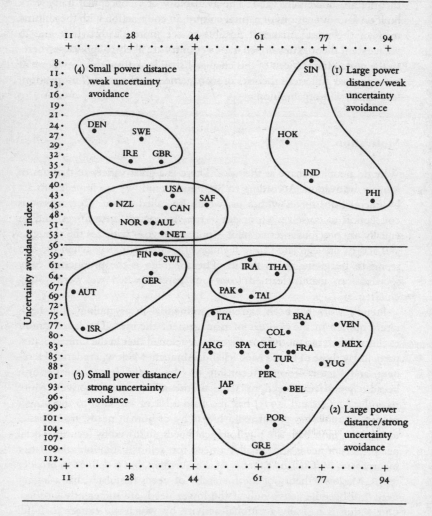

Figure 1 The position of the forty countries on the Power Distance and Uncertainty Avoidance scales

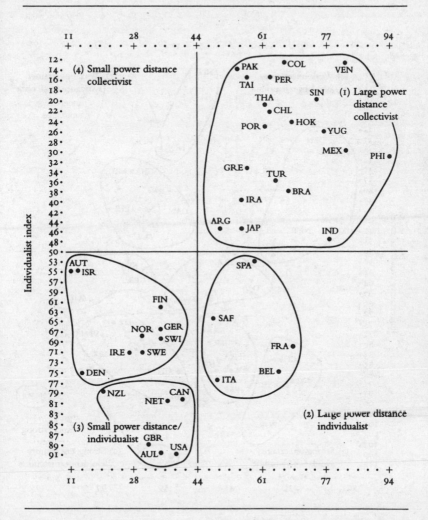

Figure 2   The position of the forty countries on the Power Distance and Individualism scales

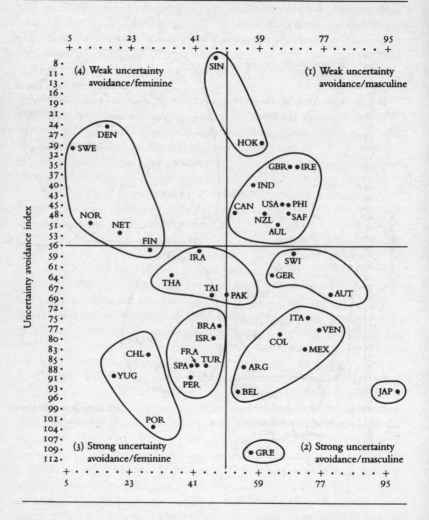

Figure 3   The position of the forty countries on the Uncertainty Avoidance and Masculinity scales

motivators (Maslow's higher needs – esteem, self-actualization); the hygiene factors have only the potential to motivate negatively (demotivate – they are necessary but not sufficient conditions), while only the motivators have the potential to motivate positively. Vroom has formalized the role of 'expectancy' in motivation; he contrasts 'expectancy' theories and 'drive' theories. The former see people as being *pulled* by the expectancy of some kind of result from their acts, mostly consciously. The latter (in accordance with Freud's theories) see people as *pushed* by inside forces – often unconscious ones.

Let us now look at these theories through culture-conscious glasses. Why has Freudian thinking never become popular in US management theory, as has the thinking of McClelland, Maslow, Herzberg, and Vroom? To what extent do these theories reflect different cultural patterns? Freud was part of an Austrian middle-class culture at the turn of the century. If we compare present-day Austria and the United States on our cultural maps, we find the following: Austria scores considerably lower on Power Distance; Austria scores considerably higher on Uncertainty Avoidance; Austria scores considerably lower on Individualism; Austria scores considerably higher on Masculinity.

We do not know to what extent Austrian culture has changed since Freud's time, but evidence suggests that cultural patterns change very slowly. It is, therefore, not likely to have been much different from today's culture. The most striking thing about present-day Austrian culture is that it combines a fairly high Uncertainty Avoidance with a very low Power Distance (see Figure 1). Somehow the combination of high Uncertainty Avoidance with high Power Distance is more comfortable (we find this in Japan and in all Latin American and Mediterranean countries – see Figure 1). Having a powerful superior whom we can both praise and blame is one way of satisfying a strong need for avoiding uncertainty. The Austrian culture, however (together with the German, Swiss, Israeli, and Finnish cultures), cannot rely on an external boss to absorb its uncertainty. Thus Freud's superego acts naturally as an inner uncertainty-absorbing device, an internalized boss. For strong Uncertainty Avoidance countries like Austria, working hard is caused by an inner urge – it is a way of relieving stress. (See Table 2.) The Austrian superego is reinforced by the country's relatively low level of Individualism (see Figure 2). The inner feeling of obligation to society plays a much stronger role in Austria than in the United States. The ultrahigh Individualism of the United States leads to a need to explain every act in terms of self-interest, and expectancy theories of motivation do provide this explanation – we always do something *because* we expect to obtain the satisfaction of some need. The high Masculinity score of Austria (Figure 3) may be one reason why Freud paid such a considerable amount of attention to the sexual instinct as a motivation.

The comparison between Austrian and US culture has so far justified the popularity of expectancy theories of motivation in the United States. The combination in the United States of weak Uncertainty Avoidance and relatively high Masculinity can tell us more about why the achievement motive has become so popular in that country. David McClelland (1976) sets up scores reflecting how strong achievement need is in many countries by analyzing the content of children's stories used in those countries to each the young to read. It now appears that there is a strong relationship between McClelland's need for achievement country scores and the combination of weak Uncertainty Avoidance and strong Masculinity charted in Figure 3.[3]

Countries in the upper right-hand corner of Figure 3 received mostly high scores on achievement need in McClelland's book; countries in the lower left-hand corner of Figure 3 received low scores. This leads us to the conclusion that the concept of the achievement motive presupposes two cultural choices – a willingness to accept risk (equivalent to weak Uncertainty Avoidance; see Table 2) and a concern with performance (equivalent to strong Masculinity; see Table 4). This combination is found exclusively in countries in the Anglo-American group and in some of their former colonies (Figure 3). One striking thing about the concept of achievement is that the word itself is hardly translatable into any language other than English; for this reason, the word could not be used in the questionnaire of the multinational corporation used in my research. The English-speaking countries all appear in the upper right-hand corner of Figure 3.

If this is so, there is reason to reconsider Maslow's hierarchy of human needs in the light of the map shown in Figure 3. Quadrant 1 (upper right-hand corner) in Figure 3 stands for *achievement motivation*, as we have seen (performance plus risk). Quadrant 2 distinguishes itself from quadrant 1 by strong Uncertainty Avoidance, which means *security motivation* (performance plus security). The countries on the feminine side of Figure 3 distinguish themselves by a focusing on quality of life rather than on per-

---

3. McClelland's data were collected for two historic years – 1925 and 1950 – but only his 1925 data relate to the cultural map in Figure 3. It is likely that the 1925 stories were more traditional, reflecting deep underlying cultural currents; the choice of stories in 1950 in most countries may have been affected by modernization currents in education, often imported from abroad.

formance and on relationships between people rather than on money and things (see Table 4). This means *social motivation*: quality of life plus security in quadrant 3, and quality of life plus risk in quadrant 4. Now, Maslow's hierarchy puts self-actualization (achievement) plus esteem above social needs above security needs. This, however, is not the description of a universal human motivation process – it is the description of a value system, the value system of the US middle class to which the author belonged. I suggest that if we want to continue thinking in terms of a hierarchy for countries in the lower right-hand corner of Figure 3 (quadrant 2), security needs should rank at the top; for countries in the upper left-hand corner (quadrant 4), social needs should rank at the top, and for countries in the lower left-hand corner (quadrant 3) *both* security and social needs should rank at the top.

One practical outcome of presenting motivation theories is the movement toward humanization of work: an attempt to make work more intrinsically interesting to the workers. There are two main currents in humanization of work. One, developed in the United States and called *job enrichment*, aims at restructuring individual jobs. A chief proponent of job enrichment is Frederick Herzberg. The other current, developed in Europe and applied mainly in Sweden and Norway, aims at restructuring work into group work, forming, for example, such semiautonomous teams as those seen in the experiments at Volvo. Why the difference in approaches? What is seen as a 'human' job depends on a society's prevailing model of humankind. In a more masculine society like the United States, humanization takes the form of masculinization, allowing individual performance. In the more feminine societies of Sweden and Norway, humanization takes the form of feminization: it is a means toward more wholesome interpersonal relationships in its de-emphasis of interindividual competition.

Leadership

One of the oldest theorists of leadership in world literature is Machiavelli (1468–1527). He described certain effective techniques for manipulation and remaining in power (including deceit, bribery, and murder) that gave him a bad reputation in later centuries. Machiavelli wrote in the context of the Italy of his day, and what he described is clearly a large Power Distance situation. We still find Italy on the larger Power Distance side of Figure 1 (with Latin American and other Mediterranean countries), and we can assume from historical evidence that Power Distances in Italy during the sixteenth century were considerably larger than they are now. When we compare Machiavelli's work with that of his contemporary, Sir Thomas More (1478–1535), we find cultural differences between ways of thinking in different countries even in the sixteenth century. The English More described in *Utopia* a state based on consensus as a 'model' to criticize the political situation of his day. But practice did not always follow theory, of course: More was beheaded by order of King Henry VIII for refusing to conform, while Machiavelli the realist managed to die peacefully in his bed. The difference in theories is nonetheless remarkable.

In the United States a current of leadership theories has developed. Some of the best known were put forth by the late Douglas McGregor (Theory X versus Theory Y, cf. McGregor, 1960), Rensis Likert (System 4 management, 1967), and Robert R. Blake with Jane S. Mouton (the managerial grid, 1978). What these theories have in common is that they all advocate participation in the manager's decisions by his/her subordinates (participative management); however, the initiative toward participation is supposed to be taken by the manager. In a worldwide perspective (Figure 1), we can understand these theories from the middle position of the United States on the Power Distance side (rank 25 out of 40 countries). Had the culture been one of larger Power Distance, we could have expected more 'Machiavellian' theories of leadership. In fact, in the management literature of another country with a larger Power Distance index score, France, there is little concern with American-style participative management, but great concern with who has the power. However, in countries with smaller Power Distances than the United States (Sweden, Norway, Germany, Israel), there is considerable sympathy for models of management in which even the initiatives are taken by the subordinates (forms of industrial democracy) which meet with little sympathy in the United States. In the approaches toward 'industrial democracy' taken in these countries, we notice their differences on the second dimension, Uncertainty Avoidance. In weak Uncertainty Avoidance countries like Sweden, industrial democracy was started in the form of local experiments and only later was given a legislative framework. In strong Uncertainty Avoidance countries like Germany, industrial democracy was brought about by legislation first and then had to be brought alive in the organizations (*Mitbestimmung*).

The crucial fact about leadership in any culture is that it is a complement to subordinateship. The Power Distance Index scores in Figure 1 are, in fact, based on the values of people as *subordinates*, not on the value of superiors. Whatever a naïve literature on leadership may give us to understand, leaders cannot choose their styles at will; what is feasible depends to a large extent on the cultural conditioning of a leader's subordinates. Along these lines, Table 5 describes the type of subordinateship that, other things being equal, a leader can expect to meet in societies at three different levels of Power Distance – subordinateship to which a leader must respond. The middle level represents what is most likely found in the United States.

Neither McGregor, nor Likert, nor Blake and Mouton allow for this type of cultural proviso – all three tend to be prescriptive with regard to a leadership style that, at best, will work with US subordinates and with those in cultures – such as Canada or Australia – that have not too different Power Distance levels (Figure 1). In fact, my research shows that subordinates in larger Power Distance countries tend to agree more frequently with McGregor's Theory X, while those in smaller Power Distance countries agree more frequently with Theory Y.

Table 5. Subordinacy for three levels of Power Distance

Small Power Distance	Medium Power Distance (United States)	Large Power Distance
Subordinates have weak dependence needs.	Subordinates have medium dependence needs.	Subordinates have strong dependence needs.
Superiors have weak dependence needs toward their superiors.	Superiors have medium dependence needs toward their superiors.	Superiors have strong dependence needs toward their superiors.
Subordinates expect superiors to consult them and may rebel or strike if superiors are not seen as staying within their legitimate role.	Subordinates expect superiors to consult them but will accept autocratic behavior as well.	Subordinates expect superiors to act autocratically.
Ideal superior to most is a loyal democrat.	Ideal superior to most is a resourceful democrat.	Ideal superior to most is a benevolent autocrat or paternalist.
Laws and rules apply to all and privileges for superiors are not considered acceptable.	Laws and rules apply to all, but a certain level of privileges for superiors is considered normal.	Everybody expects superiors to enjoy privileges; laws and rules differ for superiors and subordinates.
Status symbols are frowned upon and will easily come under attack from subordinates.	Status symbols for superiors contribute moderately to their authority and will be accepted by subordinates.	Status symbols are very important and contribute strongly to the superior's authority with the subordinates.

A US theory of leadership that allows for a certain amount of cultural relativity, although indirectly, is Fred Fiedler's contingency theory of leadership. Fiedler states that different leader personalities are needed for 'difficult' and 'easy' situations, and that a cultural gap between superior and subordinates is one of the factors that makes a situation 'difficult'. However, this theory does not address the kind of cultural gap in question.

In practice, the adaptation of managers to higher Power Distance environments does not seem to present too many problems. Although this is an unpopular message – one seldom professed in management-development courses – managers moving to a larger Power Distance culture soon learn that they have to behave more autocratically in order to be effective, and tend to do so. This is borne out by the colonial history of most Western countries. But it is interesting that the Western ex-colonial power with the highest Power Distance norm – France – seems to be most appreciated by its former colonies and seems to maintain the best postcolonial relationships with most of them. This suggests that subordinates in a large Power Distance culture feel even more comfortable with superiors who are real autocrats than with those whose assumed autocratic stance is out of national character.

The operation of a manager in an environment with a Power Distance norm lower than his or her own is more problematic. US managers tend to find it difficult to collaborate wholeheartedly in the 'industrial democracy' processes of such countries as Sweden, Germany, and even the Netherlands. US citizens tend to consider their country as the example of democracy, and find it difficult to accept that other countries might wish to develop forms of democracy for which they feel no need and that make major inroads upon managers' (or leaders') prerogatives. However, the very idea of management prerogatives is not accepted in very low Power Distance countries. This is, perhaps, best illustrated by a remark a Scandinavian social scientist is supposed to have made to Herzberg in a seminar: 'You are against participation for the very reason we are in favour of it – one doesn't know where it will stop. We think that is good.' (From D. Jenkins, 1973, p. 258.)

One way in which the US approach to leadership has been packaged and formalized is management by objectives (MBO), first advocated by Peter Drucker (1954). In the United States, MBO has been used to spread a pragmatic results orientation throughout the organization. It has been considerably more successful where results are objectively measurable than where they can only be interpreted subjectively, and, even in the United States, it has been criticized heavily (H. Levinson, 1970). Still, it has been perhaps the single most popular management technique 'made in USA'. Therefore, it can be accepted as fitting US culture. MBO presupposes:

1. That subordinates are sufficiently independent to negotiate meaningfully with the boss (not-too-large Power Distance).

2. That both are willing to take risks (weak Uncertainty Avoidance).

3. That performance is seen as important by both (high Masculinity).

Let us now take the case of Germany, a below-average Power Distance country. Here, the dialogue element in MBO should present no problem. However, since Germany scores considerably higher on Uncertainty Avoidance, the tendency toward accepting risk and ambiguity will not exist to the same extent. The idea of replacing the arbitrary authority of the boss with the impersonal authority of mutually agreed-upon objectives, however, fits the small Power Distance/strong Uncertainty Avoidance cultural cluster very well. The objectives become the subordinates' 'superego'. In a book of case studies about MBO in Germany, Ian R. G. Ferguson (1973) states that 'MBO has acquired a different flavour in the German-speaking area, not least because in these countries the societal and political pressure towards increasing the value of man in the organization on the right to co-determination has become quite clear. Thence, MBO has been transliterated into Management by Joint Goal Setting (*Führung durch Zielvereinbarung*).' Ferguson's view of MBO fits the ideological needs of present-day German-speaking countries. The case studies in his book show elaborate formal systems with extensive ideological justification; the stress on *team* objectives is quite strong, which is in line with the lower individualism in these countries.

The other area in which specific information on MBO is available is France. MBO was first introduced in France in the early 1960s, but it became extremely popular for a time after the 1968 student revolt. People expected that this new technique would lead to the long-overdue democratization of organizations. DPO (*Direction par Objectifs* – the French name for MBO) became DPPO (*Direction Participative par Objectifs*). So in France, too, societal developments affected the MBO system. However, DPPO remained, in general, as much a vain slogan as did *Liberté, Egalité, Fraternité* after the 1789 revolt. G. Franck (1973) wrote: '. . . I think that the career of DPPO is terminated, or rather that it has never started, and it won't ever start as long as we continue in France our tendency to confound ideology and reality . . .' In a postscript to Franck's article, the editors of *Le Management* wrote: 'French blue- and white-collar workers, lower-level and higher-level managers, and "patrons" all belong to the same cultural system which maintains dependency relations from level to level. Only the deviants really dislike this system. The hierarchical structure protects against anxiety; DPO, however, generates anxiety. . . .' The reason for the anxiety in the French cultural context is that MBO presupposes a depersonalized authority in the form of internalized objectives; but French people, from their early childhood onward, are accustomed to large Power Distances, to an authority that is highly personalized. And in spite of all attempts to introduce Anglo-Saxon management methods, French superiors do not easily decentralize and do not stop short-circuiting intermediate hierarchical levels, nor do French subordinates expect them to. The developments of the 1970s have severely discredited DPPO, which probably does injustice to the cases in which individual French organizations or units, starting from less exaggerated expectations, have benefited from it.

In the examples used thus far in this section, the cultural context of leadership may look rather obvious to the reader. But it also works in more subtle, less obvious ways. Here's an example from the area of management decision-making. A prestigious US consulting firm was asked to analyze the decision-making processes in a large Scandinavian 'XYZ' corporation. Their report criticized the corporation's decision-making style, which they characterized as being, among other things, 'intuitive' and 'consensus based.' They compared 'observations of traditional' 'XYZ' 'practices' with 'selected examples of practices in other companies'. These 'selected examples,' offered as a model, were evidently taken from their US clients and reflect the US textbook norm: 'fact based' rather than intuitive management, and 'fast decisions based on clear responsibilities' rather than the use of informal, personal contacts and the concern for consensus.

Is this consulting firm doing its Scandinavian clients a service? It follows from Figure 3 that where the United States and the Scandinavian culture are wide apart is on the Masculinity dimension. The use of intuition and the concern for consensus in Scandinavia are 'feminine' characteristics of the culture, well embedded in the total texture of these societies. Stressing 'facts' and 'clear responsibilities' fits the 'masculine' US culture. From a neutral viewpoint, the reasons for criticizing the US decision-making style are as good as those for criticizing the Scandinavian style. In complex decision-making situations, 'facts' no longer exist independently from the people who define them, so 'fact-based management' becomes a misleading slogan. Intuition may not be a bad method of deciding in such cases at all. And if the implementation of decisions requires the commitment of many people, even a consensus process that takes more time is an asset rather than a liability. But the essential element overlooked by the consultant is that decisions have to be made in a way that corresponds to the values of the environment in which they have to be effective. People in this consulting firm lacked insight into their own culture biases. This does not mean that the Scandinavian corporation's management need not improve its decision-making and could not learn from the consultant's experience. But this can be done only through a mutual recognition of cultural differences, not by ignoring them. As one 'XYZ' manager put it: 'They looked at us through American glasses and determined that we don't operate the American way. What did they expect?'

Organization

The Power Distance by Uncertainty Avoidance map (Figure 1) is of vital importance for structuring organizations that will work best in different countries. For example, one US-based multinational corporation has a worldwide policy that salary-increase proposals should be initiated by the employee's direct superior. However, the French management of its French subsidiary interpreted this policy in such a way that the superior's superior's superior – three levels above – was the one to initiate salary proposals. This way of working was regarded as quite natural by both superiors and subordinates in France. Other factors being equal, people in large Power Distance cultures prefer that decisions be centralized because even superiors have strong dependency needs in relation to their superiors; this tends to move decisions up as far as they can go (see Table 5). People in small Power Distance cultures want decisions to be decentralized.

While Power Distance relates to centralization, Uncertainty Avoidance relates to formalization – the need for formal rules and specialization, the assignment of tasks to experts. My former colleague O. J. Stevens at INSEAD has done an interesting research project (as yet unpublished) with MBA students from Germany, Great Britain, and France. He asked them to write their own diagnosis and solution for a small case study of an organizational problem: a conflict in one company between the sales and product development departments. The majority of the French referred the problem to the next higher authority (the president of the company); the Germans attributed it to the lack of a written policy, and proposed establishing one; the British attributed it to a lack of interpersonal communication, to be cured by some kind of group training.

Stevens concludes that the 'implicit model' of the organization for most French was a pyramid (both centralized and formal); for most Germans, a well-oiled machine (formalized but not centralized); and for most British, a village market (neither formalized nor centralized). This covers three quadrants (2, 3, and 4) in Figure 1. What is missing is an 'implicit model' for quadrant 1, which contains four Asian countries, including India. A discussion with an Indian colleague leads me to place the family (centralized, but not formalized) in this quadrant as the 'implicit model' of the organization. In fact, Indian organizations tend to be formalized as far as relationships between people go (this is related to Power Distance), but not as far as workflow goes (this is Uncertainty Avoidance).

The 'well-oiled machine' model for Germany reminds us of the fact that Max Weber, author of the first theory of bureaucracy, was a German. Weber pictures bureaucracy as a highly formalized system (strong Uncertainty Avoidance), in which, however, the rules protect the lower-ranking members against abuse of power by their superiors. The superiors have no power by themselves, only the power that their bureaucratic roles have given them as incumbents of the roles: the power is in the role, not in the person (small Power Distance).

The United States is found fairly close to the center of the map in Figure 1, taking an intermediate position between the 'pyramid,' 'machine,' and 'market' implicit models – a position that may help explain the success of US business operations in very different cultures. However, according to the common US conception of organization, we might say that *hierarchy is not a goal by itself* (as it is in France) and that *rules are not a goal by themselves*. Both are means toward obtaining results, to be changed if needed. A breaking away from hierarchic and bureaucratic traditions is found in the development toward matrix organizations and similar temporary or flexible organization systems.

Another INSEAD colleague, André Laurent, has shown that French managers strongly disbelieve in the feasibility of matrix organizations, because they see them as violating the 'holy' principle of unity of command. However, in the French subsidiary of a multinational corporation that has a long history of successful matrix management, the French managers were quite positive toward it; obviously, then, cultural barriers to organizational innovation can be overcome. German managers are not too favorably disposed toward matrix organizations either, feeling that they tend to frustrate their need for organizational clarity. This means that matrix organizations will be accepted *if* the roles of individuals within the organization can be defined without ambiguity.

The extreme position of the United States on the Individualism scale leads to other potential conflicts between the US way of thinking about organizations and the values dominant in other parts of the world. In the US Individualist conception, the relationship between the individual and the organization is essentially calculative, being based on enlightened self-interest. In fact, there is a strong historical and cultural link between Individualism and capitalism. The capitalist system – based on self-interest and the market mechanism – was 'invented' in Great Britain, which is still among the top three most Individualist countries in the world. In more Collectivist societies, however, the link between individuals and their traditional organizations is not calculative, but moral: it is based not on self-interest, but on the individual's loyalty toward the clan, organization, or society, which is supposedly the best guarantee of that individual's ultimate interest. 'Collectivism' is a bad word in the United States, but 'individualism' is as much a bad word in the writings of Mao Tse-tung, who writes from a strongly Collectivist cultural tradition (see Figure 2 for the Collectivist scores of the Chinese majority countries Taiwan, Hong Kong, and Singapore). This means that US organizations may get themselves into considerable trouble in more Collectivist environments if they do not recognize their local employees' needs for ties of mutual loyalty between company and employee. 'Hire and fire' is very ill perceived in these countries, if firing isn't prohibited by law altogether. Given the value position of people in more Collectivist cultures, it should not be seen as surprising if they prefer other types of economic order to capitalism, if capitalism cannot get rid of its Individualist range.

Consequences for policy

So far we have seriously questioned the universal validity of management theories developed in one country, in most instances here, the United States.

On a practical level, this has the least consequence for organizations operating entirely within the country in which the theories were born. As long as the theories apply within the United States, US organizations can base their policies for motivating employees, leadership, and organization development on these policies. Still, some caution is due. If differences in environmental culture can be shown to exist between countries, and if these constrain the validity of management theories, what about the subcultures and countercultures within the country? To what extent do the familiar theories apply when the organization employs people for whom the theories were not originally conceived, such as members of minority groups with different educational backgrounds, or belonging to a different generation? If culture matters, an organization's policies can lose their effectiveness when its cultural environment changes.

No doubt, however, the consequences of the cultural relativity of management theories are more serious for the multinational organization. The cultural maps in Figures 1, 2, and 3 can help predict the kind of culture difference between subsidiaries and mother company that will need to be met. An important implication is that identical personnel policies may have very different effects in different countries, and within countries for different subgroups of employees. This is not only a matter of different employee values; there are also, of course, differences in government policies and legislation (which usually reflect quite clearly the country's different cultural position). And there are differences in labor market situations and labor union power positions. These differences – tangible as well as intangible – may have consequences for performance, attention to quality, cost, labor turnover, and absenteeism. Typical universal policies that may work out quite differently in different countries are those dealing with financial incentives, promotion paths, and grievance channels.

The dilemma for the organization operating abroad is whether to adapt to the local culture or try to change it. There are examples of companies that have successfully changed local habits, such as in the earlier mention of the introduction of matrix organization in France. Many Third World countries want to import new technologies from more economically advanced countries. If they are to work at all, these technologies must presuppose values that may run counter to local traditions, such as a certain discretion of subordinates allowed by superiors (lower Power Distance) or of individuals allowed by in-groups (more Individualism). In such a case, the local culture has to be changed; this is a difficult task that should not be taken on lightly. Since it calls for a conscious strategy based on insight into the local culture, it's logical to involve acculturated locals in strategy formulations. Often, the original policy will have to be adapted to fit local culture and lead to the desired effect. We saw earlier how, in the case of MBO, this has succeeded in Germany, but generally failed in France.

A final area in which the cultural boundaries of home-country management theories are important is the training of managers for assignments abroad. For managers who have to operate in an unfamiliar culture, training based on home-country theories is of very limited use and may even do more harm than good. Of more importance is a thorough familiarization with the other culture, for which the organization can use the services of specialized crosscultural training institutes, or it can develop its own program by using host-country personnel as teachers.

References

BLAKE, R. R., and MOUTON, J. S. (1978), *The New Managerial Grid*, Gulf Publishing Co.

DRUCKER, P. (1954), *The Practice of Management*, Harper & Row

FERGUSON, I. R. G. (1973), *Management by Objectives in Deutschland*, Herder und Herder

FRANCK, G. (1973), 'Epitaphe pour la DPO', *Le Management*, November

JENKINS, D. (1973), *Job Power: Blue and White Collar Democracy*, Doubleday

LEVINSON, H. (1970), 'Management by whose objectives?', *Harvard Business Review*, no. 4

LIKERT, R. (1967), *The Human Organization: Its Management and Value*, McGraw-Hill

McCLELLAND, D. C. (1975), *Power: The Inner Experience*, Irvington

McCLELLAND, D. C. (1976), *The Achieving Society*, Irvington

McGREGOR, D. (1960), 'Theory X: the traditional view of direction and control' and 'Theory Y: the integration of individual and organizational goals', *The Human Side of Enterprise*, McGraw-Hill, chapters 3 and 4

Further reading

The first US book about the cultural relativity of US management theories is still to be written, I believe – which lack in itself indicates how difficult it is to recognize one's own cultural biases. One of the few US books describing the process of cultural conditioning for a management readership is Edward T. Hall's *The Silent Language*, Fawcett, 1959, but reprinted since. Good reading also is Hall's article 'The silent language in overseas business', *Harvard Business Review*, May–June 1960. Hall is an anthropologist and therefore a specialist in the study of culture. Very readable on the same subject are two books by the British anthropologist Mary Douglas, *Natural Symbols: Exploration in Cosmology*, Vintage, 1973, and the reader *Rules and Meanings: The Anthropology of Everyday Knowledge*, Penguin, 1973. Another excellent reader is Theodore D. Weinshall's *Culture and Management*, Penguin, 1977.

On the concept of national character, some well-written professional literature is Margaret Mead's 'National character', in the reader by Sol Tax, *Anthropology Today*, University of Chicago Press, 1962, and Alex Inkeles and D. J. Levinson's 'National Character', in Lindzey and Aronson's *Handbook of Social Psychology*, second edition, volume 4, Addison-Wesley, 1969. Critique on the implicit claims of universal validity of management theories comes from some foreign authors. An important article is Michel Brossard and Marc Maurice's 'Is there a universal model of organization structure?' *International Studies of Management and Organization*, fall 1976. This journal is a journal of translations from non-American literature, based in New York, that often contains important articles on management issues by non-US authors that take issue with the dominant theories. Another article is Gunnar Hjelholt's 'Europe is different', in Geert Hofstede and M. Sami Kassem's reader, *European Contributions to Organization Theory*, Von Gorcum, 1976.

Geert Hofstede's study of national cultures has been published in his book, *Culture's Consequences: International Differences in Work-Related Values*, Sage Publications, 1980.

PART THREE
Management and Decision-making

All organizations have to be managed, and the tasks and the processes which this involves have been the subject of much thought. In particular, attempts have been made to generalize the analyses so that they may be of use to managers in a large variety of organizations in their attempts to manage better. The contributors to this section have tried to present overall principles distilled from their experience and their studies, all of which have attracted much support and much criticism.

Fayol (Reading 12) was the first of the modern management writers to propound a theoretical analysis of what managers have to do and by what principles they have to do it; an analysis which has withstood eighty years of critical discussion. His principles of authority and responsibility, unity of command, good order, *esprit de corps*, etc. are the common currency of management parlance.

Taylor (Reading 13) set out to challenge management with his 'scientific management' approach, which promised increased efficiency through extreme specialization and tight control of tasks (including those of managers as well as workers). His ideas made him a controversial figure in his own day, and he has remained so since, but from him has come the approach to management through time study, work study and industrial engineering, which are important parts of the control procedures of many organizations.

Mintzberg (Reading 14) conducted a detailed empirical study of the actual job that top managers have to do. This leads him to suggest a new way of classifying managerial work. It consists of *interpersonal, informational* and *decisional* sets of tasks.

Kanter (Reading 15) underlines the importance of the correct use of managerial power in achieving effective organizational performance, and draws a distinction between productive and oppressive uses of power.

March (Reading 16) maintains that decision-making is the key distinctive activity of managers. He argues that because of the complex nature of organizational reality managers should not always strive for rationality in their decisions since this could hamper flexibility and innovation. Playfulness and foolishness also have a part to play.

12   H. Fayol

General Principles of Management

From *General and Industrial Management*, Pitman, 1949, chapter 4, trans. Constance Storrs (reprinted 1987 by the Center for Effective Performance, Inc., Atlanta GA). (French original published in 1916)

The managerial function finds its only outlet through the members of the organization (body corporate). Whilst the other functions bring into play material and machines, the managerial function operates only on the personnel. The soundness and good working order of the body corporate depend on a certain number of conditions termed indiscriminately principles, laws, rules. For preference I shall adopt the term principles whilst dissociating it from any suggestion of rigidity, for there is nothing rigid or absolute in management affairs, it is all a question of proportion. Seldom do we have to apply the same principle twice in identical conditions; allowance must be made for different changing circumstances, for men just as different and changing and for many other variable elements.

Therefore principles are flexible and capable of adaptation to every need; it is a matter of knowing how to make use of them, which is a difficult art requiring intelligence, experience, decision and proportion. Compounded of tact and experience, proportion is one of the foremost attributes of the manager. There is no limit to the number of principles of management, every rule or managerial procedure which strengthens the body corporate or facilitates its functioning has a place among the principles so long, at least, as experience confirms its worthiness. A change in the state of affairs can be responsible for a change of rules which had been engendered by that state.

I am going to review some of the principles of management which I have most frequently had to apply, viz.

1. Division of work.
2. Authority.
3. Discipline.

253

4. Unity of command.
5. Unity of direction.
6. Subordination of individual interest to the general interest.
7. Remuneration.
8. Centralization.
9. Scalar chain (line of authority).
10. Order.
11. Equity.
12. Stability of tenure of personnel.
13. Initiative.
14. *Esprit de corps*.

Division of work

Specialization belongs to the natural order; it is observable in the animal world, where the more highly developed the creature the more highly differentiated its organs; it is observable in human societies, where the more important the body corporate[1] the closer is the relationship between structure and function. As society grows, so new organs develop destined to replace the single one performing all functions in the primitive state.

The object of division of work is to produce more and better work with the same effort. The worker always on the same part, the manager concerned always with the same matters, acquire an ability, sureness and accuracy which increase their output. Each change of work brings in its train an adaptation which reduces output. Division of work permits of reduction in the number of objects to which attention and effort must be directed and has been recognized as the best means of making use of individuals and of groups of people. It is not merely applicable to technical work, but without exception to all work involving a more or less considerable number of people and demanding abilities of various types, and it results in specialization of functions and separation of powers. Although its advantages are universally recognized and although possibility of progress is inconceivable without the specialized work of learned men and artists,

---

1. '*Body corporate*'. Fayol's term '*Corps social*', meaning all those engaged in a given corporate activity in any sphere, is best rendered by this somewhat unusual term because (a) it retains his implied biological metaphor; (b) it represents the structure as distinct from the process of organization.

The term will be retained in all contexts where these two requirements have to be met (Translator's note).

yet division of work has its limits which experience and a sense of proportion teach us may not be exceeded.

Authority and responsibility

Authority is the right to give orders and the power to exact obedience. Distinction must be made between a manager's official authority deriving from office and personal authority, compounded of intelligence, experience, moral worth, ability to lead, past services, etc. In the make-up of a good head personal authority is the indispensable complement of official authority. Authority is not to be conceived of apart from responsibility, that is apart from sanction – reward or penalty – which goes with the exercise of power. Responsibility is a corollary of authority, it is its natural consequence and essential counterpart, and wheresoever authority is exercised responsibility arises.

The need for sanction, which has its origin in a sense of justice, is strengthened and increased by this consideration, that in the general interest useful actions have to be encouraged and their opposite discouraged. Application of sanction to acts of authority forms part of the conditions essential for good management, but it is generally difficult to effect, especially in large concerns. First, the degree of responsibility must be established and then the weight of the sanction. Now, it is relatively easy to establish a workman's responsibility for his acts and a scale of corresponding sanctions; in the case of a foreman it is somewhat difficult, and proportionately as one goes up the scalar chain of business, as work grows more complex, as the number of workers involved increases, as the final result is more remote, it is increasingly difficult to isolate the share of the initial act of authority in the ultimate result and to establish the degree of responsibility of the manager. The measurement of this responsibility and its equivalent in material terms elude all calculation.

Sanction, then, is a question of kind, custom, convention, and judging it one must take into account the action itself, the attendant circumstances and potential repercussions. Judgment demands high moral character, impartiality and firmness. If all these conditions are not fulfilled there is a danger that the sense of responsibility may disappear from the concern.

Responsibility valiantly undertaken and borne merits some consideration; it is a kind of courage everywhere much appreciated. Tangible proof of this exists in the salary level of some industrial leaders, which is much higher than that of civil servants of comparable rank but carrying no responsibility. Nevertheless, generally speaking, responsibility is feared as much as authority is sought after, and fear of responsibility paralyses much initiative and destroys many good qualities. A good leader should possess and infuse into those around him courage to accept responsibility.

The best safeguard against abuse of authority and against weakness on the part of a higher manager is personal integrity and particularly high moral character of such a manager, and this integrity, it is well known, is conferred neither by election nor ownership.

Discipline

Discipline is in essence obedience, application, energy, behaviour and outward marks of respect observed in accordance with the standing agreements between the firm and its employees, whether these agreements have been freely debated or accepted without prior discussion, whether they be written or implicit, whether they derive from the wish of the parties to them or from rules and customs, it is these agreements which determine the formalities of discipline.

Discipline, being the outcome of different varying agreements, naturally appears under the most diverse forms; obligations of obedience, application, energy, behaviour, vary, in effect, from one firm to another, from one group of employees to another, from one time to another. Nevertheless, general opinion is deeply convinced that discipline is absolutely essential for the smooth running of business and that without discipline no enterprise could prosper.

This sentiment is very forcibly expressed in military handbooks, where it runs that 'Discipline constitutes the chief strength of armies'. I would approve unreservedly of this aphorism were it followed by this other, 'Discipline is what leaders make it'. The first one inspires respect for discipline, which is a good thing, but it tends to eclipse from view the responsibility of leaders, which is undesirable, for the state of discipline of any group of people depends essentially on the worthiness of its leaders.

When a defect in discipline is apparent or when relations between superiors and subordinates leave much to be desired, responsibility for this must not be cast heedlessly, and without going further afield, on the poor state of the team, because the ill mostly results from the ineptitude of the leaders. That, at all events, is what I have noted in various parts of France, for I have always found French workmen obedient and loyal provided they are ably led.

In the matter of influence upon discipline, agreements must be set side by side with command. It is important that they be clear and, as far as is possible afford satisfaction to both sides. This is not easy. Proof of that exists in the great strikes of miners, railwaymen and civil servants which, in these latter years, have jeopardized national life at home and elsewhere and which arose out of agreements in dispute or inadequate legislation.

For half a century a considerable change has been effected in the mode of agreements between a concern and its employees. The agreements of former days fixed by the employer alone are being replaced, in ever increasing measure, by understandings arrived at by discussion between an owner or group of owners and workers' associations. Thus each individual owner's responsibility has been reduced and is further diminished by increasingly frequent State intervention in labour problems. Nevertheless, the setting up of agreements binding a firm and its employees, from which disciplinary formalities emanate, should remain one of the chief preoccupations of industrial heads.

The well-being of the concern does not permit, in cases of offence against discipline, of the neglect of certain sanctions capable of preventing or minimizing their recurrence. Experience and tact on the part of a manager are put to the proof in the choice and degree of sanctions to be used, such as remonstrances, warnings, fines, suspensions, demotion, dismissal. Individual people and attendant circumstances must be taken into account. In fine, discipline is respect for agreements which are directed at achieving obedience, application, energy, and the outward marks of respect. It is incumbent upon managers at high levels as much as upon humble employees, and the best means of establishing and maintaining it are:

1. Good superiors at all levels.
2. Agreements as clear and fair as possible.
3. Sanctions (penalties) judiciously applied.

Unity of command

For any action whatsoever, an employee should receive orders from one superior only. Such is the rule of unity of command, arising from general and ever-present necessity and wielding an influence on the conduct of affairs which, to my way of thinking, is at least equal to any other principle whatsoever. Should it be violated, authority is undermined, discipline is in jeopardy, order disturbed and stability threatened. This rule seems fundamental to me and so I have given it the rank of principle. As soon as two superiors wield their authority over the same person or department, uneasiness makes itself felt and should the cause persist, the disorder increases, the malady takes on the appearance of an animal organism troubled by a foreign body, and the following consequences are to be observed: either the dual command ends in disappearance or elimination of one of the superiors and organic well-being is restored, or else the organism continues to wither away. In no case is there adaptation of the social organism to dual command.

Now dual command is extremely common and wreaks havoc in all concerns, large or small, in home and in State. The evil is all the more to be feared in that it worms its way into the social organism on the most plausible pretexts. For instance:

1. In the hope of being better understood or gaining time or to put a stop forthwith to an undesirable practice, a superior S^2 may give orders directly to an employee E without going via the superior S^1. If this mistake is repeated there is dual command with its consequences, viz., hesitation on the part of the subordinate, irritation and dissatisfaction on the part of the superior set aside, and disorder in the work. It will be seen later that it is possible to by-pass the scalar chain when necessary, whilst avoiding the drawbacks of dual command.

2. The desire to get away from the immediate necessity of dividing up authority as between two colleagues, two friends, two members of one family, results at times in dual command reigning at the top of a concern right from the outset. Exercising the same powers and having the same authority over the same men, the two colleagues end up inevitably with dual command and its consequences. Despite harsh lessons, instances of this sort are still numerous. New colleagues count on their mutual regard, common interest and good sense to save them from every conflict, every serious disagreement and, save for rare exceptions, the illusion is short-lived. First an awkwardness makes itself felt, then a certain irritation and, in time, if dual command exists, even hatred. Men cannot bear dual command. A judicious assignment of duties would have reduced the danger without entirely banishing it, for between two superiors on the same footing there must always be some question ill-defined. But it is riding for a fall to set up a business organization with two superiors on equal footing without assigning duties and demarcating authority.

3. Imperfect demarcation of departments also leads to dual command: two

superiors issuing orders in a sphere which each thinks his own, constitutes dual command.

4. Constant linking up as between different departments, natural intermeshing of functions, duties often badly defined, create an ever-present danger of dual command. If a knowledgeable superior does not put it in order, footholds are established which later upset and compromise the conduct of affairs.

In all human associations, in industry, commerce, army, home, State, dual command is a perpetual source of conflicts, very grave sometimes, which have special claim on the attention of superiors of all ranks.

Unity of direction

This principle is expressed as: one head and one plan for a group of activities having the same objective. It is the condition essential to unity of action, coordination of strength and focusing of effort. A body with two heads is in the social as in the animal sphere a monster, and has difficulty in surviving. Unity of direction (one head one plan) must not be confused with unity of command (one employee to have orders from one superior only). Unity of direction is provided for by sound organization of the body corporate, unity of command turns on the functioning of the personnel. Unity of command cannot exist without unity of direction, but does not flow from it.

Subordination of individual interest to general interest

This principle calls to mind the fact that in a business the interest of one employee or group of employees should not prevail over that of the concern, that the interest of the home should come before that of its members and that the interest of the State should have pride of place over that of one citizen or group of citizens.

It seems that such an admonition should not need calling to mind. But ignorance, ambition, selfishness, laziness, weakness, and all human passions tend to cause the general interest to be lost sight of in favour of individual interest and a perpetual struggle has to be waged against them. Two interests of a different order, but claiming equal respect, confront each other and means must be found to reconcile them. That represents one of the great difficulties of management. Means of effecting it are:

1. Firmness and good example on the part of superiors.
2. Agreements as fair as is possible.
3. Constant supervision.

Remuneration of personnel

Remuneration of personnel is the price of services rendered. It should be fair and, as far as is possible, afford satisfaction both to personnel and firm (employee and employer). The rate of remuneration depends, firstly, on circumstances independent of the employer's will and employee's worth, viz. cost of living, abundance or shortage of personnel, general business conditions, the economic position of the business, and after that it depends on the value of the employee and mode of payment adopted. Appreciation of the factors dependent on the employer's will and on the value of employees, demands a fairly good knowledge of business, judgment, and impartiality. Later on in connection with selecting personnel we shall deal with assessing the value of employees; here only the mode of payment is under consideration as a factor operating on remuneration. The method of payment can exercise considerable influence on business progress, so the choice of this method is an important problem. It is also a thorny problem which in practice has been solved in widely different ways, of which so far none has proved satisfactory. What is generally looked for in the methods of payment is that:

1. It shall assure fair remuneration.
2. It shall encourage keenness by rewarding well-directed effort.
3. It shall not lead to over-payment going beyond reasonable limits.

I am going to examine briefly the modes of payment in use for workers, junior managers, and higher managers.

Workers

The various modes of payment in use for workers are:

1. Time rates.
2. Job rates.
3. Piece rates.

These three modes of payment may be combined and give rise to important variations by the introduction of bonuses, profit-sharing schemes, payment in kind, and non-financial incentives.

1. *Time rates.* Under this system the workman sells the employer, in return for a predetermined sum, a day's work under definite conditions. This system has the disadvantage of conducing to negligence and of demanding constant supervision. It is inevitable where the work done is not susceptible to measurement and in effect it is very common.

2. *Job rates.* Here payment made turns upon the execution of a definite job set in advance and may be independent of the length of the job. When payment is due only on condition that the job be completed during the normal work spell, this method merges into time rate. Payment by daily job does not require as close a supervision as payment by the day. But it has the drawback of levelling the output of good workers down to that of mediocre ones. The good ones are not satisfied, because they feel that they could earn more; the mediocre ones find the task set too heavy.

3. *Piece rates.* Here payment is related to work done and there is no limit. This system is often used in workshops where a large number of similar articles have to be made, and is found where the product can be measured by weight, length or cubic capacity, and in general is used wherever possible. It is criticized on the grounds of emphasizing quantity at the expense of quality and of provoking disagreements when rates have to be revised in the light of manufacturing improvements. Piecework becomes contract work when applied to an important unit of work. To reduce the contractor's risk, sometimes there is added to the contract price a payment for each day's work done.

Generally, piece rates give rise to increased earnings which act for some time as a stimulus, then finally a system prevails in which this mode of payment gradually approximates to time rates for a pre-arranged sum.

The above three modes of payment are found in all large concerns; sometimes time rates prevail, sometimes one of the other two. In a workshop the same workman may be seen working now on piece rates, now on time rates. Each one of these methods has its advantages and drawbacks, and their effectiveness depends on circumstances and the ability of superiors. Neither method nor rate of payment absolves management from competence and tact, and keenness of workers and peaceful atmosphere of the workshop depend largely upon it.

Bonuses

To arouse the worker's interest in the smooth running of the business, sometimes an increment in the nature of a bonus is added to the time, job or piece rate: for good time keeping, hard work, freedom from machine breakdown, output, cleanliness, etc. The relative importance, nature and qualifying conditions of these bonuses are very varied. There are to be found the small daily supplement, the monthly sum, the annual award, shares or portions of shares distributed to the most meritorious, and also even profit-sharing schemes such as, for example, certain monetary allocations distributed annually among workers in some large firms. Several French collieries started some years back the granting of a bonus proportional to profits distributed or to extra profits. No contract is required from the workers save that the earning of the bonus is subject to certain conditions, for instance, that there shall have been no strike during the year, or that absenteeism shall not have exceeded a given number of days. This type of bonus introduced an element of profit-sharing into miners' wages without any prior discussion as between workers and employer. The workman did not refuse a gift, largely gratuitous, on the part of the employer, that is, the contract was a unilateral one. Thanks to a successful trading period the yearly wages have been appreciably increased by the operation of the bonus. But what is to happen in lean times? This interesting procedure is as yet too new to be judged, but obviously it is no general solution of the problem.

In the mining industry there is another type of bonus, dependent upon the selling price of coal. The sliding scale of wages depending on a basic rate plus a bonus proportionate to the local selling price, which had long flourished in Wales, but was discontinued when minimum wages legislation came into force, is today the principle regulating the payment of miners in the Nord and Pas de Calais *départements*, and has also been adopted in the Loire region. This system established a certain fixed relationship between the prosperity of the colliery and the miner's wage. It is criticized on the grounds that it conduces to limitation of production in order to raise selling price. So we see that it is necessary to have recourse to a variety of methods in order to settle wages questions. The problem is far from being settled to everyone's satisfaction and all solutions are hazardous.

Profit-sharing

Workers. The idea of making workers share in profits is a very attractive one and it would seem that it is from there that harmony as between Capital and Labour should come. But the practical formula for such sharing has not yet been found. Workers' profit-sharing has hitherto come up against insurmountable difficulties of application in the case of large concerns. Firstly, let us note that it cannot exist in enterprises having no monetary objective (State services, religions, philanthropic, scientific societies) and also that it is not possible in the case of businesses running at a loss. Thus profit-sharing is excluded from a great number of concerns. There remain the prosperous business concerns and of these latter the desire to reconcile and harmonize workers' and employers' interests is nowhere so great as in French mining and metallurgical industries. Now, in these industries I know of no clear application of workers' profit-sharing, whence it may be concluded forthwith that the matter is difficult, if not impossible. It is very difficult indeed. Whether a business is making a profit or not the worker must have an immediate wage assured him, and a system which would make workers' payment depend entirely on eventual future profit is unworkable. But perhaps a part of wages might come from business profits. Let us see. Viewing all contingent factors, the worker's greater or lesser share of activity or ability in the final outcome of a large concern is impossible to assess and is, moreover, quite insignificant. The portion accruing to him of distributed dividend would at the most be a few centimes on a wage of five francs for instance, that is to say the smallest extra effort, the stroke of a pick or of a file operating directly on his wage, would prove of greater advantage to him. Hence the worker has no interest in being rewarded by a share in profits proportionate to the effect he has upon profits. It is worthy of note that, in most large concerns, wage increases, operative now for some twenty years, represent a total sum greater than the amount of capital shared out. In effect, unmodified real profit-sharing by workers of large concerns has not yet entered the sphere of practical business politics.

Junior managers. Profit-sharing for foremen, superintendents, engineers, is scarcely more advanced than for workers. Nevertheless, the influence of these employees on the results of a business is quite considerable, and if they are not consistently interested in profits the only reason is that the basis for participation is difficult to establish. Doubtless managers have no need of monetary incentive to carry out their duties, but they are not indifferent to material satisfactions and it must be acknowledged that the hope of extra profit is capable of arousing their enthusiasm. So employees at middle levels should, where possible, be induced to have an interest in profits. It is relatively easy in businesses which are starting out or on trial, where exceptional effort can yield outstanding results. Sharing may then be applied to overall business profits or merely to the running of the particular department of the employee in question. When the business is of long standing and well run the zeal of a junior manager is scarcely apparent in the general outcome, and it is very hard to establish a useful basis on which he may participate. In fact, profit-sharing among junior managers in France is very rare in large concerns. Production or workshop output bonuses – not to be confused with profit-sharing – are much more common.

Higher managers. It is necessary to go right to the top management to find a class of employee with frequent interest in the profits of large-scale French concerns. The head of the business, in view of his knowledge, ideas and actions, exerts considerable influence on general results, so it is quite natural to try and provide him with an interest in them. Sometimes it is possible to establish a close connection between his personal activity and its effects. Nevertheless, generally speaking, there exist other influences quite independent of the personal capability of the manager which can influence results to a greater extent than can his personal activity. If the manager's salary were exclusively dependent upon profits, it might at times be reduced to nothing. There are, besides, businesses being built up, wound up or merely passing through temporary crisis, wherein management depends no less on talent than in the case of prosperous ones, and wherein profit-sharing cannot be a basis for remuneration for the manager. In fine, senior civil servants cannot be paid on a profit-sharing basis. Profit-sharing, then, for either higher managers or workers, is not a general rule of remuneration. To sum up, then: profit-sharing is a mode of payment capable of giving excellent results in certain cases, but is not a general rule. It does not seem to me possible, at least for the present, to count on this mode of payment for appeasing conflict between Capital and Labour. Fortunately, there are other means which hitherto have been sufficient to maintain relative social quiet. Such methods have not lost their power and it is up to managers to study them, apply them, and make them work well.

Payment in kind, welfare work, non-financial incentives

Whether wages are made up of money only or whether they include various additions such as heating, light, housing, food, is of little consequence provided that the employee be satisfied.

From another point of view, there is no doubt that a business will be better served in proportion as its employees are more energetic, better educated, more conscientious and more permanent. The employer should have regard, if merely in the interests of the business, for the health, strength, education, morale, and stability of his personnel. These elements of smooth running are not acquired in the workshop alone, they are formed and developed as well, and particularly, outside it, in the home and school, in civil and religious life. Therefore, the employer comes to be concerned with his employees outside the works and here the question of proportion comes up again. Opinion is greatly divided on this point. Certain unfortunate experiments have resulted in some employers stopping short their interest at the works gate and at the regulation of wages. The majority consider that the employer's activity may be used to good purpose outside the factory confines provided that there be discretion and prudence, that it be sought after rather than imposed, be in keeping with the general level of education and taste of those concerned and that it have absolute respect for their liberty. It must be benevolent collaboration, not tyrannical stewardship, and therein lies an indispensable condition of success.

The employer's welfare activities may be of various kinds. In the works they bear on matters of hygiene and comfort: ventilation, lighting, cleanliness, canteen facilities. Outside the works they bear on housing accommodation, feeding, education, and training. Provident schemes come under this head.

Non-financial incentives only come in the case of large scale concerns and may be said to be almost exclusively in the realm of government work. Every mode of payment likely to make the personnel more valuable and improve its lot in life, and also to inspire keenness on the part of employees at all levels, should be a matter for managers' constant attention.

Centralization

Like division of work, centralization belongs to the natural order; this turns on the fact that in every organism, animal or social, sensations converge towards the brain or directive part, and from the brain or directive part orders are sent out which set all parts of the organism in movement. Centralization is not a system of management good or bad of itself, capable of being adopted or discarded at the whim of managers or of circumstances; it is always present to a greater or lesser extent. The question of centralization or decentralization, is a simple question of proportion, it is a matter of finding the optimum degree for the particular concern. In small firms, where the manager's orders go directly to subordinates, there is absolute centralization; in large concerns, where a long scalar chain is interposed between manager and lower grades, orders and counter-information, too, have to go through a series of intermediaries. Each employee, intentionally or unintentionally, puts something of himself into the transmission and execution of orders and of information received too. He does not operate merely as a cog in a machine. What appropriate share of initiative may be left to intermediaries depends on the personal character of the manager, on his moral worth, on the reliability of his subordinates, and also on the condition of the business. The degree of centralization must vary according to different cases. The objective to pursue is the optimum utilization of all faculties of the personnel.

If the moral worth of the manager, his strength, intelligence, experience and swiftness of thought allow him to have a wide span of activities he will be able to carry centralization quite far and reduce his seconds in command to mere executive agents. If, conversely, he prefers to have greater recourse to the experience, opinions, and counsel of his colleagues whilst reserving to himself the privilege of giving general directives, he can effect considerable decentralization.

Seeing that both absolute and relative values of manager and employees are constantly changing, it is understandable that the degree of centralization or decentralization may itself vary constantly. It is a problem to be solved according to circumstances, to the best satisfaction of the interests involved. It arises, not only in the case of higher authority, but for superiors at all levels and not one but can extend or confine, to some extent, his subordinates' initiative.

The finding of the measure which shall give the best overall yield: that is the problem of centralization or decentralization. Everything which goes to increase the importance of the subordinate's role is decentralization, everything which goes to reduce it is centralization.

Scalar chain

The scalar chain is the chain of superiors ranging from the ultimate authority to the lowest ranks. The line of authority is the route followed – via every link in the chain – by all communications which start from or go to the ultimate authority. This path is dictated both by the need for some transmission and by the principle of unity of command, but it is not always the swiftest. It is even at times disastrously lengthy in large concerns, notably in governmental ones. Now, there are many activities whose success turns on speedy execution, hence respect for the line of authority must be reconciled with the need for swift action.

Let us imagine that section F has to be put into contact with section P in a business whose scalar chain is represented by the double ladder G-A-Q thus

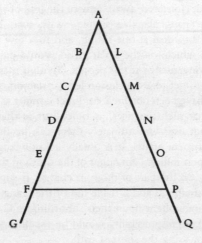

By following the line of authority the ladder must be climbed from F to A and then descended from A to P, stopping at each rung, then ascended again from P to A, and descended once more from A to F, in order to get back to the starting point. Evidently it is much simpler and quicker to go directly from F to P by making use of FP as a 'gang plank' and that is what is most often done. The scalar principle will be safeguarded if managers E and O have authorized their respective subordinates F and P to treat directly, and the position will be fully regularized if F and P inform their respective superior forthwith of what they have agreed upon. So long as

F and P remain in agreement, and so long as their actions are approved by their immediate superiors, direct contact may be maintained, but from the instant that agreement ceases or there is no approval from the superiors direct contact comes to an end, and the scalar chain is straightway resumed. Such is the actual procedure to be observed in the great majority of businesses. It provides for the usual exercise of some measure of initiative at all levels of authority. In the small concern, the general interest, viz. that of the concern proper, is easy to grasp, and the employer is present to recall this interest to those tempted to lose sight of it. In government enterprise the general interest is such a complex, vast, remote thing, that it is not easy to get a clear idea of it, and for the majority of civil servants the employer is somewhat mythical and unless the sentiment of general interest be constantly revived by higher authority, it becomes blurred and weakened and each section tends to regard itself as its own aim and end and forgets that it is only a cog in a big machine, all of whose parts must work in concert. It becomes isolated, cloistered, aware only of the line of authority.

The use of the 'gang plank' is simple, swift, sure. It allows the two employees F and P to deal at one sitting, and in a few hours, with some question or other which via the scalar chain would pass through twenty transmissions, inconvenience many people, involve masses of paper, lose weeks or months to get to a conclusion less satisfactory generally than the one which could have been obtained via direct contact as between F and P.

Is it possible that such practices, as ridiculous as they are devastating, could be in current use? Unfortunately there can be little doubt of it in government department affairs. It is usually acknowledged that the chief cause is fear of responsibility. I am rather of the opinion that it is insufficient executive capacity on the part of those in charge. If supreme authority A insisted that his assistants B and L made use of the 'gang plank' themselves and made its use incumbent upon their subordinates C and M, the habit and courage of taking responsibility would be established and at the same time the custom of using the shortest path.

It is an error to depart needlessly from the line of authority, but it is an even greater one to keep to it when detriment to the business ensues. The latter may attain extreme gravity in certain conditions. When an employee is obliged to choose between the two practices, and it is impossible for him to take advice from his superior, he should be courageous enough and feel free enough to adopt the line dictated by the general interest. But for him to be in this frame of mind there must have been previous precedent, and his superiors must have set him the example — for example must always come from above.

Order

The formula is known in the case of material things: 'A place for everything and everything in its place'. The formula is the same for human order: 'A place for everyone and everyone in his place'.

Material order

In accordance with the preceding definition, so that material order shall prevail, there must be a place appointed for each thing and each thing must be in its appointed place. Is that enough? Is it not also necessary that the place shall have been well chosen? The object of order must be avoidance of loss of material, and for this object to be completely realized not only must things be in their place suitably arranged but also the place must have been chosen so as to facilitate all activities as much as possible. If this last condition be unfulfilled, there is merely the appearance of order. Appearance of order may cover over real disorder. I have seen a works yard used as a store for steel ingots in which the material was well stacked, evenly arranged and clean and which gave a pleasing impression of orderliness. On close inspection it could be noted that the same heap included five or six types of steel intended for different manufacture all mixed up together. Whence useless handling, lost time, risk of mistakes because each thing was not in its place. It happens, on the other hand, that the appearance of disorder may actually be true order. Such is the case with papers scattered about at a master's whim which a well-meaning but incompetent servant rearranges and stacks in neat piles. The master can no longer find his way about them. Perfect order presupposes a judiciously chosen place and the appearance of order is merely a false or imperfect image of real order Cleanliness is a corollary of orderliness, there is no appointed place for dirt. A diagram representing the entire premises divided up into as many sections as there are employees responsible facilitates considerably the establishing and control of order.

Social order

For social order to prevail in a concern there must, in accordance with the definition, be an appointed place for every employee and every employee be in his appointed place. Perfect order requires, further, that the place be suitable for the employee and the employee for the place – in English idiom, 'The right man in the right place'.

Thus understood, social order presupposes the successful execution of the two most difficult managerial activities: good organization and good selection. Once the posts essential to the smooth running of the business have been decided upon and those to fill such posts have been selected, each employee occupies that post wherein he can render most service. Such is perfect social order: 'A place for each one and each one in his place'. That appears simple, and naturally we are so anxious for it to be so that when we hear for the twentieth time a government departmental head assert this principle, we conjure up straightaway a concept of perfect administration. This is a mirage.

Social order demands precise knowledge of the human requirements and resources of the concern and a constant balance between these requirements and resources. Now this balance is most difficult to establish and maintain and all the more difficult the bigger the business, and when it has been upset and individual interests resulted in neglect or sacrifice of the general interest, when ambition, nepotism, favouritism, or merely ignorance, has multiplied positions without good reason or filled them with incompetent employees, much talent and strength of will and more persistence than current instability of ministerial appointments presupposes are required in order to sweep away abuses and restore order.

As applied to government enterprise the principle of order 'A place for each one and each one in his place' takes on an astounding breadth. It means national responsibility towards each and all, everyone's destiny mapped out, national solidarity, the whole problem of society. I will stay no longer over this disturbing extension of the principle of order. In private business and especially in those of restricted scope it is easier to maintain proportion as between selection and requirements. As in the case of orderly material arrangement, a chart or plan makes the establishment and control of human arrangement much easier. This represents the personnel in entirety, and all sections of the concern together with the people occupying them. This chart will come up again in the chapter on Organization [not included].

Equity

Why equity and not justice? Justice is putting into execution established conventions, but conventions cannot foresee everything, they need to be interpreted or their inadequacy supplemented. For the personnel to be encouraged to carry out its duties with all the devotion and loyalty of which it is capable it must be treated with kindliness, and equity results from the combination of kindliness and justice. Equity excludes neither forcefulness nor sternness and the application of it requires much good sense, experience and good nature.

Desire for equity and equality of treatment are aspirations to be taken into account in dealing with employees. In order to satisfy these requirements as much as possible without neglecting any principle or losing sight of the general interest, the head of the business must frequently summon up his highest faculties. He should strive to instil sense of equity throughout all levels of the scalar chain.

Stability of tenure of personnel

Time is required for an employee to get used to new work and succeed in doing it well, always assuming that he possesses the requisite abilities. If when he has got used to it, or before then, he is removed, he will not have had time to render worthwhile service. If this be repeated indefinitely the work will never be properly done. The undesirable consequences of such insecurity of tenure are especially to be feared in large concerns, where the settling in of managers is generally a lengthy matter. Much time is needed to get to know men and things in a large concern in order to be in a position to decide on a plan of action, to gain confidence in oneself and inspire it in others. Hence it has often been recorded that a mediocre manager who stays is infinitely preferable to outstanding managers who merely come and go.

Generally the managerial personnel of prosperous concerns is stable, that of unsuccessful ones is unstable. Instability of tenure is at one and the same time cause and effect of bad running. The apprenticeship of a higher manager is generally a costly matter. Nevertheless, changes of personnel are inevitable; age, illness, retirement, death, disturb the human make-up of the firm; certain employees are no longer capable of carrying out their duties, whilst others become fit to assume greater responsibilities. In common with all the other principles, therefore, stability of tenure of personnel is also a question of proportion.

Initiative

Thinking out a plan and ensuring its success is one of the keenest satisfactions for an intelligent man to experience. It is also one of the most powerful stimulants of human endeavour. This power of thinking out and executing is what is called initiative, and freedom to propose and to execute belongs, too, each in its way, to initiative. At all levels of the organizational ladder zeal and energy on the part of employees are augmented by initiative. The initiative of all, added to that of the manager, and supplementing it if need be, represents a great source for strength for business. This is particularly apparent at difficult times; hence it is essential to encourage and develop this capacity to the full.

Much tact and some integrity are required to inspire and maintain everyone's initiative, within the limits imposed by respect for authority and for discipline. The manager must be able to sacrifice some personal vanity in order to grant this sort of satisfaction to subordinates. Other things being equal, moreover, a manager able to permit the exercise of initiative on the part of subordinates is infinitely superior to one who cannot do so.

Esprit de corps

'Union is strength'. Business heads would do well to ponder on this proverb. Harmony, union among the personnel of a concern, is great strength in that concern. Effort, then, should be made to establish it. Among the countless methods in use I will single out specially one principle to be observed and two pitfalls to be avoided. The principle to be observed is unity of command; the dangers to be avoided are (1) a misguided interpretation of the motto 'divide and rule', (2) the abuse of written communications.

1 *Personnel must not be split up*

Dividing enemy forces to weaken them is clever, but dividing one's own team is a grave sin against the business. Whether this error results from inadequate managerial capacity or imperfect grasp of things, or from egoism which sacrifices general interest to personal interest, it is always reprehensible because harmful to the business. There is no merit in sowing dissension among subordinates; any beginner can do it. On the contrary, real talent is needed to coordinate effort, encourage keenness, use each man's abilities, and reward each one's merit without arousing possible jealousies and disturbing harmonious relations.

2 Abuse of written communications

In dealing with a business matter or giving an order which requires explanation to complete it, usually it is simpler and quicker to do so verbally than in writing. Besides, it is well known that differences and misunderstandings which a conversation could clear up grow more bitter in writing. Thence it follows that, wherever possible, contacts should be verbal; there is a gain in speed, clarity and harmony. Nevertheless, it happens in some firms that employees of neighbouring departments with numerous points of contact, or even employees within a department, who could quite easily meet, only communicate with each other in writing. Hence arise increased work and complications and delays harmful to the business. At the same time, there is to be observed a certain animosity prevailing between different departments or different employees within a department. The system of written communications usually brings this result. There is a way of putting an end to this deplorable system and that is to forbid all communications in writing which could easily and advantageously be replaced by verbal ones. There again, we come up against a question of proportion.

It is not merely by the satisfactory results of harmony obtaining as between employees of the same department that the power of unity is shown: commercial agreements, unions, associations of every kind, play an important part in business management.

The part played by association has increased remarkably in half a century. I remember, in 1860, workers of primary industries without cohesion, without common bond, a veritable cloud of individual dust particles; and out of that the union has produced collective associations, meeting employers on equal terms. At that same time, bitter rivalry prevailed between large firms, closely similar, which has given place gradually to friendly relations, permitting of the settlement of most common interests by joint agreement. It is the beginning of a new era which already has profoundly modified both habits and ideas, and industrial heads should take this development into account.

There I bring to an end this review of principles, not because the list is exhausted – this list has no precise limits – but because to me it seems at the moment especially useful to endow management theory with a dozen or so well-established principles, on which it is appropriate to concentrate general discussion. The foregoing principles are those to which I have most often had recourse. I have simply expressed my personal opinion in connection with them. Are they to have a place in the management code which is to be built up? General discussion will show.

This code is indispensable. Be it a case of commerce, industry, politics, religion, war or philanthropy, in every concern there is a management function to be performed, and for its performance there must be principles, that is to say acknowledged truths regarded as proven on which to rely. And it is the code which represents the sum total of these truths at any given moment.

Surprise might be expressed at the outset that the eternal moral principles, the laws of the Decalogue and Commandments of the Church are not sufficient guide for the manager, and that a special code is needed. The explanation is this: the higher laws of religious or moral order envisage the individual only, or else interests which are not of this world, whereas management principles aim at the success of associations of individuals and at the satisfying of economic interests. Given that the aim is different, it is not surprising that the means are not the same. There is no identity, so there is no contradiction. Without principles one is in darkness and chaos; interest, experience and proportion are still very handicapped, even with the best principles. The principle is the lighthouse fixing the bearings but it can only serve those who already know the way into port.

13 F. W. Taylor

Scientific Management[1]

From *Scientific Management*, Harper & Row, 1947, pp. 39–73

What I want to try to prove to you and make clear to you is that the principles of scientific management when properly applied, and when a sufficient amount of time has been given to make them really effective, must in all cases produce far larger and better results, both for the employer and the employees, than can possibly be obtained under even this very rare type of management which I have been outlining, namely, the management of 'initiative and incentive', in which those on the management's side deliberately give a very large incentive to their workmen, and in return the workmen respond by working to the very best of their ability at all times in the interest of their employers.

I want to show you that scientific management is even far better than this rare type of management.

The first great advantage which scientific management has over the management of initiative and incentive is that under scientific management the initiative of the workmen – that is, their hard work, their good will, their ingenuity – is obtained practically with absolute regularity, while under even the best of the older type of management this initiative is only obtained spasmodically and somewhat irregularly. This obtaining, however, of the initiative of the workmen is the lesser of the two great causes which make scientific management better for both sides than the older type of management. By far the greater gain under scientific management comes from the new, the very great and the extraordinary burdens and duties which are voluntarily assumed by those on the management's side.

These new burdens and new duties are so unusual and so great that they are to the men used to managing under the old school almost inconceivable.

1. Testimony to the House of Representatives Committee, 1912.

These duties and burdens voluntarily assumed under scientific management, by those on the management's side, have been divided and classified into four different groups and these four types of new duties assumed by the management have (rightly or wrongly) been called the 'principles of scientific management'.

The first of these four groups of duties taken over by the management is the deliberate gathering in on the part of those on the management's side of all of the great mass of traditional knowledge, which in the past has been in the heads of the workmen, and in the physical skill and knack of the workmen, which they have acquired through years of experience. The duty of gathering in of all this great mass of traditional knowledge and then recording it, tabulating it and, in many cases, finally reducing it to laws, rules and even to mathematical formulae, is voluntarily assumed by the scientific managers. And later, when these laws, rules and formulae are applied to the everyday work of all the workmen of the establishment, through the intimate and hearty cooperation of those on the management's side, they invariably result, first, in producing a very much larger output per man, as well as an output of a better and higher quality; and, second, in enabling the company to pay much higher wages to their workmen; and, third, in giving to the company a larger profit. The first of these principles, then, may be called the development of a science to replace the old rule-of-thumb knowledge of the workmen; that is, the knowledge which the workmen had, and which was, in many cases, quite as exact as that which is finally obtained by the management, but which the workmen nevertheless in nine hundred and ninety-nine cases out of a thousand kept in their heads, and of which there was no permanent or complete record.

A very serious objection has been made to the use of the word 'science' in this connection. I am much amused to find that this objection comes chiefly from the professors of this country. They resent the use of the word science for anything quite so trivial as the ordinary, every-day affairs of life. I think the proper answer to this criticism is to quote the definition recently given by a professor who is, perhaps, as generally recognized as a thorough scientist as any man in the country – President McLaurin, of the Institute of Technology, of Boston. He recently defined the word science as 'classified or organized knowledge of any kind'. And surely the gathering in of knowledge which, as previously stated, has existed, but which was in an unclassified condition in the minds of workmen, and then the reducing of this knowledge to laws and rules and formulae, certainly represents the organization and classification of knowledge, even though it may not meet with the approval of some people to have it called science.

The second group of duties which are voluntarily assumed by those on the management's side, under scientific management, is the scientific selection and then the progressive development of the workmen. It becomes the duty of those on the management's side to deliberately study the character, the nature, and the performance of each workman with a view to finding out his limitations on the one hand, but even more important, his possibilities for development on the other hand; and then, as deliberately and as systematically to train and help and teach this workman, giving him, wherever it is possible, those opportunities for advancement which will finally enable him to do the highest and most interesting and most profitable class of work for which his natural abilities fit him, and which are open to him in the particular company in which he is employed. This scientific selection of the workman and his development is not a single act; it goes on from year to year and is the subject of continual study on the part of the management.

The third of the principles of scientific management is the bringing of the science and the scientifically selected and trained workmen together. I say 'bringing together' advisedly, because you may develop all the science that you please, and you may scientifically select and train workmen just as much as you please, but unless some man or some men bring the science and the workman together all your labor will be lost. We are all of us so constituted that about three-quarters of the time we will work according to whatever method suits us best; that is, we will practice the science or we will not practice it; we will do our work in accordance with the laws of the science or in our own old way, just as we see fit unless someone is there to see that we do it in accordance with the principles of the science. Therefore I use advisedly the words 'bringing the science and the workman together'. It is unfortunate, however, that this word 'bringing' has rather a disagreeable sound, a rather forceful sound; and, in a way, when it is first heard it puts one out of touch with what we have come to look upon as the modern tendency. The time for using the word 'bringing', with a sense of forcing, in relation to most matters, has gone by; but I think that I may soften this word down in its use in this particular case by saying that nine-tenths of the trouble with those of us who have been engaged in helping people to change from the older type of management to the new management – that is, to scientific management – that nine-tenths of our trouble has been to 'bring' those on the management's side to do their fair share of the work and only one-tenth of our trouble has come on the workman's side. Invariably we find very great opposition on the part of those on the management's side to do their new duties and comparatively little opposition on the part of the workmen to cooperate in doing their new duties. So that the word 'bringing' applies much more forcefully to those on the management's side than to those on the workman's side.

The fourth of the principles of scientific management is perhaps the most difficult of all of the four principles of scientific management for the average man to understand. It consists of an almost equal division of the actual work of the establishment between the workmen, on the one hand, and the management, on the other hand. That is, the work which under the old type of management practically all was done by the workman, under the new is divided into two great divisions, and one of these divisions is deliberately handed over to those on the management's side. This new division of work, this new share of the work assumed by those on the management's side, is so great that you will, I think, be able to understand it better in a numerical way when I tell you that in a machine shop, which, for instance, is doing an intricate business – I do not refer to a manufacturing company, but, rather, to an engineering company; that is, a machine shop which builds a variety of machines and is not engaged in manufacturing them, but, rather, in constructing them – will have one man on the management's side to every three workmen; that is, this immense share of the work – one-third – has been deliberately taken out of the workman's hands and handed over to those on the management's side. And it is due to this actual sharing of the work between the two sides more than to any other one element that there has never (until this last summer) been a single strike under scientific management. In a machine shop, again, under this new type of management there is hardly a single act or piece of work done by any workman in the shop which is not preceded and followed by some act on the part of one of the men in management. All day long every workman's acts are dovetailed in between corresponding acts of the management. First, the workman does something, and then a man on the management's side does something, and then the workman does something; and under this intimate, close, personal cooperation between the two sides it becomes practically impossible to have a serious quarrel.

Of course I do not wish to be understood [as saying] that there are never any quarrels under scientific management. There are some, but they are the very great exception, not the rule. And it is perfectly evident that while the workmen are learning to work under this new system, and while the management is learning to work under this new system, while they are both learning, each side to cooperate in this intimate way with the other, there is plenty of chance for disagreement and for quarrels and misunderstandings, but after both sides realize that it is utterly impossible to turn out the work of the establishment at the proper rate of speed and have it correct without this intimate, personal cooperation, when both sides realize that it is utterly impossible for either one to be successful without the intimate, brotherly cooperation of the other, the friction, the disagreements, and quarrels are reduced to a minimum. So I think that scientific management can be justly and truthfully characterized as management in which harmony is the rule rather than discord.

There is one illustration of the application of the principles of scientific management with which all of us are familiar and with which most of us have been familiar since we were small boys, and I think this instance represents one of the best illustrations of the application of the principles of scientific management. I refer to the management of a first-class American baseball team. In such a team you will find almost all of the elements of scientific management.

You will see that the science of doing every little act that is done by every player on the baseball field has been developed. Every single element of the game of baseball has been the subject of the most intimate, the closest study of many men, and finally, the best way of doing each act that takes place on the baseball field has been fairly well agreed upon and established as a standard throughout the country. The players have not only been told the best way of making each important motion or play, but they have been taught, coached and trained to it through months of drilling. And I think that every man who has watched first-class play, or who knows anything of the management of the modern baseball team, realizes fully the utter impossibility of winning with the best team of individual players that was ever gotten together unless every man on the team obeys the signals or orders of the coach and obeys them at once when the coach gives those orders; that is, without the intimate cooperation between all members of the team and the management, which is characteristic of scientific management.

Now, I have so far merely made assertions; I have merely stated facts in a dogmatic way. The most important assertion I have made is that when a company, when the men of a company and the management of a company have undergone the mental revolution that I have referred to earlier in my testimony, and that when the principles of scientific management have been applied in a correct way in any particular occupation or industry that the results must, inevitably, in all cases, be far greater and better than they could possibly be under the best of the older types of management, even under the especially fine management of 'initiative and incentive', which I have tried to outline.

I want to try and prove the above-stated fact to you gentlemen. I want to try now and make good in this assertion. My only hope of doing so lies in showing you that whenever these four principles are correctly applied to work, either large or small, to work which is either of the most elementary or the more intricate character, that inevitably results follow which are not only greater, but enormously greater, than it is possible to accomplish under the old type of management. Now, in order to make this clear I want to show the application of the four principles first to the most elementary, the simplest kind of work that I know of, and then to give a series of further illustrations of one class of work after another, each a little more difficult and a little more intricate than the work which preceded it, until I shall finally come to an illustration of the application of these same principles to about the most intricate type of mechanical work that I know of. And in all of these illustrations I hope that you will look for and see the application of the four principles I have described. Other elements of the stories may interest you, but the thing that I hope you will see and have before you in all cases is the effect of the four following elements in each particular case: First, the development of the science, i.e. the gathering in on the part of those on the management's side of all the knowledge which in the past has been kept in the heads of the workmen; second, the scientific selection and the progressive development of the workmen; third, the bringing of the science and the scientifically selected and trained men together; and, fourth, the constant and intimate cooperation which always occurs between the men on the management's side and the workmen.

I ordinarily begin with a description of the pig-iron handler. For some reason, I don't know exactly why, this illustration has been talked about a great deal, so much, in fact, that some people seem to think that the whole of scientific management consists in handling pig-iron. The only reason that I ever gave this illustration, however, was that pig-iron handling is the simplest kind of human effort; I know of nothing that is quite so simple as handling pig-iron. A man simply stoops down and with his hands picks up a piece of iron, and then walks a short distance and drops it on the ground. Now, it doesn't look as if there was very much room for the development of a science; it doesn't seem as if there was much room here for the scientific selection of the man nor for his progressive training, nor for cooperation between the two sides; but, I can say, without the slightest hesitation, that the science of handling pig-iron is so great that the man who is fit to handle pig-iron as his daily work cannot possibly understand that science; the man who is physically able to handle pig-iron and is sufficiently phlegmatic and stupid to choose this for his occupation is rarely able to comprehend the science of handling pig-iron; and this inability of the man who is fit to do the work to understand the science of doing his work becomes more and more evident as the work becomes more complicated, all the way up the scale. I assert, without the slightest hesitation, that the high-class mechanic has a far smaller chance of ever thoroughly understanding the science of his work than the pig-iron handler has of understanding the science of his work, and I am going to try and prove to your satisfaction, gentlemen, that the law is almost universal – not entirely so, but nearly so – that the man who is fit to work at any particular trade is unable to understand the science of that trade without the kindly help and cooperation of men of a totally different type of education, men whose education is not necessarily higher but a different type from his own.

I dare say most of you gentlemen are familiar with pig-iron handling and with the illustration I have used in connection with it, so I won't take up any of your time with that. But I want to show you how these principles may be applied to some one of the lower classes of work. You may think I am a little highfalutin when I speak about what may be called the atmosphere of scientific management, the relations that ought to exist between both sides, the intimate and friendly relations that should exist between employee and employer. I want, however, to emphasize this as one of the most important features of scientific management, and I can hardly do so without going into detail, without explaining minutely the duties of both sides, and for this reason I want to take some of your time in explaining the application of these four principles of scientific management to one of the cheaper kinds of work, for instance, to shoveling. This is one of the simplest kinds of work, and I want to give you an illustration of the application of these principles to it.

Now, gentlemen, shoveling is a great science compared with pig-iron handling. I dare say that most of you gentlemen know that a good many pig-iron handlers can never learn to shovel right; the ordinary pig-iron handler is not the type of man well suited to shoveling. He is too stupid; there is too much mental strain, too much knack required of a shoveler for the pig-iron handler to take kindly to shoveling.

You gentlemen may laugh, but that is true, all right; it sounds ridiculous, I know, but it is a fact. Now, if the problem were put up to any of you men to develop the science of shoveling as it was put up to us, that is, to a group of men who had deliberately set out to develop the science of doing all kinds of laboring work, where do you think you would begin? When you started to study the science of shoveling I make the assertion that you would be within two days – just as we were within two days – well on the way toward development of the science of shoveling. At least you would have outlined in your minds those elements which required careful, scientific study in order to understand the science of shoveling. I do not want to go into all the details of shoveling, but I will give you some of the elements, one or two of the most important elements of the science of shoveling; that is, the elements that reach further and have more serious consequences than any other. Probably the most important element in the science of shoveling is this: there must be some shovel load at which a first-class shoveler will do his biggest day's work. What is that load? To illustrate: when we went to the Bethlehem Steel Works and observed the shovelers in the yard of that company, we found that each of the good shovelers in that yard owned his own shovel; they preferred to buy their own shovels rather than to have the company furnish them. There was a larger tonnage of ore shoveled in that works than of any other material and rice coal came next in tonnage. We would see a first-class shoveler go from shoveling rice coal with a load of $3\frac{1}{2}$ pounds to the shovel to handling ore from the Massaba Range, with 38 pounds to the shovel. Now, is $3\frac{1}{2}$ pounds the proper shovel load or is 38 pounds the proper shovel load? They cannot both be right. Under scientific management the answer to this question is not a matter of anyone's opinion; it is a question for accurate, careful, scientific investigation.

Under the old system you would call in a first-rate shoveler and say, 'See here, Pat, how much ought you to take on at one shovel load?' And if a couple of fellows agreed, you would say that's about the right load and let it go at that. But under scientific management absolutely every element in the work of every man in your establishment, sooner or later, becomes the subject of exact, precise, scientific investigation and knowledge to replace the old, 'I believe so', and 'I guess so'. Every motion, every small fact becomes the subject of careful, scientific investigation.

What we did was to call in a number of men to pick from, and from these we selected two first-class shovelers. Gentlemen, the words I used were 'first-class shovelers'. I want to emphasize that. Not poor shovelers. Not men unsuited to their work, but first-class shovelers. These men were then talked to in about this way, 'See here, Pat and Mike, you fellows understand your job all right; both of you fellows are first-class men; you know what we think of you; you are all right now; but we want to pay you fellows double wages. We are going to ask you to do a lot of damn fool things, and when you are doing them there is going to be someone out alongside of you all the time, a young chap with a piece of paper and a stop watch and pencil, and all day long he will tell you to do these fool things, and he will be writing down what you are doing and snapping the watch on you and all that sort of business. Now, we just want to know whether you fellows want to go into that bargain or not? If you want double wages while that is going on all right, we will pay you double; if you don't, all right, you needn't take the job unless you want to; we just called you in to see whether you want to work this way or not.

'Let me tell you fellows just one thing: If you go into this bargain, if you go at it, just remember that on your side we want no monkey business of any kind; you fellows will have to play square; you fellows will have to do just what you are supposed to be doing; not a damn bit of soldiering on your part; you must do a fair day's work; we don't want any rushing, only a fair day's work and you know what that is as well as we do. Now, don't take this job unless you agree to these conditions, because if you start to try to fool this same young chap with the pencil and paper he will be onto you in fifteen minutes from the time you try to fool him, and just as surely as he reports you fellows as soldiering you will go out of this works and you will never get in again. Now, don't take this job unless you want to accept these conditions; you need not do it unless you want to; but if you do, play fair.'

Well, these fellows agreed to it, and, as I have found almost universally to be the case, they kept their word absolutely and faithfully. My experience with workmen has been that their word is just as good as the word of any other set of men that I know of, and all you have to do is to have a clear, straight, square understanding with them and you will get just as straight and fair a deal from them as from any other set of men. In this way the shoveling experiment was started. My rememberance is that we first started them on work that was very heavy, work requiring a very heavy shovel load. What we did was to give them a certain kind of heavy material ore, I think, to handle with a certain size of shovel. We sent these two men into different parts of the yards, with two different men to time and study them, both sets of men being engaged on the same class of work. We made all the conditions the same for both pairs of men, so as to be sure that there was no error in judgement on the part of either of the observers and that they were normal, first-class men.

The number of shovel loads which each man handled in the course of the day was counted and written down. At the end of the day the total tonnage of the material handled by each man was weighed and this weight was divided by the number of shovel loads handled, and in that way, my remembrance is, our first experiment showed that the average shovel load handled was thirty-eight pounds, and that with this load on the shovel the man handled, say, about twenty-five tons per day. We then cut the shovel off, making it somewhat shorter, so that instead of shoveling a load of thirty-eight pounds it held a load of approximately thirty-four pounds. The average, then, with the thirty-four pound load, of each man went up, and instead of handling twenty-five he had handled thirty tons per day. These figures are merely relative, used to illustrate the general principles, and I do not mean that they were the exact figures. The shovel was again cut off, and the load made approximately thirty pounds, and again the tonnage ran up, and again the shovel load was reduced, and the tonnage handled per day increased, until at about twenty-one or twenty-two pounds per shovel we found that these men were doing their largest day's work. If you cut the shovel load off still more, say until it averages eighteen pounds instead of twenty-one and a half, the tonnage handled per day will begin to fall off, and at sixteen pounds it will be still lower, and so on right down. Very well; we now have developed the scientific fact that a workman well suited to his job, what we call a first-class shoveler, will do his largest day's work when he has a shovel load of twenty-one and a half pounds.

Now, what does that fact amount to? At first it may not look to be a fact of much importance, but let us see what it amounted to right there in the yard of the Bethlehem Steel Co. Under the old system, as I said before, the workmen owned their shovels, and the shovel was the same size whatever the kind of work. Now, as a matter of common sense, we saw at once that it was necessary to furnish each workman each day with a shovel which would hold just twenty-one and a half pounds of the particular material which he was called upon to shovel. A small shovel for the heavy material, such as ore, and a large scoop for light material, such as ashes. That meant, also, the building of a large shovel room, where all kinds of laborers' implements were stored. It meant having an ample supply of each type of shovel, so that all the men who might be called upon to use a certain type in any one day could be supplied with a shovel of the size desired that would hold just twenty-one and a half pounds. It meant, further, that each day each laborer should be given a particular kind of work to which he was suited, and that he must be provided with a particular shovel suited to that kind of work, whereas in the past all the laborers in the yard of the Bethlehem Steel Co. had been handled in masses, or in great groups of men, by the old-fashioned foreman, who had from twenty-five to one hundred men under him and walked them from one part of the yard to another. You must realize that the yard of the Bethlehem Steel Co. at that time was a very large yard. I should say that it was at least one and a half or two miles long and, we will say, a quarter to a half mile wide, so it was a good large yard; and in that yard at all times an immense variety of shoveling was going on.

There was comparatively little standard shoveling which went on uniformly from day to day. Each man was likely to be moved from place to place about the yard several times in the course of the day. All of this involved keeping in the shovel room ten or fifteen kinds of shovels, ranging from a very small flat shovel for handling ore up to immense scoops for handling rice coal, and forks with which to handle the coke, which, as you know, is very light. It meant the study and development of the implement best suited to each type of material to be shoveled, and assigning, with the minimum of trouble, the proper shovel to each one of the four to six hundred laborers at work in that yard. Now, that meant mechanism, human mechanism. It meant organizing and planning work at least a day in advance. And, gentlemen, here is an important fact, that the greatest difficulty which we met with in this planning did not come from the workmen. It came from the management's side. Our greatest difficulty was to get the heads of the various departments each day to inform the men in the labor office what kind of work and how much of it was to be done on the following day.

This planning the work one day ahead involved the building of a labor office where before there was no such thing. It also involved the equipping of that office with large maps showing the layout of the yards so that the movements of the men from one part of the yard to another could be laid out in advance, so that we could assign to this little spot in the yard a certain number of men and to another part of the yard another set of men, each group to do a certain kind of work. It was practically like playing a game of chess in which four to six hundred men were moved about so as to be in the right place at the right time. And all this, gentlemen, follows from the one idea of developing the science of shoveling; the idea that you must give each workman each day a job to which he is well suited and provide him with just that implement which will enable him to do his biggest day's work. All this, as I have tried to make clear to you, is the result that followed from the one act of developing the science of shoveling.

In order that our workmen should get their share of the good that came from the development of the science of shoveling and that we should do what we set out to do with our laborers – namely, pay them 60 per cent higher wages than were paid to any similar workmen around the whole district. Before we could pay them these extra high wages it was necessary for us to be sure that we had first-class men and that each laborer was well suited to his job, because the only way in which you can pay wages 60 per cent higher than other people pay and not overwork your men is by having each man properly suited and well trained to his job. Therefore, it became necessary to carefully select these yard laborers; and in order that the men should join with us heartily and help us in their selection it became necessary for us to make it possible for each man to know each morning as he came in to work that on the previous day he had earned his 60 per cent premium, or that he had failed to do so. So here again comes in a lot of work to be done by the management that had not been done before. The first thing each workman did when he came into the yard in the morning – and I may say that a good many of them could not read and write – was to take two pieces of paper out of his pigeonhole; if they were both white slips of paper, the workman knew he was all right. One of those slips of paper informed the man in charge of the tool room what implement the workman was to use on his first job and also in what part of the yard he was to work. It was in this way that each one of the 600 men in that yard received his orders for the kind of work he was to do and the implement with which he was to do it, and he was also sent right to the part of the yard where he was to work, without any delay whatever. The old-fashioned way was for the workmen to wait until the foreman got good and ready and had found out by asking some of the heads of departments what work he was to do, and then he would lead the gang off to some part of the yard and go to work. Under the new method each man gets his orders almost automatically; he goes right to the tool room, gets the proper implement for the work he is to do, and goes right to the spot where he is to work without any delay.

The second piece of paper, if it was a white piece of paper, showed this man that he had earned his 60 per cent higher wages; if it was a yellow piece of paper the workman knew that he had not earned enough to be a first-class man, and that within two or three days something would happen, and he was absolutely certain what this something would be. Every one of them knew that after he had received three or four yellow slips a teacher would be sent down to him from the labor office. Now, gentlemen, this teacher was no college professor. He was a teacher of shoveling; he understood the science of shoveling; he was a good shoveler himself, and he knew how to teach other men to be good shovelers. This is the sort of man who was sent out of the labor office. I want to emphasize the following point, gentlemen: The workman, instead of hating the teacher who came to him – instead of looking askance at him and saying to himself, 'Here comes one of those damn nigger drivers to drive me to work' – looked upon him as one of the best friends he had around there. He knew that he came out there to help him, not to nigger drive him. Now, let me show you what happens. The teacher comes, in every case, not to bulldoze the man, not to drive him to harder work than he can do, but to try in a friendly, brotherly way to help him, so he says, 'Now, Pat, something has gone wrong with you. You know no workman who is not a high-priced workman can stay on this gang, and you will have to get off of it if we can't find out what is the matter with you. I believe you have forgotten how to shovel right. I think that's all there is the matter with you. Go ahead and let me watch you awhile. I want to see if you know how to do the damn thing, anyway.'

Now, gentlemen, I know you will laugh when I talk again about the science of shoveling. I dare say some of you have done some shoveling. Whether you have or not, I am going to try to show you something about the science of shoveling, and if any of you have done much shoveling, you will understand that there is a good deal of science about it.

There is a good deal of refractory stuff to shovel around a steel works; take ore, or ordinary bituminous coal, for instance. It takes a good deal of effort to force the shovel down into either of these materials from the top of the pile, as you have to when you are unloading a car. There is one right way of forcing the shovel into materials of this sort, and many wrong ways. Now, the way to shovel refractory stuff is to press the forearm hard against the upper part of the right leg just below the thigh, like this (indicating), take the end of the shovel in your right hand and when you push the shovel into the pile, instead of using the muscular effort of your arms, which is tiresome, throw the weight of your body on the shovel like this (indicating); that pushes your shovel in the pile with hardly any exertion and without tiring the arms in the least. Nine out of ten workmen who try to push a shovel in a pile of that sort will use the strength of their arms, which involves more than twice the necessary exertion. Any of you men who don't know this fact just try it. This is one illustration of what I mean when I speak of the science of shoveling, and there are many similar elements of this science. Now, this teacher would find, time and time again, that the shoveler had simply forgotten how to shovel; that he had drifted back to his old wrong and inefficient way of shoveling, which prevented him from earning his 60 per cent higher wages. So he would say to him, 'I see all that is the matter with you is that you have forgotten how to shovel; you have forgotten what I showed you about shoveling some time ago. Now, watch me,' he says, 'this is the way to do the thing.' And the teacher would stay by him, two, three, four or five days, if necessary, until he got the man back again into the habit of shoveling right.

Now, gentlemen, I want you to see clearly that, because that is one of the characteristic features of scientific management; this is not nigger driving; this is kindness; this is teaching; this is doing what I would like mighty well to have done to me if I were a boy trying to learn how to do something. This is not a case of cracking a whip over a man and saying, 'Damn you, get there'. The old way of treating with workmen, on the other hand, even with a good foreman, would have been something like this: 'See here, Pat, I have sent for you to come up here to the office to see me; four or five times now you have not earned your 60 per cent increase in wages; you know that every workman in this place has got to earn 60 per cent more wages than they pay in any other place around here, but you're no good and that's all there is to it; now, get out of this.' That's the old way. 'You are no good; we have given you a fair chance; get out of this', and the workman is pretty lucky if it isn't 'get to hell out of this', instead of 'get out of this'.

The new way is to teach and help your man as you would a brother; to try to teach him the best way and show him the easiest way to do his work. This is the new mental attitude of the management toward the men, and that is the reason I have taken so much of your time in describing this cheap work of shoveling. It may seem to you a matter of very little consequence, but I want you to see, if I can, that this new mental attitude is the very essence of scientific management; that the mechanism is nothing if you have not got the right sentiment, the right attitude in the minds of the men, both on the management's side and on the workman's side. Because this helps to explain the fact that until this summer there has never been a strike under scientific management.

The men who developed the science of shoveling spent, I should say, four or five months studying the subject and during that time they investigated not only the best and most efficient movements that the men should make when they are shoveling right, but they also studied the proper time for doing each of the elements of the science of shoveling. There are many other elements which go to make up this science, but I will not take up your time describing them.

Now, all of this costs money. To pay the salaries of men who are studying the science of shoveling is an expensive thing. As I remember it there were two college men who studied this science of shoveling and also the science of doing many other kinds of laboring work during a period of about three years; then there were a lot of men in the labor office whose wages had to be paid, men who were planning the work which each laborer was to do at least a day in advance; clerks who worked all night so that each workman might know the next morning when he went to work just what he had accomplished and what he had earned the day before; men who wrote out the proper instructions for the day's work for each workman. All of this costs money; it costs money to measure or weigh up the materials handled by each man each day. Under the old method the work of fifty or sixty men was weighed up together; the work done by a whole gang was measured together. But under scientific management we are dealing with individual men and not with gangs of men. And in order to study and develop each man you must measure accurately each man's work. At first we were told that this would be impossible. The former managers of this work told me 'You cannot possibly measure up the work of each individual laborer in this yard; you might be able to do it in a small yard, but our work is of such an intricate nature that it is impossible to do it here.'

I want to say that we had almost no trouble in finding some cheap way of measuring up each man's work, not only in that yard but throughout the entire plant.

But all of that costs money, and it is a very proper question to ask whether it pays or whether it doesn't pay, because, let me tell you, gentlemen, at once, and I want to be emphatic about it, scientific management has nothing in it that is philanthropic; I am not objecting to philanthropy, but any scheme of management which has philanthropy as one of its elements ought to fail; philanthropy has no part in any scheme of management. No self-respecting workman wants to be given things, every man wants to earn things, and scientific management is no scheme for giving people something they do not earn. So, if the principles of scientific management do not pay, then this is a miserable system. The final test of any system is, does it pay?

At the end of some three and a half years we had the opportunity of proving whether or not scientific management did pay in its application to yard labor. When we went to the Bethlehem Steel Co. we found from 400 to 600 men at work in that yard, and when we got through 140 men were doing the work of the 400 to 600, and these men handled several million tons of material a year.

We were very fortunate to be able to get accurate statistics as to the cost of handling a ton of materials in that yard under the old system and under the new. Under the old system the cost of handling a ton of materials had been running between seven and eight cents, and all you gentlemen familiar with railroad work know that this is a low figure for handling materials. Now, after paying for all the clerical work which was necessary under the new system for the time study and the teachers, for building and running the labor office and the implement room, for constructing a telephone system for moving men about the yard, for a great variety of duties not performed under the old system, after paying for all these things incident to the development of the science of shoveling and managing the men the new way, and including the wages of the workmen, the cost of handling a ton of material was brought down from between seven and eight cents to between three and four cents, and the actual saving, during the last six months of the three and one-half years I was there, was at the rate of $78,000 a year. That is what the company got out of it; while the men who were on the labor gang received an average of sixty per cent more wages than their brothers got or could get anywhere around that part of the country. And none of them were overworked, for it is no part of scientific management ever to overwork any man; certainly overworking these men could not have been done with the knowledge of anyone connected with scientific management, because one of the first requirements of scientific management is that no man shall ever be given a job which he cannot do and thrive under through a long term of years. It is no part of scientific management to drive anyone. At the end of three years we had men talk to and investigate all of these yard laborers and we found that they were almost universally satisfied with their jobs.

Of course certain men are permanent grouches and when we run across that kind we all know what to expect. But, in the main, they were the most satisfied and contented set of laborers I have ever seen anywhere; they lived better than they did before, and most of them were saving a little money; their families lived better, and as to having any grouch against their employers, those fellows, every one, looked upon them as the best friends they ever had, because they taught them how to earn 60 per cent more wages than they had ever earned before. This is the round-up of both sides of this question. If the use of the system does not make both sides happier, then it is no good.

To give you one illustration of the application of scientific management to a rather high class of work, gentlemen, bricklaying, so far as I know, is one of the oldest of the trades, and it is a truly extraordinary fact that bricks are now laid just about as they were two thousand years before Christ. In

England they are laid almost exactly as they were then; in England the scaffold is still built with timbers lashed together – in many cases with the bark still on it – just as we see that the scaffolds were made in old stone-cut pictures of bricklaying before the Christian era. In this country we have gone beyond the lashed scaffold, and yet in most respects it is almost literally true that bricks are still laid as they were four thousand years ago. Virtually the same trowel, virtually the same brick, virtually the same mortar, and, from the way in which they were laid, according to one of my friends, who is a brick work contractor and a student of the subject, who took the trouble to take down some bricks laid four thousand years ago to study the way in which the mortar was spread, etc., it appears that they even spread the mortar in the same way then as we do now. If, then, there is any trade in which one would say that the principles of scientific management would produce but small results, that the development of the science would do little good, it would be in a trade which thousands and thousands of men through successive generations had worked and had apparently reached, as far as methods and principles were concerned, the highest limit of efficiency four thousand years ago. In bricklaying this would seem to be true since practically no progress has been made in this art since that time. Therefore, viewed broadly, one would say that there was a smaller probability that the principles of scientific management could accomplish notable results in this trade than in almost any other.

Mr Frank Gilbreth is a man who in his youth worked as a bricklayer; he was an educated man and is now a very successful contractor. He said to me, some years ago, 'Now, Taylor, I am a contractor, putting up all sorts of buildings, and if there is one thing I know it is bricklaying; I can go out right now, and I am not afraid to back myself, to beat any man I know of laying bricks for ten minutes, both as to speed and accuracy; you may think I am blowing, but that is one way I got up in the world. I cannot stand it now for more than ten minutes; I'm soft; my hands are tender, I haven't been handling bricks for years, but for ten minutes I will back myself against anyone. I want to ask you about this scientific management; do you think it can be applied to bricklaying? Do you believe that these things you have been shouting about (at that time it was called the 'task system'), do you believe these principles can be applied to bricklaying?' 'Certainly,' I said, 'some day some fellow will make the same kind of study about bricklaying that we have made of other things, and he will get the same results.' 'Well,' he said, 'if you really think so, I will just tell you who is going to do it, his name is Frank Gilbreth.'

I think it was about three years later that he came to me and said: 'Now,

I'm going to show you something about bricklaying. I have spent three years making a motion and time study of bricklaying, and not I alone did it; my wife has also spent almost the same amount of her time studying the problems of bricklaying, and I think she has made her full share of the progress which has been made in the science of bricklaying.' Then he said, 'I will show you just how we went to work at it. Let us assume that I am now standing on the scaffold in the position that the bricklayer occupies when he is ready to begin work. The wall is here on my left, the bricks are there in a pile on the scaffold to my right, and the mortar is here on the mortar-board alongside of the bricks. Now, I take my stand as a bricklayer and am ready to start to lay bricks, and I said to myself, "What is the first movement that I make when I start to lay bricks?" I take a step to the right with the right foot. Well, is that movement necessary? It took me a year and a half to cut out that motion – that step to the right – and I will tell you later how I cut it out. Now, what motion do I make next? I stoop down to the floor to the pile of bricks and disentangle a brick from the pile and pick it up off the pile. "My God," I said, "that is nothing short of barbarous." Think of it! Here I am a man weighing over 250 pounds, and every time I stoop down to pick up a brick I lower 250 pounds of weight down two feet so as to pick up a brick weighing four pounds, and then raise my 250 pounds of weight up again, and all of this to lift up a brick weighing four pounds. Think of this waste of effort. It is monstrous. It took me – it may seem to you a pretty long while – but it took a year and a half of thought and work to cut out that motion; when I finally cut it out, however, it was done in such a simple way that anyone in looking at the method which I adopted would say, "There is no invention in that, any fool could do that; why did you take a year and a half to do a little thing like that?" Well, all I did was to put a table on the scaffold right alongside of me here on my right side and put the bricks and mortar on it, so as to keep them at all times at the right height, thus making it unnecessary to stoop down in picking them up. This table was placed in the middle of the scaffold with the bricklayer on one side of it, and with a walkway on the other side along which the bricks were brought by wheelbarrow or by hod to be placed on the table without interfering with the bricklayer or even getting in his way.' Then Mr Gilbreth made his whole scaffold adjustable, and a laborer was detailed to keep all of the scaffolds at all times at such a height that as the wall goes up the bricks, the mortar, and the men will occupy that position in which the work can be done with the least effort.

Mr Gilbreth has studied out the best position for each of the bricklayer's feet and for every type of bricklaying the exact position for the feet is fixed so that the man can do his work without unnecessary movements. As a result of further study both on the part of Mr and Mrs Gilbreth, after the bricks are unloaded from the cars and before bringing them to the bricklayer they are carefully sorted by a laborer and placed with their best edges up on a simple wooden frame, constructed so as to enable him to take hold of each brick in the quickest time and in the most advantageous position. In this way the bricklayer avoids either having to turn the brick over or end for end to examine it before laying it, and he saves also the time taken in deciding which is the best edge and end to place on the outside of the wall. In most cases, also, he saves the time taken in disentangling the brick from a disorderly pile on the scaffold. This 'pack of bricks', as Mr Gilbreth calls his loaded wooden frames, is placed by the helper in its proper position on the adjustable scaffold close to the mortar box.

We have all been used to seeing bricklayers tap each brick after it is placed on its bed of mortar several times with the end of the handle of the trowel so as to secure the right thickness for the joint. Mr Gilbreth found that by tempering the mortar just right the bricks could be readily bedded to the proper depth by a downward pressure of the hand which lays them. He insisted that the mortar mixers should give special attention to tempering the mortar and so save the time consumed in tapping the brick.

In addition to this he taught his bricklayers to make simple motions with both hands at the same time, where before they completed a motion with the right hand before they followed it later with one made by the left hand. For example, Mr Gilbreth taught his ᴜicklayers to pick up a brick in the left hand at the same time that he takes a trowel of mortar with the right hand. This work with two hands at the same time is, of course, made possible by substituting a deep mortar box for the old mortar-board, on which the mortar used to spread out so thin that a step or two had to be taken to reach it, and then placing the mortar box and the brick pile close together and at the proper height on his new scaffold.

Now, what was the practical outcome of all this study? To sum it up he finally succeeded in teaching his bricklayers, when working under the new method, to lay bricks with five motions per brick, while with the old method they used eighteen motions per brick. And, in fact, in one exceedingly simple type of bricklaying he reduced the motions of his bricklayers from eighteen to two motions per brick. But in the ordinary bricklaying he reduced the motions from eighteen to five. When he first came to me, after he had made this long and elaborate study of the motions of bricklayers, he had accomplished nothing in a practical way through this study, and he said, 'You know, Fred, I have been showing all my friends these new methods of laying bricks and they say to me, "Well, Frank, this is a beautiful thing to talk about, but what in the devil do you think it amounts to? You know perfectly well the unions have forbidden their members to lay more than so many bricks per day; you know they won't allow this thing to be carried out." ' But Gilbreth said, 'Now, my dear boy, that doesn't make an iota of difference to me. I'm just going to see that the bricklayers do the right thing. I belong to the bricklayers' union in Boston, and the next job that I get in Boston this thing goes through. I'm not going to do it in any underhanded way. Everyone knows that I have always paid higher wages than the union scale in Boston. I've got a lot of friends at the head of the unions in Boston, and I'm not afraid of having any trouble.'

He got his job near Boston, and he went to the leaders of the union and told them just what you can tell any set of sensible men. He said to them, 'I want to tell you fellows some things that you ought to know. Most of my contracts around here used to be brick jobs; now, most of my work is in reinforced concrete or some other type of construction, but I am first and last a bricklayer; that is what I am interested in, and if you have any sense you will just keep your hands off and let me show you bricklayers how to compete with the reinforced concrete men. I will handle the bricklayers myself. All I want of you leaders is to keep your hands off and I will show you how bricklayers can compete with reinforced concrete or any other type of construction that comes along.'

Well, the leaders of the union thought that sounded all right, and then he went to the workmen and said to them, 'No fellow can work for me for less than $6·50 a day – the union rate was $5 a day – but every man who gets on this job has got to lay bricks my way; I will put a teacher on the job to show you all my way of laying bricks and I will give every man plenty of time to learn, but after a bricklayer has had a sufficient trial at this thing, if he won't do my way or cannot do my way, he must get off the job.' Any number of bricklayers were found to be only too glad to try the job, and I think he said that before the first storey of the building was up he had the whole gang trained to work in the new way, and all getting their $6·50 a day when before they only received $5 per day; I believe those are the correct figures; I am not absolutely sure about that, but at least he paid them a very liberal premium above the average bricklayer's pay.

It is one of the principles of scientific management to ask men to do things in the right way, to learn something new, to change their ways in accordance with the science, and in return to receive an increase of from 30 to 100 per cent in pay, which varies according to the nature of the business in which they are engaged.

14 H. Mintzberg

The Manager's Job: Folklore and Fact

From *Harvard Business Review*, July–August 1975, pp. 49–61

If you ask a manager what he does, he will most likely tell you that he plans, organizes, coordinates, and controls. Then watch what he does. Don't be surprised if you can't relate what you see to these four words.

When he is rung up and told that one of his factories has just burned down, and he advises the caller to see whether temporary arrangements can be made to supply customers through a foreign subsidiary, is he planning, organizing, coordinating, or controlling? What about when he presents a gold watch to a retiring employee? Or when he attends a conference to meet people in the trade? Or, on returning from that conference, when he tells one of his employees about an interesting product idea he picked up there? The fact is that these four words, which have dominated management vocabulary since the French industrialist Henri Fayol first introduced them in 1916, tell us little about what managers actually do. At best, they indicate some vague objectives managers have when they work.

The field of management, so devoted to progress and change, has for more than half a century not seriously addressed the basic question, 'What do managers do?' Without a proper answer, how can we teach management? How can we design planning or information systems for managers? How can we improve the practice of management at all?

Our ignorance of the nature of managerial work shows up in various ways in the modern organization – in the boast by the successful manager that he has never spent a single day in a management-training program; in the turnover of corporate planners who have never quite understood what it is the manager wants; in the computer consoles gathering dust in the back room because the managers never use the fancy on-line MIS some analyst thought they needed. Perhaps most importantly, our ignorance shows up in the inability of our large public organizations to come to grips with some of their most serious policy problems.

Somehow, in the rush to automate production, to use management science in the functional areas of marketing and finance, and to apply the skills of the behavioral scientist to the problem of worker motivation, the manager – that person in charge of the organization or one of its subunits – has been forgotten.

My intention in this article is simple: to break the reader away from Fayol's words and to introduce him to a more supportable, and what I believe to be a more useful, description of managerial work. This description derives from my review and synthesis of the available research on how various managers have spent their time.

In some studies, managers were observed intensively ('shadowed' is the word some of them used); in a number of others, they kept detailed diaries of their activities; in a few studies, their records were analysed. All kinds of managers were studied – foremen, factory supervisors, staff managers, field sales managers, hospital administrators, presidents of companies and nations, and even street gang leaders. These 'managers' worked in the United States, Canada, Sweden and Great Britain. At the end of this article I have given a brief review of the major studies that I found most useful in developing this description, including my own study of five American chief-executive officers.

A synthesis of these findings paints an interesting picture, one as different from Fayol's classical view as a cubist abstract is from a Renaissance painting. In a sense this picture will be obvious to anyone who has ever spent a day in a manager's office, whether in front of the desk or behind it. Yet at the same time this picture may turn out to be revolutionary, in that it throws doubt upon so much of the folklore that we have accepted about the manager's work.

I will first discuss some of this folklore and contrast it with some of the discoveries of systematic research – the hard facts about how managers spend their time. I will then synthesize these research findings in a description of ten roles that seem to describe the essential content of all managers' jobs. In a concluding section, I will discuss a number of implications of this synthesis for those trying to achieve more effective management, both in classrooms and in the business world.

Some folklore and facts about managerial work

There are four myths about the manager's job that do not withstand careful scrutiny of the facts.

1. *Folklore: 'The manager is a reflective, systematic planner.'* The evidence on this issue is overwhelming, but not a shred of it supports this statement.

Fact: study after study has shown that managers work at an unrelenting pace, that their activities are characterized by brevity, variety and discontinuity, and that they are strongly orientated towards action and dislike reflective activities. Consider the following evidence.

Half the activities engaged in by the five chief executives of my study lasted less than nine minutes and only 10 per cent exceeded one hour (all the data from my study can be found in Mintzberg, 1973). A study of fifty-six US foremen found that they averaged 583 activities per eight-hour shift, an average of one every forty-eight seconds (R. H. Guest, 1956). The work pace for both chief executives and foremen was unrelenting. The chief executives met a steady stream of callers and mail from the moment they arrived in the morning until they left in the evening. Coffee breaks and lunches were inevitably work-related, and ever-present subordinates seemed to usurp any free moment. A diary study of 160 British middle and top managers found that they worked for half an hour or more without interruption about once every two days (R. Stewart, 1967; see also S. Carlson, 1951, the first of the diary studies).

Of the verbal contacts of the chief executives in my study, 93 per cent were arranged on an ad hoc basis. Only 1 per cent of the executives' time was spent in open-ended observational tours. Only one out of 368 verbal contacts was unrelated to a specific issue and could be called general planning. Another researcher finds that '*in not one single case* did a manager report the obtaining of important external information from a general conversation or other undirected personal communication' (F. J. Aguilar, 1967, p. 102). No study has found important patterns in the way managers schedule their time. They seem to jump from issue to issue, continually responding to the needs of the moment.

Is this the planner that the classical view describes? Hardly. How, then, can we explain this behaviour? The manager is simply responding to the pressures of his job. I found that my chief executives terminated many of their own activities, often leaving meetings before the end, and interrupted their desk work to call in subordinates. One president not only placed his desk so that he could look down a long hallway but also left his door open when he was alone – an invitation for subordinates to come in and interrupt him.

Clearly, these managers wanted to encourage the flow of current information. But more significantly, they seemed to be conditioned by their own work loads. They appreciated the opportunity cost of their own time, and they were continually aware of their ever-present obligations: mail to be answered, callers to attend to, and so on. It seems that no matter what he is doing, the manager is plagued by both what he might do and what he must do.

When the manager must plan, he seems to do so implicitly in the context of daily actions, not in some abstract process reserved for two weeks in the organization's mountain retreat. The plans of the chief executives I studied seemed to exist only in their heads – as flexible, but often specific, intentions. The traditional literature notwithstanding, the job of managing does not breed reflective planners; the manager responds to stimuli as an individual who is conditioned by his job to prefer live to delayed action.

2. *Folklore: 'The effective manager has no regular duties to perform.'* Managers are constantly being told to spend more time planning and delegating, and less time seeing customers and engaging in negotiations. These are not, after all, the true tasks of the manager. To use the popular analogy, the good manager, like the good conductor, carefully orchestrates everything in advance, then sits back to enjoy the fruits of his labor, responding occasionally to an unforeseeable exception. But here again the pleasant abstraction just does not seem to hold. We had better take a closer look at those activities in which managers feel compelled to engage before we arbitrarily define them away.

Fact: in addition to handling exceptions, managerial work involves performing a number of regular duties, including ritual and ceremony, negotiations, and processing soft information that links the organization with its environment. Consider some evidence from the research studies.

A study of the work of the presidents of small companies found that they engaged in routine activities because their companies could not afford staff specialists and were so thin on operating personnel that a single absence often required the president to substitute.[1] One study of field sales managers

---

1. Unpublished study by Irving Choran, reported in Mintzberg (1973).

and another of chief executives suggest that it is a natural part of both jobs to see important customers, assuming the managers wish to keep those customers (R. T. Davis, 1957, and G. H. Copeman, 1963).

Someone once described the manager only half in jest as that person who sees visitors so that everyone else can get his work done. In my study, I found that certain ceremonial duties – meeting visiting dignitaries, giving out gold watches, presiding at Christmas dinners – were an intrinsic part of the chief executive's job.

Studies of managers' information-flow suggest that managers play a key role in securing 'soft' external information (much of it available only to them because of their status) and passing it along to their subordinates.

3. Folklore: 'The senior manager needs aggregated information, which a formal management-information system best provides.' Not too long ago, the words total-information system were everywhere in the management literature. In keeping with the classical view of the manager as that individual perched at the apex of the regulated, hierarchical system, the literature's manager was to receive all his important information from a giant, comprehensive MIS.

Lately, however, as it has become increasingly evident that these giant MIS systems are not working – that managers are simply not using them – the enthusiasm has waned. A look at how managers actually process information makes the reason quite clear. Managers have five media at their command – documents, telephone calls, scheduled and unscheduled meetings, and observational tours.

Fact: 'Managers strongly favor the verbal media – namely, telephone calls and meetings.' The evidence comes from every single study of managerial work. Consider the following.

In two British studies, managers spent an average of 66 per cent and 80 per cent of their time in verbal (oral) communication (R. Stewart, 1967, and T. Burns, 1954). In my study of five American chief executives, the figure was 78 per cent. These five chief executives treated mail processing as a burden to be dispensed with. One came in on Saturday morning to process 142 pieces of mail in just over three hours, to 'get rid of all the stuff'. This same manager looked at the first piece of 'hard' mail he had received all week, a standard cost report, and put it aside with the comment 'I never look at this'.

These same five chief executives responded immediately to two of the forty routine reports they received during the five weeks of my study and to four items in the 104 periodicals. They skimmed most of these periodicals in seconds, almost ritualistically. In all, these chief executives of sizeable organizations initiated on their own – that is, not in response to something else – a grand total of twenty-five pieces of mail during the twenty-five days I observed them.

An analysis of the mail the executives received reveals an interesting picture – only 13 per cent was of specific and immediate use. So now we have another piece in the puzzle: not much of the mail provides live, current information – the action of a competitor, the mood of a government legislator, or the rating of last night's television show. Yet this is the information that drove the managers, interrupting their meetings and rescheduling their workdays.

Consider another interesting finding. Managers seem to cherish 'soft' information, especially gossip, hearsay, and speculation. Why? The reason is its timeliness: today's gossip may be tomorrow's fact. The manager who is not accessible for the telephone call informing him that his biggest customer was seen golfing with his main competitor may read about a dramatic drop in sales in the next quarterly report. But by then it's too late.

To assess the value of historical, aggregated, 'hard' MIS information, consider two of the manager's prime uses for his information: to identify problems and opportunities and to build his own mental models of the things around him (e.g. how his organization's budget system works, how his customers buy his product, how changes in the economy affect his organization, and so on. See H. E. Wrapp, 1967).[2] Every bit of evidence suggests that the manager identifies decision situations and builds models not with the aggregated abstractions an MIS provides, but with specific titbits of data.

Consider the words of Richard Neustadt (1960, pp. 153–4), who studied the information-collecting habits of Presidents Roosevelt, Truman, and Eisenhower:

> It is not information of a general sort that helps a President see personal stakes; not summaries, not surveys, not the *bland amalgams*. Rather . . . it is the odds and ends of *tangible detail* that pieced together in his mind illuminate the underside of issues put before him. To help himself he must reach out as widely as he can for every scrap of fact, opinion, gossip, bearing on his interests and relationships as President. He must become his own director of his own central intelligence.

2. Wrapp refers to this as spotting opportunities and relationships in the stream of operating problems and decisions; Wrapp raises a number of excellent points related to this analysis in his article.

The manager's emphasis on verbal media raises two important points.

First, verbal information is stored in people's brains. Only when people write this information down can it be stored in the files of the organization – whether in metal cabinets or on magnetic tape – and managers apparently do not write down much of what they hear. Thus the strategic data-bank of the organization is not in the memory of its computers but in the minds of its managers.

Second, the manager's extensive use of verbal media helps to explain why he is reluctant to delegate tasks. When we note that most of the manager's important information comes in verbal form and is stored in his head, we can well appreciate his reluctance. It is not as if he can hand a dossier over to someone; he must take the time to 'dump memory' – to tell someone all he knows about the subject. But this could take so long that the manager may find it easier to do the task himself. Thus the manager is damned by his own information system to a 'dilemma of delegation' – to do too much himself or to delegate to his subordinates with inadequate briefing.

4. *Folklore: 'Management is, or at least is quickly becoming, a science and a profession.'* By almost any definitions of *science* and *profession*, this statement is false. Brief observation of any manager will quickly lay to rest the notion that managers practise a science. A science involves the enaction of systematic, analytically determined procedures or programs. If we do not even know what procedures managers use, how can we prescribe them by scientific analysis? And how can we call management a profession if we cannot specify what managers are to learn? For, after all, a profession involves 'knowledge of some department of learning of science' (*Random House Dictionary*).[3]

Fact: the managers' programs – to schedule time, process information, make decisions, and so on – remain locked deep inside their brains. Thus, to describe these programs, we rely on words like *judgment* and intuition, seldom stopping to realize that they are merely labels for our ignorance.

I was struck during my study by the fact that the executives I was observing – all very competent by any standard – were fundamentally indistinguishable from their counterparts of a hundred years ago (or a thousand years ago, for that matter). The information they need differs, but they seek it in the same way: by word of mouth. Their decisions

3. For a more thorough, though rather different, discussion of this issue, see K. R. Andrews (1969).

concern modern technology, but the procedures they use are the same as the procedures of the nineteenth-century manager. Even the computer, so important for the specialized work of the organization, has apparently had no influence on the work procedures of general managers. In fact, the manager is in a kind of loop, with increasingly heavy work pressures but no aid forthcoming from management science.

Considering the facts about managerial work, we can see that the manager's job is enormously complicated and difficult. The manager is overburdened with obligations; yet he cannot easily delegate his tasks. As a result, he is driven to overwork and is forced to do many tasks superficially. Brevity, fragmentation, and verbal communication characterize his work. Yet these are the very characteristics of managerial work that have impeded scientific attempts to improve it. As a result, the management scientist has concentrated his efforts on the specialized functions of the organization, where he could more easily analyze the procedures and quantify the relevant information.[4]

But the pressures of the manager's job are becoming worse. Where before he needed only to respond to owners and directors, now he finds that his subordinates with democratic norms continually reduce his freedom to issue unexplained orders, and a growing number of outside influences (consumer groups, government agencies, and so on) expect his attention. And the manager has nowhere to turn for help. The first step in providing the manager with some help is to find out what his job really is.

Back to a basic description of managerial work

Now let us try to put some of the pieces of this puzzle together. Earlier I defined the manager as that person in charge of an organization or one of its subunits. Besides chief-executive officers, this definition would include vice-presidents, bishops, foremen, hockey coaches, and prime ministers. Can all these people have anything in common? Indeed they can. To begin with, all are vested with formal authority over an organizational unit. From formal authority comes status, which leads to various interpersonal relations, and from these comes access to information. Information, in turn, enables the manager to make decisions and construct strategies for his unit.

The manager's job can be described in terms of various 'roles', or

---

4. C. J. Grayson, Jr (1973) explains in similar terms why, as chairman of the Price Commission, he did not use those very techniques that he himself promoted in his earlier career as a management scientist.

organized sets of behaviors identified with a position. My description, shown in Figure 1, comprises ten roles. As we shall see, formal authority gives rise to the three interpersonal roles, which in turn give rise to the three informational roles; these two sets of roles enable the manager to play the four decisional roles.

Interpersonal roles

Three of the manager's roles arise directly from his formal authority and involve basic interpersonal relationships.

1. The first is the *figurehead* role. By virtue of his position as head of an organizational unit, every manager must perform some duties of a ceremonial nature. The president greets the touring dignitaries, the foreman attends the wedding of a lathe operator, and the sales manager takes an important customer to lunch.

The chief executives of my study spent 12 per cent of their contact time on ceremonial duties; 17 per cent of their incoming mail dealt with acknowledgements and requests related to their status. For example, a letter to a company president requested free merchandise for a crippled schoolchild; diplomas were put on the desk of the school superintendent for his signature.

Duties that involve interpersonal roles may sometimes be routine, involving little serious communication and no important decision-making. Nevertheless, they are important to the smooth functioning of an organization and cannot be ignored by the manager.

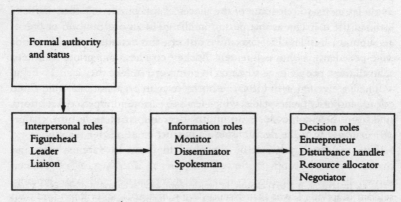

Figure 1   The manager's roles

2. Because he is in charge of an organizational unit, the manager is responsible for the work of the people of that unit. His actions in this regard constitute the *leader* role. Some of these actions involve leadership directly – for example, in most organizations the manager is normally responsible for hiring and training his own staff.

In addition, there is the indirect exercise of the leader role. Every manager must motivate and encourage his employees, somehow reconciling their individual needs with the goals of the organization. In virtually every contact the manager has with his employees, subordinates seeking leadership clues probe his actions: 'Does he approve?' 'How would he like the report to turn out?' 'Is he more interested in market share than high profits?'

The influence of the manager is most clearly seen in the leader role. Formal authority vests him with great potential power; leadership determines in large part how much of it he will realize.

3. The literature of management has always recognized the leader role, particularly those aspects of it related to motivation. By comparison, until recently it has hardly mentioned the *liaison* role, in which the manager makes contacts outside his vertical chain of command. This is remarkable in the light of the finding of virtually every study of managerial work that managers spend as much time with peers and other people outside their units as they do with their own subordinates, and surprisingly little time with their own superiors.

In Rosemary Stewart's diary study (R. Stewart, 1967), the 160 British middle and top managers spent 47 per cent of their time with peers, 41 per cent of their time with people outside their unit, and only 12 per cent of their time with their superiors. For Robert H. Guest's study of US foremen (R. H. Guest, 1956), the figures were 44 per cent, 46 per cent, and 10 per cent. The chief executives of my study averaged 44 per cent of their contact time with people outside their organization, 48 per cent with subordinates, and 7 per cent with directors and trustees.

The contacts the five CEOs made were with an incredibly wide range of people: subordinates; clients; business associates and suppliers; and peers (managers of similar organizations, government- and trade-organization officials, fellow directors on outside boards, and independents with no relevant organizational affiliations). The chief executives' time with and mail from these groups is shown in Figure 2. Guest's study of foremen shows, likewise, that their contacts were numerous and wide ranging, seldom involving fewer than twenty-five individuals, and often more than fifty.

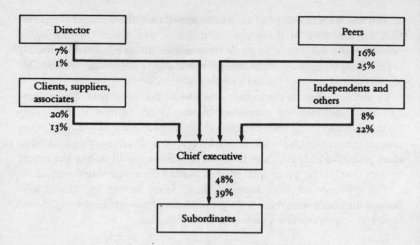

Note: the top figure indicates the proportion of total contact time spent with each group and the bottom figure, the proportion of mail from each group.

Figure 2 The chief executives' contacts

As we shall see shortly, the manager cultivates such contacts largely to find information. In effect, the liaison role is devoted to building up the manager's own external information system – informal, private, verbal, but nevertheless effective.

Informational roles

By virtue of his interpersonal contacts, both with his subordinates and with his network of contacts, the manager emerges as the nerve center of his organizational unit. He may not know everything, but he typically knows more than any member of his staff.

Studies have shown this relationship to hold for all managers, from street gang leaders to US presidents. In *The Human Group*, George C. Homans explains how, because they were at the center of the information-flow of their own gangs and were also in close touch with other gang leaders, street gang leaders were better informed than any of their followers (G. C. Homans, 1950, based on W. F. Whyte, 1955). And Richard Neustadt (1960, p. 157) gives the following account from his study of Franklin D. Roosevelt:

The essence of Roosevelt's technique for information-gathering was competition. 'He would call you in,' one of his aides once told me, 'and he'd ask you to get the story on some complicated business, and you'd come back after a couple of days of hard labor and present the juicy morsel you'd uncovered under a stone somewhere, and *then* you'd find out he knew all about it, along with something else you didn't know. Where he got this information from he wouldn't mention, usually, but after he had done this to you once or twice you got damn careful about your information.'

We can see where Roosevelt 'got this information' when we consider the relationship between the interpersonal and the informational roles. As leader, the manager has formal and easy access to every member of his staff. Hence, as noted earlier, he tends to know more about his own unit than anyone else does. In addition, his liaison contacts expose the manager to external information to which his subordinates often lack access. Many of these contacts are with other managers of equal status, who are themselves nerve centers in their own organization. In this way the manager develops a powerful data base of information.

The processing of information is a key part of the manager's job. In my study, the chief executives spent 40 per cent of their contact time on activities devoted exclusively to the transmission of information; 70 per cent of their incoming mail was purely informational (as opposed to request for action). The manager does not leave meetings or hang up the telephone in order to get back to work. In large part, communication *is* his work. Three roles describe these informational aspects of managerial work.

1. As *monitor*, the manager perpetually scans his environment for information, interrogates his liaison contacts and his subordinates, and receives unsolicited information, much of it as a result of the network of personal contacts he has developed. Remember that a good part of the information the manager collects in his monitor role arrives in verbal form, often as gossip, hearsay, and speculation. By virtue of his contacts, the manager has a natural advantage in collecting this soft information for his organization.

2. He must share and distribute much of this information. Information he gleans from outside personal contacts may be needed within his organization. In his *disseminator* role, the manager passes some of his privileged information directly to his subordinates, who would otherwise have no access to it. When his subordinates lack easy contact with one another, the manager will sometimes pass information from one to another.

3. In his *spokesman* role, the manager sends some of his information to people outside his unit – a president makes a speech to a lobby for an

organization cause, or a foreman suggests a product modification to a supplier. In addition, as part of his role as spokesman, every manager must inform and satisfy the influential people who control his organizational unit. For the foreman, this may simply involve keeping the plant manager informed about the flow of work through the shop.

The president of a large corporation, however, may spend a great deal of his time dealing with a host of influences. Directors and shareholders must be advised about financial performance; consumer groups must be assured that the organization is fulfilling its social responsibilities; and government officials must be satisfied that the organization is abiding by the law.

Decisional roles

Information is not, of course, an end in itself; it is the basic input to decision-making. One thing is clear in this study of managerial work: the manager plays the major role in his unit's decision-making system. As its formal authority, only he can commit the unit to important new courses of action; and as its nerve center, only he has full and current information to make the set of decisions that determine the unit's strategy. Four roles describe the manager as decision-maker.

1. As *entrepreneur*, the manager seeks to improve his unit and to adapt it to changing conditions in the environment. In his monitor role, the president is constantly on the lookout for new ideas. When a good one appears, he initiates a development project that he may supervise himself or delegate to an employee (perhaps with the stipulation that he must approve the final proposal).

There are two interesting features about these development projects at the chief-executive level. First, these projects do not involve single decisions or even unified clusters of decisions. Rather, they emerge as a series of small decisions and actions sequenced over time. Apparently, the chief executive prolongs each project so that he can fit it bit by bit into his busy, disjointed schedule and so that he can gradually come to comprehend the issue, if it is a complex one.

Second, the chief executives I studied supervised as many as fifty of these projects at the same time. Some projects entailed new products or processes; others involved public-relations campaigns, improvement of the cash position, reorganization of a weak department, resolution of a morale problem in a foreign division, integration of computer operations, various acquisitions at different stages of development, and so on.

The chief executive appears to maintain a kind of inventory of the development projects that he himself supervises – projects that are at various stages of development, some active and some in limbo. Like a juggler, he keeps a number of projects in the air: periodically one comes down, is given a new burst of energy, and is sent back into orbit. At various intervals, he puts new projects on-stream and discards old ones.

2. While the entrepreneurial role describes the manager as the voluntary initiator of change, the *disturbance handler* role depicts the manager involuntarily responding to pressures. Here change is beyond the manager's control. He must act because the pressures of the situation are too severe to be ignored: a strike looms, a major customer has gone bankrupt, or a supplier reneges on his contract.

It has been fashionable, I noted earlier, to compare the manager to an orchestra conductor, just as Peter F. Drucker (1954, pp. 341–2) wrote in *The Practice of Management*:

> The manager has the task of creating a true whole that is larger than the sum of its parts, a productive entity that turns out more than the sum of the resources put into it. One analogy is the conductor of a symphony orchestra, through whose effort, vision and leadership individual instrumental parts that are so much noise by themselves become the living whole of music. But the conductor has the composer's score; he is only interpreter. The manager is both composer and conductor.

Now consider the words of Leonard R. Sayles (1964, p. 162), who has carried out systematic research on the manager's job:

> (The manager) is like a symphony orchestra conductor, endeavouring to maintain a melodious performance in which the contributions of the various instruments are coordinated and sequenced, patterned and paced, while the orchestra members are having various personal difficulties, stage hands are moving music stands, alternating excessive heat and cold are creating audience and instrument problems, and the sponsor of the concert is insisting on irrational changes in the program.

In effect, every manager must spend a good part of his time responding to high-pressure disturbances. No organization can be so well run, so standardized, that it has conducted in advance every contingency in the uncertain environment. Disturbances arise not only because poor managers ignore situations until they reach crisis proportions, but also because good managers cannot possibly anticipate all the consequences of the actions they take.

3. The third decisional role is that of *resource allocator*. To the manager falls

the responsibility of deciding who will receive what in his organizational unit. Perhaps the most important resource the manager allocates is his own time. Access to the manager constitutes exposure to the unit's nerve center and decision-maker. The manager is also charged with designing his unit's structure, that pattern of formal relationships that determines how work is to be divided and coordinated.

Also in his role as resource allocator the manager authorizes the important decisions of his unit before they are implemented. By retaining this power, the manager can ensure that decisions are interrelated; all must pass through a single brain. To fragment this power is to encourage discontinuous decision-making and disjointed strategy.

There are a number of interesting features about the manager's authorizing others' decisions. First, despite the widespread use of capital-budgeting procedures – a means of authorizing various capital expenditures at one time – executives in my study made a great many authorization decisions on an ad hoc basis. Apparently, many projects cannot wait or simply do not have the quantifiable costs and benefits that capital budgeting requires.

Second, I found that the chief executives faced incredibly complex choices. They had to consider the impact of each decision on other decisions and on the organization's strategy. They had to ensure that the decision would be acceptable to those who influence the organization as well as ensuring that resources would not be overextended. They had to understand the various costs and benefits as well as the feasibility of the proposal. They also had to consider questions of timing. All this was necessary for the simple approval of someone else's proposal. At the same time, however, delay could cost time, while quick approval could be ill considered and quick rejection might discourage the subordinate who had spent months developing a pet project.

One common solution to approving projects is to pick the man instead of the proposal. That is, the manager authorizes those projects presented to him by people whose judgment he trusts. But he cannot always use this simple dodge.

4. The final decisional role is that of *negotiator*. Studies of managerial work at all levels indicate that managers spend considerable time in negotiations: the president of the football team is called in to work out a contract with the holdout superstar; the corporation president leads his company's contingent to negotiate a new strike issue; the foreman argues a grievance problem to its conclusion with the shop steward. As Leonard Sayles puts it, negotiations are a 'way of life' for the sophisticated manager.

These negotiations are duties of the manager's job; perhaps routine, they are not to be shirked. They are an integral part of his job, for only he has the authority to commit organizational resources in 'real time', and only he has the nerve-center information that important negotiations require.

The integrated job

It should be clear by now that the ten roles I have been describing are not easily separable. In the terminology of the psychologist, they form a *gestalt*, an integrated whole. No role can be pulled out of the framework leaving the job intact. For example, a manager without liaison contact lacks external information. As a result, he can neither disseminate the information his employees need nor make decisions that adequately reflect external conditions. (In fact, this is a problem for the new person in a managerial position, since he cannot make effective decisions until he has built up his network of contacts.)

Here lies a clue to the problems of team management.[5] Two or three people cannot share a single managerial position unless they can act as one entity. This means they cannot divide up the ten roles unless they can very carefully integrate them. The real difficulty lies with the information roles. Unless there can be a full sharing of managerial information – and, as I pointed out earlier, it is primarily verbal – team management breaks down. A single managerial job cannot be arbitrarily split, for example, into internal and external roles, for information from both sources must be brought to bear on the same decisions.

To say that the ten roles form a *gestalt* is not to say that all managers give equal attention to each role. In fact, I found in my review of the various research studies that:

1. Sales managers seem to spend relatively more of their time in the interpersonal roles, presumably a reflection of the extrovert nature of the marketing activity.
2. Production managers give relatively more attention to the decisional roles, presumably a reflection of their concern with efficient work flow.
3. Staff managers spend the most time in the informational roles, since they are experts who manage departments that advise other parts of the organization.

5. See R. C. Hodgson, D. J. Levinson, and A. Zaleznik, 1965, for a discussion of the sharing of roles.

Nevertheless, in all cases the interpersonal, informational and decisional roles remain inseparable.

Towards more effective management

What are the messages for management in this description? I believe, first and foremost, that this description of managerial work should prove more important to managers than any prescription they might derive from it. That is to say, *the manager's effectiveness is significantly influenced by his insight into his own work.* His performance depends on how well he understands and responds to the pressures and dilemmas of the job. Thus managers who can be introspective about their work are likely to be effective at their jobs. Table 1 offers fourteen groups of self-study questions for managers. Some may sound rhetorical; none is meant to be. Even though the questions cannot be answered simply, the manager should address himself to them.

Let us take a look at three specific areas of concern. For the most part, the managerial log-jams – the dilemmas of delegation, the data base centralized in one brain, the problems of working with the management scientist – revolve around the verbal nature of the manager's information. There are great dangers in centralizing the organization's data bank in the minds of its managers. When they leave they take their memory with them. And when subordinates are out of convenient verbal reach of the manager, they are at an informational disadvantage.

1. *The manager is challenged to find systematic ways to share his privileged information.* A regular debriefing session with key subordinates, a weekly memory dump on the dictating machine, the maintaining of a diary of important information for limited circulation, or other similar methods may ease the log-jam of work considerably. Time spent disseminating this information will be more than regained when decisions must be made. Of course, some will raise the question of confidentiality. But managers would do well to weigh the risks of exposing privileged information against having subordinates who can make effective decisions.

If there is a single theme that runs through this article, it is that the pressures of his job drive the manager to be superficial in his actions – to overload himself with work, encourage interruption, respond quickly to every stimulus, seek the tangible and avoid the abstract, make decisions in small increments, and do everything abruptly.

2. *Here again the manager is challenged to deal consciously with the pressures of superficiality by giving serious attention to the issues that require it, by stepping back from his tangible bits of information in order to see a broad picture, and by making use of analytical inputs.* Although effective managers do have to be adept at responding quickly to numerous and varying problems, the danger in managerial work is that they will respond to every issue equally (and that means abruptly) and that they will never work the tangible bits and pieces of informational input into a comprehensive picture of their work.

As I noted earlier, the manager uses these bits of information to build models of his world. But the manager can also avail himself of the models of the specialists. Economists describe the functioning of markets, operations researchers stimulate financial flow processes, and behavioral scientists explain the needs and goals of people. The best of these models can be sought out and learned.

In dealing with complex issues, the senior manager has much to gain from a close relationship with the management scientists of his own organization. They have something important that he lacks: time to probe complex issues. An effective working relationship hinges on the resolution of what a colleague and I have called 'the planning dilemma' (J. S. Hekimian and H. Mintzberg, 1968, p. 4). Managers have the information and the authority, analysts have the time and the technology. A successful working relationship between the two will be effected when the manager learns to share his information and the analyst learns to adapt to the manager's needs. For the analyst, adaptation means worrying less about the elegance of the method and more about its speed and flexibility.

It seems to me that analysis can especially help the top manager to schedule his time, feed in analytical information, monitor projects under his supervision, develop models to aid in making choices, design contingency plans for disturbances that can be anticipated, and conduct 'quick-and-dirty' analysis for those that cannot. But there can be no cooperation if the analysts are out of the mainstream of the manager's information flow.

3. *The manager is challenged to gain control of his own time by turning obligations to his advantage and by turning those things he wishes to do into obligations.* The chief executives of my study initiated only 32 per cent of their own contacts (and another 5 per cent by mutual agreement). And yet to a considerable extent they seemed to control their time. There were two key factors that enabled them to do so.

First, the manager has to spend so much time discharging obligations that if he were to view them as just that, he would leave no mark on his

Table 1. Self-study questions for managers

1. Where do I get my information, and how? Can I make greater use of my contacts to get information? Can other people do some of my scanning for me? In what area is my knowledge weakest, and how can I get others to provide me with the information I need? Do I have powerful enough mental models of those things I must understand within the organization and in its environment?

2. What information do I disseminate in my organization? How important is it that my subordinates get my information? Do I keep too much information to myself because dissemination of it is time consuming or inconvenient? How can I get more information to others so they can make better decisions?

3. Do I balance information collecting with action taking? Do I tend to act before information is in? Or do I wait so long for all the information that opportunities pass me by and I become a bottleneck in my organization?

4. What pace of change am I asking my organization to tolerate? Is this change balanced so that our operations are neither excessively static nor overly disrupted? Have we sufficiently analysed the impact of this change on the future of our organization?

5. Am I sufficiently well informed to pass judgement on the proposals that my subordinates make? Is it possible to leave final authorization for more of the proposals with subordinates? Do we have problems of coordination because subordinates in fact now make too many of these decisions independently?

6. What is my vision of direction for this organization? Are these plans primarily in my own mind in loose form? Should I make them explicit in order to guide the decisions of others in the organization better? Or do I need flexibility to change them at will?

7. How do my subordinates react to my managerial style? Am I sufficiently sensitive to the powerful influence my actions have on them? Do I fully understand their reactions to my actions? Do I find an appropriate balance between encouragement and pressure? Do I stifle their initiative?

8. What kind of external relationships do I maintain, and how? Do I spend too much of my time maintaining these relationships? Are there certain types of people whom I should get to know better?

9. Is there any system to my scheduling, or am I just reacting to the pressures of the moment? Do I find the appropriate mix of activities, or do I tend to concentrate on one particular function or one type of problem just because I find it interesting? Am I more efficient with particular kinds of work at special times of the day or week? Does my schedule reflect this? Can someone else (in addition to my secretary) take responsibility for much of my scheduling and do it more systematically?

10. Do I overwork? What effect does my work load have on my efficiency? Should I force myself to take breaks or to reduce the pace of my activity?

11. Am I too superficial in what I do? Can I really shift moods as quickly and frequently as my work patterns require? Should I attempt to decrease the amount of fragmentation and interruption in my work?

12. Do I orientate myself too much towards current, tangible activities? Am I slave to the action and excitement of my work, so that I am no longer able to concentrate on

issues? Do key problems receive the attention they deserve? Should I spend more time reading and probing into certain issues? Could I be more reflective? Should I be?

13. Do I use the different media appropriately? Do I know how to make the most of written communication? Do I rely excessively on face-to-face communication, thereby putting all but a few of my subordinates at an informational disadvantage? Do I schedule enough of my meetings on a regular basis? Do I spend enough time touring my organization to observe activity first hand? Am I too detached from the heart of my organization's activities, seeing things only in an abstract way?

14. How do I blend my personal rights and duties? Do my obligations consume all my time? How can I free myself sufficiently from obligations to ensure that I am taking this organization where I want it to go? How can I turn my obligations to my advantage?

---

organization. The unsuccessful manager blames failure on the obligations; the effective manager turns his obligations to his own advantage. A speech is a chance to lobby for a cause; a meeting is a chance to reorganize a weak department; a visit to an important customer is a chance to extract trade information.

Second, the manager frees some of his time to do those things that he (and perhaps no one else) thinks important by turning them into obligations. Free time is made, not found, in the manager's job; it is forced into the schedule. Hoping to leave some time open for contemplation or general planning is tantamount to hoping that the pressures of the job will go away. The manager who wants to innovate initiates a project and obligates others to report back to him; the manager who needs certain environmental information establishes channels that will automatically keep him informed; the manager who has to tour facilities commits himself publicly.

The educator's job

Finally, a word about the training of managers. Our management schools have done an admirable job of training the organization's specialists – management scientists, marketing researchers, accountants, and organizational development specialists. But for the most part they have not trained managers (see J. S. Livingston, 1971, p. 79).

Management schools will begin the serious training of managers when skill training takes a serious place next to cognitive learning. Cognitive learning is detached and informational, like reading a book or listening to a lecture. No doubt much more important cognitive material must be assimilated by the manager-to-be. But cognitive learning no more makes a manager than it does a swimmer. The latter will drown the first time he jumps into the water if his coach never takes him out of the lecture hall, gets him wet, and gives him feedback on his performance.

In other words, we are taught a skill through practice plus feedback, whether in a real or a simulated situation. Our management schools need to identify the skills managers use, select students who show potential in these skills, put the students into situations where these skills can be practiced, and then give them a systematic feedback on their performance.

My description of managerial work suggests a number of important managerial skills – developing peer relationships, carrying out negotiations, motivating subordinates, resolving conflicts, establishing information networks and subsequently disseminating information, making decisions in conditions of extreme ambiguity, and allocating resources. Above all, the manager needs to be introspective about this work so that he may continue to learn on the job. Many of the manager's skills can, in fact, be practiced using techniques that range from role playing to videotaping real meetings. And our management schools can enhance the entrepreneurial skills by designing programs that encourage sensible risk taking and innovation.

No job is more vital to our society than that of the manager. It is the manager who determines whether our social institutions serve us well or whether they squander our talents and resources. It is time to strip away the folklore about managerial work, and time to study it realistically so that we can begin the difficult task of making significant improvements in its performance.

Research on managerial work

Considering its central importance to every aspect of management, there has been surprisingly little research on the manager's work, and virtually no systematic building up of knowledge from one group of studies to another. In seeking to describe managerial work, I conducted my own research and also scanned the literature widely to integrate the findings of studies from many diverse sources with my own. These studies focused on two very different aspects of managerial work. Some were concerned with the characteristics of the work – how long managers work, where, at what pace and with what interruptions, with whom they work and through what media they communicate. Other studies were more concerned with the essential content of the work – what activities the managers actually carry out and why. Thus, after a meeting, one researcher might note that the manager spent forty-five minutes with three government officials in their Washington office, while another might record that he presented his company's stand on some proposed legislation in order to change a regulation.

A few of the studies of managerial work are widely known, but most have remained buried as single journal articles or isolated books. Among the more important ones I cite are the following.

Sune Carlson developed the diary method to study the work characteristics of nine Swedish managing directors. Each kept a detailed log of his activities. Carlson's results are reported in his book *Executive Behavior*. A number of British researchers, notably Rosemary Stewart, have subsequently used Carlson's method. In *Managers and Their Jobs* she describes the study of 160 top and middle managers of British companies during four weeks, with particular attention to the differences in their work.

Leonard Sayles's book *Managerial Behavior* is another important source of reference. Using a method he refers to as 'anthropological', Sayles studied the work content of middle- and lower-level managers in a large US corporation. Sayles moved freely in the company, collecting whatever information struck him as important.

Perhaps the best-known source is *Presidential Power*, in which Richard Neustadt analyzes the power and managerial behavior of Presidents Roosevelt, Truman and, Eisenhower. Neustadt used secondary sources – documents and interviews with other parties – to generate his data.

Robert H. Guest, in *Personnel*, reports on a study of the foreman's working day. Fifty-six US foremen were observed and each of their activities recorded during one eight-hour shift.

Richard C. Hodgson, Daniel J. Levinson, and Abraham Zaleznik studied a team of three top executives of a US hospital. From that study they wrote *The Executive Role Constellation*. These researchers addressed in particular the way in which work and socio-emotional roles were divided among the three managers.

William F. Whyte, from his study of a street gang during the Depression, wrote *Street Corner Society*. His findings about the gang's leadership, which George C. Homans analysed in *The Human Group*, suggest some interesting similarities of job content between street gang leaders and corporate managers.

My own study involved five American CEOs of middle- to large-sized organizations – a consulting firm, a technology company, a hospital, a consumer-goods company, and a school system. Using a method called 'structural observation', during one intensive week of observation for each executive I recorded various aspects of every piece of mail and every verbal contact. My method was designed to capture data on both work characteristics and job content. In all, I analysed 890 pieces of incoming and outgoing mail and 368 verbal contacts.

References

AGUILAR, F. J. (1967), *Scanning the Business Environment*, Macmillan

ANDREWS, K. R. (1969), 'Towards professionalism in business management', *Harvard Business Review*, March–April

BURNS, T. (1954), 'The directions of activity and communication in a departmental executive group', *Human Relations*, 7, no. 1

CARLSON, S. (1951), *Executive Behaviour*, Strombergs

COPEMAN, G. H. (1963), *The Role of the Managing Director*, Business Publications

DAVIS, R. T. (1957), *Performance and Development of Field Sales Managers*, Boston Division of Research, Harvard Business School

DRUCKER, P. F. (1954), *The Practice of Management*, Harper & Row

GRAYSON, Jr, C. J. (1973), 'Management science and business practice', *Harvard Business Review*, July–August

GUEST, R. H. (1956), 'Of time and the foreman', *Personnel*, May

HEKIMIAN, J. S., and MINTZBERG, H. (1968), 'The planning dilemma', *The Management Review*, May

HODGSON, R. C., LEVINSON, D. J., and ZALEZNIK, A. (1965), *The Executive Role Constellation*, Boston Division of Research, Harvard Business School

HOMANS, G. C. (1950), *The Human Group*, Harcourt, Brace & World

LIVINGSTON, J. S. (1971), 'Myth of the well-educated manager', *Harvard Business Review*, January–February

MINTZBERG, H. (1973), *The Nature of Managerial Work*, Harper & Row

NEUSTADT, R. E. (1960), *Presidential Power*, Wiley

SAYLES, L. R. (1964), *Managerial Behavior*, McGraw-Hill

STEWART, R. (1967), *Managers and Their Jobs*, Macmillan

WHYTE, W. F. (1955), *Street Corner Society*, rev. ed., University of Chicago Press

WRAPP, H. E. (1967), 'Good managers don't make policy decisions', *Harvard Business Review*, September–October

15 R. M. Kanter

Power Failure in Management Circuits

From *Harvard Business Review*, July–August 1979, pp. 65–75

Power is America's last dirty word. It is easier to talk about money – and much easier to talk about sex – than it is to talk about power. People who have it deny it; people who want it do not want to appear to hunger for it; and people who engage in its machinations do so secretly.

Yet, because it turns out to be a critical element in effective managerial behavior, power should come out from under cover. Having searched for years for those styles or skills that would identify capable organization leaders, many analysts, like myself, are rejecting individual traits or situational appropriateness as key and finding the sources of a leader's real power.

Access to resources and information and the ability to act quickly make it possible to accomplish more and to pass on more resources and information to subordinates. For this reason, people tend to prefer bosses with 'clout'. When employees perceive their manager as influential upward and outward, their status is enhanced by association and they generally have high morale and feel less critical or resistant to their boss (D. C. Pelz, 1952, p. 209). More powerful leaders are also more likely to delegate (they are too busy to do it all themselves), to reward talent and to build a team that places subordinates in significant positions.

Powerlessness, in contrast, tends to breed bossiness rather than true leadership. In large organizations, at least, it is powerlessness that often creates ineffective, desultory management and petty, dictatorial, rules-minded managerial styles. Accountability without power – responsibility for results without the resources to get them – creates frustration and failure. People who see themselves as weak and powerlessness and find their subordinates resisting or discounting them tend to use more punishing forms of influence. If organizational power can 'ennoble', then, recent

319

research shows, organizational powerlessness can (with apologies to Lord Acton) 'corrupt' (R. M. Kanter, 1977, pp. 164–205; D. Kipnis, 1976).

So perhaps power, in the organization at least, does not deserve such a bad reputation. Rather than connoting only dominance, control, and oppression, power can mean efficacy and capacity – something managers and executives need to move the organization toward its goals. Power in organizations is analogous in simple terms to physical power: it is the ability to mobilize resources (human and material) to get things done. The true sign of power, then, is accomplishment – not fear, terror, or tyranny. Where the power is 'on', the system can be productive; where the power is 'off', the system bogs down.

But saying that people need power to be effective in organizations does not tell us where it comes from or why some people, in some jobs, seem to have more of it than others. In this article I want to show that to discover the sources of productive power, we have to look not at the person – as conventional classifications of effective managers and employees do – but at the position the person occupies in the organization.

Where does power come from?

The effectiveness that power brings evolves from two kinds of capacities: first, access to the resources, information, and support necessary to carry out a task; and, second, ability to get cooperation in doing what is necessary. (Exhibit 1 identifies some symbols of an individual manager's power.)

Both capacities derive not so much from a leader's style and skill as from his or her location in the formal and informal systems of the organization – in both job definition and connection to other important people in the company. Even the ability to get cooperation from subordinates is strongly defined by the manager's clout outward. People are more responsive to bosses who look as if they can get more for them from the organization.

We can regard the uniquely organizational sources of power as consisting of three 'lines':

1. *Lines of supply*. Influence outward, over the environment, means that managers have the capacity to bring in the things that their own organizational domain needs – materials, money, resources to distribute as rewards, and perhaps even prestige.

2. *Lines of information*. To be effective, managers need to be 'in the know' in both the formal and the informal sense.

Exhibit I. Some common symbols of a manager's organizational power (influence upward and outward)

To what extent a manager can:
Intercede favorably on behalf of someone in trouble with the organization
Get a desirable placement for a talented subordinate
Get approval for expenditures beyond the budget
Get above-average salary increases for subordinates
Get items on the agenda at policy meetings
Get fast access to top decision-makers
Get regular, frequent access to top decision-makers
Get early information about decisions and policy shifts

3. *Lines of support.* In a formal framework, a manager's job parameters need to allow for nonordinary action, for a show of discretion or exercise of judgment. Thus managers need to know that they can assume innovative, risk-taking activities without having to go through the stifling multilayered approval process. And, informally, managers need the backing of other important figures in the organization whose tacit approval becomes another resource they bring to their own work unit as well as a sign of the manager's being 'in'.

Note that productive power has to do with *connections* with other parts of a system. Such systemic aspects of power derive from two sources – job activities and political alliances:

1. Power is most easily accumulated when one has a job that is designed and located to allow *discretion* (nonroutinized action permitting flexible, adaptive, and creative contributions), *recognition* (visibility and notice), and *relevance* (being central to pressing organizational problems).

2. Power also comes when one has relatively close contact with *sponsors* (higher-level people who confer approval, prestige, or backing), *peer networks* (circles of acquaintanceship that provide reputation and information, the grapevine often being faster than formal communication channels), and *subordinates* (who can be developed to relieve managers of some of their burdens and to represent the manager's point of view).

Exhibit II. Ways organizational factors contribute to power or powerlessness

Factors	Generates power when factor is	Generates powerlessness when factor is
Rules inherent in the job	few	many
Predecessors in the job	few	many
Established routines	few	many
Task variety	high	low
Rewards for reliability/predictability	few	many
Rewards for unusual performance/innovation	many	few
Flexibility around use of people	high	low
Approvals needed for nonroutine decisions	few	many
Physical location	central	distant
Publicity about job activities	high	low
Relation of tasks to current problem areas	central	peripheral
Focus of tasks	outside work unit	inside work unit
Interpersonal contact in the job	high	low
Contact with senior officials	high	low
Participation in programs, conferences, meetings	high	low
Participation in problem-solving task forces	high	low
Advancement prospects of subordinates	high	low

When managers are in powerful situations, it is easier for them to accomplish more. Because the tools are there, they are likely to be highly motivated and, in turn, to be able to motivate subordinates. Their activities are more likely to be on target and to net them successes. They can flexibly interpret or shape policy to meet the needs of particular areas, emergent situations, or sudden environmental shifts. They gain the respect and cooperation that attributed power brings. Subordinates' talents are resources rather than threats. And, because powerful managers have so many lines of connection and thus are oriented outward, they tend to let go of control downward, developing more independently functioning lieutenants.

The powerless live in a different world. Lacking the supplies, information, or support to make things happen easily, they may turn instead to the ultimate weapon of those who lack productive power – oppressive power: holding others back and punishing with whatever threats they can muster.

Exhibit II summarizes some of the major ways in which variables in the organization and in job design contribute to either power or powerlessness.

Positions of powerlessness

Understanding what it takes to have power and recognizing the classic behavior of the powerless can immediately help managers make sense out of a number of familiar organizational problems that are usually attributed to inadequate people: the ineffectiveness of first-line supervisors, the petty-interest protection and conservatism of staff professionals, and the crises of leadership at the top.

Instead of blaming the individuals involved in organizational problems, let us look at the positions people occupy. Of course, power or powerlessness in a position may not be all of the problem. Sometimes incapable people *are* at fault and need to be retrained or replaced. (See the appendix on page 335 for a discussion of women and power.) But where patterns emerge, where the troubles associated with some units persist, organizational power failures could be the reason. Then, as Volvo President Pehr Gyllenhammar (1977, p. 133) concludes, we should treat the powerless not as 'villains' causing headaches for everyone else but as 'victims'.

First-line supervisors

Because an employee's most important work relationship is with his or her supervisor, when many of them talk about 'the company', they mean their immediate boss. Thus a supervisor's behavior is an important determinant of the average employee's relationship to work and is in itself a critical link in the production chain.

Yet I know of no US corporate management entirely satisfied with the performance of its supervisors. Most see them as supervising too closely and not training their people. In one manufacturing company where direct laborers were asked on a survey how they learned their job, on a list of seven possibilities 'from my supervisor' ranked next to last. (Only company training programs ranked worse.) Also, it is said that supervisors do not translate company policies into practice – for instance, that they do not carry out the right of every employee to frequent performance reviews or to career counseling.

In court cases charging race or sex discrimination, first-line supervisors are frequently cited as the 'discriminating official' (W. E. Fulmer, 1976, p. 40). And, in studies in innovative work redesign and quality of work life projects, they often appear as the implied villains; they are the ones who are said to undermine the program or interfere with its effectiveness. In short, they are often seen as 'not sufficiently managerial'.

The problem affects white-collar as well as blue-collar supervisors. In one large government agency, supervisors in field offices were seen as the source of problems concerning morale and the flow of information to and from headquarters. 'Their attitudes are negative,' said a senior official. 'They turn people against the agency; they put down senior management. They build themselves up by always complaining about headquarters; but prevent their staff from getting any information directly. We can't afford to have such attitudes communicated to field staff.'

Is the problem that supervisors need more management training programs or that incompetent people are invariably attracted to the job? Neither explanation suffices. A large part of the problem lies in the position itself – one that almost universally creates powerlessness.

First-line supervisors are 'people in the middle', and that has been seen as the source of many of their problems. (See 'Life in the middle: getting in, getting up, and getting along' in R. M. Kanter and B. A. Stein (eds.), 1979.) But by recognizing that first-line supervisors are caught between higher management and workers, we only begin to skim the surface of the problem. There is practically no other organizational category as subject to powerlessness.

First, these supervisors may be at a virtual dead end in their careers. Even in companies where the job used to be a stepping stone to higher-level management jobs, it is now common practice to bring in MBAs from the outside for those positions. Thus moving from the ranks of direct labor into supervision may mean, essentially, getting 'stuck' rather than moving upward. Because employees do not perceive supervisors as eventually joining the leadership circles of the organization, they may see them as lacking the high-level contacts needed to have clout. Indeed, sometimes turnover among supervisors is so high that workers feel they can outwait – and outwit – any boss.

Second, although they lack clout, with little in the way of support from above, supervisors are forced to administer programs or explain policies that they have no hand in shaping. In one company, as part of a new personnel program, supervisors were required to conduct counseling interviews with employees. But supervisors were not trained to do this and were given no incentives to get involved. Counseling was just another obligation. Then managers suddenly encouraged the workers to bypass their supervisors or to put pressure on them. The personnel staff brought them together and told them to demand such interviews as a basic right. If supervisors had not felt powerless before, they did after that squeeze from below, engineered from above.

The people they supervise can also make life hard for them in numerous ways. This often happens when a supervisor has himself or herself risen up from the ranks. Peers that have not made it are resentful or derisive of their former colleague, whom they now see as trying to lord it over them. Often it is easy for workers to break rules and let a lot of things slip.

Yet first-line supervisors are frequently judged according to rules and regulations while being limited by other regulations in what disciplinary actions they can take. They often lack the resources to influence or reward people; after all, workers are guaranteed their pay and benefits by someone other than their supervisors. Supervisors cannot easily control events; rather, they must react to them.

In one factory, for instance, supervisors complained that performance of their job was out of their control: they could fill production quotas only if they had the supplies, but they had no way to influence the people controlling supplies.

The lack of support for many first-line managers, particularly in large organizations, was made dramatically clear in another company. When asked if contact with executives higher in the organization who had the potential for offering support, information, and alliances diminished their own feelings of career vulnerability and the number of headaches they experienced on the job, supervisors in five out of seven work units responded positively. For them *contact* was indeed related to a greater feeling of acceptance at work and membership in the organization.

But in the two other work units where there was greater contact, people perceived more, not less, career vulnerability. Further investigation showed that supervisors in these business units got attention only when they were in trouble. Otherwise, no one bothered to talk to them. To these particular supervisors, hearing from a higher-level manager was a sign not of recognition or potential support but of danger.

It is not surprising, then, that supervisors frequently manifest symptoms of powerlessness: overly close supervision, rules-mindedness, and a tendency to do the job themselves rather than to train their people (since job skills may be one of the few remaining things they feel good about). Perhaps this is why they sometimes stand as roadblocks between their subordinates and the higher reaches of the company.

Staff professionals

Also working under conditions that can lead to organizational powerlessness are the staff specialists. As advisers behind the scenes, staff people must sell their programs and bargain for resources, but unless they get themselves entrenched in organizational power networks, they have little in the way of favors to exchange. They are seen as useful adjuncts to the primary tasks of the organization but inessential in a day-to-day operating sense. This disenfranchisement occurs particularly when staff jobs consist of easily routinized administrative functions which are out of the mainstream of the currently relevant areas and involve little innovative decision-making.

Furthermore, in some organizations, unless they have had previous line experience, staff people tend to be limited in the number of jobs into which they can move. Specialists' ladders are often very short, and professionals are just as likely to get 'stuck' in such jobs as people are in less prestigious clerical or factory positions.

Staff people, unlike those who are being groomed for important line positions, may be hired because of a special expertise or particular background. But management rarely pays any attention to developing them into more general organizational resources. Lacking growth prospects themselves and working alone or in very small teams, they are not in a position to develop others or pass on power to them. They miss out on an important way by which power can be accumulated.

Sometimes staff specialists, such as house counsel or organization development people, find their work being farmed out to consultants. Management considers them fine for the routine work, but the minute the activities involve risk or something problematic, they bring in outside experts. This treatment says something not only about their expertise but also about the status of their function. Since the company can always hire talent on a temporary basis, it is unclear whether or not the management really needs to have, or considers important, its own staff for these functions.

And, because staff professionals are often seen as adjuncts to primary tasks, their effectiveness and therefore their contribution to the organization are often hard to measure. Thus visibility and recognition, as well as risk taking and relevance, may be denied to people in staff jobs.

Staff people tend to act out their powerlessness by becoming 'turf-minded'. They create islands within the organization. They set themselves up as the only ones who can control professional standards and judge their own work. They create sometimes false distinctions between themselves as experts (no one else could possibly do what they do) and lay people, and this continues to keep them out of the mainstream.

One form such distinctions take is a combination of disdain when line managers attempt to act in areas the professionals think are their preserve and of subtle refusal to support the managers' efforts. Or staff groups battle with each other for control of new 'problem areas', with the result that no one really handles the issue at all. To cope with their essential power-lessness, staff groups may try to elevate their own status and draw boundaries between themselves and others.

When staff jobs are treated as final resting places for people who have reached their level of competence in the organization – a good shelf on which to dump managers who are too old to go anywhere but too young to retire – then staff groups can also become pockets of conservatism, resistant to change. Their own exclusion from the risk-taking actions may make them resist *anyone's* innovative proposals. In the past, personnel departments, for example, have sometimes been the last in their organiz-ation to know about innovations in human resource development or to be interested in applying them.

Top executives

Despite the great resources and responsibilities concentrated at the top of an organization, leaders can be powerless for reasons that are not very different from those that affect staff and supervisors: lack of supplies, infor-mation, and support.

We have faith in leaders because of their ability to make things happen in the larger world, to create possibilities for everyone else, and to attract resources to the organization. These are their supplies. But influence out-ward – the source of much credibility downward – can diminish as environ-ments change, setting terms and conditions out of the control of the leaders. Regardless of top management's grand plans for the organization, the environment presses. At the very least, things going on outside the organiz-ation can deflect a leader's attention and drain energy. And, more detrimen-tally, decisions made elsewhere can have severe consequences for the organization and affect top management's sense of power and thus its operating style inside.

In the go-go years of the mid-1960s, for example, nearly every corporation officer or university president could look – and therefore feel – successful. Visible success gave leaders a great deal of credibility inside the organization, which in turn gave them the power to put new things in motion.

In the past few years, the environment has been strikingly different and the capacity of many organization leaders to do anything about it has been severely limited. New 'players' have flexed their power muscles: the Arab oil bloc, government regulators, and congressional investigating committees. And managing economic decline is quite different from managing growth. It is no accident that when top leaders personally feel out of control the control function in a corporation grows.

As powerlessness in lower levels of organizations can manifest itself in overly routinized jobs where performance measures are oriented to rules and absence of change, so it can at upper levels as well. Routine work often drives out nonroutine work. Accomplishment becomes a question of nailing down details. Short-term results provide immediate gratifications and satisfy stockholders or other constituencies with limited interests.

It takes a powerful leader to be willing to risk short-term deprivations in order to bring about desired long-term outcomes. Much as first-line supervisors are tempted to focus on daily adherence to rules, leaders are tempted to focus on short-term fluctuations and lose sight of long-term objectives. The dynamics of such a situation are self-reinforcing. The more the long-term goals go unattended, the more a leader feels powerless and the greater the scramble to prove that he or she is in control of daily events at least. The more he is involved in the organization as a short-term Mr Fix-it, the more out of control of long-term objectives he is, and the more ultimately powerless he is likely to be.

Credibility for top executives often comes from doing the extraordinary: exercising discretion, creating, inventing, planning, and acting in nonroutine ways. But since routine problems look easier and more manageable, require less change and consent on the part of anyone else, and lend themselves to instant solutions that can make any leader look good temporarily, leaders may avoid the risky by taking over what their subordinates should be doing. Ultimately, a leader may succeed in getting all the trivial problems dumped on his or her desk. This can establish expectations even for leaders attempting more challenging tasks. When Warren Bennis was president of the University of Cincinnati, a professor called him when the heat was down in a classroom. In writing about this incident, Bennis (1976) commented, 'I suppose he expected me to grab a wrench and fix it.'

People at the top need to insulate themselves from the routine operations of the organization in order to develop and exercise power. But this very insulation can lead to another source of powerlessness – lack of information. In one multinational corporation, top executives who are sealed off in a large, distant office, flattered and virtually babied by aides, are frustrated by their distance from the real action. (See 'How the top is different', in R. M. Kanter and B. A. Stein (eds.), 1979.)

At the top, the concern for secrecy and privacy is mixed with real loneliness. In one bank, organization members were so accustomed to never seeing the top leaders that when a new senior vice-president went to the branch offices to look around, they had suspicion, even fear, about his intentions.

Thus leaders who are cut out of an organization's information networks understand neither what is really going on at lower levels nor that their own isolation may be having negative effects. All too often top executives design 'beneficial' new employee programs or declare a new humanitarian policy (e.g. 'Participatory management is now our style') only to find the policy ignored or mistrusted because it is perceived as coming from uncaring bosses.

The information gap has more serious consequences when executives are so insulated from the rest of the organization or from other decision-makers that, as Nixon so dramatically did, they fail to see their own impending downfall. Such insulation is partly a matter of organizational position and, in some cases, of executive style.

For example, leaders may create closed inner circles consisting of '*doppelgängers*', people just like themselves, who are their principal sources of organizational information and tell them only what they want to know. The reasons for the distortions are varied: key aides want to relieve the leader of burdens, they think just like the leader, they want to protect their own positions of power, or the familiar 'kill the messenger' syndrome makes people close to top executives reluctant to be the bearers of bad news.

Finally, just as supervisors and lower-level managers need their supporters in order to be and feel powerful, so do top executives. But for them sponsorship may not be so much a matter of individual endorsement as an issue of support by larger sources of legitimacy in the society. For top executives the problem is not to fit in among peers; rather, the question

Exhibit III. Common symptoms and sources of powerlessness for three key organizational positions

Position	Symptoms	Sources
First-line supervisors	Close, rules-minded supervision Tendency to do things oneself, blocking of subordinates' development and information Resistant, underproducing subordinates	Routine, rules-minded jobs with little control over lines of supply Limited lines of information Limited advancement or involvement prospects for oneself/subordinates
Staff professionals	Turf protection, information control Retreat into professionalism Conservative resistance to change	Routine tasks seen as peripheral to 'real tasks' of line organization Blocked careers Easy replacement by outside experts
Top executives	Focus on internal cutting, short-term results, 'punishing' Dictatorial top-down communications Retreat to comfort of like-minded lieutenants	Uncontrollable lines of supply because of environment changes Limited or blocked lines of information about lower levels of organization Diminished lines of support because of challenges to legitimacy (e.g. from the public or special interest groups)

is whether the public at large and other organization members perceive a common interest which they see the executives as promoting.

If, however, public sources of support are withdrawn and leaders are open to public attack or if inside constituencies fragment and employees see their interests better aligned with pressure groups than with organizational leadership, then powerlessness begins to set in.

When common purpose is lost, the system's own politics may reduce the capacity of those at the top to act. Just as managing decline seems to create a much more passive and reactive stance than managing growth, so does mediating among conflicting interests. When what is happening outside and inside their organizations is out of their control, many people at the top turn into decline managers and dispute mediators. Neither is a particularly empowering role.

Thus when top executives lose their own lines of supply, lines of information, and lines of support, they too suffer from a kind of powerlessness. The temptation for them then is to pull in every shred of power they can and to decrease the power available to other people to act. Innovation loses out in favor of control. Limits rather than targets are set. Financial goals are met by reducing 'overhead' (people) rather than by giving people the tools and discretion to increase their own productive capacity. Dictatorial statements come down from the top, spreading the mentality of powerlessness farther until the whole organization becomes sluggish and people concentrate on protecting what they have rather than on producing what they can.

When everyone is playing 'king of the mountain', guarding his or her turf jealously, then king of the mountain becomes the only game in town.

To expand power, share it

In no case am I saying that people in the three hierarchical levels described are always powerless, but they are susceptible to common conditions that can contribute to powerlessness. Exhibit III summarizes the most common symptoms of powerlessness for each level and some typical sources of that behavior.

I am also distinguishing the tremendous concentration of economic and political power in large corporations themselves from the powerlessness that can beset individuals even in the highest positions in such organizations. What grows with organizational position in hierarchical levels is not necessarily the power to accomplish – productive power – but the power to punish, to prevent, to sell off, to reduce, to fire, all without appropriate concern for consequences. It is that kind of power – oppressive power – that we often say corrupts.

The absence of ways to prevent individual and social harm causes the policy to feel it must surround people in power with constraints, regulations, and laws that limit the arbitrary use of their authority. But if oppressive power corrupts, then so does the absence of productive power. In large organizations, powerlessness can be a bigger problem than power.

David C. McClelland (1975, p. 263) makes a similar distinction between oppressive and productive power:

'The negative . . . face of power is characterized by the dominance–submission mode: if I win, you lose. . . . It leads to simple and direct means of feeling powerful [such as being aggressive]. It does not often lead to effective social leadership for the reason that such a person tends to treat other people as pawns. People who feel they are pawns tend to be passive and useless to the leader who gets his satisfaction from dominating them. Slaves are the most inefficient form of labor ever devised by man. If a leader wants to have far-reaching influence, he must make his followers feel powerful and able to accomplish things on their own. . . . Even the most dictatorial leader does not succeed if he has not instilled in at least some of his followers a sense of power and the strength to pursue the goals he has set.'

Organizational power can grow, in part, by being shared. We do not yet know enough about new organizational forms to say whether productive power is infinitely expandable or where we reach the point of diminishing returns. But we do know that sharing power is different from giving or throwing it away. Delegation does not mean abdication.

Some basic lessons could be translated from the field of economics to the realm of organizations and management. Capital investment in plants and equipment is not the only key to productivity. The productive capacity of nations, like organizations, grows if the skill base is upgraded. People with the tools, information, and support to make more informed decisions and act more quickly can often accomplish more. By empowering others, a leader does not decrease his power; instead he may increase it – especially if the whole organization performs better.

This analysis leads to some counterintuitive conclusions. In a certain tautological sense, the principal problem of the powerless is that they lack power. Powerless people are usually the last ones to whom anyone wants to entrust more power, for fear of its dissipation or abuse. But those people are precisely the ones who might benefit most from an injection of power and whose behavior is likely to change as new options open up to them.

Also, if the powerless bosses could be encouraged to share some of the power they do have, their power would grow. Yet, of course, only those leaders who feel secure about their own power outward – their lines of supply, information, and support – can see empowering subordinates as a gain rather than a loss. The two sides of power (getting it and giving it) are closely connected.

There are important lessons here for both subordinates and those who want to change organizations, whether executives or change agents. Instead of resisting or criticizing a powerless boss, which only increases the boss's feeling of powerlessness and need to control, subordinates instead might concentrate on helping the boss become more powerful. Managers might make pockets of ineffectiveness in the organization more productive not by training or replacing individuals but by structural solutions such as opening supply and support lines.

Similarly, organizational change agents who want a new program or policy to succeed should make sure that the change itself does not render any other level of the organization powerless. In making changes, it is wise to make sure that the key people in the level or two directly above and in neighboring functions are sufficiently involved, informed, and taken into account, so that the program can be used to build their own sense of power also. If such involvement is impossible, then it is better to move these people out of the territory altogether than to leave behind a group from whom some power has been removed and who might resist and undercut the program.

In part, of course, spreading power means educating people to this new definition of it. But words alone will not make the difference; managers will need the real experience of a new way of managing.

Here is how the associate director of a large corporate professional department phrased the lessons that he learned in the transition to a team-oriented, participatory, power-sharing management process:

'Get in the habit of involving your own managers in decision-making and approvals. But don't abdicate! Tell them what you want and where you're coming from. Don't go for a one-boss grass roots "democracy". Make the management hierarchy work for you in participation. . . .

'Hang in there, baby, and don't give up. Try not to "revert" just because everything seems to go sour on a particular day. Open up – talk to people and tell them how you feel. They'll want to get you back on track and will do things to make that happen – because they don't really want to go back to the way it was. . . . Subordinates will push you to "act more like a boss", but their interest is usually more in seeing someone else brought to heel than getting bossed themselves.'

Naturally, people need to have power before they can learn to share it. Exhorting managers to change their leadership styles is rarely useful by itself. In one large plant of a major electronics company, first-line production supervisors were the source of numerous complaints from managers who saw them as major roadblocks to overall plant productivity and as insufficiently skilled supervisors. So the plant-personnel staff undertook two pilot programs to increase the supervisors' effectiveness. The first program was based on a traditional competency and training model aimed at teaching the specific skills of successful supervisors. The second program, in contrast, was designed to empower the supervisors by directly affecting their flexibility, access to resources, connections with higher-level officials, and control over working conditions.

After an initial gathering of data from supervisors and their subordinates, the personnel staff held meetings where all the supervisors were given tools for developing action plans for sharing the data with their people and collaborating on solutions to perceived problems. But then, in a departure from common practice in this organization, task forces of supervisors were formed to develop new systems for handling job and career issues common to them and their people. These task forces were given budgets, consultants, representation on a plantwide project steering committee alongside managers at much higher levels, and wide latitude in defining the nature and scope of the changes they wished to make. In short, lines of supply, information, and support were opened to them.

As the task forces progressed in their activities, it became clear to the plant management that the hoped-for changes in supervisory effectiveness were taking place much more rapidly through these structural changes in power than through conventional management training; so the conventional training was dropped. Not only did the pilot groups design useful new procedures for the plant, astonishing senior management in several cases with their knowledge and capabilities, but also, significantly, they learned to manage their own people better.

Several groups decided to involve shop-floor workers in their task forces; they could now see from their own experience the benefits of involving subordinates in solving job-related problems. Other supervisors began to experiment with ways to implement 'participatory management' by giving subordinates more control and influence without relinquishing their own authority.

Soon the 'problem supervisors' in the 'most troubled plant in the company' were getting the highest possible performance ratings and were considered models for direct production management. The sharing of organizational power from the top made possible the productive use of power below.

One might wonder why more organizations do not adopt such empowering strategies. There are standard answers: that giving up control is threatening to people who have fought for every shred of it; that people do not want to share power with those they look down on; that managers fear losing their own place and special privileges in the system; that 'predictability' often rates higher than 'flexibility' as an organizational value; and so forth.

But I would also put skepticism about employee abilities high on the list. Many modern bureaucratic systems are designed to minimize dependence on individual intelligence by making routine as many decisions as possible. So it often comes as a genuine surprise to top executives that people doing the more routine jobs could, indeed, make sophisticated decisions or use resources entrusted to them in intelligent ways.

In the same electronics company just mentioned, at the end of a quarter the pilot supervisory task forces were asked to report results and plans to senior management in order to have their new budget requests approved. The task forces made sure they were well prepared, and the high-level executives were duly impressed. In fact, they were *so* impressed that they kept interrupting the presentations with compliments, remarking that the supervisors could easily be doing sophisticated personnel work.

At first the supervisors were flattered. Such praise from upper management could only be taken well. But when the first glow wore off, several of them became very angry. They saw the excessive praise as patronizing and insulting: 'Didn't they think we could think? Didn't they imagine we were capable of doing this kind of work?' one asked. 'They must have seen us as just a bunch of animals. No wonder they gave us such limited jobs.'

As far as these supervisors were concerned, their abilities had always been there, in latent form perhaps, but still there. They as individuals had not changed – just their organizational power.

Women managers experience special power failures

The traditional problems of women in management are illustrative of how formal and informal practices can combine to engender powerlessness. Historically, women in management have found their opportunities in more routine, low-profile jobs. In staff positions, where they serve in support capacities to line managers but have no line responsibilities of their own, or in supervisory jobs managing 'stuck' subordinates, they are not in a position either to take the kinds of risks that build credibility or to develop their own team by pushing bright subordinates.

Such jobs, which have few favors to trade, tend to keep women out of the mainstream of the organization. This lack of clout, coupled with the greater difficulty anyone who is 'different' has in getting into the information and support networks, has meant that merely by organizational situation women in management have been more likely than men to be rendered structurally powerless. This is one reason those women who have achieved power have often had family connections that put them in the mainstream of the organization's social circles.

A disproportionate number of women managers are found among first-line supervisors or staff professionals; and they, like men in those circumstances, are likely to be organizationally powerless. But the behavior of other managers can contribute to the powerlessness of women in management in a number of less obvious ways.

One way other managers can make a woman powerless is by patronizingly overprotecting her: putting her in 'a safe job', not giving her enough to do to prove herself, and not suggesting her for high-risk, visible assignments. This protectiveness is sometimes born of 'good' intentions to give her every chance to succeed (why stack the deck against her?). Out of managerial concerns, out of awareness that a woman may be up against situations that men simply do not have to face, some very well-meaning managers protect their female managers ('It's a jungle, so why send her into it?').

Overprotectiveness can also mask a manager's fear of association with a woman should she fail. One senior bank official at a level below vice-president told me about his concerns with respect to a high-performing, financially experienced woman reporting to him. Despite *his* overwhelmingly positive work experiences with her, he was still afraid to recommend her for other assignments because he felt it was a personal risk. 'What if other managers are not as accepting of women as I am?' he asked. 'I know I'd be sticking my neck out; they would take her more because of my endorsement than her qualifications. And what if she doesn't make it? My judgment will be on the line.'

Overprotection is relatively benign compared with rendering a person powerless by providing obvious signs of lack of managerial support. For example, allowing someone supposedly in authority to be bypassed easily means that no one else has to take him or her seriously. If a woman's immediate supervisor or other managers listen willingly to criticism of her and show they are concerned every time a negative comment comes up and that they assume she must be at fault, then they are helping to undercut her. If managers let other people know that they have concerns about this person or that they are testing her to see how she does, then they are inviting other people to look for signs of inadequacy or failure.

Furthermore, people assume they can afford to bypass women because they 'must be uninformed' or 'don't know the ropes'. Even though women may be respected for their competence or expertise, they are not necessarily seen as being informed beyond the technical requirements of the job. There may be a grain of historical truth in this. Many women come to senior management positions as 'outsiders' rather than up through the usual channels.

Also, because until very recently men have not felt comfortable seeing women as business-people (business clubs have traditionally excluded women), they have tended to seek each other out for informal socializing. Anyone, male or female, seen as organizationally naïve and lacking sources of 'inside dope' will find his or her own lines of information limited.

Finally, even when women are able to achieve some power on their own, they have not necessarily been able to translate such personal credibility into an organizational power base. To create a network of supporters out of individual clout requires that a person pass on and share power, that subordinates and peers be empowered by virtue of their connection with that person. Traditionally, neither men nor women have seen women as capable of sponsoring others, even though they may be capable of achieving and succeeding on their own. Women have been viewed as the *recipients* of sponsorship rather than as the sponsors themselves.

(As more women prove themselves in organizations and think more self-consciously about bringing along young people, this situation may change. However, I still hear many more questions from women managers about how they can benefit from mentors, sponsors, or peer networks than about how they themselves can start to pass on favors and make use of their own resources to benefit others.)

Viewing managers in terms of power and powerlessness helps explain two familiar stereotypes about women and leadership in organizations: that no one wants a woman boss (although studies show that anyone who has ever had a woman boss is likely to have had a positive experience), and that the reason no one wants a woman boss is that women are 'too controlling, rules-minded, and petty'.

The first stereotype simply makes clear that power is important to leadership. Underneath the preference for men is the assumption that, given the current distribution of people in organizational leadership positions, men are more likely than women to be in positions to achieve power and, therefore, to share their power with others. Similarly, the 'bossy woman boss' stereotype is a perfect picture of powerlessness. All of those traits are just as characteristic of men who are powerless, but because of circumstances I have mentioned, women are slightly more likely to find themselves powerless than are men. Women with power in the organization are just as effective – and preferred – as men.

Recent interviews conducted with about 600 bank managers show that, when a woman exhibits the petty traits of powerlessness, people assume that she does so 'because she is a woman'. A striking difference is that, when a man engages in the same behavior, people assume the behavior is a matter of his own individual style and characteristics and do not conclude that it reflects on the suitability of men for management.

References

BENNIS, W. (1976), *The Unconscious Conspiracy: Why Leaders Can't Lead*, AMACOM

FULMER, W. E. (1976), 'Supervisory selection: the acid test of affirmative action', *Personnel*, November–December

GYLLENHAMMAR, P. G. (1977), *People at Work*, Addison-Wesley

KANTER, R. M. (1977), *Men and Women of the Corporation*, Basic Books

KANTER, R. M., and STEIN, B. A. (eds.) (1979), *Life in Organizations*, Basic Books

KIPNIS, D. (1976), *The Powerholders*, University of Chicago Press

McCLELLAND, D. C. (1975), *Power: The Inner Experience*, Irvington Publishers
PELZ, D. C. (1952), 'Influence: a key to effective leadership in the first-line supervisor', *Personnel*, November

16 J. G. March

The Technology of Foolishness

From J. G. March and J. P. Olsen, *Ambiguity and Choice in Organizations*, Universitetsförlaget, 1976, chapter 5

Choice and rationality

The concept of choice as a focus for interpreting and guiding human behavior has rarely had an easy time in the realm of ideas. It is beset by theological disputations over free will, by the dilemmas of absurdism, by the doubts of psychological behaviorism, by the claims of historical, economic, social, and demographic determinism. Nevertheless, the idea that humans make choices has proven robust enough to become a major matter of faith in important segments of contemporary western civilization. It is a faith that is professed by virtually all theories of social policy making.

The major tenets of this faith run something like this. Human beings make choices. If done properly, choices are made by evaluating alternatives in terms of goals on the basis of information currently available. The alternative that is most attractive in terms of the goals is chosen. The process of making choices can be improved by using the technology of choice. Through the paraphernalia of modern techniques, we can improve the quality of the search for alternatives, the quality of information, and the quality of the analysis used to evaluate alternatives. Although actual choice may fall short of this ideal in various ways, it is an attractive model of how choices should be made by individuals, organizations, and social systems.

These articles of faith have been built upon, and have stimulated, some scripture. It is the scripture of theories of decision-making. The scripture is partly a codification of received doctrine and partly a source for that doctrine. As a result, our cultural ideas of intelligence and our theories of

339

choice bear some substantial resemblance. In particular, they share three conspicuous interrelated ideas.

The first idea is the *pre-existence of purpose*. We find it natural to base an interpretation of human choice behavior on a presumption of human purpose. We have, in fact, invented one of the most elaborate terminologies in the professional literature: 'values', 'needs', 'wants', 'goods', 'tastes', 'preferences', 'utility', 'objectives', 'goals', 'aspirations', 'drives'. All of these reflect a strong tendency to believe that a useful interpretation of human behavior involves defining a set of objectives that (a) are prior attributes of the system, and (b) make the observed behavior in some sense intelligent vis-à-vis those objectives.

Whether we are talking about individuals or about organizations, purpose is an obvious presumption of the discussion. An organization is often defined in terms of its purpose. It is seen by some as the largest collectivity directed by a purpose. Action within an organization is justified (or criticized) in terms of the purpose. Individuals explain their own behavior, as well as the behavior of others, in terms of a set of value premises that are presumed to be antecedent to the behavior. Normative theories of choice begin with an assumption of a pre-existent preference-ordering defined over the possible outcomes of a choice.

The second idea is the *necessity of consistency*. We have come to recognize consistency both as an important property of human behavior and as a prerequisite for normative models of choice. Dissonance theory, balance theory, theories of congruency in attitudes, statuses, and performances have all served to remind us of the possibilities for interpreting human behavior in terms of the consistency requirements of a limited-capacity information-processing system.

At the same time, consistency is a cultural and theoretical virtue. Action should be made consistent with belief. Actions taken by different parts of an organization should be consistent with each other. Individual and organizational activities are seen as connected with each other in terms of their consequences for some consistent set of purposes. In an organization, the structural manifestation of a dictum of consistency is the hierarchy with its obligations of coordination and control. In the individual, the structural manifestation is a set of values that generates a consistent preference-ordering.

The third idea is the *primacy of rationality*. By rationality I mean a procedure for deciding what is correct behavior by relating consequences systematically to objectives. By placing primary emphasis on rational techniques, we implicitly have rejected – or seriously impaired – two other procedures for choice: (a) the processes of intuition, by means of which people may do things without fully understanding why and (b) the processes of tradition and faith, through which people do things because that is the way they are done.

Both within the theory and within the culture we insist on the ethic of rationality. We justify individual and organizational action in terms of an analysis of means and ends. Impulse, intuition, faith, and tradition are outside that system and viewed as antithetical to it. Faith may be seen as a possible source of values. Intuition may be seen as a possible source of ideas about alternatives. But the analysis and justification of action lie within the context of reason.

These ideas are obviously deeply embedded in the culture. The roots extend into ideas that have conditioned much of modern western history and interpretations of that history. Their general acceptance is probably highly correlated with the permeation of rationalism and individualism into the style of thinking within the culture. The ideas are even more obviously embedded in modern theories of choice. It is fundamental to those theories that thinking should precede action; that action should serve a purpose; that purpose should be defined in terms of a consistent set of pre-existent goals; and that choice should be based on a consistent theory of the relation between action and its consequences.

Every tool of management decision that is currently a part of management science, operations research, or decision theory assumes the prior existence of a set of consistent goals. Almost the entire structure of microeconomic theory builds on the assumption that there exists a well-defined, stable, and consistent preference-ordering. Most theories of individual or organizational choice behavior accept the idea that goals exist and that (in some sense) an individual or organization acts on those goals, choosing from among some alternatives on the basis of available information. Discussions of educational policy, for example, with the emphasis on goal setting, evaluation, and accountability, are directly in this tradition.

From the perspective of all of man's history, the ideas of purpose, consistency, and rationality are relatively new. Much of the technology currently available to implement them is extremely new. Over the past few centuries, and conspicuously over the past few decades, we have substantially improved man's capability for acting purposively, consistently, and rationally. We have substantially increased his propensity to think of himself as doing so. It is an impressive victory, won — where it has been won — by a happy combination of timing, performance, ideology, and persistence. It is a battle yet to be concluded, or even engaged, in many cultures of the world; but within most of the western world, individuals and organizations see themselves as making choices.

The problem of goals

The tools of intelligence as they are fashioned in modern theories of choice are necessary to any reasonable behavior in contemporary society. It is difficult to see how we could, and inconceivable that we would, fail to continue their development, refinement, and extension. As might be expected, however, a theory and ideology of choice built on the ideas outlined above is deficient in some obvious, elementary ways, most conspicuously in the treatment of human goals.

Goals are thrust upon the intelligent man. We ask that he act in the name of goals. We ask that he keep his goals consistent. We ask that his actions be oriented to his goals. We ask that a social system amalgamate individual goals into a collective goal. But we do not concern ourselves with the origin of goals. Theories of individual organizational and social choice assume actors with pre-existent values.

Since it is obvious that goals change over time and that the character of those changes affects both the richness of personal and social development and the outcome of choice behavior, a theory of choice must somehow justify ignoring the phenomena. Although it is unreasonable to ask a theory of choice to solve all of the problems of man and his development, it is reasonable to ask how something as conspicuous as the fluidity and ambiguity of objectives can plausibly be ignored in a theory that is offered as a guide to human choice behavior.

There are three classic justifications. The first is that goal development and choice are independent processes, conceptually and behaviorally. The second is that the model of choice is never satisfied in fact and that deviations from the model accommodate the problems of introducing change. The third is that the idea of changing goals is so intractable in a normative theory of choice that nothing can be said about it. Since I am unpersuaded of the first and second justifications, my optimism with respect to the third is somewhat greater than most of my fellows'.

The argument that goal development and choice are independent behaviorally seems clearly false. It seems to me perfectly obvious that a description that assumes goals come first and action comes later is frequently radically wrong. Human choice behavior is at least as much a process for discovering goals as for acting on them. Although it is true enough that goals and decisions are 'conceptually' distinct, that is simply a statement of the theory. It is not a defence of it. They are conceptually distinct if we choose to make them so.

The argument that the model is incomplete is more persuasive. There do appear to be some critical 'holes' in the system of intelligence as described by standard theories of choice. There is incomplete information, incomplete goal consistency, and a variety of external processes impinging on goal development – including intuition and tradition. What is somewhat disconcerting about the argument, however, is that it makes the efficacy of the concepts of intelligent choice dependent on their inadequacy. As we become more competent in the techniques of the mode, and more committed to it, the 'holes' become smaller. As the model becomes more accepted, our obligation to modify it increases.

The final argument seems to me sensible as a general principle, but misleading here. Why are we more reluctant to ask how human beings might find 'good' goals than we are to ask how they might make 'good' decisions? The second question appears to be a relatively technical problem. The first seems more pretentious. It claims to say something about alternative virtues. The appearance of pretense, however, stems directly from the theory and the ideology associated with it.

In fact, the conscious introduction of goal discovery as a consideration in theories of human choice is not unknown to modern man. For example, we have two kinds of theories of choice behavior in human beings. One is a theory of children. The other is a theory of adults. In the theory of childhood, we emphasize choices as leading to experiences that develop the child's scope, his complexity, his awareness of the world. As parents, or psychologists, we try to lead the child to do things that are inconsistent with his present goals because we know (or believe) that he can only develop into an interesting person by coming to appreciate objects of experience that he initially rejects.

In the theory of adulthood, we emphasize choices as a consequence of our intentions. As adults, or economists, we try to take actions that (within the limits of scarce resources) come as close as possible to achieving our goals. We try to find improved ways of making decisions consistent with our perceptions of what is valuable in the world.

The asymmetry in these models is conspicuous. Adults have constructed a model world in which adults know what is good for themselves, but children do not. It is hard to react positively to the conceit. The asymmetry has, in fact, stimulated a rather large number of ideologies and reforms designed to allow children the same moral prerogative granted to adults –

the right to imagine that they know what they want. The efforts have cut deeply into traditional childrearing, traditional educational policies, traditional politics, and traditional consumer economics.

In my judgment, the asymmetry between models of choice for adults and models of choice for children is awkward; but the solution we have adopted is precisely wrong-headed. Instead of trying to adapt the model of adults to children, we might better adapt the model of children to adults. For many purposes, our model of children is better. Of course, children know what they want. Everyone does. The critical question is whether they are encouraged to develop more interesting 'wants'. Values change. People become more interesting as those values and the interconnections made among them change.

One of the most obvious things in the world turns out to be hard for us to accommodate in our theory of choice: a child of two will almost always have a less interesting set of values (yes, indeed, a *worse* set of values) than a child of twelve. The same is true of adults. Values develop through experience. Although one of the main natural arenas for the modification of human values is the area of choice, our theories of adult and organizational decision making ignore the phenomenon entirely.

Introducing ambiguity and fluidity to the interpretation of individual, organizational, and societal goals obviously has implications for behavioral theories of decision-making. The main point here, however, is not to consider how we might describe the behavior of systems that are discovering goals as they act. Rather, it is to examine how we might improve the quality of that behavior, how we might aid the development of interesting goals.

We know how to advise a society, an organization, or an individual if we are first given a consistent set of preferences. Under some conditions, we can suggest how to make decisions if the preferences are only consistent up to the point of specifying a series of independent constraints on the choice. But what about a normative theory of goal-finding behavior? What do we say when our client tells us that he is not sure his present set of values is the set of values in terms of which he wants to act? It is a question familiar to many aspects of ordinary life. It is a question that friends, associates, students, college presidents, business managers, voters, and children ask at least as frequently as they ask how they should act within a set of consistent and stable values.

Within the context of the normative theory of choice as it exists, the answer we give is: first determine the values, then act. The advice is frequently useful. Moreover, we have developed ways in which we can use conventional techniques for decision analysis to help discover value premises and to expose value inconsistencies. These techniques involve testing the decision implications of some successive approximations to a set of preferences. The object is to find a consistent set of preferences with implications that are acceptable to the person or organization making the decisions. Variations on such techniques are used routinely in operations research, as well as in personal counseling and analysis. The utility of such techniques, however, apparently depends on the assumption that a primary problem is the amalgamation or excavation of pre-existent values. The metaphors – 'finding oneself', 'goal clarification', 'self-discovery', 'social-welfare function', 'revealed preference' – are metaphors of search. If our value premises are to be 'constructed' rather than 'discovered', our standard procedures may be useful; but we have no a priori reason for assuming they will.

Perhaps we should explore a somewhat different approach to the normative question of how we ought to behave when our value premises are not yet (and never will be) fully determined. Suppose we treat action as a way of creating interesting goals at the same time as we treat goals as a way of justifying action. It is an intuitively plausible and simple idea, but one that is not immediately within the domain of standard normative theories of intelligent choice.

Interesting people and interesting organizations construct complicated theories of themselves. In order to do this, they need to supplement the technology of reason with a technology of foolishness. Individuals and organizations need ways of doing things for which they have no good reason. Not always. Not usually. But sometimes. They need to act before they think.

Sensible foolishness

In order to use the act of intelligent choice as a planned occasion for discovering new goals, we apparently require some idea of sensible foolishness. Which of the many foolish things that we might do now will lead to attractive value consequences? The question is almost inconceivable. Not only does it ask us to predict the value consequences of action, it asks us to evaluate them. In what terms can we talk about 'good' changes in goals?

In effect, we are asked either to specify a set of super-goals in terms of which alternative goals are evaluated, or to choose among alternatives *now* in terms of the unknown set of values we will have at some future time (or the distribution over time of that unknown set of future values). The former alternative moves us back to the original situation of a fixed set of values – now called 'super-goals' – and hardly seems an important step in the direction of inventing procedures for discovering new goals. The latter alternative seems fundamental enough, but it violates severely our sense of temporal order. To say that we make decisions now in terms of goals that will only be knowable later is nonsensical – as long as we accept the basic framework of the theory of choice and its presumptions of pre-existent goals.

I do not know in detail what is required, but I think it will be substantial. As we challenge the dogma of pre-existent goals, we will be forced to re-examine some of our most precious prejudices: the strictures against imitation, coercion, and rationalization. Each of those honorable prohib- itions depends on the view of man and human choice imposed on us by conventional theories of choice.

Imitation is not necessarily a sign of moral weakness. It is a prediction. It is a prediction that if we duplicate the behavior or attitudes of someone else, the chances of our discovering attractive new goals for ourselves are relatively high. In order for imitation to be normatively attractive we need a better theory of who should be imitated. Such a theory seems to be eminently feasible. For example, what are the conditions for effectiveness of a rule that you should imitate another person whose values are close to yours? How do the chances of discovering interesting goals through imita- tion change as the number of other people exhibiting the behavior to be imitated increases?

Coercion is not necessarily an assault on individual autonomy. It can be a device for stimulating individuality. We recognize this when we talk about parents and children (at least sometimes). What has always been difficult with coercion is the possibility for perversion that it involves, not its obvious capability for stimulating change. What we require is a theory of the circumstances under which entry into a coercive system produces behavior that leads to the discovery of interesting goals. We are all familiar with the tactic. We use it in imposing deadlines, entering contracts, making commitments. What are the conditions for its effective use? In particular, what are the conditions for coercion in social systems?

Rationalization is not necessarily a way of evading morality. It can be a test for the feasibility of a goal change. When deciding among alternative actions for which we have no good reason, it may be sensible to develop some definition of how 'near' to intelligence alternative 'unintelligent' actions lie. Effective rationalization permits this kind of incremental approach to changes in values. To use it effectively, however, we require a better idea of the kinds of metrics that might be possible in measuring value distances. At the same time, rationalization is the major procedure for integrating newly discovered goals into an existing structure of values. It provides the organization of complexity without which complexity itself becomes indistinguishable from randomness.

There are dangers in imitation, coercion, and rationalization. The risks are too familiar to elaborate. We should, indeed, be able to develop better techniques. Whatever those techniques may be, however, they will almost certainly undermine the superstructure of biases erected on purpose, consistency, and rationality. They will involve some way of thinking about action now as occurring in terms of a set of unknown future values.

Play and reason

A second requirement for a technology of foolishness is some strategy for suspending rational imperatives toward consistency. Even if we know which of several foolish things we want to do, we still need a mechanism for allowing us to do it. How do we escape the logic of our reason?

Here, I think, we are closer to understanding what we need. It is playfulness. Playfulness is the deliberate, temporary relaxation of rules in order to explore the possibilities of alternative rules. When we are playful, we challenge the necessity of consistency. In effect, we announce – in advance – our rejection of the usual objections to behavior that does not fit the standard model of intelligence. Playfulness allows experimentation. At the same time, it acknowledges reason. It accepts an obligation that at some point either the playful behavior will be stopped or it will be integrated into the structure of intelligence in some way that makes sense. The suspension of the rules is temporary.

The idea of play may suggest three things that are, to my mind, quite erroneous in the present context. First, play may be seen as a kind of Mardi Gras for reason, a release of emotional tensions of virtue. Although it is possible that play performs some such function, that is not the function with which I am concerned. Second, play may be seen as part of some mystical balance of spiritual principles: fire and water, hot and cold, weak and strong. The intention here is much narrower than a general mystique of balance. Third, play may be seen as an antithesis of intelligence, so that the emphasis on the importance of play becomes a support for simple self-indulgence. My present intent is to propose play as an instrument of intelligence, not a substitute.

Playfulness is a natural outgrowth of our standard view of reason. A strict insistence on purpose, consistency, and rationality limits our ability to find new purposes. Play relaxes that insistence to allow us to act 'unintelligently' or 'irrationally', or 'foolishly' to explore alternative ideas of possible purposes and alternative concepts of behavioral consistency. And it does this while maintaining our basic commitment to the necessity of intelligence.

Although play and reason are in this way functional complements, they are often behavioral competitors. They are alternative styles and alternative orientations to the same situation. There is no guarantee that the styles will be equally well-developed. There is no guarantee that all individuals, all organizations, or all societies will be equally adept in both styles. There is no guarantee that all cultures will be equally encouraging to both. Our design problem is either to specify the best mix of styles or, failing that, to assure that most people and most organizations most of the time use an alternation of strategies rather than persevering in either one. It is a difficult problem. The optimization problem looks extremely difficult on the face of it, and the learning situations that will produce alternation in behavior appear to be somewhat less common than those that produce perseverance.

Consider, for example, the difficulty of sustaining playfulness as a style within contemporary American society. Individuals who are good at consistent rationality are rewarded early and heavily. We define it as intelligence, and the educational rewards of society are associated strongly with it. Social norms press in the same direction, particularly for men. Many of the demands of modern organizational life reinforce the same abilities and style preferences. The result is that many of the most influential, best-educated, and best-placed citizens have experienced a powerful over-learning with respect to rationality. They are exceptionally good at maintaining consistent pictures of themselves, of relating action to purposes. They are exceptionally poor at a playful attitude toward their own beliefs, toward the logic of consistency, or toward the way they see things as being connected in the world. The dictates of manliness, forcefulness, independence, and intelligence are intolerant of playful urges if they arise. The playful urges that arise are weak ones.

The picture is probably overdrawn, but not, I believe, the implications. For societies, for organizations, and for individuals reason and intelligence have had the unnecessary consequence of inhibiting the development of purpose into more complicated forms of consistency. In order to move away from that position, we need to find some ways of helping individuals and organizations to experiment with doing things for which they have no good reason, to be playful with their conception of themselves. It is a facility that requires more careful attention than I can give it, but I would suggest five things as a small beginning:

First, we can treat *goals* as *hypotheses*. Conventional decision theory allows us to entertain doubts about almost everything except the thing about which we frequently have the greatest doubt – our objectives. Suppose we define the decision process as a time for the sequential testing of hypotheses about goals. If we can experiment with alternative goals, we stand some chance of discovering complicated and interesting combinations of good values that none of us previously imagined.

Second, we can treat *intuition* as *real*. I do not know what intuition is, or even if it is any one thing. Perhaps it is simply an excuse for doing something we cannot justify in terms of present values or for refusing to follow the logic of our own beliefs. Perhaps it is an inexplicable way of consulting that part of our intelligence that is not organized in a way anticipated by standard theories of choice. In either case, intuition permits us to see some possible actions that are outside our present scheme for justifying behavior.

Third, we can treat *hypocrisy* as a *transition*. Hypocrisy is an inconsistency between expressed values and behavior. Negative attitudes about hypocrisy stem from two major things. The first is a general onus against inconsistency. The second is a sentiment against combining the pleasures of vice with the appearance of virtue. Apparently, that is an unfair way of allowing evil to escape temporal punishment. Whatever the merits of such a position as ethics, it seems to be distinctly inhibiting towards change. A bad man with good intentions may be a man experimenting with the possibility of becoming good. Somehow it seems to me more sensible to encourage the experimentation than to insult it.

Fourth, we can treat *memory* as an *enemy*. The rules of consistency and rationality require a technology of memory. For most purposes, good memories make good choices. But the ability to forget, or overlook, is also useful. If I do not know what I did yesterday or what other people in the organization are doing today, I can act within the system of reason and still do things that are foolish.

Fifth, we can treat *experience* as a *theory*. Learning can be viewed as a series of conclusions based on concepts of action and consequences that we have invented. Experience can be changed retrospectively. By changing our interpretive concepts now, we modify what we learned earlier. Thus, we expose the possibility of experimenting with alternative histories. The usual strictures against 'self-deception' in experience need occasionally to be tempered with an awareness of the extent to which all experience is an interpretation subject to conscious revision. Personal histories, and national histories, need to be rewritten continuously as a base for the retrospective learning of new self-conceptions.

Each of these procedures represents a way in which we temporarily suspend the operation of the system of reasoned intelligence. They are playful. They make greatest sense in situations in which there has been an overlearning of virtues of conventional rationality. They are possibly dangerous applications of powerful devices more familiar to the study of behavioral pathology than to the investigation of human development. But they offer a few techniques for introducing change within current concepts of choice.

The argument extends easily to the problems of social organization. If we knew more about the normative theory of 'acting before you think', we could say more intelligent things about the functions of management and leadership when organizations or societies do not know what they are doing. Consider, for example, the following general implications.

First, we need to re-examine the functions of management decision. One of the primary ways in which the goals of an organization are developed is by interpreting the decisions it makes, and one feature of good managerial decisions is that they lead to the development of more interesting value premises for the organization. As a result, decisions should not be seen as flowing directly or strictly from a pre-existent set of objectives. Managers who make decisions might well view that function somewhat less as a process of deduction or a process of political negotiation and somewhat more as a process of gently upsetting preconceptions of what the organization is doing.

Second, we need a modified view of planning. Planning in organizations has many virtues, but a plan can often be more effective as an interpretation of past decisions than as a program for future ones. It can be used as a part of the efforts of the organization to develop a new consistent theory of itself that incorporates the mix of recent actions into a moderately comprehensive structure of goals. Procedures for interpreting the meaning of most past events are familiar to the memoirs of retired generals, prime ministers, business leaders, and movie stars. They suffer from the company they keep. In an organization that wants to continue to develop new objectives, a manager needs to be relatively tolerant of the idea that he will discover the meaning of yesterday's action in the experiences and interpretations of today.

Third, we need to reconsider evaluation. As nearly as I can determine, there is nothing in a formal theory of evaluation that requires that the criterion function for evaluation be specified in advance. In particular, the evaluation of social experiments need not be in terms of the degree to which they have fulfilled our a priori expectations. Rather, we can examine what they did in terms of what we now believe to be important. The prior specification of criteria and the prior specification of evaluational procedures that depend on such criteria are common presumptions in contemporary social policy making. They are presumptions that inhibit the serendipitous discovery of new criteria. Experience should be used explicitly as an occasion for evaluating our values as well as our actions.

Fourth, we need a reconsideration of social accountability. Individual preferences and social action need to be consistent in some way. But the process of pursuing consistency is one in which both the preferences and the actions change over time. Imagination in social policy formation involves systematically adapting to and influencing preferences. It would be unfortunate if our theories of social action encouraged leaders to ignore their responsibilities for anticipating public preferences through action and for providing social experiences that modify individual expectations.

Fifth, we need to accept playfulness in social organizations. The design of organizations should attend to the problems of maintaining both playfulness and reason as aspects of intelligent choice. Since much of the literature on social design is concerned with strengthening the rationality of decisions, managers are likely to overlook the importance of play. This is partly a matter of making the individuals within an organization more playful by encouraging the attitudes and skills of inconsistency. It is also a matter of making organizational structure and organizational procedure more playful. Organizations can be playful even when the participants in them are not. The managerial devices for maintaining consistency can be varied. We encourage organizational play by permitting (and insisting on) some temporary relief from control, coordination, and communication.

Intelligence and foolishness

Contemporary theories of decision-making and the technology of reason have considerably strengthened our capabilities for effective social action. The conversion of the simple ideas of choice into an extensive technology is a major achievement. It is, however, an achievement that has reinforced some biases in the underlying models of choice in individuals and groups.

In particular, it has reinforced the uncritical acceptance of a static interpretation of human goals.

There is little magic in the world, and foolishness in people and organizations is one of the many things that fail to produce miracles. Under certain conditions, it is one of several ways in which some of the problems of our current theories of intelligence can be overcome. It may be a good way. It preserves the virtues of consistency while stimulating change. If we had a good technology of foolishness, it might (in combination with the technology of reason) help in a small way to develop the unusual combinations of attitudes and behaviors that describe the interesting people, interesting organizations, and interesting societies of the world.

PART FOUR
People in Organizations

Organizations are systems of interdependent human beings. From some points of view the members of an organization may be considered as a resource, but they are a special kind of resource in that they are directly involved in all the functioning processes of the organization and can affect its aims as well as the methods used to accomplish them. The contributors to this section are concerned to analyse the behaviour of people as they affect, and are affected by, organization processes.

Mayo (Reading 17) was the inspirer of the famous Hawthorne studies and the 'founding father' of the human relations movement – the first major impact of social science on management thinking. He emphasized that workers must first be understood as people if they are to be understood as organization members. From his work have followed a large number of studies which demonstrate the social processes which inevitably surround the formal management system: the informal organization which is part of every organization's infrastructure.

Herzberg (Reading 18) challenges existing views on motivation, maintaining that as well as economic needs human beings have psychological needs for autonomy, responsibility and development which have to be satisfied in work. He advocates the 'enrichment' of jobs through additional responsibility and authority in order to promote improved performance and increased mental health.

Schein (Reading 19) has been concerned to understand the relationship between the individual's career and the organization's culture. He describes the 'career anchors' developed by people that provide the attitudes through which they see themselves, their jobs and their relationship to the organization.

Weick (Reading 20) focuses on the way in which individuals 'enact' (i.e. create for themselves) their understanding of organizational situations based upon subjective preconceptions. These attempts at 'sensemaking' are a particular concern in complex crisis situations. There is then a trade-off between dangerous action which improves understanding and safe inaction

353

which produces confusion. As an example, he analyses the Union Carbide catastrophe in Bhopal, India.

Argyris (Reading 21) points to the power of 'defensive routines'. These are psychological blocks to development, which limit an organization's ability to draw on the full potential of its members. He suggests ways in which they might be overcome to produce an organization more open to change and able to participate in innovative 'double-loop' learning.

17 E. Mayo

Hawthorne and the Western Electric Company

From *The Social Problems of an Industrial Civilization*, Routledge, 1949, chapter 4

A highly competent group of Western Electric engineers refused to accept defeat when experiments to demonstrate the effect of illumination on work seemed to lead nowhere. The conditions of scientific experiment had apparently been fulfilled – experimental room, control room; changes introduced one at a time; all other conditions held steady. And the results were perplexing: Roethlisberger gives two instances – lighting improved in the experimental room, production went up; but it rose also in the control room. The opposite of this: lighting diminished from ten to three foot-candles in the experimental room and production again went up; simultaneously in the control room, with illumination constant, production also rose (F. J. Roethlisberger, 1941). Many other experiments, and all inconclusive; yet it had seemed so easy to determine the effect of illumination on work.

In matters of mechanics or chemistry the modern engineer knows how to set about the improvement of process or the redress of error. But the determination of optimum working conditions for the human being is left largely to dogma and tradition, guess, or quasi-philosophical argument. In modern large-scale industry the three persistent problems of management are:

1. The application of science and technical skill to some material good or product.
2. The systematic ordering of operations.
3. The organization of teamwork – that is, of sustained cooperation.

The last must take account of the need for continual reorganization of teamwork as operating conditions are changed in an *adaptive* society.

355

The first of these holds enormous prestige and interest and is the subject of continuous experiment. The second is well developed in practice. The third, by comparison with the other two, is almost wholly neglected. Yet it remains true that if these three are out of balance, the organization as a whole will not be successful. The first two operate to make an industry *effective*, in Chester Barnard's phrase, the third, to make it *efficient*. For the larger and more complex the institution, the more dependent is it upon the wholehearted cooperation of every member of the group.

This was not altogether the attitude of Mr G. A. Pennock and his colleagues when they set up the experimental 'test room'. But the illumination fiasco had made them alert to the need that very careful records should be kept of everything that happened in the room in addition to the obvious engineering and industrial devices.[1] Their observations therefore included not only records of industrial and engineering changes but also records of physiological or medical changes, and, in a sense, of social and anthropological. This last took the form of a 'log' that gave as full an account as possible of the actual events of every day, a record that proved most useful to Whitehead when he was re-measuring the recording tapes and re-calculating the changes in productive output. He was able to relate eccentricities of the output curve to the actual situation at a given time – that is to say, to the events of a specific day or week.

First phase – the test room

The facts are by now well known. Briefly restated, the test room began its inquiry by first attempting to secure the active collaboration of the workers. This took some time but was gradually successful, especially after the retirement of the original first and second workers and after the new worker at the second bench had assumed informal leadership of the group. From this point on, the evidence presented by Whitehead or Roethlisberger and Dickson seems to show that the individual workers became a team, wholeheartedly committed to the project. Second, the conditions of work were changed one at a time: rest periods of different numbers and length, shorter working day, shorter working week, food with soup or coffee in the morning break. And the results seemed satisfactory: slowly at first, but

1. For a full account of the experimental setup, see F. J. Roethlisberger and W. J. Dickson (1939) and T. North Whitehead, *The Industrial Worker*, vol. 1 (1938), Harvard University Press.

later with increasing certainty, the output record (used as an index of well-being) mounted. Simultaneously the girls claimed that they felt less fatigued, felt that they were not making any special effort. Whether these claims were accurate or no, they at least indicated increased contentment with the general situation in the test room by comparison with the department outside. At every point in the programme, the workers had been consulted with respect to proposed changes; they had arrived at the point of free expression of ideas and feelings to management. And it had been arranged thus that the twelfth experimental change should be a return to the original conditions of work – no rest periods, no mid-morning lunch, no shortened day or week. It had also been arranged that, after twelve weeks of this, the group should return to the conditions of period 7, a fifteen-minute mid-morning break with lunch and a ten-minute mid-afternoon rest. The story is now well known: in period 12 the daily and weekly output rose to a point higher than at any other time (the hourly rate adjusted itself downward by a small fraction), and in the whole twelve weeks 'there was no downward trend'. In the following period, the return to the conditions of work as in the seventh experimental change, the output curve soared to even greater heights: this thirteenth period lasted for thirty-one weeks.

These periods, 12 and 13, made it evident that increments of production could not be related point for point to the experimental changes introduced. Some major change was taking place that was chiefly responsible for the index of improved conditions – the steadily increasing output. Period 12 – but for minor qualifications, such as 'personal time out' – ignored the nominal return to original conditions of work and the output curve continued its upward passage. Put in other words, there was no actual return to original conditions. This served to bring another fact to the attention of the observers. Periods 7, 10 and 13 had nominally the same working conditions, as above described – fifteen-minute rest and lunch in mid-morning, ten-minute rest in the afternoon. But the average weekly output for each girl was:

Period 7 – 2,500 units
Period 10 – 2,800 units
Period 13 – 3,000 units

Periods 3 and 12 resembled each other also in that both required a full day's work without rest periods. But here also the difference of average weekly output for each girl was:

Period 3 – less than 2,500 units
Period 12 – more than 2,900 units.

Here then was a situation comparable perhaps with the illumination experiment, certainly suggestive of the Philadelphia experience where improved conditions for one team of mule spinners were reflected in improved morale not only in the experimental team but in the two other teams who had received no such benefit.

This interesting, and indeed amusing, result has been so often discussed that I need make no mystery of it now. I have often heard my colleague Roethlisberger declare that the major experimental change was introduced when those in charge sought to hold the situation humanly steady (in the interest of critical changes to be introduced) by getting the cooperation of the workers. What actually happened was that six individuals became a team and the team gave itself wholeheartedly and spontaneously to cooperation in the experiment. The consequence was that they felt themselves to be participating freely and without afterthought, and were happy in the knowledge that they were working without coercion from above or limitation from below. They were themselves astonished at the consequence, for they felt that they were working under less pressure than ever before: and in this, their feelings and performance echoed that of the mule spinners.

Here then are two topics which deserve the closest attention of all those engaged in administrative work – the organization of working teams and the free participation of such teams in the task and purpose of the organization as it directly affects them in their daily round.

Second phase – the interview programme

But such conclusions were not possible at the time: the major change, the question as to the exact difference between conditions of work in the test room and in the plant departments, remained something of a mystery. Officers of the company determined to 'take another look' at departments outside the test room – this, with the idea that something quite important was there to be observed, something to which the experiment should have made them alert. So the interview programme was introduced.

It was speedily discovered that the question–and–answer type of interview was useless in the situation. Workers wished to talk, and to talk freely under the seal of professional confidence (which was never abused) to someone who seemed representative of the company or who seemed, by his very attitude, to carry authority. The experience itself was unusual; there are few people in this world who have had the experience of finding someone intelligent, attentive and eager to listen without interruption to all that he or she has to say. But to arrive at this point it became necessary to train interviewers how to listen, how to avoid interruption or the giving of advice, how generally to avoid anything that might put an end to free expression in an individual instance. Some approximate rules to guide the interviewer in his work were therefore set down. These were, more or less, as follows:[2]

1. Give your whole attention to the person interviewed, and make it evident that you are doing so.
2. Listen — don't talk.
3. Never argue; never give advice.
4. Listen to:
   (a) What he wants to say.
   (b) What he does not want to say.
   (c) What he cannot say without help.
5. As you listen, plot out tentatively and for subsequent correction the pattern (personal) that is being set before you. To test this, from time to time summarize what has been said and present for comment (e.g. 'Is this what you are telling me?'). Always do this with the greatest caution, that is, clarify but do not add or distort.
6. Remember that everything said must be considered a personal confidence and not divulged to anyone. (This does not prevent discussion of a situation between professional colleagues. Nor does it prevent some form of public report when due precaution has been taken.)

It must not be thought that this type of interviewing is easily learned. It is true that some persons, men and women alike, have a natural flair for the work, but, even with them, there tends to be an early period of discouragement, a feeling of futility, through which the experience and coaching of a senior interviewer must carry them. The important rules in the interview (important, that is, for the development of high skill) are two. First, rule 4 indicates the need to help the individual interviewed to articulate expression of an idea or attitude that he has not before expressed; and, second, rule 5 which indicates the need from time to time to summarize what has been said and to present it for comment. Once equipped

2. For a full discussion of this type of interview, see F. J. Roethlisberger and W. J. Dickson (1939), chapter 13. For a more summary and perhaps less technical discussion, see Homans (1941).

to do this effectively, interviewers develop very considerable skill. But, let me say again, this skill is not easily acquired. It demands of the interviewer a real capacity to follow the contours of another person's thinking, to understand the meaning for him of what he says.

I do not believe that any member of the research group or its associates had anticipated the immediate response that would be forthcoming to this introduction of such an interview programme. Such comments as 'This is the best thing the Company has ever done', or 'The Company should have done this long ago', were frequently heard. It was as if workers had been awaiting an opportunity for expressing freely and without afterthought their feelings on a great variety of modern situations, not by any means limited to the various departments of the plant. To find an intelligent person who was not only eager to listen but also anxious to help to give expression to ideas and feelings but dimly understood – this, for many thousand persons, was an experience without precedent in the modern world.

In a former statement (E. Mayo, 1933, p. 114) I named two questions that inevitably presented themselves to the interviewing group in these early stages of the study:

1. Is some experience which might be described as an experience of personal futility a common incident of industrial organization for work?
2. Does life in a modern industrial city, in some unrealized way, predispose workers to obsessive response?

And I said that these two questions 'in some form' continued to preoccupy those in charge of the research until the conclusion of the study.

After twelve years of further study (not yet concluded), there are certain developments that demand attention. For example, I had not fully realized in 1932, when the above was written, how profoundly the social structure of civilization has been shaken by scientific, engineering and industrial development. This radical change – the passage from an *established* to an *adaptive* social order – has brought into being a host of new and unanticipated problems for management and for the individual worker. The management problem appears at its acutest in the work of the supervisor. No longer does the supervisor work with a team of persons that he has known for many years or perhaps a lifetime; he is a leader of a group of individuals that forms and disappears almost as he watches it. Now it is difficult, if not impossible, to relate oneself to a working group one by one; it is relatively easy to do so if they are already a fully constituted team. A communication from the supervisor, for example, in the latter instance has to be made to one person only with the appropriate instructions; the individual will pass it on and work it out with the team. In the former instance, it has to be repeated to every individual and may often be misunderstood.

But for the individual worker the problem is really much more serious. He has suffered a profound loss of security and certainty in his actual living and in the background of his thinking. For all of us the feeling of security and certainty derives always from assured membership of a group. If this is lost, no monetary gain, no job guarantee, can be sufficient compensation. Where groups change ceaselessly, as jobs and mechanical processes change, the individual inevitably experiences a sense of void, of emptiness, where his fathers knew the joy of comradeship and security. And in such situation, his anxieties – many, no doubt, irrational or ill-founded – increase and he becomes more difficult both to fellow workers and to supervisor. The extreme of this is perhaps rarely encountered as yet, but increasingly we move in this direction as the tempo of industrial change is speeded by scientific and technical discovery.

I have claimed that scientific method has a dual approach – represented in medicine by the clinic and the laboratory. In the clinic one studies the whole situation with two ends in view: first, to develop intimate knowledge of and skill in handling the facts, and, second, on the basis of such a skill to separate those aspects of the situation that skill has shown to be closely related for detailed laboratory study. When a study based upon laboratory method fails, or partially fails, because some essential factor has been unknowingly and arbitrarily excluded, the investigator, if he is wise, returns to clinical study of the entire situation to get some hint as to the nature of the excluded determinant. The members of the research division at Hawthorne, after the twelfth experimental period in the test room, were faced by just such a situation and knew it. The so-called interview programme represented for them a return from the laboratory to clinical study. And, as in all clinical study, there was no immediate and welcome revelation of a single discarded determinant: there was rather a slow progress from one observation to another, all of them important – but only gradually building up into a single complex finding. This slow development has been elsewhere described in *Management and the Worker*; one can however attempt a succinct résumé of the various observations, more or less as they occurred.

Officers of the company had prepared a short statement, a few sentences, to be repeated to the individual interviewed before the conversation began. This statement was designed to assure the worker that nothing he said would be repeated to his supervisors or to any company official outside the interviewing group. In many instances, the worker waved this aside and began to talk freely and at once. What doubts there were seemed to be resident in the interviewers rather than in those interviewed. Many workers, I cannot say the majority for we have no statistics, seemed to have something 'on their minds', in ordinary phrase, about which they wished to talk freely to a competent listener. And these topics were by no means confined to matters affecting the company. This was, I think, the first observation that emerged from the mass of interviews reported daily. The research group began to talk about the need for *emotional release* and the great advantage that accrued to the individual when he had 'talked off' his problem. The topics varied greatly. One worker two years before had been sharply reprimanded by his supervisor for not working as usual: in interview he wished to explain that on the night preceding the day of the incident his wife and child had both died, apparently unexpectedly. At the time he was unable to explain; afterwards he had no opportunity to do so. He told the story dramatically and in great detail; there was no doubt whatever that telling it thus benefited him greatly. But this story, naturally, was exceptional; more often a worker would speak of his family and domestic situation, of his church, of his relations with other members of the working group – quite usually the topic of which he spoke presented itself to him as a problem difficult for him to resolve. This led to the next successive illumination for the inquiry. It became manifest that, whatever the problem, it was partly, and sometimes wholly, determined by the attitude of the individual worker. And this defect or distortion of attitude was consequent on his past experience or his present situation, or, more usually, on both at once. One woman worker, for example, discovered for herself during an interview that her dislike of a certain supervisor was based upon a fancied resemblance to a detested stepfather. Small wonder that the same supervisor had warned the interviewer that she was 'difficult to handle'. But the discovery by the worker that her dislike was wholly irrational eased the situation considerably (F. J. Roethlisberger and W. J. Dickson, 1939, pp. 307–10). This type of case led the interviewing group to study carefully each worker's *personal situation* and attitude. These two phrases 'emotional release' and 'personal situation' became convenient titles for the first phases of observation and seemed to resume for the interviewers the effective work that they were doing. It was at this point that a change began to show itself in the study and in the conception of the study.

The original interviewers, in these days, after sixteen years of industrial experience, are emphatic on the point that the first cases singled out for report were special cases – individuals – and not representative either of the working group or of the interviews generally. It is estimated that such cases did not number more than an approximate 2 per cent of the twenty thousand persons originally interviewed. Probably this error of emphasis was inevitable and for two reasons: first, the dramatic changes that occur in such instances seemed good evidence of the efficacy of the method, and, second, this type of interviewing had to be insisted upon as *necessary to the training of a skilled interviewer*. This last still holds good; a skilled interviewer must have passed through the stage of careful and observant listening to what an individual says and to all that he says. This stage of an interviewing programme closely resembles the therapeutic method and its triumphs are apt to be therapeutic. And I do not believe that the study would have been equipped to advance further if it had failed to observe the great benefit of emotional release and the extent to which every individual's problems are conditioned by his personal history and situation. Indeed, even when one has advanced beyond the merely psychotherapeutic study of individuals to study of industrial groups, one has to beware of distortions similar in kind to those named; one has to know how to deal with such problems. The first phase of the interview programme cannot therefore be discarded; it still retains its original importance. But industrial studies must nevertheless move beyond the individual in need of therapy. And this is the more true when the change from established routines to adaptive changes of routine seems generally to carry a consequence of loss of security for many persons.

A change of attitude in the research group came gradually. The close study of individuals continued, but in combination with an equally close study of groups. An early incident did much to set the new pattern for inquiry. One of the earliest questions proposed before the original test-room experiment began was a question as to the fatigue involved in this or that type of work. Later a foreman of high reputation, no doubt with this in mind, came to the research group, now for the most part engaged in interviewing, and asserted that the girls in his department worked hard all day at their machines and must be considerably fatigued by the evening; he wanted an inquiry. Now the interviewers had discovered that this working group claimed a habit of doing most of their work in the morning period and 'taking things easy' during the afternoon. The foreman obviously realized nothing of this, and it was therefore fortunate that the two possibilities could be directly tested. The officer in charge of the research made a quiet arrangement with the engineers to measure during a period the amount of electric current used by the group to operate its machines; this quantity indicated the overall amount of work being done. The results of this test wholly supported the statements made by the girls in interview; far more current was used in the morning period than during the afternoon. And the attention of the research group was, by this and other incidents, thus redirected to a fact already known to them, namely, that the working group as a whole actually determined the output of individual workers by reference to a standard, pre-determined but never clearly stated, that represented the group conception of a fair day's work. This standard was rarely, if ever, in accord with the standards of the efficiency engineers.

The final experiment, reported under the title of the Bank Wiring Observation Room, was set up to extend and confirm these observations (F. J. Roethlisberger and W. J. Dickson, 1939, part 4, p. 379 ff.). Simultaneously it was realized that these facts did not in any way imply low working morale as suggested by such phrases as 'restriction of output'. On the contrary, the failure of free communication between management and workers in modern large-scale industry leads inevitably to the exercise of caution by the working group until such time as it knows clearly the range and meaning of changes imposed from above. The enthusiasm of the efficiency engineer for the organization of operations is excellent; his attempt to subsume problems of cooperation under this heading is not. At the moment, he attempts to solve the many human difficulties involved in whole-hearted cooperation by organizing the organization without any reference whatever to workers themselves. This procedure inevitably blocks communication and defeats his own admirable purpose.[3]

This observation, important as it is, was not however the leading point for the interviewers. The existence and influence of the group – those in active daily relationship with one another – became the important fact. The industrial interviewer must learn to distinguish and specify, as he listens to what a worker says, references to 'personal' or group situations. More often than not, the special case, the individual who talks himself out of a gross distortion, is a solitary – one who has not 'made the team'. The usual interview, on the other hand, though not by any means free from distortion, is speaking as much for the working group as for the person. The influence of the communication in the interview, therefore, is not limited to the individual but extends to the group.

Two girl workers in a large industry were recently offered 'upgrading'; to accept would mean leaving their group and taking a job in another department: they refused. Then representatives of the union put some

3. For further evidence on this point, see S. B. Mathewson (1931) and also E. Mayo (1933), pp. 119–21.

pressure on them, claiming that, if they continued to refuse, the union organizers 'might just as well give up' their efforts. With reluctance the girls reversed their decision and accepted the upgrading. Both girls at once needed the attention of an interviewer: they had liked the former group in which they had earned informal membership. Both felt adjustment to a new group and a novel situation as involving effort and private discontent. From both much was learned of the intimate organization and common practices of their groups, and their adjustments to their new groups were eased, thereby effectively helping to reconstitute the teamwork in those groups.

In another recent interview a girl of eighteen protested to an interviewer that her mother was continually urging her to ask Mr X, her supervisor, for a 'raise'. She had refused, but her loyalty to her mother and the pressure the latter exerted were affecting her work and her relations at work. She talked her situation out with an interviewer, and it became clear to her a 'raise' would mean departure from her daily companions and associates. Although not immediately relevant, it is interesting to note that, after explaining the situation at length to the interviewer, she was able to present her case dispassionately to her mother – without exaggeration or protest. The mother immediately understood and abandoned pressure for advancement, and the girl returned to effective work. This last instance illustrates one way in which the interview clears lines of communication of emotional blockage – within as without the plant. But this is not my immediate topic; my point is rather that the age-old human desire for persistence of human association will seriously complicate the development of an adaptive society if we cannot devise systematic methods of easing individuals from one group of associates into another.

But such an observation was not possible in the earliest inquiry. The important fact brought to the attention of the research division was that the ordinary conception of management–worker relation as existing between company officials, on the one hand, and an unspecified number of individuals, on the other, is utterly mistaken. Management, in any continuously successful plant, is not related to single workers, but always to working groups. In every department that continues to operate, the workers have – whether aware of it or not – formed themselves into a group with appropriate customs, duties, routines, even rituals; and management succeeds (or fails) in proportion as it is accepted without reservation by the group as authority and leader. This, for example, occurred in the relay-assembly test room at Hawthorne. Management, by consultation with the girl workers, by clear explanation of the proposed experiments and the reasons for them, by accepting the workers' verdict in special instances unwittingly scored a success in two most important human matters – the girls became a self-governing team, and a team that cooperated whole-heartedly with management. The test room was responsible for many important findings – rest periods, hours of work, food, and the like: but the most important finding of all was unquestionably in the general area of teamwork and cooperation.

It was at this time that the research division published, for private circulation within the company, a monograph entitled 'Complaints and Grievances'. Careful description of many varied situations within the interviewers' experience showed that an articulate complaint only rarely, if ever, gave any logical clue to the grievance in which it had origin; this applied at least as strongly to groups as to individuals. Whereas economists and industry generally *tend to concentrate upon the complaint and upon logical inferences from its articulate statement* as an appropriate procedure, the interviewing group had learned almost to ignore, except as symptom, the – sometimes noisy – manifestation of discomfort and to study the situation anew to gain knowledge of its source. Diagnosis rather than argument became the proper method of procedure.

It is possible to quote an illustration from a recently published book, *China Enters the Machine Age* (Shih Kuo-heng, 1944). When industries had to be moved, during this war, from Shanghai and the Chinese coast to Kunming in the interior of China, the actual operation of an industry still depended for the most part on skilled workers who were refugees from Shanghai and elsewhere. These skilled workers knew their importance to the work and gained considerable prestige from it; nevertheless discontent was rife among them. Evidence of this was manifested by the continual, deliberate breaking of crockery in the company mess hall and complaints about the quality of the food provided. Yet this food was much better than could have been obtained outside the plant – especially at the prices charged. And in interview the individual workers admitted freely that the food was good and could not rightly be made the subject of complaint. But the relationship between the skilled workers as a group and the *Chih Yuan* – the executive and supervisory officers – was exceedingly unsatisfactory.

Many of these officers – the *Chih Yuan* – have been trained in the United States – enough at least to set a pattern for the whole group. Now in America we have learned in actual practice to accept the rabble hypothesis with reservations. But the logical Chinese student of engineering or economics, knowing nothing of these practical reservations, returns to his own country convinced that the workman who is not wholly responsive to the 'financial incentive' is a troublemaker and a nuisance. And the Chinese worker lives up to this conviction by breaking plates.[4] Acceptance of the complaint about the food and collective bargaining of a logical type conducted at that level would surely have been useless.

Yet this is what industry, not only in China, does every day, with the high sanction of State authority and the alleged aid of lawyers and economists. In their behaviour and their statements, economists indicate that they accept the rabble hypothesis and its dismal corollary of financial incentive as the only effective human motive. They substitute a logical hypothesis of small practical value for the actual facts.

The insight gained by the interviewing group, on the other hand, cannot be described as substituting irrational for rational motive, emotion for logic. On the contrary, it implies a need for competent study of complaints and the grievances that provoke them, a need for knowledge of the actual facts rather than acceptance of an outdated theory. It is amusing that certain industrialists, rigidly disciplined in economic theory, attempt to shrug off the Hawthorne studies as 'theoretic'. Actually the shoe is on the other foot; Hawthorne has restudied the facts without prejudice, whereas the critics have unquestioningly accepted that theory of man which had its vogue in the nineteenth century and has already outlived its usefulness.

The Hawthorne interview programme has moved far since its beginning in 1929. Originally designed to study the comfort of workers in their work as a mass of individuals, it has come to clear specification of the relation of working groups to management as one of the fundamental problems of large-scale industry. It was indeed this study that first enabled us to assert that the third major preoccupation of management must be that of organizing teamwork, that is to say, of developing and sustaining cooperation.

References

BARNARD, C. (1938), 'The executive functions', *The Functions of the Executive*, Harvard University Press, chapter 15, pp. 215–34
HOMANS, G. C. (1941), *Fatigue of Workers*, Reinhold
MATHEWSON, S. B. (1931), *Restriction of Output among Unorganized Workers*, Viking
MAYO, E. (1933), *The Human Problems of an Industrial Civilization*, Macmillan Co.
ROETHLISBERGER, F. J. (1941), *Management and Morale*, Harvard University Press, pp. 9–10

4. Shih Kuo-heng (1944), chapter 8, pp. 111–27; also chapter 10, pp. 151–3.

ROETHLISBERGER, F. J., and DICKSON, W. J. (1939), *Management and the Worker*, Harvard University Press, pp. 379–510

SHIH KUO-HENG (1944), *China Enters the Machine Age*, Harvard University Press

18   F. Herzberg

The Motivation—Hygiene Theory

From *Work and the Nature of Man*, World Publishing Co., 1966, chapter 6

With the duality of man's nature in mind, it is well to return to the significance of these essays to industry by reviewing the motivation—hygiene concept of job attitudes as it was reported in Herzberg, Mausner and Snyderman (1959). This study was designed to test the concept that man has two sets of needs: his need as an animal to avoid pain and his need as a human to grow psychologically.

For those who have not read *The Motivation to Work* (Herzberg, Mausner and Snyderman, 1959), I will summarize the highlights of that study. Two hundred engineers and accountants, who represented a cross-section of Pittsburgh industry, were interviewed. They were asked about events they had experienced at work which either had resulted in a marked improvement in their job satisfaction or had led to a marked reduction in job satisfaction.

The interviewers began by asking the engineers and accountants to recall a time when they had felt exceptionally good about their jobs. Keeping in mind the time that had brought about the good feelings, the interviewers proceeded to probe for the reasons why the engineers and accountants felt as they did. The workers were asked also if the feelings of satisfaction in regard to their work had affected their performance, their personal relationships and their well-being.

Finally, the nature of the sequence of events that served to return the workers' attitudes to 'normal' was elicited. Following the narration of a sequence of events, the interview was repeated, but this time the subjects were asked to describe a sequence of events that resulted in negative feelings about their jobs. As many sequences as the respondents were able to give

369

were recorded within the criteria of an acceptable sequence. These were the criteria.

First, the sequence must revolve around an event or series of events; that is, there must be some objective happening. The report cannot be concerned entirely with the respondent's psychological reactions or feelings.

Second, the sequence of events must be found by time; it should have a beginning that can be identified, a middle and, unless the events are still in process, some sort of identifiable ending (although the cessation of events does not have to be dramatic or abrupt).

Third, the sequence of events must have taken place during a period in which feelings about the job were either exceptionally good or exceptionally bad.

Fourth, the story must be centered on a period in the respondent's life when he held a position that fell within the limits of our sample. However, there were a few exceptions. Stories involving aspirations to professional work or transitions from subprofessional to professional levels were included.

Fifth, the story must be about a situation in which the respondent's feelings about his job were directly affected, not about a sequence of events unrelated to the job that caused high or low spirits.

Figure 1, reproduced from *The Motivation to Work*, shows the major findings of this study. The factors listed are a kind of shorthand for summarizing the 'objective' events that each respondent described. The length of each box represents the frequency with which the factor appeared in the events presented. The width of the box indicates the period in which the good or bad job attitude lasted, in terms of a classification of short duration and long duration. A short duration of attitude change did not last longer than two weeks, while a long duration of attitude change may have lasted for years.

Five factors stand out as strong determiners of job satisfaction – *achievement*, *recognition*, *work itself*, *responsibility* and *advancement* – the last three being of greater importance for lasting change of attitudes. These five factors appeared very infrequently when the respondents described events that paralleled job dissatisfaction feelings. A further word on *recognition*: when it appeared in a 'high' sequence of events, it referred to recognition for achievement rather than to recognition as a human-relations tool divorced from any accomplishment. The latter type of recognition does not serve as a 'satisfier'.

When the factors involved in the job dissatisfaction events were coded, an entirely different set of factors evolved. These factors were similar to

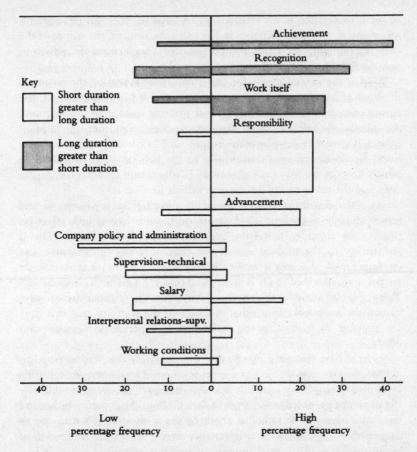

Figure 1 Comparison of satisfiers and dissatisfiers (reproduced from Herzberg, Mausner and Snyderman, 1959, by permission of the publishers)

the satisfiers in their unidimensional effect. This time, however, they served only to bring about job dissatisfaction and were rarely involved in events that led to positive job attitudes. Also, unlike the 'satisfiers', the 'dissatisfiers' consistently produced short-term changes in job attitudes. The major dissatisfiers were *company policy and administration, supervision, salary, interpersonal relations* and *working conditions*.

What is the explanation of such results? Do the two sets of factors have two separate themes? It appears so, for the factors on the right of Figure 1 all seem to describe man's relationship to what he does: his job content, achievement on a task, recognition for task achievement, the nature of the task, responsibility for a task and professional advancement or growth in task capability.

What is the central theme for the dissatisfiers? Restating the factors as the kind of administration and supervision received in doing the job, the nature of interpersonal relationships and working conditions that surround the job and the effect of salary suggests the distinction from the 'satisfier' factors. Rather than describe man's relationship to what he does, the 'dissatisfier' factors describe his relationship to the context or environment in which he does his job. One cluster of factors relates to what the person does and the other to the situation in which he does it.

Since the dissatisfier factors essentially describe the environment and serve primarily to prevent job dissatisfaction, while having little effect on positive job attitudes, they have been named the *hygiene* factors. This is an analogy to the medical use of the term meaning 'preventative and environmental'. Another term for these factors in current use is *maintenance* factors. I am indebted to Dr Robert Ford of the American Telephone and Telegraph Company for this excellent synonym. The 'satisfier' factors were named the *motivators*, since other findings of the study suggest that they are effective in motivating the individual to superior performance and effort.

So far, I have described that part of the interview that was restricted to determining the actual objective events as reported by the respondents (first level of analysis). They were also asked to interpret the events, to tell why the particular event led to a change in their feelings about their jobs (second level of analysis). The principal result of the analysis of this data was to suggest that the hygiene or maintenance events led to job dissatisfaction because of a need to *avoid* unpleasantness; the motivator events led to job satisfaction because of a need for growth or self-actualization. At the psychological level, the two dimensions of job attitudes reflected a two-dimensional need structure: one need system for the avoidance of unpleasantness and a parallel need system for personal growth.

The discussion so far has paved the way for the explanation of the duality of job-attitude results. Why do the hygiene factors serve as dissatisfiers? They represent the environment to which man the animal is constantly trying to adjust, for the environment is the source of Adam's suffering. The hygiene factors listed are the major environmental aspects of work.

Why do the motivators affect motivation in the positive direction? An analogy drawn from a familiar example of psychological growth in children may be useful. When a child learns to ride a bicycle, he is becoming more competent, increasing the repertory of his behavior, expanding his skills – psychologically growing. In the process of the child's learning to master a bicycle, the parents can love him with all the zeal and compassion of the most devoted mother and father. They can safeguard the child from injury by providing the safest and most hygienic area in which to practice; they can offer all kinds of incentives and rewards, and they can provide the most expert instructions. But the child will never, never learn to ride the bicycle – unless he is given a bicycle! The hygiene factors are not a valid contributor to psychological growth. The substance of a task is required to achieve growth goals. Similarly, you cannot love an engineer into creativity, although by this approach you can avoid his dissatisfactions with the way you treat him. Creativity will require a potentially creative task to do.

In summary, two essential findings were derived from this study. First, the factors involved in producing job satisfaction were *separate* and *distinct* from the factors that led to job dissatisfaction. Since separate factors needed to be considered, depending on whether job satisfaction or job dissatisfaction was involved, it followed that these two feelings were not the obverse of each other. Thus, the opposite of job satisfaction would not be job dissatisfaction, but rather *no* job satisfaction; similarly, the opposite of job dissatisfaction is *no* job dissatisfaction, not satisfaction with one's job. The fact that job satisfaction is made up of two unipolar traits is not unique, but it remains a difficult concept to grasp.

Perhaps another analogy will help explain this new way of thinking about job attitudes. Let us characterize job satisfaction as vision and job dissatisfaction as hearing. It is readily seen that we are talking about two separate dimensions, since the stimulus for vision is light, and increasing and decreasing light will have no effect on man's hearing. The stimulus for audition is sound, and, in a similar fashion, increasing or decreasing loudness will have no effect on vision.

Man's basic needs can be diagrammed as two parallel arrows pointing in opposite directions. One arrow depicts his Animal–Adam nature, which is concerned with avoidance of pain stemming from the environment, and for man the psychological environment is the major source of this pain. The other arrow represents man's Human–Abraham nature, which is concerned with approaching self-fulfillment or psychological growth through the accomplishment of tasks.

◄ Animal–Adam: avoidance of pain from environment

Human–Abraham: seeking growth from tasks ►

The problem of establishing a zero point in psychology, with the procedural necessity of using instead a bench mark (e.g. the mean of a population) from which to start our measurement, has led to the conception that psychological traits are bipolar. Recent empirical investigations, however, have cast some shadows on the assumptions of bipolarity for many psychological attributes, in addition to job attitudes, as shown in *The Motivation to Work*.

Thus, the hypothesis with which the study of motivation began appears to be verified. The factors on the right of Figure 1 that led to satisfaction (*achievement, recognition, work itself, responsibility* and *advancement*) are mainly unipolar; that is, they contribute very little to job dissatisfaction. Conversely, the dissatisfiers (*company policy and administration, supervision, interpersonal relations, working conditions* and *salary*) contribute very little to job satisfaction.

Sixteen separate job–attitude factors were investigated in the original study dealing with accountants and engineers. Only those motivators and hygiene factors that were found to differentiate statistically between positive and negative job attitudes were presented. However, the other factors have similarly been shown to fall into one category or the other in the follow-up studies to be described in subsequent chapters. These factors are *possibility of growth*, a task-centered motivator, and the hygiene factors, *salary, status, job security* and *effect on personal life*.

If we are to be able to define a human being, the following sections represent an attempt to organize man's needs in order to reach such a definition. Since man is capable of such a variety of behavior and still can survive, it is little wonder that so many ways of acting can be declared normal, dependent on their cultural acceptance. In this sense, a prominent difference between cultures lies in the kinds of pathology that are declared normal. At this point, the theory of job motivation will be expanded to a greater concept of mental health, and this in turn will allow for a culture-free definition of mental illness.

Just as there are two sets of needs at work – hygiene needs and motivator needs – and two continua to represent them, so we may speak of two continua in mental health: a mental-illness continuum and a mental-health continuum. We have seen that a conceptual shift in viewpoint regarding job attitudes has been made in order to incorporate the two-dimensional motivation–hygiene theory. Essentially the same shift might well lead to an equally important change in theory and research on mental health.

The argument for this generalization has been presented in two papers by Dr Roy Hamlin of the Veterans Administration and myself. The implications for mental health are best introduced by recalling the subjective reactions of the employees as to why the various factors affected them as they did. For the job-dissatisfied situation the subjects reported that they were made unhappy mostly because they felt they were being treated unfairly or that they found the situation unpleasant or painful. On the other hand, the common denominator for the reasons for positive job attitudes seemed to be variations on the theme of feelings or psychological growth, the fulfillment of self-actualizing needs. There was an approach-avoidance dichotomy with respect to job adjustment. A need to avoid unpleasant job environments led to job dissatisfaction; the need for self-realization led to job satisfaction when the opportunity for self-realization was afforded.

A 'hygienic' environment prevents discontent with a job, but such an environment cannot lead the individual beyond a minimal adjustment consisting of the absence of dissatisfaction. A positive 'happiness' seems to require some attainment of psychological growth.

It is clear why the hygiene factors fail to provide for positive satisfactions; they do not possess the characteristics necessary for giving an individual a sense of growth. To feel that one has grown depends on achievement in tasks that have meaning to the individual, and since the hygiene factors do not relate to the task, they are powerless to give such meaning to the individual. Growth is dependent on some achievements, but achievement requires a task. The motivators are task factors and thus are necessary for growth; they provide the psychological stimulation by which the individual can be activated toward his self-realization needs.

To generalize from job attitudes to mental attitudes, we can think of two types of adjustment for mental equilibrium. First, an adjustment to the environment, which is mainly an avoidance adjustment; second, an adjustment to oneself, which is dependent on the successful striving for psychological growth, self-actualization, self-realization or, most simply, being psychologically more than one has been in the past.

Traditionally, mental health has been regarded as the obverse of mental illness. Mental health, in this sense, is the mere *absence* of mental illness. At one time, the psychiatrist anticipated that mental health would be automatically *released* when the conflicts of mental illness were resolved. And, currently, the biochemist hopes that mental health will bloom once neuro-enzymes are properly balanced and optimally distributed in the brain.

In essence, this traditional view ignores *mental health*. In general, the focus has been on mental illness – on anxiety, anxiety-reducing mechanisms, past frustrations, childhood trauma, distressing interpersonal relations, disturbing ideas and worries, current patterns of inefficiency and stressful present environment. Except for sporadic lip service, positive attitudes and experiences have been considered chiefly in an atmosphere of alleviating distress and dependency.

The factors that determine mental illness are *not the obverse* of the mental health factors. Rather, the mental illness factors belong to the category of hygiene factors, which describe the environment of man and serve to cause illness when they are deficient but effect little positive increase in mental health. They are factors that cause avoidance behavior; yet, as will be explained, only in the 'sick' individual is there an attempt to activate approach behavior. The implications of the conceptual shift for job satisfaction has been discussed. Traditional research on job attitudes has focused almost exclusively on only one set of factors, on the hygiene or job-context factors. The motivating factors, the positive or self-actualizing factors, have been largely neglected. The thesis holds that a very similar neglect has characterized traditional research on mental health.

Specifically, the resolution of conflicts, the correction of biochemical imbalance and the modification of psychic defenses might all be assigned to the attempts to modify the hygiene or avoidance needs of the individual. The positive motivating factors – self-actualization and personal growth – have received treatment of two sorts. Either they have been neglected or dismissed as irrelevant, or they have been regarded as so individually sacred and vague as to defy research analysis. At best, the mental health factors have been looked upon as important *forces* that might be released by the removal of mental illness factors.

The motivation–hygiene concept stresses three points regarding mental adjustment. The first is the proposition that mental illness and mental health are not of the same dimensions. Contrary to classical psychiatric belief, there are degrees of sickness and there are degrees of health. The degree of sickness reflects an individual's reaction to the hygiene factors, while the degree of mental health represents his reaction to the motivator factors.

Second, the motivator–mental-health aspect of personal adjustment has been sadly neglected in theory, in research and in application. The positive side of personal adjustment has been considered to be a dividend or consequence of successful attention to the 'negative maladjustment' side.

The third point is a new definition or idea of mental illness. The new definition derives from the first proposition that mental illness is not the opposite of mental health, as is suggested by some of the data on job satisfaction.

While the incidents in which job satisfaction were reported almost always contained the factors that related to the job task – the motivators – there were some individuals who reported receiving job satisfaction solely from hygiene factors, that is, from some aspect of the job environment. Commenting on this reversal, the authors of *The Motivation to Work* suggest that 'there may be individuals who because of their training and because of the things that have happened to them have learned to react positively to the factors associated with the *context* of their jobs'. The hygiene seekers are primarily attracted to things that usually serve only to prevent dissatisfaction, not to be a source of positive feelings. The hygiene seekers have not reached a stage of personality development at which self-actualizing needs are active. From this point of view, they are fixated at a less mature level of personal adjustment.

Implied in *The Motivation to Work* is the admonition to industry that the lack of 'motivators' in jobs will increase the sensitivity of employees to real or imagined bad job hygiene, and consequently the amount and quality of hygiene given to employees must be constantly improved. There is also the reported finding that the relief from job dissatisfaction by hygiene factors has only a temporary effect and therefore adds to the necessity for more frequent attention to the job environment. The graphs shown in Figure 1 indicate that the hygiene factors stem from short-range events, as contrasted with the longer range of motivator events. Animal or hygiene drives, being cyclical, are only temporarily satisfied. The cyclical nature of these drives is necessary in order to sustain life. The hygiene factors on the job partake of the quality of briefly acting analgesics for meaningless work; the individual becomes unhappy without them, but is relieved only temporarily with them, for their effects soon wear off and the hygiene seeker is left chronically dissatisfied.

A hygiene seeker is not merely a victim of circumstances, but is *motivated* in the direction of temporary satisfaction. It is not that his job offers little opportunity for self-actualization; rather, it is that his needs lie predominantly in another direction, that of satisfying avoidance needs. He is seeking positive happiness via the route of avoidance behavior, and this his resultant chronic dissatisfaction is an illness of motivation. Chronic unhappiness, a motivation pattern that ensures continual dissatisfaction, a failure to grow or to want to grow – these characteristics add up to a neurotic personality.

So it appears that the neurotic is an individual with a lifetime pattern of hygiene seeking and that the definition of a neurotic, in terms of defenses against anxiety arising from early psychological conflicts, represents at best the *origin* of his hygiene seeking. The motivation–hygiene view of a neurotic adjustment is free of substantial ties with any theory of etiology, and therefore the thesis is independent of conceptualizations regarding the traditional dynamics of personality development and adjustment. The neurotic motivation pattern of hygiene-seeking is mostly a learned process that arises from the value systems endemic in society.

Since total adaptation depends on the gratification of two separate types of needs, a rough operational categorization of adjustment can be made by examining the sources of a person's satisfactions.

A first category is characterized by positive mental health. Persons in this category show a preponderance of lifetime contentment stemming from situations in which the motivator factors are paramount. These factors are necessary in providing them with a sense of personal growth. They can be identified as directly involving the individual in some task, project or activity in which achievement or the consequences of achievement are possible. Those factors found meaningful for industrial job satisfaction may not be complete or may not be sufficiently descriptive to encompass the total life picture of an individual.

Other factors may be necessary to describe the motivators in this larger sense. Whatever they may be, the criteria for their selection must include activity on the part of an individual – some task, episode, adventure or activity in which the individual achieves a growth experience and without which the individual *will not* feel unhappy, dissatisfied or uncomfortable. In addition, to belong to this positive category the individual must have frequent opportunity for the gratification of these motivator needs. How frequent and how challenging the growth opportunities must be will depend on the level of ability (both genetic and learned) of the individual and, secondly, on his tolerance for delayed success. This tolerance, too, may be constitutional, learned or governed by dynamic conflicts; the source does not really matter to the argument.

The motivation–hygiene concept may seem to involve certain paradoxes. For example, is all achievement work and no play? Is the individual of limited ability doomed to be a nonachiever, and therefore a hygiene seeker?

In regard to work and play, achievements include all personal growth experience. While it is true that *The Motivation to Work* focuses on industrial production, as demanded by society or company policy, the satisfying sequences reported are rich in examples of creativity and individual initiative. Artistic and scholarly interests, receptive openness to new insights, true relaxation and regrouping of growth potentials (as contrasted with plain laziness) are all achievement or elements in achievement. Nowhere is the balanced work–play growth element in achievement more apparent than in the mentally healthy individual.

In regard to limitations resulting from meager ability, the motivating history of achievement depends to an important degree on a realistic attitude. The individual who concerns himself largely with vague aspiration, completely unrelated to his abilities and to the actual situation, is simply one kind of hygiene seeker. He does not seek satisfaction in the job itself, but rather in those surrounding conditions that include such cultural noises as 'any American boy can be president' or 'every young man should have a college degree'. The quotation by Carl Jung bears repetition: 'The supreme goal of man is to fulfil himself as a creative, *unique* individual according to his own *innate potentialities* and within the *limits of reality*.' (Italics supplied.)

A final condition for membership in this mentally healthy group would be a good life environment or the successful avoidance of poor hygiene factors. Again, those conditions mentioned previously for the work situation may not suffice for all the environments of the individual.

Three conditions, then, will serve to define a mentally healthy individual: seeking life satisfaction through personal growth experiences (experiences defined as containing the motivator factors); sufficient success, commensurate with ability and tolerance for delay, to give direct evidence of growth, and, finally, successful avoidance of discomfort from poor hygiene.

If the hygiene is poor, the mental health is not affected, but obviously the individual becomes unhappy. This second category of adjustment – self-fulfillment, accompanied by dissatisfaction with the rewards of life – perhaps characterizes that large segment of the population that continues to do a good job despite reason for complaint. There is research evidence to support the idea that a motivator seeker who is effective in his performance will be listed among the gripers in a company. This is not surprising, for he feels justified in his criticism because he earns his right to complain and is perhaps bright enough to see reasons for his ill temper.

A third category consists of individuals characterized by symptom-free adjustment. Individuals grouped in this category would also have sought and obtained their satisfactions primarily from the motivator factors. However, their growth needs will be much less reinforced during their life because of lack of opportunity. Such individuals will not have achieved a complete sense of accomplishment because of circumstances extrinsic to their motivation. Routine jobs and routine life-experiences attenuate the growth of these individuals, not their motivation. Because their motivation is healthy, we do not place these persons on the sick continuum. In addition, those in this category must have sufficient satisfactions of their hygiene needs.

It is not unusual, though it is infrequent, to find that a respondent in the job-attitude investigations will stress one or more of the motivator factors as contributing to his job dissatisfaction. In other words, a satisfier acts as a dissatisfier. This occurrence most frequently includes the factors of failure of advancement, lack of recognition, lack of responsibility and uninteresting work. Closer inspection of these incidents reveals that many are insincere protestations covering a more latent hygiene desire. For example, the respondent who declares that his unhappiest time on the job occurred when his boss did not recognize his work is often saying that he misses the comfort and security of an accepting supervisor. His hygiene needs are simply wrapped in motivator clothing.

However, there are some highly growth-oriented persons who so desire the motivators and seek so very much a positive aspect for their lives that deprivation in this area may be interpreted by them as pain. In this case, their inversion of a motivator for a dissatisfaction episode is legitimate, but it represents a misinterpretation of their feelings. Their lack of happiness is felt as unhappiness, although it is qualitatively quite different from the unhappiness they experience because of the lack of the 'hygiene' factors. Often these people summarize their job-attitude feelings by saying, 'I really can't complain, but I sure don't like what I am doing' or 'as a job goes, this isn't bad, but I'm not getting anywhere.'

The fourth category of essentially health-oriented people includes those who, paradoxically, are miserable. These are the motivator seekers who are denied any psychological growth opportunities and, in addition, find themselves with their hygiene needs simultaneously deprived. However miserable they might be, they are differentiated from the next three categories by their reluctance to adopt neurotic or psychotic defense mechanisms to allay their dual pain.

The next category represents a qualitative jump from the mental health dimension to the mental illness dimension. This category may be called the *maladjusted*. The basic characteristic of persons in this group is that they have sought positive satisfaction from the hygiene factors. There is an inversion of motivation away from the approach behavior of growth to the avoidance behavior of comfortable environments. Members of this group are the hygiene seekers, whose maladjustment is defined by the direction of their motivation and is evidenced by the environmental source of their satisfactions.

Many in this category will have had a significant number of personal achievements that result in no growth experience. It has been noted that hygiene satisfactions are short-lived and partake of the characteristics of opiates. The environmental satisfactions for persons whom we call maladjusted must be rather frequent and of substantial quality. It is the satisfactions of their hygiene needs that differentiate the maladjusted from the next category in our system – the mentally ill.

The mentally ill are lifetime hygiene seekers with poor hygiene satisfactions (as perceived by the individual). This poor hygiene may be realistic or it may reflect mostly the accentuated sensitivity to hygiene deprivation because of the inversion of motivation.

One of the extremes to which the 'hygiene or maintenance' seeker resorts is to deny his hygiene needs altogether. This is termed the 'monastic' defense. Seemingly, this line of reasoning asserts that the denial of man's animal nature will reward the individual with happiness, because the proponents of the 'monastic' view of man's nature have discovered that no amount of hygiene rewards lead to human happiness. This sometime revered approach to the human dilemma now emerges as the blatant non sequitur that it is. How can psychological growth be achieved by denying hygiene realities? The illness is at two levels. The primary sickness is the denial of man's animal nature. Second, psychological growth and happiness depend on two separate factors, and no denial of irrelevant factors will serve man in his pursuit of happiness.

The motivation–hygiene concept holds that mental health depends on the individual's history or past experience. The history of the healthy individual shows success in growth achievements. In contrast, mental illness depends on a different pattern of past experience. The unhealthy individual has concerned himself with surrounding conditions. His search for satisfaction has focused on the limitations imposed by objective reality and by other individuals, including society and culture.

In the usual job situation these limitations consist of company policy, supervision, interpersonal relations and the like. In broader life adjustments the surrounding conditions include cultural taboos, social demands for material production and limited native ability. The hygiene seeker devotes his energies to concern with the surrounding limitations, to 'defenses' in the Freudian sense. He seeks satisfaction, or mental health, in a policy of 'defense'. No personal growth occurs and his search for health is fruitless, for it leads to ever more intricate maneuvers of defense or hygiene seeking.

Mental illness is an inversion – the attempt to accentuate or deny one set of needs in the hope of obtaining the other set.

To reiterate, mankind has two sets of needs. Think about man twice: once about events that cause him pain and, secondly, about events that make him happy. Those who seek only to gratify the needs of their animal natures are doomed to live in dreadful anticipation of pain and suffering. This is the fate of those human beings who want to satisfy only their biological needs. But some men have become aware of the advantage humans have over their animal brothers. In addition to the compulsion to avoid pain, the human being has been blessed with the potentiality to achieve happiness. And, as I hope I have demonstrated, man can be happy only by seeking to satisfy both his animal need to avoid pain and his human need to grow psychologically.

The seven classifications of adjustment continua are shown in Figure 2, using the motivation–hygiene theory frame of reference of parallel and diverging arrows. Within each category, the top arrow depicts the mental-illness continuum and the bottom arrow the mental-health continuum. The triangle signifies the scale on which the individual is operating and the degree of his gratification with the factors of that scale.

Category I: The healthy motivator seeker is shown to be on both the mental-illness and the mental-health continua, and he is successful in achieving the motivator (mental health) needs and in avoiding the pain of the hygiene (mental illness) needs.

Category II: The unhappy motivator seeker is depicted as obtaining human significance from his job but receiving little amelioration of his animal-avoidance pains.

Category III: This shows the motivator seeker searching for gratification of both sets of needs but being successful only in avoiding hygiene deprivation.

Category IV: The miserable motivator seeker is illustrated as basically healthy but, unfortunately, with neither need system being serviced.

Category V: The hygiene seeker who is motivated only by his hygiene needs is indicated here. He is successful at avoiding mental illness but debarred from achieving mental health.

Category VI: These people are the true mentally ill. They are the hygiene seekers who fail in their hygiene gratification.

Category VII: Finally, there is that interesting form of hygiene seeker, the 'monastic', who also is living by only one need system and is fulfilling his

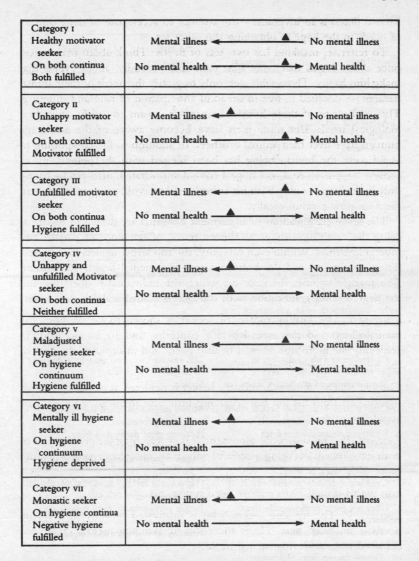

Figure 2   Seven categories of adjustment continua

hygiene requirements by denying them. Familiar examples are the no-talent beatnik, the sacrificing mother, the severe disciplinarian in the military world and, less often today, his counterpart in industry.

Table 1. Types of adjustments

Classification	Orientation	Motivator satisfaction	Hygiene satisfaction
Mental Health	Motivator	Yes	Yes
Unhappy	Motivator	Yes	No
Unfulfilled	Motivator	No	Yes
Unhappy and unfulfilled	Motivator	No	No
Maladjusted	Hygiene	Not pertinent	Yes
Mental illness	Hygiene	Not pertinent	No
Monastic	Hygiene	Not pertinent	Denied

Table 2. Characteristics of hygiene and motivator seekers

Hygiene seeker	Motivator seeker
1. Motivated by nature of the environment	Motivated by nature of the task
2. Chronic and heightened dissatisfaction with various aspects of his job context, e.g. salary, supervision, working conditions, status, job security, company policy and administration, fellow employees	Higher tolerance for poor hygiene factors
3. Overreaction with satisfaction to improvement in hygiene factors	Less reaction to improvement in hygiene factors
4. Short duration of satisfaction when the hygiene factors are improved	Similar
5. Overreaction with dissatisfaction when hygiene factors are not improved	Milder discontent when hygiene factors need improvement
6. Realizes little satisfaction from accomplishments	Realizes great satisfaction from accomplishments
7. Shows little interest in the kind and quality of the work he does	Shows capacity to enjoy the kind of work he does
8. Cynicism regarding positive virtues of work and life in general	Has positive feelings toward work and life in general
9. Does not profit professionally from experience	Profits professionally from experience
10. Prone to cultural noises (*a*) Ultraliberal, ultraconservative (*b*) Parrots management philosophy (*c*) Acts more like top management than top management does	Belief systems sincere and considered
11. May be successful on the job because of talent	May be an overachiever

These types are summarized in Table 1.

Can we identify the people on jobs who are the healthy individuals, that is, who are the motivator seekers, as distinguished from the hygiene seekers? What are the consequences to companies that select and reinforce hygiene seekers? These questions will be examined in the final chapter, but at this point a brief description of hygiene seekers and of the consequences to the company hiring them will be useful.

The hygiene seeker, as opposed to the motivator seeker, is motivated by the nature of the environment of his job rather than by his tasks. He suffers from a chronic and heightened dissatisfaction with his job hygiene. Why? Because he lives by it. He has an overreaction to improvement in hygiene factors. You give him a salary raise and you become the most wonderful boss in the world; he is in the most wonderful company in the world – he protests too much. In other words, you have given him a shot in the arm. But the satisfaction of hygiene factors are of short duration – and the short action applies as well to the motivator seeker, because this is the nature of the beast.

The hygiene seeker realizes little satisfaction from accomplishments and consequently shows little interest in the kind and quality of the work he does. Why? Since he is basically an avoidance-oriented organism, how can he have a positive outlook on life? He does not profit professionally from experience. The only profit he desires is a more comfortable environment. 'What did you learn?' 'Nothing, it was a complete waste of time.' Obviously, there was no definite reward. In other words, even though you can stimulate him for a temporary action, he does not have his own generator. And I think, also, that many companies feel they have to keep doing his stimulating.

The hygiene seeker is ultraliberal or ultraconservative. He parrots management's philosophy. As a means of reducing ambiguity he acts more like top management than top management does. The question arises whether he may be successful on the job because of talent. The question is then legitimately asked: If a man does well on the job because of hygiene satisfactions, what difference does it make?

The answer is twofold. I believe that hygiene seekers will let the company down when their talents are most needed. They are motivated only for short times and only when there is an external reward to be obtained. It is just when an emergency situation arises, and when the organization cannot be bothered with hygiene, that these key men may fail to do their jobs. In the army they are known as 'barracks soldiers'.

The second answer I suggest, and one that I believe to be of more serious import, is that hygiene seekers offer their own motivational characteristics as the pattern to be instilled in their subordinates. They become the template from which the new recruit to industry learns his motivational pattern. Hygiene seekers in key positions set the extrinsic reward atmosphere for the units of the company that they control. Because of the talent they possess, their influence on conditioning the atmosphere is generally out of proportion to their long-term effectiveness to the company.

If we accept the notion that one of the most important functions of a manager is the development of future managers, the teaching of hygiene motivations becomes a serious defect to the company. This, I believe, is one of the major implications that the motivation—hygiene theory has for modern personnel practices. Previous research knowledge has strongly indicated that the effectiveness of management development is attuned to its congruence with the company atmosphere, as it is manifested in the superior's beliefs and behavior. The superior who is a hygiene seeker cannot but have an adverse effect on management development, which is aimed at the personal growth and actualization of subordinates.

Reference

HERZBERG, F., MAUSNER, B., and SNYDERMAN, B. B. (1959), *The Motivation to Work*, Wiley

19 E. H. Schein

Career Anchors

From *Career Anchors: Discovering Your Real Values*, Pfeiffer, 1993, pp. 11–26

The word *career* is used in many different ways and has many connotations. Sometimes 'having a career' is used to apply only to someone who has a profession or whose occupational life is well-structured and involves steady advancement. In the context of career anchors, *career* includes how any individual's work life develops over time and how it is perceived by that person.

One might consider this to be the 'internal career,' to distinguish it from what others might view that person's work life to be. Everyone has some kind of picture of his or her work life and role in that life. It is this internal picture that will be explored here in some detail in discussing the concept of career anchors.

To distinguish 'internal career' from other uses of the word, we will use 'external career' to refer to the actual steps that are required by an occupation or an organization for progress through that occupation. A physician must complete medical school, internship, residency, specialty board examinations, and so on. In some organizations a general manager has to go through several business functions, have experience in supervising people, take on a functional management job, rotate through the international division, and serve on the corporate staff before being given a true generalist job as a division general manager. Some organizations talk of career paths, which define the necessary – or at least desirable – steps for the career occupant to take along the way to some goal job.

What follows is an outline of the major stages of the external career and some of the dimensions along which one can measure career movement or progress. Next is a description of the evolution of the internal career and the concept of career anchor, the self-image that a person develops

387

around his or her career which comes to be a guide as well as a constraint on career decisions. The implications of the career anchor concept for human resource management will be explored from the individual career occupant's point of view as well as from the point of view of the supervisor.

Major stages of the career[1]

From the individual's point of view, a career consists of several meaningful units or stages that are recognized both by the person and by society, although the length of time associated with each unit or stage varies immensely according to the occupation and the individual within it. These ten stages are described in the sections that follow and are depicted in Figure 1.

Stage 1: Growth, fantasy, and exploration. In this period, usually associated with childhood and early adolescence, an occupation is a mere thought, and a career has little meaning except in terms of occupational stereotypes and a general goal of 'success.' The person at this stage prepares to enter the necessary training or educational process for whatever occupation is tentatively chosen.

Stage 2: Education and training. Depending on the occupation, this process can be very elaborate or very minimal, lasting anywhere from a few months to twenty or more years. There are many choice points during this stage as occupational goals are clarified and changed. In some occupations (such as medicine), the external career stages require early decision making to ensure that all of the prerequisites for later entry are achieved during the period of education.

Stage 3: Entry into the world of work. For most people, regardless of their levels of preparation, this is a time of major adjustment as they learn about the realities of work and their own reactions. In particular, the educational process rarely prepares people for the seemingly irrational and political side of organizational life or for the fact that much of the work in every occupation involves not only logic and reason but also working with people and their feelings. Major personal learning begins at this point, and an occupational self-concept begins to evolve as the career incumbent begins to test his or her own talents, motives, and values in the crucible of real work.

1. The stages outlined here are drawn from the seminal work of Donald Super and are expanded on the basis of the author's own research (see E. H. Schein, *Career Dynamics: Matching Individual and Organizational Needs*, Addison-Wesley, 1978).

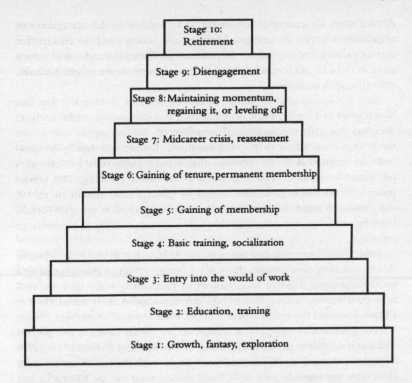

Figure 1 Major stages of the career

Stage 4: Basic training and socialization. The length and the intensity of this period differ by occupation, organization, complexity of the work, the organization's assumptions about the importance of teaching elements of the culture to the new members, and the degree of responsibility that society assigns to the occupation. The more responsible the occupation, the longer and more intense the socialization period. This stage is a major source of personal learning because the organization now begins to make demands to which the individual must respond. The career occupant is faced with real choices about whether or not to remain in the occupation and/or the organization, depending on how he or she responds to the socialization process.

Stage 5: Gaining of membership. At some point an individual recognizes through formal rituals or the kinds of assignments received that he or she has passed beyond the trainee stage and has been accepted as a full contributor.

At this stage a meaningful self-image as a member of the occupation or organization begins to emerge. Motives and values begin to be clarified through seeing one's responses to different challenging situations in which choices must be made. One begins to have a better sense of one's talents, strengths, and weaknesses.

Stage 6: Gaining of tenure and permanent membership. Within the first five to ten years of a career, most organizations and occupations make a tenure decision that tells the individual whether or not he or she can count on a long-term future in the organization. Tenure is formally or symbolically granted with the proviso that tenure exists only so long as a job exists. In some occupations (such as university teaching), the tenure process forces the organization either to grant formal tenure or to ask the person to leave. In most organizations the process is not that formalized but operates, nevertheless, through norms pertaining to seniority or layoffs.

Stage 7: Midcareer crisis and reassessment. Although it is not clear whether this is a crisis or even a stage, there is mounting evidence that most people go through some kind of reassessment of themselves when they are well into their careers, asking themselves questions about their initial choices ('Have I entered the right career?'), about their levels of attainment ('Have I accomplished all I hoped to accomplish?' or 'What have I accomplished and was it worth the sacrifices?'), and about their futures ('Should I continue or make a change?' or 'What do I want to do with the rest of my life, and how does my work fit into it?'). Such reassessment can be traumatic, but many people find it to be normal and relatively painless, often leading to a rediscovery or reaffirmation of goals that have been present but not salient. When people make such goals more prominent, they sometimes appear to be making major career changes. However, such changes rarely are experienced as big events by the career occupant. Rather, they tend to be experienced as 'Finally I am doing more of what I really want to do with my life!'

Stage 8: Maintaining momentum, regaining it, or leveling off. The insights that result from reassessment result in decisions about how the remainder of one's career will be pursued. Each person at this stage develops a personal solution that will guide his or her next steps. For some this is a determination to climb the ladder as far as possible; for some it is a redefining of the areas of work they wish to pursue; and for many it involves a complex assessment of how to balance the demands of work, family, and personal concerns. Those whose talents force them to level off may face a difficult psychological adjustment. However, for many people at this stage, leveling off is a choice based on the realization that one's talents, motives, and values do not require one to aspire any further.

Stage 9: Disengagement. Inevitably a person slows down, becomes less involved, begins to think about retirement, and prepares for that stage. However, some people deal with potential retirement by aggressively denying its reality, by continuing business as usual, and by actively avoiding the attempts of others to get them involved in such preparation.

Stage 10: Retirement. Whether or not the individual has prepared for it, inevitably the organization or occupation no longer makes a meaningful role available, and the individual must adjust. What happens to occupational self-image at this time varies greatly from person to person. Some people retire early because the occupation encourages it (for example, the military or professional sports) or because they want to and are able to enter different kinds of occupations early enough in life to develop second careers. For others, retirement is traumatic, resulting in loss of physical or psychological health, sometimes to the point of premature death.

These stages provide a kind of internal timetable for every person. However, the stages can be long or short, can repeat themselves if the person moves from one career to another, and are not related in any necessary fashion to age. Within a given occupation, stage may correlate with age, but the relationship between stages and age for a doctor, a clerk, a manager, a storekeeper, an engineer, and a consultant all differ.

Career movement, progress, or success

The standards by which an individual measures his or her own success may be quite different from those used by another person or by society at large. In fact, the subjective definition of success largely reflects one's career anchor or internal career definition. All progress can be measured along three basic dimensions, which correspond to the movement within an organization or occupation. These dimensions are shown in Figure 2 as an organizational cone.

Cross-functional horizontal movement: growth in abilities and skills

As people move into careers, they change in terms of what they are able to do and how well they are able to do it. Such development may be the result of their own efforts or may be correlated with specified training or development, opportunities provided by the employer or profession. This

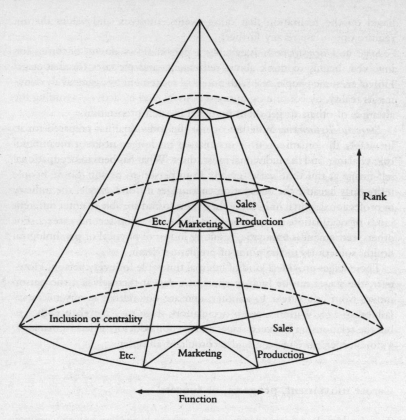

Figure 2   A three-dimensional model of an organization[2]

kind of movement corresponds to cross-functional rotation or formal training and development, and it results in changes in the work an individual does. It also reflects the growing tendency for workers to trade jobs and to be certified in a number of different skills. Pay systems acknowledge this form of organizational movement in the trend to pay workers for the number of skills they use.

2. From E. H. Schein, 'The individual, the organization and the career: a conceptual scheme', *Journal of Applied Behavioural Science*, 1971, 7, p. 404.

Cross-level hierarchical movement: up the ladder

Every occupation or organization maintains some hierarchy or system of ranks and titles by which a career occupant can judge his or her progress. Success then is a function of attaining or surpassing the level to which a person aspires.

Again, the assessments of others may differ from those of the individual. One entrepreneur who made two-million dollars felt like a failure because his friends all owned 300-million-dollar companies. Another person who leveled off in middle management felt very successful because he went so far beyond the level that his father had attained.

Without knowing a person's aspiration level, one cannot judge that person's subjective feelings of success. Level of aspiration is influenced by how society defines success, resulting in some correlation between aspirations and external criteria. Yet the external criteria will be those relevant within a given occupation, not just those of society as a whole. Money may be a general indicator of success in the United States, but engineers may judge the number of patents to be more important. For professors, the prestige of the university and fame among colleagues may matter more than money. Managers often put more value on the size of the budgets they control than on their actual salaries. To understand an individual's criteria for success, one must understand what that individual views as his or her reference group.

Movement in: attaining influence and power

One important criterion used to judge success is the extent to which an individual feels that he or she has penetrated the inner circle of an organization or occupation. Such penetration often is correlated with hierarchical movement, but it may be achieved independently. For example, an employee who has leveled off, but who is consulted by more senior, high-ranking people by virtue of his or her experience, seniority, or personality, still influences policy. Many technical people in organizations enjoy this kind of influence. Often, secretaries have power and influence far beyond their formal positions, resulting from informal contacts that have been built over the years.

Because such movement is invisible, judging its impact is difficult without talking to the individual. A person may feel very successful because of the sense of being in the inner circle and having influence; unless others ask about this, they may misjudge that person's sense of success. Sometimes one even encounters anomalies. For example, success may hinge on a carefully built network of contacts. Such a network might lead an individual to refuse a promotion if such a promotion would destroy the network and move the person up but out.

In summary, career movement can be seen to occur along horizontal, lateral, and vertical lines, and career paths can be viewed as complex interactions of these three kinds of movement. People are highly sensitive to the kind of movement that job shifts represent because of their differing aspirations and self-images. The career anchor concept is one way of describing such self-images within the internal career.

Development of a career anchor

As a career evolves, the person develops a self-concept that includes some explicit answers to these questions:

1. What are my talents, skills, and areas of competence? What are my strengths and weaknesses?

2. What are my main motives, needs, drives, and goals in life? What do I want or not want, either because I have never wanted it or because I have reached a point of insight and no longer want it?

3. What are my values – the main criteria by which I judge what I am doing? Am I in an organization or job that is congruent with my values? How good do I feel about what I am doing? How proud or ashamed am I of my work and career?

This self-concept builds on whatever self-insight an individual has acquired from the experiences of youth and education. However, it cannot be a mature self-concept until a career occupant has had enough real occupational experience to know his or her talents, motives, and values. Such learning may require up to ten years or more of actual work experience. If the person has many varied experiences and gets meaningful feedback in each one, a self-concept develops more quickly. If a person has only a few jobs in the early years of the career or obtains minimal feedback, it may take much longer.

Talents, motives, and values become intertwined. People learn to be better at those things they value and are motivated to do, and they learn to value and be motivated by those things they happen to do well. They also gradually learn to avoid those things that they do not do well; although without clear feedback, they may cling to illusions about themselves that set them up for repeated failures. Talents without motivation gradually atrophy. Conversely, new challenges can reveal latent or hidden talents that simply had not had an opportunity to appear earlier.

People differ as to whether talents, motives, or values initially dominate their self-concepts and provide central themes to their careers. As time goes on, however, a need for congruence causes people to seek consistency and integration among the different elements of self-concept. How is this consistency learned? People first enter the world of work with many ambitions, hopes, fears, and illusions but with relatively little good information about themselves, especially about their abilities and talents. Through testing and counseling they get an idea of their interests, motives, and values as well as their intellectual and motor skills, but they cannot really determine how good they will be at a certain kind of work or how they will react to it emotionally.

Nowhere is this more true than in management, because of the difficulty of simulating some of its key skills and abilities. Until a person actually feels the responsibility of committing large sums of money, of hiring and firing people, of saying 'no' to a valued subordinate, that person cannot tell whether he or she will be able to do it or will like doing it. This principle applies to many other occupations: a person cannot tell if he or she has a talent in or likes the job without actually performing that job.

The early years in an occupation are a crucial time of learning – learning about the occupation or organization and learning about oneself in relation to the demands of the job. This process often is painful and full of surprises because of the many misconceptions and illusions with which people typically enter their early work situations. Many of people's dreams about who they are and what their work will be like may be inconsistent with their work experiences, causing 'reality shock,' a phenomenon that is observed in all occupations in the early years.

As people accumulate work experience, they have the opportunity to make choices; from these choices they begin to ascertain what they really find important. For each person, dominant themes emerge – critical skills or abilities that an individual wants to exercise or crucial needs or values that dominate one's orientation toward life. Previously, a person may have had a vague sense of these elements; but in the absence of actual life experience, he or she does not know how important they are or how any given talent, motive, or value relates in a subjective hierarchy to other elements of the total personality. Only when he or she is confronted with difficult choices does a person begin to decide what is really important to him or her.

With accumulation of work experience and feedback come clarification and insight, providing a basis for more rational and empowered career decisions. The self-concept begins to function more and more as a guidance system and as an anchor that constrains career choices. A person begins to have a sense of what is 'me' and what is 'not me.' This knowledge keeps a person on course or in a safe harbor. As people recount their career choices, they increasingly refer to 'being pulled back' to things they have strayed from or 'figuring out' what they really want to do or 'finding' themselves.

The career anchor, as defined here, is that one element in a person's self-concept that he or she will not give up, even in the face of difficult choices. People typically manage to fulfill a broad range of needs in any given career, but those needs are not all equally important. If all needs cannot be met, it is important to know which ones have highest priority.

A person's career anchor may not always match what he or she is doing occupationally because of external constraints over which the person has no control. For example, economic circumstances or family illness could prevent someone from pursuing something that his or her self-image dictates. If interviewed, that person would explain that what he or she currently is doing is 'not really me, not really what I would like to be doing or am capable of doing.' These are not just idle illusions talking; in many cases people have actualized their self-concepts the moment the external constraints were lifted.

The career anchor is the self-image; it can remain remarkably stable even without the opportunity to exercise it, as in the case of the starving artist who drives a cab. Self-image will change if the person obtains systematic experience and feedback that make it impossible to maintain an illusion, as in the case of the artist who repeatedly fails to produce art that meets even his or her own standards. However, self-image may not change if the constraint is seen as merely external and temporary.

Early in a career, each person confronts the issue of how to integrate work, family, and personal priorities. Some will decide to de-emphasize work, considering it merely instrumental to survival. For such a person, experience is shaped primarily by what might be called a 'life anchor.' For purposes of discussion, the focus here initially will be on those people for whom work and career are important enough to warrant speaking of career anchors. For many younger people the concept of life anchor may make more sense, and for many older people career commitments may be reassessed, decreasing the importance of career anchors.

Origin of the concept 'career anchor'

The concept of 'career anchor' originally arose from a study designed to better understand how managerial careers evolved and how people learned the values and procedures of their employing organizations. A longitudinal study of forty-four alumni of the Master's program at the Sloan School of Management, Massachusetts Institute of Technology, began in 1961. The initial interviews and surveys of values and attitudes were conducted in 1961, 1962, and 1963 while the respondents were second-year students in the two-year Master's program. All were interviewed at their places of work six months after graduation and again one year after graduation. These interviews revealed a great deal about the problems of making the transition from school to work organizations.

All respondents completed questionnaires five years after graduation and had follow-up interviews in 1973, after they were approximately ten to twelve years into their careers. From these sources came insights into how the internal career evolves. The 1973 interviews elicited a detailed chronological career history, asking respondents not only to identify key choices and events but also to speculate about why they had made those particular choices and how they felt about each change. The interview format was essentially the same as that used in this book.

The actual events of the career histories proved to be highly varied, but the reasons that respondents gave for their choices and the pattern of their feelings about events proved to be surprisingly consistent. For each individual, underlying themes – of which he or she often had been unaware – reflected a growing sense of self, based on the learnings of the early years. When these people tried jobs that did not feel right to them, they referred to the image of being pulled back to something that fitted better – hence the metaphor of an anchor.

Types of career anchors

Based on this longitudinal study and on subsequent career-history interviews of several hundred people in various career stages, eight career anchor categories were identified:

– Technical/Functional competence
– General managerial competence

- Autonomy/Independence
- Security/Stability
- Entrepreneurial creativity
- Service/Dedication to a cause
- Pure challenge
- Lifestyle

Every person is concerned to some degree with each of these issues. The label 'career anchor' indicates an area of such paramount importance to a person that he or she would not give it up. The person comes to define his or her basic self-image in terms of that concern, and it becomes an overriding issue at every stage of the career.

20 K. E. Weick

Enacted Sensemaking in Crisis Situations

From 'Enacted Sensemaking in Crisis Situations', *Journal of Management Studies*, 1988, vol. 25, pp. 305–17

Introduction

Crises are characterized by low probability/high consequence events that threaten the most fundamental goals of an organization. Because of their low probability, these events defy interpretations and impose severe demands on sensemaking. The less adequate the sensemaking process directed at a crisis, the more likely it is that the crisis will get out of control. That straightforward proposition conceals a difficult dilemma because people think by acting. To sort out a crisis as it unfolds often requires action which simultaneously generates the raw material that is used for sensemaking and affects the unfolding crisis itself. There is a delicate tradeoff between dangerous action which produces understanding and safe inaction which produces confusion. The purpose of this article is to explore the complications of that tension.

Two exhibits highlight the central issue. The first involves explorers, the second involves the last paragraph of Union Carbide's procedure for dealing with gas leaks.

(1) 'An explorer can never know what he is exploring until it has been explored' (Bateson, 1972, p. xvi).

(2) 'The [Bhopal] plant's operating manual for methyl isocyanate offered little guidance in the event of a large leak. After telling the operators to dump the gas into a spare tank if a leak in a storage tank cannot be stopped or isolated, the manual says: "There may be other situations not covered above. The situation will determine the appropriate action. We will learn more and more as we gain actual experience"' (Diamond, 28 January 1985, p. 7).

399

Bateson's description of exploring illustrates the key point about sensemaking. The explorer cannot know what he is facing until he faces it, and then looks back over the episode to sort out what happened, a sequence that involves retrospective sensemaking. But the act of exploring itself has an impact on what is being explored, which means that parts of what the explorer discovers retrospectively are consequences of his own making. Furthermore, the exploring itself is guided by preconceptions of some kind, even though they may be generic preconceptions such as 'this will have made sense once I explore it although right now it seems senseless' (Weick, Gilfillan and Keith, 1973).

The explorer who enacts a sensible environment is no different from the operator of a console in a chemical plant control room who confronts a puzzling assortment of dials, lights and sounds and discovers, through action, what the problem is, but in doing so, shapes the problem itself (see McHugh, 1968, for an analogue). Both the explorer and the control room operator understand the problem they face only after they have faced it and only after their actions have become inextricably wound into it.

Imagine that the control room operator faces a gas leak and the admonition from the Union Carbide procedure cited above. Carbide is right when it says experience is the source of learning, but it is wrong when it says, 'The situation will determine the appropriate action'. People often don't know what the 'appropriate action' is until they take some action and see what happens. Thus, actions determine the situation. Furthermore, it is less often true that 'situations' determine appropriate action than that 'preconceptions' determine appropriate action. Finally, the judgement of 'appropriateness' is likely to be a motivated assessment constructed partially to validate earlier reasoning. These corrections show not so much that Carbide's statement is in error, as that Carbide's assessment is incomplete because it misrepresents the contribution of action to human understanding.

Understanding is facilitated by action, but action affects events and can make things worse. Action during crisis is not just an issue of control, it is an epistemological issue. If action is a means to get feedback, learn, and build an understanding of unknown environments, then a reluctance to act could be associated with less understanding and more errors.

In the remainder of this article I will enlarge these introductory ideas in three ways. First, I will describe the concept of enactment that drives this analysis. Second, I will discuss how cognition and understanding are affected by commitment, capacity, and expectations during crises. I conclude with a brief survey of implications for crisis management.

The enactment perspective

Assumptions of the enactment perspective

The concept of enactment is a synthesis, tailored for organizational settings, of four lines of scholarship: self-fulfilling prophecies (E. E. Jones, 1986; R. A. Jones, 1977; Snyder, 1984), retrospective sensemaking (Staw, 1980; Weick, 1979), commitment (Salancik, 1977; Staw, 1982), and social information processing (Salancik and Pfeffer, 1978). The term 'enactment' is used to preserve the central point that when people act, they bring events and structures into existence and set them in motion. People who act in organizations often produce structures, constraints and opportunities that were not there before they took action.

Enactment involves both a process, enactment, and a product, an enacted environment.

Enactment is the social process by which a 'material and symbolic record of action' (Smircich and Stubbart, 1985, p. 726) is laid down. The process occurs in two steps. First, portions of the field of experience are bracketed and singled out for closer attention on the basis of preconceptions. Second, people act within the context of these bracketed elements, under the guidance of preconceptions, and often shape these elements in the direction of preconceptions (Powers, 1973). Thus, action tends to confirm preconceptions.

An enacted environment is the residuum of changes produced by enactment. The world 'residuum' is preferred to the word 'residue' because residuum emphasizes that what is left after a process cannot be ignored or left out of account because it has potential significance (Webster's Dictionary of Synonyms, 1951, p. 694). The product of enactment is not an accident, an afterthought, or a byproduct. Instead, it is an orderly, material, social construction that is subject to multiple interpretations. Enacted environments contain real objects such as reactors, pipes and valves. The existence of these objects is not questioned, but their significance, meaning, and content is. These objects are inconsequential until they are acted upon and then incorporated retrospectively into events, situations, and explanations.

The external residuum of enacted changes is summarized internally by people in the form of a plausible map by which observed actions produced observed consequences. Since the summary map contains if–then assertions, it is called a cause map (Weick and Bougon, 1986) and is the source of expectations for future action. When we assert that the organization and the environment are in the mind of the actor, this means two things. It means that cause maps affect the construction of new experience through the mechanism of expectations and it means that cause maps affect the interpretation of old experience through the mechanism of labelling.

Thus, an enacted environment has both a public and a private face. Publicly, it is a construction that is usually visible to observers other than the actor. Privately, it is a map of if–then assertions in which actions are related to outcomes. These assertions serve as expectations about what will happen in the future.

At the heart of enactment is the idea that cognition lies in the path of the action. Action precedes cognition and focuses cognition. The sensemaking sequence implied in the phrase, 'How can I know what I think until I see what I say?' involves the action of talking, which lays down traces that are examined, so that cognitions can be inferred. These inferred cognitions then become preconceptions which partially affect the next episode of talk, which means the next set of traces deposited by talk are affected partially by previous labels and partially by current context. These earlier inferences also affect how the next episode of talk is examined and what is seen. This sensemaking sequence has the potential to become closed and detached from the context in which it occurs. However, that potential is seldom realized because preconceptions are usually weak, actions are usually novel, and memories are usually flawed.

Relationship of enactment perspective to crisis literature

The enactment perspective is applied to crisis situations in this article in an attempt to address Shrivastava's (1987, p. 118) observation that we do not yet understand much about how individual actions can cause an industrial crisis. The analysis of enactment suggests that individual actions involved in sensemaking can cause a crisis, but also manage it to lower levels of danger. Actions often construct the reasons for their occurrence as they unfold, which means their consequences are difficult to forecast in advance. Our actions are always a little further along than is our understanding of those actions, which means we can intensify crises literally before we know what we are doing. Unwitting escalation of crises is especially likely when technologies are complex, highly interactive, non-routine, and poorly understood. The very action which enables people to gain some understanding of these complex technologies can also cause those technologies to escalate and kill.

To learn more about how sensemaking can be decoupled from escalation, we focus on triggered events: 'a specific event that is identifiable in time and place and traceable to specific man-made causes' (Shrivastava, 1987, p. 8). Triggered events are placed where interventions can have an effect, these events involve judgement which can deteriorate when pressure increases (Staw, Sandelands and Dutton, 1981), and these events can escalate into a crisis.

The enactment perspective is about both crisis prevention and crisis management. We share with Ayres and Rohatgi (1987, p. 41) the assumption that 'while the probability of operator error can often be reduced, there is no evidence whatever that it can be eliminated altogether . . . Human errors are fundamentally "caused" by human variability, which cannot be designed away'. This assumption suggests to us that errors are inevitable, so the key issue is how to keep errors from enlarging. Errors are less likely to enlarge if they are understood more fully, more quickly. If we can understand the process of sensemaking during a crisis, then we can help people to prevent larger crises by smarter management of small crises. It is this sense in which enactment blurs the line between crisis prevention and crisis management. By understanding triggering events and the ways in which small sensemaking actions can grow into large senseless disasters, we hope to develop a better understanding of how crises can be isolated and contained.

The enactment approach shares an interest with Billings, Milburn, and Schaalman (1980) in triggering events, and complements their analysis by emphasizing that action is instrumental to crisis perception. The enactment perspective focuses on 'proactive crisis management' in Mitroff, Shrivastava, and Udwadia (1987) and develops specifically the activities of pre-assessment, prevention, preparation, and coping. The threat-rigidity cycle (Staw, Sandelands and Dutton, 1981) is in the background throughout our analysis since we assume that action often manages threat toward lower levels of intensity thereby reducing the tendency toward rigid problem solving.

Crises obviously are overdetermined and human sensemaking may play only a small part in their development. Nevertheless, crises engage human action, human action can amplify small deviations into major crises, and in any search for causes, we invariably can find some human act which may have set the crisis in motion. It is our contention that actions devoted to sensemaking play a central role in the genesis of crises and therefore need to be understood if we are to manage and prevent crises.

The enacted quality of crises

Shrivastava's (1987) analysis of Bhopal can be read for themes of enactment, as when he observes that 'the initial response to the crisis sets the tone for the rest of the effort' (p. 134). From the standpoint of enactment, initial responses do more than set the tone; they determine the trajectory of the crisis. Since people know what they have done only after they do it, people and their actions rapidly become part of the crisis. That is unavoidable. To become part of the problem means that people enact some of the environment they face. Had they not acted or had they acted differently, they would face a different set of problems, opportunities and constraints.

All crises have an enacted quality once a person takes the first action. Suppose that a gauge shows an unexpected increase in temperature. That is not enactment. Suppose further that in response to the unexpected temperature increase people tap the gauge or call the supervisor or proceed with a tea break or walk out to look at the tank whose temperature is being measured. That still is not enactment, because all that exists so far is a simple stimulus and response. But the response of tapping, calling, drinking, or walking produces a new stimulus that would not have been there had the first been ignored. The 'second stimulus' is now a partial construction. The assumptions that underlie the choice of that first response contribute to enactment and the second stimulus. As action continues through more cycles, the human responses which stimulate further action become increasingly important components of the crisis. 'When a triggering event occurs, spontaneous reactions by different stakeholders solve some of the immediate problems, but they also create new problems – thus prolonging the crisis and making it worse' (Shrivastava, 1987, p. 24).

Thus, from the perspective of enactment, what is striking is that crises can have small, volitional beginnings in human action. Small events are carried forward, cumulate with other events, and over time systematically construct an environment that is a rare combination of unexpected simultaneous failures.

Shrivastava (1987, p. 42) identified 'the leakage of toxic gas' as the triggering event at Bhopal, but my choice would be the failure to insert a slip blind into a pipe being cleaned, which allowed water to back up and enter the MIC tank and catalyse a complex chemical interaction (Ayres and Rohatgi, 1987, p. 32; Shrivastava, 1987, p. 46). The slip blind oversight occurred in close proximity to the 'leakage of toxic gas'; it was a small deviation that amplified because MIC was stored in 60 ton tanks rather than 55 gallon drums, and it resulted from a proximate combination of preconceptions about a job and its safety, inadequate supervision, and inadequate training.

It is not sufficient to deal with the enacted quality of crises by striving to make the technology operator-proof. All that does is move the dynamics of enactment to an earlier point in time where incomplete designs are enacted into unreliable technology by fallible designers who believe they can bypass the very human variability that has already been exhibited by their design process.

The enacted quality of crises is especially visible when we apply the concepts of commitment, capacity, and expectations to crisis conditions.

Enactment and commitment

The importance of commitment (Salancik, 1977) for enactment is straight-forward. Normally, when people act, their reasons for doing things are either self-evident or uninteresting, especially when the actions themselves can be undone, minimized, or disowned. Actions that are neither visible nor permanent can be explained with casual, transient explanations. As those actions become more public and irrevocable, however, they become harder to undo; and when those same actions are also volitional, they become harder to disown. When action is irrevocable, public and volitional, the search for explanations becomes less casual because more is at stake. Explanations that are developed retrospectively to justify committed actions are often stronger than beliefs developed under other, less involving, con-ditions. A tenacious justification can produce selective attention, confident action, and self-confirmation. Tenacious justifications prefigure both per-ception and action, which means they are often self-confirming.

Tenacious justifications can be forces for good or evil in crises. They are forces for good because they generate meaning in times of ambiguity, surprise, and confusion (Staw, 1980). Justifications provide sufficient struc-ture for people to get their bearings and then create fuller, more accurate views of what is happening and what their options are.

The dark side of commitment is that it produces blind spots. Once a person becomes committed to an action, and then builds an explanation that justifies that action, the explanation tends to persist and become trans-formed into an assumption that is taken for granted. Once this transforma-tion has occurred it is unlikely that the assumption will be readily viewed as a potential contributor to a crisis.

For example, the public, irrevocable choice at Bhopal to keep the dangerous process of MIC production secret, was justified in terms of competitive advantage and the prevention of 'unnecessary' alarm. As a result, the commitment to secrecy was one of the last assumptions workers considered as a contributor to the crisis. To minimize alarm, the warning siren at Bhopal was not turned on until gas actually started to leak into the atmosphere, the siren was turned off after 5 minutes, and it was not restarted until gas had been escaping for 90 minutes. The commitment to secrecy induced a blind spot toward a partial solution, necessary alarm.

As another example, the public, irrevocable decision by Bhopal management to announce that all safety violations reported to them in a September 1982 report, had been corrected (Ayres and Rohatgi, 1987, p. 36), was justified by actions which took safety for granted and inadvertently allowed it to deteriorate steadily in several different places. Thus, the eventual public, irrevocable choice to disconnect the refrigeration equipment that kept MIC temperature under control, was justified as a relatively safe means to save electricity, reduce costs, and recover freon which could be used elsewhere in the plant. It was the uncontrolled heating of MIT in Tank 610 that led to rupture of the safety valves and venting of the gas.

When people make a public commitment that an operating gauge is inoperative, the last thing they will consider during a crisis is that the gauge is operating. Had they not made the commitment, the blind spot would not be so persistent. When a person becomes committed to the view that fluctuations in electricity cause 90 per cent of the variances that are seen in gauges, the possibility that a much different percentage is more accurate will not be entertained until the crisis is at an advanced stage.

Given the effects of commitments on attention, practitioners and researchers alike might learn more about crisis potential (Mitroff, Shrivastava and Udwadia, 1987, p. 290) if they see which people are 'on record' as making irreversible assertions about technology, operators, and capabilities. Those assertions, and their associated justifications, will have been shielded from scrutiny more than other assertions in which less is at stake. The practices and assumptions that those justifications shield may be significant contributors to crisis.

Enactment and capacity

Action in the form of capacity can affect crisis management through perception, distribution of competence and control within a hierarchy, and number and diversity of actors.

Capacity and response repertoire affect crisis perception, because people see those events they feel they have the capacity to do something about. As capacities change, so too do perceptions and actions. This relationship is one of the crucial leverage points to improve crisis management.

The rationale for these relationships has been described by Jervis (1976, pp. 374–5). '(T)he predisposition to perceive a threat varies with the person's beliefs about his ability to take effective counteraction if he perceives the danger ... Whether they are vigilant or defensive depends in large part on whether they think they can act effectively on the undesired information'.

If people think they can do lots of things, then they can afford to pay attention to a wider variety of inputs because, whatever they see, they will have some way to cope with it. The more a person sees of any situation, the higher the probability that the person will see the specific change that needs to be made to dampen the crisis. Accuracy in perception comes from an expanded response capacity. Perrow (1984) argues that operators who have specialized expertise do not see the 'big picture' as crises develop and therefore miss key events. That scenario is consistent with the proposition that capacity affects perception. Specialists can do a few things well, which means that they search the world to see if it needs what they can do. If it doesn't, they do nothing else because they see nothing else.

If people are aware that volitional action may enact conditions that intensify or de-escalate crises, and if they are also aware of their actions and capacities, this heightened awareness could allow them to see more of a developing crisis. Seeing more of the developing crisis, people should then be able to see more places where they could intervene and make an actual difference in what is developing. The joint beliefs, 'I have capacity' and 'capacity makes a difference', should reduce defensive perception and allow people to see more. As they see more, there is a greater probability that they will see some place where their intervention can make a difference.

Capacity can also affect crisis management by the way in which it is distributed in a hierarchy. Perrow (1984, p. 10) notes that 'operators need to be able to take independent and creative action because they are closest to the system, yet centralization, tight coupling, and prescribed steps prevent decentralized action'.

Action of any kind may be prevented or slowed in a centralized system. Hermann (1963) has noted when crises occur, authority becomes contracted in one of three ways: it moves to higher levels of the hierarchy, fewer people exercise authority, or there is an increase in the number of occasions when authority is exercised even though the number of units exercising it remain constant (p. 70).

The danger in centralization and contraction of authority is that there may be a reduction in the level of competence directed at the problem as well as an overall reduction in the use of action to develop meaning. For example, Bhopal had relatively unsophisticated sensing devices and had to rely on workers to sense problems by means of the 'tear gas effect of the vapor' (Diamond, 28 January, 1985, p. 6). But the presence of that vivid indicator was still not enough because the tearing was given little attention by authorities. Furthermore, if people had moved around at Bhopal, they would have heard gurgling and rumbling in the MIC tank, seen drops of water near the tank, and felt tearing in their eyes.

The person in authority is not necessarily the most competent person to deal with a crisis, so a contraction of authority leads either to less action or more confusion. Career ladders in crisis-prone organizations are crucial antecedents for coping. People who come up through the technical ranks have hands-on experience and the requisite knowledge to sense variations in the technological environment they face. Those who administer without a technical background have less requisite expertise and miss more.

Diamond (30 January, 1985, p. 6), in his account of Bhopal, noted that during the crisis, 'K. V. Shetty, the plant superintendent for the shift, had come racing over from the main gate on a bicycle, workers said. "He came in pretty much in a panic", Mr Day said. "He said, 'what should we do?' " Mr Shetty, who declined to be interviewed, was on the administrative and not the technical side of the factory, the workers said'.

Capacity can also affect crisis potential through staffing decisions that affect the diversity of acts that are available. Enactment is labour-intensive, which means understaffing has serious effects. Even though the Bhopal plant had few automated controls, high manual control over processes, and a potentially large amount of action data from which understanding could be built, these potential assets were neutralized because operating staffs had been cut from 12 to 6 people per shift. Thus, knowledge was reduced, not because of automation, but because of understaffing. If action is the means to understanding, then the number and quality of actors available to do that acting and interpretation become crucial variables.

Turnover is as much a threat to capacity as is understaffing, but for a different reason. Institutional memory is an important component of crisis management. People can see only those categories and assumptions that they store in cause maps built up from previous experience. If those cause maps are varied and rich, people should see more, and good institutional memory would be an asset. However, if cause maps are filled with only a handful of overworked justifications, then perception should be limited and inaccurate, and a good memory would be a liability.

Shrivastava (1987, p. 52) reported that there was no institutional memory at Bhopal because turnover in top management was high and Smith (1984, p. 908) made the same observation about crisis management in the US government. In both cases, there are few beliefs that control seeing. It might seem desirable for a few preconceptions to be carried in institutional memory because then people will perceive more of what is 'really there'. Perception, however, is never free of preconceptions, and when people perceive without institutional memories, they are likely to be influenced by salient distractions (e.g. Kirwan, 1987) or by experience gained in settings that are irrelevant to present problems.

If more people are in constant touch with the system, this will make it easier to detect and correct anomalies and also to implant more reliable environments. These outcomes should be especially likely when the people doing the enactment have diverse experience, novel categories and justifications, and diverse activities at which they are skilled and in terms of which they perceive the world. We are not talking about specialists isolated from one another. Instead, we are talking about heterogeneous teams of diverse people with sufficient mutual respect that they maintain dense interaction with one another. Teams able to meet these demands are scarce, do not come cheap, and may be most likely to form if high levels of professionalism are associated with them.

Enactment and expectations

The assumptions that top management make about components within the firm often influence enactment in a manner similar to the mechanism of self-fulfilling prophecy. Many of these assumptions can increase or decrease the likelihood that small errors will escalate into major crises. Thus, assumptions are an important source of crisis prevention.

This mechanism is clearly visible in Bhopal where top management assumed that the Bhopal plant was unimportant and therefore allocated limited resources to maintain it. That assumption of unimportance set in motion a self-confirming vicious circle in which worker indifference and management cost-cutting became mutually reinforcing and resulted in deteriorating conditions that became more dangerous. ' "The whole industrial culture of Union Carbide at Bhopal went down the drain", said Mr Pareek, the former project engineer. "The plant was losing money, and top management decided that saving money was more important than safety. Maintenance practices became poor, and things generally got sloppy. The plant didn't seem to have a future, and a lot of skilled people became depressed and left as a result" ' (Diamond, 28 January, 1985, p. 6).

A plant perceived as unimportant proceeds to act out, through turnover, sloppy procedures, inattention to details, and lower standards, the prophecy implied in top management's expectations. A vicious circle is created and conditions become increasingly dangerous. Notice that the most crucial assumption does not involve safety directly. Instead, the crucial assumptions focus on themes of competence, importance, and value. Susceptibility to crisis varies as a function of top management assumptions about which units are important.

When cost cutting is focused on less important units, it is not just decreased maintenance which raises susceptibility to crisis. Instead, it is all of the indirect effects on workers of the perception that their unit doesn't matter. This perception results in increased inattention, indifference, turnover, low cost improvisation, and working-to-rule, all of which remove slack, lower the threshold at which a crisis will escalate, and increase the number of separate places at which a crisis could start. As slack decreases, the technology becomes more interactively complex (Perrow, 1984), which means there are more places where a minor lapse can escalate just when there are more minor lapses occurring.

The point is, this scenario starts with top management perceptions that set in motion enactments that confirm the perceptions. Furthermore, the initial perceptions were concerned with strategy, not safety. Strategy became an inadvertent source of crisis through its effects on realities constructed by disheartened workers. The realities they enacted removed buffers, dampers, and controls between steps in the technology, made it harder for errors to be contained, and easier for errors to get started.

Implications for crisis management

Crisis management is often portrayed as reactive activity directed at problems that are already escalating. That portrait is too narrow and I have tried to show why.

Perrow (1984) captured the core issue in crisis management, but did so in a way that exhibited rather than remedied the blind spot that concerns us. He observed that 'our ability to organize does not match the inherent hazards of some of our organized activities' (p. 10). The potential blindspot in that otherwise tight description is the reference to 'inherent hazard'.

Hazards are not given nor do they necessarily inhere in organized activity. Instead, they are often constructed and put into place by human actors. Their development is indeterminant rather than fixed, and crisis management can mean quick action that deflects a triggering event as it unfolds rather than delayed action that mops up after the triggering event has run its course. These possibilities are more likely to be seen if we think of large crises as the outcome of smaller scale enactments.

When the enactment perspective is applied to crisis situations, several aspects stand out that are normally overlooked.

To look for enactment themes in crises, for example, is to listen for verbs of enactment, words like manual control, intervene, cope, probe, alter, design, solve, decouple, try, peek and poke (Perrow, 1984, p. 333), talk, disregard, and improvise. These verbs may signify actions that have the potential to construct or limit later stages in an unfolding crisis.

To look for enactment themes in crisis is also to assess the forcefulness of actions and the ambiguity of the situation (Perrow, 1984, p. 83) in which those actions occur. As forcefulness and ambiguity increase, enactment is more consequential, and more of the unfolding crisis is under the direct control of human action. Conversely, as action becomes more tentative and situations become more clearly structured, enactment processes will play a smaller role in crisis development and management. Enactment, therefore, will have most effect on those portions of a crisis which are loosely coupled. If pipe cleaning procedures are not standardized, if supervision is intermittent, if job specifications are vague, or if warning devices are activated capriciously, then these loosely coupled activities will be susceptible to alteration through enactment. Human action will produce environments involving pipes, supervision, specifications, and alarms, either in dangerous or safe combinations, because these are the most influencible elements. Loose coupling does not guarantee safety. Instead, it guarantees susceptibility to human action, and those actions can either reduce or increase hazards.

Enactment affects crisis management through several means such as the psychology of control, effects of action on stress levels, speed of interactions, and ideology.

An enactment perspective suggests that crisis events are more controllable than was first thought. That suggestion, by itself, can be self-affirming because as perceptions of control increase, stress decreases, and as stress decreases, perceptual narrowing also decreases which means people see more when they inspect any display (George, 1986). As people see more, they are more likely to notice things they can do something about, which confirms the perception of control and also reduces crisis intensity to lower levels by virtue of early intervention in its development.

Enactment can also reduce the perceptual narrowing produced by stress in another way. When people take some action, they often transform a more complex task into a simpler task. This occurs because action clarifies what the problem may be, specific action renders many cues and options irrelevant, and action consolidates an otherwise unorganized set of environmental elements. All of these simplifications gain significance in the context of stress because there is good evidence that stress has less adverse effects on performance of simple tasks than on performance of complex tasks (Eysenck, 1982). Since stress is an accompaniment of all crises, and since many crises escalate because of the secondary effects of crisis induced stress, the beneficial effect of action in the form of task simplification is important.

Not only does action simplify tasks, it also often slows down the effects of one variable on another. Perrow (1984) has shown tight coupling, in the presence of interactive complexity, leads to rapid escalation of crisis events. Action such as rearrangements of traffic patterns by air traffic controllers (Weick, 1987) often dampens the tight coupling between variables and reduces both the speed and magnitude with which connected variables affect one another. Especially if a controller becomes a step in a process (Perrow, 1984, p. 331), the actions of that controller can slow the speed with which the process unfolds and can also slow the speed with which unanticipated interactions occur.

Perhaps the most important implication of enactment is that it might serve as the basis for an ideology of crisis prevention and management. By ideology, we mean a 'relatively coherent set of beliefs that bind people together and explain their worlds in terms of cause-and-effect relations' (Beyer, 1981, p. 166). Enactment leverages human involvement in systems and, as a coherent set of beliefs about the form and outcomes of such involvement, could elicit self-control and voluntary co-operation similar to that elicited by more formal structures designed to do the same thing (Meyer, 1982, p. 55).

An ideology built around the preceding ideas would mean that people have a fuller idea of how individuals generate their own environments including crisis environments, have an appreciation that the strength of commitments is a manipulable variable that has tangible environment effects, see the importance of expertise in action and the value of multiple small actions, understand how structures can accelerate or decelerate responsive action, and see more potential cause of crises and more places where interventions are possible, while maintaining an awareness of the necessity to balance dangerous action with safe inaction in the interest of diagnosis.

If these beliefs were adopted as a component of crisis management, people could think about crises in ways that highlight their own actions and decisions as determinants of the conditions they want to prevent.

The activity of crisis management, viewed through the lens of enactment, involves such things as managing crises to lower levels of intensity, increasing skill levels and heightening the awareness of existing skill levels in the interest of expanded perception, appreciation of the ways in which small interventions can amplify, and being exquisitely aware of commitments that may bias diagnoses.

Perrow (1984) has, I think, correctly identified a new cause of human-made catastrophes, 'interactive complexity in the presence of tight coupling, producing a system accident' (p. 11). Recent benchmark catastrophes such as Chernobyl, Bhopal, and Challenger all fit this recipe. The way to counteract catastrophes, therefore, is to reduce tight coupling and interactive complexity. To do this, it seems important not to blame technology, but rather to look for and exaggerate all possible human contributions to crises in the hope that we can spot some previously unnoticed contributions where we can exert leverage. Therefore, even if the relative importance of enactment is exaggerated and borders on hyperbole, the important outcome of such exaggeration could be discovery of unexpected places to gain control over crises. The enactment perspective urges people to include their own actions more prominently in the mental experiments they run to discover potential crises of which they may be the chief agents.

Note

I acknowledge with appreciation the comments of Barbara Kelly, Reuben McDaniel, and Douglas Orton on an early version of this manuscript.

References

AYRES, R. U., and ROHATGI, P. K. (1987), 'Bhopal: lessons for technological decision-makers', *Technology in Society*, 9, pp. 19–45

BATESON, G. (1972), *Steps to an Ecology of Mind*, New York, Ballantine

BEYER, J. M. (1981), 'Ideologies, values, and decision-making in organizations', in: Nystrom, P. C., and Starbuck, W. H. (eds.), *Handbook of Organizational Design*, vol. 2, pp. 166–202, New York, Oxford University Press

BILLINGS, R. S., MILBURN, T. W., and SCHAALMAN, M. L. (1980), 'A model of crisis perception: a theoretical analysis', *Administrative Science Quarterly*, 25, pp. 300–16

DIAMOND, S. (1985), 'The Bhopal disaster: how it happened', *New York Times*, 28 January, pp. 1, 6, 7

DIAMOND, S. (1985), 'The disaster in Bhopal: workers recall horror', *New York Times*, 30 January, pp. 1, 6

EYSENCK, M. S. (1982), *Attention and Arousal*, New York, Springer-Verlag

GEORGE, A. L. (1986), 'The impact of crisis-induced stress on decision-making', in: Solomon, F., and Marston, R. Q. (eds.), *The Medical Implications of Nuclear War*, Washington DC, National Academy of Sciences Press

HERMANN, C. F. (1963), 'Some consequences of crisis which limit the viability of organizations', *Administrative Science Quarterly*, 8, pp. 61–82

JERVIS, R. (1976), *Perception and Misperception in International Politics*, Princeton, NJ, Princeton University Press

JONES, E. E. (1986), 'Interpreting interpersonal behavior: the effects of expectancies', *Science*, 234, pp. 41–6

JONES, R. A. (1977), *Self-fulfilling Prophecies*, Hillside, NJ, Erlbaum

KIRWAN, B. (1987), 'Human reliability analysis of an offshore emergency blowdown system', *Applied Ergonomics*, 18, pp. 23–33

McHUGH, P. (1968), *Defining the Situation*, Indianapolis, Bobbs-Merrill

MEYER, A. D. (1982), 'How ideologies supplant formal structures and shape responses to environment', *Journal of Management Studies*, 19, pp. 45–61

MITROFF, I. I., SHRIVASTAVA, P., and UDWADIA, F. (1987), 'Effective crisis management', *Executive*, 1, pp. 283–92

PERROW, C. (1984), *Normal Accidents*, New York, Basic Books

POWERS, W. T. (1973), *Behavior: The Control of Perception*, Chicago, Aldine

SALANCIK, G. R. (1977), 'Commitment and the control of organizational behavior and belief', in: Staw, B. M., and Salancik, G. R. (eds.), *New Directions in Organizational Behavior*, pp. 1–54, Chicago, St Clair

SALANCIK, G. R., and PFEFFER, J. (1978), 'A social information processing approach to job attitude and task design', *Administrative Science Quarterly*, 23, pp. 224–53

SHRIVASTAVA, P. (1987), *Bhopal: Anatomy of a Crisis*, Cambridge, Mass., Ballinger

SMIRCICH, L., and STUBBART, C. (1985), 'Strategic management in an enacted world', *Academy of Management Review*, 10, pp. 724–36

SMITH, R. J. (1984), 'Crisis management under strain', *Science*, 225, pp. 907–9

SNYDER, M. (1984), 'When belief creates reality', in: Berkowitz, L. (ed.), *Advances in Experimental Social Psychology*, vol. 18, pp. 247–305, New York, Academic Press

STAW, B. M. (1980), 'Rationality and justification in organizational life', in:

Cummings, L., and Staw, B. (eds.), *Research in Organizational Behavior*, vol. 2, pp. 45–80, Greenwich, Conn., JAI Press

STAW, B. M. (1982), 'Counterforces to change', in: Goodman, P. S., and Associates (eds.), *Change in Organizations: New Perspectives on Theory, Research, and Practice*, pp. 87–121, San Francisco, Jossey-Bass

STAW, B. M., SANDELANDS, L. E., and DUTTON, J. E. (1981), 'Threat-rigidity effects in organizational behavior: a multi-level analysis', *Administrative Science Quarterly*, 26, pp. 501–24

WEBSTER'S DICTIONARY OF SYNONYMS, 1st edn (1951), Springfield, Mass., Merriam

WEICK, K. E. (1979), *The Social Psychology of Organizing*, 2nd edn, Reading, Mass., Addison-Wesley

WEICK, K. E. (1987), 'Organizational culture as a source of high reliability', *California Management Review*, 29, 2, pp. 112–27

WEICK, K. E., and BOUGON, M. G. (1986), 'Organizations as cause maps', in: Sims, H. P., Jr, and Gioia, D. A. (eds.), *Social Cognition in Organizations*, pp. 102–35, San Francisco, Jossey-Bass

WEICK, K. E., GILFILLAN, D. P., and KEITH, T. (1973), 'The effect of composer credibility on orchestra performance', *Sociometry*, 36, pp. 435–62

21   C. Argyris

Defensive Routines

From 'Summary and implications', *Strategy, Change and Defensive Routines*, Pitman, 1985, chapter 12

Defensive routines are powerful

Defensive routines exist in most organizations. The routines most dangerous to organizational learning and effectiveness are those that are used in the name of support, concern, strength, humanism, and realism. These ideas are culturally taught and accepted to be true.

Threat is dealt with by defensive reasoning and a defensive-prone theory in use. This, in turn, produces learning systems in organizations that are actually against understanding how to deal with threatening issues so they can be eliminated.

The three resources upon which practitioners can understandably depend for guidance also reinforce these conditions. The researchers on strategy implementation and, indeed, management in general, acknowledge the danger/threat posed by defensive routines yet provide advice that is fraught with defensive reasoning, defensive theories in use, and defensive organizational cultures. The second source – the consulting firms – are, for the most part, not much different. They appear to deal with threat primarily in ways that bypass these defensive routines. Finally, the same may be true for most university and executive programs. They may teach that defensive routines exist, but we know of no course that is dedicated to helping us become aware of our defensive reasoning or our theories in use and how to provide opportunity to change them.

Thus, a multitiered set of defensive loops exists, to my knowledge, throughout the world, that reinforces defensive routines. It is for this reason, I believe, that defensive routines can be acknowledged as one of the most powerful factors that inhibit organizational learning and learning how to learn. However, teachers do not discuss them; organizations have no formal rules to support them, and, to my knowledge, most strategy or management consultants do not deal with them in the name of being realistic, the art of the possible, and holding on to their clients.

What makes it possible for organizations to be productive under these conditions? First, much that goes on in organizations does not contain threat, or where threat does exist, there are times when it cannot be hidden and ignored. By the way, the dream of many management information systems designers is to design a tamper-proof, guaranteed-to-catch-the-culprit information system. If they succeed, they will also succeed in super-imposing on defensive routines a control system that will call the individuals to new heights of creativity on how to bypass the threatening features of the information system. The strategy most often used by systems designers is to translate nonroutine, difficult problems into routine ones. Once this is done, a good deal of threat is supposed to be taken out of the system. Again, this could work in the short term and still create a long-term danger. The long-term danger is that the routine, easily programmable mentality takes over. This not only may drive out creativity but also may become so rigid and inflexible that the most threatening challenge is to change the routine.

A second reason why organizations can get on with their business is that there are useful bypass solutions. In strategy, for example, defining a sound planning process, defining the new roles and the new structure, creating new management information systems, and rewarding the individuals can help keep the organization effective.

The problem is that an increasing number of organizations that do these things well still find themselves crippled by defensive routines. Moreover, these defensive routines eventually become immune to any corrective features that may be taken to eliminate them. This is related to the most important fear expressed by top management and first-rate consultants. They do not fear designing and putting in place all these corrective actions. Their biggest fear is once this has been done, the corrective actions will work for a while and eventually lose a good deal (but not all) of their effectiveness.

This fear is realistic for a fundamental reason. Whenever new jobs are defined, new structures, new management information systems, they are designed with the explicit or tacit assumption that threat is ruled out. If you examine the written material that makes any of these solutions operative, you will probably find little about how to deal with distortions and cover-ups.

The implicit assumption in most organizations is that employees, especially managers and professional contributors, are intendedly rational, have a sense of their stewardship, and are loyal. These characteristics are expected to combine to create an ongoing monitoring system against distortion and cover-up. This assumption is partially valid. The difficulty is that when threat occurs, defensive routines are created by individuals because such actions appear to them to be rational, indicating their keen sense of stewardship (they are trying to keep the place afloat), which therefore means they are loyal.

In addition, the designs are often developed with individuals knowing they were partially a cover-up. Recall the university that created the job of provost to separate the president from the faculty, the firm that created a corporate planning office because they gave up on divisional planners, and the organizations that demanded of their strategy professionals new planning processes and simultaneously gave tacit or explicit clues that they did not wish to touch the defensive routines with a ten-foot pole. Again, the intentions are clear. Top management believes that to change defensive routines is the equivalent of changing the world, a belief that I share with them. They conclude that the most realistic solution is to bypass them – a conclusion I see as understandable, shortsighted, and leaving a polluted organization to the managers of future organizations.

A third reason why some organizations perform in spite of defensive routines is that they may have dedicated hard-working management, especially at the top. Once they create new structures and policies, they keep driving home their point that they value risk takers, individuals who blow whistles, people who keep organizations flexible, and so on. This is consistent with the fundamental messages of the recent best seller on organizational excellence (Peters and Waterman, 1984): organizations should tend to their knitting and keep strategies that depend on their proven skills, listen to their customers (who can give feedback of the kind that defensive routines dread), and have a CEO who will take on the defensive loops in a multilevel, continual, unabating offensive. The long-range cost of this advice may be to burn out those dedicated individuals and to allow the defensive routines to flourish.

Defensive routines are alterable

The second lesson we are learning about defensive routines is that they are changeable. It is surprising but true that, given a commitment to change defensive routines, change can be made relatively easily compared to the staying and proliferating power of defensive routines. I believe the long-term barrier to progress will not be appropriate change technology but whether society will encourage and whether individuals will take the initiative to tackle the challenge.

There are many forces that make tackling defensive routines realistic. First, it is not necessary – indeed, it may be counterproductive – to think in terms of massive change programs. Recall our advice to start small and at the top.

Second, the change technology being developed places the control over the direction and pace in the hands of the players. There is little danger of things going out of control. The advice is to move slowly and iteratively. Let the organization learn from each experiment so it can make the next one even more successful and build up organizational intelligence on these change processes that can be disseminated throughout the organization. Each attempt should be focused on a real, technical problem. For example, designing a planning process or pricing strategies are types of changes that require careful inquiry, experimentation, and iterative learning.

Third, it is not necessary to have executives or consultants completely educated and highly skilled in changing defensive routines. In several situations in which I was involved, the top executives or the consultants were learning as they were doing. Most of them had experience of appreciation learning seminars. Most had experience in trying out the new ideas and skills in small and manageable activities.

Be they line or consultants, individuals should be able to use publicly compelling and testable reasoning when dealing with defensive routines, be able to minimize the use of their own defenses to protect themselves or to protect the client, be able to translate an error into an opportunity for new learning, and be smart enough to design programs within these competencies and not to overpromise (which would make them feel anxious and the client wary).

In most cases, the executives and consultants made up for their gaps in knowledge and skills by learning while they were doing (with the help of a professional more competent than them). For example, the consultants described previously were able to learn and stay ahead of their clients by spending several hours working with an adviser after every session with the client and then designing what to do next.

I was particularly impressed how quickly the participants learned to identify and correct errors, how good they become at designing new encounters, how little they forgot so they could use their knowledge, not only in their own work but also in helping others, and how, after six months or a year of such efforts, some of them began to design interventions and examine current practice in ways that contributed to new advances in practice and theory.

I am sure that not all executives or consultants can learn as easily and as fast as those with whom I have been involved. I am also quite confident that, because of my lack of knowledge and competence about teaching the new competences, some of those who appeared to be slower learners were not. Also inhibiting their learning was the lack of sound theory about such interventions that they could read and that would answer their burning questions.

As our knowledge increases, I believe that we will be able to help an increasingly larger number of individuals to become competent and to become so more quickly than is presently the case. The same knowledge should also help us to identify where it is unlikely that we can be of help either to individuals or to organizations. My belief is that if there are limits they will be related more to individuals than to organizations because it is more likely that the latter will have a wide variety of individuals and, hence, some who can learn the new ideas and competencies.

Another encouraging sign is that although changes usually start very slowly, they are often additive and spread throughout the organization. Moreover, they appear to deepen and be resilient to defensive routines that are threatened by changes. Even in very defensive organizations where the changes were suppressed by anxious senior executives, the competencies were not forgotten. A year or longer after the organization became more supportive, the individuals were able to take out of mothballs their skills and the conditions they had begun to develop, and place them into action relatively easily and quickly.

New skills can be used in situations where change is not being considered

We often meet executives and consultants who, after learning the skills in our seminars, believe that their organizations or their clients are not ready for engaging defensive routines. These individuals tell us that the ideas and competencies they learn are still very useful, however.

For example, in a survey, clients who used strategy consultants identified five criteria that were important in selecting the consultants with whom they worked:

1. A tough, analytically rigorous mind accompanied with high standards.
2. A continual concern for implementation.
3. A capacity to train the organization in the skills they use for strategy formulation and implementation.
4. Experience in the business.
5. The ability to create conditions where the top management could feel comfortable to think out loud, make errors, feel stupid, and in general work with them as they were growing.

It is interesting to note that relative experience was overwhelmingly voted as the least important attribute and that working in an effective personal relationship was the most important one.

The knowledge and skills that individuals learn to cope with defensive routines are very helpful in establishing close, enduring relationships with the clients (peers or subordinates in the case of line executives) where there is little thought, at the outset, of engaging defensive routines. These skills can also help the individual become a more effective diagnostician of organizational routines and of the routines the players use to bypass them. They lead to a much richer picture of what is reality, as well as what can or cannot be done to begin to sensitize the organization toward the need to change.

Along with a more realistic picture of the scope and depth of defensive routines, the individual is also able to be more empathic and patient about change. Change agents can be less defensive about dealing with others' defensive routines. There is less anger toward clients who genuinely do not wish to change or are ambivalent about doing so.

Another payoff is that any recommendations for change that are developed will tend to be more valid as well as more realistic about what can and cannot be done. Finally, all these combine to make it more likely that the individual can help the clients who are not ready for change at least not to get into worse difficulties.

Defensive routines and changing the status quo

It is possible to use the concept of defensive routines to explain one of the most persistent consequences of trying to change the status quo in organizations. I refer to the fact that such change rarely lasts. Every time I dig into the histories of attempts to change organizations significantly, I find that during the early stages, especially with the help of a driven, charismatic leader (and financial resources), changes are made. The problems arise when the players begin to face dilemmas, paradoxes, and threats; that is when defensive routines come into play. The knowledge and competencies people have to deal with them are not only inadequate but also create regressions to the status quo.

Take schools as an example. A decade ago, many alternative schools cropped up that were creative experiments to change the status quo. To my knowledge, most have not succeeded in doing so. I examined several where the schools had funding, the teachers and students had volunteered, the curriculum was jointly controlled, and the players were left alone to create their brave new world. In all cases they failed. When I dug into why this was the case, the key factors were related to defensive routines. For example, as long as the teachers and students were designing the easy aspects of the curriculum or the easy features of the school culture, everything went well; but when the difficult issues such as evaluations of performance, the choice of standards, and the level of commitment to learning the academic disciplines had to be faced, then all sorts of conflicts arose. Moreover, the students became as authoritarian and manipulative as they had accused teachers of being previously. The teachers, who had volunteered, were deeply shocked and hurt because they believed that they could eliminate unilateral control and manipulation. The teachers tended to withdraw and become depressed. The students were left with their manipulative tendencies, which they then turned on each other (Argyris, 1974). In another case, we observed a dedicated, bright group of faculty trying to create a democratic culture in an inner-city school in order to raise the level of moral development (which, in turn, might help the educational performance). The students who 'bought' the dream dealt with the dilemmas and paradoxes by acting not only Model I but also Model I cubed! The teachers eventually became discouraged and withdrew (Argyris and Argyris, 1979).[1]

The same problems exist in the area of worker participation and ownership. Witte (1980) provides vivid data that experiments in worker democracy begin with an outburst of enthusiasm that soon begins to wane. He concludes that one of the causes of the regression is the lack of effective leadership and authority to ensure stability. When one digs into his rich data, it is possible to see why such leadership is lacking. For example, the dynamics of the planning councils are full of competitive, win/lose activities or easing-in diplomatic activities. As we have seen throughout this book, the groups are faced with threat; some members react aggressively while others react passively. The groups never deal with the tension between the two reactions. The result is often misunderstanding coupled with compromises that cover up the misunderstanding and cover up the cover-up.

Witte (1980) wonders whether genuine equality will be possible. He notes that often management dominates the conversation not because they have a dominating style (although some do) but because they have the relevant information. Workers are quite willing to speak less and listen more if they believe they do not have the relevant technical information to get on with the job. It is interesting to note that management in Yugoslavia dominates more than does the management studied in the United States (p. 73).

Bradley and Hill (1982) report similar problems in their study of Japanese and Western management styles. They studied the introduction of quality circles in two relatively comparable chemical and pharmaceutical firms, one in the United Kingdom and the other in the United States. They found, for example, that despite the introduction of quality circles, managers could not be regarded as pursuing high-trust relations when it came to providing the information the employee needed. Managers, at times, acted to keep the quality circles off subjects they did not want discussed even if it meant reducing the quality of the discussions. Another approach was to frustrate either the initial formulation or the subsequent implementation of circle suggestions that were seen as threatening (p. 303).

Quality circles did improve communications and social relations, but they failed to allay suspicions of management or the awareness that the interests of management and labor were not the same. Another consequence was the emergence of an insider–outsider division between members and

---

1. Model I is the author's term for the view of the world held by those whose aim is to defend themselves from change and impose it upon others – Ed.

nonmembers as the result of quality circles that, as far as I could tell, were not engaged by the respective firms.

Bradley and Hill (1982) conclude that quality circles do produce efficiency gains with quantifiable financial returns. The biggest gains are made in the early period. There is little positive impact on the employee–employer mistrust partially, I suggest, because both sides attempt to manipulate each other when difficult issues arise. It is interesting that similar results were reported in attempts to gain worker participation in India (Pylee, 1975).

Finally, Raelin (1984) conducted research among professionals to show how they tend to deal with the problem of mismatch between what they are seeking from work and what is available to them on the job. He finds that professionals may use a wide variety of defensive routines to deal with the mismatch that, I believe, they are likely to cover up. For example, on the job, they may engage in projects that will benefit their personal career but not the organization, they believe they are too busy to get to the things that might prove more useful to the organization, or they do exactly what is required of them, never more and never less. They may combine these actions with feelings that they are burning out and becoming distanced from the organization. These consequences are accompanied by seeking greater autonomy, requesting professional privileges like attending professional meetings, and searching for new employment.

In all these examples, the theme is the same. Whenever threat is generated, the defensive routines individuals use are counterproductive, they tend to be bypassed by the players, the bypass is covered up, which means that the players begin to feel that they are not in control. Disenchantment and disappointment follow, and these, in turn, are not discussed.

Defensive routines and the media

Defensive routines are especially powerful in the media. What makes it difficult to deal with them is that the media people often use a tails-you-lose, heads-I-win strategy to argue their point, and when they see that this is no longer working, they revert to a defense that is even more profound. They claim, in effect, that their defensive routines should be protected by the First Amendment and, hence, by the courts.

For example, in a study of a newspaper, I found that reporters would describe their colleagues (and themselves) as 'highly competitive', 'partially paranoid', 'out to show the emperor to be without clothes', 'willing to commit substantial shady acts to get a story', 'people who, when under stress, magnify reality', and as people who are almost always under stress. Building upon their descriptions, I would then ask if such predispositions had any influence on the way these newspeople might perceive and report reality. The response was immediate: the press must be protected by the First Amendment and any exploration of these issues by citizens could lead to the loss of their freedom. The ultimate advocate of the latter argument that I have heard was the Nieman Foundation adviser who remarked that even the irresponsibility of the media people should be protected by the courts.

In another example, I observed a long discussion among reporters, columnists, and editors. The editors were trying to find ways to deal fairly with the issue of subjective—objective reporting and to define the conditions under which each was appropriate. The essence of the reporters' and columnists' arguments was that all reporting is subjective because it is all selective and, when published, highly incomplete. They polarized the issue so they could argue that nothing could be done.

As I listened to the reporters and columnists, I attributed to them a sense of fear and anguish about having to face the daily responsibility of writing minimally distorted stories under the pressure of deadlines. I empathized with the problem because it is one that I face in my work as a diagnostician of individuals, groups, and organizations (though I am rarely under the same time-pressures). But what impressed me was that they fought any attempt to define ways to increase the validity of their reporting. The social scientists in my field would never get away with such a response because it is basically against learning. Much evidence has been accumulated that indicates that social scientists who are against such learning also tend to distort reality without realizing what they do.

Let us dig a bit deeper. In previous interviews, all the reporters and columnists had identified two reporters who were models of what they called 'old-fashioned objective reporting'. They admired the abilities of these two reporters to write a 'straight story'. The only trouble was that their stories had little color. These data appear to illustrate that some objectivity is possible. The result admittedly was colorless stories. But if they did not value colorless stories, how could they speak of these two senior reporters with such admiration and warmth? Further discussion surfaced the fact that the reporters themselves were ambivalent on this issue. On the one hand, they could see that the two straight reporters were a valid model of objective reporting. On the other hand, they believed that such reporting ignored the responsibility of newspapers to discover injustice.

This led to the discovery of another pattern of motivations and attitudes. On the one hand, many of the reporters had a very strong desire to identify and correct society's ills – especially since these ills were created by powerful individuals in powerful private or public organizations. On the other hand, all but one admitted that they would 'be fearful as hell' to take a position in which they would be responsible for curing some of these ills. They enjoyed discovering the ills, but they feared taking a position where they would be responsible for correcting them.

Could these fears and this ambivalence influence the intensity of color in the story? 'Yes, I suppose so,' was the most frequent response that I was given. However, none of the reporters wanted to explore ways of identifying and correcting the possible distortions that could come from these defenses.

People who are fearful of taking action may also attribute to themselves a degree of cowardice. It is difficult to live with such feelings. One way to overcome the implied injustice of having cowardly behavior protected by the job is to escalate investigative reporting and dig out injustice. When injustice is discovered, report it relatively accurately but with color enough so that you can justify your fear of taking on the job required to correct these errors.

Perhaps this explanation may be overdrawn. Consider the following experience. A Nieman fellow described how he (and his newspaper) had paid to obtain information that led to the jailing of a banker. A distinguished professor of constitutional law who heard the story asked the reporter why he did not turn over the data to a grand jury. The reporter replied that he did not trust the courts. Someone asked why not reproduce the material, give it to the courts, and give them some sort of deadline. Before the reporter could reply, another Nieman fellow said, in effect, 'Let's be honest, he published the story because he was hoping for a Pulitzer Prize and the editor published it because he had paid for it.' Neither the reporter nor any other Nieman present rejected that possibility.

Back to the newspaper. I can recall vividly the elation and euphoria in the newsroom when the difficulties of the Nixon White House were being discovered and published. Many statements were made in the stories, and even more in the newsroom, that a milieu had developed at the upper levels of the White House that had caused the President and his chief advisers to distort aspects of reality and to be blind to that fact.

I was able to show that the innards of the newspaper had many of the same dynamics of the White House. I found the same kinds of interpersonal dynamics and internal politics, the same mistrust and win/lose competitiveness. The same deception and miscommunication existed among the reporters, between the reporters and their immediate editors, and between the reporters and the top editors. These similarities were confirmed by the reporters and editors. But the moment I suggested that the distortion of reality created in the White House (which they believed was caused by mistrust, deception, and win/lose competitiveness) could also exist in their organization (due to the same factors), their reaction was an immediate closing off of inquiry (back to the high road).

Role of consulting firms

The biggest nemesis to professional firms that consult with organizations in any field where implementation is the name of the game is the defensive routines in each system and the more encompassing defensive loops in which they are found. Immediately after competence in their respective domain of service is the capacity to engage defensive routines wherever they exist in order to reduce them. We have seen how defensive routines lead consultants to hedge on their diagnoses and advice in precisely the areas in which the clients are most blind and defensive. This may even lead to a first class piece of analysis and conceptualization being reduced in quality in order to bypass the client's defensive routines.

I am not suggesting that consultants should not modify their proposals in order to implement them. I am suggesting that they first test their attributions that they must bypass, either with their client or with some outside professional who may act as reviewers of their practice. I have illustrated that the former can be done without serious danger to the client relationship. To my knowledge, the latter is rare. I am a consultant, for example, to several consulting firms where I periodically review several cases to evaluate how they are dealing with defensive routines. The results, I believe, have helped the firms to redesign certain aspects of their practice. They are also used to develop some ongoing reflection on why they did not see what the outsider saw that has led to changes in the ways these firms manage themselves and their case teams. Finally, the results produce case material used in the ongoing re-education of their professionals.

Another important reason why consulting firms should consider seriously engaging defensive routines is that clients must have professionals who can help them intervene in the organizational factors that lead to slow deterioration in a way that is reminiscent of entropy. Defensive routines pollute the system and undermine it the same way air pollution undermines our lives. Consulting firms are to organizations what medical doctors are to individual health. Part of their stewardship is to detect those features that harm organizations, especially features that the players may resist examining. I say especially because organizations require individuals who will protect them from self-destructive defensive routines.

Consulting firms also have a responsibility to the societies from which they derive their practice to examine how that society may be structured to create the very problems that organizations must overcome. The massive defensive loops must be interrupted and altered if societies are not to have their capacity for learning impaired.

Another reason why consulting firms should develop competencies to deal with defensive routines is that the practice is self-regenerative of the professionals. I have watched consultants, who are economists, statisticians, applied mathematicians, and management experts, who found that after a decade of active work, some of their practice was becoming routine and not as exciting as it used to be. However, this same practice was a financial necessity to them as individuals and to the firm.

Learning to deal with defensive routines and integrating this knowledge with consultants' practice have several positive consequences. First, they help to reduce client conservatism and make it possible to conduct even more challenging studies in their technical field. Second, they reduce the probability that defensive routines from the client, or even from their own case team, will blunt the implementation of the more exciting technical results. Third, it becomes easier for consultants to reduce the burnout factors in their lives that come from the dilemmas, conflicts, and double binds that defensive routines would create. An extension of this consequence is that the consultants (and their firm) find themselves increasingly more reflective and innovative. They report feeling more at the forefront of their practice.

To my knowledge, the consultants or academics who can genuinely integrate recommendations and implementation in their specific fields by engaging defensive routines are very few in number. Some such professionals exist in the firms within which I have worked. More may be in consulting firms whom I have missed because they do not publish much about their practice.

Two of the first consultants to develop a genuinely integrated developmental strategy are Gisele and Göran Asplund. They have published a thoughtful analytical account of how they have integrated fields such as strategy, marketing, and management consulting by engaging defensive routines at the upper levels of management. They are also candid about their own defensive routines and how they tried to overcome them. It is a model of how practice can contribute to theory (Asplund and Asplund, 1982a, 1982b).

The Asplunds describe, for example, the case of the Eagle Corporation that was not able to market effectively the many new products it produced. Salespeople blamed the prices, and manufacturing blamed poor marketing. The situation was self-reinforcing. Using an integrative format, the Asplunds were able to show that the divisional managers mistrusted the capability of the sales companies when it came to more sophisticated marketing of the products and that prices were set for all products by using a conventional cost-plus-pricing method.

These two revelations seemed trivial and everybody knew about them. The problem was they contradicted the espoused theories of the company on marketing and pricing. This means that everyone knew something was going on that was contradictory to policies and that either they were unable to stop the counterproductive behavior or they did not wish to do so. The Asplunds present data that it was more the former than the latter. A set of nested cover-up activities was created that had to be covered up. This cover-up led the players to avoid the real issues. Examples of the cover-ups were some individuals' covering up facts about the profitability of certain products and others' letting it happen without comment. When someone estimated a topic to be threatening, he or she played down these estimations in order not to hurt anyone.

The initial reaction of the top was to make jokes about the findings. As they dug into the defensive routines, however, they unearthed important ineffective business policies and organizational activities such as rigid control systems, incorrect segmentation criteria, and product innovation that was not market oriented. The Asplunds helped the clients to alter these counter-productive practices and to explore the behavioral and cultural features that made them possible. The result was a restructuring of the research and development and marketing departments, which has led to improved performance.

Upping the ante

The most fundamental professional and moral responsibility of managers is their stewardship to the organization. In order to fulfill the stewardship, managers at all levels must understand and act within and upon the world in which they operate. Underlying understanding and action is reasoning. The reasoning required for effective leadership is productive reasoning.

Organizations are blessed with people who act as their agents. Human beings make organizations come alive. Unfortunately, people also can lead organizations to wither and die. They carry the seeds of organizational illness through their tendency to use defensive reasoning, especially when threat is involved.

Defensive reasoning produces defensive routines. Defensive routines combine to produce the equivalent of an organizational pollutant that makes it increasingly difficult for organizations to manage themselves as well as to design and be in control of their destiny. As is true of most pollutants, defensive reasoning and defensive routines are by-products of everyday actions that are required to run organizations. It is therefore difficult to see how they can be reduced and eliminated without opening up Pandora's box.

Eliminating defensive routines represents one of the most basic challenges to consulting professionals. How can consultants help organizations to reduce their defensive reasoning and routines no matter what the business or organizational problem? Providing this help is not easy for at least two reasons. First, we are being taught, around the world, that defensive reasoning is humane because it helps us to bypass threat. What we are not being taught is that bypass activities have profound unintended consequences. They may reduce threat or pain temporarily, but they harness the organization with increasingly comprehensive and deepening defensive loops. The legacy of bypass activities is slow but sure strangulation of productive reasoning and effective action.

The second reason why providing this help will be difficult is that as defensive loops become more comprehensive, not able to be influenced, and difficult to manage, the less likely clients will wish to take the risks to overcome the defensive reasoning and routines. As this fear becomes more prominent, then a self-fulfilling prophecy is created because it is precisely this kind of fear that reinforces defensive loops.

To my mind, we cannot bypass this dilemma. Management is increasingly being influenced by the information science technology that makes it possible to process amounts of information that hitherto was deemed unlikely. This possibility usually translates, in the minds of senior executives, into a demand from those who monitor their stewardship to have the information required to manage the organization effectively. The assumption is that having access to valid information helps.

Observers have pointed out that the information science revolution can provide the organization with too much information. I do not believe, strictly speaking, that this is a valid explanation. It is not the information science capabilities that produce too much information but the defensive routines surrounding the production and use of the information. The underlying assumption of information science is that truth is a good idea. The underlying assumption of human beings is that truth is a good idea when it is not threatening.

It is the task of consulting firms to have as one of their underlying values the production of valid information. Without it, the basis for their help will be threatened. The concepts, analytical activities, models, and metaphors that inform their practice all assume the existence of valid information. The success of consulting firms will depend very much on their being able to reduce defensive reasoning when it infects the chances of productive actions.

The conclusion, I believe, is inescapable. Consultants will have to take the lead in overcoming defensive reasoning in their clients and in themselves if they are to use the knowledge that will be increasingly available. As progress is made in understanding organizations, defensive reasoning will no longer be accepted in the name of caring, being realistic, or playing it safe. It will be seen for what it is: a poor, if not dangerous, second choice. I realize this questions many of the ideas of good currency. That is why we are upping the ante.

References

ARGYRIS, C. (1974), *Behind the Front Page*, Jossey-Bass

ARGYRIS, C., and ARGYRIS, D. (1979), 'Moral reasoning and moral action: some preliminary questions', mimeographed, Harvard University

ASPLUND, G., and ASPLUND, G. (1982a), 'Increasing innovativeness through integrated development strategy', Erhvervs Økonomist Tidsskrift (Stockholm), FDC no. 1–2, pp. 15–28

ASPLUND, G., and ASPLUND, G. (1982b), *An Integrated Development Strategy*, Wiley

BRADLEY, K., and HILL, S. (1982), 'After Japan: the quality circle transplant and productive efficiency', *British Journal of Industrial Relations*, 21, pp. 291–311

PETERS, T. M., and WATERMAN, R. H., Jr (1984), *In Search of Excellence*, Warner

PYLEE, M. V. (1975), *Worker Participation in Management*, NV Publications (New Delhi)

RAELIN, J. A. (1984), 'An examination of deviant/adaptive behaviors in the organizational careers of professionals', *Academy of Management Review*, 9, pp. 413–27

WITTE, J. F. (1980), *Democracy, Authority and Alienation in Work*, University of Chicago Press

PART FIVE
Organizational Change and Learning

Organizations change, and the ways in which they do are affected by many factors. The context and the environment of the organization appear both to impel particular changes to occur and also set constraints on what is possible. The contributors to this section emphasize the important part that managers play in the change process. Appropriate change which assists the organization to become more effective only comes about through considerable effort on the part of its managers. They have to understand the need for change and be consciously working to achieve it. In addition, modern organizations are in situations which require continuous development. They not only need to change; they have to acquire a capacity for learning.

DiMaggio and Powell (Reading 22) maintain that organizations change primarily to be more like each other. They argue that pressures from the state, from other institutions and from professional standards require managers to conform to accepted practice. This is the most important mark of their success.

Pettigrew (Reading 23) underlines the specific complexity of achieving strategic change. He analyses the interacting factors of context, content and process with which managers have to grapple, often over long periods, if they are to execute an effective change.

Senge (Reading 24) is concerned to establish the characteristics of a 'learning organization', i.e. one which through a systems approach is able to change continuously, because it had learned how to change effectively. Managers need to accept a number of disciplines in their thinking about change if they are to achieve this.

Morgan (Reading 25) maintains that understanding an organization is greatly helped if managers apply a range of different images to it. This 'imaginization' is the key to being better able to conceive possible changes. As an example of a useful image, he asks what topics would be raised if you imagined your organization as *a spider plant*. He then suggests some new questions and some ideas for organizational improvement which stem from this image.

433

Peters (Reading 26) argues that the most important characteristic of a modern organization is that it should be an exciting place to work in. It should embrace change, seek out unusual work, and, above all, fight dullness. Success will then follow. He suggests a number of steps which managers have to take to create such a 'curious corporation'.

22   P. J. DiMaggio and W. W. Powell*

Institutional Isomorphism

From 'The iron cage revisited: institutional isomorphism and collective rationality in organizational fields', *American Sociological Review*, 1983, vol. 48, pp. 147–60

In *The Protestant Ethic and the Spirit of Capitalism*, Max Weber warned that the rationalist spirit ushered in by asceticism had achieved a momentum of its own and that, under capitalism, the rationalist order had become an iron cage in which humanity was, save for the possibility of prophetic revival, imprisoned 'perhaps until the last ton of fossilized coal is burnt' (Weber, 1952, pp. 181–2). In his essay on bureaucracy, Weber returned to this theme, contending that bureaucracy, the rational spirit's organizational manifestation, was so efficient and powerful a means of controlling men and women that, once established, the momentum of bureaucratization was irreversible (Weber, 1968).

The imagery of the iron cage has haunted students of society as the tempo of bureaucratization has quickened. But while bureaucracy has spread continuously in the eighty years since Weber wrote, we suggest that the engine of organizational rationalization has shifted. For Weber, bureaucratization resulted from three related causes: competition among capitalist firms in the marketplace; competition among states, increasing rulers' need to control their staff and citizenry; and bourgeois demands for equal protection under the law. Of these three, the most important was the competitive marketplace. 'Today,' Weber (1968, p. 974) wrote:

it is primarily the capitalist market economy which demands that the official business of administration be discharged precisely, unambiguously, continuously, and with as much speed as possible. Normally, the very large, modern capitalist enterprises are themselves unequalled models of strict bureaucratic organization.

* The authors' names are listed in alphabetical order for convenience. This was a fully collaborative effort.

435

We argue that the causes of bureaucratization and rationalization have changed. The bureaucratization of the corporation and the state have been achieved. Organizations are still becoming more homogeneous, and bureaucracy remains the common organizational form. Today, however, structural change in organizations seems less and less driven by competition or by the need for efficiency. Instead, we will contend, bureaucratization and other forms of organizational change occur as the result of processes that make organizations more similar without necessarily making them more efficient. Bureaucratization and other forms of homogenization emerge, we argue, out of the structuration (Giddens, 1979) of organizational fields. This process, in turn, is effected largely by the state and the professions, which have become the great rationalizers of the second half of the twentieth century. For reasons that we will explain, highly structured organizational fields provide a context in which individual efforts to deal rationally with uncertainty and constraint often lead, in the aggregate, to homogeneity in structure, culture, and output.

Organizational theory and organizational diversity

Much of modern organizational theory posits a diverse and differentiated world of organizations and seeks to explain variation among organizations in structure and behavior (e.g., Woodward, 1965; Child and Kieser, 1981). Hannan and Freeman begin a major theoretical paper (1977) with the question, 'Why are there so many kinds of organizations?' Even our investigatory technologies (for example, those based on least-squares techniques) are geared towards explaining variation rather than its absence.

We ask, instead, why there is such startling homogeneity of organizational forms and practices; and we seek to explain homogeneity, not variation. In the initial stages of their life cycle, organizational fields display considerable diversity in approach and form. Once a field becomes well established, however, there is an inexorable push towards homogenization.

Coser, Kadushin, and Powell (1982) describe the evolution of American college textbook publishing from a period of initial diversity to the current hegemony of only two models, the large bureaucratic generalist and the small specialist. Rothman (1980) describes the winnowing of several competing models of legal education into two dominant approaches. Starr (1980) provides evidence of mimicry in the development of the hospital field; Tyack (1974) and Katz (1975) show a similar process in public schools; Barnouw (1966–68) describes the development of dominant forms in the radio industry; and DiMaggio (1981) depicts the emergence of dominant organizational models for the provision of high culture in the late nineteenth century.

What we see in each of these cases is the emergence and structuration of an organizational field as a result of the activities of a diverse set of organizations; and, second, the homogenization of these organizations, and of new entrants as well, once the field is established.

By organizational field, we mean those organizations that, in the aggregate, constitute a recognized area of institutional life: key suppliers, resource and product consumers, regulatory agencies, and other organizations that produce similar services or products. The virtue of this unit of analysis is that it directs our attention not simply to competing firms, as does the population approach of Hannan and Freeman (1977), or to networks of organizations that actually interact, as does the interorganizational network approach of Laumann et al. (1978), but to the totality of relevant actors. In doing this, the field idea comprehends the importance of both *connectedness* (see Laumann et al., 1978) and *structural equivalence* (White et al., 1976).[2]

The structure of an organizational field cannot be determined a priori but must be defined on the basis of empirical investigation. Fields only exist to the extent that they are institutionally defined. The process of institutional definition, or 'structuration,' consists of four parts: an increase in the extent of interaction among organizations in the field; the emergence of sharply defined interorganizational structures of domination and patterns of coalition: an increase in the information load with which organizations in a field must contend; and the development of a mutual awareness among participants in a set of organizations that they are involved in a common enterprise (DiMaggio, 1982).

Once disparate organizations in the same line of business are structured into an actual field (as we shall argue, by competition, the state, or the professions), powerful forces emerge that lead them to become more similar to one another. Organizations may change their goals or develop new

1. By *connectedness* we mean the existence of transactions tying organizations to one another: such transactions might include formal contractual relationships, participation of personnel in common enterprises such as professional associations, labor unions, or boards of directors, or informal organizational-level ties like personnel flows. A set of organizations that are strongly connected to one another and only weakly connected to other organizations constitutes a *clique*. By *structural equivalence* we refer to similarity of position in a network structure: for example, two organizations are structurally equivalent if they have ties of the same kind to the same set of other organizations, even if they themselves are not connected: here the key structure is the *role* or *block*.

practices, and new organizations enter the field. But, in the long run, organizational actors making rational decisions construct around themselves an environment that constrains their ability to change further in later years. Early adopters of organizational innovations are commonly driven by a desire to improve performance. But new practices can become, in Selznick's words (1957, p. 17), 'infused with value beyond the technical requirements of the task at hand.' As an innovation spreads, a threshold is reached beyond which adoption provides legitimacy rather than improves performance (Meyer and Rowan, 1977). Strategies that are rational for individual organizations may not be rational if adopted by large numbers. Yet the very fact that they are normatively sanctioned increases the likelihood of their adoption. Thus organizations may try to change constantly; but, after a certain point in the structuration of an organizational field, the aggregate effect of individual change is to lessen the extent of diversity within the field.[2] Organizations in a structured field, to paraphrase Schelling (1978, p. 14), respond to an environment that consists of other organizations responding to their environment, which consists of organizations responding to an environment of organizations' responses.

Zucker and Tolbert's (1981) work on the adoption of civil-service reform in the United States illustrates this process. Early adoption of civil-service reforms was related to internal governmental needs, and strongly predicted by such city characteristics as the size of immigrant population, political reform movements, socioeconomic composition, and city size. Later adoption, however, is not predicted by city characteristics, but is related to institutional definitions of the legitimate structural form for municipal administration.[3] Marshall Meyer's (1981) study of the bureaucratization of

2. By organizational change, we refer to change in formal structure, organizational culture, and goals, program, or mission. Organizational change varies in its responsiveness to technical conditions. In this paper we are most interested in processes that affect organizations in a given field: in most cases these organizations employ similar technical bases; thus we do not attempt to partial out the relative importance of technically functional versus other forms of organizational change. While we shall cite many examples of organizational change as we go along, our purpose here is to identify a widespread class of organizational processes relevant to a broad range of substantive problems, rather than to identify deterministically the causes of specific organizational arrangements.

3. Knoke (1982), in a careful event-history analysis of the spread of municipal reform, refutes the conventional explanations of culture clash or hierarchal diffusion and finds but modest support for modernization theory. His major finding is that regional differences in municipal reform adoption arise not from social compositional differences, 'but from some type of imitation or contagion effects as represented by the level of neighboring regional cities previously adopting reform government' (p. 1337).

urban fiscal agencies has yielded similar findings: strong relationships between city characteristics and organizational attributes at the turn of the century, null relationships in recent years. Carroll and Delacroix's (1982) findings on the birth and death rates of newspapers support the view that selection acts with great force only in the early years of an industry's existence.[4] Freeman (1982, p. 14) suggests that older, larger organizations reach a point where they can dominate their environments rather than adjust to them.

The concept that best captures the process of homogenization is *isomorphism*. In Hawley's (1968) description, isomorphism is a constraining process that forces one unit in a population to resemble other units that face the same set of environmental conditions. At the population level, such an approach suggests that organizational characteristics are modified in the direction of increasing compatibility with environmental characteristics; the number of organizations in a population is a function of environmental carrying capacity; and the diversity of organizational forms is isomorphic to environmental diversity. Hannan and Freeman (1977) have significantly extended Hawley's ideas. They argue that isomorphism can result because nonoptimal forms are selected out of a population of organizations *or* because organizational decision makers learn appropriate responses and adjust their behavior accordingly. Hannan and Freeman's focus is almost solely on the first process: selection.[5]

Following Meyer (1979) and Fennell (1980), we maintain that there

4. A wide range of factors – interorganizational commitments, elite sponsorship, and government support in form of open-ended contracts, subsidy, tariff barriers and import quotas, or favorable tax laws – reduce selection pressures even in competitive organizational fields. An expanding or a stable, protected market can also mitigate the forces of selection.

5. In contrast to Hannan and Freeman, we emphasize adaptation, but we are not suggesting that managers' actions are necessarily strategic in a long-range sense. Indeed, two of the three forms of isomorphism, described below – mimetic and normative – involve managerial behaviors at the level of taken-for-granted assumptions rather than consciously strategic choices. In general, we question the utility of arguments about the motivations of actors that suggest a polarity between the rational and the nonrational. Goal-oriented behavior may be reflexive or prerational in the sense that it reflects deeply embedded predispositions, scripts, schema, or classifications; and behavior oriented to a goal may be reinforced without contributing to the accomplishment of that goal. While isomorphic change may often be mediated by the desires of managers to increase the effectiveness of their organizations, we are more concerned with the menu of possible options that managers consider than with their motives for choosing particular alternatives. In other words, we freely concede that actors' understandings of their own behaviors are interpretable in rational terms. The theory of isomorphism addresses not the psychological states of actors but the structural determinants of the range of choices that actors perceive as rational or prudent.

are two types of isomorphism: competitive and institutional. Hannan and Freeman's classic paper (1977), and much of their recent work, deals with competitive isomorphism, assuming a system rationality that emphasizes market competition, niche change, and fitness measures. Such a view, we suggest, is most relevant for those fields in which free and open competition exists. It explains parts of the process of bureaucratization that Weber observed, and may apply to early adoption of innovation, but it does not present a fully adequate picture of the modern world of organizations. For this purpose it must be supplemented by an institutional view of isomorphism of the sort introduced by Kanter (1972, pp. 152–4) in her discussion of the forces pressing communes toward accommodation with the outside world. As Aldrich (1979, p. 265) has argued, 'the major factors that organizations must take into account are other organizations.' Organizations compete not just for resources and customers, but for political power and institutional legitimacy, for social as well as economic fitness.[6] The concept of institutional isomorphism is a useful tool for understanding the politics and ceremony that pervade much modern organizational life.

Three mechanisms of institutional isomorphic change

We identify three mechanisms through which institutional isomorphic change occurs, each with its own antecedents: (1) *coercive* isomorphism that stems from political influence and the problem of legitimacy; (2) *mimetic* isomorphism resulting from standard responses to uncertainty; and (3) *normative* isomorphism, associated with professionalization. This typology is an analytic one: the types are not always empirically distinct. For example, external actors may induce an organization to conform to its peers by requiring it to perform a particular task and specifying the professional responsible for its performance. Or mimetic change may reflect environmentally constructed uncertainties.[7] Yet, while the three types intermingle in empirical setting, they tend to derive from different conditions and may lead to different outcomes.

Coercive isomorphism. Coercive isomorphism results from both formal and informal pressures exerted on organizations by other organizations upon which they are dependent and by cultural expectations in the society within which organizations function. Such pressures may be felt as force,

6. Carroll and Delacroix (1982) clearly recognize this and include political and institutional legitimacy as a major resource. Aldrich (1979) has argued that the population perspective must attend to historical trends and changes in legal and political institutions.

7. This point was suggested by John Meyer.

as persuasion, or as invitations to join in collusion. In some circumstances, organizational change is a direct response to government mandate: manufacturers adopt new pollution control technologies to conform to environmental regulations; nonprofits maintain accounts, and hire accountants, in order to meet tax law requirements; and organizations employ affirmative-action officers to fend off allegations of discrimination. Schools mainstream special students and hire special education teachers, cultivate PTAs and administrators who get along with them, and promulgate curricula that conform with state standards (Meyer et al., 1981). The fact that these changes may be largely ceremonial does not mean that they are inconsequential. As Ritti and Goldner (1979) have argued, staff become involved in advocacy for their functions that can alter power relations within organizations over the long run.

The existence of a common legal environment affects many aspects of an organization's behavior and structure. Weber pointed out the profound impact of a complex, rationalized system of contract law that requires the necessary organizational controls to honor legal commitments. Other legal and technical requirements of the state − the vicissitudes of the budget cycle, the ubiquity of certain fiscal years, annual reports, and financial reporting requirements that ensure eligibility for the receipt of federal contracts or funds − also shape organizations in similar ways. Pfeffer and Salancik (1978, pp. 188−224) have discussed how organizations faced with unmanageable interdependence seek to use the greater power of the larger social system and its government to eliminate difficulties or provide for needs. They observe that politically constructed environments have two characteristic features: political decisionmakers often do not experience directly the consequences of their actions; and political decisions are applied across the board to entire classes of organizations, thus making such decisions less adaptive and less flexible.

Meyer and Rowan (1977) have argued persuasively that as rationalized states and other large rational organizations expand their dominance over more arenas of social life, organizational structures increasingly come to reflect rules institutionalized and legitimated by and within the state (also see Meyer and Hannan, 1979). As a result, organizations are increasingly homogeneous within given domains and increasingly organized around rituals of conformity to wider institutions. At the same time, organizations are decreasingly structurally determined by the constraints posed by technical activities, and decreasingly held together by output controls. Under such circumstances, organizations employ ritualized controls of credentials and group solidarity.

Direct imposition of standard operating procedures and legitimated rules and structures also occurs outside the governmental arena. Michael Sedlak (1981) has documented the ways that United Charities in the 1930s altered and homogenized the structures, methods, and philosophies of the social service agencies that depended upon them for support. As conglomerate corporations increase in size and scope, standard performance criteria are not necessarily imposed on subsidiaries, but it is common for subsidiaries to be subject to standardized reporting mechanisms (Coser *et al.*, 1982). Subsidiaries must adopt accounting practices, performance evaluations, and budgetary plans that are compatible with the policies of the parent corporation. A variety of service infrastructures, often provided by monopolistic firms – for example, telecommunications and transportation – exert common pressures over the organizations that use them. Thus, the expansion of the central state, the centralization of capital, and the coordination of philanthropy all support the homogenization of organizational models through direct authority relationships.

We have so far referred only to the direct and explicit imposition of organizational models on dependent organizations. Coercive isomorphism, however, may be more subtle and less explicit than these examples suggest. Milofsky (1981) has described the ways in which neighborhood organizations in urban communities, many of which are committed to participatory democracy, are driven to developing organizational hierarchies in order to gain support from more hierarchically organized donor organizations. Similarly, Swidler (1979) describes the tensions created in the free schools she studied by the need to have a 'principal' to negotiate with the district superintendent and to represent the school to outside agencies. In general, the need to lodge responsibility and managerial authority at least ceremonially in a formally defined role in order to interact with hierarchical organizations is a constant obstacle to the maintenance of egalitarian or collectivist organizational forms (Kanter, 1972; Rothschild-Whitt, 1979).

Mimetic processes. Not all institutional isomorphism, however, derives from coercive authority. Uncertainty is also a powerful force that encourages imitation. When organizational technologies are poorly understood (March and Olsen, 1976), when goals are ambiguous, or when the environment creates symbolic uncertainty, organizations may model themselves on other organizations. The advantages of mimetic behavior in the economy of human action are considerable; when an organization faces a problem with ambiguous causes or unclear solutions, problemistic search may yield a viable solution with little expense (Cyert and March, 1963).

Modeling, as we use the term, is a response to uncertainty. The modeled organization may be unaware of the modeling or may have no desire to be copied; it merely serves as a convenient source of practices that the borrowing organization may use. Models may be diffused unintentionally, indirectly through employee transfer or turnover, or explicitly by organizations such as consulting firms or industry trade associations. Even innovation can be accounted for by organizational modeling. As Alchian (1950) has observed:

While there certainly are those who consciously innovate, there are those who, in their imperfect attempts to imitate others, unconsciously innovate by unwittingly acquiring some unexpected or unsought unique attributes which under the prevailing circumstances prove partly responsible for the success. Others, in turn, will attempt to copy the uniqueness, and the innovation–imitation process continues.

One of the most dramatic instances of modeling was the effort of Japan's modernizers in the late nineteenth century to model new governmental initiatives on apparently successful western prototypes. Thus, the imperial government sent its officers to study the courts, Army, and police in France, the Navy and postal system in Great Britain, and banking and art education in the United States (see Westney, forthcoming). American corporations are now returning the compliment by implementing (their perceptions of) Japanese models to cope with thorny productivity and personnel problems in their own firms. The rapid proliferation of quality circles and quality-of-work-life issues in American firms is, at least in part, an attempt to model Japanese and European successes. These developments also have a ritual aspect; companies adopt these 'innovations' to enhance their legitimacy, to demonstrate they are at least trying to improve working conditions. More generally, the wider the population of personnel employed by, or customers served by, an organization, the stronger the pressure felt by the organization to provide the programs and services offered by other organizations. Thus, either a skilled labor force or a broad customer base may encourage mimetic isomorphism.

Much homogeneity in organizational structures stems from the fact that despite considerable search for diversity there is relatively little variation to be selected from. New organizations are modeled upon old ones throughout the economy, and managers actively seek models upon which to build (Kimberly, 1980). Thus, in the arts one can find textbooks on how to organize a community arts council or how to start a symphony women's guild. Large organizations choose from a relatively small set of major consulting firms, which, like Johnny Appleseeds, spread a few organizational models throughout the land. Such models are powerful because structural changes are observable, whereas changes in policy and strategy are less easily noticed. With the advice of a major consulting firm, a large metropolitan public television station switched from a functional design to a multidivisional structure. The stations' executives were skeptical that the new structure was more efficient; in fact, some services were now duplicated across divisions. But they were convinced that the new design would carry a powerful message to the for-profit firms with whom the station regularly dealt. These firms, whether in the role of corporate underwriters or as potential partners in joint ventures, would view the reorganization as a sign that 'the sleepy nonprofit station was becoming more business-minded' (Powell, forthcoming). The history of management reform in American government agencies, which are noted for their goal ambiguity, is almost a textbook case of isomorphic modeling, from the PPPB of the McNamara era to the zero-based budgeting of the Carter administration.

Organizations tend to model themselves after similar organizations in their field that they perceive to be more legitimate or successful. The ubiquity of certain kinds of structural arrangements can more likely be credited to the universality of mimetic processes than to any concrete evidence that the adopted models enhance efficiency. John Meyer (1981) contends that it is easy to predict the organization of a newly emerging nation's administration without knowing anything about the nation itself, since 'peripheral nations are far more isomorphic – in administrative form and economic pattern – than any theory of the world system of economic division of labor would lead one to expect.'

Normative pressures. A third source of isomorphic organizational change is normative and stems primarily from professionalization. Following Larson (1977) and Collins (1979), we interpret professionalization as the collective struggle of members of an occupation to define the conditions and methods of their work, to control 'the production of producers' (Larson, 1977, pp. 49–52), and to establish a cognitive base and legitimation for their occupational autonomy. As Larson points out, the professional project is rarely achieved with complete success. Professionals must compromise with nonprofessional clients, bosses, or regulators. The major recent growth in the professions has been among organizational professionals, particularly managers and specialized staff of large organizations. The increased professionalization of workers whose futures are inextricably bound up with the fortunes of the organizations that employ them has rendered obsolescent (if not obsolete) the dichotomy between organizational commitment and professional allegiance that characterized traditional professionals in earlier organizations (Hall, 1968). Professions are subject to the same coercive and mimetic pressures as are organizations. Moreover, while various kinds of professionals within an organization may differ from one another, they exhibit much similarity to their professional counterparts in other organizations. In addition, in many cases, professional power is as much assigned by the state as it is created by the activities of the professions.

Two aspects of professionalization are important sources of isomorphism. One is the resting of formal education and of legitimation in a cognitive base produced by university specialists; the second is the growth and elaboration of professional networks that span organizations and across which new models diffuse rapidly. Universities and professional training institutions are important centers for the development of organizational norms among professional managers and their staff. Professional and trace associations are another vehicle for the definition and promulgation of normative rules about organizational and professional behavior. Such mechanisms create a pool of almost interchangeable individuals who occupy similar positions across a range of organizations and possess a similarity of orientation and disposition that may override variations in tradition and control that might otherwise shape organizational behavior (Perrow, 1974).

One important mechanism for encouraging normative isomorphism is the filtering of personnel. Within many organizational fields filtering occurs through the hiring of individuals from firms with the same industry; through the recruitment of fast-track staff from a narrow range of training institutions; through common promotion practices, such as always hiring top executives from financial or legal departments; and from skill-level requirements for particular jobs. Many professional career tracks are so closely guarded, both at the entry level and throughout the career progression, that individuals who make it to the top are virtually indistinguishable. March and March (1977) found that individuals who attained the position of school superintendent in Wisconsin were so alike in background and orientation as to make further career advancement random and unpredictable. Hirsch and Whisler (1982) find a similar absence of variation among *Fortune* 500 board members. In addition, individuals in an organizational field undergo anticipatory socialization to common expectations about their personal behavior, appropriate style of dress, organizational vocabularies (Cicourel, 1970; Williamson, 1975) and standard methods of speaking, joking, or addressing others (Ouchi, 1980). Particularly in industries with a service or financial orientation (Collins, 1979, argues that the importance of credentials is strongest in these areas), the filtering of personnel approaches what Kanter (1977) refers to as the 'homosexual reproduction of management.' To the extent managers and key staff are drawn from the same universities and filtered on a common set of attributes, they will tend to view problems in a similar fashion, see the same policies, procedures and structures as normatively sanctioned and legitimated, and approach decisions in much the same way.

Entrants to professional career tracks who somehow escape the filtering process – for example, Jewish naval officers, woman stockbrokers, or Black insurance executives – are likely to be subjected to pervasive on-the-job socialization. To the extent that organizations in a field differ and primary socialization occurs on the job, socialization could reinforce, not erode, differences among organizations. But when organizations in a field are similar and occupational socialization is carried out in trade association workshops, in-service educational programs, consultant arrangements, employer-professional school networks, and in the pages of trade magazines, socialization acts as an isomorphic force.

The professionalization of management tends to proceed in tandem with the structuration of organizational fields. The exchange of information among professionals helps contribute to a commonly recognized hierarchy of status, of center and periphery, that becomes a matrix for information flows and personnel movement across organizations. This status ordering occurs through both formal and informal means. The designation of a few large firms in an industry as key bargaining agents in union-management negotiations may make these central firms pivotal in other respects as well. Government recognition of key firms or organizations through the grant or contract process may give these organizations legitimacy and visibility and lead competing firms to copy aspects of their structure or operating procedures in hope of obtaining similar rewards. Professional and trade associations provide other arenas in which center organizations are recognized and their personnel given positions of substantive or ceremonial influence. Managers in highly visible organizations may in turn have their stature reinforced by representation on the boards of other organizations, participation in industry-wide or inter-industry councils, and consultation by agencies of government (Useem, 1979). In the nonprofit sector, where legal barriers to collusion do not exist, structuration may proceed even more rapidly. Thus executive producers or artistic directors of leading theatres head trade or professional association committees, sit on government and foundation grant-award panels, or consult as government- or foundation-financed management advisors to smaller theatres, or sit on smaller organizations' boards, even as their stature is reinforced and enlarged by the grants their theatres receive from government, corporate, and foundation funding sources (DiMaggio, 1982).

Such central organizations serve as both active and passive models; their policies and structures will be copied throughout their fields. Their centrality is reinforced as upwardly mobile managers and staff seek to secure positions in these central organizations in order to further their own careers. Aspiring managers may undergo anticipatory socialization into the norms and mores of the organizations they hope to join. Career paths may also involve movement from entry positions in the center organizations to middle-management positions in peripheral organizations. Personnel flows within an organizational field are further encouraged by structural homogenization, for example the existence of common career titles and paths (such as assistant, associate, and full professor) with meanings that are commonly understood.

It is important to note that each of the institutional isomorphic processes can be expected to proceed in the absence of evidence that they increase internal organizational efficiency. To the extent that organizational effectiveness is enhanced, the reason will often be that organizations are rewarded for being similar to other organizations in their fields. This similarity can make it easier for organizations to transact with other organizations, to attract career-minded staff, to be acknowledged as legitimate and reputable, and to fit into administrative categories that define eligibility for public and private grants and contracts. None of this, however, insures that conformist organizations do what they do more efficiently than do their more deviant peers.

Pressures for competitive efficiency are also mitigated in many fields because the number of organizations is limited and there are strong fiscal and legal barriers to entry and exit. Lee (1971, p. 51) maintains this is why hospital administrators are less concerned with the efficient use of resources and more concerned with status competition and parity in prestige. Fennell (1980) notes that hospitals are a poor market system because patients lack the needed knowledge of potential exchange partners and prices. She argues that physicians and hospital administrators are the actual consumers. Competition among hospitals is based on 'attracting physicians, who, in turn, bring their patients to the hospital.' Fennell (p. 505) concludes that:

Hospitals operate according to a norm of social legitimation that frequently conflicts with market considerations of efficiency and system rationality. Apparently, hospitals can increase their range of services not because there is an actual need for a particular service or facility within the patient population, but because they will be defined as fit only if they can offer everything other hospitals in the area offer.

These results suggest a more general pattern. Organizational fields that include a large professionally trained labor force will be driven primarily by status competition. Organizational prestige and resources are key elements in attracting professionals. This process encourages homogenization as organizations seek to ensure that they can provide the same benefits and services as their competitors.

Predictors of isomorphic change

It follows from our discussion of the mechanism by which isomorphic change occurs that we should be able to predict empirically which organizational fields will be most homogeneous in structure, process, and behavior. While an empirical test of such predictions is beyond the scope of this paper, the ultimate value of our perspective will lie in its predictive utility. The hypotheses discussed below are not meant to exhaust the universe of predictors, but merely to suggest several hypotheses that may be pursued using data on the characteristics of organizations in a field, either cross-sectionally or, preferably, over time. The hypotheses are implicitly governed by *ceteris paribus* assumptions, particularly with regard to size, technology, and centralization of external resources.

A. *Organizational-level predictors.* There is variability in the extent to and rate at which organizations in a field change to become more like their peers. Some organizations respond to external pressures quickly; others change only after a long period of resistance. The first two hypotheses derive from our discussion of coercive isomorphism and constraint.

Hypothesis A-1: *The greater the dependence of an organization on another organization, the more similar it will become to that organization in structure, climate, and behavioral focus.* Following Thompson (1957) and Pfeffer and Salancik (1978), this proposition recognizes the greater ability of organizations to resist the demands of organizations on whom they are not dependent. A position of dependence leads to isomorphic change. Coercive pressures are built into exchange relationships. As Williamson (1979) has shown, exchanges are characterized by transaction-specific investments in both knowledge and equipment. Once an organization chooses a specific supplier or distributor for particular parts or services, the supplier or distributor develops expertise in the performance of the task as well as idiosyncratic knowledge about the exchange relationship. The organization comes to rely on the supplier or distributor and such transaction-specific investments give the supplier or distributor considerable advantages in any subsequent competition with other suppliers or distributors.

Hypothesis A-2: *The greater the centralization of organization A's resource supply, the greater the extent to which organization A will change isomorphically to resemble the organizations on which it depends for resources.* As Thompson (1967) notes, organizations that depend on the same sources for funding, personnel, and legitimacy will be more subject to the whims of resource suppliers than will organizations that can play one source of support off against another. In cases where alternative sources are either not readily available or require effort to locate, the stronger party to the transaction can coerce the weaker party to adopt its practices in order to accommodate the stronger party's needs (see Powell, 1983).

The third and fourth hypotheses derive from our discussion of mimetic isomorphism, modeling, and uncertainty.

Hypothesis A-3: *The more uncertain the relationship between means and ends the greater the extent to which an organization will model itself after organizations it perceives to be successful.* The mimetic thought process involved in the search for models is characteristic of change in organizations in which key technologies are only poorly understood (March and Cohen, 1974). Here our prediction diverges somewhat from Meyer and Rowan (1977) who argue, as we do, that organizations which lack well-defined technologies will import institutionalized rules and practices. Meyer and Rowan posit a loose coupling between legitimated external practices and internal organizational behavior. From an ecologist's point of view, loosely coupled organizations are more likely to vary internally. In contrast, we expect substantive internal changes in tandem with more ceremonial practices, thus greater homogeneity and less variation and change. Internal consistency of this sort is an important means of interorganizational coordination. It also increases organizational stability.

Hypothesis A-4: *The more ambiguous the goals of an organization, the greater the extent to which the organization will model itself after organizations that it perceives to be successful.* There are two reasons for this. First, organizations with ambiguous or disputed goals are likely to be highly dependent upon appearances for legitimacy. Such organizations may find it to their advantage to meet the expectations of important constituencies about how they should be designed and run. In contrast to our view, ecologists would argue that organizations that copy other organizations usually have no competitive advantage. We contend that, in most situations, reliance on established, legitimated procedures enhances organizational legitimacy and survival characteristics. A second reason for modeling behavior is found in situations where conflict over organizational goals is repressed in the interest of harmony; thus participants find it easier to mimic other organizations than to make decisions on the basis of systematic analyses of goals since such analyses would prove painful or disruptive.

The fifth and sixth hypotheses are based on our discussion of normative processes found in professional organizations.

Hypothesis A-5: *The greater the reliance on academic credentials in choosing managerial and staff personnel, the greater the extent to which an organization will become like other organizations in its field.* Applicants with academic credentials have already undergone a socialization process in university programs, and are thus more likely than others to have internalized reigning norms and dominant organizational models.

Hypothesis A-6: *The greater the participation of organizational managers in trade and professional associations, the more likely the organization will be, or will become, like other organizations in its field.* This hypothesis is parallel to the institutional view that the more elaborate the relational networks among organizations and their members, the greater the collective organization of the environment (Meyer and Rowan, 1977).

B. *Field-level predictors.* The following six hypotheses describe the expected effects of several characteristics of organizational fields on the extent of isomorphism in a particular field. Since the effect of institutional isomorphism is homogenization, the best indicator of isomorphic change is a decrease in variation and diversity, which could be measured by lower standard deviations of the values of selected indicators in a set of organizations. The key indicators would vary with the nature of the field and the interests of the investigator. In all cases, however, field-level measures are expected to affect organizations in a field regardless of each organization's scores on related organizational-level measures.

Hypothesis B-1: *The greater the extent to which an organizational field is dependent upon a single (or several similar) source of support for vital resources, the higher the level of isomorphism.* The centralization of resources within a field both directly causes homogenization by placing organizations under similar pressures from resource suppliers, and interacts with uncertainty and goal ambiguity to increase their impact. This hypothesis is congruent with the ecologists' argument that the number of organizational forms is determined by the distribution of resources in the environment and the terms on which resources are available.

Hypothesis B-2: *The greater the extent to which the organizations in a field transact with agencies of the state, the greater the extent of isomorphism in the field as a whole.* This follows not just from the previous hypothesis, but from two elements of state/private-sector transactions: their rule-boundedness and formal rationality, and the emphasis of government actors on institutional rules. Moreover, the federal government routinely designates industry standards for an entire field which require adoption by all competing firms. John Meyer (1979) argues convincingly that the aspects of an organization which are affected by state transactions differ to the extent that state participation is unitary or fragmented among several public agencies.

The third and fourth hypotheses follow from our discussion of isomorphic change resulting from uncertainty and modeling.

Hypothesis B-3: *The fewer the number of visible alternative organizational models in a field, the faster the rate of isomorphism in that field.* The predictions of this hypothesis are less specific than those of others and require further refinement; but our argument is that for any relevant dimension of organizational strategies or structures in an organizational field there will be a threshold level, or a tipping point, beyond which adoption of the dominant form will proceed with increasing speed (Granovetter, 1978; Boorman and Leavitt, 1979).

Hypothesis B-4: *The greater the extent to which technologies are uncertain or goals are ambiguous within a field, the greater the rate of isomorphic change.* Somewhat counterintuitively, abrupt increases in uncertainty and ambiguity should, after brief periods of ideologically motivated experimentation, lead to rapid isomorphic change. As in the case of A-4, ambiguity and uncertainty may be a function of environmental definition, and, in any case, interact both with centralization of resources (A-1, A-2, B-1, B-2) and with professionalization and structuration (A-5, A-6, B-5, B-6). Moreover, in fields characterized by a high degree of uncertainty, new entrants, which could serve as sources of innovation and variation, will seek to overcome the liability of newness by imitating established practices within the field.

The two final hypotheses in this section follow from our discussion of professional filtering, socialization, and structuration.

Hypothesis B-5: *The greater the extent of professionalization in a field, the greater the amount of institutional isomorphic change.* Professionalization may be measured by the universality of credential requirements, the robustness of graduate training programs, or the vitality of professional and trade associations.

Hypothesis B-6: *The greater the extent of structuration of a field, the greater the degree of isomorphics.* Fields that have stable and broadly acknowledged centers, peripheries, and status orders will be more homogeneous both because the diffusion structure for new models and norms is more routine and because the level of interaction among organizations in the field is higher. While structuration may not lend itself to easy measurement, it might be tapped crudely with the use of such familiar measures as concentration ratios, reputational interview studies, or data on network characteristics.

This rather schematic exposition of a dozen hypotheses relating the extent of isomorphism to selected attributes of organizations and of organizational fields does not constitute a complete agenda for empirical assessment of our perspective. We have not discussed the expected nonlinearities and ceiling effects in the relationships that we have posited. Nor have we addressed the issue of the indicators that one must use to measure homogeneity. Organizations in a field may be highly diverse on some dimensions, yet extremely homogeneous on others. While we suspect, in general, that the rate at which the standard deviations of structural or behavioral indicators approach zero will vary with the nature of an organizational field's technology and environment, we will not develop these ideas here. The point of this section is to suggest that the theoretical discussion is susceptible to empirical test, and to lay out a few testable propositions that may guide future analyses.

Implications for social theory

A comparison of macrosocial theories of functionalist or Marxist orientation with theoretical and empirical work in the study of organizations yields a paradoxical conclusion. Societies (or elites), so it seems, are smart, while organizations are dumb. Societies comprise institutions that mesh together comfortably in the interests of efficiency (Clark, 1962), the dominant value system (Parsons, 1951), or, in the Marxist version, capitalists (Domhoff, 1967; Althusser, 1969). Organizations, by contrast, are either anarchies (Cohen et al., 1972), federations of loosely coupled parts (Weick, 1976), or autonomy-seeking agents (Gouldner, 1954) laboring under such formidable constraints as bounded rationality (March and Simon, 1958), uncertain or contested goals (Sills, 1957), and unclear technologies (March and Cohen, 1974).

Despite the findings of organizational research, the image of society as consisting of tightly and rationally coupled institutions persists throughout much of modern social theory. Rational administration pushes out non-bureaucratic forms, schools assume the structure of the workplace, hospital and university administrations come to resemble the management of for-profit firms, and the modernization of the world economy proceeds unabated. Weberians point to the continuing homogenization of organizational structures as the formal rationality of bureaucracy extends to the limits of contemporary organizational life. Functionalists describe the rational adaptation of the structure of firms, schools, and states to the values and needs of modern society (Chandler, 1977; Parsons, 1977). Marxists attribute changes in such organizations as welfare agencies (Pivan and Cloward, 1971) and schools (Bowles and Gintis, 1976) to the logic of the accumulation process.

We find it difficult to square the extant literature on organizations with these macrosocial views. How can it be that the confused and contentious bumblers that populate the pages of organizational case studies and theories combine to construct the elaborate and well-proportioned social edifice that macrotheorists describe?

The conventional answer to this paradox has been that some version of natural selection occurs in which selection mechanisms operate to weed out those organizational forms that are less fit. Such arguments, as we have contended, are difficult to mesh with organizational realities. Less efficient organizational forms do persist. In some contexts efficiency or productivity cannot even be measured. In government agencies or in faltering corporations selection may occur on political rather than economic grounds. In other contexts, for example the Metropolitan Opera or the Bohemian Grove, supporters are far more concerned with noneconomic values like aesthetic quality or social status than with efficiency per se. Even in the for-profit sector, where competitive arguments would promise to bear the greatest fruit, Nelson and Winter's work (Winter, 1964, 1975; Nelson and Winter, 1982) demonstrates that the invisible hand operates with, at best, a light touch.

A second approach to the paradox that we have identified comes from Marxists and theorists who assert that key elites guide and control the social system through their command of crucial positions in major organizations (e.g., the financial institutions that dominate monopoly capitalism). In this view, while organizational actors ordinarily proceed undisturbed through mazes of standard operating procedures, at key turning points capitalist elites get their way by intervening in decisions that set the course of an institution for years to come (Katz, 1975).

While evidence suggests that this is, in fact, sometimes the case – Barnouw's account of the early days of broadcasting or Weinstein's (1968) work on the Progressives are good examples – other historians have been less successful in their search for class-conscious elites. In such cases as the development of the New Deal programs (Hawley, 1966) or the expansion of the Vietnamese conflict (Halperin, 1974), the capitalist class appears to have been muddled and disunited.

Moreover, without constant monitoring, individuals pursuing parochial organizational or subunit interests can quickly undo the work that even the most prescient elites have accomplished. Perrow (1976, p. 21) has noted that despite superior resources and sanctioning power, organizational elites are often unable to maximize their preferences because 'the complexity of modern organizations makes control difficult.' Moreover, organizations have increasingly become the vehicle for numerous 'gratifications, necessities, and preferences so that many groups within and without the organization seek to use it for ends that restrict the return to masters.'

We reject neither the natural-selection nor the elite-control arguments out of hand. Elites do exercise considerable influence over modern life and aberrant or inefficient organizations sometimes do expire. But we contend that neither of these processes is sufficient to explain the extent to which organizations have become structurally more similar. We argue that a theory of institutional isomorphism may help explain the observations that organizations are becoming more homogeneous, and that elites often get their way, while at the same time enabling us to understand the irrationality, the frustration of power, and the lack of innovation that are so commonplace in organizational life. What is more, our approach is more consonant with the ethnographic and theoretical literature on how organizations work than are either functionalist or elite theories of organizational change.

A focus on institutional isomorphism can also add a much needed perspective on the political struggle for organizational power and survival that is missing from much of population ecology. The institutionalization approach associated with John Meyer and his students posits the importance of myths and ceremony but does not ask how these models arise and whose interests they initially serve. Explicit attention to the genesis of legitimated models and to the definition and elaboration of organizational fields should answer this question. Examination of the diffusion of similar organizational strategies and structures should be a productive means for assessing the influence of elite interests. A consideration of isomorphic processes also leads us to a bifocal view of power and its application in modern politics. To the extent that organizational change is unplanned and goes on largely behind the backs of groups that wish to influence it, our attention should be directed to two forms of power. The first, as March and Simon (1958) and Simon (1957) pointed out years ago, is the power to set premises, to define the norms and standards which shape and channel behavior. The second is the point of critical intervention (Domhoff, 1979) at which elites can define appropriate models of organizational structure and policy which then go unquestioned for years to come (see Katz, 1975). Such a view is consonant with some of the best recent work on power (see Lukes, 1974); research on the structuration of organizational fields and on isomorphic processes may help give it more empirical flesh.

Finally, a more developed theory of organizational isomorphism may have important implications for social policy in those fields in which the state works through private organizations. To the extent that pluralism is a guiding value in public policy deliberations, we need to discover new forms of intersectoral coordination that will encourage diversification rather than hastening homogenization. An understanding of the manner in which fields become more homogeneous would prevent policy makers and analysts from confusing the disappearance of an organizational form with its substantive failure. Current efforts to encourage diversity tend to be conducted in an organizational vacuum. Policy makers concerned with pluralism should consider the impact of their programs on the structure of organizational fields as a whole, and not simply on the programs of individual organizations.

We believe there is much to be gained by attending to similarity as well as to variation among organizations and, in particular, to change in the degree of homogeneity or variation over time. Our approach seeks to study incremental change as well as selection. We take seriously the observations of organizational theorists about the role of change, ambiguity, and constraint and point to the implications of these organizational characteristics for the social structure as a whole. The foci and motive forces of bureaucratization (and, more broadly, homogenization in general) have, as we argued, changed since Weber's time. But the importance of understanding the trends to which he called attention has never been more immediate.

References

ALCHIAN, A. (1950), 'Uncertainty, evolution, and economic theory,' *Journal of Political Economy*, 58, pp. 211–21

ALDRICH, H. (1979), *Organizations and Environments*, Englewood Cliffs, NJ, Prentice-Hall

ALTHUSSER, L. (1969), *For Marx*, London, Allen Lane

BARNOUW, E. (1966–8), *A History of Broadcasting in the United States*, 3 vols., New York, Oxford University Press

BOORMAN, S. A., and LEVITT, R. (1979), *The Cascade Principle for General Disequilibrium Dynamics*, Cambridge/New Haven, Harvard–Yale Preprints in Mathematical Sociology 15

BOWLES, S., and GINTIS, H. (1976), *Schooling in Capitalist America*, New York, Basic Books

CARROLL, G. R., and DELACROIX, J. (1982), 'Organizational mortality in the newspaper industries of Argentina and Ireland: an ecological approach,' *Administrative Science Quarterly*, 27, pp. 169–98

CHANDLER, A. D. (1977), *The Visible Hand: The Managerial Revolution in American Business*, Cambridge, Harvard University Press

CHILD, J., and KIESER, A. (1981), 'Development of organizations over time,' pp. 28–64 in: P. C. Nystrom and W. H. Starbuck (eds.), *Handbook of Organizational Design*, New York, Oxford University Press

CICOUREL, A. (1970), 'The acquisition of social structure: toward a developmental sociology of language,' pp. 136–88 in: Jack D. Douglas (ed.), *Understanding Everyday Life*, Chicago, Aldine

CLARK, B. R. (1962), *Educating the Expert Society*, San Francisco, Chandler

COHEN, M. D., MARCH, J. G., and OLSEN, P. (1972), 'A garbage can model of organizational choice,' *Administrative Science Quarterly*, 17, pp. 1–25

COLLINS, R. (1979), *The Credential Society*, New York, Academic Press

COSER, L., KADUSHIN, C., and POWELL, W. (1982), *Books: The Culture and Commerce of Book Publishing*, New York, Basic Books

CYERT, R. M., and MARCH, J. G. (1963), *A Behavioral Theory of the Firm*, Englewood Cliffs, NJ, Prentice-Hall

DiMAGGIO, P. (1981), 'Cultural entrepreneurship in nineteenth-century Boston. Part I: The creation of an organizational base for high culture in America,' *Media, Culture and Society*, 4, pp. 33–50

DiMAGGIO, P. (1982), 'The structural of organizational fields: an analytical approach and policy implications,' paper prepared for *SUNY-Albany Conference on Organizational Theory and Public Policy, April 1 and 2*

DOMHOFF, J. W. (1967), *Who Rules America?*, Englewood Cliffs, NJ, Prentice-Hall

DOMHOFF, J. W. (1979), *The Powers That Be: Processes of Ruling Class Domination in America*, New York, Random House

FENNELL, M. L. (1980), 'The effects of environmental characteristics on the structure of hospital clusters,' *Administrative Science Quarterly*, 25, 484–510

FREEMAN, J. H. (1982), 'Organizational life cycles and natural selection processes,' pp. 1–32 in: Barry Staw and Larry Cummings (eds.), *Research in Organizational Behavior*, vol. 4. Greenwich, Conn., JAI Press

GIDDENS, A. (1979), *Central Problems in Social Theory: Action, Structure, and Contradiction in Social Analysis*, Berkeley, Calif., University of California Press

GOULDNER, A. W. (1954), *Patterns of Industrial Bureaucracy*, Glencoe, Ill., Free Press

GRANOVETTER, M. (1978), 'Threshold models of collective behavior,' *American Journal of Sociology*, 83, pp. 1420–43

HALL, R. (1968), 'Professionalization and bureaucratization,' *American Sociological Review*, 33, pp. 92–104

HALPERIN, M. H. (1974), *Bureaucratic Politics and Foreign Policy*, Washington DC, The Brookings Institution

HANNAN, M. T., and FREEMAN, J. H. (1977), 'The population ecology of organizations,' *American Journal of Sociology*, 82, pp. 929–64

HAWLEY, A. (1968), 'Human ecology,' pp. 328–37 in: D. L. Sills (ed.), *International Encyclopedia of the Social Sciences*, New York, Macmillan

HAWLEY, E. W. (1966), *The New Deal and the Problem of Monopoly: A Study in Economic Ambivalence*, Princeton, Princeton University Press

HIRSCH, P. and WHISLER, T. (1982), 'The view from the boardroom,' paper presented at Academy of Management meeting, New York, NY

KANTER, R. M. (1972), *Commitment and Community*, Cambridge, Mass., Harvard University Press

KANTER, R. M. (1977), *Men and Women of the Corporation*, New York, Basic Books

KATZ, M. B. (1975), *Class, Bureaucracy, and Schools: The Illusion of Educational Change in America*, New York, Praeger

KIMBERLY, J. (1980), 'Initiation, innovation and institutionalization in the creation process,' pp. 180–43 in: J. Kimberly and R. B. Miles (eds.), *The Organizational Life Cycle*, San Francisco, Jossey-Bass

KNOKE, D. (1982), 'The spread of municipal reform: temporal, spatial, and social dynamics,' *American Journal of Sociology*, 87, pp. 1314–39

LARSON, M. S. (1977), *The Rise of Professionalism: A Sociological Analysis*, Berkeley, Calif., University of California Press

LAUMANN, E. O., GALASKIEWICZ, J., and MARSDEN, P. (1978), 'Community structure as interorganizational linkage,' *Annual Review of Sociology*, 4, pp. 455–84

LEE, M. L. (1971), 'A conspicuous production theory of hospital behavior,' *Southern Economic Journal*, 38, pp. 48–58

LUKES, S. (1974), *Power: A Radical View*, London, Macmillan

MARCH, J. C., and MARCH, J. G. (1977), 'Almost random careers: the Wisconsin school superintendency, 1940–72,' *Administrative Science Quarterly*, 22, pp. 378–409

MARCH, J. G., and COHEN, M. (1974), *Leadership and Ambiguity: The American College President*, New York, McGraw-Hill

MARCH, J. G., and OLSEN, J. P. (1976), *Ambiguity and Choice in Organizations*, Bergen, Norway, Universitetsförlaget

MARCH, J. G., and SIMON, H. A. (1958), *Organizations*, New York, Wiley

MEYER, J. W. (1979), *The Impact of the Centralization of Educational Funding and Control on State and Local Organizational Governance*, Stanford, Calif., Institute for Research on Educational Finance and Governance, Stanford University, Program Report 79–B20

MEYER, J. W. (1981), Remarks at ASA session on *The Present Crisis and the Decline in World Hegemony*, Toronto, Canada

458 ORGANIZATIONAL CHANGE AND LEARNING

MEYER, J. W., and HANNAN, M. (1979), *National Development and the World System: Educational, Economic, and Political Change*, Chicago, University of Chicago Press

MEYER, J. W., and ROWAN, B. (1977), 'Institutionalized organizations: formal structure as myth and ceremony,' *American Journal of Sociology*, 83, pp. 340–63

MEYER, J. W., SCOTT, W. R., and DEAL, T. C. (1981), 'Institutional and technical sources of organizational structure explaining the structure of educational organizations,' in: Herman Stein (ed.), *Organizations and the Human Services: Cross-Disciplinary Reflections*, Philadelphia, Pa, Temple University Press

MEYER, M. (1981), 'Persistence and change in bureaucratic structures,' paper presented at the annual meeting of the American Sociological Association, Toronto, Canada

MILOFSKY, C. (1981), *Structure and Process in Community Self-help Organizations*, New Haven, Yale Program on Non-Profit Organizations, Working Paper 17

NELSON, R. R., and WINTER, S. (1982), *An Evolutionary Theory of Economic Change*, Cambridge, Harvard University Press

OUCHI, W. G. (1980), 'Markets, bureaucracies, and clans,' *Administrative Science Quarterly*, 25, pp. 129–41

PARSONS, T. (1951), *The Social System*, Glencoe, Ill., Free Press

PARSONS, T. (1977), *The Evolution of Societies*, Englewood Cliffs, NJ, Prentice-Hall

PERROW, C. (1974), 'Is business really changing?' *Organizational Dynamics*, summer, pp. 31–44

PERROW, C. (1976), 'Control in organizations,' paper presented at American Sociological Association annual meetings, New York, NY

PFEFFER, J., and SALANCIK, G. (1978), *The External Control of Organizations: A Resource Dependence Perspective*, New York, Harper & Row

PIVEN, F. F., and CLOWARD, R. A. (1971), *Regulating the Poor: The Functions of Public Welfare*, New York, Pantheon

POWELL, W. W. (forthcoming), 'The political economy of public television,' New Haven, Program on Non-Profit Organizations

POWELL, W. W. (1983), 'New solutions to perennial problems of bookselling: whither the local bookstore?', *Daedalus*, winter

RITTI, R. R., and GOLDNER, F. H. (1979), 'Professional pluralism in an industrial organization,' *Management Science*, 16, pp. 233–46

ROTHMAN, M. (1980), 'The evolution of forms of legal education,' unpublished manuscript, Department of Sociology, Yale University, New Haven, Conn.

ROTHSCHILD-WHITT, J. (1979), 'The collectivist organization: an alternative to rational bureaucratic models,' *American Sociological Review*, 44, pp. 509–27

SCHELLING, T. (1978), *Micromotives and Macrobehavior*, New York, W. W. Norton

SEDLAK, M. W. (1981), 'Youth policy and young women, 1950–1972: the impact of private-sector programs for pregnant and wayward girls on public policy,' paper presented at *National Institute for Education Youth Policy Research Conference*, Washington, D.C.

SELZNICK, P. (1957), *Leadership in Administration*, New York, Harper & Row

SILLS, D. L. (1957), *The Volunteers: Means and Ends in a National Organization*, Glencoe, Ill., Free Press

SIMON, H. A. (1957), *Administrative Behavior*, New York, Free Press

STARR, P. (1980), 'Medical care and the boundaries of capitalist organization,' unpublished manuscript, Program on Non-Profit Organizations, Yale University, New Haven, Conn.

SWIDLER, A. (1979), *Organization without Authority: Dilemmas of Social Control of Free Schools*, Cambridge, Harvard University Press

THOMPSON, J. (1967), *Organizations in Action*, New York, McGraw-Hill

TYACK, D. (1974), *The One Best System: A History of American Urban Education*, Cambridge, Mass., Harvard University Press

USEEM, M. (1979), 'The social organization of the American business elite and participation of corporation directors in the governance of American institutions,' *American Sociological Review*, 44, pp. 553–72

WEBER, M. (1952), *The Protestant Ethic and the Spirit of Capitalism*, New York, Scribner

WEBER, M. (1968), *Economy and Society: An Outline of Interpretive Sociology*, 3 vols., New York, Bedminster

WEICK, K. (1976), 'Educational organizations as loosely coupled systems,' *Administrative Science Quarterly*, 21, pp. 1–19

WEINSTEIN, J. (1968), *The Corporate Ideal in the Liberal State, 1900–1918*, Boston, Beacon Press

WESTNEY, D. E. (forthcoming), Organizational Development and Social Change in Meiji Japan

WHITE, H. C., BOORMAN, S. A., and BREIGER, R. L. (1976), 'Social structure from multiple networks. I. Blockmodels of roles and positions,' *American Journal of Sociology*, 81, pp. 730–80

WILLIAMSON, O. E. (1975), *Markets and Hierarchies, Analysis and Antitrust Implications: A Study of the Economics of Internal Organization*, New York, Free Press

WILLIAMSON, O. E. (1979), 'Transaction-cost economics: the governance of contractual relations,' *Journal of Law and Economics*, 22, pp. 233–61

WINTER, S. G. (1964), 'Economic "natural selection" and the theory of the firm,' *Yale Economic Essays*, 4, pp. 224–72

WINTER, S. G. (1975), 'Optimization and evolution in the theory of the firm,' pp. 73–118 in: Richard H. Day and Theodore Graves (eds.), *Adaptive Economic Models*, New York, Academic Press

WOODWARD, J. (1965), *Industrial Organization, Theory and Practice*, London, Oxford University Press

ZUCKER, L. G., and TOLBERT, P. S. (1981), 'Institutional sources of change in the formal structure of organizations: the diffusion of civil service reform, 1880–1935,' paper presented at American Sociological Association annual meeting, Toronto, Canada

23 A. M. Pettigrew

Context and Action in the Transformation of the Firm[1]

From the *Journal of Management Studies*, vol. 24, no. 6, 1987, pp. 649–70

Introduction

It is perfectly natural that in an era of rapid economic, social and organizational change there should be a revival of academic interest in the subject of leadership. In times of uncertainty it is comforting to believe that individuals in leadership positions can make a difference. There is, however, a large gap between belief and assertions about the potency of leaders in changing circumstances and the need empirically to demonstrate through careful research the what, why, and how of translating executive intentions into realized change. While there are many facets of leadership behaviour worthy of attention, this article follows James MacGregor Burns's assertion that 'ultimately the effectiveness of leaders as leaders will be tested by the achievement of purpose in the form of real and intended social change' (Burns, 1978, p. 251). But Burns and many other students of leadership and change recognize the theoretical and analytical complexities of the easy use of words such as purpose, intention, and effectiveness in linking behaviour to the processes and outcomes of transformation, whether at the societal or organizational levels of analysis.

Behind any worthwhile attempt to explain change processes and outcomes, at least partially in terms of leadership behaviour, lies a whole range of practical analytic questions. There is the problem of perspective. Where we sit not only influences where we stand, but also what we see. Few social scientists would claim to enter the field with empty minds waiting to be gradually filled by evidence. At a time when there are now available a whole range of perspectives for interpreting change processes, ranging from incrementalism, Quinn (1980) to garbage can, March and Olsen

(1976), to political and cultural views of process, Pettigrew (1985a), Johnson (1987), the perspective of the author is important. Time itself sets a frame of reference for what changes are seen and how those changes are explained. The more we look at present-day events the easier it is to identify change and see the visible hand of leadership. The longer we stay with an emergent process and the further back we go to disentangle its origins, the more we can identify continuities. Empirically and theoretically, change and continuity need one another. Action and structure are inextricably linked.

If we start with the premise that leadership and action are important, need we also drift into the assumption that human history and social change are about chaps and nothing else? Gellner's (1973) view is that history is about chaps, but he is quick to point out that it does not follow that its explanations are always in terms of chaps. Societies are what people do, but social scientists are not biographers *en grande série*. So we are drawn into deep questions about the content of change under investigation; the models of man and theory or theories of process being used; the time frame of the analysis; a need to examine action and structure and explain continuity and change, together with a requirement to explore exogenous and endogenous sources of change. All this takes us well away from any simple-minded link between leadership and change.

Interesting as the recent normative writings of Bass (1985), Bennis and Nanus (1985), and Tichy and Ulrich (1984) are about the role of transformational leadership in effecting major change, one remains fundamentally sceptical about their message and the form in which it is presented thus far. This is not to say that prominent business leaders have not played a critical role in reorientating major firms, indeed there is considerable evidence from the ICI case reported in this article of a key transformational role played by ICI's then chairman, Sir John Harvey-Jones. However, focusing on the behaviour of so called transformational leaders may prematurely disable research on strategic change from producing the kind of practical theory Bennis and Bass are seeking to generate. The approach in this article, therefore, is to conceptualize major transformations of the firm in terms of linkages between the content of change and its context and process and to regard leadership behaviour as a central ingredient but only one of the ingredients, in a complex analytical, political, and cultural process of challenging and changing the core beliefs, structure, and strategy of the firm.

The issue is not prematurely to downplay the explanatory role of leadership behaviour in any theory of strategic change but to address questions about leadership within a sufficiently broad analytical approach. This means treating leadership as a continuous process in context; where context refers to the antecedent conditions of change, the internal structure, cultural, and political context within which leadership occurs, as well as broad features of the outer context of the firm from which much of the legitimacy for change is derived.

The starting point here, therefore, is to beware the singular theory of process or indeed, of social and organizational change. Look for continuity and change, patterns and idiosyncrasies, the actions of individuals and groups, and processes of structuring. Give history and social processes the chance to reveal their untidiness. To understand change, examine the juxtaposition of the analytical and the political, the role of exceptional people and extreme circumstances, the enabling and constraining forces of the environment and explore some of the conditions in which mixtures of these occur.

This article has four sections. Section one gives an outline of some of the current literature connecting leadership to strategic changes in the firm. The middle two sections in turn present the theoretical and analytical underpinnings of a major longitudinal study of strategic change processes in Imperial Chemical Industries, Pettigrew (1985a), and then a highly synoptic account of the principal findings of the study. The fourth and final section interprets the ICI empirical findings in terms of processes of change and briefly outlines the developing body of research on strategic change processes now under way at the Centre for Corporate Strategy and Change, University of Warwick.

Leadership and the transformation of the firm

This is not the place to attempt a comprehensive review of recent literature on leadership in organizational contexts. Rather, the purpose of this section is to reveal some of the strengths and weaknesses and trends in current leadership writing in so far as it bears on the study of strategic change processes in organizations. In exploring this writing attention will be given to the evaluative summaries of research on leadership offered by writers such as Bryman (1986), Hunt *et al.* (1984), McCall and Lombardo (1978) and Stogdill (1974). Particular focus will be given to current interest in transformational leadership (Bass, 1985; Bennis and Nanus, 1985; Burns, 1978; and Tichy and Ulrich, 1984), as well as those writers who have contributed to theoretical and empirical debates about the effects of leadership on organizational performance (Lieberson and O'Connor, 1972; Smith *et al.*, 1984 and Weiner and Mahoney, 1981). The section ends by drawing on the important recent work by Romanelli and Tushman (1983), and Tushman and Romanelli (1985) which explicitly connects the character and contribution of leaders to evolutionary periods in the development of the firm.

For those scholars who have invested their time in the study of leadership the recent reviews of the field cannot have made a comfortable read. The comments vary from the coolly apologetic statements of Stogdill (1974, p. vii) 'the endless accumulation of empirical data has not produced an integrated understanding of leadership', to the apocalyptic and impatient assertion of Bennis and Nanus (1985, p. 4) that 'never have so many labored so long to say so little'. Bass (1985), like Stogdill a long devotee of the subject, calmly talks of the repetitive narrowness of social and organizational psychology work on leadership with the continuing circling around of directive *versus* participative, initiation *versus* consideration, and variations of the theme of situational differences in understanding leadership effectiveness. It was partly this repetitive recycling which encouraged Miner (1975) ten years ago to argue that the way forward in this area was to abandon the concept of leadership, and for Bryman (1986, p. 198) recently to use adjectives such as 'disappointment' to characterize the past and 'clutching at straws' to denote current attempts to break out of the old paradigm.

All this critical reflection has, of course, begun to open up the field. Appropriately enough an institution outside the university sector, the Center for Creative Leadership, Greensboro, North Carolina, has made its contribution to facilitating new directions in leadership research. The McCall and Lombardo (1978) book based on a Center Conference drew together a group of scholars not normally associated with leadership to explore new concepts, new methodologies, and new topic areas for study under the leadership banner. McCall and Lombardo (1978) extracted from these papers a number of conclusions germane to the theme of this article. Approaches to leadership should be less short-range and atomistic – less reductionist. Leaders should be studied in natural settings using observational and other qualitative methodologies. Leadership should be examined through the holistic study of actual behaviour rather than breaking the activities of leaders and the responses of followers into categories of independent and dependent variables. Finally and crucially, McCall and Lombardo argue there is a need to study corporate leaders, not the middle managers and supervisors so often the focus of empirical research in this area.

The developing concern in the late 1970s to link leader behaviour to managerial behaviour in organizational settings became reflected in the ever widening topic range and disciplinary participation at the Leadership Symposia organized, amongst others, by J. G. Hunt. The recent outputs from these symposia, Hunt, Sekaran, Schriesheim (1982), and Hunt *et al.* (1984), reflect differences in academic traditions between North America and Europe, but also more general trends which cross the Atlantic and are beginning to impact the study of leadership. Amongst what one reads as a nervousness about a breaking up of the dominant paradigm in leadership research, Hunt *et al.* (1984) are able to report greater attention being paid to 'subjective assessments of social situations, in idiographic approaches, and in the social contexts of action and interaction' (1984, p. 424).

While in the latest Leadership Symposia output, Hunt *et al.* (1984) picks up the current interest in corporate culture and its links to the seminal writing of Selznick (1957), there is only one reference in the symposia volume to Burns's (1978) treatise on political leadership from which current writing on transformational leadership is derived. Burns's (1978) book is a work of great synthesis and scholarship. It is also important in the present context because it directly links leadership behaviour to large system change and does it in a way that draws attention to the context and process of leadership. To Burns, leadership and followership are inextricably linked. Transactional leadership he sees as an exchange relationship between leader and follower whereby compliance is agreed, explicitly or implicitly, through reciprocal exchange. Transformational leadership is a more uplifting process with higher order goals. Here the leader looks for potential motives in followers, seeks to satisfy higher order needs so that through a process of mutual stimulation they 'unite in the pursuit of higher goals, the realization of which is tested by achievement of significant change' (1978, p. 425). Thus to Burns leadership is a mobilization process by persons with motives and values, various 'resources in a context of competition and conflict, in order to realize goals independently or mutually held by leaders and followers' (1978, p. 425).

Six years after the publication of Burns's work, and with the intervening effects of the Iranian oil shock, a world-wide economic recession, and accelerated rates of change in many large firms in mature industries, the language of transformational leadership has passed over into prescriptive writing about management, by Allaire and Firsirotu (1985), Bass (1985), Bennis and Nanus (1985), Tichy and Ulrich (1984), and others. What is the message in this writing and what contribution does it make to the study of leadership and change?

The message is well encapsulated in the slogan wrapped around the Bennis and Nanus book, 'managers are people who do things right and leaders are people who do the right thing' (1985, p. 21). Here is a direct appeal to the vanity of corporate leaders. While managers may be fixated by a concern with 'moving organizations along historical tracks' Tichy and Ulrich (1984, p. 5a), the transformational leader is 'causative . . . can invent and create institutions . . . can choose purposes and visions . . . can create the social architecture that supports them . . . can move followers to higher degrees of consciousness, such as liberty, freedom, justice, and self-actualization' (Bennis and Nanus, 1985, p. 218). Even with Warren Bennis's undoubted sincerity and humanity this is hard to take, either as a description of what corporate leaders do, or a guide to what they might do.

The Bass (1985) book is more carefully written. Here there is less appeal to the vanity of corporate leaders, more willingness to recognize that the complexities of organizational life require senior executives to vary their performance and display in varying amounts and intensities aspects of transitional and transformational objectives and behaviour patterns. The value of the Tichy and Ulrich (1984) writing is the attempt to connect transformational leader behaviour to conceptualizations of the change process and indeed to the technical, political and cultural resistances to fundamental changes in the firm. But apart from instant cameos of contemporary performances by, for example, Iacocca in Chrysler, or Roger Smith in General Motors, there is no sustained attempt to test the concepts and assumptions behind transformational leadership through sustained empirical inquiry. The potential of examining top level change processes through the construction and mobilization of vision and purpose, the use of metaphors and other potent symbols to manage meaning, and through the encouragement of destructive and constructive processes of organizational learning will have to await the attention of others.

There is, of course, a tradition of writing on leadership which is sceptical of any link between leader behaviour and firm performance. In a much quoted article, Pfeffer (1977) argues that leadership has become a repository for unexplained variance much in a way that culture is used in cross cultural studies of organizations. Boal and Bryson (1986) argue that much of the difficulty in studying leadership surrounds the appropriate definitions, measurements, units of analysis and methods for its study. Certainly questions of measurement and method have got tied up into the arguments for and against the proposition that leadership impacts performance outcomes. The study of Lieberson and O'Connor (1972) is most often cited as evidence for the inability of leaders to effect performance, but follow-up work using a similar methodology by Weiner (1978), and a modified methodology by Weiner and Mahoney (1981), has left this stream of research with inconclusive results. However, the larger stream of research on the effects of managerial succession on performance, for example, Brown (1982) and Grusky (1963), seems to point to little successor effect on performance, but most of these studies measure performance within a year of the succession event and this may be structuring the consistent findings. The strength and importance of this tradition of research lies in its desire to bring context back in. Lieberson and O'Connor (1972) make this point with force, but their chosen methodology and analytical framework does not allow them to realize their objective; 'in emphasizing the effects of leadership we may be overlooking far more powerful environmental influences. Unless leadership is studied as part of a total set of forces, one cannot gauge its impact'. As we shall see, one critical aspect of exploring those total sets of forces is to see them over considerable periods of time. The temporal study of leadership processes is one of the reasons for the critical attention given to research by Romanelli and Tushman (1983).

In a series of theoretical papers, Romanelli and Tushman (1983), and Tushman and Romanelli (1985), help to integrate a broad range of literature on leadership and change around what they describe as a metamorphosis model of organizational evolution. In a later empirical piece (Tushman and Anderson, forthcoming), aspects of this model are tested against time series data. They propose that organizations evolve through convergent periods punctuated by strategic reorientations (or re-creations). Convergent periods are relatively long periods of incremental change when a particular strategic focus is elaborated. Such periods may or may not be eras of high performance. Strategic reorientations occur in discontinuous fashion, may involve changes in strategy, power, and structure, and are regularly triggered by environment pressure. However 'only executive leadership is able to initiate and implement strategic reorientations' (Tushman and Romanelli, 1985, p. 214). The character of the leadership task changes from convergent to reorientation periods. 'During convergent periods executive leadership emphasizes symbolic activities and incremental change, while during re-creations, executive leadership engages in major substantive as well as symbolic activities' (1985, p. 214). Here leadership is context sensitive and time sensitive. Here also there is an attempt being made to analyse the variable expression of leadership behaviour in relation to a more general theory of the evolution of the firm in its industry and economic context. Even without theoretical ideas and empirical data about the *processes* through which this may occur, it is possible to see the strength of the Tushman and Romanelli approach to inform inquiry about leadership and the transformation of the firm.

Context, process and organizational changing

The above highly partial review has raised a number of doubts about linking leadership behaviour to the transformation of the firm. As yet the absence of sustained empirical inquiry into the activities of corporate leaders suggests an over confident and over simple view of their role in organizational transformation. Part of the difficulty here is a rush into prescriptive writing before description and analysis (Bennis and Nanus, 1985), but more important are the analytical deficiencies underlying much of the research on leadership behaviour in the firm. These analytical difficulties include a concentration on leadership episodes rather than long-term leadership processes, a tendency to explore leader–follower relations without reference to the antecedent conditions which may influence their expression, and more significantly, the limited attempts to place leader behaviour in the context of political and cultural forces within the organization, and the wider economic and competitive forces with which the firm must operate.

These deficiencies in the study of corporate leadership are not unique to that sphere of social science inquiry. In a broad review of the literature on organization change made elsewhere (Pettigrew, 1985a), the point is made that, with a few limited and noteworthy exceptions (Berg, 1979; Kervasdoue and Kimberly, 1979), much research on organization change is ahistorical, aprocessual, and acontextual in character. In this respect, the area of organization change merely reflects the biases inherent in the social sciences generally and in the study of organizations in particular. There are remarkably few studies of change that actually allow the change process to reveal itself in any kind of substantially temporal or contextual manner. Where the change project is treated as the unit of analysis the focus is on a single event or a set of discrete episodes somehow separate from the immediate and more distant antecedents that give those events form, meaning, and substance. Such episodic views of change not only treat innovations as if they had a clear beginning and a clear end but also, where they limit themselves to snapshot time–series data, fail to provide data on the mechanisms and processes through which changes are created. Studies of transformation are, therefore, often preoccupied with the intricacies of narrow *changes* rather than the holistic and dynamic analysis of *changing*.

The suggestion made here is that one way to respond to the above weaknesses in the literature on leadership and on change is to encourage a form of research which is contextualist and processual in character (Pettigrew, 1985b). A contextualist analysis of a process such as leadership and change draws on phenomena at vertical and horizontal levels of analysis and the interconnections between those levels through time. The vertical level refers to the interdependencies between higher or lower levels of analysis upon phenomena to be explained at some further level; for example, the impact of a changing socioeconomic context on features of intraorganizational context and interest-group behaviour. The horizontal level refers to the sequential interconnectedness among phenomena in historical, present, and future time. An approach that offers both multilevel, or vertical analysis and processual, or horizontal, analysis is said to be contextualist in character. Any wholly contextualist analysis would have the following characteristics:

(1) It would require a clearly delineated but theoretically and empirically connectable set of levels of analysis. Within each level of analysis, of course, depending upon the focus of explanation, there would be specified a set of cross-sectional categories.

(2) It would require a clear description of the process or processes under examination. Basic to the notion of a processual analysis is that an organization or any other social system may profitably be explored as a continuing system, with a past, a present and a future. Sound theory must, therefore, take into account the history and future of a system and relate them to the present. The process itself is seen as a continuous, interdependent sequence of actions and events that is being used to explain the origins, continuance, and outcome of some phenomenon. At the level of the actor, the language of process is most obviously characterized in terms of the verb forms interacting, acting, reacting, responding, and adapting, while at the system level, the interest is in emerging, elaborating, mobilizing, continuing, changing, dissolving, and transforming. The focus is on the language systems of becoming rather than of being – of actors and systems in motion.

Any processual analysis of this form requires as a preliminary the set of cross-sectional categories identified in point (1). Change processes can be identified and studied only against a background of structure or relative constancy. Figure needs ground.

(3) The processual analysis requires a motor, or theory or theories, to drive the process, part of which will require the specification of the model of human beings underlying the research. Within this research on change, strong emphasis is given both to people's capacity and desire to adjust social conditions to meet their ends and to the part played by power relationships in the emergence and ongoing development of the processes being examined.

(4) Crucial, however, to this whole approach to contextualist analysis is the way that the contextual variables in the vertical analysis are linked to the processes under observation in the horizontal analysis. The view taken here is that it is not sufficient to treat context either just as descriptive background or as an eclectic list of antecedents that somehow shape the process. Neither, of course, given the dangers of simple determinism, should structure or context be seen as just constraining process. Rather, this approach recognizes that processes both are constrained by structures and shape structures, either in the direction of preserving them or in altering them. In the past, structural analyses emphasizing abstract dimensions and contextual constraints have been regarded as incompatible with processual analyses stressing action and strategic conduct. Here an attempt is being made to combine these two forms of description and analysis, first of all, by conceptualizing structure and context not just as a barrier to action but as essentially involved in its production (Giddens, 1979; Ranson, Hinings, and Greenwood, 1980) and, secondly, by demonstrating how aspects of structure and context are mobilized or activated by actors and groups as they seek to obtain outcomes important to them.

In this analytical approach to understanding the origins, development, and implementation of organizational change, the interest, therefore, is in multilevel theory construction. An attempt will be made to formulate models of higher-level factors and processes, lower-level factors and processes, and the manner in which they interact. It is recognized that each level often has its own properties, processes, and relationships – its own momentum – and that, while phenomena at one level are not reducible to or cannot be inferred from those at another level, a key to the analysis is tracking the interactions between levels through time. But as applied to strategic change[2] or major transformations in the firm, what kind of more detailed study questions would such a form of contextualist inquiry involve? They would first of all involve questions about the *content*, *context*, and *process* of change, together with the inter-connections between those three broad analytical categories.

The starting point for this analysis of strategic change is the notion that formulating the *content* of any new strategy inevitably entails managing its *context* and *process*. Outer context refers to the social, economic, political, and competitive environment in which the firm operates. Inner context refers to the structure, corporate culture, and political context within the firm through which ideas for change have to proceed. Content refers to the particular areas of transformation under examination. Thus the firm

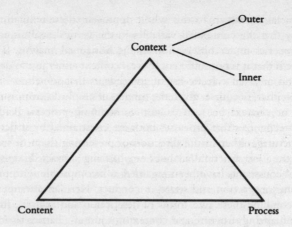

Figure 1 The broad framework guiding the research

may be seeking to change technology, manpower, products, geographical positioning, or indeed corporate culture. The process of change refers to the actions, reactions, and interactions from the various interested parties as they seek to move the firm from its present to its future state. Thus broadly speaking, the 'what' of change is encapsulated under the label content, much of the 'why' of change is derived from an analysis of inner and outer context, and the 'how' of change can be understood from an analysis of process.

The frame of reference used to guide this research on strategic change is a continuation and development of the author's previous work on organizations as political and cultural systems (Pettigrew, 1973, 1977, 1979). There is no pretence to see strategic change as a rational analytical process of analysing environments, resources, and gaps, revealing and assessing strategic alternatives, and choosing and implementing carefully analysed and well thought through outcomes (Andrews, 1971; King and Cleland, 1978). Rather, in the manner of Bower (1970), Mintzberg (1978) and Burgelman (1983) the transformation of the firm is seen as an iterative, multilevel process, with outcomes emerging not merely as a product of rational or boundedly rational debates, but also shaped by the interests and commitments of individuals and groups, the forces of bureaucratic momentum, gross changes in the environment, and the manipulation of the structural context around decisions. Taking this view the focus of attention is on seeing change as a multilevel and continuous process in context, where leadership is expressed through understanding and tactical skill as well as the purposive force of mobilizing often imprecise and inarticulate visions, which are used in challenge dominating beliefs and institutional arrangements.

In this contextualist view of strategic change the analyst has a choice of alternative process modes. Although on the surface the custom and practice of persuasion may dictate that initiatives for change are publicly justified on the weight of technical evidence and analysis, or more narrowly in terms of managerial drives for efficiency and effectiveness, it is too narrow to see change just as a rational and linear problem-solving process. Explanations of change have to be able to deal with continuity and change, actions and structures, endogenous and exogenous factors, as well as the role of chance and surprise. Although there is force in Poggi's (1965, p. 284) stricture 'that a way of seeing is a way of not seeing', there is also a trap in trying to be over eclectic, trying to see everything and thus to see nothing. In this author's view, and indeed in the theoretical writing and empirical research of others (Greenwood and Hinings, 1986; Hardy, 1985; Johnson, 1987; Normann, 1977; Pfeffer, 1981), a view of process combining political and cultural elements evidently has real power in explaining continuity and change.

The interest in culture directs attention to sources of coherence and consistency in organizational life, to the dominating beliefs or ideologies which provide the systems of meaning and interpretation which filter in and filter out environmental and intra-organizational signals. The recognition that culture can shape and not merely reflect organizational power relationships directs attention both to the ground rules which structure the character of political processes in the firm, and the assumptions and interests which powerful groups shield and lesser groups may only with fortitude challenge.

The acts and processes associated with politics as the management of meaning represent conceptually the overlap between a concern with the political and cultural analyses of organizations. A central concept linking political and cultural analyses essential to the understanding of continuity and change is legitimacy. The management of meaning refers to a process of symbol construction and value use designed to create legitimacy for one's ideas, actions, and demands, and to delegitimate the demands of one's opponents. If one sees strategic change processes at least partially as a contest about ideas and rationalities between individuals and groups, then the mechanisms used to legitimate and delegitimate particular ideas or broader ideologies are obviously critical in such an analysis. Equally well, the resolution of such contests about ideas need to be sensitive to questions of power and control in the firm.

Building on Lukes (1974) and Pfeffer (1981), Hardy (1985) has recently argued that a concern with power and control as explanations of strategic choice and change processes would in effect correspond to two uses of power. Power used to defeat competition in a choice or change process, and power used to prevent competition in a choice or change process. In both of these processes there would be an explanatory role for unobtrusive systems of power derived from the generation and manipulation of symbols, language, belief and ideology – from culture creation; and from the more public face of power expressed through the possession, control, and tactical use of overt sources of power such as position, rewards or sanctions, or expertise.

There are two further essential points to derive from the above way of thinking about process. The first is that structures, cultures, and strategies are not just being treated here as neutral, functional constructs connectable to some system need such as efficiency or adaptability; those constructs are viewed as capable of serving to protect the interests of dominant groups. Thus the biases existing in structures and cultures can protect dominant groups by reducing the chances of challenge, and features of inner and outer context can be mobilized by dominant or aspiring groups to legitimate the existing order, or indeed to help create a new order. These points are as pertinent to understanding processes of strategic change as they are to achieving practical outcomes in strategic change. As Normann (1977, p. 161) has so aptly put it, 'the only way to bring about lasting change and to foster an ability to deal with new situations is by influencing the conditions that determine the interpretation of situations and the regulation of ideas'.

The above political and cultural view of process gives a central place to the processes and mechanisms through which strategic changes are legitimated or delegitimated. The content of strategic change is thus ultimately a product of a legitimation process shaped by political/cultural considerations, though often expressed in rational/analytical terms. This recognition that transformation in the firm may involve a challenge for the dominating ideology, cultures, systems of meaning and power relationships in the organization, makes it clear why and how the processes of sensing, justifying, creating, and stabilizing major change can be so tortuous and long. How long and how tortuous, even with high-level and consistent leadership pressure for change, will become evident from the case study of ICI which follows.

Some patterns in a process of strategic change: the case of ICI

Researchers who choose to conduct processual analyses have usually decided to trade off generality over actors and systems for realism of context and scope for theoretical interpretation. What they have usually also committed themselves to is presenting their findings in book-length form, especially if the research was conducted on a comparative and longitudinal basis. What follows is a thoroughly limited treatment of the context, content, and process of strategic change in ICI. There is space here only to present some of the patterns in the data plus a limited interpretation of the study findings. The reader interested in the complete presentation of the methods, data, and theoretical interpretation should consult Pettigrew (1985a, 1985b, 1985c).

ICI is one of Britain's largest manufacturing firms and in 1981 was ranked the fifth largest of the world's chemical companies in terms of sales in US dollars (after Du Pont and the big German three of Hoechst, Bayer, and BASF). The study described in this article examines ICI's attempts to change its strategy, structure, technology, organizational culture, and the quality of union–management relationships over the period 1960–84. An important and unusual feature of the research strategy has been the collection of comparative and longitudinal data. Interview, documentary, and observational data are available from what, in 1980, were ICI's four largest divisions, and from the corporate headquarters. Crucially these data have been assembled on a continuous real-time basis since 1975, through retrospective analysis of the period 1960–74; and, in the case of the divisional studies, by probing into the traditions and culture of each division established long before the last two decades.

The study explores two linked continuous processes. The initial focus of the research was to examine the birth, evolution, demise, and development of the groups of internal and external organization development consultants employed by ICI in order to help initiate and implement organization change. This analysis of specialist-led attempts to facilitate change prompted and opened the way for a broader analysis of strategic change in ICI as seen through the activities of the main board of the company and the boards of the Agricultural, Mond, Petrochemicals, and Plastics Divisions. Five cases of strategic change are compared and contrasted in the study (Pettigrew, 1985a). Here it is feasible to discuss only one of those five cases – the one relating to the strategic development of the whole ICI group. No reference is made here to that part of the study dealing with the use and fate of organization development consultants.

Over the period 1975 to 1983, 134 people were interviewed from the ICI corporate headquarters and the 4 divisions under study. Some of these individuals were interviewed on a number of occasions and the total number of interviews for the research amounted to 175. All the interviews except one were tape recorded. Those interviewed included main board and division directors, senior, middle, and supervisory levels of management, internal and external OD consultants, and shop stewards and shop floor employees. Extensive and high level archival material was consulted along with relevant secondary sources on the UK and world-wide chemical industries and on ICI and their major competitors. Company archival materials provided valuable information in their own right, as well as cross-validation for statements made in interviews and conversations. The study is rare in its use of high level and high quality data collected for 9 years in real time and more than 16 years historically. For those scholars who raise doubts about the validity of longitudinal studies of change using only retrospective data, here is a study where the change process was followed for considerable periods of real and retrospective time.

Aspects of the context and content of strategic change in ICI

This case illustrates how much the formulation of the content of strategic change is dependent upon managing its context and process. The process skills at the most general level involve the legitimation of the content of strategy in the evolving inner and outer context of the firm. The ICI data illustrates the deep-seated organizational cultural and political roots of strategy, and the existence of dominating rationalities or core beliefs inside the firm that provide the frame of reference by which individuals and groups make sense of changing features of their inner and outer context. The case also points to the enormous difficulties of breaking down such core beliefs once a particular marriage of content, context, and process has become established. The breaking down of such core beliefs is seen as a long-term conditioning process – a political learning process, influenced by the interest and, above all, the persistence of visionary leaders, the changing pattern of competition between individuals and groups representing different rationalities, the massive enabling opportunity created by changes in outer context, and ultimately a subtle process of connecting what are perceived to be coherent solutions at particular points in time to legitimate problems.

But what are some of the key features of the context of ICI during the 1960s and 1970s and what strategic changes did occur over the period 1960 to 1983?

In 1972, ICI was not only Britain's biggest industrial company, it was, according to prevailing rates of exchange, the biggest chemical company in the world. ICI had scale and scope. They were product-wise one of the most diversified chemical companies in the world, had 350 subsidiaries and were active in all major industrial and most non-industrial countries. However, in spite of this international spread, ICI was in culture and management almost entirely British. The British factories were by far the most important part of ICI's manufacturing interests. In 1972 63 per cent of total sales were derived from UK assets. Counting subsidiaries, ICI employed 132,000 people in 1972. About two thirds of the total work force were employed in Britain.

ICI was divided into nine largely autonomous and profit accountable divisions, answering to the main board and monitored through a system of policy and planning and budget controls. ICI's head office was and still is at Millbank, London SW1. The main board and executive directors were resident at Millbank and maintained effective strategic control at the centre over the divisions and subsidiaries through two main elements of reserve powers. The main board had final say over the investment decisions that determined ICI's future shape and also was the final arbiter of personnel policy.

ICI's competitive position in 1970 was partly a function of acquiring scale and scope early in the development of the chemical industry. Their position had also been ensured by the pre-Second World War cartels in the industry and their success as technological innovators. Immediately after the Second World War, with the cartels and agreements dissolved, and in the 1950s a wide range of new and expanding entrants into the world chemical industry fast building new and larger plant, ICI found themselves in a more international and a more competitive industry. Spurred by the increasing success of the large US chemical companies in European markets, the platform for growth in Europe created by the birth of the EEC, pressures from within ICI for innovation from some of the newer divisions and activities such as organics, plastics, synthetic fibres, and pharmaceuticals, and some inauspicious financial results in 1958 and 1961, ICI began the decade of the 1960s in an atmosphere of challenge and change. Thus around the early 1960s ICI began to cohere around four strategic changes which it was hoped would improve their international competitive position. These changes required a dramatic improvement in the size and efficiency of ICI's manufacturing technology; energetic attempts to improve labour productivity; a strategic thrust to reposition ICI's market focus away from Britain and the old Empire markets towards Europe and then North America; and finally and crucially attempts to change ICI's management culture and organization towards a greater concern with marketing and financial competences and away from a technological focus within a purely functional bureaucracy.

Not all the above strategic changes were realized with the purpose and energy some people in and outside ICI would have liked. As ICI entered the 1970s, Anthony Sampson had placed the jibe 'slumbering giant' around ICI's neck. During the 1970s ICI slowly came to terms with the dependence on an inflation-ridden and declining British economy, and a world wide chemical industry where the premium of chemical growth over general rates was reduced and in some sectors eliminated.

By the end of the 1970s there was a massive over-capacity in the European fibres, petrochemicals and plastics industries, and throughout the 1970s, ICI, like all other large British manufacturing firms, had to learn to live with the increasingly confident use of trade union power and government intervention in business affairs. Finally, the arrival of the Thatcher government in 1979, pursuing strict monetarist economic policies, meant high interest rates, a recession in industrial production, and mounting unemployment. The further fall in ICI's United Kingdom customer base and, worse still, the sharply rising value of sterling in 1980 and 1981 in relation to the US dollar and deutsche mark meant cheaper chemical imports from Europe and North America and a trend for British chemical prices to move out of line with those in continental Europe. The net effect of all this was a dramatic worsening of ICI's business performance and profitability in the years 1980 to 1983, and an end to the belief that competitive success could come from creating capital investment in huge and efficient complexes for the production of heavy chemicals.

The early 1980s thus became the second era of strategic change in the last two-and-a-half decades of ICI's history. The content of those changes was a mixture of culture, structure, and business strategy. A new Chairman, Sir John Harvey-Jones, and other key executives sought to replace the old beliefs about the potency of capital expenditure, cash management, and a risk aversive, consensual, and operational style of top management with a new ideology. This new ideology emphasized a sharpening of market focus, a greater entrepreneurial emphasis to more decentralized units, a lessening of bureaucracy and central control, and a change in the mode and style of operation of the main board. These attempts at cultural change were linked to major changes in structure, systems, rewards, and manpower. Assets in the two biggest loss-making divisions, Petrochemicals and Plastics were closed, and then in 1981 the two divisions were merged under a single smaller board. Mond, Fibres, and Organics divisions all lost assets and manpower. Service functions such as engineering, R&D, purchasing, and personnel were rationalized. ICI's UK employees fell by 31 per cent from 89,400 to 61,800 between 1979 and 1983. This process of structural change reached its fruition in 1986 with the merging of all the UK heavy chemicals divisions, Agricultural, Fibres, Mond, Petrochemicals, and Plastics into one group, ICI Chemicals and Polymers. This will allow further fixed costs to be taken out.

As these changes in culture and structure are implemented, business strategy changes are becoming evident. These are to realize the intentions of the 1970s to increase the proportion of the group's business in high added value products; to consolidate its position in Europe, and to build up its presence in the US. In addition, acquisitions are being sought and ICI is cultivating high growth markets in the Pacific Basin.

The overall pattern: revolution and incremental adjustment

One of the important contributions of the McGill research on strategic change (Miller and Friesen, 1982; Mintzberg, 1978; Mintzberg and Waters, 1982) has been to identify both the ebb and flow of strategic concentrations in the firm and also the existence of periods of revolutionary and evolutionary change. What these authors do less precisely is to develop a process theory which explains the timing, relative intensity and mechanisms for producing such revolutionary and evolutionary periods. An approach, again relying on a crisis theory of change which does have more to say about precrisis, crisis and stabilization, and thus the linkages between revolutionary and evolutionary periods, is that offered by Brunsson (1982), Jonsson and Lundin (1977), and Starbuck, Greve and Hedberg (1978). Crucially Brunsson argues that the periods when ideological shifts are in process, i.e. when the dominant ideology has not yet been debunked and when any aspiring new ideology still lacks a critical mass of support, are poor contexts for action. This is because ideological inconsistencies increase uncertainty and make it difficult to marshal the strong commitments and high levels of motivation and energy which are necessary to create radical organizational changes. Thus, he argues, an ideological shift has to be completed before radical action in the change sphere can begin.

This study of ICI corroborates the phenomenon of radical periods of change interspersed with periods of incremental adjustment, and also changes in core beliefs to precede structural and business strategy change. In brief, the corporate development of ICI over the period from 1969 to 1986 indicates the following patterns:

(1) Change did not occur as a continuous incremental process.

(2) The pattern of change was for radical eras of change to occur at periodic intervals. Of the three periods of high levels of change activity, two, the ones between 1960 and 1964 and 1980 to 1986 could be sensibly labelled as revolutionary in that they featured substantial ideological, structural, and business strategy change. The third period between 1970 and 1982, was a period of substantial if lesser change when further structural change was made and elements of the ideological and business strategy changes made ten years earlier were accelerated or de-emphasized. The periods between these packages of changes were occasions for implementing and stabilizing changes, and most notably between 1973 and 1980, eras of organizational learning when ideological justification was prepared for the revolutionary break between 1980 and 1986.

(3) Each of these periods of high levels of change activity was associated with world economic recessions, with their associated effects on world chemical production, markets, and prices, and in turn on ICI's relative business performance. In other words, ICI made substantial changes only when it was in severe economic difficulties. However, a critical facet of these change periods was not only the perception and reality of business pressure, but also the active strategies by managers to construct a climate for change around the performance difficulties. Mobilizing the outer content in order to provide the legitimacy and justification for change was a critical part of the political learning process of change.

(4) The revolutionary periods of change were also connected with changes in leadership and power in ICI. The era of change in the early 1960s was associated with the appearance of Sir Paul Chambers. In the early 1980s, Sir John Harvey-Jones has also supplied radical leadership. Chambers was the first 'outsider' to become Chairman of ICI. Harvey-Jones joined ICI in his early thirties from a career in Naval Intelligence. Significantly neither man had spent his whole career in the ICI culture.

(5) Finally, within the eras of revolutionary change there was little evidence to support Chandler's (1962) dictum that structure follows strategy. Rather the pattern of change in ICI was a complex mixture of adjustment in core beliefs of the top decision-makers, followed by changes in structure,

systems, and rewards, with the business strategy changes emerging and being implemented rather more slowly after the changes in beliefs, structure, systems, and rewards had been legitimated and implemented.

Interpreting the ICI case: summary and conclusion

The above highly synoptic account of some patterns of ICI's corporate development has revealed an association between environmental change and pressure and internal strategic change. As such, the view so far of strategic change is that real change requires crisis conditions; and, by implication, senior executives who may be pushing for change in pre-crisis circumstances do not have sufficient leverage to break through the pattern of inertia in their organization. However, although the above brief analysis does reveal periodic eras of high levels of change activity precipitated by crisis, it is not being argued that the process and content of strategic changes can be explained solely by economic and business-related environmental disturbance. Clearly, a potential danger of an analysis that might infer too simply a relation between economic and business crisis and organizational change is that the firm may thus end up being seen just 'bobbing on the economic waves, as so many corks on the economic bathtub' (Boswell, 1983, p. 15).

As I have already noted, no such brand of simple economic determinism is intended here. Behind the periodic strategic reorientations in ICI are not just economic and business events but also processes of managerial perception, choice, and action influenced by and influencing perceptions of the operating environment of the firm and its structure, culture, and systems of power and control. Crucial to the character and content of the package of structural and then business strategy changes made at the revolutionary points when those changes are actually delivered are the antecedent factors and processes of the precrisis period. Crucial in the precrisis period is the process through which the dominating ideology nurtured in earlier contexts is first challenged and then changed. Since business strategies are likely to be rooted in the idea systems that are institutionalized in an industry sector at any point of time (Grinyer and Spender, 1979; Huff, 1982) and are represented in the values, structures, and systems of powerful groups who control the firms in any sector, a change in business strategies has to involve a process of ideological and political change, which eventually releases a new concept of strategy that is ideologically acceptable within a newly appreciated context. Because this precrisis era of ideological change represents a fundamental challenge to the dominating ideas and power groups of the organization, such eras of ideological challenge are often thwarted, sidetracked, or otherwise immobilized, leaving many who have attempted to champion new ideas faced with stereotyping as oddballs, moral entrepreneurs, or folk devils. Posed in this way, the development of strategic change in the firm takes on the character of a political learning process, a long-term conditioning and influence process designed to establish the dominating legitimacy of a different pattern of relation between strategic content, context, and process. The ICI case illustrates that the real problem of strategic change is anchoring new concepts of reality, new issues for attention, and new ideas for debate and resolution and mobilizing concern, energy, and enthusiasm, often in an additive and evolutionary fashion, to ensure that these thoughts initially considered as illegitimate gain powerful support and eventually result in contextually appropriate action. The ICI case also indicates the contribution of corporate leaders to long-term change processes though not in the apocalyptic and acontextual fashion suggested by, for example, Bennis and Nanus (1985). Lord Beeching departed rapidly from ICI in 1967 for sensing problem areas and recommending action which his board colleagues could neither appreciate nor act on. Many of Beeching's recommendations made in 1967 were not to be implemented until a dozen or more years later. John Harvey-Jones arrived on the main board of ICI in 1973 and spent much of the 1970s orchestrating an educational process – trying to open up ICI to change. Critical to this process was a need to change the mode, style, composition, and problem solving processes on the main board. This required persistence and patience as well as the articulation of an imprecise vision of a better future for ICI. Harvey-Jones had no simple minded and clear cut vision for ICI. In so far as there was a vision amongst Harvey-Jones and the 'for change caucus' on the main board, it was clarified through additive implementation. Whilst that was going on there was the crucial requirement for the visionary leader to keep one foot in the present whilst pushing on into the future. Or as Harvey-Jones put it, to push for change using illegitimate methods whilst 'never missing a chance to make the point that I'm basically an operator'.

Another important feature of managerial action in strategic change is the necessity to alter the structural context in which strategy changes are being articulated. These attempts to change inner context included the use of new ideological posturing to challenge traditional ways of thinking and acting, setting up management-development programmes to focus attention on the needs for new management capabilities and skills, and creating permanent and temporary changes in administrative mechanisms and working groups to build energy and commitment around particular problems and their solution. These activities did not occur in the ICI cases as part of some grand process design. Instead, opportunities were taken as they presented themselves to break any emerging global vision of a better future into manageable bits, to find small steps on the way to larger breaks, and to use any political momentum created by a number of complementary moves to bind a critical mass of powerful people around a set of principles that eventually would allow a series of pieces in the jigsaw to be moved simultaneously.

These processes required understanding and skill in intervening in the organization's structure, culture, and political processes. As Selznick (1957, p. 70) has argued, 'a wise leader faces up to the character of his organization, although he may do so only as a prelude to designing a strategy that will alter it'. This kind of process management also necessitated patience and perseverance. It required waiting for people to retire to exploit any policy vacuum so created; introducing known sympathizers as replacements for known sceptics or opponents; using succession occasions to combine portfolios and responsibilities and integrate thought and action in an otherwise previously factious and deadlocked area of change; and backing off and waiting or moving the pressure point for change into another area where continuing downright opposition might have endangered the success of the whole change exercise.

One swallow doesn't make a summer, and certainly one, even comprehensive case study, cannot on its own prove a point. However, the ICI study reported more fully in Pettigrew (1985a) is able to corroborate the above findings across five cases of strategic change. Through this comparative analysis the fuller study is also able to demonstrate how and why variability in context may influence the pace, timing, and direction of change processes.

There are a number of ways of taking forward this kind of contextual and processual research on the transformation of the firm. Some of these ways are now being tested at the Centre for Corporate Strategy and Change, University of Warwick. Research is underway seeking to connect the capability of firms to effect strategic and operational changes and the maintenance and improvement of their competitive performance. Data are being collected in the automobile, merchant banking, insurance, and book publishing sectors and early findings are reported in Pettigrew et al. (forthcoming) and Whipp et al. (1987). A related research project is examining the links between corporate strategy change and human resource management in office automation, engineering, commercial banking, and retailing sectors (Hendry and Pettigrew, 1987; Sparrow and Pettigrew, 1987). Both of the above studies are looking at the interactive effects of firm level and industry sector level variables in explaining the content and processes of change. Finally, a major study of the National Health Service is utilizing a similar methodology and conceptual approach to investigate the context, content, and process of change at the district level in the National Health Service (Pettigrew et al., 1987). Through such comparative and longitudinal case study research we believe additive and reliable empirical findings on the transformation of the firm will emerge.

Notes

[1] The research reported in this article was partly supported by the *Economic and Social Research Council*.

[2] Strategic change or transformation are descriptive of magnitude in alteration in, for example, the culture, or strategy, and structure of the firm, recognizing the second order effects, or multiple consequences of any such changes.

References

ALLAIRE, Y., and FIRSIROTU, M. (1985), 'How to implement radical strategies in large organizations', *Sloan Management Review*, spring, pp. 19-33

ANDREWS, K. (1971), *The Concept of Corporate Strategy*, Homewood, Ill., Irwin

BASS, B. M. (1985), *Leadership and Performance Beyond Expectations*, New York, Free Press

BENNIS, W., and NANUS, B. (1985), *Leaders: The Strategies for Taking Charge*, New York, Harper & Row

BERG, P. O. (1979), *Emotional Structures in Organizations: A Study of the Process of Change in a Swedish Company*, Lund, Student Literature

BOAL, K. B. and BRYSON, J. M. (1986), 'Charismatic leadership: a phenomenological and structural approach', in J. G. Hunt et al. (eds.), *Emerging Leadership Vistas*, New York, Pergamon Press

BOSWELL, J. S. (1983), *Business Policies in the Making*, London, Allen & Unwin

BOWER, J. L. (1970), *Managing the Resource Allocation Process*, Cambridge, Harvard University Press

BROWN, M. C. (1982), 'Administrative succession and organizational performance: the succession effect', *Administrative Science Quarterly*, 27, pp. 1-16

BRUNSSON, N. (1982), 'The irrationality of action and action rationality: decisions, ideologies and organizational action', *Journal of Management Studies*, 19, 1, pp. 29-44

BRYMAN, A. (1986), *Leadership and Organizations*, London, Routledge & Kegan Paul

BURGELMAN, R. A. (1983), 'A model of the interaction of strategic behaviour, corporate context and the concept of strategy', *Academy of Management Review*, 8, 1, pp. 61-70

BURNS, J. M. (1978), *Leadership*, New York, Harper & Row

CHANDLER, A. J. (1962), *Strategy and Structure: Chapters in the History of the American Industrial Enterprise*, Cambridge, Mass., MIT Press

GELLNER, E. (1973), *Cause and Meaning in the Social Sciences*, London, Routledge & Kegan Paul

GIDDENS, A. (1979), *Central Problems in Social Theory*, London, Macmillan

GREENWOOD, R., and HININGS, C. R. (1986), 'Organizational design types, tracks and the dynamics of change', Working Paper, Department of Organizational Analysis, University of Alberta

GRINYER, P. A., and SPENDER, J. C. (1979), *Turnaround: the Fall and Rise of the Newton Chambers Group*, London, Associated Business Press

GRUSKY, O. (1963), 'Management succession', *American Journal of Sociology*, 49, pp. 21-31

HARDY, C. (1985), *Managing Organizational Closure*, Aldershot, Gower

HENDRY, C., and PETTIGREW, A. M. (1987), 'The practice of strategic human resource management', *Personnel Review*, 15, 5, pp. 3-8

HUFF, A. S. (1982), 'Industry influences on strategy reformulation', *Strategic Management Journal*, 3, pp. 119-31

HUNT, J. G., SEKARAN, U., and SCHRIESHEIM, C. A. (eds.) (1982), *Leadership Beyond Established Views*, Carbondale, Ill., Southern Illinois University Press

HUNT, J. G., HOSKING, D. M., SCHRIESHEIM, C. A., and STEWART, R. (eds.) (1984), *Leaders and Managers: International Perspectives on Managerial Behavior and Leadership*, New York, Pergamon Press

JOHNSON, G. (1987), *Strategic Change and the Management Process*, Oxford, Blackwell

JONSSON, S. A., and LUNDIN, R. A. (1977), 'Myths and wishful thinking as management tools', in P. C. Nystrom and W. H. Starbuck (eds.), *Prescriptive Models of Organizations*, Amsterdam, North Holland

KANTER, R. M. (1983), *The Change Masters: Innovation for Productivity in the American Corporation*, New York, Simon & Schuster

KERVASDOUE, J., and KIMBERLY, J. R. (1979), 'Are organization structures culture free?', in G. England *et al.* (eds.), *Organizational Functioning in a Cross-Cultural Perspective*. Kent State University Press

KING, W. R., and CLELAND, D. T. (1978), *Strategic Planning and Policy*, New York, Van Nostrand

LIEBERSON, S., and O'CONNOR, J. F. (1972), 'Leadership and organizational performance: a study of large corporations', *American Sociological Review*, 37, pp. 117-30

LUKES, S. (1974), *Power: A Radical View*, London, Macmillan

McCALL, M. W., and LOMBARDO, M. M. (1978), *Leadership – Where Else Can We Go?*, Durham, NC, Duke University Press

MARCH, J. G., and OLSEN, J. P. (1976), *Ambiguity and Choice in Organizations*, Bergen, Universitetsførlaget

MILLER, D., and FRIESEN, P. (1982), 'Structural change and performance: quantum vs piecemeal incremental approaches', *Academy of Management Journal*, 25, 4, pp. 867–92

MINER, J. B. (1975), 'The uncertain future of the leadership concept: an overview', in: J. G. Hunt and L. C. Larson (eds.), *Leadership Frontiers*, Kent, Ohio, Kent State University Press

MINTZBERG, H. (1978), 'Patterns of strategy formation', *Management Science*, 24, 9, pp. 934—48

MINTZBERG, H., and WATERS, J. (1982), 'Tracking strategy in an entrepreneurial firm', *Academy of Management Journal*, 25, 3, pp. 465–99

NORMANN, R. (1977), *Management for Growth*, London, Wiley

PETTIGREW, A. M. (1973), *The Politics of Organizational Decision Making*, London, Tavistock

PETTIGREW, A. M. (1977), 'Strategy formulation as a political process', *International Studies of Management and Organization*, 7, 2, pp. 78–87

PETTIGREW, A. M. (1979), 'On studying organizational cultures', *Administrative Science Quarterly*, 24, 4, pp. 570–81

PETTIGREW, A. M. (1985a), *The Awakening Giant: Continuity and Change in Imperial Chemical Industries*, Oxford, Blackwell

PETTIGREW, A. M. (1985b), 'Contextualist research: a natural way to link theory and practice', in E. Lawler (ed.), *Doing Research That is Useful in Theory and Practice*, San Francisco, Jossey-Bass

PETTIGREW, A. M. (1985c), 'Examining change in the long term context of culture and politics', in: J. M. Pennings (ed.), *Organizational Strategy and Change*, San Francisco, Jossey-Bass

PETTIGREW, A. M., McKEE, L., and FERLIE, E. (1987), 'Understanding change in the NHS: a review and research agenda', Working Paper, Centre for Corporate Strategy and Change, University of Warwick

PETTIGREW, A. M., WHIPP, R., and ROSENFELD, R. (forthcoming). 'Competitiveness and the management of strategic change processes: a research agenda', in: P. K. M. Tharakan and A. Francis (eds.), *The Competitiveness of European Industry: Country Policies and Company Strategies*

PFEFFER, J. (1977), 'The ambiguity of leadership', *Academy of Management Review*, 2, pp. 104–12

PFEFFER, J. (1981), *Power in Organizations*, Marshfield, Mass., Pitman

POGGI, G. (1965), 'A main theme of contemporary sociological analysis: achievements and eliminations', *British Journal of Sociology*, 16, pp. 283–94

QUINN, J. B. (1980), *Strategies for Change: Logical Incrementalism*, Homewood, Ill., Irwin

RANSON, S., HININGS, C. R., and GREENWOOD, R. (1980), 'The structuring of organizational structures', *Administrative Science Quarterly*, 25, 1, pp. 1–18

ROMANELLI, E., and TUSHMAN, M. L. (1983), 'Executive leadership and organizational outcomes: an evolutionary perspective', Working Paper 508A, Columbia University

SELZNICK, P. (1957), *Leadership in Administration: A Sociological Interpretation*, New York, Harper & Row

SMITH, J. E., CARSON, K. P., and ALEXANDER, R. A. (1984), 'Leadership, it can make a difference', *Academy of Management Journal*, 27, pp. 765–76

SPARROW, P. R., and PETTIGREW, A. M. (1987), 'Britain's training problems: the search for a strategic human resources management approach', *Human Resource Management*, 26, 1, pp. 109–28

STARBUCK, W., GREVE, A., and HEDBERG, B. L. T. (1978), 'Responding to crises', *Journal of Business Administration*, 9, 2, pp. 111–37

STOGDILL, R. M. (1974), *Handbook of Leadership: a Survey of Theory and Research*, New York, Free Press

TICHY, N. M., and ULRICH, D. O. (1984), 'SMR Forum; the leadership challenge – a call for the transformational leader', *Sloan Management Review*, fall, pp. 59–68

TUSHMAN, M. L., and ROMANELLI, R. (1985), 'Organizational evolution: a metamorphosis model of convergence and reorientation', in: L. L. Cummings and B. Staw (eds.), *Research in Organizational Behavior*, 7, Greenwich, Conn., JAI Press

TUSHMAN, M. L., and ANDERSON, P. (forthcoming), 'Technological discontinuities and organization environments', in: A. M. Pettigrew (ed.), *Managing Strategic Change Processes*, Oxford, Blackwell

WEINER, N. (1978), 'Situational and leadership influence on organizational performance', *Proceedings of the Academy of Management*, pp. 230–4

WEINER, N., and MAHONEY, T. A. (1981), 'A model of corporate performance as a function of environmental, organizational and leadership influences', *Academy of Management Journal*, 24, pp. 453–70

WHIPP, R., ROSENFELD, R., and PETTIGREW, A. M. (forthcoming), 'Understanding strategic change processes: some preliminary British findings', in: A. M. Pettigrew (ed.), *Managing Strategic Change Processes*, Oxford, Blackwell

WILSON, D. C., BUTLER, R. J., CRAY, D., HICKSON, D. J., and MALLORY, G. R. (1986), 'Breaking the bounds of organization in strategic decision making', *Human Relations*, 39, 4, pp. 309–32

24 P. Senge

Building Learning Organizations

From 'The leader's new work: building learning organizations', *Sloan Management Review*, fall 1990, pp. 7–23

Human beings are designed for learning. No one has to teach an infant to walk, or talk, or master the spatial relationships needed to stack eight building blocks that don't topple. Children come fully equipped with an insatiable drive to explore and experiment. Unfortunately, the primary institutions of our society are oriented predominantly toward controlling rather than learning, rewarding individuals for performing for others rather than for cultivating their natural curiosity and impulse to learn. The young child entering school discovers quickly that the name of the game is getting the right answer and avoiding mistakes – a mandate no less compelling to the aspiring manager.

'Our prevailing system of management has destroyed our people,' writes W. Edwards Deming, leader in the quality movement.[1] 'People are born with intrinsic motivation, self-esteem, dignity, curiosity to learn, joy in learning. The forces of destruction begin with toddlers – a prize for the best Halloween costume, grades in school, gold stars, and on up through the university. On the job, people, teams, divisions are ranked – reward for the one at the top, punishment at the bottom. MBO, quotas, incentive pay, business plans, put together separately, division by division, cause further loss, unknown and unknowable.'

Ironically, by focusing on performing for someone else's approval, corporations create the very conditions that predestine them to mediocre performance. Over the long run, superior performance depends on superior learning. A Shell study showed that, according to former planning director Arie de Geus, 'a full one-third of the Fortune "500" industrials listed in 1970 had vanished by 1983.'[2] Today, the average lifetime of the largest industrial enterprises is probably less than *half* the average lifetime of a person

486

in an industrial society. On the other hand, de Geus and his colleagues at Shell also found a small number of companies that survived for seventy-five years or longer. Interestingly, the key to their survival was the ability to run 'experiments in the margin,' to continually explore new business and organizational opportunities that create potential new sources of growth.

If anything, the need for understanding how organizations learn and accelerating that learning is greater today than ever before. The old days when a Henry Ford, Alfred Sloan, or Tom Watson *learned for the organization* are gone. In an increasingly dynamic, interdependent, and unpredictable world, it is simply no longer possible for anyone to 'figure it all out at the top.' The old model, 'the top thinks and the local acts,' must now give way to integrating thinking and acting at all levels. While the challenge is great, so is the potential payoff. 'The person who figures out how to harness the collective genius of the people in his or her organization,' according to former Citibank CEO Walter Wriston, 'is going to blow the competition away.'

Adaptive learning and generative learning

The prevailing view of learning organizations emphasizes increased adaptability. Given the accelerating pace of change, or so the standard view goes, 'the most successful corporation of the 1990s,' according to *Fortune* magazine, 'will be something called a learning organization, a consummately adaptive enterprise.'[3] As the Shell study shows, examples of traditional authoritarian bureaucracies that responded too slowly to survive in changing business environments are legion.

But increasing adaptiveness is only the first stage in moving toward learning organizations. The impulse to learn in children goes deeper than desires to respond and adapt more effectively to environmental change. The impulse to learn, at its heart, is an impulse to be generative, to expand our capability. This is why leading corporations are focusing on *generative* learning, which is about creating, as well as *adaptive* learning, which is about coping.[4]

The total quality movement in Japan illustrates the evolution from adaptive to generative learning. With its emphasis on continuous experimentation and feedback, the total quality movement has been the first wave in building learning organizations. But Japanese firms' view of serving the customer has evolved. In the early years of total quality, the focus was on 'fitness to standard,' making a product reliably so that it would do what its designers intended it to do and what the firm told its customers it would do. Then came a focus on 'fitness to need,' understanding better what the customer wanted and then providing products that reliably met those needs. Today, leading edge firms seek to understand and meet the 'latent need' of the customer – what customers might truly value but have never experienced or would never think to ask for. As one Detroit executive commented recently, 'You could never produce the Mazda Miata solely from market research. It required a leap of imagination to see what the customer *might* want.'[5]

Generative learning, unlike adaptive learning, requires new ways of looking at the world, whether in understanding customers or in understanding how to better manage a business. For years, US manufacturers sought competitive advantage in aggressive controls on inventories, incentives against overproduction, and rigid adherence to production forecasts. Despite these incentives, their performance was eventually eclipsed by Japanese firms who saw the challenges of manufacturing differently. They realized that eliminating delays in the production process was the key to reducing instability and improving cost, productivity, and service. They worked to build networks of relationships with trusted suppliers and to redesign physical production processes so as to reduce delays in materials procurement, production set up, and in-process inventory – a much higher-leverage approach to improving both cost and customer loyalty.

As Boston Consulting Group's George Stalk has observed, the Japanese saw the significance of delays because they saw the process of order entry, production scheduling, materials procurement, production, and distribution *as an integrated system.* 'What distorts the system so badly is time,' observed Stalk – the multiple delays between events and responses. 'These distortions reverberate throughout the system, producing disruptions, waste, and inefficiency.'[6] Generative learning requires seeing the systems that control events. When we fail to grasp the systemic source of problems, we are left to 'push on' symptoms rather than eliminate underlying causes. The best we can ever do is adaptive learning.

The leader's new work

'I talk with people all over the country about learning organizations, and the response is always very positive,' says William O'Brien, CEO of the Hanover Insurance companies. 'If this type of organization is so widely preferred, why don't people create such organizations? I think the answer is leadership. People have no real comprehension of the type of commitment it requires to build such an organization.'[7]

Our traditional view of leaders – as special people who set the direction, make the key decisions, and energize the troops – is deeply rooted in an individualistic and nonsystemic worldview. Especially in the West, leaders are *heroes* – great men (and occasionally women) who rise to the fore in times of crisis. So long as such myths prevail, they reinforce a focus on short-term events and charismatic heroes rather than on systemic forces and collective learning.

Leadership in learning organizations centers on subtler and ultimately more important work. In a learning organization, leaders' roles differ dramatically from that of the charismatic decision maker. Leaders are designers, teachers, and stewards. These roles require new skills: the ability to build shared vision, to bring to the surface and challenge prevailing mental models, and to foster more systemic patterns of thinking. In short, leaders in learning organizations are responsible for *building organizations* where people are continually expanding their capabilities to shape their future – that is, leaders are responsible for learning.

Creative tension: the integrating principle

Leadership in a learning organization starts with the principle of creative tension.[8] Creative tension comes from seeing clearly where we want to be, our 'vision,' and telling the truth about where we are, our 'current reality.' The gap between the two generates a natural tension (see Figure 1).

Creative tension can be resolved in two basic ways: by raising current reality toward the vision, or by lowering the vision toward current reality. Individuals, groups, and organizations who learn how to work with creative tension learn how to use the energy it generates to move reality more reliably toward their visions.

The principle of creative tension has long been recognized by leaders. Martin Luther King, Jr, once said, 'Just as Socrates felt that it was necessary to create a tension in the mind, so that individuals could rise from the bondage of myths and half truths . . . so must we . . . create the kind of tension in society that will help men rise from the dark depths of prejudice and racism.'[9]

Without vision there is no creative tension. Creative tension cannot be generated from current reality alone. All the analysis in the world will never generate a vision. Many who are otherwise qualified to lead fail to do so because they try to substitute analysis for vision. They believe that, if only people understood current reality, they would surely feel the

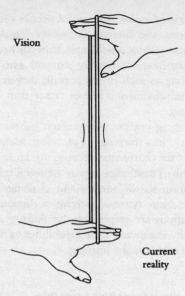

Vision

Current
reality

Figure 1. The principle of creative tension

motivation to change. They are then disappointed to discover that people 'resist' the personal and organizational changes that must be made to alter reality. What they never grasp is that the natural energy for changing reality comes from holding a picture of what might be that is more important to people than what is.

But creative tension cannot be generated from vision alone; it demands an accurate picture of current reality as well. Just as King had a dream, so too did he continually strive to 'dramatize the shameful conditions' of racism and prejudice so that they could no longer be ignored. Vision without an understanding of current reality will more likely foster cynicism than creativity. The principle of creative tension teaches that *an accurate picture of current reality is just as important as a compelling picture of a desired future.*

Leading through creative tension is different than solving problems. In problem solving, the energy for change comes from attempting to get away from an aspect of current reality that is undesirable. With creative tension, the energy for change comes from the vision, from what we want to create, juxtaposed with current reality. While the distinction may seem small, the consequences are not. Many people and organizations find themselves motivated to change only when their problems are bad enough to cause them to change. This works for a while, but the change process runs out of steam as soon as the problems driving the change become less pressing. With problem solving, the motivation for change is extrinsic. With creative tension, the motivation is intrinsic. This distinction mirrors the distinction between adaptive and generative learning.

New roles

The traditional authoritarian image of the leader as 'the boss calling the shots' has been recognized as oversimplified and inadequate for some time. According to Edgar Schein, 'Leadership is intertwined with culture formation.' Building an organization's culture and shaping its evolution is the 'unique and essential function' of leadership.[10] In a learning organization, the critical roles of leadership – designer, teacher, and steward – have antecedents in the ways leaders have contributed to building organizations in the past. But each role takes on new meaning in the learning organization and, as will be seen in the following sections, demands new skills and tools.

Leader as designer

Imagine that your organization is an ocean liner and that you are 'the leader.' What is your role?

I have asked this question of groups of managers many times. The most common answer, not surprisingly, is 'the captain.' Others say, 'The navigator, setting the direction.' Still others say, 'The helmsman, actually controlling the direction,' or, 'The engineer down there stoking the fire, providing energy,' or, 'The social director, making sure everybody's enrolled, involved, and communicating.' While these are legitimate leadership roles, there is another which, in many ways, eclipses them all in importance. Yet rarely does anyone mention it.

The neglected leadership role is the *designer* of the ship. No one has a more sweeping influence than the designer. What good does it do for the captain to say, 'Turn starboard 30 degrees,' when the designer has built a rudder that will only turn to port, or which takes six hours to turn to starboard? It's fruitless to be the leader in an organization that is poorly designed.

The functions of design, or what some have called 'social architecture,' are rarely visible; they take place behind the scenes. The consequences that appear today are the result of work done long in the past, and work today will show its benefits far in the future. Those who aspire to lead out of a desire to control, or gain fame, or simply to be at the center of the action, will find little to attract them to the quiet design work of leadership.

But what, specifically, is involved in organizational design? 'Organization design is widely misconstrued as moving around boxes and lines,' says Hanover's O'Brien. 'The first task of organization design concerns designing the governing ideas of purpose, vision, and core values by which people will live.' Few acts of leadership have a more enduring impact on an organization than building a foundation of purpose and core values.

In 1982, Johnson & Johnson found itself facing a corporate nightmare when bottles of its best-selling Tylenol were tampered with, resulting in several deaths. The corporation's immediate response was to pull all Tylenol off the shelves of retail outlets. Thirty-one million capsules were destroyed, even though they were tested and found safe. Although the immediate cost was significant, no other action was possible given the firm's credo. Authored almost forty years earlier by president Robert Wood Johnson, Johnson & Johnson's credo states that permanent success is possible only when modern industry realizes that:
– service to its customers comes first;
– service to its employees and management comes second;
– service to the community comes third; and
– service to its stockholders, last.

Such statements might seem like motherhood and apple pie to those who have not seen the way a clear sense of purpose and values can affect key business decisions. Johnson & Johnson's crisis management in this case was based on that credo. It was simple, it was right, and it worked.

If governing ideas constitute the first design task of leadership, the second design task involves the policies, strategies, and structures that translate guiding ideas into business decisions. Leadership theorist Philip Selznick calls policy and structure the 'institutional embodiment of purpose.'[11] 'Policy making (the rules that guide decisions) ought to be separated from decision making,' says Jay Forrester.[12] 'Otherwise, short-term pressures will usurp time from policy creation.'

Traditionally, writers like Selznick and Forrester have tended to see policy making and implementation as the work of a small number of senior managers. But that view is changing. Both the dynamic business environment and the mandate of the learning organization to engage people at all levels now make it clear that this second design task is more subtle.

Henry Mintzberg has argued that strategy is less a rational plan arrived at in the abstract and implemented throughout the organization than an 'emergent phenomenon.' Successful organizations 'craft strategy' according to Mintzberg, as they continually learn about shifting business conditions and balance what is desired and what is possible.[13] The key is not getting the right strategy but fostering strategic thinking. 'The choice of individual action is only part of . . . the policymaker's need,' according to Mason and Mitroff.[14] 'More important is the need to achieve insight into the nature of the complexity and to formulate concepts and world views for coping with it.'

Behind appropriate policies, strategies, and structures are effective learning processes; their creation is the third key design responsibility in learning organizations. This does not absolve senior managers of their strategic responsibilities. Actually, it deepens and extends those responsibilities. Now, they are not only responsible for ensuring that an organization have well-developed strategies and policies, but also for ensuring that processes exist whereby these are continually improved.

In the early 1970s, Shell was the weakest of the big seven oil companies. Today, Shell and Exxon are arguably the strongest, both in size and financial health. Shell's ascendance began with frustration. Around 1971 members of Shell's 'Group Planning' in London began to foresee dramatic change and unpredictability in world oil markets. However, it proved impossible to persuade managers that the stable world of steady growth in oil demand and supply they had known for twenty years was about to change. Despite brilliant analysis and artful presentation, Shell's planners realized, in the words of Pierre Wack, that they 'had failed to change behavior in much of the Shell organization.'[15] Progress would probably have ended there, had the frustration not given way to a radically new view of corporate planning.

As they pondered this failure, the planners' view of their basic task shifted: 'We no longer saw our task as producing a documented view of the future business environment five or ten years ahead. Our real target was the microcosm (the 'mental model') of our decision makers.' Only when the planners reconceptualized their basic task as fostering learning rather than devising plans did their insights begin to have an impact. The initial tool used was 'scenario analysis,' through which planners encouraged operating managers to think through how they would manage in the future under different possible scenarios. It mattered not that the managers believed the planners' scenarios absolutely, only that they became engaged in ferreting out the implications. In this way, Shell's planners conditioned managers to be mentally prepared for a shift from low prices to high prices and from stability to instability. The results were significant. When OPEC became a reality, Shell quickly responded by increasing local operating company control (to enhance maneuverability in the new political environment), building buffer stocks, and accelerating development of non-OPEC sources – actions that its competitors took much more slowly or not at all.

Somewhat inadvertently, Shell planners had discovered the leverage of designing institutional learning processes, whereby, in the words of former planning director de Geus, 'Management teams change their shared mental models of their company, their markets, and their competitors.'[16] Since then, 'planning as learning' has become a byword at Shell, and Group Planning has continually sought out new learning tools that can be integrated into the planning process. Some of these are described below.

Leader as teacher

'The first responsibility of a leader,' writes retired Herman Miller CEO Max de Pree, 'is to define reality.'[17] Much of the leverage leaders can actually exert lies in helping people achieve more accurate, more insightful, and more *empowering* views of reality.

Leader as teacher does *not* mean leader as authoritarian expert whose job it is to teach people the 'correct' view of reality. Rather, it is about helping everyone in the organization, oneself included, to gain more insightful views of current reality. This is in line with a popular emerging view of leaders as coaches, guides, or facilitators.[18] In learning organizations, this teaching role is developed further by virtue of explicit attention to people's mental models and by the influence of the systems perspective.

The role of leader as teacher starts with bringing to the surface people's mental models of important issues. No one carries an organization, a market, or a state of technology in his or her head. What we carry in our heads are assumptions. These mental pictures of how the world works have a significant influence on how we perceive problems and opportunities, identify courses of action, and make choices.

One reason that mental models are so deeply entrenched is that they are largely tacit. Ian Mitroff, in his study of General Motors, argues that an assumption that prevailed for years was that, in the United States, 'Cars are status symbols. Styling is therefore more important than quality.'[19] The Detroit automakers didn't say, 'We have a *mental model* that all people care about is styling.' Few actual managers would even say publicly that all people care about is styling. So long as the view remained unexpressed, there was little possibility of challenging its validity or forming more accurate assumptions.

But working with mental models goes beyond revealing hidden assumptions. 'Reality,' as perceived by most people in most organizations, means pressures that must be borne, crises that must be reacted to, and limitations that must be accepted. Leaders as teachers help people *restructure their views of reality* to see beyond the superficial conditions and events into the underlying causes of problems – and therefore to see new possibilities for shaping the future.

Specifically, leaders can influence people to view reality at three distinct levels: events, patterns of behavior, and systemic structure.

Systemic structure
(Generative)
↓
Patterns of behavior
(Responsive)
↓
Events
(Reactive)

The key question becomes *where do leaders predominantly focus their own and their organization's attention?*

Contemporary society focuses predominantly on events. The media reinforces this perspective, with almost exclusive attention to short-term, dramatic events. This focus leads naturally to explaining what happens in terms of those events: 'The Dow Jones average went up sixteen points because high fourth-quarter profits were announced yesterday.'

Pattern-of-behavior explanations are rarer, in contemporary culture, than event explanations, but they do occur. 'Trend analysis' is an example of seeing patterns of behavior. A good editorial that interprets a set of current events in the context of long-term historical changes is another example. Systemic, structural explanations go even further by addressing the question, 'What causes the patterns of behavior?'

In some sense, all three levels of explanation are equally true. But their usefulness is quite different. Event explanations – who did what to whom – doom their holders to a reactive stance toward change. Pattern-of-behavior explanations focus on identifying long-term trends and assessing their implications. They at least suggest how, over time, we can respond to shifting conditions. Structural explanations are the most powerful. Only they address the underlying causes of behavior at a level such that patterns of behavior can be changed.

By and large, leaders of our current institutions focus their attention on events and patterns of behavior, and, under their influence, their organizations do likewise. That is why contemporary organizations are predominantly reactive, or at best responsive – rarely generative. On the other hand, leaders in learning organizations pay attention to all three levels, but focus especially on systemic structure; largely by example, they teach people throughout the organization to do likewise.

Leader as steward

This is the subtlest role of leadership. Unlike the roles of designer and teacher, it is almost solely a matter of attitude. It is an attitude critical to learning organizations.

While stewardship has long been recognized as an aspect of leadership, its source is still not widely understood. I believe Robert Greenleaf came closest to explaining real stewardship, in his seminal book *Servant Leadership*.[20] There, Greenleaf argues that 'The servant leader *is* servant first . . . It begins with the natural feeling that one wants to serve, to serve *first*. This conscious choice brings one to aspire to lead. That person is sharply different from one who is leader first, perhaps because of the need to assuage an unusual power drive or to acquire material possessions.'

Leaders' sense of stewardship operates on two levels: stewardship for the people they lead and stewardship for the larger purpose or mission that underlies the enterprise. The first type arises from a keen appreciation of the impact one's leadership can have on others. People can suffer economically, emotionally, and spiritually under inept leadership. If anything, people in a learning organization are more vulnerable because of their commitment and sense of shared ownership. Appreciating this naturally instills a sense of responsibility in leaders. The second type of stewardship arises from a leader's sense of personal purpose and commitment to the organization's larger mission. People's natural impulse to learn is unleashed when they are engaged in an endeavor they consider worthy of their fullest commitment. Or, as Lawrence Miller puts it, 'Achieving return on equity does not, as a goal, mobilize the most noble forces of our soul.'[21]

Leaders engaged in building learning organizations naturally feel part of a larger purpose that goes beyond their organization. They are part of changing the way businesses operate, not from a vague philanthropic urge, but from a conviction that their efforts will produce more productive organizations, capable of achieving higher levels of organizational success and personal satisfaction than more traditional organizations. Their sense of stewardship was succinctly captured by George Bernard Shaw when he said,

This is the true joy in life, the being used for a purpose you consider a mighty one, the being a force of nature rather than a feverish, selfish clod of ailments and grievances complaining that the world will not devote itself to making you happy.

New skills

New leadership roles require new leadership skills. These skills can only be developed, in my judgment, through a lifelong commitment. It is not enough for one or two individuals to develop these skills. They must be distributed widely throughout the organization. This is one reason that understanding the *disciplines* of a learning organization is so important. These disciplines embody the principles and practices that can widely foster leadership development.

Three critical areas of skills (disciplines) are building shared vision, surfacing and challenging mental models, and engaging in systems thinking.[22]

Building shared vision

How do individual visions come together to create shared visions? A useful metaphor is the hologram, the three-dimensional image created by interacting light sources.

If you cut a photograph in half, each half shows only part of the whole image. But if you divide a hologram, each part, no matter how small, shows the whole image intact. Likewise, when a group of people come to share a vision for an organization, each person sees an individual picture of the organization at its best. Each shares responsibility for the whole, not just for one piece. But the component pieces of the hologram are not identical. Each represents the whole image from a different point of view. It's something like poking holes in a window shade; each hole offers a unique angle for viewing the whole image. So, too, is each individual's vision unique.

When you add up the pieces of a hologram, something interesting happens. The image becomes more intense, more lifelike. When more people come to share a vision, the vision becomes more real in the sense of a mental reality that people can truly imagine achieving. They now have partners, co-creators; the vision no longer rests on their shoulders alone. Early on, when they are nurturing an individual vision, people may say it is 'my vision.' But, as the shared vision develops, it becomes both 'my vision' and 'our vision.'

The skills involved in building shared vision include the following:

– *Encouraging personal vision.* Shared visions emerge from personal visions. It is not that people only care about their own self-interest – in fact, people's values usually include dimensions that concern family, organiz- ation, community, and even the world. Rather, it is that people's capacity for caring is *personal.*

– *Communicating and asking for support.* Leaders must be willing to continually share their own vision, rather than being the official representative of the corporate vision. They also must be prepared to ask, 'Is this vision worthy of your commitment?' This can be difficult for a person used to setting goals and presuming compliance.

– *Visioning as an ongoing process.* Building shared vision is a never-ending process. At any one point there will be a particular image of the future that is predominant, but that image will evolve. Today, too many managers want to dispense with the 'vision business' by going off and writing the Official Vision Statement. Such statements almost always lack the vitality, freshness, and excitement of a genuine vision that comes from people asking, 'What do we really want to achieve?'

– *Blending extrinsic and intrinsic visions.* Many energizing visions are extrinsic – that is, they focus on achieving something relative to an outsider, such as a competitor. But a goal that is limited to defeating an opponent can, once the vision is achieved, easily become a defensive posture. In contrast, intrinsic goals like creating a new type of product, taking an established product to a new level, or setting a new standard for customer satisfaction can call forth a new level of creativity and innovation. Intrinsic and extrinsic visions need to coexist; a vision solely predicated on defeating an adversary will eventually weaken an organization.

– *Distinguishing positive from negative visions.* Many organizations only truly pull together when their survival is threatened. Similarly, most social move- ments aim at eliminating what people don't want: for example, anti-drugs, anti-smoking, or anti-nuclear arms movements. Negative visions carry a subtle message of powerlessness: people will only pull together when there is sufficient threat. Negative visions also tend to be short term. Two funda- mental sources of energy can motivate organizations: fear and aspiration.

Fear, the energy source behind negative visions, can produce extraordinary changes in short periods, but aspiration endures as a continuing source of learning and growth.

Surfacing and testing mental models

Many of the best ideas in organizations never get put into practice. One reason is that new insights and initiatives often conflict with established mental models. The leadership task of challenging assumptions without invoking defensiveness requires reflection and inquiry skills possessed by few leaders in traditional controlling organizations.[23]

– *Seeing leaps of abstraction.* Our minds literally move at lightning speed. Ironically, this often slows our learning, because we leap to generalizations so quickly that we never think to test them. We then confuse our generalizations with the observable data upon which they are based, treating the generalizations *as if they were data.* The frustrated sales rep reports to the home office that 'customers don't really care about quality, price is what matters,' when what actually happened was that three consecutive large customers refused to place an order unless a larger discount was offered. The sales rep treats her generalization, 'customers care only about price,' as if it were absolute fact rather than an assumption (very likely an assumption reflecting her own views of customers and the market). This thwarts future learning because she starts to focus on how to offer attractive discounts rather than probing behind the customers' statements. For example, the customers may have been so disgruntled with the firm's delivery or customer service that they are unwilling to purchase again without larger discounts.

– *Balancing inquiry and advocacy.* Most managers are skilled at articulating their views and presenting them persuasively. While important, advocacy skills can become counterproductive as managers rise in responsibility and confront increasingly complex issues that require collaborative learning among different, equally knowledgeable people. Leaders in learning organizations need to have both inquiry *and* advocacy skills.[24]

Specifically, when advocating a view, they need to be able to:
– explain the reasoning and data that led to their view;
– encourage others to test their view (e.g., Do you see gaps in my reasoning? Do you disagree with the data upon which my view is based?); and
– encourage others to provide different views (e.g., Do you have either different data, different conclusions, or both?).

When inquiring into another's view, they need to:

– actively seek to understand the other's view, rather than simply restating their own view and how it differs from the other's view; and
– make their attributions about the other and the other's view explicit (e.g., Based on your statement that . . . ; I am assuming that you believe . . . ; Am I representing your views fairly?).

If they reach an impasse (others no longer appear open to inquiry), they need to:
– ask what data or logic might unfreeze the impasse, or if an experiment (or some other inquiry) might be designed to provide new information.
– *Distinguishing espoused theory from theory in use.* We all like to think that we hold certain views, but often our actions reveal deeper views. For example, I may proclaim that people are trustworthy, but never lend friends money and jealously guard my possessions. Obviously, my deeper mental model (my theory in use) differs from my espoused theory. Recognizing gaps between espoused views and theories in use (which often requires the help of others) can be pivotal to deeper learning.
– *Recognizing and defusing defensive routines.* As one CEO in our research program puts it, 'Nobody ever talks about an issue at the 8:00 business meeting exactly the same way they talk about it at home that evening or over drinks at the end of the day.' The reason is what Chris Argyris calls 'defensive routines,' entrenched habits used to protect ourselves from the embarrassment and threat that come with exposing our thinking. For most of us, such defenses began to build early in life in response to pressures to have the right answers in school or at home. Organizations add new levels of performance anxiety and thereby amplify and exacerbate this defensiveness. Ironically, this makes it even more difficult to expose hidden mental models, and thereby lessens learning.

The first challenge is to recognize defensive routines, then to inquire into their operation. Those who are best at revealing and defusing defensive routines operate with a high degree of self-disclosure regarding their own defensiveness (e.g., I notice that I am feeling uneasy about how this conversation is going. Perhaps I don't understand it or it is threatening to me in ways I don't yet see. Can you help me see this better?).

Systems thinking

We all know that leaders should help people see the big picture. But the actual skills whereby leaders are supposed to achieve this are not well understood. In my experience, successful leaders often *are* 'systems thinkers' to a considerable extent. They focus less on day-to-day events and more on underlying trends and forces of change. But they do this almost completely intuitively. The consequence is that they are often unable to explain their intuitions to others and feel frustrated that others cannot see the world the way they do.

One of the most significant developments in management science today is the gradual coalescence of managerial systems thinking as a field of study and practice. This field suggests some key skills for future leaders:

– *Seeing interrelationships, not things, and processes, not snapshots.* Most of us have been conditioned throughout our lives to focus on things and to see the world in static images. This leads us to linear explanations of systemic phenomenon. For instance, in an arms race each party is convinced that the other is *the cause* of problems. They react to each new move as an isolated event, not as part of a process. So long as they fail to see the interrelationships of these actions, they are trapped.

– *Moving beyond blame.* We tend to blame each other or outside circumstances for our problems. But it is poorly designed systems, not incompetent or unmotivated individuals, that cause most organizational problems. Systems thinking shows us that there is no outside – that you and the cause of your problems are part of a single system.

– *Distinguishing detail complexity from dynamic complexity.* Some types of complexity are more important strategically than others. Detail complexity arises when there are many variables. Dynamic complexity arises when cause and effect are distant in time and space, and when the consequences over time of interventions are subtle and not obvious to many participants in the system. The leverage in most management situations lies in understanding dynamic complexity, not detail complexity.

– *Focusing on areas of high leverage.* Some have called systems thinking the 'new dismal science' because it teaches that most obvious solutions don't work – at best, they improve matters in the short run, only to make things worse in the long run. But there is another side to the story. Systems thinking also shows that small, well-focused actions can produce significant, enduring improvements, if they are in the right place. Systems thinkers refer to this idea as the principle of 'leverage.' Tackling a difficult problem is often a matter of seeing where the high leverage lies, where a change – with a minimum of effort – would lead to lasting, significant improvement.

– *Avoiding symptomatic solutions.* The pressures to intervene in management systems that are going awry can be overwhelming. Unfortunately, given the linear thinking that predominates in most organizations, interventions usually focus on symptomatic fixes, not underlying causes. This results in only temporary relief, and it tends to create still more pressures later on for further, low-leverage intervention. If leaders acquiesce to these pressures, they can be sucked into an endless spiral of increasing intervention. Sometimes the most difficult leadership acts are to refrain from intervening through popular quick fixes and to keep the pressure on everyone to identify more enduring solutions.

While leaders who can articulate systemic explanations are rare, those who *can* will leave their stamp on an organization. One person who had this gift was Bill Gore, the founder and long-time CEO of W. L. Gore and Associates (makers of Gore-Tex and other synthetic fiber products). Bill Gore was adept at telling stories that showed how the organization's core values of freedom and individual responsibility required particular operating policies. He was proud of his egalitarian organization, in which there were (and still are) no 'employees,' only 'associates,' all of whom own shares in the company and participate in its management. At one talk, he explained the company's policy of controlled growth: 'Our limitation is not financial resources. Our limitation is the rate at which we can bring in new associates. Our experience has been that if we try to bring in more than a 25 percent per year increase, we begin to bog down. Twenty-five percent per year growth is a real limitation; you can do much better than that with an authoritarian organization.' As Gore tells the story, one of the associates, Esther Baum, went home after this talk and reported the limitation to her husband. As it happened, he was an astronomer and mathematician at Lowell Observatory. He said, 'That's a very interesting figure.' He took out a pencil and paper and calculated and said, 'Do you realize that in only fifty-seven and a half years, everyone in the world will be working for Gore?'

Through this story, Gore explains the systemic rationale behind a key policy, limited growth rate – a policy that undoubtedly caused a lot of stress in the organization. He suggests that, at larger rates of growth, the adverse effects of attempting to integrate too many new people too rapidly would begin to dominate. (This is the 'limits to growth' systems archetype explained below.) The story also reaffirms the organization's commitment to creating a unique environment for its associates and illustrates the types of sacrifices that the firm is prepared to make in order to remain true to its vision. The last part of the story shows that, despite the self-imposed limit, the company is still very much a growth company.

The consequences of leaders who lack systems thinking skills can be devastating. Many charismatic leaders manage almost exclusively at the level of events. They deal in visions and in crises, and little in between. Under their leadership, an organization hurtles from crisis to crisis. Eventually, the worldview of people in the organization becomes dominated by events and reactiveness. Many, especially those who are deeply committed, become burned out. Eventually, cynicism comes to pervade the organization. People have no control over their time, let alone their destiny.

Similar problems arise with the 'visionary strategist,' the leader with vision who sees both patterns of change and events. This leader is better prepared to manage change. He or she can explain strategies in terms of emerging trends, and thereby foster a climate that is less reactive. But such leaders still impart a responsive orientation rather than a generative one.

Many talented leaders have rich, highly systemic intuitions but cannot explain those intuitions to others. Ironically, they often end up being authoritarian leaders, even if they don't want to, because only they see the decisions that need to be made. They are unable to conceptualize their strategic insights so that these can become public knowledge, open to challenge and further improvement.

New tools

Developing the skills described above requires new tools – tools that will enhance leaders' conceptual abilities and foster communication and collaborative inquiry. What follows is a sampling of tools starting to find use in learning organizations.

Systems archetypes

One of the insights of the budding, managerial systems-thinking field is that certain types of systemic structures recur again and again. Countless systems grow for a period, then encounter problems and cease to grow (or even collapse) well before they have reached intrinsic limits to growth. Many other systems get locked in runaway vicious spirals where every actor has to run faster and faster to stay in the same place. Still others lure individual actors into doing what seems right locally, yet which eventually causes suffering for all.[25]

Some of the system archetypes that have the broadest relevance include:
– *Balancing process with delay.* In this archetype, decision makers fail to appreciate the time delays involved as they move toward a goal. As a result, they overshoot the goal and may even produce recurring cycles. Classic example: Real estate developers who keep starting new projects until the

market has gone soft, by which time an eventual glut is guaranteed by the properties still under construction.

– *Limits to growth*. A reinforcing cycle of growth grinds to a halt, and may even reverse itself, as limits are approached. The limits can be resource constraints, or external or internal responses to growth. Classic examples: Product life cycles that peak prematurely due to poor quality or service, the growth and decline of communication in a management team, and the spread of a new movement.

– *Shifting the burden*. A short-term 'solution' is used to correct a problem, with seemingly happy immediate results. As this correction is used more and more, fundamental long-term corrective measures are used less. Over time, the mechanisms of the fundamental solution may atrophy or become disabled, leading to even greater reliance on the symptomatic solution. Classic example: Using corporate human resource staff to solve local personnel problems, thereby keeping managers from developing their own interpersonal skills.

– *Eroding goals*. When all else fails, lower your standards. This is like 'shifting the burden,' except that the short-term solution involves letting a fundamental goal, such as quality standards or employee morale standards, atrophy. Classic example: A company that responds to delivery problems by continually upping its quoted delivery times.

– *Escalation*. Two people or two organizations, who each see their welfare as depending on a relative advantage over the other, continually react to the other's advances. Whenever one side gets ahead, the other is threatened, leading it to act more aggressively to reestablish its advantage, which threatens the first, and so on. Classic examples: Arms race, gang warfare, price wars.

– *Tragedy of the commons*.[26] Individuals keep intensifying their use of a commonly available but limited resource until all individuals start to experience severely diminishing returns. Classic examples: Sheepherders who keep increasing their flocks until they overgraze the common pasture; divisions in a firm that share a common salesforce and compete for the use of sales reps by upping their sales targets, until the salesforce burns out from overextension.

– *Growth and underinvestment*. Rapid growth approaches a limit that could be eliminated or pushed into the future, but only by aggressive investment in physical and human capacity. Eroding goals or standards cause investment that is too weak, or too slow, and customers get increasingly unhappy, slowing demand growth and thereby making the needed investment (apparently) unnecessary or impossible. Classic example: Countless once-successful growth firms that allowed product or service quality to erode, and were unable to generate enough revenues to invest in remedies.

The Archetype template is a specific tool that is helping managers identify archetypes operating in their own strategic areas (see Figure 2).[27] The template shows the basic structural form of the archetype but lets managers fill in the variables of their own situation. For example, the shifting the burden template involves two balancing processes ('B') that compete for control of a problem symptom. The upper, symptomatic solution provides a short-term fix that will make the problem symptom go away for a while. The lower, fundamental solution provides a more enduring solution. The side effect feedback ('R') around the outside of the diagram identifies unintended exacerbating effects of the symptomatic solution, which, over time, make it more and more difficult to invoke the fundamental solution.

Several years ago, a team of managers from a leading consumer goods

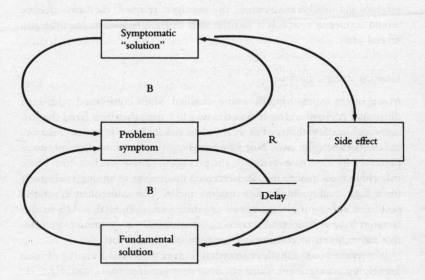

In the 'shifting the burden' template, two balancing processes (B) compete for control of a problem symptom. Both solutions affect the symptom, but only the fundamental solution treats the cause. The symptomatic 'solution' creates the additional side effect (R) of deferring the fundamental solution, making it harder and harder to achieve.

Figure 2. 'Shifting the burden' archetype template

producer used the shifting the burden archetype in a revealing way. The problem they focused on was financial stress, which could be dealt with in two different ways: by running marketing promotions (the symptomatic solution) or by product innovation (the fundamental solution). Marketing promotions were fast. The company was expert in their design and implementation. The results were highly predictable. Product innovation was slow and much less predictable, and the company had a history over the past ten years of product-innovation mismanagement. Yet only through innovation could they retain a leadership position in their industry, which had slid over the past ten to twenty years. What the managers saw clearly was that the more skillful they became at promotions, the more they shifted the burden away from product innovation. But what really struck home was when one member identified the unintended side effect: the last three CEOs had all come from the advertising function, which had become the politically dominant function in the corporation, thereby institutionalizing the symptomatic solution. Unless the political values shifted back toward product and process innovation, the managers realized, the firm's decline would accelerate – which is just the shift that has happened over the past several years.

Charting strategic dilemmas

Management teams typically come unglued when confronted with core dilemmas. A classic example was the way US manufacturers faced the low cost–high quality choice. For years, most assumed that it was necessary to choose between the two. Not surprisingly, given the short-term pressures perceived by most managements, the prevailing choice was low cost. Firms that chose high quality usually perceived themselves as aiming exclusively for a high quality, high price market niche. The consequences of this perceived either–or choice have been disastrous, even fatal, as US manufacturers have encountered increasing international competition from firms that have chosen to consistently improve quality *and* cost.

In a recent book, Charles Hampden-Turner presented a variety of tools for helping management teams confront strategic dilemmas creatively.[28] He summarizes the process in seven steps:

– *Eliciting the dilemmas.* Identifying the opposed values that form the 'horns' of the dilemma, for example, cost as opposed to quality, or local initiative as opposed to central coordination and control. Hampden-Turner suggests that humor can be a distinct asset in this process since 'the admission that dilemmas even exist tends to be difficult for some companies.'

– *Mapping*. Locating the opposing values as two axes and helping managers identify where they see themselves, or their organization, along the axes.

– *Processing*. Getting rid of nouns to describe the axes of the dilemma. Present participles formed by adding 'ing' convert rigid nouns into processes that imply movement. For example, central control versus local control becomes 'strengthening national office' and 'growing local initiatives.' This loosens the bound of implied opposition between the two values. For example, it becomes possible to think of 'strengthening national services from which local branches can benefit.'

– *Framing contextualizing*. Further softening the adversarial structure among different values by letting 'each side in turn be the frame or context for the other.' This shifting of the 'figure–ground' relationship undermines any implicit attempts to hold one value as intrinsically superior to the other, and thereby to become mentally closed to creative strategies for continuous improvement of both.

– *Sequencing*. Breaking the hold of static thinking. Very often, values like low cost and high quality appear to be in opposition because we think in terms of a point in time, not in terms of an ongoing process. For example, a strategy of investing in new process technology and developing a new production-floor culture of worker responsibility may take time and money in the near term, yet reap significant long-term financial rewards.

– *Waving/cycling*. Sometimes the strategic path toward improving both values involves cycles where both values will get 'worse' for a time. Yet, at a deeper level, learning is occurring that will cause the next cycle to be at a higher plateau for both values.

– *Synergizing*. Achieving synergy where significant improvement is occurring along all axes of all relevant dilemmas. (This is the ultimate goal, of course.) Synergy, as Hampden-Turner points out, is a uniquely systemic notion, coming from the Greek *syn-ergo* or 'work together.'

'The left-hand column': surfacing mental models

The idea that mental models can dominate business decisions and that these models are often tacit and even contradictory to what people espouse can be very threatening to managers who pride themselves on rationality and judicious decision making. It is important to have tools to help managers discover for themselves how their mental models operate to undermine their own intentions.

One tool that has worked consistently to help managers see their own mental models in action is the 'left-hand column' exercise developed by

Chris Argyris and his colleagues. This tool is especially helpful in showing how we leap from data to generalization without testing the validity of our generalizations.

When working with managers, I start this exercise by selecting a specific situation in which I am interacting with other people in a way that is not working, that is not producing the learning that is needed. I write out a sample of the exchange, with the script on the right-hand side of the page.

The left-hand column: an exercise

Imagine my exchange with a colleague, Bill, after he made a big presentation to our boss on a project we are doing together. I had to miss the presentation, but I've heard that it was poorly received.

Me: How did the presentation go?

Bill: Well, I don't know. It's really too early to say. Besides, we're breaking new ground here.

Me: Well, what do you think we should do? I believe that the issues you were raising are important.

Bill: I'm not so sure. Let's just wait and see what happens.

Me: You may be right, but I think we may need to do more than just wait.

Now, here is what the exchange looks like with my 'left-hand column':

What I'm thinking	What is said
Everyone says the presentation was a bomb.	*Me*: How did the presentation go?
Does he really not know how bad it was? Or is he not willing to face up to it?	*Bill*: Well, I don't know. It's too early to say. Besides, we're breaking new ground here.
	Me: Well, what do you think we should do? I believe that the issues you were raising are important.
He really is afraid to see the truth. If he only had more confidence, he could probably learn from a situation like this.	*Bill*: I'm not so sure. Let's just wait and see what happens.
I can't believe he doesn't realize how disastrous that presentation was to our moving ahead.	*Me*: You may be right, but I think we may need to do more than just wait.
I've got to find some way to light a fire under the guy.	

On the left-hand side, I write what I am thinking but not saying at each stage in the exchange (see sidebar).

The left-hand column exercise not only brings hidden assumptions to the surface, it shows how they influence behavior. In the example, I make two key assumptions about Bill: he lacks confidence and he lacks initiative. Neither may be literally true, but both are evident in my internal dialogue, and both influence the way I handle the situation. Believing that he lacks confidence, I skirt the fact that I've heard the presentation was a bomb. I'm afraid that if I say it directly, he will lose what little confidence he has, or he will see me as unsupportive. So I bring up the subject of the presentation obliquely. When I ask Bill what we should do next, he gives no specific course of action. Believing he lacks initiative, I take this as evidence of his laziness; he is content to do nothing when action is definitely required. I conclude that I will have to manufacture some form of pressure to motivate him, or else I will simply have to take matters into my own hands.

The exercise reveals the elaborate webs of assumptions we weave, within which we become our own victims. Rather than dealing directly with my assumptions about Bill and the situation, we talk around the subject. The reasons for my avoidance are self-evident: I assume that if I raised my doubts, I would provoke a defensive reaction that would only make matters worse. But the price of avoiding the issue is high. Instead of determining how to move forward to resolve our problems, we end our exchange with no clear course of action. My assumptions about Bill's limitations have been reinforced. I resort to a manipulative strategy to move things forward.

The exercise not only reveals the need for skills in surfacing assumptions, but that we are the ones most in need of help. There is no one right way to handle difficult situations like my exchange with Bill, but any productive strategy revolves around a high level of self-disclosure and willingness to have my views challenged. I need to recognize my own leaps of abstraction regarding Bill, share the events and reasoning that are leading to my concern over the project, and be open to Bill's views on both. The skills to carry on such conversations without invoking defensiveness take time to develop. But if both parties in a learning impasse start by doing their own left-hand column exercise and sharing them with each other, it is remarkable how quickly everyone recognizes their contribution to the impasse and progress starts to be made.

Learning at Hanover Insurance

Hanover Insurance has gone from the bottom of the property and liability industry to a position among the top 36 percent of US insurance companies over the past twenty years, largely through the efforts of CEO William O'Brien and his predecessor Jack Adam. The following comments are excerpted from a series of interviews Senge conducted with O'Brien as background for his book.
Senge: Why do you think there is so much change occurring in management and organizations today? Is it primarily because of increased competitive pressures?
O'Brien: That's a factor, but not the most significant factor. The ferment in management will continue until we find models that are more congruent with human nature.

One of the great insights of modern psychology is the hierarchy of human needs. As Maslow expressed this idea, the most basic needs are food and shelter. Then comes belonging. Once these three basic needs are satisfied, people begin to aspire toward self-respect and esteem, and toward self-actualization – the fourth- and fifth-order needs.

Our traditional hierarchical organizations are designed to provide for the first three levels, but not the fourth and fifth. These first three levels are now widely available to members of industrial society, but our organizations do not offer people sufficient opportunities for growth.
Senge: How would you assess Hanover's progress to date?
O'Brien: We have been on a long journey away from a traditional hierarchical culture. The journey began with everyone understanding some guiding ideas about purpose, vision, and values as a basis for participative management. This is a better way to begin building a participative culture than by simply 'letting people in on decision making.' Before there can be meaningful participation, people must share certain values and pictures about where we are trying to go. We discovered that people have a real need to feel that they're part of an enobling mission. But developing shared visions and values is not the end, only the beginning.

Next we had to get beyond mechanical, linear thinking. The essence of our jobs as managers is to deal with 'divergent' problems – problems that have no simple answer. 'Convergent' problems – problems that have a 'right' answer – should be solved locally. Yet we are deeply conditioned to see the world in terms of convergent problems. Most managers try to force-fit simplistic solutions and undermine the potential for learning when divergent problems arise. Since everyone handles the linear issues fairly well, companies that learn how to handle divergent issues will have a great advantage.

The next basic stage in our progression was coming to understand inquiry and advocacy. We learned that real openness is rooted in people's ability to continually inquire into their own thinking. This requires exposing yourself to being wrong – not something that most managers are rewarded for. But learning is very difficult if you cannot look for errors or incompleteness in your own ideas.

What all this builds to is the capability throughout an organization to manage mental models. In a locally controlled organization, you have the fundamental challenge of learning how to help people make good decisions without coercing them into making *particular* decisions. By managing mental models, we create 'self-concluding' decisions – decisions that people come to themselves – which will result in deeper conviction, better implementation, and the ability to make better adjustments when the situation changes.

Senge: What concrete steps can top managers take to begin moving toward learning organizations?

O'Brien: Look at the signals you send through the organization. For example, one critical signal is how you spend your time. It's hard to build a learning organization if people are unable to take the time to think through important matters. I rarely set up an appointment for less than one hour. If the subject is not worth an hour, it shouldn't be on my calendar.

Senge: Why is this so hard for so many managers?

O'Brien: It comes back to what you believe about the nature of your work. The authoritarian manager has a 'chain gang' mental model: 'The speed of the boss is the speed of the gang. I've got to keep things moving fast, because I've got to keep people working.' In a learning organization, the manager shoulders an almost sacred responsibility to create conditions that enable people to have happy and productive lives. If you understand the effects the ideas we are discussing can have on the lives of people in your organization, you will take the time.

Learning laboratories: practice fields for management teams

One of the most promising new tools is the learning laboratory or 'microworld': constructed microcosms of real-life settings in which management teams can learn how to learn together.

The rationale behind learning laboratories can best be explained by analogy. Although most management teams have great difficulty learning (enhancing their collective intelligence and capacity to create), in other domains team learning is the norm rather than the exception – team sports and the performing arts, for example. Great basketball teams do not start off great. They learn. But the process by which these teams learn is, by and large, absent from modern organizations. The process is a continual movement between practice and performance.

The vision guiding current research in management learning laboratories is to design and construct effective practice fields for management teams. Much remains to be done, but the broad outlines are emerging.

First, since team learning in organizations is an individual-to-individual and individual-to-system phenomenon, learning laboratories must combine meaningful business issues with meaningful interpersonal dynamics. Either alone is incomplete.

Second, the factors that thwart learning about complex business issues must be eliminated in the learning lab. Chief among these is the inability to experience the long-term, systemic consequences of key strategic decisions. We all learn best from experience, but we are unable to experience the consequences of many important organizational decisions.

Learning laboratories remove this constraint through system dynamics simulation games that compress time and space.

Third, new learning skills must be developed. One constraint on learning is the inability of managers to reflect insightfully on their assumptions, and to inquire effectively into each other's assumptions. Both skills can be enhanced in a learning laboratory, where people can practice surfacing assumptions in a low-risk setting. A note of caution: It is far easier to design an entertaining learning laboratory than it is to have an impact on real management practices and firm traditions outside the learning lab. Research on management simulations has shown that they often have greater entertainment value than education value. One of the reasons appears to be that many simulations do not offer deep insights into systemic structures causing business problems. Another reason is that they do not foster new learning skills. Also, there is no connection between experiments in the learning lab and real life experiments. These are significant problems that research on learning laboratory design is now addressing.

Developing leaders and learning organizations

In a recently published retrospective on organization development in the 1980s, Marshall Shashkin and N. Warner Burke observe the return of an emphasis on developing leaders who can develop organizations.[29] They also note Schein's critique that most top executives are not qualified for the task of developing culture.[30] Learning organizations represent a potentially significant evolution of organizational culture. So it should come as no surprise that such organizations will remain a distant vision until the leadership capabilities they demand are developed. 'The 1990s may be the period,' suggest Sashkin and Burke, 'during which organization development and (a new sort of) management development are reconnected.'

I believe that this new sort of management development will focus on the roles, skills, and tools for leadership in learning organizations. Undoubtedly, the ideas offered above are only a rough approximation of this new territory. The sooner we begin seriously exploring the territory, the sooner the initial map can be improved – and the sooner we will realize an age-old vision of leadership:

> The wicked leader is he who the people despise.
> The good leader is he who the people revere.
> The great leader is he who the people say, 'We did it ourselves.'
>
> – Lao Tsu

References

1. P. SENGE, *The Fifth Discipline: The Art and Practice of the Learning Organization*, New York, Doubleday/Currency, 1990
2. A. P. DE GEUS, 'Planning as learning,' *Harvard Business Review*, March–April 1988, pp. 70–74
3. B. DOMAIN, *Fortune*, 3 July 1989, pp. 48–62
4. The distinction between adaptive and generative learning has its roots in the distinction between what Argyris and Schon have called their 'single-loop' learning, in which individuals or groups adjust their behavior relative to fixed goals, norms, and assumptions, and 'double-loop' learning, in which goals, norms, and assumptions, as well as behavior, are open to change (e.g., see C. ARGYRIS and D. SCHON, *Organizational Learning: A Theory-in-Action Perspective*, Reading, Mass., Addison-Wesley, 1978).
5. All unattributed quotes are from personal communications with the author.
6. G. STALK, Jr, 'Time: the next source of competitive advantage,' *Harvard Business Review*, July–August 1988, pp. 41–51
7. SENGE, 1990
8. The principle of creative tension comes from Robert Fritz' work on creativity. See R. FRITZ, *The Path of Least Resistance*, New York, Ballantine, 1989, and *Creating*, New York, Ballantine, 1990.
9. M. L. KING, Jr, 'Letter from Birmingham Jail,' *American Visions*, January–February 1986, pp. 52–9
10. E. SCHEIN, *Organizational Culture and Leadership*, San Francisco, Jossey-Bass, 1985. Similar views have been expressed by many leadership theorists. For example, see: P. SELZNICK, *Leadership in Administration*, New York, Harper & Row, 1957; W. BENNIS and B. NANUS, *Leaders*, New York, Harper & Row, 1985; and N. M. TICHY and M. A. DEVANNA, *The Transformational Leader*, New York, John Wiley & Sons, 1986.
11. SELZNICK, 1957
12. J. W. FORRESTER, 'A new corporate design,' *Sloan Management Review* (formerly *Industrial Management Review*), fall 1965, pp. 5–17
13. See, for example, H. MINTZBERG, 'Crafting strategy,' *Harvard Business Review*, July–August 1987, pp. 66–75
14. R. MASON and I. MITROFF, *Challenging Strategic Planning Assumptions*, New York, John Wiley & Sons, 1981, p. 16
15. P. WACK, 'Scenarios: uncharted waters ahead,' *Harvard Business Review*, September–October 1985, pp. 73–89
16. DE GEUS, 1988
17. M. DE PREE, *Leadership Is an Art*, New York, Doubleday, 1989, p. 9
18. For example, see T. PETERS and N. AUSTIN, *A Passion for Excellence*, New York, Random House, 1985, and J. M. KOUZES and B. Z. POSNER, *The Leadership Challenge*, San Francisco, Jossey-Bass, 1987

19. I. MITROFF, *Break-away Thinking*, New York, John Wiley & Sons, 1988, pp. 66—7
20. R. K. GREENLEAF, *Servant Leadership: A Journey into the Nature of Legitimate Power and Greatness*, New York, Paulist Press, 1977
21. L. MILLER, *American Spirit: Visions of New Corporate Culture*, New York, William Morrow, 1984, p. 15
22. These points are condensed from the practices of the five disciplines examined in SENGE, 1990.
23. The ideas below are based to a considerable extent on the work of Chris Argyris, Donald Schon, and their Action Science colleagues: C. ARGYRIS and D. SCHON, *Organizational Learning: A Theory-in-Action Perspective*, Reading, Mass., Addison-Wesley, 1978; C. ARGYRIS, R. PUTNAM, and D. SMITH, *Action Science*, San Francisco, Jossey-Bass, 1985; C. ARGYRIS, *Strategy, Change, and Defensive Routines*, Boston, Pitman, 1985; and C. ARGYRIS, *Overcoming Organizational Defenses*, Englewood Cliffs, NJ, Prentice-Hall, 1990.
24. I am indebted to Diana Smith for the summary points below.
25. The system archetypes are one of several systems diagraming and communication tools. See D. H. KIM, *Toward Learning Organizations: Integrating Total Quality Control and Systems Thinking*, Cambridge, Mass., MIT Sloan School of Management, Working Paper 3037-89-BPS, June 1989.
26. This archetype is closely associated with the work of ecologist Garrett Hardin, who coined its label: G. HARDIN, 'The tragedy of the commons,' *Science*, 13 December 1968.
27. These templates were originally developed by Jennifer Kemeny, Charles Kiefer, and Michael Goodman of Innovation Associates Inc., Framingham, Mass.
28. C. HAMPDEN-TURNER, *Charting the Corporate Mind*, New York, The Free Press, 1990
29. M. SASHKIN and W. W. BURKE, 'Organization development in the 1980s' and 'An end-of-the-eighties retrospective,' in *Advances in Organization Development*, ed. F. MASARIK, Norwood, NJ, Ablex, 1990
30. E. SCHEIN, 1985

25 G. Morgan

Imaginization: On Spider Plants

From *Imaginization*, Sage, 1994, chapter 4

It's impossible to develop new styles of organization and management while continuing to think in old ways.

As I have suggested, numerous organizations are now facing the challenge of finding more flexible, adaptive forms. Decentralization and a flattening of hierarchies are key priorities. But the influence of old thinking often constrains what can occur.

In this chapter, I offer the image of a spider plant as a way of rethinking organizational design and managerial styles to promote flexible, decentralized modes of operation. I have structured my discussion around an exercise inviting you to think about your organization in these terms. See it as just one example of how we can imaginize alternatives to the mechanical 'blueprints' shaping so much organizational design and find ways of managing multiple decentralized teams, projects, and other organizational units in a controlled yet self-organizing manner.

For many of us, the process of designing a new organizational initiative usually involves reaching for a blank piece of paper and sketching an organization chart. Before we know it, we find ourselves drawing boxes and lines linking people and the activities they are expected to perform. This mapping can prove very useful. But it can also be incredibly limiting, as the lines and boxes become constraints, locking us into linear and rather reductive patterns of thought. As we sketch, we split and shape complex activities into neat and tidy parts, tying the process of organization to a variation of the mechanistic-bureaucratic mode.

To break free, we need to develop new images of organization that can help us imaginize new forms. This is especially important in an era of rapid change, where free-flowing, organic images that have more in common with brains, webs, cells, balloons, bubbles, and umbilical cords are more likely to be relevant than the static blueprints found in typical organization charts.

To illustrate, have you ever thought about your organization as a spider plant (Exhibit 4.1)? If not, you may find it instructive to do so. On the following pages, I invite you to engage in a short exercise using this metaphor. This is followed by a discussion of some of the insights that emerge when managers use the metaphor to gain fresh perspective on the management and design of their organizations. If you are going to do the exercise, I suggest that you do so *before* reading the account that follows. It will be much more meaningful that way!

The spider-plant exercise

Part I

(a) Select an organization for the purpose of this exercise, preferably the one with which you are most involved at this time. If you wish, you can focus on a subunit or department within a larger organization or network of organizations.

Exhibit 4.1   The spider plant

(b) Now, describe the organization or unit as a spider plant. Feel free to let your imagination run wild! What parallels can you find with the image presented in Exhibit 4.1? List them below.

Characteristics of the spider plant   Parallels in my organization

_____   _____

_____   _____

_____   _____

_____   _____

_____   _____

(c) How well does the image fit? Does it grasp the nature of your organization? Does it create any new insights?

_____

Part II
(a) Now use the spider plant to think about how your organization or unit *could* be.

In other words, use the image – interpreted in whatever way you wish – as the basis for a new organizational design. If you had the opportunity to design your organization (or subunit) as a spider plant, how would it be? Use the method of drawing parallels between the spider-plant image and characteristics of the new organization as a means of developing your design.

Spider-plant characteristics   Parallels in the new design

_____   _____

_____   _____

_____   _____

_____   _____

_____   _____

(b) What are the differences between the new organization and the one you described in Part I of this exercise?

Do any new insights for shaping the management process emerge?

I have used variations of this exercise on organizational change projects and in numerous management seminars.

The 'graffiti boards' on pages 520–23 present some typical responses and some creative adaptations of the images that emerge when the possibilities are explored.

Responses to the exercise vary according to the organization or situation one has in mind. If one's managing in a tight, centralized bureaucracy, the image of the spider plant may seem to have little relevance. One may 'push' one's imagination and see that one is working in a large 'pot,' reinterpret the spider plant as a form of hierarchy where the stems or tentacles define lines of control and resource flows, see how the whole system is dependent on power 'in the pot.' But, all in all, the exercise often seems hollow or contrived. It does little more than reinterpret the existing hierarchy.

If, on the other hand, one is working in a more decentralized situation, or in a centralized organization that is trying to launch new initiatives in a more decentralized style, the metaphor resonates much more readily. As reflected in the 'graffiti board' images and quotes, many interesting questions come to mind:

What is the role of the central pot?

How large should it be?

How should 'offshoot' businesses or departments be linked to the pot?

How should the stems or 'umbilical cords' be defined?

How can one use these umbilical cords to create autonomy for decentralized, self-managing units (the offshoots) while securing integration and accountability in the system as a whole?

How can one use the spider plant as a model for managing multiple projects or decentralized teams in a 'hands off' way?

And so on!

If you examine the images and quotations presented on following pages, I think you'll find a storehouse of ideas about how the spider plant can create fresh dialogue and insight about the problems of designing and managing decentralized initiatives.

Here are four key ideas that frequently emerge with managers interested in pursuing the implications of the metaphor.

Idea 1. We must break the constraints set by large 'central pots'

Spider plants begin to spin off tentacles and new offshoots when they outgrow their pots: It's part of the attempt to find new ground in which to grow.

But what do our organizations do when they want to grow?

They usually find a bigger pot!

This is the core dilemma facing so many organizations. They want to grow, but they can't shake free of the idea that they are an integrated organization. Hence the small office grows into a series of offices occupying the whole floor of a building. Eventually, they spread onto three floors. Then the company takes over the whole building. Eventually, the building gets too small, so they move to a larger one. Then growth spills into neighboring offices. The company eventually occupies an 'industrial park,' and so on.

Organizations grow. Then size becomes a barrier to flexibility.

The message of the spider plants is this: Why grow in this way?

Because you can grow large while staying small!

You can grow by replicating yourself in a decentralized fashion. Franchising and retailing systems have mastered the art. But the principle can be applied in other contexts as well.

In times of rapid change, large 'central pots' can be a liability. They tend to be expensive, slow and inflexible. Perhaps there are ways of 'shrinking the pot' by spinning off different elements of one's business, so that they stand as quasi-autonomous units.

Perhaps one can 'spin off' HRD, MIS, and other functional departments into separate businesses with the mandate of generating 75 per cent of their revenues from outside the established organization in five years' time.

Perhaps there are ways of building one's activities around a large number of small, highly differentiated pots, in different regions or different businesses, or of pursuing some of the other ideas presented in the mosaic of images and ideas presented on the graffiti boards.

Try thinking about them and see!

OUR PRESENT ORGANIZATION . .

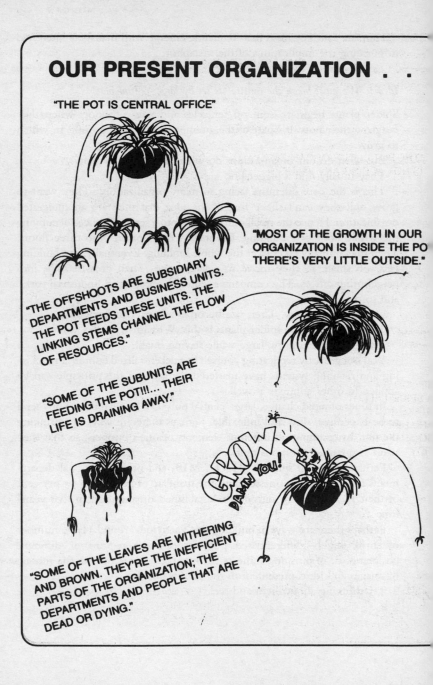

"THE POT IS CENTRAL OFFICE"

"THE OFFSHOOTS ARE SUBSIDIARY DEPARTMENTS AND BUSINESS UNITS. THE POT FEEDS THESE UNITS. THE LINKING STEMS CHANNEL THE FLOW OF RESOURCES."

"MOST OF THE GROWTH IN OUR ORGANIZATION IS INSIDE THE PO THERE'S VERY LITTLE OUTSIDE."

"SOME OF THE SUBUNITS ARE FEEDING THE POT!!!... THEIR LIFE IS DRAINING AWAY."

GROW DAMN YOU!

"SOME OF THE LEAVES ARE WITHERING AND BROWN. THEY'RE THE INEFFICIENT PARTS OF THE ORGANIZATION; THE DEPARTMENTS AND PEOPLE THAT ARE DEAD OR DYING."

. . . AS A SPIDER PLANT

"WE HAVE A NUMBER OF DIFFERENT POTS."

"THE POT IN OUR ORGANIZATION IS NOT ADDING ANY VALUE."

"OUR OFFSHOOTS ARE DANGLING IN MIDAIR. THEY'RE NOT ROOTED. THEY'RE DETACHED FROM REALITY. THEY'RE NOT FULLY LINKED WITH THE CUSTOMERS AND RESOURCES NEEDED FOR SURVIVAL."

WHO FEEDS THE POT?

"IF OUR ORGANIZATION WAS LIKE A SPIDER PLANT, THEY'D DRIVE A STAKE IN THE CENTER OF THE POT AND PROP UP ALL THE OFFSHOOTS SO THAT THE GARDEN IS NEAT AND TIDY."

"THE IMAGE CAN BE USED TO RE-CREATE HIERARCHY OR BREAK INTO NEW THINKING."

DESIGNING OUR ORGANIZATION . . .

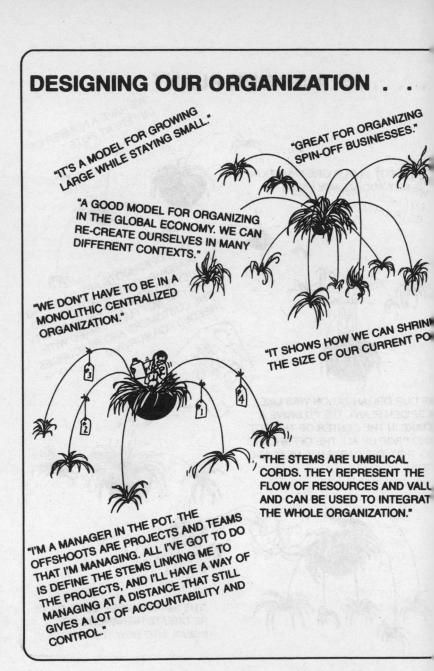

"IT'S A MODEL FOR GROWING LARGE WHILE STAYING SMALL."

"GREAT FOR ORGANIZING SPIN-OFF BUSINESSES."

"A GOOD MODEL FOR ORGANIZING IN THE GLOBAL ECONOMY. WE CAN RE-CREATE OURSELVES IN MANY DIFFERENT CONTEXTS."

"WE DON'T HAVE TO BE IN A MONOLITHIC CENTRALIZED ORGANIZATION."

"IT SHOWS HOW WE CAN SHRIN[K] THE SIZE OF OUR CURRENT PO[...]

"THE STEMS ARE UMBILICAL CORDS. THEY REPRESENT THE FLOW OF RESOURCES AND VALU[...] AND CAN BE USED TO INTEGRAT[E] THE WHOLE ORGANIZATION."

"I'M A MANAGER IN THE POT. THE OFFSHOOTS ARE PROJECTS AND TEAMS THAT I'M MANAGING. ALL I'VE GOT TO DO IS DEFINE THE STEMS LINKING ME TO THE PROJECTS, AND I'LL HAVE A WAY OF MANAGING AT A DISTANCE THAT STILL GIVES A LOT OF ACCOUNTABILITY AND CONTROL."

. . . AS A SPIDER PLANT

"A GREAT IMAGE FOR DESCRIBING AND DESIGNING FRANCHISING SYSTEMS WITH OUTLETS LIKE MCDONALDS, BUT MOST ORGANIZATIONS HAVE TO BE MUCH MORE DIVERSIFIED."

"YOU HAVE TO BUILD PAIN AND PLEASURE INTO THE SPIDER PLANT – THE PAIN OF ACCOUNTABILITY AND THE PLEASURE OF REWARDS AND SUCCESS."

"LET'S GET MORE TEAMS AND PROJECTS OUTSIDE THE POT SO THEY HAVE SPACE TO DEVELOP."

"WE NEED TO THROW MORE FUNCTIONS AND BUSINESSES OUT OF THE POT."

"WHEN THE TIME IS RIGHT, WE CAN SNIP THE STEMS AND LET SELECTED UNITS DEVELOP ON NEW GROUND."

"IT'S DIFFICULT TO KNOW HOW MUCH LATITUDE TO GIVE THE NEW OFFSHOOTS. HOW DEPENDENT SHOULD THEY BE ON THE POT? HOW LONG SHOULD YOU HELP THEM TO SURVIVE OUT THERE BEFORE CUTTING THEM OFF, OR BRINGING THEM BACK IN?"

FROM THIS:

TO THIS:

Idea 2. Successful decentralization depends on the development of good 'umbilical cords'

Umbilical cords are lifelines. As the spider plant reaches out and searches for new ground, it receives nourishment from the mother plant. When it 'roots,' and is able to sustain itself, the cord is no longer necessary.

There is a message for our organizations here.

Many are struggling with processes of decentralization or of spawning new entrepreneurial initiatives. They desperately want to create more flexible, innovative units, but they get hamstrung by traditional patterns of thinking about control and accountability. As a result, the new units get enmeshed in report-writing and rule-following requirements and other hierarchical requirements that make them extensions of the central bureaucracy.

Yet, if those in the central bureaucratic 'pot' could think in terms of 'umbilical cords,' like those of a 'spider plant,' they'd have a means of reconciling the contradictory demands of creating decentralization while sustaining control and accountability.

Decentralization is basically an umbilical cord activity.

Why do organizations want to decentralize? Because they cannot manage from the center. Because they want to create a local presence. Because they want to give local units the power, control, and autonomy that will allow them to flourish in their local niches. Because they want to give space for some kind of self-organizing activity. The whole thrust behind decentralization is to create local nodes of activity that can flourish by tapping local resources, by meeting the needs of customers, by adapting to the variations of local environments, and so on.

The problem is to do this while retaining a measure of central control that prevents the decentralization from becoming an anarchic process. The local units have to be accountable to the center in some way. If you're a franchise producing identical pizzas or hamburgers, or replacing mufflers in cars, this can be achieved bureaucratically, using rules, manuals, and controls to define the 'umbilical cord' in almost every detail. But, if you're in a business or other activity that demands more local initiative and creativity, then the umbilical cords need to be defined more flexibly.

Try thinking about some different situations. For example: You are a factory manager responsible for a manufacturing unit employing autonomous work groups. You want to give the groups autonomy and space to move. You recognize that you can't be a 'hands on' manager exercising close control. How should you design the umbilical cords between you and the work groups? Are you going to impose a degree of uniformity? Or are you going to have a different 'cord' for each group?

You are a project manager responsible for seven separate project teams. How do you define your relationship with each team?

You are the head of a business unit producing and marketing multiple products. What umbilical cords should you develop with the managers responsible for the different units?

You are a chief executive of a company with five different business divisions. How do you define the umbilical cord with each division?

I've witnessed many situations where this kind of umbilical cord thinking has created instant transformations in a manager's ability to focus on key tasks and key relationships. For what could be easier than thinking about management as a 'cord' concept. Typically, managers get overwhelmed by detail and ideas about what they should or should not be delegating and controlling. As a result, it's difficult to see the forest for the trees.

In these circumstances, it is useful to:

Step back and see the spider plant.

See oneself or one's office as the pot.

See one's projects, one's teams, or one's business as the offshoots.

Think about the connecting 'umbilical cords' and what they should look like.

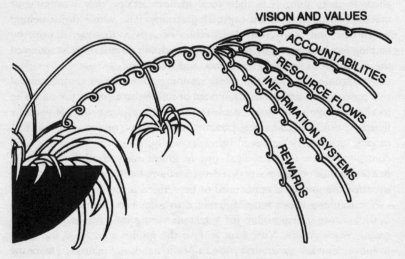

Exhibit 4.2 'Umbilical cords' may have many strands

Think about their different dimensions.

Are the cords one thick, solid strand: a well-defined control system?

Or do they comprise many strands, as illustrated in Exhibit 4.2?

Reflect on why you are defining the cord and on what you are trying to do.

Are you trying to achieve a 'tight rein' where you can control and stay on top of everything?

Or do you want to define a set of principles and parameters that will create a controlled space that allows people in the decentralized units to self-organize on their own initiative?

How is each cord going to be defined?

Are you going to define it yourself?

Or are you going to do so by creating dialogue between both ends?

There are many questions, and the answers depend on the details of the situation one is managing. They can result in the re-creation of a bureaucratic style of tight control or a more open-ended style of collaborative management. They can result in a cord with fixed characteristics or in one that evolves and changes over time.

If one is dealing with a tight franchising situation where one knows *exactly* what one wants to do, and how to do it, cords can usually be predesigned. But, when one is dealing with more open-ended situations, dialogue and learning are the key priorities.

My favored approach in such situations is to get 'both ends' of the cord together, to arrive at a definition of mutual needs. What is the manager 'in the pot' trying to realize through the project, autonomous work group, or business representing the offshoot? What help does the offshoot need to flourish? What are the mutual requirements for sustaining and developing the health and growth of the whole plant?

The dimensions of the 'cord' illustrated in Exhibit 4.2 were the outcome of a 'designing the umbilical cord session' involving a manager and a new business initiative. The session resulted in a 'cord agreement' defining five strands:

Strand a. A shared sense of overall vision and values. What is it that we are ultimately trying to achieve?

What are the philosophies and values shaping basic do's and don'ts?

What is the territory within which a new business unit can feel free to roam, *knowing* that it has the support of 'the pot'?

Agreement on these issues serves to create space within which the unit can move without detailed control or encumbrance. With a shared understanding of the vision and direction in which the overall system is trying to move, the various parties can self-organize their activities autonomously, yet in an integrated way. They know when they are working within agreed-upon parameters. They know when they are stepping outside. They know when further discussion and consultation will be necessary. The offshoots remain autonomous yet connected!

Strand b. Agreement on accountabilities. Autonomy requires accountability. So what are the responsibilities on both sides?

The unit is being given space. What is it going to deliver?

How are results going to be assessed?

How is 'the pot' going to be responsive to local needs?

A broad sense of agreement on these issues helps to clarify the operational parameters and general obligations through which activities are discharged on a daily basis.

Strand c. Resource flows in both directions. What are the key resources that will be exchanged?

What financial and other support will the offshoot receive from the pot?

What will it provide in return?

What are the time frames in which these arrangements will operate?

What contingencies will require a fresh agreement?

Shared understandings here create a sense of the financial and other resource realities shaping the project.

Strand d. Information systems. What information and information systems can 'the pot' provide the offshoot?

What information does 'the pot' need from the offshoot?

How is it going to be made available?

Agreements here help to ensure that the new unit receives all the information it requires to be effective and that the pot will develop 'early warning systems' and other indications of when further dialogue or intervention may be appropriate or necessary. Such information systems are crucial for developing 'hands off' styles of management that still lend a measure of control.

Strand e. Rewards. There's the 'pain' of accountability, and there should be the pleasure of appropriate rewards.

How will the offshoot and the pot share the success of new ventures?

Will the new unit be able to retain a substantial share of its profits, or, as is often the case, will it be 'drained' by the pot?

Also, how can members of the new unit be rewarded at a personal or team level?

How can accomplishments be recognized and celebrated?

How can rewards be used to sustain the vitality of the new enterprise?

The understandings and agreements struck through this kind of 'cord dialogue' are crucial in creating a shared frame of reference through which 'the pot' and 'offshoots' can operate in harmony *without direct control*. Whenever one engages in decentralized activity, there is always a danger of the decentralized units lurching in directions that violate the spirit or principles of the enterprise as a whole. The bureaucrat tries to protect against this by minimizing the space for maneuver through the creation of hierarchy, rules, and top-down management. The umbilical cord manager looks to shared understandings as a means of creating integration while *maximizing*

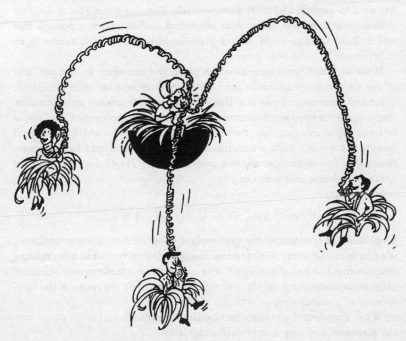

Exhibit 4.3 'Cord dialogue'

the space, autonomy, and self-organizing capacities of the units being controlled. Minimum, rather than maximum, specifications and controls are the order of the day.

I can't overemphasize the importance of this point, because the familiar pathology in most organizations is that of over-control. The managers at the center tend to define too much and impose too many requirements. The focus is on maximum specification rather than 'minimum specs'! The challenge in developing innovative self-organizing initiatives is to have minimal yet highly effective control, to give as much space as possible. The idea of managing through umbilical cords provides an excellent means of doing this.

Clearly, the attitude that shapes the definition of an umbilical cord is crucial. If one is trying to create a decentralized yet controlled pattern of self-organization, umbilical cords need to be approached flexibly, with learning in mind. Cord dialogue sessions should not be seen as negotiating sessions with binding results or as attempts to push the other party into a fixed position. They should be based on a process of genuine dialogue designed to explore and meet mutual needs. The aim should be to develop shared understandings rather than blueprints and to create a process that will help to manage conflicts and produce linkages that can evolve with experience.

With an initial 'cord agreement' in place, the managers in 'the pot' and in the decentralized offshoots are in a position to operate with maximum space and autonomy. So long as they watch for the warnings and anomalies that suggest the cord agreement may be becoming inappropriate, and needs to be reshaped in some way, they can create a context in which the overall system can evolve with a minimum of direct control and intervention. Anomalies in this context are not problems; they create opportunities for genuine dialogue and learning.

Idea 3. Develop different 'cords' for managing different situations

One frequent reaction to the spider-plant image is that 'it's too uniform'; it's a 'system of clones'; 'OK for describing McDonalds . . . but our organization is much more diversified!' The point is an excellent one, because most organizations are highly diversified. They don't always have the uniformity of a franchising or retailing chain.

Why, therefore, be constrained by the metaphor?

Imaginize! Develop a hybrid (Exhibit 4.4)!

The image has important implications. The different 'flowers' have

Exhibit 4.4 The hybrid 'spider plant'

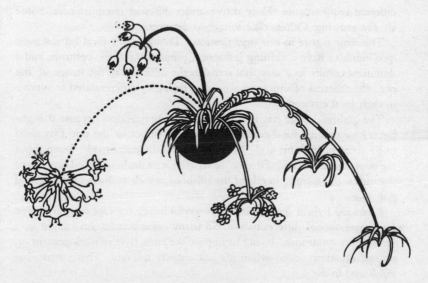

Exhibit 4.5 Different 'cords' for different situations

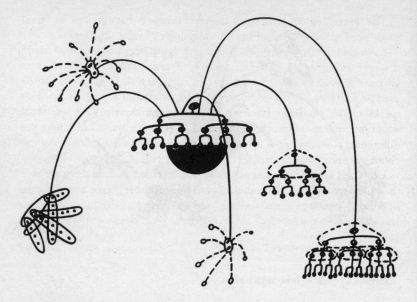

Exhibit 4.6 'Six model' spider plant

different requirements. They thrive under different circumstances. Some are fast growing. Others take longer to develop.

The same is true in our organizations. Though the typical bureaucratic 'pot' tends to have a cloning influence, propagating rules, controls, and a dominant culture in a way that remakes the offshoots in the image of 'the pot,' the different offshoots may need to be highly differentiated to survive in their local environments.

The 'hybrid' image has important design implications, because it highlights how the umbilical cords linking each offshoot to 'the pot' may need to be different (Exhibit 4.5). This underscores the point made above about the importance of 'cord dialogue' in arriving at an umbilical cord agreement that meets the specific needs of the offshoot as well as those of the central pot.

I find the hybrid spider plant a powerful image for capturing the need for organizational differentiation. So many organizations get caught in a 'uniformity syndrome,' trying to impose the same style of management on diverse situations, even when it's not entirely relevant. That's what 'big pots' tend to do!

The 'hybrid' spider plant sends the clear message that different umbilical cords need to be adapted to the contingencies of local situations.

I also find the 'hybrid' image useful in helping organizations understand the role and need for different models of organization, as discussed in Chapter 7. For example, the 'six models' approach discussed there can be used to create a new 'hybrid' spider plant, as illustrated in Exhibit 4.6. This speaks to the challenge faced in so many organizations. They need to adopt different styles of organization and have to find ways of keeping the differences alive under the subtle but ever present cloning influence of the culture of the dominant model in the central pot.

Umbilical cords to the rescue! If the managers in the central pot are able to appreciate and use the umbilical cord concept, they have a new means of defining parameters and controls in a way that will help to manage the relations between internal and external environments and give new initiatives the space needed for success.

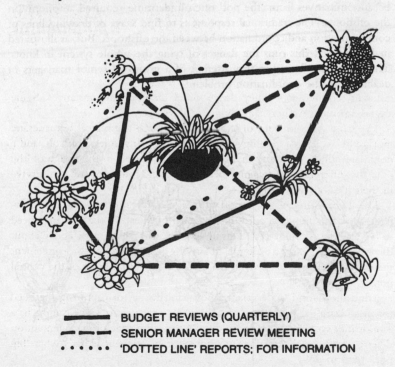

▬▬▬▬ BUDGET REVIEWS (QUARTERLY)
▬ ▬ ▬ SENIOR MANAGER REVIEW MEETING
• • • • • • 'DOTTED LINE' REPORTS; FOR INFORMATION

Exhibit 4.7   Beware of knots!

Idea 4. Encourage bumblebees

The 'hybrid' overcomes the uniformity or 'cloning' problems of the spider plant.

But there is another problem that's frequently raised.

Doesn't the spider plant imply a system that's too decentralized?

What about lost synergies and potential coordination between the offshoots?

The umbilical cords tie the offshoots to the pot. But they're not integrated with anything else.

These are important issues, for the problem in many decentralized organizations is that, as each part works in isolation, each occupies a world of its own and doesn't learn anything from the others.

The difficulty, however, is to find a way of coordinating and integrating potential benefits while avoiding the pitfalls of further bureaucratization, because initiatives from 'the pot' often undermine required autonomy in the offshoots. The traditional response is to find ways of drawing lines of communication and coordination between the offshoots. But, as illustrated in Exhibit 4.7, this runs the danger of tying the whole system in knots. The drawing reflects the first attempt of a group of senior managers in dealing with the coordination problem!

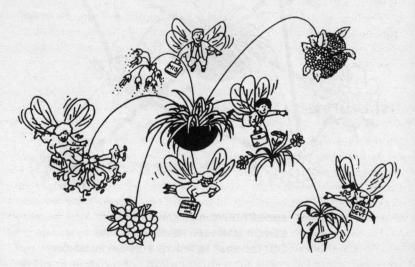

Exhibit 4.8   Organizational bumblebees

Another approach rests in building requirements for coordination into the umbilical cords. For example, managers in the offshoots could be mandated to collaborate and coordinate across the whole system and be encouraged to disseminate information, ideas, and innovations on a regular basis. 'The pot' could facilitate the process and to fund and 'resource' meetings that will help to achieve the desired results.

But, if we stretch our imagination, there is another way in which synergies and integration can be achieved: by introducing 'organizational bumblebees' that fly around and create the required cross-pollination (Exhibit 4.8)!

There's a new role here for managers who used to be located in the pot. Every decentralized organization needs a few good bumblebees flying 'from plant to plant,' keeping in touch with what's going on, spotting synergies, highlighting needs and linking them with resources, identifying 'best practice,' making connections, and disseminating what's learned. Many HRD, MIS, and other organizational development functions can probably be served much more effectively in this free-floating mode than from departments in the central pot.

Of course, the style of the bumblebee is crucial. As one executive expressed the problem, 'We have lots of bumblebees in our organization. The trouble is, they're killer bees.' And, as another executive put it, 'They're also swarming!'

The bees needed to pollinate a spider-plant organization must be facilitators, orchestrators, and coordinators who are at the service of the offshoots. They need to be welcome and 'invited in.' They should not be making forced entries!

The spider plant as imaginization

In the foregoing pages, I have tried to push the spider plant to its limits.

At first glance, there may seem absolutely no parallels between one's organization and a spider plant. The metaphor seems almost absurd. But, as we 'push' and explore, it's amazing how our minds can *create* meaningful linkages and how we can merrily end our discussion on the role of 'bumblebees' in managing decentralized organizations.

For the process to work, one must feel free to play with the metaphor's strengths and limitations, letting links and ideas unfold in whatever way they will. When I introduce the spider-plant image in change interventions or in workshops on the new management skills, especially when I move from the ordinary representation in Exhibit 4.1 to the hybrid in Exhibit 4.4, many managers see an instant relevance. They're immediately thinking about the 'umbilical cords' and how they can use them for managing their teams, projects, or businesses in new ways. But for other people the process is more strained. They may see the spider plant as just another way of thinking about hierarchy or, perhaps, remark on how the image presented in Exhibit 4.1 is too perfect: 'Spider plants often have dry, brown, withered leaves!'

Yet it's amazing what this kind of comment can evoke. People start thinking about brown, withered leaves and find themselves seeing them in their organization. Smiles go around the group. Everyone knows who or where the brown leaves are. They know why they're withering!

This is the power of imaginization. It creates space for new thinking, free of the usual patterns of dialogue. We start by talking about a spider plant and, before we know it, we are talking about 'withering leaves' in Department X or Y. The process can have a powerful impact!

It is difficult to overemphasize the evocative role of metaphor. When it resonates and 'flies,' it really flies and can develop in many unexpected ways. Sometimes it goes nowhere. But, more often than not, it unleashes a flood of ideas, some of which eventually will be forgotten while others stick.

Sometimes it will just result in the identification of one key issue. For example, in one 'spider-plant session' with the top management team of a growing and highly diversified company, the relevance of the metaphor was immediately recognized:

'That's us.'

'That's what we're doing.'

'We're the spider plant!'

But the core discussion returned to one basic question: 'How can we find the right people to manage the offshoots?'

That was the critical business problem: finding the right people! As one of the executives went on to say: 'We interview hundreds of highly qualified candidates, and still have difficulty getting the right one . . . The spider plant is fine in theory. But it only works if you can find the right people to manage the offshoots!'

As a result of this observation, which basically questioned the utility of the model, discussion focused on current recruitment practices for top management and on stories of recent successes and failures. The system, professionally, was impeccable. Everything was being done as it should be.

'But do you know what's missing?' asked one of the senior vice presidents. 'We don't play poker with them.'

The new metaphor placed the selection problem in a new frame. The potential new managers were subject to all the usual recruitment tests for aptitude, personality, and other skills. But they were never tested with their sleeves rolled up in the thick of battle.

The problem: How does one create a surrogate of 'playing poker' in the selection process?

The progress from spider plant to poker is probably a one of a kind event. But it serves to illustrate a central point that I observe time and again. A powerful new image can set people thinking on a new track – creating new insights or reinforcing or rejuvenating older ones. The point is that we must let the process go. Encourage, but don't force. Let it lead where it will. Even when people focus on the limitations and weaknesses of a metaphor, this doesn't necessarily lead to dead ends.

In writing this chapter, I have tried to illustrate and model the same process. Witness, for example, the way we have jumped from the spider plant in Exhibit 4.1 to the 'hybrid' in Exhibit 4.4, to the variation in organizational styles illustrated in Exhibit 4.6. The potential *weakness* of the uniform or clonelike nature of the original image, which created insights for franchising but not for diversified organizations, was used as a springboard for elaborating the image in completely new ways. Note how the 'stems' or 'tentacles' became 'umbilical cords' and how the 'cords' were then elaborated in a completely new way to generate new insights, for example, through the multiple strands illustrated in Exhibit 4.2. This is a distortion of the umbilical cord concept but one that leads to new developments. Note how the lack of synergy between the offshoots of a spider plant, another potential limitation of the metaphor from a management standpoint, was used to generate the idea of bumblebees. And so on.

This, for me, is what the process of imaginization is all about. It's about pursuing the implications of a resonant image or metaphor to develop new insights that can help us organize in new ways. It is a process that allows us to break free of the constraints of traditional thinking and to create the opportunity for new behaviors rooted in a new image of what one is doing.

The development of new images through which one can see, rationalize, and understand new actions and behaviors is crucial for establishing genuine change. One of the reasons bureaucratic thinking is so robust and enduring in situations where it doesn't produce desired effects rests in the fact that the managers do not have alternative models for rethinking and reshaping their behaviors. The calls to be faster, more flexible, more innovative, and more creative just don't cut the ice, because you can't be all these things if you're stuck in old ways. It's through new resonant images, like the spider plant, that we can create a new conception of what we need to do.

As I have tried to show, it provides us with a completely new way of thinking about organizational issues, encouraging us to see how we are often 'hooked' by the concept of a large central pot and the hierarchical forms of management to which it gives rise. It shows how it's possible to grow large while staying small, that one can control and create accountability while giving space through well-designed umbilical cords, that one can unleash organic growth through local processes of self-organization while avoiding anarchic development, that one can be a large organization that still keeps in touch with the demands of many local environments. It provides a lifeline for managers who want to delegate authority to teams and project groups by combining a 'hands on' and 'hands off' style of management.

The metaphor has great relevance for decentralization in business and government. It provides a way of reshaping the management of education and other social services, so that they are 'driven' and managed at local as well as more centralized levels. It provides a way of mobilizing 'grass-roots' activity on environmental and social problems, building around the needs of families, neighborhoods, and communities. The model can serve the needs of the chief executive who is thinking about the structure of her total organization. It can help the factory manager who wishes to use umbilical cords to sustain the self-organizing capacities of autonomous work teams.

But, when all is said and done, we have to remember that the spider plant is just a metaphor. As such, it will resonate in certain circumstances more than others. Like all metaphors, it has strengths, and, as we have seen, it also has limitations.

The important point to remember, and this cuts to the core of imaginization as an approach to management, is that it provides just *one* example of the many ways in which we can use metaphor to create new insights about organization and management.

As demonstrated through the other chapters in this book, there are virtually no limits on the process. Hence the aim of this chapter is not to get *everyone* going back to their offices and managing their projects or designing their organizations like a spider plant, though this may be appropriate. Rather, the purpose is to model and illustrate the basic and potential elements of a process that can help us to reshape old thinking, old managerial styles, and old organizational designs in many different ways. Often, it's a question of finding an appropriate metaphor for reshaping what we do.

Organizations are never changed just by changing structures. They're changed by changing thinking, and this is where imaginization can be of help. Our organizations have been dominated by the mechanical thinking underpinning bureaucracy. Perhaps it's now time to open ourselves to thinking based on spider plants or other organic, growthful imagery that will provide the basis for more innovative, flexible, and humane modes of practice.

So, open yourselves to new images of organization.

Don't worry too much about finding 'the right one' or 'the wrong one.'

Don't feel constrained by your starting point.

Just let the process unfold. Feel free to grasp, elaborate, and shape resonant insights. Use them to create a basis for new dialogue about the needs at hand. Feel free to change, modify, develop, and distort metaphors when appropriate. Openness and receptivity to the creative process count! Ultimately, imaginization is about finding creative ways of dealing with the problems, challenges, and difficulties we face. Maybe your spider-plant thinking will only lead to 'poker.' But, if poker is the critical problem, you may be on a new path to an all-important solution.

26 T. Peters

Creating the Curious Corporation

From *The Tom Peters Seminar*, Vintage Books, 1994, chapter 7

'More intellect, less materials.' 'Only factory asset is the human imagination.' I'm repeatedly drawn back (as you know) to those words and the line from Wal-Mart CEO David Glass about the 'absolute dearth' of exciting, fashion-forward products. More products, yes. Developed faster than ever, yes. But most of them aren't exactly scintillating, to put it mildly.

So we've created new corporations, virtual corporations, and corporate virtual workspaces. So we've turned the average person into a businessperson, placed her or him within a moderate-size unit, and networked her or him with everyone from everywhere. So we've worried ourselves to death about leveraging knowledge.

But is *it* (whatever our company is about) interesting?

Is *it* exciting?

Bored stiff

Most organizations bore me stiff. I can't imagine working in one of them. I'd be sad if my children chose to. Most organizations, large and even small, are bland as bean curd.

Ugly thoughts? They're terrifying thoughts, when we realize we're relying on these organizations to be and remain commercially viable in a marketplace gone bonkers.

'What a distressing contrast there is between the radiant intelligence of the child and the feeble mentality of the average adult,' Sigmund Freud once said. Sorry to say, Freud was right. So is turnaround executive Victor Palmieri: 'Strategies are okayed in boardrooms that even a child would say are bound to fail. The problem is, there's never a child in the boardroom.'

What do you do about a bland organization? How do you get a child (virtual child?) into the boardroom? It's obvious: Build a curious corporation. But how? Can we get our arms around such a . . . curious term? Are we willing to try? Are we willing even to use the words? In public?

A list, no more and no less

What follows is a list, and not all that great a list. Fact is, I hastily sketched it out a while back, then immediately transferred it to 35-mm slides. On the slides it looks great, it looks tidy. But the list wasn't meant to be great, certainly not tidy. Its only purpose is to show that one can make such a list. Okay, how do you create a curious corporation? Try these fourteen ideas:

1. *Hire curious people.* Yes, it's that simple. Except that it flies in the face of conventional wisdom. I sometimes think Rule No. 1 in the corporate recruiting manual is, 'Thou shalt not hire anyone who has as much as a nanosecond's gap in her or his résumé between nursery school and now.'

Whom do we hire? The person with the perfect grade-point average, who didn't miss a day of class in kindergarten, elementary school, or junior high. Perfect folks. Blemishless. And unspeakably dull. Never a hair out of place, never done a thing wrong. But they haven't done much interesting, either. Curious? I doubt it. After all, the curious kids are the ones, age six or sixty-six, who are constantly in trouble. Right?

I'm not alone, if not in a majority, in these observations. Stanley Bing, writing in *Esquire*, offers this marvelous snapshot of an encounter with a job candidate that went nowhere:

He comes in and seats himself carefully on the edge of my guest chair. He is staring at the toys on my desk, trying to suppress the realization that I am an infantile nit whose job he could probably do much better . . . Of course he does not play with the toys . . . He looks out my window instead. 'Nice view,' he says rather perfunctorily, but he does not say, 'Wow!' – which is what my view of the canyons and spires of high-mercantile capitalism deserves . . .

'I'm looking for an entry-level position in public relations. Maybe corporate marketing, if I get lucky,' he says.

'Really?' I say. 'Like, out of the entire realm of human possibility, that's what you want to be doing?' I'm sorry. He's really starting to tweeze my bumpus. What twenty-four-year-old really and truly wants to be in *corporate marketing*, for God's sake? . . . I look him over as he burbles on about targeting demos or retrofitting corporate superstructures or some frigging thing like that. The guy makes me want to stand up on my desk and yell, 'Booga-booga!' Instead, I say, 'Didn't you ever want to be a rock musician or a forest ranger or anything?' He looks at me like I have a banana peel on the end of my nose. It's quite clear to me that, since he was in high school, he's been preparing to be a . . . communicator. That's actually what he says.

Screw it. There is no poetry in this dude. No soul. No surf or wind or whalebone in his eye. He's . . . desiccated. He makes me sad. I kick him out of my office.

Is Bing on the money? 'Fraid so. Too harsh? I don't think so. Whom do I suggest we hire? A dude with poetry? A gal with soul? Absolutely. I suggest we search for the young woman who went to MIT to study computer science, was doing fine, and then mysteriously dropped out midway in her sophomore year, said the place was the dreariest institution ever created, and took off around the world, maybe to work with Mother Teresa, maybe just to hang out. We really don't know.

Why would I hire her? I'll tell you. She's demonstrated – at least at one point in her life – the gumption to do something exciting, something extraordinary, something that breaks the mold. Maybe we'll get lucky – and she'll do it again. For us.

VCW, Inc., of Kansas City, Missouri, is in what would hardly be labeled a glamorous, 'happening' business. Or so it would seem. Peddling insurance to independent truckers? Yawn. But founder Cheryl Womack, Fortune reports, has turned her firm into a high-growth, high-profit gem. Hiring is key. 'We look for passion, flexibility, and excitement,' Womack asserts. I like that. And I'm dead serious when I suggest we make the first line in the corporate recruitment manual: 'Thou shalt not consider for employment anyone who does not have a gap and a couple of glitches in his or her résumé.' How about it? Got the nerve? I doubt it. But then I suspect your company is among those routinely offering me-too products and services. (Hey, I'm only saying that because the odds are on my side and long.)

2. Hire a few genuine off-the-wall sorts – collect some weirdos. Curious and the occasional gap in the resume are not enough. We need some real kooks. If we want original products, they're likely to come from original people. What else would you call Ted Turner, George Lucas, Steve Jobs, Anita Roddick? Original they are, oddballs they are. And they've given us breakthrough products and services.

I swiped this idea from Gary Withers, head of the brash British marketing-services firm, Imagination. Some have called Withers Britain's Walt Disney. He makes his money by creating fabulous events, marketing campaigns, and corporate culture makeovers, for clients wild and not so wild. His personal key, he told me, is looking for flaky sorts who have insatiable 'appetites for adventure.' It doesn't matter one whit whether there's a job for them or not. He says he comes in contact with a lot of zesty nuts, and if he hits it off with them, he hires them. If they're as good as he thinks they are, they'll make a special niche for themselves in the company, and take Imagination someplace it's never been (praise be, since 'topping our last' is the company's strategy). Collecting weirdos sounds to me like one dandy idea.

Civil War historian Shelby Foote reports that General Ulysses S. Grant was once relieved from high command because of his boozing. General William T. Sherman was also once relieved – because of 'suspicion of insanity.' Yet these two ended up saving the Union, whereas their predecessors, who had boot-licked their way to the top, were disasters when times got tough. What if Lincoln had stuck with the squeaky-clean résumé, had failed to take the plunge for weird?

Words are revealing. How about weird? Withers has no problem with it. Do you? How about maniac? One Nintendo exec says that's what his firm wants – 'maniacs.' Listen to Guy Kawasaki, the former Apple software executive. He begs us to 'turn everyone into raging, inexorable thunder lizard evangelists.' Can you imagine that rolling off your tongue while talking with your boss's boss? In a personnel manual? If the times are upside down, the language must be, too. And believe it or not, the choice of words and images is near the center of business strategy.

3. *Weed out the dullards, nurture the nuts.* Power to the peculiar! Mike Koelker, creative director at Foote, Cone & Belding, says, tongue nowhere near his cheek, that he's 'learned to predict the future. Anyone who comes to see you more than once every two years to discuss their "career path" probably doesn't have one.' On the other hand, he insists that 'without exception, the people in the account group and creative department who I find the most brilliant will have the hardest time fitting into . . . the agency structure.' It's his job No. 1 to nurture these misfits.

Advertising legend David Ogilvy doubtless would nod in agreement. One listless soul, he said in his official statement of agency philosophy, can infect a cast of hundreds. (Or more.) Out they (should, must) go. Vamooski! – you don't want the wet noodles dragging down the live wires.

You've seen it. I've seen it. We unconsciously learned it at age seven, when we first observed leadership in Sunday School, or with Brownies or Cub Scouts. There's that person (leader) who walks into the room, things are going moderately well, but the whole place clams up and goes stiff.

Then there's that other person (leader) who walks in, and even if things are going badly, you feel just a little bit better, there's a little more buzz in the air, just because of his or her presence. We know all this, we know what it means. We even agree on it. But we don't use the dull-is-deadly, cherish-the-live-wires criterion in hiring and especially in promoting. I suggest we do. I suggest we must. Again, the point is strategic, not peripheral.

4. *Go for youth.* One big reason PepsiCo stays vital at $25 billion in revenues is that it's willing to place big bets on exciting people that others would veto as untested. Time after time, you'll find the company has appointed a twenty-eight-, twenty-nine- or thirty-year-old to run a big part of the business. (Hey, Thomas Jefferson penned the Declaration of Independence at age thirty-three. It's held up pretty well.)

The eighty-five-year-old *New Republic* magazine, though respected, was in a rut. In 1991, the owner, Martin Peretz, appointed twenty-seven-year-old Andrew Sullivan as editor of the venerable publication. He shook things up. 'I can't imagine a forty-five-year-old having the effect he's had,' said staffer Jacob Weisberg. Why? 'The younger people are much more irresponsible and more willing to do things on the edge,' staffer Michael Lewis explains.

I like that: the pursuit of irresponsible greenhorns. How many of your company's leadership cadre are under thirty-five? Thirty? . . . Twenty-five? (You'd be amazed at the number of companies that refer to the appointment of someone forty-five years old as part of a youth movement.)

5. *Insist that everyone takes vacations.* When you're blessed with phenomenal growth or extraordinary problems, people, especially in key positions, tend to work thirteen-hour days, six or seven days a week. They think they're strong, tough, invincible – and as fresh as ever. They may be strong as oxen. But fresh? That's a bunch of baloney. People need to rejuvenate themselves, especially these upside-down days.

I had a good friend at McKinsey, one of the cleverest folks I ever worked with, who each summer took a month's vacation. We were a macho, type-A organization. I couldn't imagine why he did it. At any rate, I knew that I didn't need a month off, I of boundless energy. Then one year I spent August at a cabin on the Northern California coast. When I got back, I was immediately aware of what a burned-out shell I'd been. Let me say it – to toughen up, lighten up.

6. *Support generous sabbaticals.* For refreshing the overtilled soil. And reinventing ourselves. Vacations, aye. But unless we go farther and occasionally take megabreaks, of several months (or more), to radically ream out and

retool, the chances of hitting a second home run (if we've been lucky enough to hit the first one) are very low indeed. Been on the job for five years without a three-month (six-month) break? You're flat. Trust me.

7. *Foster new interaction patterns.* Create a physical environment that (a) lets people express their personalities, (b) allows project teams to form at a moment's notice, (c) encourages getting together and hanging out, and (d) aggressively snubs traditional functional groupings.

Space reflects (and shapes) corporate culture, spirited or blah, like no other variable. Managers, by a wide margin, don't take it seriously enough. And, in these pages, we don't either (wait until the next book). 'We need to change underlying beliefs about how we view and perform white-collar jobs,' designer Duncan Sutherland told *Industry Week*. 'It's still typical to view offices as information factories or places that produce data. So our traditional response has been to see how much we can produce – how many keystrokes we can coax out of workers, or how many memos. But the purpose of an office is to create knowledge. That is an intellectual process, not a production process.' Most offices bore the hell out of me. And if they bore me – I've learned, almost unfailingly – nothing very interesting is going to happen there.

It's the tiny telltale signs, too. Does your company have a clean-desk policy? If so, the company's nuts – and, frankly, you're nuts to stay there. (Yes, based on that criterion alone.) Oh, how many businesses have I visited where you'd never guess at human habitation! Then we wonder why they produce another dozen copycat products (even if they're quick copycats, TQM'd to a fare-thee-well).

8. *Establish clubs, bring in outsiders, support offbeat educational programs.* Don't invite Tom Peters or Peter Drucker, damn it! Invite Steven Spielberg or Kenneth Branagh or Tim Burton. Or your favorite science-fiction writer – how about William Gibson? Invite somebody who's doing something beyond the pale, clearly contrary to the ordinary corporate usage. P-L-E-A-S-E!

9. *Measure curiosity.* Yes, I'm serious. Time for semiannual performance reviews? Consider having each employee submit a one-page essay on (a) the oddest thing I've done this year off the job, (b) the craziest idea I've tried at work, (c) my most original screw-up on the job, and off, or (d) the five stupidest rules we have around here.

Hey, I'm not kidding. (I stole this idea, though not the questions, from Herman Miller's very special boss, Max DePree. He asks execs to answer queries that force them way out of the box.) Why not? We're trying to get people to explode from the traces that hold them back. At the very least, this will make the reading of performance reviews more fun. And it might even do some good.

10. *Seek out odd work.* Imagination's Withers says he won't take a job, even if it means forgoing megabucks, unless he figures out some way to make it exciting – some way it can force him to push his company's performance to new heights.

11. *Look in the mirror.* If the chief ain't curious, the troops ain't likely to be. (And that's an understatement.) How many times have I seen the video on 'culture change' featuring the CEO? Dressed in black, at least it seems so. The office tidy (i.e., sterile). His animation zilch. And he's telling us (droning on) to get more excited. It doesn't get through. He's a stiff. And then he wonders why his talk doesn't ignite the troops, why they don't race out and do some absolutely madcap stuff. If you're not zany (I don't mean loud, I mean infectiously enthusiastic), then the joint's not going to be zany. By the way, I'm talking to supervisors running eight-person accounting operations as well as CEOs running 100,000-person corporations.

12. *Teach curiosity.* Brainstorming is not *the* answer to creativity. But it is *an* answer. There are time-tested techniques for milking people's wackier ideas (you'd do no better than to attend one of creativity guru Edward de Bono's seminars); invest heavily in using such techniques to solve all problems – from purchasing and accounting to quality and marketing.

All, as in solving *all* problems. The curiosity mandate does not just apply to marketing or research and development. Curiosity applies to everything, especially if you think of the company, as I suggested in Chapter 5, as 'packages of services.' Curiosity is at least as important in accounting, purchasing, and logistics as it is in science and design.

13. *Make it fun.* Not ha-ha fun. (Though there's nothing wrong with that from time to time.) But fun as in enjoyable, or refreshing . . . you know what I mean. A place that makes you smile and makes you want to go to work on Monday morning, even if you had a terrific weekend – that's the ticket. And it is possible.

'We've always said that Silicon Graphics is all about making technology fun and usable,' says CEO Ed McCracken, 'and that means that working here should be fun. Too many corporations in the United States and Japan have cut the fun out of their businesses . . . Fun and irreverence also make change less scary.' McCracken doesn't have trouble with the three-letter F-word. Can you say the same? (And live it?)

14. *Change pace.* Go to work next Thursday and declare it miniature-golf day. Showing a training film this afternoon? Order popcorn. Hotter than

hell on an August morning? Buy 10 water guns, the good ones, at lunch – and go back and start a water-gun fight in the accounting department. (I stole this one from a software company – yup, the part about the accounting department, too.) Curiosity has a lot to do with perpetually looking at the world through slightly cockeyed glasses.

I'm sure that if you and a few of your colleagues, running a group of six or sixty or 600 people, got together for half an hour, you'd come up with a different – and better – list than mine. The important thing is to understand that you can turn this mushy – and strategic – idea of 'creating the curious corporation' into hard, doable suggestions.

And, by the way, while I don't think my list is great, I do earnestly believe that every idea on it makes sense. In these wacky times . . . only asset imagination . . .

Whoops, I plumb forgot item number 15. While I'm against adding staff slots in this Age of Lean, I will make an exception: How about a Vicar of Vitality, Grand Panjandrum of Pandemonium, Crown Prince of Curiosity, Master of Madness? And even if you don't add the slot, how about at least changing your job title on your business card, including the Japanese-language version, to one of the above? I'll say it again. I'm serious about all this. As for you, admit it. When was the last time you kicked up your heels in the corridor? Danced the length of the cafeteria? Your place of work bores you silly, too – and it's costing you. Right?

Innocence renewed

'One of the lessons you learned in becoming an adult,' John Seabrook wrote in the *New Yorker*, 'is that it doesn't always pay to be curious. Some people learn to avoid curiosity altogether. [Microsoft's Bill] Gates appears to have completely failed to absorb this lesson.' Gates is not alone. Harvard psychology professor Howard Gardner discovered that geniuses in general lived on the margins of society (perpetually skeptical of conventional wisdom and its purveyors) and maintained, throughout life, 'intellectual innocence.'

Most of us aren't geniuses, aren't Bill Gates. But at least we can create corporate cultures, and workplaces, that nurture innocence and don't actively stomp out curiosity.

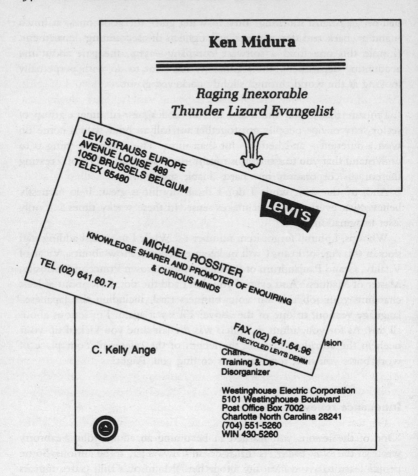

Ken Midura

Raging Inexorable Thunder Lizard Evangelist

LEVI STRAUSS EUROPE
AVENUE LOUISE 489
1050 BRUSSELS BELGIUM
TELEX 65480

Levi's

MICHAEL ROSSITER
KNOWLEDGE SHARER AND PROMOTER OF ENQUIRING
& CURIOUS MINDS

TEL (02) 641.60.71

FAX (02) 641.64.96
RECYCLED LEVI'S DENIM

C. Kelly Ange

Chan...
Training & De...
Disorganizer

Westinghouse Electric Corporation
5101 Westinghouse Boulevard
Post Office Box 7002
Charlotte North Carolina 28241
(704) 551-5260
WIN 430-5260

Snared by the great blight dullness

We grotesquely underestimate the role of physical space in setting organizational tone . . . It was urban planner-philosopher Jane Jacobs who taught me that lesson. In fact, few books have influenced me more than her *The Death and Life of Great American Cities*. 'Nobody enjoys sitting on a stoop looking out at an empty street,' Jacobs writes at one point. She claims that most significant urban problems stem from cities that are engulfed by the Great Blight of Dullness (she's very fond of capital letters), that are perfectly planned (by urban planners), but are boring up close. Her winning formula includes energetic sidewalks, short blocks, lots of old buildings, mixed uses (houses and stores and offices and bars all squeezed together). At its best it adds up, Jacobs says, to 'exuberant variety.'

Most of our corporate stoops look out on empty streets, devoid of spirit. And, oh my, I do love that phrase 'exuberant variety.' How do (a) you, (b) your unit, (c) your company score on the EVI – or Exuberant Variety Index? (A perfect 10 is Microsoft or Planet Hollywood, a stifling 1 is, still, GM.)

Which brings me to the copy of the thirty-ninth Annual Design Review edition of I.D. (International Design) that landed in my mailbox a while back. A frustrated architect, I flipped to the sections on buildings, interiors, and furniture. Without exception, I was repelled by the award winners. They deaden the human spirit.

What are spaces that enliven the spirit? They are comfortable, friendly, awake. I'm for sweatshirts and sweatpants at home and, if I can get away with it, at work. I like to be surrounded by familiar objects, to look up at 100-year-old roughhewn rafters, to gaze at trees and birds or an electric street scene. Like Esquire's Stanley Bing, perhaps, I can no more imagine an office without toys than a computer without software.

At first, as I reacted so strongly to I.D.'s winners, I wondered if I was a crank. So I did a smidgen of research.

Architect Christopher Alexander, in his widely acclaimed, Zen-ish The Timeless Way of Building, describes 'a central quality which is the root criterion of life and spirit in a man, a town, a building, or a wilderness. This quality is objective and precise, but it cannot be named.'

Nameable or not, Alexander evokes it: 'The first place I think of, when I try to tell someone about this quality, is a corner of an English country garden, where a peach tree grows against a wall. . . . The sun shines on the tree and as it warms the bricks behind the tree, the warm bricks themselves warm the peaches on the tree. It has a slightly dozy quality.'

Mark the words (remember words!) 'alive,' 'whole,' 'comfortable,' and 'eternal.' Alexander says they describe places that 'let our inner forces loose, and set us free; but when [spaces] are dead, they keep us locked in inner conflict.' I believe the same qualities are central to creating value in our companies.

Too much corporate experience is anesthetized by work environments that squash our spirits. I shake my head in wonder – and sometimes am moved to anger or sadness or both – by most facilities I enter. From reception area to research lab, they lack ferment.

Surfaces are smooth and polished. Glass-topped, chrome-legged desks are barren. Light is synthetic. 'For proven physiological reasons, people can feel ill if they work all day in artificial light,' architect Christopher Day says in *Places of the Soul*. 'Yet the light of spring can bring such joy to the heart, it can get the invalid out of bed!'

Does your workspace suck you out from under the covers in the morning? Does it up the likelihood of clever, collaborative, and energetic problem-solving?

Doubtful. The typical corporate landscape, urban stone or rural lawn, breeds hunkering and hiding, not sharing and openness.

These are, I repeat, critical issues. If value in the new economy is to come from spunk, energy, talk, collaboration, and imagination, then the places where we hang out to do commerce must reflect the principles of that new economy.

Is space everything? Of course not. But you'd be surprised at the role it plays in creating a corporate signature – curious or incurious.

(PS. In the for-what-it's-worth department, Duncan Sutherland, writing in *Design Management Journal*, reports that Benjamin Franklin did his best work in the nude and Martin Luther on the can. Supercomputer maven Seymour Cray, when stuck, digs tunnels in his backyard. What's around you is inside you.)

New realities

A different sort of character (curious) in a different sort of place (spunky) is required to create value in today's, let alone tomorrow's, marketplace. In fact, Peter Drucker wrote in the *Harvard Business Review*, 'The relationship between knowledge workers and their organization is a distinctly new phenomenon.' Drucker goes on to suggest that we should treat all knowledge workers as 'volunteers.' We can demand that people show up at work on time, especially in this problematic economic period. But we cannot demand, ever, that people bring passion along, or exuberance, or imagination. We must attract the special worker, then tap into his or her curiosity. But what, specifically, do these new knowledge workers want? In a July 1993 article, *Inc.* magazine presented this fictitious memo, which ought to be framed behind every executive's desk:

To: *Inc.* magazine
From: Determinedly Seeking the Perfect Job

I don't want to screw around anymore in a place that's badly managed, poorly run, and so stupid I'm just wasting my time. Or a place where you have to be a vice-president to get a window. I want to take my dogs to work, at least on Saturdays, and if I break into a chorus of 'Oklahoma' at 4 p.m., I want two people to harmonize with me – not look at me sideways.

I want to work cooperatively in a team. I don't care so much what industry it is, but the more socially conscious, the better. I want an environment that's honest, supportive, fair, inclusive, and playful. I'm really great at what I do, and now I'm going to find a really great place to do it in. I want flex time and exercise space and community service and lots of chances to learn. I want trees and easy parking!

Signed, Determined

Sounds reasonable to me. Mr Work-as-Conversation, Alan Webber, understands, too. He wrote in the *Harvard Business Review*, 'In the new economy, individuals at all levels of the company and in all kinds of companies are challenged to develop new knowledge and to create new value, to take responsibility for their ideas and to pursue them as far as they can go. People who manage in the new economy [must] tap into the emotional energy that comes from wrestling with their own destiny. In the end, that's a job description that most people would welcome.'

Yes, most would, but in early 1994 it's still a chimera – a long, long way from the norm.

Something great

David Sheff's *Game Over* traces the meteoric rise of Japan's controversial, unconventional Nintendo. The spirit of Nintendo is best captured by a simple exchange. A game designer, Gunpei Yokoi, asked his boss, 'What should I make?' Nintendo chief executive Hiroshi Yamauchi replied, 'Something great.'

That brief exchange made my head spin for days. Not long after, I started asking seminar participants, 'Has any boss, in your career, ever said to you, "Do/make something great"? Or, perhaps more to the point, have you ever said that to one of your subordinates?' (No rounding off allowed: not something important, good, or even nifty, but something great, or Something Great, to mimic Jane Jacobs.)

Sad to say, barely a hand has gone up. None for 500 in London. None for 200 in Frankfurt. One out of 5,000 in Sydney and Melbourne. None in Kuala Lumpur. None in large gatherings in Silicon Valley or Chicago either. One out of 1,200 in Atlanta.

What should I make? Something great. Wow! What a turn-on! What a motivator! What a challenge to the human imagination! What a wake-up call to curiosity! Recall our discussion about Tom Strange and Joe Tilli, the Rapid Deployment Team at Titeflex: Making something great is not just for software developers at Nintendo or Microsoft, chefs at Chez Panisse, or aircraft designers at Boeing. It's for hosemakers. Or a hotel's housekeeping department. 'Do something great' – I can imagine a marvelous response coming from a housekeeping department given just such a challenge. 'Make something great' is the sort of challenge we must embrace, as bosses at all levels and in all departments and in all firms, if we really do believe that imagination is the only asset, if we really do believe that economic security in developed countries is wholly dependent on leveraging knowledge.

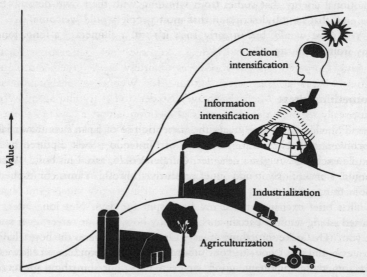

Yo, creation intensification

Drucker gets it. Nintendo's Yamauchi gets it. So does Murikami Teruyasu at Nomura Research Institute. He claims history can be divided into four epochs. First, the Age of Agriculture, which is largely behind us. Then, the Industrial Age, fast fading. Next, the Age of Information Intensification, where most of us would say we are today (in fact, most of us would say we're befuddled by it). But that's not the end of it, says our friend at Nomura. We're quickly moving into the Age of Creation Intensification.

And that's a whole new ball game. Providing and helpfully packaging information is one thing. Getting a handle on that is tough enough (most of us haven't). Ripping out layers is also one (good) thing. Reengineering is another (good) thing. But this is different: This is creation intensification. Creation of the curious corporation. Label it any way you want, it will separate tomorrow's (today's) winners from losers.

The practicality of 'correct' imagery

Words are important. Images are more important. To deal with the new era calls for new metaphors. Jazz combos (per researcher Karl Weick). Improvisational theatre (per Digital Equipment's Charles Savage). Organization as carnival (me, *Liberation Management*). Shamrock organizations (per Charles Handy). Intellectual holding companies (per Dartmouth's Brian Quinn). Corporate virtual workspaces (courtesy Steve Truett and Tom Barrett). Work as conversation (from Alan Webber). Collaboration as romance (thanks to Michael Schrage). Spider's webs (Quinn again). We must really *see* these new images. 'Competition is now a "war of movement" in which success depends on anticipation of market trends and quick response to changing customer needs,' wrote George Stalk, Philip Evans, and Lawrence Schulman in the *Harvard Business Review*. 'Successful competitors move quickly in and out of products, markets, and sometimes even entire businesses – a process more akin to an interactive video game than to chess.'

Interactive video. I like that.

'Mr Andy Grove, chairman of Intel . . . compares [Silicon Valley] to the theater business in New York, which has an itinerant workforce of actors, directors, writers and technicians, as well as experienced financial backers,' wrote Geoffrey Owen and Louise Kehoe in the *Financial Times*. 'By tapping into this network you can quickly put a production together. It might be a smash hit . . . or it might be panned by the critics. Inevitably, the number of long-running plays is small, but new creative ideas keep bubbling up.' Theater as model. Good. Think about it. Please.

Lessons learned

- Traits of the curious corporation (your list or mine)
- Loving 'weird'
- Hot words
- Staving off the Great Blight of Dullness
- Spaces with spunk
- New relationships with knowledge workers
- Make something great
- Creation intensification
- New metaphors needed
- Vicar of Vitality

Reprise: a place for your kids

In *In Search of Excellence*, Bob Waterman and I defined the measured excellence in terms of long-term financial health. Truth is, we could hardly have cared less. But we knew we needed to go through the drill to be taken seriously by the 5,000 conformists we hoped would buy the book.

Nothing wrong with financial measures, mind you. Can't live without them. But they're far from the whole picture. In recent years, for example, we've taken to measuring quality and customer service with a vengeance. (Good for us!)

But I'm thinking in other terms these days. In fact, I've got a new one-dimensional measure of excellence:

Would you want your son or daughter to work there?

What would such a place be, in order to be good enough for your kids? Ethical? Profitable? Growing? Yes. Yes. Yes.

Also, if you ask me, spirited, spunky. And curious. And a place where they're routinely told, 'Do something great!' Maybe the list for your kids is different. Somehow I bet it isn't, or not much. That's another vote for going all out to create the curious corporation as we traverse these oh-so-curious times.

TTD (things to do) and QTA (questions to answer)

1. Most important suggestion in this book: When you go to work tomorrow, try to look at 'your place' as a fearful, first-day employee would. (It's very hard to do.) Start with the parking lot, front door, or reception area. Does 'arriving' add a little spring to your (first day, remember) step? Or are you shut down a bit? Exuberance or Great Blight? Repeat this exercise with a handful of colleagues. Ask a first-day employee (if you're lucky enough to be hiring).

2. Score yourself (and colleagues) on my list of fifteen ideas for the curious corporation. How do you do? (I bet agreement among you is high.) Now create your own list. S-t-r-e-t-c-h, please. Score yourself again. Then repeat quarterly.

3. How do you do with words like 'weird'? Are you uncomfortable with them? Why? The times are weird, aren't they? (Think about it. 'More intellect . . . ,' remember. 'Only factory asset . . .' I didn't make this stuff up, dammit.)

4. Review the comments on space. Invent a 'Vitality of Space' audit, or something like it. Do your spaces turn folks (you) on? Or off?

5. Have you ever been asked to, or asked someone to, make something great? (Not good, nifty, but . . .) If not, why not? Does it actually apply to hotel housekeeping departments? If not, why not? (And if you run a hotel, is your housekeeping department great – not 'TQM good,' but zesty, zippy, zany good?)

6. Ready to sign up to be Vicar of Vitality? If you're a big cheese, why not create such a position? Or assign it to yourself for six months? (PS. If you're not interested enough, or nervy enough, to change your business card title to Master of Madness, please throw this book away promptly. It's a waste of time to keep reading and sorry to have bothered you to this point.)

Notes

p. 540 'What a distressing . . . the average adult': Robert Bly, *Iron John: A Book About Men* (Reading, Mass., Addison-Wesley, 1990), p. 7

p. 540 'Strategies are okayed . . . child in the boardroom': Victor Palmieri, 'Now hear this,' *Fortune*, February 24, 1992, p. 18

pp. 541–2   'Stanley Bing . . . of my office': Stanley Bing, 'Dudes! Get a life!', *Esquire*, May 1993, pp. 76–7

p. 542   'VCW, Inc. . . . Womack asserts': Charles Burck, 'Succeeding with tough love,' *Fortune*, November 29, 1993, p. 188

p. 543   'General William . . . of insanity': Shelby Foote, *Shiloh* (New York, Dial Press, 1952), p. 39

p. 543   'Guy Kawasaki . . . thunder lizard evangelists': Michelle Moreno, 'Product evangelists make customers into believers,' *On Achieving Excellence*, January 1993, p. 5

p. 543   'Mike Koelker . . . the agency structure': Mike Moreno, 'A creative man shares (some of) what he's learned,' *Advertising Age*, December 13, 1993, p. F-8

p. 543   'David Ogilvy . . . cast of hundreds': David Ogilvy, *Principles of Management* (New York, Ogilvy & Mather, 1968)

p. 544   'The 85-year old . . . Lewis explains': Walter Kim, 'The editor as gap model,' *The New York Times Magazine*, March 7, 1993, p. 56

p. 545   'We need to . . . production process': Charles R. Day Jr., 'First factories, now offices,' *Industry Week*, September 7, 1992, p. 7

p. 546   'We've always said . . . change less scary': Prokesch, *Harvard Business Review*, November–December 1993, p. 142

p. 547   'One of the . . . absorb this lesson': John Seabrook, 'E-mail from Bill,' *The New Yorker*, January 10, 1994, p. 56

p. 547   'Harvard psychology professor . . . intellectual innocence': Howard Gardner, *Creating Minds* (New York, Basic Books, 1993)

pp. 548–9   'Nobody enjoys . . . exuberant variety': Jane Jacobs, *The Death and Life of Great American Cities* (New York, Random House, 1961), p. 161

p. 549   'Architect Christopher Alexander . . . in inner conflict': Christopher Alexander, *The Timeless Way of Building* (New York, Oxford University Press, 1979), pp. ix–x, 25

p. 550   'For proven physiological . . . out of bed': Christopher Day, *Places of the Soul: Architecture and Environmental Designs as a Healing Art* (London, Harper-Collins, 1990), p. 50

p. 550   'Duncan Sutherland . . . in his backyard': Duncan B. Sutherland Jr, 'Technology and the contemporary design firm; reflections on time, space, tools, and the mind's work,' *Design Management Journal*, spring, 1993, pp. 38–9

p. 550   'The relationship between . . . new phenomenon': Peter Drucker, 'The new society of organizations,' *Harvard Business Review*, September–October 1992, p. 101

p. 551   'To: *Inc.* . . . Signed, Determined': John Kerr, 'The best small companies to work for in America,' *Inc.*, July 1993, p. 51

p. 551   'In the new . . . people would welcome': Webber, *Harvard Business Review*, January–February 1993, p. 42

p. 551   'A game designer . . . something great': David Sheff, *Game Over: How Nintendo Zapped An American Industry, Captured Your Dollars, and Enslaved Your Children* (New York, Random House, 1993), p. 21

p. 553 'Competition is now . . . than to chess': George Stalk, Philip Evans, and Lawrence E. Shulman, 'Competing on capabilities: the new rules of corporate strategy,' *Harvard Business Review*, March–April 1992, p. 62

p. 553 'Mr Andy Grove . . . keep bubbling up': Geoffrey Owen and Louise Kehoe, 'A hotbed of high-tech,' *Financial Times*, June 28, 1992, p. 20

Acknowledgements

Permission to reprint the readings in this volume is acknowledged to the following sources:

1 Free Press, a division of Simon & Schuster
2 *Organizational Dynamics*
3 Free Press, a division of Simon & Schuster
4 *Sloan Management Review*
5 *Harvard Business Review*
6 Tom Burns
7 Harvard Business School Press
8 Addison-Wesley Educational Publishers Inc.
9 *California Management Review*
10 Michael Hannen and University of Chicago Press
11 Geert Hofstede
12 The Centre for Effective Performance, Inc.
13 Harper Collins Publishers Inc. and Macmillan Ltd
14 Harvard Business School Publishing
15 *Harvard Business Review*
16 Universitetsförlaget
17 Routledge
18 Transaction Publishers
19 Pfeiffer & Company
20 Blackwell Publishers
21 Chris Argyris
22 American Sociological Review
23 Blackwell Publishers
24 *Sloan Management Review*
25 Sage Publications
26 Vintage Books, a division of Random House Inc.

Author Index

Subject Index

READ MORE IN PENGUIN

BUSINESS AND ECONOMICS

Webonomics Evan I. Schwartz

In *Webonomics*, Evan I. Schwartz defines nine essential principles for growing your business on the Web. Using case studies of corporations such as IBM and Volvo, as well as smaller companies and web-based start-ups, Schwartz documents both the tremendous failures and the successes on the Web in a multitude of industries.

Inside Organizations Charles B. Handy

Whatever we do, whatever our profession, organizing is a part of our lives. This book brings together twenty-one ideas which show you how to work with and through other people. There are also questions at the end of each chapter to get you thinking on your own and in a group.

Lloyds Bank Small Business Guide Sara Williams

This long-running guide to making a success of your small business deals with real issues in a practical way. 'As comprehensive an introduction to setting up a business as anyone could need' *Daily Telegraph*

Teach Yourself to Think Edward de Bono

Edward de Bono's masterly book offers a structure that broadens our ability to respond to and cope with a vast range of situations. *Teach Yourself to Think* is software for the brain, turning it into a successful thinking mechanism, and, as such, will prove of immense value to us all.

The Road Ahead Bill Gates

Bill Gates – the man who built Microsoft – takes us back to when he dropped out of Harvard to start his own software company and discusses how we stand on the brink of a new technology revolution that will for ever change and enhance the way we buy, work, learn and communicate with each other.

READ MORE IN PENGUIN

BUSINESS

Corporate Strategy	Igor Ansoff
Atlas of Management Thinking	Edward de Bono
The 5-Day Course in Thinking	
Lateral Thinking for Management	
Water Logic	
Opportunities	
Wordpower	
Accidental Empires	Robert Cringely
Offensive Marketing	Hugh Davidson
Even More Offensive Marketing	
Commercial Law	R. M. Goode
Cosmopolitan Guide to Working in Finance	Robert Gray
New Marketing Practice	David Mercer
Understanding Company Financial Statements	R. H. Parker
Cosmopolitan Guide to Working in Retail	Elaine Robertson
An Insight into Management Accounting	John Sizer
Corporate Recovery	Stuart Slatter
The Art of Japanese Management	Richard Tanner Pascale and Anthony Athos
Management and Motivation	Victor H. Vroom and Edward L. Deci
The Manager's Casebook	Woods and Thomas